Social Connectionism

Many of our thoughts and decisions occur without us being conscious of them taking place; connectionism attempts to reveal the internal hidden dynamics that drive the thoughts and actions of both individuals and groups. Connectionist modeling is a radically innovative approach to theorizing in psychology, and more recently in the field of social psychology. The connectionist perspective interprets human cognition as a dynamic and adaptive system that learns from its own direct experiences or through indirect communication from others.

Social Connectionism offers an overview of the most recent theoretical developments of connectionist models in social psychology. The volume is divided into four sections, beginning with an introduction and overview of social connectionism. This is followed by chapters on causal attribution, person and group impression formation, and attitudes. Each chapter is followed by simulation exercises that can be carried out using the FIT simulation program; these guided exercises allow the reader to reproduce published results.

Social Connectionism will be invaluable to graduate students and researchers primarily in the field of social psychology, but also in cognitive psychology and connectionist modeling.

For FIT software and other information, please see: www.vub.ac.be/FIT

Frank Van Overwalle is a full professor affiliated with the Department of Psychology at the Vrije Universiteit Brussel. He got his MSc in psychology in 1980, and defended his PhD in 1987, for which he received the Tobie Jonckheere Award of the Belgian Royal Academy of Sciences, Letters and Arts. Recently, he has developed artificial neural network models of social cognition, and has authored some 35 peer-refereed scientific publications in leading journals.

Social Connectionism
A reader and handbook for simulations

Frank Van Overwalle

Psychology Press
Taylor & Francis Group
LONDON AND NEW YORK

Published 2007 by Psychology Press
27 Church Road, Hove, East Sussex, BN3 2FA

Simultaneously published in the USA and Canada
by Psychology Press
711 Third Avenue, New York, NY 10017

First issued in paperback 2015

*Psychology Press is an imprint of the Taylor & Francis Group,
an informa business*

© 2007 Psychology Press

The FIT software is the sole responsibility of Frank Van Overwalle and
is not affiliated with Psychology Press, inc. For technical support issues,
please contact Frank Van Overwalle directly at
Frank.

Typeset in Times by RefineCatch Limited, Bungay, Suffolk
Cover design by Design Deluxe

British Library Cataloguing in Publication Data
A catalogue record for this book is available from the British Library

Library of Congress Cataloging in Publication Data
Overwalle, Frank van, 1957–
    Social connectionism : a reader and handbook for simulations /
Frank Van Overwalle.
        p. cm.
    Includes bibliographical references and index.
    ISBN-13: 978–1–84169–665–2
    1. Social interaction. 2. Social exchange. 3. Social interaction—
Simulation methods. 4. Social exchange—Simulation methods. I. Title.
    HM1111.O94 2007
    302.01′13—dc22

                                                    2006023113

ISBN13: 978-1-138-87759-7 (pbk)
ISBN13: 978-1-84169-665-2 (hbk)

This book is dedicated to Kristine and our children

He writes that early on, he already embraced the idea of humans 'as a machine', an expression that typified the dream of that age on rationality. He used the expression literally; and only the human organism created mind, emotions, good and bad (translated from Per Olov Enquist, 1999, *Het bezoek van de lijfarts*, p. 100. Ambo: Amsterdam).

The FIT program was written by Frank Van Overwalle, using StringGrid © features from TmsSoftware and TeeChart © from Steema. The FIT program can be freely used. Although many efforts have been made to avoid bugs, it is possible that some program errors remain. The author is not responsible for any possible damage done due to the use of this code.

Contents

Tables

Figures

Appendix

About the author

Frank Van Overwalle is a full professor affiliated with the Department of Psychology at the Vrije Universiteit Brussel. He worked first as research assistant in the VUB department for new media and computer technology in education, then as a PostDoc at the University of California at Los Angeles (1988–1989), and finally as a PostDoc and tenured professor at the VUB psychology department.

He got his MSc in psychology in 1980 and defended his PhD in 1987 on "Causes of success and failure of freshmen at university: An attributional approach", for which he received the Tobie Jonckheere Award of the Belgian Royal Academy of Sciences, Letters and Arts. He continued to work on attribution and social cognition, and then applied his and others' research to the development of artificial neural network models of social cognition. He has received several grants from his university and the Fund for Scientific Research-Flanders to test some of the unique predictions derived from these theoretical proposals.

Frank Van Overwalle has authored some 35 peer-refereed scientific publications, in the domain of social cognition. His recent research focuses on artificial neural network models of various phenomena in the general domain of social cognition, to demonstrate the common cognitive processes underlying many social findings. The aim is to enrich ad-hoc hypothesis-building, which is currently very flourishing in social psychology with a more general cognitive theory encompassing the whole of social cognition, in line with general theories of psychological information processing. His work is receiving a wide and growing international recognition from peers and has resulted in a number of publications in top-ranking journals, which are part of this book.

Acknowledgements

Preparation of this book would not have been possible without the support received from many people. The research described in the original articles (co)-authored by Frank Van Overwalle was made possible by grants from the OZR-VUB (Research Council of the Vrije Universiteit Brussel) and the FWO (Research Foundation—Flanders) Writing this book was made possible by grant OZR941. I am indebted to Tim Vanhoomissen, Axel Cleeremans, Dick Eiser, Gerd Bohner, Frank Siebler, and Claudia Toma, who provided invaluable assistance in proofreading or testing the simulations.

Copyright permissions

Part 1
Basics

1 Introduction and overview

Frank Van Overwalle

WHAT IS THIS BOOK ABOUT?

This book is a reader of recent original work on connectionist modeling of social phenomena, together with exercises and a computer program to run the connectionist simulations that are described in these articles. The original articles were all published in 1998 or later, so that the book gives an overview of the most recent developments and discoveries in the field. Connectionist modeling is a radically novel approach to theorizing in psychology and, more recently, also in the field of social psychology. In general, a connectionist perspective interprets human cognition as a dynamic, everchanging and adaptive system that learns from its own direct experiences or indirect communication by others. It assumes that cognitive processes are not immediately accessible, as it is becoming increasingly evident that many of our thoughts and decisions occur outside our awareness. Thus, the connectionist approach attempts to elucidate the internally generated cognitive dynamics that are hidden but that drive the thoughts and actions of individuals or groups.

Although many books have been written on connectionism, this is book is unique:

- The book covers the vast domain of social psychology and, more particularly, it includes practically all areas of *social cognition* (how people perceive and interpret their social world, that is, other people or groups; how they understand themselves and their attitudes; and how they causally interpret the actions and behaviors of themselves or others).
- It is a collection of (abridged) *published articles* covering the most recent theoretical developments of connectionist modeling in many domains of social psychology. Although in an edited format, it strives for coherence in its introduction of conceptual and theoretical underpinnings (it includes only feedforward or recurrent network models used predominantly in the field). It can thus be used as a handbook to introduce students in the field.
- The book includes *exercises* of all the simulations described in these original articles (with step-by-step instructions and simulation files), as

well as the *FIT simulation program*, which allows you to run these original simulations on your own. A new version of the program, with a completely novel user interface, makes it even more accessible to users with little experience in the field (i.e. the typical researcher or student in social psychology). The new input now requires users to have no more than minimal computer expertise to specify the simulations in a sort of spreadsheet. The FIT program manual is available in the Appendix to this book.

- *Web extras*: the book provides supplementary web access to the FIT program (for PC only) and the files for running all simulation exercises. The web access also provides you with regular updates of the FIT program.

WHAT IS CONNECTIONISM?

To appreciate what connectionism is and what a radical shift in theorizing it brought to psychology, let us briefly take a look at how human thinking was portrayed in previous decades in social psychology.

What it is not: Traditional views on human cognition

Traditional views on human information processing were inspired by a computer analogy. Memory was seen as a sort of filing cabinet or storage bin, where each piece of information was a symbolic concept of some sort that was left in this memory storage so that it could be retrieved for later use. Retrieval consisted of a sequential search through this storage space until the correct piece of symbolic information was found. In more recent notions of *activation-spreading networks*, human memory was seen as a network of symbolic units connected to each other. (This approach is also termed *associative networks* but, to avoid confusion with adaptive learning models of an associate nature discussed later, this term is avoided in this book.) In these models, retrieval is easier because the activation flowing through the networks "wakes up", or activates, some memory traces in parallel. In all these approaches, however, thinking was seen as accessing information from memory or from the outside environment, and modifying it by taking it through various processing steps, sometimes referred to as if–then production rules or semantic comprehension processes. The processed information was then ready for social judgment or action, and could be stored again in memory for later use.

However, many of the production and comprehension processes in traditional models were left unspecified, so that the essence of human thinking was still a mystery. Also unexplained was why this computer-inspired, rational view of human thinking and memory so often went astray, resulting in a plethora of judgment errors and biases. One popular solution to this paradox in social psychology was the idea that humans avoid excessive mental effort and use mental short-cuts or *heuristics*. To stress this point, researchers termed social perceivers either "cognitive misers" or "motivated tacticians" because they used whatever mental means—either heuristics or mental effort—to make their decisions. But this, again, failed to explain what was making these tactical decisions in the brain, another paradox known as the *homunculus* problem. Who or what in the brain decided that a given heuristic was the optimal tool from our mental heuristic "toolbox" to solve a given social question?

Connectionism: The essentials

The connectionist approach avoids many of the earlier traps that traditional models could not escape from. Crucially, it starts from a radically different view of human thinking and memory, based on an analogy with the architecture and working of a natural human brain. The basic feature of a connectionist network is that it consists of units (representing symbolic and non-symbolic concepts) and connections between the units along which activation is spread. In terms of the brain analogy, the units are analogous to neurons and the connections are analogous to synapses, which differ in strength or permeability for the spread of signals in the nervous system. The activation of each unit in the network is determined by the total activation received from other units along the connections. Connectionist models determine how activation spreads across the connections (in the short term) and also compute how the strength of these connections between units changes over time (in the long term). It is this latter feature—the ability to change the strength of the connections—that makes connectionist approaches so powerful as learning devices. Since the publication in 1986 of the two volumes on *Parallel Distributed Processing* by Rumelhart and McClelland (1986) and McClelland and Rumelhart (1986), this approach has emerged as one of the leading paradigms in the study of cognitive processes, including social cognition.

Many of the paradoxes and mysteries of older theories can immediately be solved by the connectionist approach, especially when it involves routine social thinking. If you plan on reading this book, I hope to convey to you two key messages that result from a connectionist perspective:

1. This book sees humans as "implicit cognizers", who rely in most of their decisions and judgments on the automatic generation and reactivation of novel knowledge. Automatic processes play a prominent role in everyday social thinking, perhaps more than we are aware of because they are hidden from our conscious experience. What is the reason for believing that such unconscious processes exist? This is based on the logic that, in the evolutionary past, the human brain developed novel functions and, while doing so, it typically did not discard old structures that

were still functioning but reused them for similar or slightly adjusted functions. Thus, from an evolutionary point of view, it is highly plausible that primitive associative or connectionist-like mechanisms are still of use. If most of human social behavior can be explained by a simple bunch of interconnected brain-like units, why assume anything more complicated?

2. Human social behavior involves adapting to a constantly changing social world. People move around, friends and colleagues change, new groups pop up or their members change, and, on top of this, people's interests, goals and even their more deeply engrained traits change over time. Every one of us has to deal with these short- and long-term social changes in a fluent and efficient way. This is only possible if our capacity to deal with change is somehow built-in to our cognitive system. And this is exactly what connectionist systems are particularly good at. An inherent part of these systems is a learning algorithm that adjusts to flows of change in the external environment, so that the cognitive system is appropriately prepared to understand and anticipate a novel state of the external environment.

Connectionism: A deeper look inside

If you are convinced that these are important preconditions for a cognitive system to survive in a social environment, then you might wonder: What are the characteristics of a connectionist system that accomplish all that? Below I highlight the most important ones for theorizing in social cognition.

- In a connectionist network, units create *representations of single individuals or groups of people*, together with elements of their social context and their reactions and behaviors. The connections between these elements represent the associations in the brain, and thus may reflect memories, judgments about other people and groups, attitudes or approach or avoidance tendencies, causal inferences and (re)actions. Hence, a single concept immediately activates related concepts, such as where you know a person from, how much you like him or her, what he or she looks like and what dispositions or talents he or she possesses.
- *Processing* in a connectionist model consists of activation spreading along the units and modifying their connection strengths. Both these processes are controlled by the units directly involved, and are computed by them in parallel. Connectionist processes, therefore, can get rid of a central executive processor to make the necessary computations. Much of our routine social thinking and reasoning that occurs largely outside our awareness can be understood by this perspective. The fact that the computations in the network occur in parallel explains why routine social thinking is very fast. However, some of our cognitive activities lie outside the scope of connectionist theories, such as when we make deliberative

choices that involve sequential steps, like making arithmetic calculations or listing all the pros and cons of a decision.

- *Memory* is not a huge cabinet where each individual piece of information is stored. Rather, memorizing involves a slow change of connection strengths so that new information about people, objects and their associated features slightly changes old memories about them. Hence, in a connectionist network, your impressions of familiar persons change slowly as you learn new information about them, and the old and new information are automatically and seamlessly integrated. Moreover, a connectionist memory is distributed among many features related to the target concept that is processed. Thus, your altered impression of a single member of a social group may generalize to the whole group and affect all members of it.

Although the connectionist approach has only recently been introduced to social psychology, tremendous progress has been made in the last decade, and many domains of social psychology have been covered by a connectionist approach. One of the leading motivations of this book is to demonstrate that the current state of affairs of theorizing in social psychology—a plethora of fragmented mini-theories, each designed to explain a limited set of findings—can be reappraised within the greater realm and framework of a connectionist approach. Connectionism provides novel insights to old research questions, and so contributes to progress in social psychology. To illustrate, several seemingly different types of thinking or biases that are traditionally interpreted as involving different processes may actually be understood by the same underlying connectionist processing principles. Because concepts and memories are distributed across the network and associated with a large pool of distinct features, you and I may access different parts of it. For instance, your attitude may be formed by paying attention to the content of some novel arguments, whereas my opinion is influenced more by the context, say the expertise of the speaker. Yet this information is governed by the same connectionist learning process. Many more of such examples are discussed in the subsequent chapters of this book.

IS THIS BOOK FOR YOU?

This book is intended for two audiences:

1. It is for anyone who wants to have the most recent advances by leading theorists in social connectionism in one handy package, so that you might use this book simply as a reader of the most important articles in the field. However, the book is not a primer on the basic workings of connectionist networks. It assumes that you have some minimal background on connectionism (e.g. have taken an introductory course

on the subject). Chapters 2 and 3 will refresh your basic knowledge of the connectionist models that are used throughout the book.

2.   More importantly, this book is for social-psychological researchers and students who want to get a closer taste of connectionism in their field. One way to do this is by running the simulations by yourself. The book is intended as a primary source in graduate-level seminars and courses, or for those researchers who want to explore connectionism in the social domain by themselves and would like to have some guidance through this novel field. In this respect, it should be emphasized that the book is not about maths or computers, but that it is firmly rooted in social psychology. The digital expertise required is at the level of a spreadsheet program (e.g. Excel). For about half of the articles in this book, the simulations were originally run with the FIT simulation program and most of the original analyses were recovered. You can now do this by yourself, just as the original researchers did. The other half of the articles were run with other programs, but the simulations are now made accessible through the FIT program as well. There is no good substitute for learning about connectionism than simply doing it yourself.

IS PRIOR KNOWLEDGE REQUIRED?

You need some basic background knowledge on connectionism for the articles in this book to make sense. Although this book includes an introduction to some basic concepts and tools in connectionist modeling, it is largely focused on the models that are treated here. Hence, it might be useful to consult some other introductory books before you begin with this one. If you want to explore the domain from a broader perspective, reading the first volume of *Parallel Distributed Processing*, by Rumelhart and McClelland (1986), is one possibility, although this book is rather tough to read for a beginner. A better choice for beginners is *Introduction to Connectionist Modeling of Cognitive Processes* by McLeod, Plunkett, and Rolls (1998). The advantages of this book are that it is very close to the original ideas of Rumelhart and McClelland, and that it offers an alternative simulation program *Tlearn*. Note, however, that this program lacks some features that simplify running the current simulations. There are, of course, other introductory books in this field, and new books on connectionism come out every year.

COMPUTER SIMULATION AS A NEW TOOL

All the articles assembled in this book contain connectionist simulations. What are the advantages of computer simulations? This book will try to convince you that developing and even understanding theories now requires that you become acquainted with the tools of computer simulation, and in particular, connectionist simulations:

- Computer simulations allow the imposition of more rigor and logic to theoretical ideas. In contrast to earlier theory building, which was based on verbal formulations, computer simulations require theorists to spell-out the necessary assumptions of their theory in great detail and scope, so that they do not miss important details that might ruin their simulation results. Indeed, a computer program computes all implications of the assumptions made, even those the theorists did not think of. This will sometimes force theorists to abandon or revise underlying assumptions, before their theory goes to print.
- Simulations may demonstrate that a novel theoretical mechanism can account for a finding that has an earlier theoretical explanation. This represents a theoretical contribution, showing that an alternative explanation may be viable. This may spur further empirical research, as it raises the obvious question of which mechanism accounts best for the phenomenon (see Smith & DeCoster, 1998).
- Simulations can demonstrate that a single mechanism can account for several known phenomena that previously required separate explanations. This contributes to theoretical parsimony and integration, because a single mechanism can do the work that required many distinct mechanisms previously. Moreover, if several phenomena follow from a single theoretical mechanism, the understanding of each phenomenon may benefit from previously unrecognized parallels with the others (see Smith & DeCoster, 1998). This gives social psychology a firmer theoretical base, not only because it unifies a diversity of social fields and insights but also because it so aligns itself with other domains of psychology where connectionist simulations are a dominant research tool to develop improved theories of human thinking and behaving. This suggests the potential for creating more general laws of social psychological processes.
- Simulations can make new predictions. Empirical confirmation of such predictions constitutes strong evidence for the new proposed theoretical explanation.
- Simulations in the social domain can spur the development of a new generation of network models that are more socially inspired and that reflect human interaction and communication. It is clear that typical networks representing the memory and brain of a single individual need to be extended toward multi-agent networks that take into account multiple representations of many individuals and the manner in which they communicate with each other (Hutchins & Hazlehurst, 1995; Van Overwalle & Heylighen, 2006).

LEARNING BY DOING: WHAT IS THE FIT SIMULATION PROGRAM?

The FIT simulation program allows you to simulate all the prominent connectionist models that are used in this book. It requires no more than minimal computer expertise at the same level as a spreadsheet or a statistical package. How exactly you use the program is explained at the end of each chapter, in the Exercises section. Moreover, the Appendix at the end of the book comprises a manual with more detailed descriptions for program use. The most recently updated version of the manual is available electronically from the program itself (using the **Help | Fit Manual** menu).

Figure 1.1 gives a view on the spreadsheet-like input from the program and some output. Next (Figure 1.2), is a view on the graphical interface to visualize the simulated data (dotted lines) and the fit with the human data (full lines):

The most unique and important features of the FIT program are:

- You can directly compare the simulation output with real observed data from actual experiments (hence its name FIT). While it is of great importance to test whether a simulated theoretical model can reproduce actual human data, this often is a tedious job in other programs. In

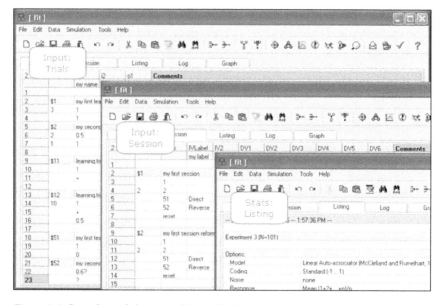

Figure 1.1 Overview of the spreadsheet-like input and some statistical output from the FIT program.

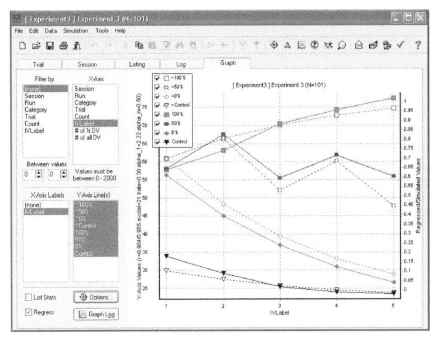

Figure 1.2 Graphical interface of the FIT program to visualize the simulated data (dashed lines) and the fit with the human data (full lines).

this program, this is the basis of the program input (although it is also possible to specify no actual data).

• In addition, you can automatically search for the parameter values of the simulated model that fit best with your human data or with your predictions.

• The program allows you to specify different categories (blocks) of trial and test data, which can be processed in a random order per category if you wish. Most importantly, each of these categories can be processed in an order that you specify in a session. This allows you to follow actual experimental procedures or fictitious learning histories in detail, without complicated script writing. This is all made easy, as you only have to select the appropriate learning histories from a drop-down list. It is even possible to specify several sessions, so that you can test different learning histories for the same data.

• You specify the data input (trial and session categories) in a user-friendly data grid, which is very similar to common spreadsheets like Excel. The simulated output is also given as grid data and can be visually inspected by graphs, or can be exported to other programs for statistical analysis and text processing.

OVERVIEW OF THE CHAPTERS

Although the connectionist perspective provides a radical shift from the past, it does not ignore earlier theories or findings. On the contrary, one of the first requirements of a connectionist approach is that it should provide at least an equally valid explanation of previous findings, with the strict rigor that is typical for computer modeling. The connectionist approach in social psychology is especially suited to deal with *social cognition*, or how humans cognize other humans and human-made objects. As you will notice, many chapters in this book involve well-known phenomena in social cognition, which are explained and simulated from this novel perspective. Thus, old theories and findings are reformulated from a connectionist framework. The original articles on these connectionist issues, as well as the computer simulations on which these articles rest, form the heart of this book.

Although the book covers a large range of domains in social cognition, the approach is particular in that it favors adaptive connectionist models. That is, the book focuses on models that are capable of changing the strength of the connections when novel information is taken in by the system. Although most connectionist models have this powerful adaptive capacity, not all of them do so. In the past, social-psychological researchers often preferred non-adaptive networks because, at that time, they were more familiar with the related idea of activation-spreading networks, whereas dynamic and adaptive systems involve concepts such as error-driven incremental learning, which were much more difficult to grasp. However, historically, these non-adaptive models were important because they paved the way to the current emphasis on the more powerful adaptive models.

This book has four major parts. Whereas the first part is mainly introductory, the last three parts include published studies and one novel chapter in which simulations are compared with empirical data. The published articles have been slightly adapted (most often abbreviated) to avoid unnecessary overlap and repetition in their introduction. The simulations in the articles are inspired either by empirical results that are generally accepted in the field or by results from some well-known illustrative experiments. In some of the articles, simulations are run to make specific predictions, which are then followed by empirical studies that confirm or disconfirm the connectionist predictions. All articles contain connectionist simulations.

To give an overview:

- The first, *Basics*, part describes the connectionist approach (Chapter 2) and then introduces the *Recurrent* and *Feedforward* networks that are used in this book in more depth (Chapter 3).
- The second part, on *Attribution*, discusses how causal strength is acquired when people observe multiple covariations between causes and effects, and how the repeated observation of this leads to effects that earlier algebraic theories could not explain (Chapter 4: Van Overwalle & Van

Rooy, 2001). Next, we further discuss the connectionist processes underlying causal reasoning (Chapter 5: Read & Montoya, 1999), and we end with a new chapter on one of the most pervasive shortcomings in causal attribution, the fundamental attribution bias (Chapter 6: by Van Overwalle).

- The third part, on *Person and Group Impression Formation*, focuses on the acquisition of stereotypes and how they generalize from one group to all its members (Chapter 7: Smith & DeCoster, 1998). Next, we discuss in more detail some well-known phenomena in person impression formation (Chapter 8: Van Overwalle & Labiouse, 2004). The last two chapters discuss a number of well-known group biases (Chapter 9: Van Rooy, Van Overwalle, Vanhoomissen, Labiouse, & French, 2003), such as subtyping of dissident minority group members (Chapter 10: Queller & Smith, 2002).
- The last part focuses on *Attitudes*. It contains one major article on attitude formation and change: How are attitudes formed when we pay attention to the content of persuasive messages, and how are we influenced by other cues in the context (Chapter 11: Van Overwalle & Siebler, 2005)? Other approaches to this topic were not included in the book, for example, on cognitive dissonance, which was not included because of space restrictions (Van Overwalle & Jordens, 2002), and reinforcement learning of attitudes during social exploration, which was not included because this approach can not at present be simulated with the FIT program (Eiser, Fazio, Stafford, & Prescott, 2003; Fazio, Eiser, & Shook, 2004; see also Chapter 2).

2 Connectionist basics

Tim Vanhoomissen and
Frank Van Overwalle

Many mainstream processes and findings in social cognition can be explained within a connectionist framework and, in many cases, explained better than by the traditional symbolic models put forward in the past by social and cognitive psychologists. What are the main characteristics of the connectionist models that accomplish this? To address this question, the general advantages of connectionist modeling, in comparison with traditional symbolic approaches, are described in this chapter. This introduction is inspired by a number of major publications in the connectionist literature (McClelland & Rumelhart, 1986; McLeod, Plunkett, & Rolls, 1998; Smith, 1996; Smith & DeCoster, 1998). It also includes fundamental highlights and clarifications on connectionism that originate from the articles that constitute the chapters in this book (and that were omitted to avoid unnecessary repetition). Thus, important common characteristics of connectionist models have been extracted from these chapters and are presented here. If you have some experience in connectionist modeling, you can skip this introductory chapter and move directly to Chapter 3, which focuses more specifically on the underlying assumptions and properties as well as on the technical specifications of the simulations applied in this book.

You might wonder in what ways connectionist models can contribute to a better understanding of social cognition. After all, should one really have to go through the effort of learning this novel approach to design new research and experiments? To obtain a deeper understanding of social behavior? Probably not; it is not crucial. One can continue doing research in the traditional manner and still contribute to the field. However, one would miss the many advantages that connectionism brings us. Connectionist models bring a unified framework, inspired by the neural working of the brain, that the traditional approach lacks and which explains why the social cognition field is replete with many unrelated and sometimes contradictory perspectives and theories. Moreover, given the nascent interest in social neuroscience and the growing empirical evidence on the place (using functional magnetic resonance imaging; fMRI) and timing (using electroencephalograms; EEGs) of brain activation, there is a need to understand how these processes are shaped in the brain. Given their neurological inspiration, connectionist models may fill this gap. They explain how content (what is learned) and process (how it is learned) proceed in parallel, unlike earlier approaches, which often see these aspects as taking place in sequential stages. Perhaps most fundamentally, connectionism views our social being as a constant learning and adaptation in a changing environment, and our memories, inferences and judgments as natural outcomes of that process.

The first section in this chapter provides a brief and non-technical introduction to how connectionist systems work, and then a more in-depth overview of the many advantages of connectionist networks and how they differ from earlier algebraic models. The next section provides a brief tour of some alternative types of connectionist network not included in this book, but which may provide intriguing insights to novel directions for the future. We end with some guidelines on how social information can be represented in a connectionist system. A more technical introduction to the connectionist models used in this book, with a worked-out example of a simple phenomenon, is given in Chapter 3.

GENERAL FEATURES OF CONNECTIONIST MODELS

Although connectionist models vary in the exact way they perform representation and learning, they all make fundamental assumptions about three basic aspects: the architecture (the units and connections), how information is processed (the flow of activation) and how information is memorized (the development of connection weights). These aspects, and their possible manifestations, are presented in the next paragraphs. A basic understanding of these connectionist characteristics is necessary before we can discuss the major advantages of them.

Architecture

A connectionist model consists of interconnected *units* or *nodes*. All of the processing in a connectionist model takes place through these units, with no need for a central processor or any other operator. The task of each unit is simply to receive activation from other units or external sources, perform a simple computation, and pass activation on to other units. Depending on their place in the process, units may be called *input units, hidden units*, or *output units*. Input units typically receive activation from sensory systems or from other sets of units, usually termed *external activation*. Output units send activation directly to motoric systems or to other sets of units. Inbetween the input and output units may be hidden units, which are connected only to input and output units from the same set. They are called "hidden" because they are "invisible" to other sets of units and receive activation only from within their own set of units. All these units are connected to each other. For reasons of clarity, a complex set of units is often structured in an input layer, output layer, and hidden layer, with only certain units from one layer connecting to certain units of another layer. In any connectionist network, units are the building blocks that actually represent the cognitive elements involved in the studied domain. There are two main types of representation:

1. A *localist* model, in which individual units can represent significant pieces of information. This is the most straightforward kind of representation, much like in most traditional symbolic models in psychology. For example, in the context of social perception, each unit would represent a concept like "person A" and "person B" (see Table 2.1A), "group C" and "category D", or even a specific piece of behavioral information like "Bert prepared some delicious snacks for his guests". However, localist models always need as many units as there are elements to represent. Therefore, they may be inefficient for modeling a lot of separate items.
2. *Distributed* models, in which single pieces of information are encoded by many units, which means that a single unit cannot represent meaningful information. This information can be abstracted from the model only by observing the pattern of activation that is spread across all units involved in encoding a specific concept. Some units in this pattern will be strongly activated, whereas others remain relatively inactive, creating a unique pattern for different concepts (see Table 2.1B). This means that more representations are possible in a distributed model than in a localist model with the same number of units. The distinction between localist and distributed representations is taken up again at the end of this chapter.

Information processing

When information is processed in a connectionist network, activation is spread through its units. This activation first reaches the input units and is passed on to the hidden units and output units. The exact way in which the activation spreads depends on the model specifications regarding the range of activation values, the activation updating, and the learning algorithm (Figure 2.1).

The activation that reaches a certain unit is expressed in numeric values. The range of these activation values may be continuous, with real values varying unlimitedly, or between a minimum and maximum. If the range is

Table 2.1 Localist (A) versus distributed (B) connectionist representation of persons "A" and "B"

(A)	Units			(B)	Units				
	1	2			1	2	3	4	5
"A"	1	0		"A"	.8	.7	.3	.4	.1
"B"	0	1		"B"	.2	.1	.8	.9	.5

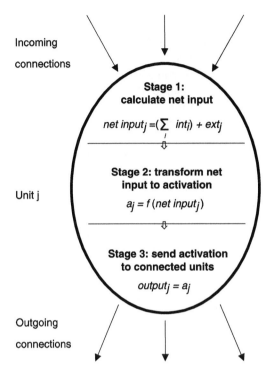

Incoming
connections

Unit j

**Stage 1:
calculate net input**

net input$_j$ =($\sum\limits_i$ int$_i$) + ext$_j$

**Stage 2: transform net
input to activation**

a$_j$ = f (net input$_j$)

**Stage 3: send activation
to connected units**

output$_j$ = a$_j$

Outgoing
connections

Figure 2.1 The processing of activation in receiving unit j in more detail. Its task can
be split up in three stages: (1) integrate activation coming from previous
units (int$_j$) and external activation (ext$_j$) into the net input; (2) transform
the net input to an activation level, according to the activation function;
(3) send the final activation level to all connected units.

discrete, most often binary values {0, 1} are used, but also a limited set of
discrete values is possible, for example {−1, 0, 1} or {1, 2, 3, 4, 5, 6}.

All the activation that is received in a certain unit is summed to form the
net input of this unit. Next, we need an *activation rule* to determine in which
way this net input will affect the activation level of the receiving unit. (This
activation rule may also take into account the current activation state of
the unit, in which case the net input is instead termed the *net activation* of
the unit.) The unit's new activation level is a function of the net input. This
function is either a linear function, which is often simply the sum, or a non-
linear function of this sum, often sigmoidal (S-like) in shape. A sigmoidal
activation function transforms the activation such that the impact of extreme
activation levels outside the typical range of −1 and +1 is reduced (that is,
brought closer to −1 and +1) and variations in the activation level between
the extremes have most impact. Furthermore, threshold functions can make
the unit change activation level only when the net input exceeds a certain
value. Activation-level changes can be positive or negative.

If the net input is strong enough to change the activation level of a certain unit, this change will be transmitted to all connected units. What is sent out by the unit is simply its activity level. Before reaching the next unit, however, this value is adjusted by the *connection weight* between both units. A high connection weight represents a strong connection between two units, which means that the sending unit will have a large effect on the receiving unit. With a small connection weight, the activation is attenuated and it will have little effect. Connection weights can be positive or negative, representing excitatory and inhibitory neurons in the brain. The final activation level is simply the product of the output activation level and the connection weight. So, a positive activation level (+.56) may be transformed to an opposite activation level (−.28) when it passes through a connection with a negative weight (−.50) Thus, an adjusted amount of activation reaches the next unit, starting the same procedure all over again. In this way, activation is spread automatically throughout all connected units, causing a new state of activation in the network. In their most straightforward form, connectionist models send activation from input units, over possible hidden units, to output units, and are hence called *feedforward* models. However, it is also possible that all units in one model act both as input and output. These models are termed *recurrent* models.

In a recurrent model, all units receive both external and internal activation. After the first phase, in which external activation is provided and the units send this activation to each other according to the connection weights, a second phase starts, in which the newly received internal activation is again sent to all connected units. This sequence may continue for a limited amount of time or *cycles*, or until the network reaches a stable state of fit with the current inputs. Although the spreading of activation in these models may seem a little more complex, there is no fundamental difference in the propagation of activity at the level of the individual units. Recurrent networks can be used to produce sequences of output after providing a single input, or can predict a next step in a sequence (for an example, see McLeod, et al., 1998, p.139). But, as is demonstrated throughout the book, they are also very useful for modeling social phenomena. The differential features of feedforward and recurrent models are further discussed in Chapter 3.

Knowledge representation and learning

In a connectionist model, knowledge is represented by the connection weights. For example, if the model "knows" that a person called "Walter" has black hair, it could contain units representing "Walter", "hair" and "black", with strong connections between them. In this way, whenever the input "Walter" is provided, the model can automatically generate the response "black hair", because those units are automatically activated. Consequently, learning occurs by changing the connection weights. For example, if a model has to learn that Walter painted his hair red, the connection weights between the units "Walter" and "black" would have to decrease, while the connection between

"Walter" and "red" should increase. These adjustments are made according to *learning algorithms*, which use a specific set of rules to calculate the exact weight change.

This view on the nature and function of memory differs radically from traditional symbolic models, which use memory as a static filing cabinet or storage bin, in which memory traces are stored, searched and retrieved. In connectionist models, memory is *distributed*. There is no discrete location for each representation or memory trace. Rather, the whole network of connection weights reflects a single representation that contains the summed information derived from many past experiences. Adding a new experience changes many weights and therefore alters the appearance of all representations, however minimal (Smith, 1996).

One of the earliest and simplest algorithms for changing the connection weights is the Hebbian learning algorithm (Hebb, 1949). According to this algorithm, the weight of the connection between two units is increased when- ever the network observes a pattern in which both units are active at the same time. This corresponds to our experience that when two things go together (e.g. the look and the taste of chocolates), they become associated in our mind and thinking of one or both will automatically activate the other. This Hebb algorithm, when applied in its most simple variant, causes connections to grow stronger without limit. This may become problematic, in that a few units can come to dominate the activation pattern in a network when they are strongly interconnected. For example, the slightest referral to chocolate can become strongly connected to salivation responses, to the extent that even entering the kitchen could activate this response. Therefore, the Hebbian learning algorithm is often extended with an additional algorithm (some- times referred to as the "anti-Hebb" rule, e.g. Houghton, 2005), which states that the weight of the connection between two units is decreased whenever the network observes a pattern in which one is active and the other is not. This also implies that this anti-Hebb algorithm can create inhibitory connections by decreasing their weights below zero.

Another, more powerful algorithm is the delta learning algorithm (McClelland & Rumelhart, 1986). In this algorithm, the output of the net- work is compared with the "correct" or "desired" external input. If the output differs from the external input, the learning algorithm will adjust the connection weights in the network. This procedure is repeated every time novel input is provided, so that the network begins to produce the correct output when it is presented with a certain input, in which case it has learned. This learning algorithm is described in detail in Chapter 3.

Because of the presence of the external input that provides the "correct" response, this kind of learning is also termed *supervised learning*. Accordingly, Hebbian learning is also known as *unsupervised learning*. However, this dis- tinction is not always justified and often irrelevant. As will be illustrated further on, from an outside point of view, a connectionist model (McClelland & Rumelhart, 1986) exhibits the same features using the delta learning algorithm as another network using the Hebb algorithm: both are provided with external input and both adjust their connection weights so as to better represent this input, without the need for an additional mechanism that "teaches" or "supervises" learning, because all adjustments happen within the units and the connections they are linked to. Moreover, Houghton (2005, p.31) showed that the delta learning algorithm can be reformulated in a such a way as to integrate the Hebb algorithm and the anti-Hebb algorithm. As this terminology appears rather superseded, the distinction will not be made in the remainder of this book.

ADVANTAGES OF CONNECTIONIST MODELS

Several characteristics of connectionist systems stand out in comparison with traditional approaches. Connectionist networks: (1) are based on a close analogy with the brain; (2) integrate process and content; (3) treat information processing as constant learning and adaptation; and (4) show memory and retrieval as a natural consequence of this. We will discuss each aspect in turn.

Neurally inspired representation

Traditional models in social and cognitive psychology are very much based on a symbolic approach to information. In symbolic models, a concept or object is represented by a number of individually meaningful symbolic entities. For example, a representation of "Mary" who "went swimming with a friend" and "invited many people to her party" is formed by linking separate entities representing the person, the individual behaviors, and (possibly) inferred characteristics such as "social". In activation-spreading models—which are closest to the connectionist models considered here—these symbolic entities are represented as nodes connected by associative links (e.g. Carlston, 1994). Such individual representations can be created, accessed, or changed without affecting other representations that are being stored simultaneously.

In connectionism, a concept or object can be represented not only by a single symbolic unit (localist encoding) but also by a pattern of activation distributed across a set of processing units, none of which necessarily have a symbolic meaning (distributed encoding). All units receive excitatory and inhibitory inputs across weighted connections from other units, sum these inputs to determine their own activation, and send the resulting output to other units. Therefore, activation levels can change rapidly and the current activation pattern reflects a transitory mental state. With this kind of representation, connectionism reaches a level of neurological plausibility that cannot be reached by symbolic models.

It is indeed known that neurons are responsible for passing information to each other, according to the level of input they receive. This information is passed over connections, whose strength is subject to change as learning takes place in the brain. To illustrate the symmetry between connectionism and neurology, consider these five assumptions about computation in the brain that inspired connectionism in its development (McLeod et al., 1998):

1. Neurons integrate information: in the brain, excitatory or inhibitory signals reach the dendrites of a neuron through synaptic connections. All incoming signals are summed and if this sum exceeds a certain threshold, the neuron will "fire". This means that it will send a signal, via its axon, to the dendrites of yet another neuron, starting another cycle.
2. When a neuron passes information, its output is systematically adjusted to the input level of information. Hence, a neuron does not just pass binary information saying that it does or does not receive input signals.
3. Information not only passes from neuron to neuron but, at a higher level, also from sets of neurons to other sets of neurons. These different sets of neurons are situated in various "layers" and all perform a certain transformation on the input of a layer. The transformed information is then sent to the input of the next layer.
4. The level of impact of one neuron on another one depends on the strength of the connections between these neurons. Neurons with strong connections between them will have more influence on each other than neurons with weak connections between them.
5. When learning occurs in the brain, the strength of the connections between neurons changes. Usually, repeated simultaneous activation of neurons will increase the strength of their mutual connections.

By adopting these principles, connectionist models provide an insight into lower levels of human mental processes, beyond what is immediately perceptible or intuitively plausible, although they do not go so deep as to describe real neural functioning. Drawing on Marr's (1982) notion of levels of information processing (see also Kashima & Kerekes, 1994), algebraic (or traditional) models are regarded as the *computational level* of human reasoning, which simply describe input–output relationships; connectionist models attempt to mimic psychological processes and therefore are considered to be the *algorithmic level*; and models that describe neural circuitry and processing that implement mental processes are regarded the *implementational level*. Thus, while it is true that connectionist models are highly simplified versions of real neural functioning and describe only the algorithmic level of mental thinking, it is commonly assumed that they reveal a number of emergent processing properties that real human brains also exhibit. One of these emergent properties is that there is no clear separation between memory and processing as there is in traditional models. Connectionist models naturally integrate long-term memory (i.e. connection weights), short-term memory (i.e. internal activation), and outside information (i.e. external activation). Even if biological constraints are not strictly adhered to in connectionist models of social judgments, there is currently an outpouring of interest in biological implementation of social inference and evaluation mechanisms (Adolphs & Damasio, 2001; Allison, Puce, & McCarthy, 2000; Cacioppo, Berntson, Sheridan, & McClintock, 2000; Ito & Cacioppo, 2001; Phelps et al., 2000; for recent overviews see Cacioppo & Berntson, 2004; Easton & Emery, 2005; Frith & Wolpert, 2004), which parallels the increasing attention paid to neurophysiological determinants of social behavior.

Integration of representation and process

Representations in symbolic models are passive and inert. They remain static and stable (although in some models they may decay over time) until processing units operate on them. The use of representations involves two operation stages. The first stage is activation or retrieval from storage. If the representation is retrieved, then it is further used by a central processor; otherwise it plays no role in processing. Given this two-stage operation, information processing in traditional models is fundamentally sequential (Smith, 1996).

In contrast, connectionist models rely on a single mechanism, the flow of activation along connections between units, for both storage and processing of information. The development of internal representations, and the processing of these representations in connectionist models, is done in parallel by simple and highly interconnected units. As a result, connectionist systems have no need for a central executive, thereby eliminating the requirement of explicit (central) processing of relevant social information. Given that a supervisory executive is superfluous in a connectionist approach of social cognition, this suggests that much of the information processing in causal attribution, impression, and attitude formation is often implicit and automatic, without recourse to explicit conscious reasoning. Consequently, many biases and shortcomings in reasoning that have been uncovered in past research (some of which are discussed in this book) are potentially due to general and normal information processes that are, in principle, working in an implicit and automatic manner without recourse to explicit awareness of their origin or conscious reasoning. This does not, of course, preclude people being aware of the outcome of these preconscious processes.

Learning and adaptation

In symbolic models, impressions or attitudes are not automatically stored somewhere in memory so that, in principle, they need to be reconstructed from their constituent components every time an object is accessed (Fishbein & Ajzen, 1975; but see Anderson, 1971). In many models, learning involves the explicit construction of new representations, much like in the process of language comprehension. For example, by combining various representations concerning Mary in the earlier example, a meaningful behavior may be constructed. Or a new representation may be constructed as a result of multiple individual experiences ("I've noticed Mary swims every day"). Earlier activation-spreading models, proposed in social psychology, can only spread activation along associations and provide no mechanism to update the weights of these associations. This lack of a learning mechanism in earlier models is a significant restriction.

Most connectionist models are not fixed models but are able to learn over time, usually by means of a simple learning algorithm that progressively modifies the strength of the connections between the units making up the network. Learning is modeled as a process of online adaptation of existing knowledge to novel information provided by the environment. Specifically, the network changes the weights of the connections between two (sets of) units, such as between an object and its characteristics, or between causes and their effects, so as to better represent the accumulated history of co-occurrences between these stimuli. Because the weights of connections are assumed to change only slowly, they are the repository of the network's long-term memory. This reflects the view that the mind is an adaptive learning mechanism that develops accurate mental representations of the world and detects statistical regularities in an ever-changing environment. This is essential for detecting and learning covariation and relationships between causes and events, or between objects and their features and evaluations.

As historic predecessors of the connectionist approach, associative learning models represent causal strength in memory as an association between two stimuli (e.g. a candidate cause and the effect, or an exemplar and a category), and describe how the weight of this association is adjusted online as new information is received (for an overview, see Allan, 1993; Shanks, 1995). One of the most popular associative learning models proposed by Rescorla and Wagner (1972) is, in fact, identical to the delta learning algorithm that is used in many connectionist models and also in the present framework. This implies that the phenomena presented in this book are naturally developed from ancient learning or conditioning processes that other organisms, besides humans, also exhibit.

In addition, connectionist networks exhibit emergent properties, such as the ability to extract prototypes from a number of exemplars (prototype extraction), to recognize exemplars based on the observation of incomplete features (pattern completion), to generalize knowledge about features to similar exemplars (generalization), to adjust to multiple constraints from the external environment (constraint satisfaction), and to lose stored knowledge only partially after damage (graceful degradation). All of these properties are extensively reviewed in Rumelhart and McClelland (1986), Smith (1996) and McLeod et al. (1998). It is clear that these characteristics are potentially useful for any account of the social phenomena studied in this book, such as causal attribution, impression formation, group stereotyping, and attitude formation.

Retrieval and accessibility

In symbolic models, a representation is retrieved from memory on the basis of its fit to a currently available set of stimulus features. The level of accessibility of the representation in memory is also important (Higgins, 1996). In some models (e.g. Wyer & Srull, 1989), accessibility is explained by *ad hoc* mechanisms, such as a "storage bin" containing multiple copies of a representation that is serially searched from the top down when a representation is sought, or a "storage battery" containing various amounts of charge attached to each representation (Smith, 1996).

In connectionism, there is no such thing as a storage space containing items to be retrieved. Instead, retrieval is the reinstatement of a previously processed activation pattern, elicited by the current inputs. This reinstatement depends largely on the weight of the connections, which thus "store" the memory. From this perspective, retrieval and judgment in connectionist models are reconstructive, in the sense that activation spreading is needed to reactivate the characteristics and evaluations associated with a stimulus object. However, this involves dramatically fewer computational steps than retrieving all constituent attributes and their evaluations and computing some sort of algebraic integration of them, as is the case in traditional algebraic models (e.g. Fishbein & Ajzen, 1975). Learning occurs incrementally after each pattern is processed. Therefore, the principle of accessibility is inherent to the network's operation, because a pattern that has recently or frequently been encountered will be reinstated more easily than other patterns (Smith, 1996; Smith & DeCoster, 1998).

OTHER CONNECTIONIST MODELS NOT INCLUDED IN THIS BOOK

A number of connectionist systems were not included in this book, although they played, or still play, an important role in social psychology. The practical reason for this is that the FIT program is not able to run some of these. A more fundamental reason is that some of these models are less powerful than the ones included in this book; this section explains why this is the case. Other models were not included because they are quite advanced. They suggest exciting novel developments in social connectionism that have recently surfaced in the literature, and which are described in this section.

Constraint satisfaction models

The constraint satisfaction perspective has long influenced the way in which social psychologists conceptualized a variety of phenomena, including causal explanation (Read & Marcus-Newhall, 1993), person perception (Read & Miller, 1993; Kunda & Thagard, 1996), cognitive dissonance (Shultz & Lepper,

1996) and attitude change (Spellman & Holyoak, 1992; Spellman, Uleman, & Holyoak, 1993; for a review see Read & Miller, 1998). In constraint satisfaction models, input information activates a number of concepts that are organized in a loose, heterogeneous network. The links or connections between these concepts are either excitatory, so that the activation of one concept increases the activation of another, or inhibitory, so that the activation of one concept decreases the activation of another. The latter occurs when concepts are inconsistent with one another, such as when explanations or attitudes are mutually inconsistent. Activation is automatically spread through all the connections in the network during a number of iterative cycles, until the network converges at a stable solution that is the best compromise among the constraints imposed by the excitatory and inhibitory connections. By this process, concepts that are not supported die out and concepts that are supported are strengthened. The most highly activated explanatory concept represents the most plausible explanation or attitude up to that point.

Perhaps the popularity of constraint satisfaction networks is due to the fact that they share important properties with the symbolic activation-spreading models used previously in social cognition. Despite their earlier theoretical impact, however, constraint satisfaction models have several important shortcomings that cast doubt on the usefulness of this perspective as a theoretical tool in social psychology. As argued by Smith (1996), "localist constraint satisfaction networks model structure only (not process). They use localist representations that are assumed to be rapidly constructed by interpretative processes ... The links do not arise from a learning process" (p.898). Thus, their major shortcoming is that the connections between the different concepts in the network are imposed by the experimenter, and do not grow as a result of learning.

Reinforcement learning

An important characteristic of a majority of connectionist networks is that they are passive receivers of input from the external environment that serves as feedback to the internal predictions of the system. Some of these connectionist networks have been extended by including a reward component so that the system has some self-interest in detecting specific information or goods. This is often accompanied by an action component so that the system can seek valued goods and feedback is contingent on the environment's response to the system's actions. This type of connectionist network is termed *reinforcement learning*. Reinforcement learning involves learning which actions to choose in order to maximize a reward or reinforcement signal. The system is not told which action to take but instead must explore the possibilities in the environment and discover which actions yield the highest reward by trying them (Sutton, 1992). Hence, reinforcement feedback is generally contingent on the system's actions and the outputs created by them. This requires a reinforcement learning system to find the appropriate balance between exploration of alternative actions to make better future choices, and exploitation of existing knowledge about earlier feedback contingencies to achieve good immediate outcomes.

Eiser and colleagues (Eiser, Fazio, Stafford, & Prescott, 2003; Fazio, Eiser, & Shook, 2004) applied the principles of reinforcement learning to the questions of how attitudes are acquired when individuals explore their social world and receive feedback from their choices. One of the things they were able to demonstrate is that people are biased, in that they learn more from their negative experiences than from their positive experiences, and typically try to avoid unfamiliar objects because they may turn out to be negative. It is evident that the inclusion of a more dynamic reward and action component is a necessary step in future models of social connectionism. Whereas the models in this book explain many of the errors and biases in judgments as naturally emerging from an organism's cognitive information processing and learning capacities, the reinforcement approach may potentially explain additional biases driven by an organism's motivation to protect its self-interests.

Multi-agent systems

A radical departure from individual systems is presented in multi-agent systems, where several agents interact to reach their individual objectives. However, the combination of their local, individual actions produces interesting social behavior that emerges at the collective level. This approach has been used to investigate complex situations, such as the emergence of cooperation and culture, and the self-organization of the different norms that govern the interactions between individuals. It manages to tackle such complex problems by means of computer simulations in which an unlimited number of software agents interact according to simple or complex protocols programmed by the researcher.

In the most common multi-agent models—*cellular automata* and *social networks*—the units represent single individuals and the connections the relationships between individuals. Thus, this type of model deals less with processes *within* an individual than *between* individuals. For instance, cellular automata consist of a number of agents (automata) arranged in a regular spatial pattern such as a checkerboard. Each automaton possesses a limited number of attributes (typically 1 or 2) that can be in a limited (often binary) number of states, such as cooperate or defect, or positive or negative opinion. Typically, individuals are linked to their neighbors, and the nature of the linkage is changed by an updating algorithm. Depending on the specific model, these links may represent different characteristics, such as persuasiveness, propensity for cooperation, decision strategies and so on (Nowak, Vallacher, & Burnstein, 1998). Cellular automata allow capturing of regularities and patterns of social norms or opinions in a group whereas individual agents update their behavior solely on the basis of local information between neighboring agents. The *social impact model* by Nowak, Szamrej, and Latané

(1990) pioneered this approach and increased our insight into the role of geographical clustering in protecting deviant minority opinions from being overthrown by a vast majority. Likewise, Axelrod's *culture* model (1997; see also Axelrod, Riolo, & Cohen, 2002; Riolo, Cohen, & Axelrod, 2000) showed that a whole population can converge to a local common culture when agents adopt their attributes on the basis of their similarity with neighboring agents. More recent work by Barr (2004) illustrates that symbolic media convergence to spatially organized systems (such as a common language or several dialects); Couzin, Krause, Franks, and Levin (2005) show that a small proportion of informed individuals can guide a group of naïve individuals towards a goal.

However, many of these multi-agent simulations are too rigid and simplistic to be psychologically plausible. The behavior of a typical software agent is strictly rule based: if a particular condition appears in the agent's environment, the agent will respond with a particular, preprogrammed action. Perhaps the most crucial limitation of many models is that the individual agents lack their own psychological interpretation and representation of the environment. As Sun (2001) deplored, multi-agent systems need ". . .better understanding and better models of individual cognition" (p.6).

To overcome this limitation, researchers have recently developed individual connectionist networks to capture an individual's psychology, and combined these into a community of networks so that the individual networks could exchange their individual information with each other. Earlier approaches (e.g. Hutchins, 1991; Shoda, LeeTiernan, & Mischel, 2002) were not very successful because the connections in these individual networks were not adaptive (i.e. they were constraint satisfaction networks, see above). More recent developments involve collections of individual nets that are adaptive, so that they can change on the basis of previous experiences. They can develop their own knowledge and memory, create opinions from novel information, and exchange them with other individual systems (Hutchins & Hazlehurst, 1995; Van Overwalle & Heylighen, 2006). One of such models, the Trust model developed by Van Overwalle and Heylighen (2006), is available in the FIT program, but is not further addressed in this book.

REPRESENTING SOCIAL INFORMATION IN A NETWORK

What does a unit in a network represent? What is the relationship between the unit's activations and the meaning of what the network is processing? These are important questions, as an appropriate representation strongly determines the efficiency of the network, or may even be the *sine qua non* to building a successful simulation. As we saw earlier, there are two basic coding schemes for representing information in the network: a localist and a distributed representation (Thorpe, 1995). Are there any advantages or normative preferences for using one of them?

Localist patterns

Many connectionist networks use a *localist representation*. This means that every unit represents a specific, meaningful entity. At a lower perceptual level, it may represent a basic perceptual form or feature, its angle and so on (e.g. horizontal stripes "—" and vertical stripes "|" as in "H", or curved forms as in "C" and "O"). Often, perceptual information is encoded at the sensory organ in a dimensional fashion, so that sensory information represents topographic vectors rather than discrete pieces of information. Figure 2.2 illustrates such a vectorial encoding for auditory information in which a "tonotopic" map transforms the pitch of a sound to a spatial

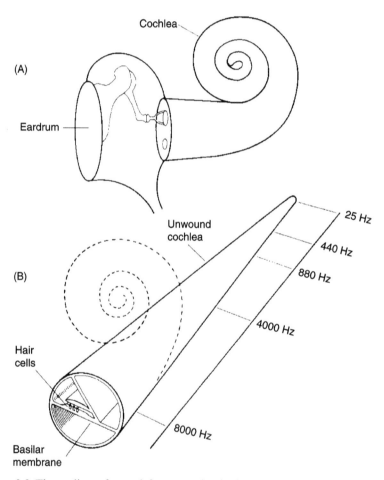

Figure 2.2 The coding of sound frequency in the human cochlea. (A) Position of the cochlea relative to the eardrum. (B) The "unrolled" cochlea. (From "Neurophilosophy: Toward a unified science of the mind/brain" by P. S. Churchland, Cambridge, MA: MIT Press, 1986, p. 126. Copyright 1986 by the MIT Press. Reprinted with permission.)

dimension along the cochlea. In these maps, the orderly mapping of neurons with sound frequencies is preserved from the cochlea to the auditory cortex. Similar topographic representations exist for the sensory and motor cortex, where a "somatotopic" map preserves the sensory and motor positions on the body (Gärdenfors, 2000).

At a higher semantic level, a unit represents the core meaning of a concept, such as "bread". This representation is discrete, in that there is no direct dimensional mapping between the neurons and meaning as in sensory organs. However, there is evidence that semantic and social meaning is also structured in an orderly fashion, traditionally referred to as a "schema" or "knowledge structure". An illustration is given in Figure 2.3, where information about a person is hierarchically structured with the person (at the top) linked directly to her or his traits (in the middle), which in turn are linked directly to the behavioral descriptions or observations (at the bottom) from which the traits are inferred (Hamilton, Driscoll, & Worth, 1989). Of course, the graphical position (top, middle, or bottom) of the hierarchy is only for convenience. What matters is the structure of the connections.

Although this latter discrete symbolic representation is an oversimplification of how the brain encodes semantic information, in the area of social psychology this is not always a significant obstacle. Localist representations have their advantages. A localist schema may simplify the representation of a network, especially when its basic processing for a given task does not depend greatly on the manner in which meaning is represented. This has the added benefit that the network is easily communicated to the social-psychological audience, even more so because it also bears resemblance with earlier activation-spreading or symbolic networks. Certainly, a distributed representation would offer more neurological plausibility but, as Hinton, McClelland, and Rumelhart (1986) argue, distributed models should be considered only if they provide an increased efficiency or processes that cannot be achieved with a localist representation. In sum, in localist models, the units both carry semantic meaning and compute the mental processes on these meanings.

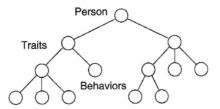

Figure 2.3 The coding of discrete knowledge structures as illustrated for the representation of a person schema involving the person, his or her traits, and episodic behaviors (based on Hamilton, Driscoll, & Worth, 1989).

Distributed patterns

Sometimes, the coding of meaning is more crucial and needs to be more realistic. In such instances, many connectionist models use a *distributed representation*, in which a semantic concept or meaningful mental state is identified by a pattern of activation across many units (McClelland & Rumelhart, 1986). Activity of a single unit has no fixed meaning independent of the pattern of which it is a part. A meaningful pattern is elicited in the network as activation is received from other units or from the external environment. The entire set of connection strengths determines the way activation flows and the activation pattern that will result from the given input. In sum, in distributed models, semantic interpretation is attached only to patterns that involve many units, whereas the actual operations of the system (the computation and spread of activation levels) occur at a lower level.

In a distributed coding, not all units contribute equally strongly to the meaning of a concept, because these concepts do not share all features. Thus, in identifying a concept, only a limited number of units receive strong external activation while the activation of the other units remains relatively low and close to 0. If this were not so, the network would suffer from the problem of *superposition*. That is, the network would not be able to discriminate between different concepts in the network because they would all involve the same features to a substantial degree. Learning about them would result in a superposition of the same connection weights for different concepts, which would become indistinguishable in the network. Consequently, although there is overlap in the activation patterns, this overlap cannot be large to avoid confounds in the identification of meaning (see Table 2.1B, p.16).

A distributed representation has many advantages over a localist representation. Not only is it closer to how the brain encodes information, but a number of important properties emerge from it. Basically, a direct consequence of a distributed representation is that it allows *generalization* of learning across similar concepts. Because similar concepts are assumed to have similar representations, learning something about one concept will influence how the network processes related concepts. Consequently, a distributed representation computes *explicit similarity* between distributed representations that represent similar concepts (e.g. the similarity of an exemplar and its prototype) and it allows the *extraction of prototypes* because the features of exemplars that are similar or central will be reinforced, whereas their differences will tend to cancel out. Consequently, a distributed representation allows *generalization* to other unknown instances on the basis of their similarity to the prototype.

A second advantage of distributed representation is that it generates *pattern completion*, so that, given a portion of a pattern as input, the network can reconstruct the whole pattern. Some connectionist networks have the ability to settle into an overall pattern, termed an *attractor*, that best fits the current input in light of stored representations of past experiences (Smolensky,

1989). This is how the network may "clean up" variations and noise in external input and end up with an identical meaningful interpretation. For instance, different pronunciations of a word may end up in the same attractor, so that we interpret it as the same word and meaning. This is similar to the pattern-completion property: the noisy input can be viewed as a partial pattern and the network computes the complete pattern that is most consistent with it.

Another advantage of a distributed representation is that it is much easier to incorporate *new concepts* into a network. In a localist network, each concept must be represented by its own unit. This means that the network itself must grow larger each time it encounters a new concept, and difficult decisions must occasionally be made as to when an input represents an instance of an existing concept versus when a new unit must be created. In a distributed network, on the other hand, the model represents every possible concept on the same units. Novel concepts induce new patterns of activity across the network, but the network's structure stays the same. More detailed elaborations on distributed representations can be found in Hinton et al. (1986), van Gelder (1991), and Thorpe (1995).

Semi-distributed representations

Some networks use a compromise between localist and distributed representations. To keep the network as simple as possible, but at the same time to encode multiple features of concepts, some models use a limited number of units to represent the core meaning of concepts, together with one or more additional units to represent their common characteristics. Thus, for instance, a specific trait can be represented by a single unit, while its evaluative meaning is encoded in positive and/or negative valence units that it shares with many more traits. Similarly, an attitude can be represented by its cognitive characteristics (that people generate when thinking about an attitude object) together with the favorable or unfavorable evaluation that it creates. These coding schemas are termed *semi-localist* or *semi-distributed*, depending on how much it resembles a purely localist or distributed representation, respectively.

3 Feedforward and recurrent connectionist networks, and their emergent properties

Frank Van Overwalle and
Tim Vanhoomissen

This is a chapter that you must read before you go on and dig deeper in the articles (unless you have read most of them already, of course) or do the exercises, even if you already have some experience in connectionist modeling. It contains the essentials for understanding many of the simulations of this book, in particular the emergent properties of the delta learning algorithm embedded in feedforward and recurrent networks. So don't skip it! In this chapter, we further explore how connectionist networks are built and function. We elaborate on the short sketch given in the previous chapter and provide a more technical (i.e. algebraic) account of connectionist processing. Don't worry, however, because we also explain how this works in a step-by-step manner, so that even the most inexperienced reader can understand the basic workings. We focus on those aspects that are most typical for feedforward and recurrent models, because these are the models that will be discussed and explored most extensively throughout this book. Next, we describe some of the most important emergent properties of these models, which drive many of the simulations explored in this book. Throughout this chapter, examples are taken from the social domain to illustrate how connectionist networks are applied in social cognition. We end the chapter with a worked-out example and guidelines on how to conduct your own simulations.

BASIC PROCESSING OF CONNECTIONISTS NETWORKS

The fundamental assumptions of connectionist models involve three different aspects: the architecture (the units and connections), how information is processed (the flow of activation), and how information is memorized (the development of connection weights). Although these steps are outlined in Chapter 2, we will now see how they are implemented in feedforward and recurrent networks.

Architecture: Units and connections

A connectionist network consists of many elementary processing units, interconnected by unidirectional links that transmit activation. These units perform a simple computation: forming a weighted algebraic sum of all their inputs (which may be positive or negative in sign) and generating output that is a function of the summed input. In contrast to the simplicity of the units, the complexity of a connectionist model resides in its overall "architecture" and in the pattern of weighted interconnections among units. Typically, the architecture of a given network is fixed. For example, the networks discussed in the book typically have two layers of units: an *input layer*, which receives input from external sources, and an *output layer*, which sends output to other cognitive subsystems or the outside world (Figure 3.1). The weights of the interconnections among units are assumed to be shaped by a learning process, as discussed below.

Processing information: Automatic spreading of activation

During the first phase of information processing, each unit receives activation from sources outside the network (for instance, from other sensory or semantic modules of the brain) which is termed the *external activation*. This activation typically ranges from a minimum value, often 0 or −1, to a maximum value of +1. Because the units are all interconnected, this activation is spread

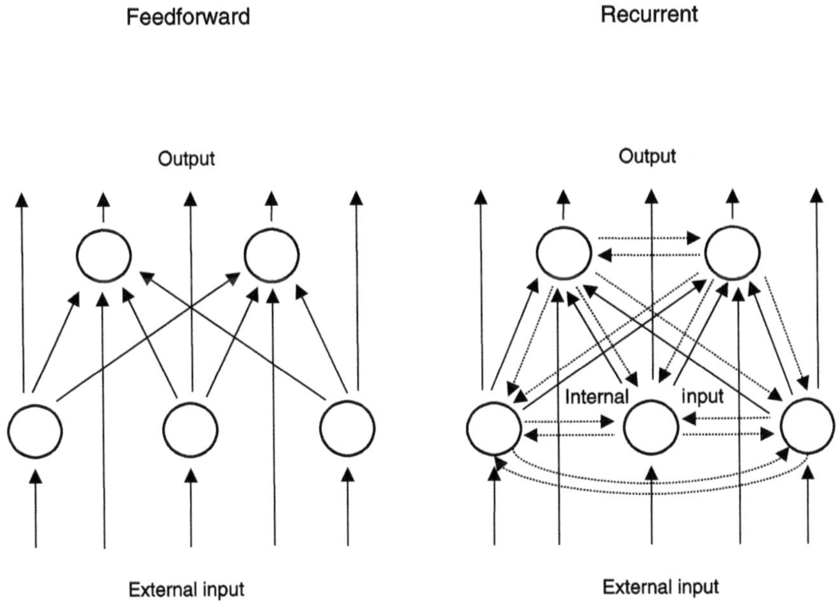

Figure 3.1 A generic feedforward and recurrent network architecture. The top layer consists of two output units, while the bottom layer consists of three input units. External activation is fed in the network at the input layer, and flows to the output layer directly (feedforward and recurrent network) or indirectly via internal connections (recurrent network only; additional connections are indicated by broken arrows).

automatically throughout the network, where it influences all other units. The activation received from other units in the network is termed the *internal activation*. Hence, a unit's current or *net activation* depends on the activation flowing to it from external sources or other units of the network over incoming links. In addition, this activation is determined by its prior activation level, which is either a resting activation level, often 0, or the remaining activation from a prior pass through the network. The external input, the internal input and the prior activation determine the net activation level of the unit. In turn, this unit sends activation over its outgoing links to other connected units. All the activation levels of all units in the network reflect the short-term memory of the network.

In mathematical terms, if the activation of unit i is denoted by a_i and the weight of the connection from unit i to unit j is denoted by w_{ij}, then the total input of unit j is:

$$input_j = \sum_i a_i * w_{ij} \qquad\qquad (3.1)$$

In most connectionist models, the unit's activation a_j is a function of this total input. In mathematical terms, the *internal activation* of a_j is:

$$int_j = f\left(\sum_i a_i * w_{ij} \right) \qquad\qquad (3.2)$$

The function f is either a *linear* function which often is simply the sum as given in the above equation, or a *non-linear* function of this sum, often sigmoidal (S-like) in shape. A sigmoidal activation function transforms the activation such that extreme activation levels outside the typical range of -1 and $+1$ are squeezed towards -1 and $+1$, so that activation levels between the extremes have most impact.

Learning and memory: Developing connection weights

The unidirectional connections in a connectionist network, which link all the units with each other, are also the very substance that stores *knowledge* in a network. When the network processes an input pattern, this pattern leads to changes in connection weights. Each single change in weights is an individual *memory trace*. Together, all memory traces encoded during prior learning are superposed, and so form a final set of weights of the network. This set of weights is the representation of the network's current knowledge.

A network learns a set of connection weights that permits it to perform some task. In virtually all the simulations described in this book, the task essentially involves the mapping of a given set of input patterns into desired outputs. For instance, in a causal attribution task, the task is to map causes to effects. The causes are encoded as the pattern of activation to the input units of the network, and the effects are encoded as the pattern of activation to the output units. Similarly, in a categorization task, the task is to map stimulus attributes to category memberships; and in an impression formation task, the goal is to map specific people to traits. The individuals are encoded as the pattern of activation to the input units of the network, and their traits are encoded as patterns of output. The network will alter its connection strengths between input and output to represent the observed relationships between cause and effect, instance and category, or person and trait. Whereas in some networks the input and output is explicitly coded (e.g. feedforward networks), in other networks the units act both as input and output (e.g. recurrent networks) so that this distinction is blurred and is only important in the computations of weight adjustments.

To perform weight adjustment, the network uses a learning algorithm to modify its connection weights. Initially, all connection weights are given a starting value, typically 0 or a random value. At each experience or *trial*, external activation is presented to the input units of the network, and the network's output activation is observed. The goal for the network is to "remember" how each external activation has generally been associated with the activation of other input units. To accomplish this, the weights must be adjusted during learning so that units that are generally concurrently active excite each other and those that tend to be active at different times inhibit each other, whereas those units in which the activations are uncorrelated show neither mutual activation nor inhibition (Smith, 1996). Researchers have developed several different learning algorithms to accomplish this (Hebb, 1949; McClelland & Rumelhart, 1986). For example, the *Hebbian learning algorithm* increases the weight of the connection between two units whenever the network observes a pattern in which both units are active at the same time and decreases it whenever the network observes a pattern in which one unit is active and the other is not (see also Chapter 2).

The *delta learning algorithm* (McClelland & Rumelhart, 1986), which is used most often in this book, performs a similar operation but accomplishes a more ambitious goal. Its overall aim is to bring the memory or internal representation of the network into close agreement with the structure of the external environment. Indeed, the better the representation in a cognitive system, the higher the chances of survival for the organism. To do this, the weights are adjusted to reduce the discrepancy at each unit between the network's predicted or internal activation and the external activation coming from the outside world (e.g. between the predicted likelihood of the effect given a cause and the actual effect that occurred). This process is repeated many times throughout a *training* or *learning history* with different stimuli (activation patterns) at the units. After enough training, or a predetermined number of trials, the weights stabilize at values that give the network's current prediction of how much the causes predict or influence the effects.

During learning, a connectionist network can combine novel input information with information derived from past experiences. If a stimulus is somehow incongruent with its past training, the learning algorithm will modify the pattern of connection weights so that it strikes a balance between prior experiences and the novel input. Depending on the *learning rate*, novel information will dominate the weight changes (when the learning rate is high) or the old background experience remains dominant (when the learning rate is low). The network carries out these functions without constructing or storing discrete representations of specific types of expected stimuli. All representations are stored together in the connection weights in the network, and all representations simultaneously influence the processing of new inputs (because all processing depends on those same weights). These assumptions contrast with those of traditional symbolic models in which different processes are assumed to construct, search for, retrieve, and use discretely stored representations (see Smith, 1996; see also Chapter 2).

Although this kind of (supervised) training is often accused of being unrealistic, in that the correct output of social events is seldom known to the observer, this is a misinterpretation. In real life, the co-occurrence between causes and effects, between stimuli and their membership or between persons and their trait-implying behavior is often given and obvious for the observer. Thus, our natural or social environment provides us many times with the "desired" output of a given input. Moreover, as we will see later, the division between input and output may become quite arbitrary, as in some models each input can act as output for other inputs, and vice versa (see Recurrent models, p.39).

Predictive and diagnostic questions: Testing the network

After learning, the network can be tested by presenting it with incomplete patterns, representing some stimuli, and observing the activation pattern generated at other units. Because of the distributed nature of the representations in a connectionist network, the separate items cannot be retrieved in precisely the same form as they were initially stored. Rather, during retrieval each stimulus is *reinstantiated* or *recreated*, instead of being *searched for* as in traditional symbolic models. Interestingly, as in humans, this re-creation will often be imperfect and subject to influence from the person's other knowledge (Smith, 1996; see also Chapter 2).

To illustrate, the predictive strength of a causal explanation is measured by reactivating the knowledge in the connections, that is, by turning on the appropriate *causal* units and reading-off the resulting activation of the *effect* units. Causal units with a strong connection will yield high activations of effect units, whereas causal units with weak connections will yield low effect activations. It is also possible to go the other way around, that is, to activate the effect units first and then to measure how much activation is received by each causal unit. The forward cause → effect activation refers how people provide explanations when given specific causal questions and thus reflects *causal estimates* or *predictions*, such as how likely it is that an abandoned campfire may set the forest on fire, or how likely it is that a disease causes a particular set of symptoms. Conversely, the backward effect → cause mechanism refers to explanations of why an effect occurred and thus reflects *diagnostic estimates*, such as what is the most likely cause of a forest fire, or what is the most likely disease underlying a set of symptoms. These two estimates are not necessarily the same (see Chapter 5). While an abandoned smoldering campfire may almost inevitably cause a forest fire, it may be so uncommon that it is a less likely candidate when trying to seek (or diagnose) the cause of a given fire. Conversely, although anger can be expressed in many behavioral ways, a slap in a loved-one's face is very diagnostic of a person's aggressive temperament. This asymmetry between causal/predictive and diagnostic inferences is very intuitive and captured by opposite unidirectional links in (recurrent) connectionist models.

Delta learning algorithm

One of the most critical aspects of a connectionist model is the learning algorithm adopted. In most simulations of this book, the *Widrow-Hoff* or *delta* learning algorithm is used (McClelland & Rumelhart, 1988). This learning algorithm is identical to the Rescorla–Wagner (Rescorla & Wagner, 1972) formulation of animal conditioning, and has also been applied in associative learning models of human learning and categorization (see Gluck & Bower, 1988a; Shanks, 1991). This provides the connectionist perspective with a strong philogenetic origin and an extensive research base from which social researchers can draw much interesting data. In addition, it has been mathematically demonstrated that, given sufficient learning experiences, this learning algorithm converges to the probabilistic norm of covariation (see Chapman & Robins, 1990; Van Overwalle, 1996). Thus, the delta learning algorithm is sensitive to actual covariation between stimuli, like causes and effects. The same learning algorithm is also capable of predicting other effects of conditioning known in the animal literature as *blocking* and *supercondi-tioning*, and which resemble discounting and augmentation, respectively, in social psychology (Van Overwalle & Van Rooy, 1998; see also Chapter 6).

In general, the delta learning algorithm predicts that the more two stimuli co-occur, the stronger their connection will grow. Thus, the specific learning history is crucial in shaping the strength of the connections in the network. How does the delta learning algorithm modify the weights in the network? As noted earlier, the basic idea is that the weights are changed so that the network better represents the observed stimuli. First, the network determines the fit between each unit's summed internal activation (see Equation 3.2) and the external activation reflecting an observed stimulus pattern. The network modifies the connection weights so that the internal activation for each unit predicts the external activation as well as possible. The error in this prediction is the difference (or delta, δ) between the internal and external activation for each unit:

$$\delta_j = ext_j - int_j \tag{3.3}$$

If this error δ_j is positive, it means that unit j is not receiving enough internal activation. For instance, the causal input predicts too little of an effect. To increase the amount of internal activation received by a unit, it is necessary to increase the weights to this unit from other units that have positive activation and to decrease the weights to this unit from other units that have negative activation. Conversely, if the error is negative, it means that the unit is receiving too much internal activation, so the weights need to be changed in the opposite direction. These weight changes (denoted by Δw_{ij}) are accomplished by the following delta learning formula:

$$\Delta w_{ij} = \varepsilon * \delta_j * a_i \tag{3.4}$$

where ε is a global parameter that determines how fast the network learns (i.e. the *learning rate* parameter). As noted earlier, a high learning rate indicates that new information has strong priority over old information and leads to radical adjustments (e.g. when a patient immediately believes the diagnosis of a medical expert), whereas a low learning rate suggests conservative adjustments, which preserve much of the knowledge acquired by old information (e.g. when people distrust new information or experiences). Thus, the delta learning algorithm will move the weights toward values that make the internal input approximate the external input for each unit. This allows the network to reconstruct its external environment on the basis of only an incomplete part of the environment. For instance, it allows the prediction of an effect on the basis of a given causal input, or the prediction of a category membership (e.g. trait) on the basis of some stimulus attributes (e.g. a person's behaviors).

TYPES OF CONNECTIONIST MODEL

Most connectionist models discussed in this book fall into two broad categories that differ mainly in their architecture and in how activation flows in the network. Let us first focus on the architecture and then discuss the activation spreading.

Architecture

Feedforward

Perhaps the most simple connectionist model used in this book is a feedforward (or pattern associative) network, as shown in the left panel of Figure 3.1

(see p.33). It has unidirectional connections from input units, sometimes by way of intervening layers of hidden units, to output units. When a stimulus (e.g. cause) is presented as external activation to the input units, activation feeds forward through the network, ultimately producing a distinct activation pattern on the output units (e.g. effects).

Recurrent

In contrast, recurrent (or autoassociative) networks are not strictly feed-forward in structure; they have a much broader architecture. They allow uni-directional links between all units of the network in all directions, except between identical units (hence $w_{ii} = 0$). Thus, they involve, beside feedforward activation, feedback of activation, either with interconnections among units in a single layer or with connections back from a later layer to another (see right panel of Figure 3.1). Recurrent connections allow units to influence and constrain each other in finding the best overall pattern that fits the input. For example, two units may have reciprocal excitatory connections and so may turn each other on even if the external input activates only one of the two.

Spreading of activation

Feedforward

In a feedforward network, given the unidirectional links, activation can flow only from the input units to the output units. As we have seen earlier, the output units' internal activation (denoted as int_j) is a function of the total activation received from other input units. In feedforward models, this is typically a *linear* function, often the sum of the receiving activation. In math-ematical terms, if the activation of input unit i is denoted by a_i and the weight of the connection from unit i to unit j is denoted by w_{ij}, then Equation 3.2 computing the final activation of output unit j can be rewritten as:

$$a_j = int_j = \Sigma \, a_i w_{ij} \tag{3.5}$$

Recurrent

In a recurrent network, because the units are all interconnected, their acti-vation flows throughout the network, where it influences all other input and output units. In mathematical terms, every unit j in the network receives external activation, termed ext_j. Every unit j also receives internal activation int_j, which is the sum of the activation from the other units i in proportion to the weight of their connection (see Equation 3.2). The external activation and internal activation are then summed to the net activation, or:

$$net_j = Estr * ext_j + Istr * int_j \tag{3.6}$$

where *Estr* and *Istr* are global parameters that reflect the degree to which the net input is determined by the external and internal input, respectively.

In recurrent models, the activation of each unit *j* may spread around, back and forth, for a limited amount of time, or *cycles*, and so further determine the internal activation of all other units. This is the typical process of *linear recurrent models*. Alternatively, activation may spread around for some time until it settles on an *attractor* state that provides an optimal fit between the various constraints represented by the between-unit connections as well as the current inputs. This is typical of *non-linear recurrent models*.

According to the linear activation algorithm, the updating of activation (denoted by Δa_j) is governed by the following equation:

$$\Delta a_j = net_j - Decay * a_j \qquad (3.7)$$

where *Decay* reflects a global parameter that sets the rate of memory decay. Subtracting *Decay* in the second part of the equation causes the activation to decay naturally toward zero. Because *Decay* is multiplied with the activation a_j, units with larger activation magnitudes experience greater decay.

In many simulations of this book, only one internal updating cycle was used with the parameter values $Decay = Istr = Estr = 1$. Given these simplifying assumptions, the final activation of unit *j* reduces simply to the sum of the external and internal input, or:

$$a_j = net_j = ext_j + int_j \qquad (3.8)$$

This linear activation function is closest to the activation function in the feedforward network (see Equation 3.5) and is actually identical for output units in a feedforward network when they receive no external activation.

Processing of the non-linear activation is somewhat more complex. According to the non-linear activation algorithm, the change in activation for unit *i* during a processing cycle is determined by the following equations:

$$\Delta a_j = net_j * (1 - a_j) - Decay * a_j \text{ if } net_j > 0 \qquad (3.9)$$

and

$$\Delta a_j = net_j * (a_j + 1) - Decay * a_j \text{ if } net_j \le 0 \qquad (3.9')$$

As these equations show, units for which the total activation is positive tend to increase their activation toward the extreme +1, whereas those that receive a negative activation will tend to decrease their activation toward the extreme −1. The equations constrain the activations within the range −1 to +1 and make it more difficult to further activate units that have activations close to +1 and more difficult to reduce the activation of units that have activations close to −1.

EMERGENT PROPERTIES OF THE DELTA
LEARNING ALGORITHM

To understand the processing mechanism underlying the simulations in this book, it is important to have some insight into how a learning history determines the growth of connection strength. Hence, we will now illustrate the workings of the delta learning algorithm step-by-step with the aid of examples. In addition, these examples will illustrate three major properties of the delta learning algorithm. An emergent property is a process that leads to the appearance of a structure not directly built-in by the constraints and specifications that control the model. Rather, over time, something new appears that was not directly specified by the equations of the model, nor was it explicitly represented in the initial and boundary conditions. These emergent properties are therefore very intriguing, because they can explain human behavior on the basis of more fundamental learning processes. These emergencies drive a great deal of the simulations in this book, so a good insight into them is a prerequisite in understanding these simulations.

To simplify this exposition, we use causes and effects to illustrate the working of the delta learning algorithm and its properties, and we use a localist encoding so that each cause or effect is represented by a single unit. Moreover, to avoid the complexity of internal activation flowing around in the network, we use a feedforward network, in which causes are represented by input units that are unidirectionally linked to effects represented by output units (Figure 3.2). Although only illustrated here with a feedforward network, all these properties also emerge from a linear recurrent network, and many even emerge from other connectionist networks.

Acquisition of connection weights and sample size effects

We begin with the simplest case where one cause, A, is always paired with one effect, E (Figure 3.2A). This example illustrates how the strength of A is incrementally acquired until it reaches the probabilistic norm of +1 (full causal strength; see Cheng & Novick, 1990; Van Overwalle, 1996).

Step 1. When cause A is present during a learning experience or trial, its input unit is turned on to the default activation level +1 (denoted by the shading in Figure 3.2). Other causes are not shown and have their activation turned off at level 0. The input activation of cause A then spreads automatically to the output (effect) unit in proportion to the weight of the connection. Because it is typically assumed that connection weights start at zero, at this point the activation sent by A and received at the output unit E is still zero (= input activation [= 1] × weight [= 0]; see Equation 3.5).

Step 2. All activations from the input units that are received at the output unit E are linearly summed to determine the activation of the output unit (see Equation 3.5). In this case, given only cause A, the activation of the output unit E is simply the activation received from cause A, which is zero at this

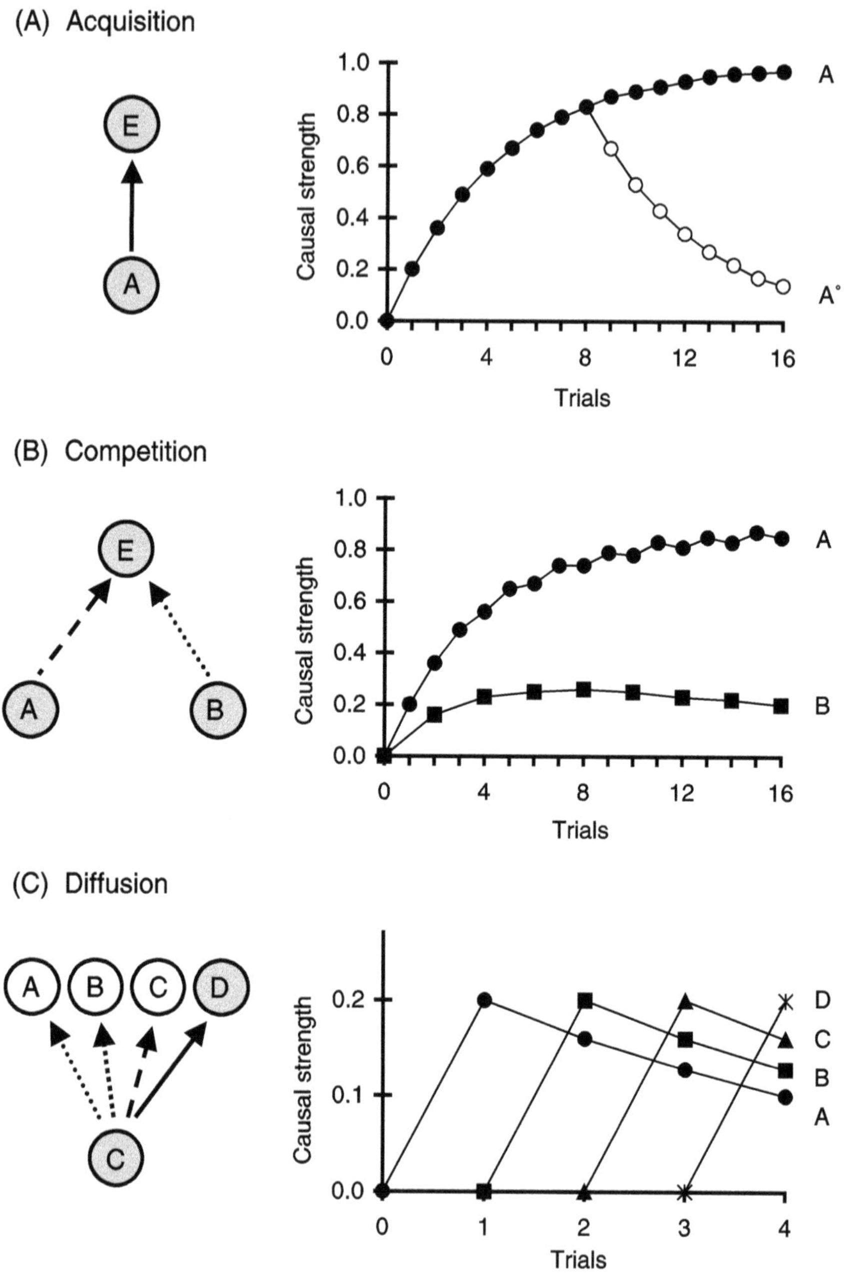

(A) Acquisition

(B) Competition

(C) Diffusion

Figure 3.2 Examples of adjustment of connection weights illustrating the property of acquisition of one cause A (panel A); of competition between a stronger cause A and a weaker cause B (panel B); and of diffusion between a single cause and effects A to D (panel C). Gray denotes an active unit, whereas white denotes a non-active unit. Full lines denote strong connectionist weights, whereas broken lines denote weaker connection weights (shorter line segments indicate weaker weights).

point. The output activation can be understood as representing the magnitude or likelihood of the effect as *predicted* by the network on the basis of the causes (or the input) present.

Step 3. The internal activation of the output unit E (predicted magnitude or likelihood of the effect) is then compared with its external activation (the *actual* occurrence of the effect). This external activation has activation level +1 when the effect is present, and 0 when the effect is absent. In our example, given that the effect is present, there is a large discrepancy or error between the internal activation = 0 (predicted outcome) and the external activation = 1 (actual outcome), which amounts to $\delta_j = 1$ (see Equation 3.3). Thus, the network at this point seriously underestimates the magnitude or likelihood of the effect.

Step 4. To achieve a faithful copy of reality, the feedforward network reduces this discrepancy by adjusting the weights of the connections in proportion to the magnitude of the discrepancy. When the effect is underestimated, the connections are adjusted upward, and when the effect is overestimated, the connections are adjusted downward. The proportion by which the connections are adjusted is specified by the *learning rate* parameter, ε, which typically varies between 0.01 and 0.30. In the example, if the learning rate is set to 0.20, then only 20% of the discrepancy will be used to make adjustments in the connection weights. This implies that the weight of A will be incremented by 0.20, so that after the first learning trial, the connection of A will reach a weight of 0.20 (see trial 1, Figure 3.2A).

By cycling through steps 1 to 4 at each trial, the weight of A will gradually increase. This process is consistent with our intuitions and experimental evidence. When we note for the first time that a particular cause and effect covary, we tend to give a rather weak causal interpretation to it; however, when our first observation is confirmed by additional co-occurrences, then we tend to give greater causal weight (see also Chapter 4). As can be seen, the weight of A slowly converges towards +1, at which point it indicates that cause A fully explains or predicts the effect. It thus takes many experiences to shape our judgments and estimates. This principle is also known as the *sample size effect*. In contrast, when A is no longer followed by the effect (e.g. see A° from trial 9, onwards), then its weight will start to decrease and converge towards 0, at which point it indicates that A° does not explain or predict the effect. Thus, the network eventually learns the best weight of the connections that predict most accurately when the effect will occur.

The effect of sample size on the acquisition of connection weights has been documented in many areas of social judgment. For instance, when receiving more supportive information, people tend to hold more extreme impressions about other persons (Anderson, 1967, 1981), make more polarized group decisions (Fiedler, 1996; Ebbesen & Bowers, 1974), endorse hypotheses more firmly (Fiedler, Walther, & Nickel, 1999), make more extreme predictions (Manis, Dovalina, Avis, & Cardoze, 1980), agree more with persuasive messages (Petty & Cacioppo, 1984), and make more extreme causal judgments

(Baker, Berbier, & Vallée-Tourangeau, 1989; Shanks, 1985, 1995; Shanks, Lopez, Darby, & Dickinson, 1996). Although most of the evidence on causal judgments comes from animal and cognitive research (but see Försterling, 1992), Van Overwalle and Van Rooy (2001a; see Chapter 4) and Van Overwalle (2003) explored the sample size or acquisition prediction in the social domain for causal and dispositional judgments.

Competition and discounting

Discounting is the general tendency to prefer a single strong cause or stimulus as an explanation at the expense of other weaker causal candidates. In a connectionist network, discounting is produced by the property of competition that naturally falls out from the delta learning algorithm (see Chapter 5 and Van Overwalle, 1998). This property gives rise to competition between connections, so that stronger connections win over weaker ones. The term "competition" stems from the associative learning literature on animal conditioning and causality judgments mentioned earlier (Rescorla & Wagner, 1972; Shanks, 1995) and should not be confused with other usages in the connectionist literature, such as competitive networks (McClelland & Rumelhart, 1988). In fact, competition also emerges from associative learning models like the Rescorla–Wagner model (Rescorla & Wagner, 1972), which— as noted earlier—is formally identical to the delta learning algorithm and in which discounting is also known as *blocking*. One of the reasons for the widespread popularity of the Rescorla–Wagner model is that it was among the first conditioning models capable of predicting competition between weaker and stronger cues.

To illustrate the principles of competition and discounting, we now turn to a second example with two causes (see Figure 3.2B, p.42). In this example, cause A and cause B always co-occur with the effect E, but cause B is only present at every other (even) trial and thus co-occurs less often with the effect E than cause A. Hence A should be a stronger explanation for the effect than B (this paradigm is known as *overshadowing* in the conditioning literature).

By applying processing steps 1 to 4 at each trial, the two causes will incrementally acquire a substantial amount of connection strength. As expected, the strength of A increases more rapidly because it is paired more often with the effect than B. Although very similar to the previous example, one important difference is that when causes A and B are jointly present, the weighted activations from *both* causes are now summed to determine the internal activation of the output unit E. Consequently, the discrepancy with the external activation will be smaller, which slows down learning. Moreover, at a certain moment during learning, the internal activation yields an overestimation of the effect (in trial 10 the output activation sums to 1.08), resulting in a downward adjustment of the connection weights (see Figure 3.2B). If this goes on for several trials, in the long run the decrement is most detrimental for cause B because it is paired less often with effect E than cause A. Hence, the strength of A will slowly increase at the expense of the strength of B. This whole process can be understood as if the two explanations compete for the available strength, which is limited to +1, or the maximum magnitude of the effect to explain. Because of this competition, the strongest cause tends to block the acquisition of other causes, resulting in the discounting of weaker causes.

Competition is a robust finding in empirical research on animal conditioning (Kamin, 1969), human causal learning (Shanks, 1985), causal attribution (Hansen & Hall, 1985; Kruglanski, Schwartz, Maides, & Hamel, 1978; Van Overwalle & Van Rooy, 2001b; Wells & Ronis, 1982), and impression formation (Gilbert & Malone, 1995; Trope & Gaunt, 2000; Van Overwalle, 2004), although the amount of discounting may often be insufficient under some circumstances. Insufficient discounting is also termed the *fundamental attribution bias* (see Chapter 6). Interestingly, many earlier algebraic and connectionist models cannot account for increasing judgments given a greater sample size of a stronger cause A and the resulting discounting of a weaker cause B. Even the Hebbian learning algorithm (see Kashima & Kerekes, 1994; Kashima et al., 2000), which is capable of simulating sample size differences, cannot reproduce competition.

Diffusion property and infrequent information

Yet another property of the delta learning algorithm is responsible for the weakening of connections when a single input unit is connected to many output units that are only occasionally activated together. Consider a disease that may cause a variety of independent symptoms (e.g. AIDS), or a personality trait that may be expressed through a variety of behavioral manifestations (e.g. kindness). We remember less the multitude of symptoms of such a disease in comparison with a disease with a single outstanding symptom. Likewise, we remember with more difficulty a multitude of behaviors expressing a person's kindness rather than the one inconsistent act that exposed the person's aggressive tendencies.

How can the increased memory for infrequent or inconsistent stimuli be explained? Traditionally, researchers in social psychology explained enhanced recall for inconsistent behavior in terms of an activation-spreading model of memory where inconsistent information is more deeply processed so that it develops stronger lateral connections with other behavior units (Hastie & Kumar, 1979). Other researchers argued that enhanced memory for unique information is due to a fan effect, where a given amount of activation is divided between the connections fanning out to other units; the more numerous the connections, the less activation each one gets (Anderson, 1976). The diffusion property proposed by Van Overwalle and Labiouse (2004; see Chapter 8) is another, fundamentally different, mechanism. While fan-out causes a division of activation, diffusion involves the division of weights.

How does this diffusion principle explain enhanced recall of inconsistent information? The diffusion effect is driven by connections linking a single cause to multiple effects (see Figure 3.2C, p.42). The basic mechanism is that during learning about the many effects generated by a cause such as multiple behavioral expressions of a trait, each unit that reflects a specific behavior is activated only once together with the trait unit, and remains inactive while other behaviors are activated with the same trait unit. This period of inactivation results in a weakening of the trait → behavior connections, and the longer this takes, the weaker the connections become. This is not due to spontaneous decay of the connection weights. Rather, the mechanism is that each behavior unit (except the last) is inactive at some moment in learning after having been active during previous learning. This inactivity of the behavior unit is not expected by the network, and therefore leads to a weakening of the trait → behavior connections. This process continues for all the behavior units, resulting in an overall weakening of the trait → behavior connections (but less so for behaviors activated more recently).

To illustrate, after observing a first behavior A, the trait → behavior connection gains some strength (by the acquisition property). When the second behavior, B, is presented, the first behavior unit A is inactive while the trait unit is still active, and consequently the strength of the first trait → behavior A connection will be reduced. This reduction continues for all the behaviors that follow, resulting in the weakest weight for the first connections (see Figure 3.2C). In contrast, imagine a deviant behavior that is expressed only occasionally and that reflects the opposite trait. In this case, because the behavior is expressed only once, there is no further inactivation of the opposite trait. This lack of diffusion leads to enhanced recall for inconsistent information.

Summary: How do people make social inferences?

The delta learning algorithm shows several types of emergent properties that seem familiar. First, according to the acquisition property, the co-occurrence between causes and events is encoded in memory under the form of incrementally adjusted input → output connections, and making a judgment or decision simply involves re-activating or re-using these existing connections. The first process involving slow incremental adjustments captures the typical trial-and-error sequence involving causal learning about *novel experiences*, whereas the re-use of existing connections captures routine explanations in everyday life, which are typically based on reactivated *prior knowledge* and hence allow a fast choice between plausible alternatives. Both processes may be combined, resulting in more deliberative social *reasoning*. Here one first considers alternatives that prior knowledge tells us are most plausible, and then additional information or arguments are taken into account, which may lead to adjustments in connections that prepare for a final judgment. These three seemingly different processes of social judgment thus originate from the same underlying connectionist system. Most learning by the delta learning algorithm occurs when the discrepancy between what is expected and what actually happens is large. This is consistent with research demonstrating that an *unexplained* effect (e.g. a disconfirmed expectancy or a failure; Weiner, 1985) instigates considerable attributional activity, which often leads to changes of causal beliefs.

Second, when multiple alternative judgments or decisions are possible, the inherent competitive nature of weight adjustment blocks the acquisition of weaker candidates in favor of stronger ones. Such *discounting* is common in human judgments, and in particular in causal inferences, as explored in cognitive and social research (e.g. Baker, Mercier, Vallée-Tourangeau, Frank, & Pan, 1993; Chapman, 1991; Chapman & Robbins, 1990; Hansen & Hall, 1985; Kruglanski et al., 1978; Shanks, 1985; Van Overwalle & Van Rooy, 2001b). Thus, connectionist modeling conceives discounting as a part of causal induction from information. This contrasts with the original spirit of Kelley (1971), who saw discounting as part of causal reasoning on the basis of minimal information. As noted above, however, in general, both processes can be captured by a connectionist approach.

Third, according to the diffusion property, multiple manifestations of a single underlying cause or trait may lead to weaker connections than a single outstanding manifestation. This is a common finding in person impression research, where inconsistent behaviors are better remembered than consistent behaviors (for a review, see Stangor & McMillan, 1992).

AN ILLUSTRATION OF LEARNING WITH THE DELTA LEARNING ALGORITHM

A simple categorization example simulated with the FIT program will further clarify the working of the delta learning algorithm in a recurrent network. This example shows how a connectionist model learns group membership by experience. A network is presented with a pattern of associations, in which some persons are associated with an ingroup while other people are associated with an outgroup. By observing this pattern, the network will learn how to reproduce the correct group when, in a test phase, only a person is provided as an input to the network.

First, let us introduce the recurrent network architecture (Figure 3.3). In this localist representation, five units embody a simple group situation in which three persons are represented by the three lower units and the two upper units represent the ingroup and the outgroup. All units are interconnected by bidirectional connections, but not all connections will be of importance for this simulation. The FIT software was run to simulate a learning history of membership of these individuals. This program allows a user to enter a network architecture, define a learning history, specify model parameters and subsequently run the model for a number of times after which the

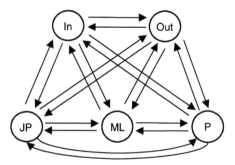

Figure 3.3 A recurrent connectionist model of group membership learning. The two upper units represent the ingroup and the outgroup. The three lower units represent three persons: JP, Jean-Paul; ML, Marie-Louise; and P, Pierluigi.

resulting or "learned" connection weights can be read off from a numeric or graphical display.

Table 3.1 shows how the training phase was represented in the FIT program. Each line in the table represents the external activation that was provided to the network at one trial. In each trial, two units were activated simultaneously (represented by "1") to indicate the association between a person and a group. As can be seen, both Jean-Paul (JP) and Marie-Louise (ML) were presented as members of the ingroup, whereas Pierluigi (P) was a member of the outgroup.

Table 3.1 Representation of the external activation to the network in the FIT program

| | Units | | | | |
Trial	JP	ML	P	In	Out
1			1		1
2	1			1	
3		1		1	

Note: empty cells represent zero activation.

Next, these trials were presented to the network. Whereas all interconnections were set to 0 initially, these connections were automatically updated after each presentation, according to the delta learning algorithm. For a clear overview of this process, the sequence of activations and weight updating for the three initial trials is given in Table 3.2.

Table 3.2A reflects the first trial in learning, where units "Pierluigi" and "Outgroup" are simultaneously activated. At the end of this trial, the connection weights in the network are updated according to the delta learning algorithm. For most connections, weight change will be 0, because the activation is 0. However, for the connection between "Pierluigi" and "Outgroup" the

Table 3.2 Activation pattern and connection weights in the network (A) after the first trial, (B) second trial and (C) third trial

(A) First trial

			JP	ML	P	in	out
	Ext		0	0	1	0	1
	Net		0	0	1	0	1

	Ext	Net		JP	ML	P	in	out
JP	0	0		0	0	0	0	0
ML	0	0		0	0	0	0	0
P	1	1		0	0	0	0	0.2
In	0	0		0	0	0	0	0
Out	1	1		0	0	0.2	0	0

(B) Second trial

			JP	ML	P	in	out
	Ext		1	0	0	1	6
	Net		1	0	0	1	0

	Ext	Net		JP	ML	P	in	out
JP	1	1		0	0	0	0.2	0
ML	0	0		0	0	0	0	0
P	0	0		0	0	0	0	0.2
In	1	1		0.2	0	0	0	0
Out	0	0		0	0	0.2	0	0

(C) Third trial

			JP	ML	P	in	out
	Ext		0	1	0	1	0
	Net		0	1	0	1	0

	Ext	Net		JP	ML	P	in	out
JP	0	0.2		0	−0.04	0	0.16	0
ML	1	1		0.04	0	0	0.2	0
P	0	0		0	0	0	0	0.2
In	1	1		0.24	0.2	0	0	0
Out	0	0		0	0	0.2	0	0

Ext, external activation; Net, net input. Weights are from top to left units.

change in weight becomes $\Delta w_{ij} = 0.2 = 0.2 * (1 - 0) * 1$, when the learning rate is set to 0.2 (see Equation 3.4).

As this is the first weight updating in the network, the weights will be updated the same way in both directions. After a few trials, however, more connections will have gained some weight and internal activation will also determine weight adjustments and, hence, weight updating will not be equal in the two directions, as can be seen from Table 3.2C.

After this first set of three trials, all trials are repeated with exactly the same external activation and calculations. The only difference is the new state of connection strengths in the network, so that the resulting values for weight updating and activation will differ from the previous simulation run. After 10 repetitions of the three learning trials, the weights pattern is as shown in

Table 3.3 Connection weights in the network after ten repetitions of the learning trials

	JP	ML	P	In	Out
JP	0	−0.62	0	0.69	0
ML	−0.53	0	0	0.77	0
P	0	0	0	0	0.98
In	0.99	0.97	0	0	0
Out	0	0	0.98	0	0

Table 3.3, and clearly shows that the network has learned which person to link with which group.

To check whether the network has really learned (i.e. whether it can generate the correct group when a person is presented), three test trials were run after each cycle. In each test trial, one person unit was activated, and the resulting activation in the ingroup-unit or outgroup-unit was read off. These results are shown in Figure 3.4. It is clear that, after ten repetitions, the network has learned to activate the correct group unit according to the person that was activated. Notice how the delta learning algorithm causes the asymptotic climb of activation values, so as not to overactivate the units.

HOW TO START YOUR OWN SIMULATIONS

Doing the exercises in this book—and especially those in this chapter (see below) and the ones on topics that interest you—is a good beginning to becoming a fluent connectionist modeler in social psychology. But then you might want to begin on your own, in a new field. How do you begin to develop your own ideas on the connectionist underpinning of a phenomenon? Although everyone has a different working style, perhaps some advice might be helpful:

- First, begin to draw the basic architecture with a few units on a piece of paper. You preferentially begin with a localist representation, as this is most easily interpretable. This drawing need not be fancy, just the bare essentials. You can make the drawing on a beer mat, a napkin, or anything that is handy when you begin to contemplate your simulation.
- Next, think how the connections might change. In this phase you could restrict yourself to the most important (usually feedforward) connections. At the start, you might want to calculate the beginning steps of a number of simulation trials by hand to see how the connections change. However, after some time, when you have done this many more

(A)

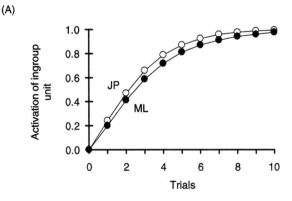

(B)

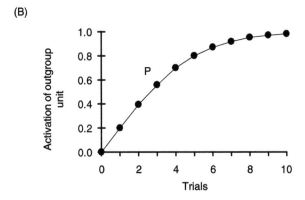

Figure 3.4 Resulting activation in ingroup (A) or outgroup (B) units for each person in function of learning (JP, Jean-Paul; ML, Marie-Louise; and P, Pierluigi).

times, you will probably have grown more confident in your understanding and intuitive predictions of weight change. Also, going through the simulations of the major emergent properties of the delta learning algorithm should help you to feel and predict how the connections change.

• After you have figured out which property might be responsible for a given phenomenon, and how the connections will develop, try it out with the FIT program. If you plan on making a number of simulations, begin with the easiest one and then go on to the more difficult phenomena.

• Although, in the early months, you might encounter some difficulties when you try to make your own simulations, when you become a more fluent connectionist modeler you will probably be able to make a simulation very quickly (in about an hour) and have a successful simulation that matches the data in about 80% of the cases. The other 20% reflect failures that can sometimes be repaired quite easily (an extra hour); but some of them require you to rethink the whole process fundamentally.

- Once your set of simulations is ready, it is now time to finalize and decide on some common parameters. Although this is not always possible, it is more convincing if you use, for instance, a common learning rate for similar phenomena. You have probably used the automatic search feature of the FIT program to figure out the most fitting parameters by now. If you want to find common parameters, you will probably start by averaging those that you used for all your simulations. Begin to test this average parameter (or something very close to this that rounds nicely to 0.05 or 0.10) with the toughest simulation and, if successful, then also test them on the easier problems. During this process, make sure that there is some reasonable psychological argument for setting your parameter at a specific value (e.g. increasing the learning rate may reflect the fact that people are quicker at learning the information given).

- It is important that the simulation is quite robust, that is, that the results you obtain are not due the specifics of your simulation. It is a good idea, therefore, to try-out other parameter values or alternative ways in which the same data can be represented (by using another type of representation for the concepts, such as a distributed encoding). You can even explore as much of the entire parameter space as possible to sort out which parameters are functionally important and which are not. My recommendation is to test the parameters values within some reasonable bounds (e.g. it makes little sense to have a learning rate beyond 0.40) and to see if this changes the results meaningfully. The articles later in this book provide several examples of these explorations into the robustness of a simulation.

- For a final publication, you need to be convinced that you thoroughly understand the underlying phenomena. This implies understanding the way the model works and which mechanisms or properties produce the results you get. Often, there is some minor variability in the simulations due to random ordering or random noise. In such cases, do not pick the simulation that best matches your data! Running more simulations to obtain a better fit would just be misleading. Try to pick the one that is most representative of your previous attempts when you were still trying them out. If you feel that the results of your simulation run are not typical of the majority of the simulations, do not use it but try to settle on the more plausible or typical simulation result. Science is a matter of replication. Hence it must be possible for other people to replicate what you have found, without too much effort.

- You are now ready to convert your simulations into a publication. The FIT program helps you to export the learning history and the graphical results into your manuscript. It also provides many statistical analyses of the simulated data, although you can also export the simulated data into your favorite statistical package.

SIMULATION EXERCISES

In these exercises, you will explore the three emergent properties of the delta learning algorithm. In addition, you can also run the illustration described in the last section of this chapter. By doing these exercises, you will become acquainted with the working of the simulation program (FIT) that was used to run these simulations. A detailed program manual is available in the Appendix at the end of the book. The text below explains only what you need to know for running the exercises on the emergent properties of the delta learning algorithm.

Start up the program. Like other programs, you do this by double clicking the FIT icon 🖳. If you are a novel user, the program will prompt you to verify the correctness of its computations. Press **OK** to test the program and wait until it signals that no errors occurred for the test Examples. Note that you should use '.' as decimal symbol, otherwise the program will signal serious computational problems.

When FIT has started up, you should see a set of menus and bars, as shown in Figure 3.5. Below the menu, you see a row of speed buttons (i.e. the speed bar). Each button is equivalent to a commonly used task in the menu and, as such, can speed-up working with the program. Below the speed bar are five tabs. By clicking one of these tabs, you can open different sheets: the **Trial** grid, the **Session** grid, the **Listing** of results, the **Log** grid or the **Graph** environment.

Figure 3.5 The menu, speed buttons and sheet tabs when opening the FIT program.

Exercise 1: Acquisition

Choose menu **File | Open Project** (Figure 3.6), search for *Acquisition.ft2* in folder *Chapter 3*, and click the **Open** button. Alternatively, you can press the 🖼 speed button.

Specifying trials

Click the **Trial** tab to open the Trial Grid. You will then see Figure 3.7. This grid defines the Trial Categories. The first two rows (in light gray) define the architecture of the network:

- In the first row, **1 : 1** indicates that there is 1 input unit and 1 output unit,

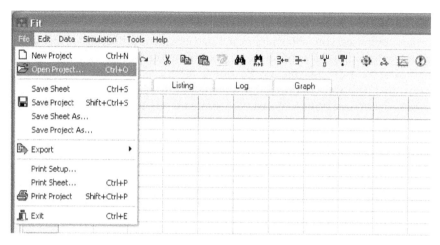

Figure 3.6 The file menu.

1:1	#	i1	o1	**Comments**
		Cause A	Effect	
1	$1	Acquisition of A		
2	20	1	1	
3				
4	$2	Acquisition of A°		
5	8	1	1	
6	8	1		
7				
8	$50	Test of Causal Infl...		
9		1	?	Cause A

Figure 3.7 The trial grid.

the **#** column contains the number of trials, the **i1** column contains the external activation levels for the input unit, and the **o1** column contains the external activation levels for the output unit. You can switch between input and output units by double clicking the top left cell of the grid containing the information **1:1** that defines the number of input and output units (alternatively, you can choose the **Data | Specify Input/Output Units** menu).

- You also have ample space to add your comments in the **Comments** column.
- In the second row, you can define a name for the units, either by double clicking, or by choosing the **Data | Column Names** menu. As you can see, the names that have been given are *Cause A* and *Effect*.

In the next rows, each of the Trial Categories defines a block of trials. These Trial Categories are denoted by a $ sign, followed by their number. You can see two Learning Trial Categories *$1* and *$2*, and one Test Trial Category *$50*. These categories are in light gray and span the whole width of the Trial Grid.

- The first Trial Category is defined as *$1* with an added description: *Acquisition of A*. The first row in this category defines 20 trials where cause A and the effect are both activated to the default level of 1. This means that cause A and the effect are always presented together, or paired together. This should lead to an increasing connection weight between cause A and the effect.
- In the second Trial Category, specified as *$2 Acquisition of A°*, after the first 8 pairings of cause A with the effect, cause A is presented alone 8 times (the activation of the effect is empty or zero). This should lead to a decrease of the connection weight between cause A and the effect.
- Finally, Trial Category *$50* provides a test of the causal strength of A. Note that all Trial Categories with number $50 or higher are considered test categories by the program. The causal strength of A is tested by prompting or priming cause A, and then reading off the resulting activation of the effect (as indicated by the *? sign*). This resulting activation will largely depend on the connection weight between cause A and the effect. For clarity, as multiple test trials are possible, the comment line provides space to label this test trial (*Cause A*).

Specifying sessions

Before you can run a simulation, you need to specify the ordering of the Learning and Test Trial Categories. Click the **Session** tab to open the Session Grid. You will then see Figure 3.8. This grid defines the order in which the Trial Categories are run for the simulation (in this case, in two different

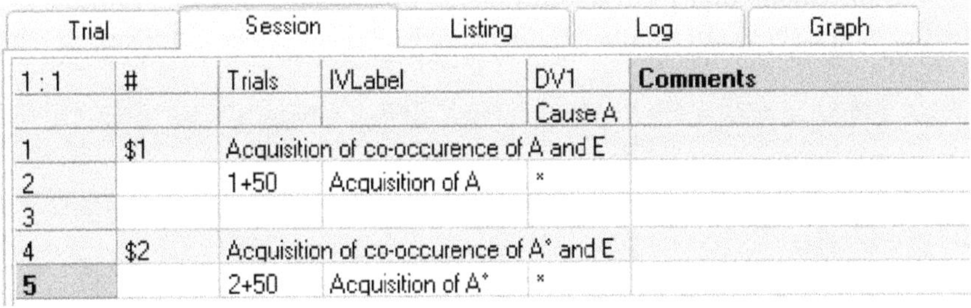

Trial		Session		Listing	Log	Graph
1:1	#	Trials	IVLabel	DV1	**Comments**	
				Cause A		
1	$1	Acquisition of co-occurence of A and E				
2		1+50	Acquisition of A	×		
3						
4	$2	Acquisition of co-occurence of A° and E				
5		2+50	Acquisition of A°	×		

Figure 3.8 The session grid.

sessions). The first two rows (in light gray) define the set up of the simulations:

- In the first row, **1 : 1** indicates that there is 1 independent variable, or IV, and 1 dependent variable, or DV; the **#** column contains the number of trials; the **Trial** column contains the trial categories that will be run; the **IVLabel** column contains the labels for the IVs; and **DV1** indicates that there is one DV. You can alter the number of IVs and DVs by double clicking the top left cell (now containing **1 : 1**; or alternatively, you can choose the **Data | Specify IV/DV Variables** menu).

  You can see that the **IVLabel** column provides a copy of the description of the Trial Categories (as just defined above) and the **DV1** column contains * symbols. This symbol is needed every time a Test Category is specified in the Trial column (in this case 50), and can be replaced by observed values that you want to predict or fit with the program (hence the name FIT). (In this latter case, the FIT program will provide correlations between these observed values and the simulated values.)

- In the second row, as in the Trial Grid, you can define a name for the IVs and DVs, either by double clicking or via the **Data | Column Names** menu. As you can see, the DV1 has been given the name *Cause A*. This label will be used throughout the simulation.

As you can see, in the next rows two sessions are specified:

- The first Session Category is defined as *$1 Acquisition of co-occurrence of A and E*. In the second row of this Session Category, the **Trial** column contains the specification *1+50*. This is a somewhat unusual input and indicates that each trial in Trial Category *$1* is immediately followed by Test Category *$50*.

- The second Session Category contains identical information, except that now Trial Category *$2* instead of *$1* is simulated.

Specifying the simulation parameters

Choose the **Simulation | Parameters** menu, or press the ⬨ speed button. In the top panel, shown in Figure 3.9, there are four drop-down list boxes, which

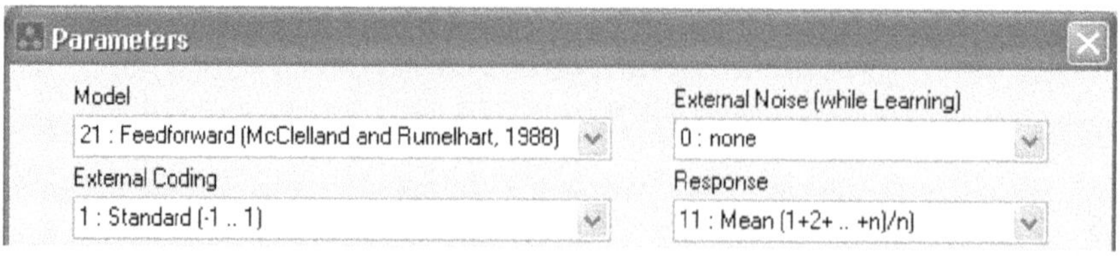

Parameters	
Model	External Noise (while Learning)
21 : Feedforward (McClelland and Rumelhart, 1988)	0 : none
External Coding	Response
1 : Standard (-1 .. 1)	11 : Mean (1+2+ .. +n)/n)

Figure 3.9 The simulation options.

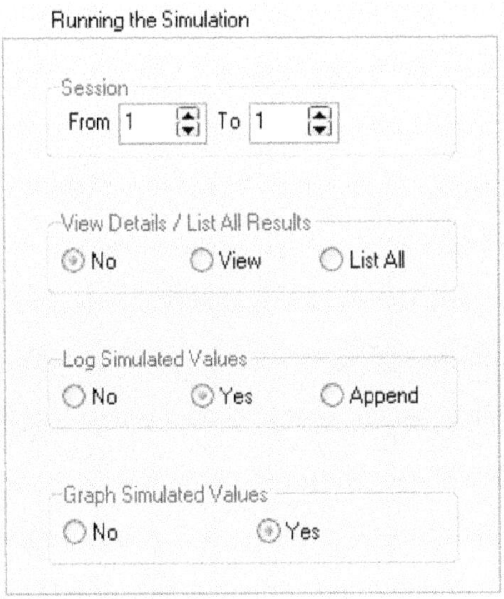

Running the Simulation

Session
From 1   To 1

View Details / List All Results
⦿ No   ○ View   ○ List All

Log Simulated Values
○ No   ⦿ Yes   ○ Append

Graph Simulated Values
○ No   ⦿ Yes

Figure 3.10 The general parameters.

list the major options. Leave them as they are but note that the model to be used is the *Feedforward* model developed by McClelland and Rumelhart (1988). Now click the **General** tab. You will see Figure 3.10. These are the parameters for running the simulation. Specify in **Session** whether you want to run session *1* or *2*, and in **Graph Simulated Values** select the button *yes* (automatically, the **Log Simulated Values** will also turn to *yes*). Leave all other parameters at *no*.

Now click the **Model** tab. As you can see in Figure 3.11, the **learning rate** is set to 0.2 (you can alter this if you want), and all other parameters are left open, or set to *auto* or *no*.

Running the simulation

To run the simulation as specified above, choose the **Simulation | Run Simulation** menu, or press the ♣ speed button. If you want to follow the simulation step by step, choose the **Simulation | Parameters** menu, press the **General** tab, and set **View Details** to *View*. Alternatively, you can hit the ᵇ speed button for a graphical display of the network with the activation levels and connections weights, or the ◯ speed button for these numerical values in a table format.

When the simulation is finished, the **Graph** tab will open automatically (see Figure 3.12). Make the following selections:

- **filter**: (*none*).
- **X-axis**: *count* (this is simply the running count of the trials).

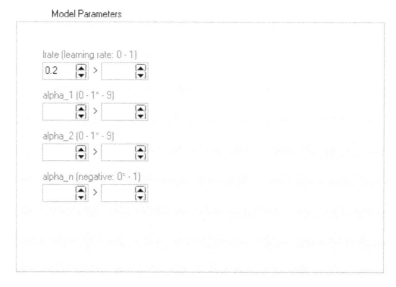

Figure 3.11 The model parameters.

- **X-axis Labels**: (*none*).
- **Y-axis Line(s)**: ~*Cause A*.

The variable names preceded by a ~ sign denote the simulated values as obtained by the Test Trial Category $50, with their name as specified in the **DV** columns of the Session Grid. After hitting the **Graph Log** button, you will see a graph of the simulation results. Part of this is shown in Figure 3.12. This is also the graph that appears in Figure 3.2A of the text. For the numerical simulation values per trial, press the **Log** tab. For the results, press the **Listing** tab. The listing is shown in Figure 3.13.

Now choose the **Simulation | Parameters** menu, press the **General** tab and select Session 2. Run the simulation by choosing **Simulation | Run Simulation**, or press the 🐆 speed button. In the graph, you will see the results of the simulation after cause A has been paired with the effect eight times, and then is presented alone eight times, as shown also in Figure 3.2A.

Exercise 2: Competition

Choose the **File | Open Project** menu or the 🖙 speed button, search for *Competition.ft2* in folder *Chapter 3*, and click the **Open** button.

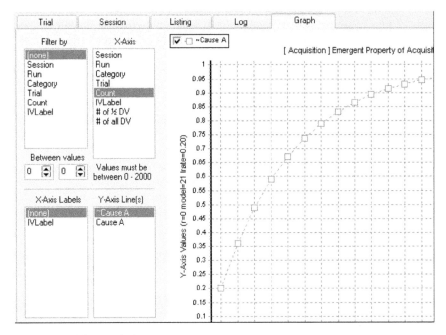

Figure 3.12 The graph sheet.

Trial	Session	Listing	Log	Graph

--- [Acquisition] --- 12/27/2005 --- 5:48:34 PM ---

Emergent Property of Acquisition

Options:
Model	Feedforward (McClelland and Rumelhart, 1988)
Coding	Standard [-1 .. 1]
Noise	none
Response	Mean (1+2+ .. +n)/n)

Parameters:
Randomized Runs	0

Model Parameters:
	lrate
Minimum	0.20
Maximum	0.20

Figure 3.13 The listing sheet.

Specifying trials and session

After clicking the **Trial** tab, you will see a learning history that is very similar to the one for the acquisition simulation. There are, however, a number of interesting differences. First, there are now two input units, labeled *Cause A* and *Cause B*. On the first row in Category *$1* only, cause A first acquires causal strength through pairing with the *Effect*, and then in the second row, cause A and cause B compete against each other in predicting the effect. No number of trials is indicated (because this will be specified later in the Session Grid), so that the program assumes only one trial each. In addition, Test Category *$50* now tests for the causal strength of both causes.

Open the Session Grid by clicking the **Session** tab. Again, this is very similar to the previous simulation, with a few noteworthy exceptions. First, the number of trials is specified here rather than in the Trial Grid. This was needed to preserve the order of the two trials (A alone, and then A with B). By specifying here the number of times Category $1 should be repeated, the whole block of trials is repeated in the same order as specified in Trial Category $1. Second, there are now two **DV**s, labeled *Cause A* and *Cause B*.

Running the simulation

Choose the **Simulation | Parameters** menu, or press the ⚙ speed button. Use the same parameters as in the previous simulation. Then choose the **Simulation | Run Simulation** menu or press the ⚒ speed button. If you want to follow the simulation step-by-step, hit the ⚒ speed button for a display of the network or the 𝒪 speed button for numerical values. The results are as shown in Figure 3.2B.

Questions

1. You can experiment a little bit with the parameters of the simulation. For instance, you can vary the number of times the Category is run (on the **Session Grid**) or the learning rate (**Model parameters** in the **Simulation | Parameters** menu). As you will see, the more trials or the faster learning, the stronger competition will be (i.e. more discounting of cause B). Conversely, with lesser trials and a slower learning rate, competition will be weaker (i.e. less discounting of cause B). Can you explain why?
2. Try the recurrent model instead of the feedforward model (choose the **Simulation | Parameters** menu and select the correct entry in the **Model options** drop-down list box). The general pattern of the result is similar to the feedforward model. Do you know why?

Exercise 3: Diffusion

Running the simulation

Open *Diffusion.ft2* in folder *Chapter 3* with the menu **File | Open Project** or the 📂 button. Basically, this simulation uses the same type of Trial and Session specifications, and also the parameters are identical. Check this by pressing the **Simulation | Parameters** menu or the ⚙ button. Run the simulation (use **Simulation | Run Simulation** menu or ♣ button). The graph shows the simulation results as shown in Figure 3.2C.

Questions

1. When you experiment with the learning rate (see the **Model parameters** in the **Simulation | Parameters** menu), you will notice that faster learning leads to more diffusion, whereas slower learning leads to diminished diffusion. Can you explain why?
2. Try the recurrent model instead of the feedforward model (see the **Model options** drop-down list box in the **Simulation | Parameters** menu). The general pattern of the result is similar to the feedforward model. Do you know why?

Exercise 4: Illustration

Running the simulation

Open *Illustration.ft2* in folder *Chapter 3* with the menu **File | Open Project** or the 📂 button. Given the extensive information about this simulation in the text, this exercise is left entirely to you to run. The parameters are set up so that you can check every step of the simulation but, if this fails, press the **Simulation | Parameters** menu or the ⊕ button. Run the simulation (use **Simulation | Run Simulation** menu or the ♣ button). The ⌕ speed button for a step-by-step progress through the simulation has already been turned on, so that you can see all the values of the model as they also appear in Tables 3.1 to 3.3. You can obtain the final weights (from Table 3.3) by pressing the **Next Run** button in the simulation details window.

Part 2

Causal attribution

4   When more observations are better than less: A connectionist account of the acquisition of causal strength *

Frank Van Overwalle and
Dirk Van Rooy

The statistical law of large numbers prescribes that estimates are more reliable and accurate when based on a larger sample of observations. This effect of sample size was investigated for causal attributions. Subjects received fixed levels of covariation, and attributions were measured after a varying number of trials. Whereas prominent statistical models of causality (e.g. Cheng & Novick, 1990; Försterling, 1992) predict no effect of sample size, adaptive connectionist models (McClelland & Rumelhart, 1988) predict that subjects will incrementally adjust causal ratings in the direction of the true covariation the more observations are made. In three experiments, sample size effects were found consistent with the connectionist prediction. Possible extensions of statistical models were considered and simulated, but none of them accommodated the data as well as connectionist models.

It is a common observation that people's judgments are often made with more confidence and accuracy when they are drawn from many cases rather than from only a few. This aspect of everyday reasoning is paralleled by the statistical law of large numbers, which prescribes that our evaluations "should be more confident when they are based on a larger number of instances" (Nisbett, Krantz, Jepson, & Kind, 1993, p.339). For instance, when making causal inferences, people make more extreme judgments after receiving more information (Baker, Berbier, & Vallée-Tourangeau, 1989; Försterling, 1992; Shanks, 1985, 1987, 1995; Shanks, Lopez, Darby, & Dickinson, 1996). Similarly, when receiving more supportive information, people tend to hold more extreme impressions about other persons (Anderson, 1967, 1981), make more polarized group decisions (Fiedler, 1996; Ebbesen & Bowers, 1974), endorse a hypothesis more firmly (Fiedler, Walther, & Nickel, 1999), make more extreme predictions (Manis, Dovalina, Avis, & Cardoze, 1980) and agree more with persuasive messages (Eagly & Chaiken, 1993). The

*   Adapted from *European Journal of Social Psychology*, *31*, 155–175. Copyright 2001 by John Wiley & Sons. Reproduced with permission of the publisher.

converging evidence in these different areas demonstrates that people have an intuitive appreciation of the law of large numbers and seem to recognize that, when making inferential judgments, more evidence is better than less.

Do people also obey the law of large numbers when they make causal judgments of social events? Most studies that documented an effect of sample size on causal explanations were conducted in the domain of experimental psychology and typically used free-operant tasks that contained little social material (Baker et al., 1989; Shanks, 1985, 1987, 1995; Shanks et al., 1996). However, in the social attribution literature, the topic of sample size has received remarkably little attention. We are aware of only one study, by Försterling (1992), who, unfortunately, did not manipulate sample size independently of covariation. Perhaps more surprising is that many major attribution models developed during the last 30 years in social psychology ignore the question of sample size altogether (e.g. Cheng & Novick, 1990; Försterling, 1989; Hewstone & Jaspars, 1987; Hilton & Slugoski, 1986; Kelley, 1967; Orvis, Cunningham, & Kelley, 1975; Read & Marcus-Newhall, 1993; but see Försterling, 1992). Even more, recent theories that explicitly claim to describe the "attribution process" (Försterling, 1989, p.624) or "causal induction" (Cheng & Novick, 1990, p.549) are silent with respect to this issue and can only account for asymptotic performance, that is, after learning has consolidated given a sufficient number of trials. Contrary to intuition, they imply that the number of observations should *not* affect people's causal estimates.

Recently, however, some models have been proposed that *do* take into account the size and order of causal information. These models either introduced an updating rule to previous statistical approaches (Busemeyer, 1991; Hogarth & Einhorn, 1992; see also Wasserman, Kao, Van Hamme, Katagiri, & Young, 1996) or are based on novel connectionist principles (Van Overwalle, 1998; Read & Montoya, 1999). Given these novel theoretical developments, the aim of this article is, first, to examine whether sample size is a reliable phenomenon in causal attribution in the social domain, and second, to evaluate how well existing models can account for this effect. Before introducing these novel approaches in some more detail, we first briefly explain why mainstream attribution models are insensitive to sample size.

STATISTICAL ATTRIBUTION MODELS

The dominant, rational view on the attribution process in social psychology is that people are intuitive statisticians who extract covariation information by tallying frequencies and applying some kind of a rule on them (e.g. Cheng & Novick, 1990; Försterling, 1989, 1992; Hewstone & Jaspars, 1987; Hilton & Slugoski, 1986; Kelley, 1967). It is assumed that perceivers tally four major types of evidence: When the cause is present and the effect is (*a*) present or (*b*) absent, and when the cause is absent and the effect is (*c*) present or (*d*) absent.

A rule is then applied on all or some of these four types of frequency (*a–d*) to estimate the degree of covariation and causality.

One of the most popular rules was formalized in the probabilistic contrast model of Cheng and Novick (1990), and "requires that people . . . estimate and compare proportions" (p.549). Because this probabilistic contrast rule closely parallels statistical measures such as χ^2, it has become widely accepted as the normative standard for computing the covariation between a cause and an effect. Other valuable statistical accounts are the Bayesian model proposed by Fales and Wasserman (1992, see also Anderson & Sheu, 1995) and Försterling's (1992) formulation of Kelley's ANOVA model, which is based on the statistical parameter of effect size (i.e. η^2).

A key element of statistical models is that the proposed rule is not based directly on raw frequencies but rather on internal proportions between these frequencies. For this reason, most of these models have difficulties explaining the effect of sample size. This can be illustrated with the following example. Take whatever values for the four types of frequencies *a–d* as discussed earlier. Now keep these frequencies fixed and repeat them a number of times. Although the overall frequencies increase, obviously, their internal proportions remain the same. Many statistical models therefore predict that the level of covariation and causality should remain identical, no matter how often these frequencies are repeated. This limitation exists for statistical models such as the probabilistic contrast model (Cheng & Novick, 1990), the Bayesian model[1] (Anderson & Sheu, 1995; Fales & Wasserman, 1992), and the ANOVA formulation (Försterling, 1992).

JUDGMENT UPDATING MODELS

Recently, a number of models have been proposed that avoid the limitations of earlier statistical approaches by incorporating some form of updating rule that makes them sensitive to sample size. These models are the step-by-step belief-adjustment model of Hogarth and Einhorn (1992) and the serial averaging strategy of Busemeyer (1991), which extends Anderson's (1981) impression formation theory into the domain of attribution. However, a major restriction is that the proposed rule involves only a single cause and

---

1 The argument that Bayesian reasoning is not influenced by sample size is based on the assumption—shared by most models—that perceivers evaluate to what extent the causal hypothesis can explain all the available data (i.e. with a probability of 1). As noted by Fales and Wasserman (1992), this assumption can be relaxed by assuming that perceivers simultaneously entertain a number of causal hypotheses with mutually exclusive degrees of causal probability, for instance, 11 hypotheses reflecting a probability of 0, 0.1, 0.2, 0.3, and so forth to 1. Because this assumption is psychologically very implausible, as it puts a great burden on human information processing, and because it is not required by any of the other models discussed, this extension is not considered in this article.

does not take into account the influence of alternative causes (e.g. discounting and augmentation). In addition, it is easy to show that these models are mathematically identical to a simplified version of the delta learning algorithm applied in connectionist models, one that deals with only one cause at a time (Wasserman et al., 1996: see also Annexe D at the end of this chapter, p.86). Because these models can be considered special instances of the more general delta learning algorithm, we ignore them for the most part and immediately turn to the connectionist approach.

A CONNECTIONIST PERSPECTIVE

A radically different approach to causal reasoning is based on connectionist principles. This perspective assumes that causal judgments are represented in memory as connections or links between the representations of causes and effects. The strength or weight of this connection reflects the perceived influence of the cause on the effect. In adaptive connectionist network models, these cause → effect connection weights vary on the basis of the evidence (Allan, 1993; McClelland & Rumelhart, 1988; Read & Montoya, 1999; Shanks, 1995; Smith, 1996; Van Overwalle, 1998).

One of the most widely accepted learning algorithms that governs this weight adjustment is the *delta learning algorithm* (McClelland & Rumelhart, 1988). This algorithm has been applied in many investigations on human categorization (see Gluck & Bower, 1988a, 1988b; Shanks, 1991) and causality (for reviews, see Allan, 1993, Shanks, 1987, 1995; Van Overwalle & Van Rooy, 1998), and is formally identical to the Rescorla–Wagner (Rescorla & Wagner, 1972) model of animal conditioning. The key assumption of the delta learning algorithm is that it attempts to reduce the error between the effect predicted (by the internal activation of the network) and the actual effect that occurred (the external activation), and it does so by adjusting the weights of the cause → effect connections. For instance, when the occurrence of the effect is underestimated, the weights are adjusted upward; and when the occurrence of the effect is overestimated, adjustments are made downward. The adjustments are made in proportion to the magnitude of the error, so that larger errors result in larger adjustments and faster causal learning (for more details, see Equations 3.3 and 3.4, p.38).

The delta learning algorithm reflects several types of well-known processes. First, the slow incremental adjustments of cause → effect connections seem to capture gradual causal learning from direct experiences, in contrast to fast routine explanations in everyday life, which are typically based on prior knowledge, that is, on the reactivation of learned connections in memory. Second, most learning in the network occurs when the discrepancy between what is expected and what actually happens is large. This is consistent with research showing that an unexplained effect (e.g. a disconfirmed expectancy or goal; Weiner, 1985) instigates considerable attributional activity, which often leads to changes of causal beliefs. Third, although the algorithm does not tally frequencies or compute statistical probabilities, it has been shown mathematically that it forces the weights to converge to Cheng and Novick's (1990) probabilistic contrast norm after a sufficient number of observations (Chapman & Robbins, 1990; Van Overwalle, 1996). Thus, the algorithm reproduces the statistical properties of covariation. The delta learning algorithm is also able to account for other familiar phenomena like discounting and augmentation (Van Overwalle & Van Rooy, 1998).

Most importantly for the present purpose, sensitivity to sample size is incorporated in the delta learning algorithm (see Acquisition of connection weights and sample size effects in Chapter 3, p.41). This can be clearly seen if we set the initial connection weights to a moderate starting value (e.g. the midpoint of the response scale). If the actual cause → effect covariation is very high, the moderate starting weight produces an underestimation of the actual effect. This error is gradually eliminated with increasing observations as each cycle through the network adjusts the connection upward toward the true (high) covariation. The same logic holds for low cause → effect covariation, which results in an overestimation and downward adjustments. Thus, the statistical law of large numbers is a natural emergent property of the delta learning algorithm.

Design and hypotheses

We have argued that people's judgments become more accurate with a growing sample size, an effect that is not anticipated by many statistical attribution formulations but that is predicted by an adaptive connectionist approach. Three experiments with a common design were devised to explore this sample size prediction. The design exploits the idea from our earlier example that simply repeating identical frequencies of information will increase sample size, but will leave unaffected statistical measures of covariation between cause and effect. This unconfounds the effect of covariation (which is kept fixed) from that of sample size (which varies).

We focus on consensus and distinctiveness covariation because they are among the prime social sources from which people infer causal attributions (cf. Kelley, 1967). Consensus refers to the extent to which behaviors or outcomes of an actor generalize to other, similar actors, whereas distinctiveness refers to the extent to which outcomes given a stimulus do *not* generalize to other, similar stimuli. High covariation of an actor is implied given low consensus (i.e. only this actor behaved in this manner) and high covariation of a stimulus is implied given high distinctiveness (i.e. the behavior occurred only with this stimulus). Conversely, low covariation is implied given the reversed patterns of high consensus or low distinctiveness. After receiving this covariation information, subjects rated the causal influence of the actor or stimulus. To examine the effect of sample size, this rating was repeated after a varying number of trials.

As noted before, existing attribution models including the probabilistic (Cheng & Novick, 1990), Bayesian (Anderson & Sheu, 1995; Fales & Wasserman, 1992) and ANOVA models (Försterling, 1992) predict that for each fixed level of covariation, the causal ratings should be identical no matter how many trials are given. In contrast, our connectionist hypothesis is that subjects will adjust their ratings incrementally in the direction of the true covariation as more evidence is given. Thus, the earlier statistical formulations essentially predict flat acquisition curves, whereas we predict increasing curves given high covariation and decreasing curves given low covariation.

EXPERIMENT 1

In the first experiment, subjects received two different levels of covariation (0% or 100%) across six blocks of trials. After each block, they rated the causal contribution of the target cause. Thus, the design of the experiment consisted of two within-subjects factors: Covariation (0% or 100%) and Block (1 to 6).

Method

Subjects

Subjects were 97 male and female freshmen from the Dutch-speaking Vrije Universiteit Brussel, who participated for a partial requirement of an introductory psychology course. They were tested in groups of one to four.

Materials

All instructions, materials and questions appeared on an IBM-compatible PC screen, and the whole experiment was monitored by MEL software. Each subject read four experimental event descriptions and four filler descriptions. Two experimental events depicted high and low consensus information involving a target actor and other comparison actors (with the same stimulus). Another two experimental events depicted high and low distinctiveness information involving a target stimulus and other comparison stimuli (with the same actor). Each event described whether the target's outcome was present or not. (To ensure correct encoding of this information, the negative wording of an outcome was always given in capitals.)

Sample size manipulation   An event description was broken down into six blocks of two trials, or 12 trials in total. The trials were presented one after the other and described as consecutive points in time. After each block of two trials, subjects had to give ratings on the target cause. Throughout all blocks of an event, the name of the target actor or stimulus remained the same, while the name of the comparison actors or stimuli differed at each block (to induce comparison with a range of comparison actors or stimuli, as is customary in social attribution research).

To illustrate, an event involving consensus manipulation of a target actor, Helen, with a comparison actor, Eva, is shown here for the first two trials. The outcome of the comparison actor was either identical or opposite (as indicated by straight brackets) depending on the covariation condition:

- Helen liked the perfume
- Eva liked [did NOT like] the perfume.

Event descriptions involving distinctiveness manipulation of a target stimulus, Corinne, with a comparison stimulus, Karen, were constructed in a similar manner as illustrated below for the first two trials:

- Jasmine deceived her friend, Corinne
- Jasmine deceived [did NOT deceive] her friend, Karen.

Level of covariation   By varying whether or not the outcome of the target actor (or stimulus) was also obtained by the comparison actors (or stimuli), covariation between target and outcome was manipulated. An illustrative summary is shown in Table 4.1. To conform to probabilistic theory (Cheng & Novick, 1990), an outcome that occurs only with the target and not with comparison cases (i.e. low consensus or high distinctiveness) is denoted by 100% covariation, while an outcome that is the same for both the target and

Table 4.1 Design of Experiment 1 illustrated for the event "Els detested the singer Karel"

		Covariation (Consensus)	
Trial Type	Actor + Stimulus	100% (Low Cs)	0% (High Cs)
Target Comparison	*Els* + Karel Ilse + Karel	Detested No	Detested Detested
		Covariation (Distinctiveness)	
Trial Type	Actor + Stimulus	100% (High Di)	0% (Low Di)
Target Comparison	Els + *Karel* Els + Peter	Detested No	Detested Detested

The target is in italics.

Cs, consensus; Di, distinctiveness; the same information in each covariation condition was repeated over six consecutive blocks with different comparison names.

comparison cases (i.e. high consensus or low distinctiveness) is denoted by 0% covariation. The level of covariation remained fixed across all blocks of an event.

The experimental events were evenly distributed over all consensus and distinctiveness conditions for each subject. The order in which they appeared was randomized for each subject, as was the order of the trials within each block. The number of action versus state verbs was counterbalanced between the events to control for potential effects of implicit causality (Rudolph & Försterling, 1997).

Procedure

Instructions appeared on the screen and the use of the rating scale was practiced. Each subject then read an event description. After each block, subjects had to rate how much influence *something special about [target actor / stimulus]* had on the outcome, using an 11-point rating scale ranging from 0 (*absolutely no influence*) to 100 (*very strong influence*), with midpoint 50 (*partial influence*). Subjects indicated their answer by moving through the scale points in steps of 10, using the left and right arrow keys. For example, to explain why "Helen liked the perfume", subjects had to judge the influence of *something special about Helen*. Similarly, to explain why "Jasmine deceived her friend, Corinne", subjects had to judge the influence of *something special about Corinne*.

Results

Because we made the same predictions for consensus and distinctiveness covariation, the ratings for the actor and stimulus target were collapsed and analyzed together. This seemed justified as preliminary multivariate analyses of variance (MANOVAs) with Measure (actor or stimulus), Covariation (0% or 100%) and Block (1 to 6) revealed that Measure did not interact with any factor. We also collapsed the target ratings in all subsequent experiments, because similar preliminary MANOVAs revealed almost no interactions with Measure.[2]

The mean attribution ratings in function of covariation condition and trial number are depicted in Figure 4.1. As expected, the ratings showed an increase over trials in the 100% covariation condition, and a decrease over trials in the 0% condition.

A repeated measures analysis of variance (ANOVA) with Covariation (0% and 100%) and Block (first vs. last) as within-subjects factors revealed

---

2   There was only one significant interaction between Measure and Block in Experiment 2, $F(3, 66) = 3.27, p < .05$, but the more relevant triple interaction including Covariation did not reach significance, $F(3, 66) < 1, p < .904$.

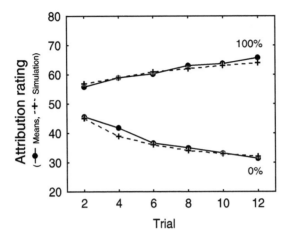

Figure 4.1 Experiment 1: Attribution ratings and feedforward simulation in function of covariation level and number of trials (100% = low consensus/high distinctiveness; 0% = high consensus/low distinctiveness).

a significant main effect of Covariation, $F(1,78) = 48.01$, $p < .0001$, indicating that subjects were very sensitive to the different levels of covariation. The main effect of Block was not significant, $F(1, 78) = 1.98$, $p = .163$. More importantly, as expected, the interaction between Covariation and Block was significant, $F(1, 78) = 35.60$, $ps < .0001$.

We predicted that sample size adjustments should occur for all levels of covariation. To verify this, we explored the interaction further by conducting trend analyses in each covariation condition. The delta learning algorithm would predict a substantial linear trend, indicating an increase or decrease across blocks, together with a smaller quadratic trend, indicating that the linear change becomes smaller toward the final rating (i.e. close to asymptote). In line with this prediction, there was a significant linear increase in the 100% condition, $F(1, 78) = 10.17$, $p < .002$, and a linear decrease in the 0% condition, $F(1, 78) = 44.72$, $p < .0001$. There was also a smaller quadratic trend in the 0% condition, $F(1, 78) = 4.77$, $p < .05$, but not in the 100% condition ($F < 1$). These results confirm our prediction that the attribution ratings were adjusted over trials as described by connectionist models.

Discussion

Our findings demonstrate that there was a reliable tendency for subjects to progressively adjust their causal ratings towards the true level of covariation with the target as more evidence was provided that confirmed their initial judgments. Given high covariation, judgments were adjusted upward; given low covariation, judgments were adjusted downward, showing an increasing sensivity to covariation given a larger sample size. This supports the connectionist model and contradicts current statistical models.

EXPERIMENT 2

Although the previous results suggest that subjects adjust their causal judgments in view of a growing sample size, a possible limitation of our procedure is that repeated ratings were requested intermittently while reading new information about the same event. It is unclear what effect this might have had on our subjects, and it might have induced a demand to change responses from trial to trial, something subjects would perhaps never do when they make spontaneous causal inferences. Moreover, this procedure is not very typical of attribution research.

To address this issue, in the next experiment we employed a design in which subjects were asked to make judgments only once at the end of the trials. The design consisted of the same within-subjects factors Covariation (0% or 100%) and Block (1 to 4) as in the previous experiment, although now the number of trials was manipulated between (rather than within) events. Our hypothesis is that subjects are sensitive to sample size even with this less contrived and demand-inducing procedure.

Method

Subjects

Subjects were 69 male and female freshmen from the Dutch-speaking Vrije Universiteit Brussel, who participated for a partial requirement of an introductory psychology course.

Materials and procedure

All instructions, materials, and questions were similar to the previous experiment, with the following modifications. Subjects read eight stories without fillers (selected randomly from a larger pool of 16 stories). Instead of interrupting the presentation of covariation information by repeated ratings, the information was presented in one whole block with a varying number of trials, and attribution ratings were requested at the end of the whole block. These blocks contained either two, four, six, or eight trials. This varying number of trials was not announced.

One other difference between the experiments deserves mentioning. Specifically, the target case in the present procedure was not repeated in each block, unlike the previous experiment where it was repeated together with the comparison case. This was done to make the task more natural and because information was not interrupted by causal ratings. As a consequence, more comparison cases were given the same total number of trials, that is, Blocks 1

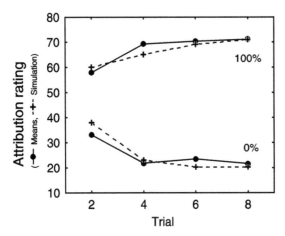

Figure 4.2 Experiment 2: Attribution ratings and feedforward simulation in function of covariation level and number of trials (100% = Low consensus/high distinctiveness; 0% = high consensus/low distinctiveness).

to 4 contained, respectively, one, three, five, and seven comparison cases, whereas they contained only one, two, three, and four comparison cases in Experiment 1. This may have facilitated the speed by which subjects adjusted their ratings.

Results

The mean attribution ratings in function of covariation condition and trial number are depicted in Figure 4.2. As expected, the target ratings showed an increase over trials in the 100% covariation condition and a decrease over trials in the 0% condition, although the ratings appear to reach asymptote more rapidly than in the previous experiment.

A repeated measures ANOVA with Covariation (0% and 100%) and Block (smallest vs. largest) as within-subjects factors revealed a significant main effect of Covariation, $F(1, 68) = 135.46$, $p < .0001$, indicating that subjects were very sensitive to the different levels of covariation. The main effect of Block was not significant, $F(1, 68) < 1$, *ns*. More importantly, as expected, the interaction between Covariation and Block was significant, $F(1, 68) = 26.93$, $ps < .0001$.

This interaction was further explored by conducting trend analyses in each covariation condition. The results revealed a significant linear increase in the 100% condition, $F(1, 68) = 12.88$, $p < .001$, as well as a linear decrease in the 0% condition, $F(1, 68) = 14.95$, $p < .0001$, together with smaller quadratic trends in the two conditions, $Fs(1, 68) = 6.60\text{--}7.84$, $p < .02$. These results confirm that causal ratings were sensitive to sample size as predicted by the delta learning algorithm.

Discussion

The results are consistent with the previous experiment and confirm that causal ratings are sensitive to sample size, even when these ratings were given only once at the end of a whole block of trials rather than repeatedly when new trial information is presented. Although we found that the causal ratings were adjusted more rapidly toward the scale extremes, this effect was presumably more apparent than real, as it might have been mainly due to a greater number of comparison cases per block in the present procedure.

EXPERIMENT 3

So far, we have seen that subjects progressively adjust their causal ratings when subsequent covariation information confirms their initial judgments. A different question is whether they would also adjust their judgments when subsequent information conflicts with their initial judgments, and how far this correction would go. This is an important question, because connectionist models have been heavily criticized on the ground that they adapt to temporal changes so rapidly and drastically that initial knowledge is fully overridden by the novel input, a feature that is known as catastrophic interference (Ratcliff, 1990).

This question was also addressed in impression formation research (Anderson, 1981). It was found that information either at the beginning or at the end of a series of items may dominate impression judgments. When judgments were made at the end of a series, initial information tended to dominate (reflecting primacy). Conversely, when judgments were given continuously while receiving novel information, final information tended to have a greater impact (reflecting recency). However, in exploring causal judgments, Wasserman et al. (1996, Experiment 3) found no primacy or recency. From a normative perspective, this latter finding is exactly what should be expected if the same amount of novel covariation information contradicts previous causal information. People should revoke previous causal judgments if there is equally strong novel information indicating that they were wrong, leading to catastrophic interference without primacy or recency.

The issue of catastrophic interference is explored in this experiment, in which subjects were given a first block of four trials in which a given target always covaried with the outcome (to build up sufficient causal strength), and then received information in a second block of four trials where the same amount of 100% covariation was given (confirming initial judgments) or was lowered to 50% (partly disconfirming initial judgments) or to 0% (entirely disconfirming initial judgments). To test whether catastrophic learning takes place in causal judgments, the latter 0% condition was compared with a control condition in which subjects received 0% covariation all the time. Attribution ratings were measured after each trial from the last trial of the first block onwards, so that the disconfirmatory process could be monitored very closely. Hence, the design consisted of two within-subjects factors Covariation (0%, 50%, 100%, or control) and Trial (4 to 8).

As before, our prediction is that the judgments will be adjusted gradually towards the novel degree of covariation, that is, a further increase of target ratings in the 100% condition, a mild decrease in the 50% condition, and a strong decrease in the 0% condition (as well as in the control condition). In addition, we predict that the disconfirming 0% information will have a catastrophic effect so that, at the end of all trials, this condition will yield the same judgments as the control condition.

In contrast, all current statistical models predict, as noted before, that consistent information over trials (100% and control condition) will not lead to changes in the attribution ratings. For inconsistent information (50% and 0% conditions), these models anticipate either no or few changes. The probabilistic contrast model predicts a sudden downward shift in the 0% condition after the first conflicting information without further changes, and a gradual decrease in the 50% condition. Likewise, the Bayesian model predicts a sudden downward shift without further changes in the 0% and 50% conditions. In contrast, the ANOVA model predicts a moderate decrease in the 50% condition, while η^2 is undetermined in the 0% condition.

Method

Subjects

Subjects were 101 male and female freshmen from the Dutch-speaking Vrije Universiteit Brussel, who participated for a partial requirement of an introductory psychology course.

Materials and procedure

All instructions, materials, and questions were similar to the first experiment, with the following modifications. Subjects read eight stories without fillers (selected randomly from a pool of 16 stories). Each story consisted of two Blocks of four trials. In the first Block, regardless of experimental condition, subjects received four trials in which the target actor or stimulus was always followed by the outcome. This allowed the target factor to acquire sufficient causal strength. In the second Block, four trials were given. These trials had a fixed covariation level. The 0% and 100% covariation conditions were similar to the first experiment, while the novel 50% covariation condition involved comparison cases, which were followed by the outcome in half of the trials (i.e. midrange consensus or distinctiveness). The design is illustrated in Table 4.2. Trial order was fixed for all subjects, as shown in the table.

In addition, there was also a control condition in which the degree of covariation was kept to 0% from the first trial. This condition involved seven comparison trials and one target trial (presented at the last trial of Block 1),

Table 4.2 Design of Experiment 3 illustrated for the event "Els detested the singer Karel"

Trial no.	Trial type	Actor + stimulus	Covariation (Consensus)		
			100% (Low Cs)	50% (Mid Cs)	0% (High Cs)
1–4	Target	*Els* + Karel	Detested	Detested	Detested
5	Comparison	Ilse + Karel	No	No	Detested
6	Comparison	Jana + Karel	No	Detested	Detested
7	Comparison	Olga + Karel	No	No	Detested
8	Comparison	Linda + Karel	No	Detested	Detested

The target is in italics.

Cs, consensus, Mid, Midrange; a similar manipulation was used for distinctiveness by varying the stimulus names instead of actor names (see also Table 4.1).

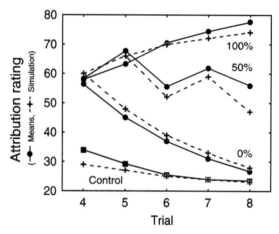

Figure 4.3 Experiment 3: Attribution ratings and feedforward simulation in function of covariation level and number of trials (100% = Low consensus/high distinctiveness; 50% = midrange consensus/distinctiveness; 0% = high consensus/low distinctiveness).

which were always followed by the outcome. For all covariation conditions, ratings of the target factor were measured after each trial, from the fourth trial (or last trial of Block 1) onwards.

Results

The mean target ratings in function of covariation conditions and trial number are depicted in Figure 4.3. As expected, the ratings showed an increase over trials in the 100% condition, a very marginal decrease in the 50% condition, and a substantial decrease in the disconfirming 0% condition which closely approached the control condition at the last trial. (The jagged-like pattern of the 50% condition is due to the fact that 50% covariation was reached on even trials only.)

A repeated measures ANOVA with Covariation (100%, 50%, 0%, and control) and Trial (fourth vs. last) as within-subjects factors revealed a significant main effect of Covariation, $F(3,98) = 94.26$, $p < .0001$, indicating again that subjects were very sensitive to the different degrees of covariation. The main effect of Trial was also significant, $F(1,100) = 20.89$, $p < .0001$, which is due to the fact that the covariation levels were not evenly distributed in the first block (they were all 100% except for the control condition). Of most importance, the predicted interaction between Covariation and Trial was significant, $F(3, 98) = 55.12$, $p < .0001$.

To explore this interaction further, and to examine whether adjustments were made after confirming trials as well after disconfirming trials, we conducted trend analyses in each covariation condition. In the confirming 100% condition, the predicted linear increase of the target ratings was significant, $F(1, 100) = 62.38$, $p < .0001$, while the quadratic trend was marginally significant, $F(1,100) = 3.86$, $p < .06$. As in the previous experiments, this result is at variance with the statistical models.

In the disconfirming 50% condition, the expected linear decrease was significant, $F(1, 100) = 4.71$, $p < .05$, although the quadratic trend was much stronger, $F(1, 100) = 11.51$, $p < .0001$, because of the jagged (non-randomized) pattern of ratings. The disconfirming 0% condition showed the predicted linear decrease, $F(1, 100) = 145.91$, $p < .0001$, just like the control condition, $F(1, 100) = 37.06$, $p < .0001$, while these two conditions also revealed a smaller quadratic trend, $Fs(1, 100) = 12.57$, $ps < .001$. More importantly, conforming to our catastrophic interference prediction, at the last trial the disconfirming 0% condition did not differ reliably from the control condition, $F(1, 100) = 2.43$, $p = .122$.

Discussion

The present results extend the previous experiments, in which covariation information confirmed initial judgments, to instances in which new information conflicts with earlier information. When subjects learned that a target covaried with an outcome, they first developed positive causal estimates. But when later information disconfirmed these earlier covariation patterns, their estimates decreased progressively the more trials were presented. When this novel information was completely opposite (as in the 0% condition), their ratings completely overrode the prior estimates, showing a typical catastrophic interference pattern and no primacy or recency. These results replicate the findings of Wasserman et al. (1996, Experiment 3) and provide further support for our connectionist hypothesis.

MODEL SIMULATIONS

The present experiments revealed adjustment effects with an increasing number of observations that can be readily explained by connectionist principles. To evaluate how closely this formulation can predict our data, we computed simulations of the present data. To simplify, we focus here on a minimalist but powerful adaptive connectionist model, known as the *feedforward* network (Van Overwalle, 1998), because this network displays the sample size effect much like more complex connectionist networks do (Read & Montoya, 1999; see also Chapter 3).

By way of comparison, we also ran simulations of two major statistical models: the probabilistic contrast (Cheng & Novick, 1990) and the ANOVA model (Försterling, 1992). However, it would be of little interest to reiterate the fact that these models fail to be sensitive to the number of observations. Therefore, we extended these existing models with additional parameters, which take into account sample size, in order to evaluate whether these extensions would be sufficient to account for the observed size effect.

Specifically, we followed the suggestion by Cheng and Holyoak (1995, p. 273) that "confidence in the assessment of a contrast is presumed to increase monotonically with the number of cases observed". That is, we weighted the major theoretical variables of the models (conditional probabilities: Cheng & Novick, 1990; sum of squares: Försterling, 1989) in proportion to the number of observations available. We allowed two such different confidence weights for frequencies that involved the presence and absence of the target cause (ω_t and ω_x, respectively). This procedure is identical to the one used recently by Lober and Shanks (2000, p.207) and parallels that of the connectionist models, where we also allowed two different learning rate parameters for target and comparison factors (ε_t and ε_x, respectively). More technical details on the model specifications are given in Annexes A–C at the end of this chapter (pp.85–86).

Method

The models were run using exactly the same order of trials and blocks as in the experiments. The connectionist model was updated after each trial and, when trial order was randomized within each block (i.e. Experiments 1 and 2), we ran 100 simulations with a random trial order within each block and averaged the results. The fit of the models was measured by taking the mean ratings for each combination of covariation level and block/trial and correlating this with the mean simulated values for those conditions. We sought the best-fitting parameters of each model by searching the maximum correlation given all admissible parameter values (Gluck & Bower, 1988a; Nosofsky, Kruschke, & McKinley, 1992). It should be noted that small changes of .05 in the obtained parameter values did not alter the results meaningfully.

To evaluate the performance of the models specifically with respect to the effect of sample size, we also computed the same correlation fit separately for each 0% and 100% covariation condition, using the same best-fitting model parameters obtained for the whole dataset.

Results and discussion

Table 4.3 displays the performance of all simulated models. The last column depicts the mean correlation across all three data sets. As can be seen in this column, all models reach substantial overall fit correlations, indicating that they accurately simulated the actual covariation to which our subjects were also very sensitive. However, the fit of the weighted ANOVA model was lowest, followed by the fit of the weighted probabilistic and connectionist models, which was about equally high. Difference tests revealed that the cor-relations of the weighted ANOVA model were significantly lower than those of the connectionist model for all three experiments ($ps < .05$, one-sided), whereas the correlations of the weighted probabilistic model were marginally lower than the connectionist model for the first two experiments ($ps < .08$ to .11, one-sided) and reached significance for the last experiment ($p < .05$, one-sided).

Of most importance are the fit correlations within the 0% and 100%

Table 4.3 Fits of the models to the data

Model	Experiment			Mean r
	1	*2*	*3*	
Weighted ANOVA				
Overall	.959	.972	.805	.912
100%	.940	.000	.748	.563
0%	.000	.000	.000	.000
	$\omega_t = .22$	$\omega_t = .10$	$\omega_t = .20$	
	$\omega_x = .40$	$\omega_x = .00$	$\omega_x = 1.00$	
Weighted probabilistic				
Overall	.988	.984	.951	.974
100%	.740	.000	.000	.247
0%	.948	.988	.993	.976
	$\omega_t = .72$	$\omega_t \geq .00$	$\omega_t = .00$	
	$\omega_x = .32$	$\omega_x = .74$	$\omega_x = .30$	
Feedforward connectionist				
Overall	.997	.992	.985	.991
100%	.985	.946	.993	.975
0%	.983	.947	1.000	.977
	$\varepsilon_t = .70$	$\varepsilon_t = .91$	$\varepsilon_t = .70$	
	$\varepsilon_x = .35$	$\varepsilon_x = .38$	$\varepsilon_x = .30$	

Cell entries are correlations between mean observed ratings and mean simulated values (over all random runs); ω_t = best-fitting weight when target is present; ω_x = when target is absent; ε_t = best-fitting learning rate for target node; ε_x = for contextual node.

conditions, because these reflect the extent to which the models are able to replicate the sample size effect. As expected, the fit was generally poor for the two statistical models; some data sets revealed zero correlations. In contrast, consistent with predictions, the connectionist model showed in all 0% and 100% conditions very high positive correlations, above 0.90 in all data sets.[3]

We predicted that Busemeyer's (1991) averaging strategy and Hogarth and Einhorn's (1992) belief-adjustment model would give similar predictions as the more general delta learning algorithm (although we used different parameters, see Annexe D, p.86). In addition, Read and Montoya (1999) argued that a recurrent network might be a better model for simulating causal judgments because it has a more extensive architecture than the feedforward network (see Annexe E, p.87). Therefore, we ran also simulations with these alternative models and found that the results were very similar to those of the feedforward network. Averaged across all conditions (i.e. Overall, 100% and 0% conditions) and all data sets, the mean correlation of the belief-adjustment model was .971 and that of the recurrent network .974, which is very close to the .981 mean correlation of the feedforward network. This suggests that it was the error-correcting delta learning algorithm, which was common to all these models, that was essential for reproducing the present data, rather than anything particular about the feedforward architecture.

To give a better appreciation of the high fit of the feedforward model, its simulation results are depicted graphically in Figures 4.1 to 4.3. Note that to visually match the simulation results with the observed data, the simulated values were regressed on the observed ratings.

GENERAL DISCUSSION

The present experiments accomplished two things. First, they demonstrated unambiguously the existence of a sample size effect in causal attribution. Second, they suggested that adaptive models using the error-correcting delta learning algorithm can account for this effect, unlike earlier statistical models (e.g. Cheng & Novick, 1990; Försterling, 1989). We now focus on each point in turn.

Sample size effect

Our findings confirm that people are quite sensitive to sample size when making causal attributions. They begin with a relatively moderate causal

3   Statistics of differential fit make little sense here because of the reduced number of observations (no higher than 10) as we computed correlations between mean observed ratings and one simulation run (for statistical models because they are independent of order) or mean simulation values (for the connectionist model).

estimate and, as more observations are made, adjust their estimate in the direction of the true covariation between cause and effect. These sample size adjustments were made when the information confirmed or disconfirmed initial judgments, and when judgments were made repeatedly during acquisition of new information or after all information was acquired.

These data suggest that people respect not only the statistical norm of covariation but also the statistical law of large numbers, that is, they are more accurate when judgments are based on a larger number of instances. This is the first study on social attributions that demonstrates people's adherence to this principle of large numbers independently from other attributional principles. A number of similar studies conducted in the past failed to unconfound the effect of sample size from covariation (Försterling, 1992) or contained material that was less rich in social content (Baker et al., 1989; Lopez and Shanks, cited in Shanks, 1995; Shanks, 1985, 1987).

However, there is a potential limitation in our research in that we did not measure subjects' confidence in their attribution ratings. Perhaps subjects would not have changed their causal ratings if given the opportunity to indicate their degree of confidence in them. If true, this would imply for Experiment 1, for instance, that after a single first piece of evidence, subjects believed that the novel cause completely influenced the outcome, but at the same time expressed uncertainty about this belief. Or, for experiment 3, it would imply that after multiple confirmatory pieces of evidence and a single disconfirmatory piece, they believed that the cause was completely irrelevant, but again expressed uncertainty about this. Such reasoning seems very implausible and anomalous. Although the present data do not directly speak to this issue, research in social attribution by Försterling (1992) did not reveal any changes in confidence ratings after manipulating sample size and covariation.[4]

Theoretical implications

Our findings may have important implications for current theories in social psychology on how people make causal attributions. Contrary to statistical models (Cheng & Novick, 1990; Försterling, 1992), our data and simulations showed that the delta learning algorithm used in adaptive connectionist models (McClelland & Rumelhart, 1988) can readily describe how people incrementally adjust their estimates when more cases are observed. This algorithm is based on the assumption that people attempt to reduce the error between their mental representation of the environment and what

---

4   This failure to find any effects of certainty measures, as well as similar failures in the experimental literature (Shanks, 1985, 1987), made us decide not to include certainty measures in the present studies.

actually happens (Read & Montoya, 1999; Smith & DeCoster, 1998; Van Overwalle, 1998).

Given this capacity, perhaps adaptive connectionist networks can simulate other judgmental biases and sample size effects, such as illusory correlation, group homogeneity, or group polarization (Ebbesen & Bowers, 1974; Fiedler, 1996), and the impact of increasing information on impression formation (Anderson, 1981), attitude change (Eagly & Chaiken, 1993), and hypothesis testing (Fiedler et al., 1999). This would place social process models in line with current conceptions of the connectionist workings of the brain (McClelland & Rumelhart, 1988; Smith, 1996).

An interesting question that arises is whether it is possible to extend mainstream statistical models with a mechanism that makes them sensitive to sample size. The simulations demonstrated that simply adding confidence weights in proportion to the number of observations, as suggested by Cheng and Holyoak (1995), does not work. Perhaps another possibility is to assume that positive (i.e. 100%) information increases confidence over trials whereas negative (i.e. 0%) information decreases confidence. However, this reasoning tends to be circular, because it confounds confidence with covariation assessment (i.e. it requires sorting-out positive from negative information independently from the model's theoretical variables that define what information is positive or negative). Moreover, it shifts the burden of proof from attribution ratings to confidence ratings, about which the statistical theories have little to say.

Another possibility is to incorporate a sort of error noise term in the statistical formulations of the probabilistic and ANOVA models and to make the assumption that increasing sample size will reduce the noise component (for a similar approach, see Fiedler, 1996). However, this extension seems implausible because the variance between subjects was typically higher at the last block than in the first block, contrary to what one would expect if noise were reduced. Taken together, we see no way of solving the sample size limitation within the boundaries of earlier statistical theories.

Perhaps a more interesting question is whether recent statistical models that incorporate an updating mechanism are more sensitive to sample size. The belief-adjustment mechanism proposed by Hogarth and Einhorn (1992), and the serial averaging strategy suggested by Busemeyer (1991), are able to accomplish this, as was documented by the simulations. However, as noted earlier, these models are limited to a single cause at the time and are therefore less powerful than the more general delta learning algorithm.

In sum, many current attribution models have difficulties in integrating and formalizing the concept of sample size, and recent proposals that have made advances on this issue are in fact identical to a restricted form of the delta learning algorithm. Whatever direction future developments of current statistical models take, our data and simulations surely highlight the need of an error-correcting learning component.

CONCLUSION

We started with the question what type of process people are using when making and adjusting causal judgments. Earlier attribution theorists used to warn that their statistical equations did not directly address the cognitive operations involved in making causal attributions, but that people probably performed a more simple, analogous reasoning (Cheng, 1997; Försterling, 1992). Although it might be argued that statistical models should be considered at a computational level (What is computed?), rather than at an algorithmic level that keeps track of the development of causal judgment (How is it computed?), the fact that the connectionist approach accommodates both levels makes this argument questionable.

We believe that connectionist models can complement or even replace earlier statistical models by providing a low-level description of the attribution process. This is consistent with the observation that causal attribution in the hustle of daily life is often effortless, preconscious, and spontaneous. The statistical models may, of course, describe causal judgments at a more explicit symbolic level, for instance, when subjects are processing verbal summary information (Baker et al., 1996; Lober & Shanks, 2000). However, recent evidence suggests that even within a verbal format, covariation information can automatically facilitate or inhibit spontaneous trait inferences (Van Overwalle, Drenth, & Marsman, 1999). Together with the present data, this seems to indicate at the very least that causal induction often proceeds without any symbolic rule.

ANNEXE

This annexe discusses how the models were specified for the simulations, and how the statistical models were extended to account for sample size.

A. Weighted probabilistic model

According to the probabilistic contrast formulation of causality (Allan, 1993; Cheng & Novick, 1990), causal strength is defined as:

$$\Delta P = P(O|T) - P(O|{\sim}T) \tag{4.1}$$

where P is a conditional probability, O is the outcome, and T is the target cause. To make the probabilistic model sensitive to the number of observations, we extended this ΔP formulation by weighting each of the conditional probabilities P with a freely estimated proportion (between 0 and 1) of the frequencies involved. That is, if ω_t denotes a proportion of the frequencies when cause T is present, and if ω_x denotes a proportion of the frequencies when cause T is absent, then the strength of a target cause can be formalized as:

$$\Delta P = \omega_t \, P(O|T) - \omega_x \, P(O|\sim T), \tag{4.2}$$

B. Weighted ANOVA model

The ANOVA formulation defines causal strength as an analog to the effect size η^2 of a standard ANOVA (Försterling, 1992), which is given by:

$$\eta^2 = SS_{between} / SS_{total} \tag{4.3}$$

where the presence of the outcome is indicated by 1 and its absence by 0 in the standard sum of squares (SS) formula. To make Försterling's (1992) model sensitive to the number of observations, we weighted η^2 with a freely estimated proportion of the frequencies involved, that is, with the same ω_t and ω_x as defined above. Thus, this becomes:

$$\eta^2 = [\omega_t \, SS_{between}] / [(\omega_t + \omega_x) \, SS_{total}] \tag{4.4}$$

C. Feedforward model

The feedforward network involves two layers of nodes (McClelland & Rumelhart, 1988). The first layer consists of two input nodes, a target node T that represents the target and a contextual node X that represents all comparison factors. The second layer consists of an output node representing the outcome. The input nodes are connected to the output nodes via weighted, unidirectional links. When a cause is present at a trial, its input node is activated to the default level 1; when a cause is missing at a trial, its input node is activated to a negative value α_n, which lies between 0 and -1 (Van Hamme & Wasserman, 1994). However, to keep the number of free parameters in all models equal, this parameter was arbitrary set at an intermediate value $\alpha_n = -.50$. Before running the simulations, the weights were set at zero starting values. We assumed that there were separate learning rates for the target node and the contextual node, denoted, respectively, by ε_t and ε_x. In addition, we also assumed that the contextual node was always activated during learning (see Van Overwalle, 1996, 1997, 1998; Van Overwalle & Van Rooy, 1998). The strength of a causal explanation is measured by activation of the cause node and reading off the resulting activation at the effect node.

D. Belief-adjustment model

We applied Equations 7a and 7b of Hogarth and Einhorn (1992) for negative and positive evidence, respectively, with learning rates as formalized in Equations 6a and 6b and hypothesis R = 0 for causal explanations. Given a subjective evaluation of 1 for positive evidence on a trial (contingency table frequencies a or $d > 0$) and an evaluation of -1 for negative evidence (frequencies b or $c > 0$), the belief-adjustment model of Hogarth and Einhorn (1992) can be restated as:

$$S_k = S_{k-1} + w_k (1 - S_{k-1}), \text{ for positive evidence} \qquad (4.5)$$

$$S_k = S_{k-1} + w_k (0 - S_{k-1}), \text{ for negative evidence} \qquad (4.6)$$

with as free parameters the initial subjective estimate, S_o, and weight adjustment rate, w_k. The serial averaging strategy of Busemeyer (1991) reduces to exactly the same set of equations. It is easy to verify that Equations 4.5 and 4.6 are a simplified version of the delta learning algorithm with only a single causal estimate, S_{k-1}, in the right-most part of the equation, whereas the delta learning algorithm incorporates the activation received from all causes (cf. int_j in Equations 3.3 and 3.4, p.38).

E. Recurrent model

For a detailed description of the recurrent model, refer to Chapter 3. The model simulations were run using the same specifications as the feedforward model, with the following additional recurrent parameters: istr = estr = decay = 1, using the linear activation rule with one internal processing cycle (McClelland & Rumelhart, 1988).

SIMULATION EXERCISES

In these exercises, we explore the feedforward simulations of the three experiments, and you can experiment yourself with the simulation of the other algebraic and connectionist models. You are expected to have some experience with the FIT program, for instance by having completed some of the exercises in Chapter 3, which explain the working of the program in somewhat more detail. The manual of the program is available in the Appendix at the end of the book.

Exercise 1: Experiment 1

Choose menu **File | Open Project**, search for *VanOverwalle+VanRooy01_1.ft2* in folder *Chapter 4*, and click the **Open** button. Alternatively, you can press the ☞ speed button.

Specifying trails

Click the **Trial** tab to open the Trial Grid, which defines the Trial Categories. The first two rows (in light gray) define the architecture of the network:

- In the first row, **2 : 1** indicates that there are 2 input units and 1 output unit, the **# column** contains the number of trials, the **i1** and **i2 columns** contain the external activation levels for the input units, and the **o1 column** contains the external activation levels for the output unit. You can switch between input and output units by double clicking the top left cell of the grid containing the **2 : 1** information, which defines the number of input and output units (alternatively, you can choose the **Data | Specify Input/Output Units** menu).
- You have also ample space to add your comments in the **Comments column**.
- In the second row, you can define a name for the units, either by double clicking, or by choosing the **Data | Edit Column Names** menu. As you can see, the names that have been given are *Target* and *Context* for the input units, and *Effect* for the output unit.

In the next rows, Trial Categories each define a block of trials. They are denoted by a $ sign, followed by their number (in light gray spanning the whole grid width). You can see two Learning Trail Categories *$1* and *$2*, one Special Learning Category *$–1*, and one Test Trial Category *$50*:

- The first Learning Category is defined as *$1*, with the description added: *100% = 100% – 0%*. The calculation stems from the probabilistic contrast model, and indicates that the target cause covariates for 100% (or always) with the effect, while the context cause(s) covariate for 0% (or never) with the effect. Hence, the net causal strength is 100%. This should also be clear from the first and second row in Trial Category $1. In the first row, the target cause (as well as the context, which is assumed to be always present) is paired with the effect, while in the second row, the context only is present and the effect is not. This should lead to an increasing connection weight between the target cause and the effect, in comparison with the context cause which loses connection weight.
- The second Learning Category is specified as *$2*, with the description added: *0% = 100% – 100%*. This calculation indicates that both the target and context cause covariate for 100% (or always) with the effect, so that the net causal strength is 0%. This can also be seen in the first and second row in Trial Category $2. In the first row, the target cause (as well as the context, which is assumed to be always present) is paired with the effect, and in the second row the context is also paired with the effect. This should lead to a decreasing connection weight between the target cause and the effect, because the context cause will gain connection weight on its own and so will lead to the discounting of the target cause (cf. emergent property of competition).
- The Special Learning Category *$–1* specifies that the target cause will receive special activation treatment by model parameter alpha_1. We will explain this in more detail later.

- Finally, Category *$50* provides a test of the causal strength of the target cause. The causal strength is tested by prompting or priming the cause, and then reading off the resulting activation of the effect (as indicated by the *? sign*). This resulting activation will largely depend on the connection weight between the cause and the effect.

Specifying sessions

Before you can run a simulation, you need to specify the ordering of the Learning and Test Trial Categories. Click the **Session** tab to open the Session Grid. The first two rows (in light gray) define the set up of the simulations:

- In the first row, **2 : 2** indicates that there are two independent variables or IVs and two dependent variables or DVs, the **# column** contains the number of trials, the **Trial column** contains the trial categories that will be run, the **IVLabel column** contains the labels for the IVs, **IV2** defines the second IV condition, and **DV1** and **DV2** define two DVs. Actually, there is only one DV (the strength of target cause), but in order to depict the two main conditions, 100% and 0%, by a different line in the Graph, we specify the results of the simulations in a different DV column. You can alter the number of IVs and DVs by double clicking the top left cell (now containing **2 : 2**) or, alternatively, you can choose the **Data | Specify IV/DV Variables** menu.
  You can see that the **IVLabel column** specifies the number of trials run so far, and one of the **DV columns** contains the observed values from Experiment 1. The program automatically matches the simulated values with the observed values in the column in which they are specified, and provides correlations between the observed and simulated values.
- In the second row, like in the Trail Grid, you can define a name for the **IVs** and **DVs**, either by double clicking, or by the **Data | Edit Column Names** menu. As you can see, the DVs have been given the name of the condition we are interested in *100%* and *0%*. This name will be used throughout the simulation and will define the labels of the graph lines as well.

As you can see, in the next rows two sessions are specified:

- The first Session Category is defined as *$1*, and provides a description of the trial information (as described in Trial Category $1) provided to the participants of Experiment 1. As you can see, this information is repeated six times. This description is first provided for condition 100% and then, after a *reset* of the network to its initial weights (see the **Trials column**), this is again provided for condition 0% using Trial Category $2.
- The second and third Session Category (defined as *$2* and *$3*) are copies of the 100% and of the 0% conditions that can be used to test these conditions separately.

Specifying the simulation parameters

Choose the **Simulation | Parameters** menu or press the ❀ speed button. In the top panel, four drop-down list boxes list the major options. Note that the model to be simulated is the *Feedforward* model developed by McClelland and Rumelhart (1988).

Now click the **General** tab. You will see the section for **Running the simulation**. Specify in **Session** that you want to run session *1*, and select in **Graph Simulated Values** the button *yes* (automatically, the **Log Simulated Values** will also turn to *yes*).

In the section on **Randomize Order for Learning Trials**, set **Randomize Order for All Learning Trials** to *yes*, and specify *100* runs. Leave the categories to which this applies to *1–49*. Set all other parameters to *no*.

Now click the **Model** tab. We will enter the parameters as specified in Table 4.3 and the Annexe. In the table, the learning rate of the target = 0.70 for the context = 0.35, and in Annexe C the negative activation for absent causes = −.50. Hence, the following values are entered:

- **learning rate**: 0.35 (for the context cause)
- **alpha_1**: 2 (to multiply with 0.35 to obtain 0.70). Only the learning rate of the target cause is multiplied by this value because in the Special Learning Category *$–1*, value *1* was specified for this cause only
- **alpha_n**: 0.5 (this will provide a negative activation of –0.50)

Leave all other parameters open, or set them to *auto* or *no*.

Now click the **Weights and Activation** tab. Because we want the alpha_1 activation parameters to impact on the learning rate only (and not on the activation of the unit as well), we need to set the **Alpa_1 & 2 determines ...** parameter to *Lrate Only*. Although the program output will act as if the activation was changed (when you follow the simulation step by step after pressing the ❀ or ◔ speed button), this parameter makes sure that only the learning rate is actually affected.

Running the simulation

To run the simulation as specified above, choose the **Simulation | Run Simulation** menu or press the ♣ speed button. If you want to follow the simulation step-by-step, choose the **Simulation | Parameters** menu, press the **General** tab, and set **View Details** to *View*. Alternatively, you can hit the ❀ speed button for a display of the network or the ◔ speed button for a tabular display.

After the simulation is finished, the **Graph** tab will open automatically (because you requested a graph). Make the following selections:

- **filter**: (*None*).
- **X-Axis**: *Condition* (the label you specified yourself for **IV2**).

- **X-Axis Labels**: *Trial* (the label you specified yourself for **IVLabel**).
- **Y-Axis Line(s)**: select all simulated and observed **DVs**.

The variable names preceded by a ~ sign denote the simulated values as obtained by Test Trial Category $50. After hitting the **Graph Log** button, you will see a graph of the simulation results, as they also appear in Figure 4.1. For the numerical results, press the **Log** tab.

Questions

1. You can experiment a little bit with the model parameters of the simulation. For instance, you can search yourself for the best-fitting model parameters. Choose the **Simulation | Parameters** menu or press the ⚙ speed button, and then press the **Model** tab. Enter as **learning rate**: 0.00 > 0.50 (in the **left box** and **right box**, respectively) and as **alpha_1**: 0.50 > 2.00 (in the **left box** and **right box**, respectively).
   The program will automatically search for the best-fitting parameters (turn **automatic search** *on* and turn **logging** *off* as requested by the program). You will probably end up with pretty much the same parameters as used above, although these best parameters and the correlation may differ slightly. This is because the random order is different for each run (you can select the same random order at each run by selecting a fixed value for **Random Seed**).
   Now choose the **Simulation | Run Best Fit and Graph** menu or press the ⬚ speed button. The program will automatically enter the best-fitting model parameters of the last run, will run the simulation once again, and will then make a graph. You can inspect the results from the Graph Sheet, which will open automatically.

2. What would happen if you do not alter the learning rate of the target cause, but simply assume that more activation (due to increased attention) is given to the target? To pursue this question, choose the **Simulation | Parameters** menu, or press the ⚙ speed button, and click the **Weights and Activation** tab. Because we want the alpha_1 activation parameters to impact on the activation instead of learning rate, we need to set the **Alpa_1 & 2 determine . . .** parameter back to *Activation*. To select a novel set of best-fitting parameters, press the **Model** tab. Enter as **learning rate**: 0.00 > 0.50 (in the **left box** and **right box**, respectively) and as **alpha_1**: 0.50 > 3.00 (in the **left box** and **right box**, respectively). After searching, choose the **Simulation | Run Best Fit and Graph** menu or press the ⬚ speed button. As you will notice, the same pattern or results will appear with different best-fitting parameters. This attests to the robustness of the feedforward simulations.

3. If you want to check the correlation for each of the conditions separately, choose the **Simulation | Parameters** menu or press the ⚙ speed button, and press the **General** tab. Now select **Sessions** *1* to *3*. Run the simulation.

After running the simulation, take a look at the **Listing sheet**, and you will find the correlation for each session (averaged for all 100 runs) in the last simulation.

4.   You can also explore other models. Choose the **Simulation | Parameters** menu or press the ✦ speed button, and select another model in the **Model** drop-down list box. For instance, as in Table 4.3, you might select the *modular probabilistic* model or the *modular Anova* model. Enter the model parameters as indicated in Table 4.3. The first model parameter **conf_c** reflects the confidence weights for the target cause, and the second model parameter **conf_x** reflects the confidence weight for the context cause(s). Then proceed as explained above (Question 1).

Exercise 2: Experiment 2

Choose the **File | Open Project** menu or the 🖙 speed button, search for *VanOverwalle+VanRooy01_2.ft2* in folder *Chapter 4*, and click the **Open** button.

Because this is a close replication of Experiment 1, many specifications are identical as before. The major difference is that the conditions were varied between rather than within participants. As a consequence, all conditions in the simulation are now specified as separate Learning Trial Categories. Thus, there is a first Category *$12* for the 100% condition with two trials, another Category *$14* for the 100% condition with four trials and so on. The reason that these categories need to be specified independently is that all trials in each condition were provided in a random order for all participants. Thus, simply repeating the same Learning Category *$12* (with randomization of only two trials) will not provide randomization across all trials.

Questions

Explore the same issues as for Exercise 1.

Exercise 3: Experiment 3

Choose the **File | Open Project** menu or the 🖙 speed button, search for *VanOverwalle+VanRooy01_3.ft2* in folder *Chapter 4*, and click the **Open** button. Because this experiment is a close replication of Experiment 1, many specifications are identical as before. The major difference is that there are now two additional conditions. As you can see, the Session Sheet follows the experimental procedure very closely (see text).

Questions

1.   The simulation as specified and published in Figure 4.3 is not entirely correct. By mistake, the order of trials in the 0% control condition was

randomized, but this was not the case in the actual experiment, in which trial order was always fixed. To follow the experimental procedure exactly, we need to turn off the randomization. Choose the **Simulation | Parameters** menu, or press the ☀ speed button, and click the **General** tab. In the section on **Randomize Order for Learning Trials**, set **Randomize Order for All Learning Trials** to *no* (instead of *yes*). To search for the best-fitting model parameters, choose the **Simulation | Parameters** menu or press the ☀ speed button, and press the **Model** tab. Enter as **learning rate**: 0.00 > 0.50 (in the **left box** and **right box**, respectively) and as **alpha_1**: 0.50 > 3.00 (in the **left box** and **right box**, respectively). Now run the simulation again. As you will see, the simulation is again very close to the observed values, and the obtained best fitting parameters are also in the same range as when random order was used.

2. In addition, you can explore the same issues as for Exercise 1.

5 An autoassociative model of causal reasoning and causal learning: Reply to Van Overwalle's (1998) critique of Read and Marcus-Newhall (1993)*

Stephen J. Read and
Jorge A. Montoya

Originally, this article was a response to Van Overwalle's (1998) critique of the explanatory coherence (ECHO) model of causal reasoning (Thagard, 1992) and its application to social reasoning (Read & Marcus-Newhall, 1993). However, some of these points of critique have since then become obsolete. Moreover, appreciating the full article would require reading and understanding these two previous articles and their underlying connectionist and simulation logic. Hence, in the interest of brevity and relevance, I have omitted several parts of the article that refer in detail to the articles by Van Overwalle and Read and Marcus-Newhall. What is left over are the most substantive simulations of the autoassociative (recurrent) model. These simulations reproduce: (1) Thagard's principles of causal explanation, including breadth (which accounts for most of the evidence), simplicity (the most parsimonious), being further explained (prefer explanations by other causes), and competition (take into account alternative explanations); (2) findings from the causal learning literature; and (3) asymmetries in reasoning between cause and effect. However, I begin here with the introductory paragraphs from the earlier article by Read and Marcus-Newhall (1993), as these give a flavor of causal reasoning processes and the basic ideas that underlie the first set of simulations.

Consider the following set of social interactions and their explanations:

- Joanne congratulates Ellen, saying that she just saw Bill in the jewelry store ordering an engagement ring. Ellen is delighted and goes off to plan the wedding.

Most of us would agree that Joanne, although perhaps a bit of a busybody, is just trying to be helpful to Ellen. Now suppose we also viewed the following:

- Janet tells Bob that she (Janet) is crazy about him and that she will agree to his earlier proposal if they elope immediately. Bob embraces Janet.

Here, most would agree that Janet did this because she wants to marry Bob. But now imagine that these two scenes, instead of involving two different couples, actually involve the same people.

- Joanne congratulates Ellen, saying that she just saw Bill in the jewelry store ordering an engagement ring. Ellen is delighted and goes off to plan the wedding.
- An hour later, Joanne tells Bill that she (Joanne) is crazy about him and that she will agree to his earlier proposal of marriage if they elope immediately. Bill embraces Joanne.

Most of us now would agree that in this interaction Joanne's behavior can be explained by a desire to hurt Ellen (and perhaps to marry Bill). But how do we arrive at this explanation so easily; and why do we prefer this explanation to alternative explanations proposed earlier, such as "Joanne is trying to help Ellen" or "Joanne is being a busybody"? After all, for neither of the two scenes in isolation would we explain Joanne's (or Janet's) behavior by a desire to hurt Ellen. Yet once the two scenes are presented together, and concern the same people, it is immediately obvious that that is what is occurring.

Several theorists (Abelson & Lalljee, 1988; Druian & Omessi, unpublished; Lalljee & Abelson, 1983; Read, 1987) have argued that in understanding and explaining social events, people use detailed theories about social and physical reality to construct a causal scenario or story from the events (also see Pennington & Hastie, 1986, 1988). This scenario identifies the goals and motives of the actors involved and the social and physical forces that influence them. To create such scenarios and connect the actions together, people must go beyond the information that is available in the interaction and use their knowledge about the social and physical worlds to make numerous inferences about the individuals involved and the meaning of their actions (Schank & Abelson, 1977).

However, as the previous example makes clear, in explaining social interactions people often have to choose among several alternative explanations.

How do they make this choice? Although a number of things are going on, we want to focus on one aspect of this process. We suggest that part of what people do in trying to explain such a sequence of behaviors is to try to find the explanation that best fits or is the most coherent with the events to be explained (Miller & Read, 1991; Pennington & Hastie, 1986, 1988; Read, 1987; Wilensky, 1983). In this article we experimentally examine the impact on explanatory goodness of four principles that have been proposed to underlie the coherence of explanations (Thagard, 1989, 1992).

The first principle we examine is that, all other things being equal, people should prefer the explanation that can account for more of the evidence (breadth). The second principle is that people should prefer the simplest or most parsimonious explanation, the one requiring the fewest assumptions (simplicity). The third principle is that people should prefer an explanation that can be explained. For example, an explanation in terms of someone's goals should be better if one can explain why they have those goals. The fourth principle we test is that the evaluation of explanations is competitive. That is, the goodness of an explanation depends on the availability of alternative explanations. This is closely akin to the discounting principle (Kelley, 1973).

The aim of this article is to study the operation of each of several principles independently and to establish whether each principle, in fact, plays a role in the evaluation of social explanations. How can the principle of breadth be tested? A strong test would be to give people a set of facts to be explained such that each fact considered in isolation has a narrow explanation that explains that fact quite well and better than an alternative, broad explanation. However, when all of the facts are considered together the broad explanation is viewed as a better explanation than each of the narrower ones.

To do this we developed scenarios in which there were several different facts to explain. These individual facts were chosen so that taken alone each fact had at least one strongly associated explanation. However, taken as a group the facts were better explained by a different, broader explanation. For example in the story about Cheryl, the fact that she felt tired can be explained by mononucleosis (mono); her weight gain can be explained by her having stopped exercising, and her upset stomach can be explained by a stomach virus. Yet the three facts taken together, being tired, gaining weight, and having an upset stomach, cannot be explained well by any of the narrow explanations but are better explained by the broad explanation that she is pregnant. Furthermore, as we discuss later, the principle of simplicity argues that the broad explanation will also be superior to a combination of the three narrow explanations. (From Read and Marcus-Newhall, 1993, pp.429–432)

SIMULATIONS WITH THE AUTOASSOCIATIVE MODEL

In the present simulations we do three things. First, we show that a non-linear autoassociative (recurrent) model with the delta learning algorithm can successfully simulate both learning and reasoning in Read and Marcus-Newhall's (1993) experiments, particularly Experiment 1, on the role of breadth and simplicity, and Experiment 2, on the effects of being explained by a further explanation.

Second, we demonstrate that such a model can also capture a number of phenomena from the classical conditioning and causal reasoning literature. The phenomena we simulate are: (1) conditioned inhibition, where one learns that a particular cause inhibits the likelihood of an effect; (2) positive patterning, where one learns that an effect occurs only in the joint presence of two causes; (3) negative patterning, where one learns that an effect does not occur when both causes are present but only when one or the other is present; (4) overshadowing, where a stimulus A gains less strength if it is reinforced simultaneously with another stimulus, compared with when A is been reinforced alone; (5) blocking, where having previously learned that cause A leads to an effect X makes it more difficult to subsequently learn that cause B leads to an effect X (some researchers, e.g. Baker, Mercier, Vallée-Tourangeau, Frank, & Pan, 1993; Shanks, 1985, 1991; Vallée-Tourangeau, Baker, & Mercier, 1994; Van Overwalle & Van Rooy, 1998 have argued that this is equivalent to discounting in the social literature); and (f) supercondi-tioning, where a cause A gains more causal strength if it is reinforced in the presence of an inhibitory cause B than if A had been reinforced alone (some researchers e.g. Shanks, 1985, 1991; Van Overwalle & Van Rooy, 1998 have argued that this parallels augmenting in the social literature). In the process of doing these simulations, we also demonstrate that recurrent networks can be appropriately sensitive to covariation information.

Third, we show that this model can learn asymmetric relations between causes and effects. Our ability to model asymmetries in causal learning and reasoning also allows us to capture what has been identified as a central distinction in causal reasoning: the difference between necessary and sufficient causes. For instance, a lit match is sufficient to set gasoline on fire, but it is not necessary because there are other ways the gasoline can be ignited. This difference can be captured in our network by assuming that the strength of a link from cause to effect captures the sufficiency of a cause; the stronger the link, the more likely the cause is to bring the effect about. In contrast, the link from effect to cause captures the necessity of a cause; the stronger the link, the more likely it is that the cause preceded the effect. A very strong link from effect to cause suggests that the effect is almost always preceded by that cause, therefore implying that the cause is necessary for the effect to come about[1]. Because it

---

1 Although the description of causal sufficiency is correct, the logic for causal necessity seems flawed. This can be demonstrated with a counterexample. Assume two effects and a single

cannot learn such asymmetries, because its links run only from cause to effect, Van Overwalle's (1998) feedforward model cannot learn or use information about this fundamental distinction between necessary and sufficient causes.

We now proceed to the simulations. We first demonstrate that this model can successfully simulate Read and Marcus-Newhall (1993). We then show that the model can simulate a number of classic findings from the learning literature. Following this, we demonstrate that it can successfully simulate asymmetries in causal learning and reasoning.

SIMULATION OF READ AND MARCUS-NEWHALL (1993)

In the interest of conserving space, only human data from the Cheryl scenario of Read and Marcus-Newhall (1993) was simulated (see the Introductory section, above). For all simulations reported in this article, learning proceeded as follows. First, an input vector or pattern was randomly selected from the set of learning vectors and input to the network. Then, the autoassociator went through 10 cycles of non-linear updating activations. The delta learning rule was used to calculate the error or discrepancy between the resulting internal activations and the original external inputs, and then the results were used to adjust the weights among the nodes. Each simulation went through 20 epochs, where each epoch corresponded to one complete presentation of all the input vectors in random order. The default parameters were .15 for decay, .15 for internal input (istr), and .15 for external input (estr). The learning rate parameter was set at .10. In these simulations, no noise was applied to the external input vectors; therefore, all reported results are based on single simulations.

Simulation of breadth and simplicity

The principle of breadth states that, all other things being equal, an explanatory hypothesis that explains more facts (broad explanation) is more coherent and therefore viewed as a better explanation than an explanation that explains fewer facts (narrow explanation). To test this principle, Read and Marcus-Newhall (1993, study 1) gave some of their subjects scenarios in which they read about only one of the three single facts, while other subjects read about all three facts. They found that the narrow explanations were rated as the best explanations for

cause that always co-occur together. Although the cause → effect connections will be very high, the effect → cause connections will be moderate due to the competition between the two effects in "predicting" the causes (this is equivalent to *overshadowing* discussed later). Although the cause was necessary in this example, the effect → cause linkages are far from high. Thus, it seems that the present recurrent approach cannot learn the causal necessity of a cause. A more adequate interpretation of cause → effect and effect → cause connections is given later in the section on *Asymmetry in Causal Learning and Reasoning*.

each fact taken alone. Despite this pattern of results, however, subjects rated the broad explanation as the best explanation for all facts together, in agreement with the principle of breadth (see Figure 5.2, top panel, p.102).

The principle of simplicity states that the simplest explanation, which requires the fewest assumptions, will be viewed as the best one. To test this principle, Read and Marcus-Newhall (1993, study 1) also asked their subjects to rate the conjunction of all three narrow explanations together (conjoint explanation) in explaining all facts. In agreement with the principle of simplicity, it was found that the conjoint explanation was rated as worse to explain all facts than the single broad explanation (again, see Figure 5.2, top panel).

The Cheryl scenario was used to simulate breadth and simplicity with a set of external input patterns similar to those used by Van Overwalle (1998) to train the network (see Figure 5.1 for Van Overwalle's feedforward network; in addition to the forward connections shown here, a recurrent network assumes also backward and lateral connections). In these simulations, each individual cause and its corresponding event were jointly activated or appeared 10 times, the broad cause appeared with all events eight times (appearing twice alone), the double conjunctive causes (two causes) and their corresponding events appeared three times, and the triple conjunctive causes (three causes) and their corresponding events appeared only once (Table 5.1). These external input patterns were presented to the network in random order.

After learning, to determine the extent to which the autoassociator network had learned the different associations, test vectors were presented to the

Table 5.1 Simulated learning experiences for the Cheryl scenario

		Event			
Causal factor	*Frequency*	*Felt tired*	*Gained weight*	*Upset stomach*	*Pregnant*
Narrow causes					
Mononucleosis (M)	10	10	0	0	
Stopped exercising (E)	10	0	10	0	
Stomach virus (V)	10	0	0	10	
Broad cause					
Pregnant	10	8	8	8	
Double conjunctions					
M and E	3	3	3	0	
M and V	3	3	0	3	
E and V	3	0	3	3	
Triple conjunction					
M and V and E	1	1	1	1	
Higher-order cause					
Husband wants children	5				5

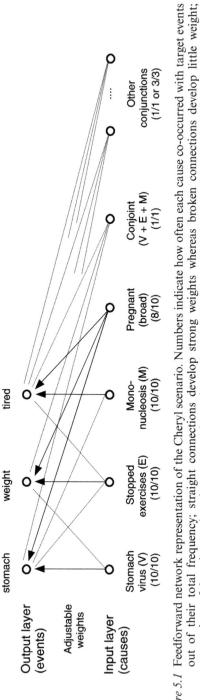

Figure 5.1 Feedforward network representation of the Cheryl scenario. Numbers indicate how often each cause co-occurred with target events out of their total frequency; straight connections develop strong weights whereas broken connections develop little weight; connections of the other conjunctions are not shown for clarity.

network and allowed to iterate for 10 cycles. As we noted earlier, because an autoassociator is a feedback (or recurrent) network, it functions as a pattern completion device, such that if a set of associations has been learned among a set of elements, when some of the nodes are activated, associated nodes are activated or "filled in". Thus, if an association has been learned between a cause and an effect, activating the cause node should lead to the activation of the effect node. Conversely, activating the effect node should lead to the activation of the associated cause node.

In these simulations, we turned on various possible effects and then looked at the resulting activation of the various causes. Test vectors contain a positive activation for the effect or effects in question, with the remaining elements set to a null activation. For instance, to test the association between fatigued and possible explanations, positive activation was provided for the fatigued element, with null activations for all other elements on the vector. We chose to do it this way because this is how Read and Marcus-Newhall (1993) did it[2].

In our model, we can choose to activate either cause or effect and see the activation of the other. Thus, we can examine reasoning in both directions between cause and effect. In contrast, Van Overwalle's (1998) feedforward model is constrained to only activating causes and examining the resulting impact on potential effects.

A test input vector results in a subsequent output pattern from the network. Consequently, if the associations between fatigued and mononucleosis, and between fatigued and pregnant, were learned, providing a test input that directly activates fatigued should also turn on or activate both mononucleosis and pregnant. However, the degree of activation of an explanation will depend on the strength of the link. If mononucleosis is more strongly associated with fatigued than is pregnancy, then turning on the fatigued node will result in greater activation of the mononucleosis node than of the pregnant node.

To test the strength of the explanations for each single fact, we had three test vectors, one for each of the individual symptoms, in which the node corresponding to that symptom was set to a positive activation and all other symptoms and causes were set to 0. To test the explanations for the multiple facts condition, we had a fourth test vector in which all of the symptoms were activated at the same time. Testing the trained network in this manner provided activation values for all of the relevant combinations of effects and possible types of explanations. The simulation results (Figure 5.2) were positively correlated with the averaged participant ratings obtained for the

---

2   It is important to note that this effect → cause testing order differs from the cause → effect order that is used in the section on *Conditioning*. The cause → effect testing order is most often used in this book, as it reflects the intuitive predictive order of antecedent causes on subsequent effects.

(A) Breadth and simplicity

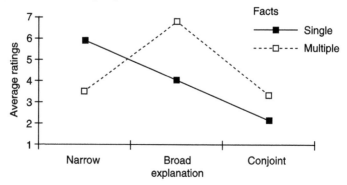

(B) Autoassociator simulation

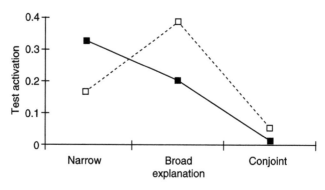

Figure 5.2 Breadth and simplicity ratings and simulations with the autoassociator with delta-rule learning.

Cheryl scenario by Read and Marcus-Newhall (1993), $r = .785, p < .001$. The averaged participant ratings for each type of explanation (narrow vs. broad vs. conjoint) for the Cheryl scenario show a clear preference for narrow causes over broad causes to explain single events (see Figure 5.2). However, in the case of multiple events, broad causes were preferred over narrow ones. Conjoint explanations for single and multiple events were the least preferred (Read & Marcus-Newhall, 1993).

These trends in the human data were captured very well by our autoassociator model, which successfully simulated both breadth and simplicity. The higher activation for the narrow explanations given single facts but higher activation for the broad explanation given multiple facts is what would be expected, given the principle of breadth. Further, the low ratings of the conjoint explanations, even in the multiple events condition, support the principle of simplicity.

Simulation of being further explained

The principle of being explained states that an explanatory hypothesis for a set of facts will be better if it can, in turn, be further explained by a higher-order explanation. To test this principle, Read and Marcus-Newhall (1993, study 2) provided half of their subjects with multiple facts scenarios in which they read about the goals of some actors, which could be interpreted as providing a higher-order explanation for the broad explanation; the other half did not read about these higher-order goals. As an example, in the Cheryl scenario, Cheryl's husband told her that he wanted children (which is most compatible with the broad pregnancy explanation). Consistent with the principle of being explained, Read and Marcus-Newhall (1993) found that subjects gave higher ratings to the broad explanation when the higher-order explanation was provided than when it was absent (Figure 5.3, top panel).

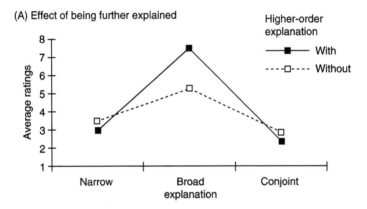

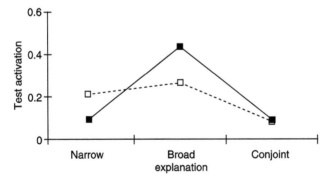

Figure 5.3 Simulations with the autoassociator of the absence and presence of a higher-order explanation for narrow, broad, and conjoint explanations.

The same set of external input patterns used for the simulation of breadth and simplicity were used for the simulation of being further explained with the addition of the higher order cause as an explanation for the event pregnant. Because we had no empirical basis for estimating the proportion of co-occurrence between a husband's wanting children and pregnancy, we decided to simply assume that the fact that a husband wants children co-occurred with his wife's being pregnant 50% of the time (see the bottom of Table 5.1)[3].

In this simulation there was only one learning history, and the impact of the higher-order explanation on pregnancy as an explanation was tested by whether it was present or absent in the test vector. We assumed that all of our participants knew the causal association between a husband's wanting children and his wife's getting pregnant, and thus the causal link should be the same in our two groups of participants. What differed between the two groups of participants in Read and Marcus-Newhall (1993) was the participants' activation of knowledge of whether the husband wanted to have children. This is best represented by whether the node corresponding to this belief is activated.

To test the strength of the pregnancy explanation for the three symptoms without the higher-order explanation, we used a test vector that had a positive activation for each of the three symptoms, but no other elements of the vector. To test the strength of the pregnancy explanation, when the higher-order explanation was added, we used a test vector that also had the higher-order explanation's node turned on. The results indicate a strong fit between the autoassociator simulation results and Read and Marcus-Newhall's (1993) participant ratings ($r = .89$, $p < .001$). As can be seen in Figure 5.3, the autoassociator model was able to capture the principle of being further explained so that the presence of the higher-order cause in the test vector resulted in greater activation for the pregnancy explanation. These results also provide a slightly stronger fit than Van Overwalle's (1998) feedforward simulation results ($r = .89$ vs. $r = .87$). Both Figures 5.2 and 5.3 show that the autoassociator with non-linear activation function and delta rule learning is able to capture participants' judgments about the Cheryl scenario.

SIMULATION OF PHENOMENA IN CONDITIONING AND CAUSAL LEARNING

We also thought it would be useful to show that the autoassociator could handle a number of classic results in the learning literature. Simulations were run using the same parameters as were used in the earlier simulations, with the learning rate set at .15. Each simulation was run with a 20-epoch limit (where 1 epoch is one complete pass through the learning set) at 10 cycles of

---

3   Table 5.1 tells another story, namely that the husband's wish to have children occurred five times and always together with pregnancy. This is also how the simulations in the exercises were set up, but the procedure as described in the text does not change the results appreciably.

updating of the network for each input pattern. In simulations where two phases were necessary, each phase was run with a 10-epoch limit. The input patterns for these simulations between units A, B, X, and sometimes the compound stimulus AB are shown in Table 5.2. The excitatory activation or

Table 5.2 Learning histories for simulations of classic learning effects

Simulation	Unit	Learning history (left to right)	Epochs
Conditioned inhibition	A	+ + + + + + + + + +	
	B	+ + + + + · · · · ·	20
	X	· · · · · + + + + +	
Positive patterning	A	+ + + + + + + + + + · · ·	
	B	+ + + + + · · · + + + + +	
	AB	+ + + + + · · · · · · · ·	20
	X	+ + + + + · · · · · · · ·	
Negative patterning	A	+ + + + + + + + + + · · ·	
	B	+ + + + + · · · + + + + +	20
	AB	+ + + + + · · · · · · · ·	
	X	· · · + + + + + + + + + +	
Overshadowing			
With B alone	A	· · · · ·	
	B	+ + + + +	20
	X	+ + + + +	
With B and A	A	+ + + + +	
	B	+ + + + +	20
	X	+ + + + +	
Blocking			
Phase 1	A	+ + + + +	
	B	· · · · ·	10
	X	+ + + + +	
Phase 2	A	+ + + + +	
	B	+ + + + +	10
	X	+ + + + +	
Superconditioning			
Phase 1	A	+ + + + + + + + + +	
	B	+ + + + + · · · · ·	10
	X	· · · · · + + + + +	
Phase 2	A	+ + + + +	
	B	+ + + + +	10
	X	+ + + + +	
Asymmetry	A	+ + · · · · · · · · ·	
	B	· · + + + + + + + + +	20
	X	+ + + + + + · · · · ·	

A plus sign represents the excitatory activation or occurrence of a unit; a dot represents the non-occurrence or null activation of a unit.

A and B, potential causes; X, effect.

occurrence of a unit is represented by pluses, whereas non-occurrence or null activation of a unit is represented by periods (i.e. full stops). If two units are excited at the same time (represented by two pluses in a column), the system learns to associate the occurrence of these two events. It is also capable of learning the lack of co-occurrence between other events (represented by a plus and a period). For example, in the learning history for asymmetry, the first column represents the presence or occurrence of A and X and the absence of B. As we read the learning history from left to right, we see that the co-occurrence among the units varies. The model is trained with a random presentation of all patterns or columns in the learning history once during each epoch.

As explained earlier, once the model learns these sets of randomly pre-sented contingencies from the learning history, it can be tested with a set of test activations composed of pluses and periods. For example, if we wished to test the impact of turning on A, we would present a vector of "+ . .", indicat-ing that A was given an input of 1 and B and X were given activations of 0. After letting the model iterate for 10 cycles, the subsequent output activations would then be examined. The resulting set of output activations after units are test activated are shown in Table 5.3.

Conditioned inhibition

The autoassociator successfully simulates conditioned inhibition, where one learns that a particular cause inhibits the likelihood of an effect. Conditioned inhibition consists of a procedure where the animal is presented with trials in which stimulus A is paired with the unconditioned stimulus X, and these trials are interspersed with trials in which stimuli A and B (the intended inhibitory cues) are presented together without the unconditioned stimulus X. This learn-ing contingency (shown in Table 5.2) gives A excitatory value over X while making B a conditioned inhibitor. Consequently, the test activations in Table 5.3 for conditioned inhibition show that A excites X (.28) but B inhibits X (−.24). Further, when we activate A and B together and look at X, we find that the inhibition from B almost totally suppresses the activation from A (.05).

Positive patterning

Positive patterning occurs in trials where the presentation of A and B together is reinforced by the occurrence of X (see Table 5.2), but neither A nor B alone is reinforced. Positive patterning is successful if one responds to the co-occurrence of A and B but does not respond to A or B alone. In modeling positive patterning and other phenomena, researchers assume that the responder develops a compound cue to represent the co-occurrence of A and B. That is, not only are A and B alone represented, but there is also a compound cue that represents their occurrence. We follow this assumption in our simulations and tests of positive and negative patterning.

Table 5.3 Resulting output activation

Simulation	Unit tested	Resulting activations			
		A	B	X	AB
Conditioned inhibition	A	.61	.28	.28	
	B	.28	.60	−.24	
	A + B	.65	.64	.05	
Positive patterning	A	.51	−.07	.05	.05
	B	−.07	.51	.06	.06
	A + B	.48	.48	.12	.12
	AB	.35	.35	.35	.56
	AB and A + B	.61	.61	.38	.59
Negative patterning	A	.56	.09	.20	.17
	B	.10	.56	.21	.17
	A + B	.59	.59	.35	.31
	AB	.30	.31	−.33	.62
	AB and A + B	.64	.64	.03	.65
Overshadowing					
With B alone	A	.48	.00	.00	
	B	.00	.58	.39	
	A + B	.48	.58	.39	
With B and A	A	.55	.29	.29	
	B	.29	.55	.29	
	A + B	.62	.62	.42	
Blocking					
Phase 2 alone	A	.55	.29	.29	
	B	.29	.55	.29	
	A + B	.62	.62	.42	
Phases 1 and 2	A	.58	.32	.39	
	B	.01	.48	.01	
	A + B	.58	.61	.39	
Superconditioning					
Phase 2 alone	A	.55	.29	.29	
	B	.29	.55	.29	
	A + B	.62	.62	.42	
Phases 1 and 2	A	.58	.41	.41	
	B	.24	.54	.11	
	A + B	.62	.65	.42	
Asymmetry	A	.56	−.19	.35	
	B	−.08	.56	.16	
	X	.27	.37	.58	

A and B, potential causes; X, effect.

Successful learning in positive patterning should produce a high output activation from X when the AB compound and the A and B components are test activated, and low output activation from X when A or B alone is test activated. Table 5.3 clearly shows that the test activation in the positive patterning simulation for A or B alone results in a low output activation from X (.05 and .06, respectively). However, the test activation of the AB compound with the A and B components produces an output activation of .38 from X. This result is not an additivity effect because this activation (AB and A+B) is considerably higher than simply adding the activation from the two separate cues.

Negative patterning

In negative patterning, one learns that A or B alone predicts X, but that A and B together do not predict X. Learning trials consist of the presentation or occurrence of A and B together without the occurrence of X but the separate presentations of A or B alone with the occurrence of X (see Table 5.2). Successful learning should produce a high output activation for X when A or B alone is test activated and essentially no output activation for X when the AB compound and A and B components are test activated. The test activation results for X (see Table 5.3) show that test activations of A or B alone produce output activations from X of .20 and .21, respectively. However, a test activation of the AB compound and the A and B components produces almost no output activation from X (.03), indicating that the compound inhibits the occurrence of X. Comparatively, activating the A and B nodes alone, without the compound, produces an activation of .35 from X. According to Miller, Barnet, and Grahame (1995), the conditioned inhibition of the AB compound (−.33) in negative patterning is not unexpected:

> Stimulus A and Stimulus B are each assumed to acquire excitatory associative strength. After many negative patterning trials, the AB unique configural stimulus is left with negative associative strength (i.e. it is a conditioned inhibitor) that is equal and opposite to the total positive associative strengths acquired by Stimulus A and Stimulus B. (p.366)

Overshadowing

Overshadowing is defined by a diminished response of X to stimulus B when B and A both occur in learning trials with X, compared with when B alone is paired with X. When A and B together co-occur with X, they essentially compete for strength with each other to predict X. In contrast, when only B co-occurs with X, it doesn't compete for strength with A. Thus, when A and B co-occur with X, because they compete they each gather less strength.

Hence, the relevant comparison in this simulation is between two learning histories, one in which A and B co-occur with stimulus X and another in which B alone co-occurs with stimulus X (see Table 5.2). Comparison of output activations for X given the learning history with B alone and the learning history with A and B together are presented in Table 5.3. When we activate the B node, the output activation from X, given a history with B alone, is higher (.39) than when B and A co-occur with X (.29), showing that B gets overshadowed by the co-occurrence of A in the second simulation.

Both overshadowing and blocking, which are discussed next, have been proposed to be quite similar to the idea of discounting (Kelley, 1971). However, as we argue in more detail later, there are some very important differences. Overshadowing and blocking deal with the initial learning of causal relationships, whereas discounting deals with the use of previously acquired causal knowledge.

Blocking

Blocking is a failure to learn an association between response X and stimulus B when B co-occurs with stimulus A, if, in previous learning trials, only stimulus A has been paired with X. In other words, the learning of an association between B and X is blocked by the previously learned association between A and X. This simulation requires two learning phases, where the first phase presents trials in which stimulus A is paired with X (Phase 1) and the second phase presents trials in which stimulus A and B are both paired with X (Phase 2; see Table 5.2). A successful simulation should produce an output activation from X when B is test activated, given Phase 2 training alone, but should produce essentially no output activation from X, given Phase 1 and 2 training. These expected results are shown in Table 5.3. As can be seen, when the simulation does not have previous experience with A and X alone (Phase 2 training alone), then the activation of X when B is activated is higher (.29) than when the simulation does have previous experience with A and X alone (Phases 1 and 2; .01).

Superconditioning

Superconditioning results when a stimulus A gains more strength when it occurs in the presence of a conditioned inhibitor B than when A occurs alone. The basic idea is that if B is a conditioned inhibitor, then for A to successfully predict X it must gain more strength to overcome the inhibitory effect of B. It requires a two-phase learning regime. Phase 1 consists of presenting A and B without the occurrence of X and presenting A alone with the occurrence of X. This leads to conditioned inhibition, which we have simulated above, and it results in B being a conditioned inhibitor. In Phase 2, A and X now co-occur in the presence of B. Successful superconditioning is evident in enhanced output activation from X when A is tested after both Phase 1 and Phase 2 have been applied successively, compared with when only Phase 2 has been presented. Table 5.3 shows that there is a stronger output activation from X when A is tested after the learning trials that consist of Phase 1 (conditioned inhibition) and Phase 2 than after the learning trials consisting of Phase 2 alone (.41 versus .29, respectively).

Thus, it is clear that this model can capture a number of classic findings in learning. Although Van Overwalle (1998) has not tested his model on these phenomena, it can probably handle them. However, in the next simulation we look at a phenomenon that Van Overwalle's feedforward model cannot capture.

ASYMMETRY IN CAUSAL LEARNING AND REASONING

Here we show that asymmetry in causal reasoning can be captured by an autoassociator with delta rule learning, something that cannot be captured by Van Overwalle's (1998) feedforward pattern associator. The autoassociator has this capability because there are two links, with opposing directions and independent weights, between each pair of nodes.

The input patterns for asymmetry at the bottom of Table 5.2 give an example of a set of learning trials that result in asymmetric learning of links. To make this concrete, assume that we are learning and reasoning about possible causes of a forest fire (X). One possibility is lightning (A), whereas another is a camp fire (B).

Although they are both plausible causes, an asymmetric direction of causality is learned by the system. Essentially, the model learns that lightning is more likely to cause a forest fire than is a camp fire. However, it also learns that if there is a forest fire and one is asked which caused it, then one is more likely to say that a camp fire is the cause. This asymmetry can be seen both in the activations when causes and effects are separately tested (see Table 5.3) and in the patterns of weights that are learned (Figure 5.4). First, we look at

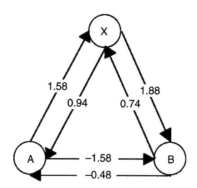

Figure 5.4 A simple, three-node autoassociator representing the learning of asymmetric weights between cause and effect. A and B, potential causes; X, effect.

the activations. We activate one possible cause A alone (lightning) and look at the other activations, and then we turn on the other cause B alone (camp fire) and look at the other activations. Cause A (lightning) alone leads to a higher activation for X (forest fire) than does B (camp fire), .35 versus .16. However, if we turn on the effect X alone (forest fire), then cause B (camp fire) is more highly activated, .37, than is cause A (lightning), .27.

The pattern of connection strengths leads to the same conclusion (see Figure 5.4). The connection from A (lightning) to X (forest fire) is stronger than the connection from B (camp fire) to X (forest fire), 1.58 versus .74. However, the connection from X (forest fire) to B (camp fire) is stronger than the connection from X (forest fire) to A (lightning), 1.88 versus .94. The model has learned that the occurrence of lightning is more likely to predict a forest fire than is the occurrence of a camp fire. However, it has also learned that if a forest fire occurs, it is more likely to have been caused by a camp fire.

Such asymmetries seem to be an important part of human causal reasoning, and our autoassociator easily captures them. Yet, because its links go only from input to output, Van Overwalle's (1998) feedforward model is completely unable to learn such asymmetries and thus is unable to reason asymmetrically.

PROBLEMS WITH VAN OVERWALLE'S (1998) PROPOSED ALTERNATIVE

A model of causal learning is not sufficient to explain causal reasoning

Van Overwalle (1998) claimed that a model of causal learning is sufficient as a model of causal reasoning as well. One does not need separate principles for learning and reasoning; rather, all one needs is an adequate model of causal learning to have a model of causal reasoning. However, there are a couple of problems with this claim.

First, it leads Van Overwalle (1998) to treat as the same thing phenomena that are related but clearly distinct. For example, he suggested that a feedforward model with delta rule learning can handle the discounting and augmenting principles identified by Kelley (1971) and Jones and Davis (1965): He claimed that discounting is the same as blocking found in studies of animal learning, and that augmenting is the same as superconditioning. Van Overwalle is not alone in this, as other authors have drawn similar parallels (e.g. Baker et al., 1993; Shanks, 1985, 1991; Vallée-Tourangeau et al., 1994; Van Overwalle & Van Rooy, 1998). However, we believe that despite their apparent similarity, in that both sets of phenomena are concerned with the allocation of confidence between causal hypotheses, the underlying processing mechanisms for the two sets of phenomena are quite different.

In blocking, when one first learns that cause A is strongly associated with effect X, if one is later presented examples of B and A covarying with X one fails to learn the new association between B and X. Once the association between A and X is strongly learned, it blocks the learning of the association between B and X. This happens because once A predicts X, B provides no new information. In terms of error-correcting learning, such as the delta rule, once X is strongly predicted by A, then when A and B are subsequently paired with X, A predicts X well enough to result in little discrepancy between the actual and predicted value of X (no error), and therefore no change is made in the weight from B to X. Learning the relationship between A and X subsequently blocks the learning of the relationship between B and X.

Although this phenomenon is similar to discounting, it is not the same thing. Blocking clearly deals with competition in the initial learning of the causal links, where initial learning of one link can prevent the learning of a different link. In contrast, discounting in the human literature clearly deals with competition among already learned causal explanations. When Kelley (1971) and Jones and Davis (1965) discussed discounting and augmenting, they were considering adults who were relying on already learned and activated knowledge. For instance, consider adults who are told that a woman behaved anxiously after being asked embarrassing questions. Because of the embarrassing questions, they should discount an anxious disposition as a cause of her anxious behavior. These adults already know that both an anxious personality trait and the embarrassing questions are possible explanations for the anxious behavior. They are not learning these relationships for the first time. Thus, in contrast to blocking, discounting does not refer to the failure to learn a causal link, but rather to reasoning on the basis of already learned causal knowledge[4].

What changes in the typical discounting situation is information about the availability or presence of a potential cause in a particular situation. As Read and Miller (1993) and Read and Marcus-Newhall (1993) have shown, discounting can be handled in an autoassociative model by assuming that there is an inhibitory link between competing explanations. As a result of the inhibitory link, increased availability of a plausible alternative will reduce the

---

4   Although discounting in the social literature indeed typically involves the question of how people make causal judgments "on the basis of already learned causal knowledge", in the recent associative learning literature (Aitken, Larkin, & Dickinson, 2001; Dickinson & Burke, 1996; Le Pelley & McLaren, 2001; Wasserman & Berglan, 1998), this phenomenon— known as backward blocking or retrospective revaluation—is also addressed from an adaptive learning perspective, captured within a single model. However, it involves a modification of recurrent models to replicate these human data. Note also that when causal reasoning is applied (e.g. as when we make causal inferences to explain a woman's anxious behavior), then we have learned something about this specific exemplar as well (e.g. this particular woman). Thus causal reasoning often implies learning about the specific exemplars on which the reasoning was applied.

activation of the other explanation. Thus, we are not looking at competition for learning of causal links, but rather at competition for the activation of concepts with previously learned causal links.

One problem with our earlier account of discounting is that we had to impose a *post hoc* negative or inhibitory link. However, one advantage of the autoassociator we use here is that it can learn the relationships among causes. Both McClure (1998) and Morris and Larrick (1995) have argued that the degree of discounting between two causes is a function of the extent to which they are positively or negatively related. For instance, Morris and Larrick (1995) showed that when two potential causes are negatively correlated one gets discounting, whereas when the causes are unrelated discounting is much weaker, and when the causes are positively correlated there is either no discounting or a tendency toward conjunctive explanations, where two causes are viewed as a better explanation than one alone[5].

Morris and Larrick (1995) made a similar distinction. They noted that in models of causal reasoning there is a distinction between induction or the initial acquisition of causal knowledge, and reasoning or attribution, the actual use of that knowledge. For instance, Kelley's (1971) analysis of variance model is a model of the acquisition of causal knowledge, whereas his causal schema model is a model of the use of preexisting knowledge for reasoning.

Van Overwalle (1998) focused almost entirely on learning, as a result of this he neglected the role that the integration of already learned causal information typically plays in causal explanation. As we have already noted, evaluating the relations among causal explanations plays a central role in causal reasoning. Scientists clearly evaluate the relation between an explanatory hypothesis and the network of theory in which it is embedded (Thagard, 1992). Also, Pennington and Hastie (1986, 1992) have shown that jurors integrate testimony and explanations in a jury trial in the form of a story that interrelates the evidence and the explanations of that evidence. Finally, consider an individual reading a novel or watching a movie. To make sense of what he or she is reading or watching, he or she must figure out how everything fits together into a causal scenario that interweaves the goals and motives of the characters (Read, 1987).

Feedforward models are inadequate as models of causal reasoning

In addition to these problems with Van Overwalle's (1998) specific proposal, there are serious shortcomings to any feedforward model of causal reasoning.

---

5   The recent studies on retrospective revaluation mentioned earlier have revealed that the relationship between causes does not matter in forward blocking, but does so in backward blocking; however, in just the opposite manner than predicted here.

First, in principle, a feedforward model does not allow one to reason in both directions between cause and effect. If causes are input nodes, as in Van Overwalle's model, then the links are from cause to effect only, and one can reason only from cause to effect. One cannot do the reverse, as there are no backward links.

Second, a feedforward model does not provide a mechanism for considering the relationships among sets of explanatory hypotheses in causal reasoning. One relatively simple example is the discounting principle. As we noted earlier, the discounting principle applies to situations in which a reasoner is dealing with the relationships among pieces of already learned causal knowledge, and what changes is information about the availability or presence of a potential cause in a particular situation. As noted above, our autoassociator can learn inhibitory links among potential causes. In contrast, there is no way for a pattern associator to learn associations among input nodes, in this case potential causes. As a result, Van Overwalle's (1998) model cannot handle the evaluation of competing explanations in already learned causal knowledge.

SIMULATION EXERCISES

These exercises enable you to explore the recurrent simulations described in the article. However, rather then using the non-linear model variant and parameters from Read and Montoya (1999), you will use the simpler linear variant for two reasons. First, the linear activation function of the recurrent model is more in line with the other simulations that you will explore in this book; it is also used in the feedforward model discussed in the previous chapter. Second, and perhaps more important, many properties of the non-linear recurrent model (the non-linear updating of the activation by cycling the activation through the network over multiple cycles) are, in fact, not necessary to make the simulations work. Hence, this becomes an interesting set of exercises, because you will learn to distinguish the essential properties of the autoassociator from those that are superfluous—at least in the present simulations.

You are expected to have some experience with the FIT program, perhaps because you have completed some of the exercises in Chapter 3 and 4. The manual of the program is available in the Appendix at the end of the book.

Exercise 1: Simulations of Read and Marcus-Newhall (1993)

Choose menu **File | Open Project**, search for *Read+Montoya99_1.ft2* in folder *Chapter* 5, and click the **Open** button. Alternatively, you can press the 🖙 speed button. This project file contains all the necessary simulation setup for all the simulations by Read and Montoya (1999) on the Read and Marcus-Newhall (1993) data, but only the results of the first simulation are shown in the Log Sheet and the Graph Sheet. The results of the other simulations can be seen in the Listing Sheet, and you can run them also by yourself.

Specifying trials

Click the **Trial** tab to open the Trial Grid, which defines the Trial Categories. The two top rows show nine input units representing the causes, and three output units representing the effects, as also listed in Table 5.1. In the second row, you can define a name for the units, either by double clicking, or by choosing the **Data | Edit Column Names** menu. You can see in Figure 5.5 the names that have been given in this project.

The Trial Categories $1 to $4 are used for the first simulation, Category $24 is additionally used for the second simulation, and Category $34 is additionally used for the third simulation:

- Learning Category $1 reflects the learning history as depicted in Table 5.1 for the first effect (Felt Tired), and Categories $2 and $3 do the same for the second effect (Gained Weight) and the third effect (Upset Stomach), respectively. These learning histories differ only to the extent that the specific effect is present or not.
- Learning Category $4 reflects the same learning history for all causes together, and differs from the previous ones with respect to the learning history involving the broader cause (Pregnant).
- Learning Category $24 is a copy of Learning Category $4, except that five trials of the higher-order cause (husband's wish to have children) was added in the last row. To avoid the unwanted effect that the three independent effects are seen as not present during these trials (while they should in fact be ignored as in Table 5.1) and so would result in a reduction of the connection weights, "i" was entered in all cells with the effect. These "i"s result in ignoring and immobilizing the weights to these effect units (for more details, see *Internal Clamp* in the help file or manual).
- Learning Category $34 is again a copy of Learning Category $4, except that now all trials with the broad cause (Pregnant) are dropped.
- The Test Categories $51 to $58 reflect forward testing (from cause to effect) by activating each relevant cause and reading off the resulting activation on the effect units. Actually, Read and Montoya (1999) used the reverse effect → cause testing direction. This direction is, however, not

Trial		Session		Listing		Log		Graph					
9:3	#	i1	i2	i3	i4	i5	i6	i7	i8	i9	o1	o2	o3
		Mono(M)	Exerc(E)	Virus(V)	Pregnant	M + E	M + V	E + V	M+V+E	Husband	Tired	Weight	Stomach

Figure 5.5 Exercise 1: Names given to the units in the trial grid.

compatible with the forward order in which their second set of simulations was tested, and with the forward order testing procedure that is generally used in simulations of causality (see the other chapters) because this order captures the intuitive idea that causes precede and predict effects.

Specifying sessions

Click the **Session** tab to open the Session Grid and to specify the ordering of the Learning and Test Trial Categories. As you can see, each single Learning Category is followed by a number of Test Categories that reflect the narrow, broad and conjoint explanations. Each of these Test Categories is given a different number (*1* to *4*) in **IV2**, and the resulting test activation is linked to **DV1** or **DV2**, which are defined as *single* and *multiple*, or alternatively, *with* and *without*. Note that for the narrow causes, only the observed values (from the study by Read & Marcus-Newhall, 1993) of its single effect were given, not those of all other narrow causes.

The above setup was chosen because it allows treating the different tests of *narrow, broad*, and *conjoint* explanation as IVs, and the single versus multiple causes as DVs (with different lines in the graph, as in Figure 5.2). In addition, in some of the Session Categories, all *narrow* explanations were put underneath each other with the same IV number, so that only their average is shown in the graph. As you can see from this and previous examples, there is much flexibility in the ways the Session Categories can be set up so that you can immediately obtain the desired Graph. However, this sometimes requires a little bit of experimenting and creativity.

In all, three Session Categories drive three simulations:

- For the first simulation *$1* on *Breadth and Simplicity*, the results of Learning Categories *$1* to *$3* (in which single causes are learned) are compared with those of *$4* (in which all causes are learned together).
- In the second simulation *$2* on *Being Further Explained*, the results of Learning Category *$24* (with higher order cause) are compared with Category *$4* (without higher order cause). Although Read and Montoya (1999) used a single learning history, you are going to use two independent histories (like in the previous simulation) to reflect the two conditions of the Read and Marcus-Newhall (1993) study. However, one could also argue that a single learning history is the better choice, as most participants know the relationship between wishing to have children and becoming pregnant. However, using a single or two histories does not change the results substantially. You can use a single learning history by changing Trial Category *$4* into *$24*.
- In the third simulation *$3* on *Competition*, the results of Learning Category *$4* (with broad cause) are compared with Category *$34* (without broad cause). This simulation was not discussed by Read and Montoya, but was part of the simulations by Van Overwalle (1998).

Specifying the simulation parameters

Choose the **Simulation | Parameters** menu, or press the ✴ speed button. In the top panel, four drop-down list boxes list the major options. In the **Model** drop-down list box, the *Linear Recurrent* model developed by McClelland and Rumelhart (1988) is chosen. If not, select that model now.

Now click the **General** tab. Specify in **Session** that you want to run session *1*, and select in **Graph Simulated Values** the button *yes* (automatically, the **Log Simulated Values** will also turn to *yes*). In addition, set **Randomize Order for All Learning Trials** to *yes*, and specify *20* runs. Leave the categories to which this applies to *1–49*. Set all other parameters to *no*.

Now click the **Model** tab. Enter a learning rate of *0.10* as in the article. Leave the other parameters blank or set them to *auto* or *no*.

Running simulation 1: Breadth and simplicity

To run the simulation as specified above, choose the **Simulation | Run Simulation** menu, or press the ♟ speed button. If you want to follow the simulation step-by-step, choose the **Simulation | Parameters** menu, press the **General** tab, and set **View Details** to *View*. Alternatively, you can hit the ♟ speed button for a display of the network or the ◯ speed button for a tabular display.

After the simulation is finished, the **Graph** tab will open automatically (because you requested a graph). Make the following selections:

- **filter**: (*none*).
- **X-Axis**: *Explanation* (or the label you specified yourself for **IV2**).
- **X-Axis Labels**: *IVLabel*.
- **Y-Axis Line(s)**: select all simulated and observed **DVs**.

The variable names preceded by a ~ sign denote the simulated values. After hitting the **Graph Log** button, you will see a graph of the simulation results. For the numerical results, press the **Log** tab.

Although we used another recurrent variant and a different testing procedure to that used by Read and Montoya (1999), the results obtained are very close to the observed data. In the Listing Sheet, you can see that the correlation originally obtained between simulated and observed means was $r = 0.933, p = 0.007$.

Running simulation 2: Being further explained

To run this simulation, you need to change a single parameter. Choose the **Simulation | Parameters** menu (or press the ✴ speed button), press the **General** tab and set **Session** to *2*.

As you can see, although you used another recurrent variant and a different testing procedure than Read and Montoya (1999), the obtained results are very close to the observed data. In the Listing Sheet, you can see that the correlation originally obtained between simulated and observed means was $r = 0.924$, $p = 0.008$.

Running simulation 3: Competition

To run this simulation, you need to change the same single parameter. Choose the **Simulation | Parameters** menu (or press the ⬆ speed button), press the **General** tab, and set **Session** to *3*.

As you can see, without the broad explanation, the other explanations gain some strength. This illustrates the principle of competition. As long as an alternative explanation (in this case, the broad explanation) was present, the other explanations were suppressed or discounted. As soon as this alternative explanation is removed, the other explanations gain more strength. The obtained results are very close to the observed data. In the Listing Sheet, you can see that the correlation originally obtained between simulated and observed means was $r = 0.929$, $p = 0.022$.

Questions

1.   For all three simulations, you can experiment with a reverse direction of testing as described in the article. To do this, open the Trial Grid by clicking the **Trial** tab. Specify in the Test Categories (*$51* and up) the effects that need to be activated (denoted by "1"), and the causes from which you read the resulting activation (denoted by "?"). The results should be close to the reported simulation results in Figure 5.2.
2.   You can also explore other models. Choose the **Simulation | Parameters** menu or press the ⬆ speed button, and select another model in the **Model** drop-down list box. For instance, you might select the *non-linear recurrent* model. Enter the model parameters as indicated in the text (**istr** = *0.15*; **estr** = *0.15*, **decay** = *0.15*, and **#cycles** = *10*). To run the simulations, choose the **Simulation | Run Simulation** menu or press the ⚘ speed button.

Exercise 2: Conditioning and causal learning

Choose menu **File | Open Project**, (or press the 📂 speed button) search for *Read+Montoya99_2.ft2* in folder *Chapter 5*, and click the **Open** button. This project file contains all the necessary simulation set-up for all the simulations by Read and Montoya (1999) on classical conditioning and causal learning phenomena. Only the results of the first simulation are shown in the Log Sheet and the Graph Sheet. The results of the other simulations can be seen in the Listing Sheet, and you can also run them yourself.

Specifying trials

Click the **Trial** tab to open the Trial Grid, which defines the Trial Categories. The two top rows show three input units representing the causes A, B, and the conjoint AB, and one output unit representing the effect X, as also listed in Table 5.2. In the second row, you can define a name for the units, either by double clicking or by choosing the **Data | Edit Column Names** menu. The names already given are, evidently, *Cause A, Cause B, Cause AB*, and *Effect X*:

- The Trial Grid follows the specifications in Table 5.2 exactly. Categories *$1* to *$10* reflect all 10 simulations in the same order. One column in the learning history of the table corresponds with one (set of) rows in the Trial Grid.
- The Test Categories *$51* to *$54* reflect the forward testing procedures (from cause to effect) by activating each relevant cause and reading off the resulting activation on the effect units. For simulation 10 on *Asymmetry*, the reverse testing direction in Test Categories *$61* to *$64* is also applied.

Specifying sessions

Click the **Session** tab to open the Session Grid and to specify the ordering of the Learning and Test Trial Categories. As you can see, each Session Category reflects the simulation of one conditioning phenomenon, followed by Test Categories of the single *cause A* and *cause B*, their *compound AB* and multiple causes *A+B*. Each of these Test Categories is given a different number (*1* to *4*) in **IV2**, and the resulting test activation is linked to **DV1** or **DV2**, which are labeled *Cause* (for forward testing) and *Indicator* (for backward testing). The term "indicator" is used to reflect a broad range of cues that serve as indictor of the "effect". A typical example is a symptom that serves as an indicator for a disease, but does not cause it.

As you have gone through the simulations for the previous exercise, you already have some experience with the flexibility in setting up Session Categories so that you can obtain the required Graph with only a little bit of trying and experimenting.

Specifying the simulation parameters

Choose the **Simulation | Parameters** menu, or press the ⚙ speed button. In the top panel, four drop-down list boxes list the major options. In the **Model** drop-down list box, the *Linear Recurrent* model developed by McClelland and Rumelhart (1988) is chosen.

Now click the **General** tab. Specify in **Session** that you want to run session *1*, and select in **Graph Simulated Values** the button *yes* (automatically, the **Log**

Simulated Values will also turn to *yes*). In addition, set **Randomize Order for All Learning Trials** to *yes*, and specify *20* runs. Leave the categories to which this applies to *1–49*. Set all other parameters to *no*.

Now click the **Model** tab. Enter a learning rate of *0.10* as in the article. Leave the other parameters blank, or set them to *auto* or *no*.

Running simulation 1: Conditioned inhibition

To run the simulation, choose the **Simulation | Run Simulation** menu or press the 🐜 speed button. If you want to follow the simulation step by step, choose the **Simulation | Parameters** menu, press the **General** tab, and set **View Details** to *View*. Alternatively, you can hit the 🐾 or ⌀ speed button.

After the simulation is finished, the **Graph** tab will open automatically (because you requested a graph). Make the following selections:

- **filter**: (*none*).
- **X-Axis**: *Condition* (or the label you specified yourself for **IV2**).
- **X-Axis Labels**: *IVLabel*.
- **Y-Axis Line(s)**: select all simulated **DVs** (preceded by a ~ sign).
- Make sure the **Regress** check box is not checked.

After hitting the **Graph Log** button, you will see a graph of the simulation results. For the numerical results, press the **Log** tab.

However, the best way to see the results of this and all other simulations is by looking at the Listing Sheet (hit the **Listing** tab to open). As you can see, cause B became an inhibitor (negative predictor of X) in comparison with cause A who was a positive predictor of X. Even using a different model than Read and Montoya (1999), the results are essentially the same.

Running simulations 2–10

By simply selecting the next Session, you now can run all simulations. Choose **Simulation | Parameters** (or press the 🌐 speed button), press the **General** tab, and set **Session** to the number required. The results confirm that:

- For *positive patterning* (Session 2), the AB compound yields higher values than either of the causes alone.
- For *negative patterning* (Session 3), the AB compound yields negative values while none of the independent causes yields negative values.
- For *overshadowing*, when A and B co-occur with X, B yields lower values (Session 4) than when A is absent (Session 5).
- For *blocking*, if A becomes a good predictor of X in Phase 1, the growth of B is blocked and reaches much lower values (Session 6) than without Phase 1 (Session 5).
- For *superconditioning*, when B become a conditioned inhibitor in Phase 1,

the value of A is augmented (Session 9) in comparison with a learning history without Phase 1 (Session 8).

- For **asymmetry** (Session 10), A (lightning) is a more certain cause of X (forest fire) than B (camp fire), but when asked what caused X (forest fire), people will come up with B (camp fire) as most likely indicator because this cause is most frequent (although it does not always cause a fire). Note that to obtain these results, the number of trials was slightly changed as can be seen in the Trial Grid Category $10 (with the number of trials as given in Table 5.2, the results of Table 5.3 could not be replicated, even with all model and parameters set identical to Read & Montoya, 1999).

Questions

1. For all simulations except the last, you can experiment with a reverse direction of testing. For this, open the Session Grid by clicking the **Session** tab. Replace the Test Categories *$51–54* with *$61–64*. As you will see, some of the effects will not replicate with this backward direction of testing.

2. You can also explore in greater depth the non-linear recurrent model. Choose the **Simulation | Parameters** menu or press the ⊕ speed button, and select the *non-linear recurrent* model in the **Model** drop-down list box. Enter the model parameters as indicated in the text (**istr** = *0.15*; **estr** = *0.15*, **decay** = *0.15*, and **#cycles** = *10*). Run the simulations by choosing **Simulation | Run Simulation** or pressing the ⚙ speed button.

6 When one explanation is enough: A connectionist view on the fundamental attribution bias

Frank Van Overwalle

This unpublished chapter reviews sources of the fundamental attribution bias, or lack of discounting, within the framework of a recurrent connectionist network model. The sources that are simulated include lack of attention to (situational) information, incomplete processing of information, increased strength of the effect, and correspondent motives. The first three sources have received considerable empirical support from previous research, and novel evidence is reviewed on the operation of the last source. The simulations point to the essential role of two emergent properties of the delta learning algorithm of the network: online acquisition of novel information and competition for associative strength given multiple causes. The discussion centers on how the present model is superior to many other computational models in attribution theory, and how it contradicts assumptions of other models that received widespread attention in the attribution literature. Novel hypotheses to test the connectionist modeling approach are discussed as well as steps to improve and unify concurrent theories in the field of social cognition.

> As Freud taught us long ago, and the modern theorists of parallel distributed processing models of cognition teach us now, many different things are going on at the same time within the typical human head (and heart). We try to serve many masters, seek many goals at the same time, and life is a continuous struggle to balance them all and find some kind of workable compromise (Funder, 2001, p.23)

One of the most fundamental mental activities of humans is to find causal structure in the activities and environment that surrounds them. To make sense of their social world, people need to relate various actions and events to the entities that cause them. An essential element in this causal analysis is discounting, or the weeding-out of less relevant conditions in favor of the most diagnostic or predictive causal factor. This selection serves cognitive economy, as it reduces the causes people need to attend to in order to predict and control their environment. Nevertheless, a plethora of studies have indicated that people can sometimes simplify their causal analysis too much, by completely ignoring some causal factors that are important. This pervasive tendency is known as the fundamental attribution bias (Ross, 1977; see also Jones & Harris, 1967): People often conclude that a person who initiated an action was predisposed to do so, and yet a full causal analysis would suggest that situational pressures also contributed a great deal. It is generally believed that this bias is partly responsible for stereotyping and discrimination of individuals. One of the continuing interests in social psychology is that, counter to layman intuitions, experiments (e.g. Festinger, 1957; Milgram, 1963) often illustrate how much people's behavior depends on the strength of social situations rather than the actor's dispositions.

It is thus crucial to psychologists to understand how the fundamental attribution bias is created and how it can be eliminated. However, earlier reports and analyses of discounting and the fundamental attribution bias (e.g. Gilbert & Malone, 1995; McClure, 1998) show a lack of theoretical integration of the different sources that contribute to this bias, resulting in what often appear as *ad hoc* hypotheses and assumptions. Moreover, the field of causal attribution has developed largely independent from other important areas in cognition at large, and in social cognition in particular, including domains such as person perception, group impression, and attitude formation. The aim of the present chapter is to describe and analyze the causes of the fundamental attribution bias from a common theoretical perspective, and in particular from a connectionist framework that potentially can explain a wider range of causes of the bias. The proposed model has already been fruitfully applied to other areas in memory and cognition (for a classic example, see McClelland & Rumelhart, 1986, p.170), including the domain of social cognition (Read & Montoya, 1999; Smith & DeCoster, 1998; Van Overwalle & Jordens, 2002; Van Overwalle & Labiouse, 2004; Van Overwalle & Siebler, 2005; Van Rooy, Van Overwalle, Vanhoomissen, Labiouse, & French, 2003; see also Chapters 4–12), where it has been applied to encompass and integrate earlier algebraic models of impression formation (Anderson, 1981) and attitude formation (Ajzen, 1991). However, this model has not always gone unchallenged and other computational models attempt to model causal attribution and discounting based on a different set of assumptions (see Chapter 5 and Read & Miller, 1993). Therefore, I will invest some time in describing the basic approach and the empirical evidence supporting it.

THEORETICAL ANALYSES OF CAUSAL ATTRIBUTION

Since Western philosophers began to wonder how people derive causal attributions, there have been many scientific attempts to understand and formalize causal induction. One of the earliest philosophers who addressed this question, John Stuart Mill (1872/1973), distinguished between the *method of difference* and the *method of agreement*. Essentially, the method of difference designates the cause to that condition that differs from other conditions (e.g. if only John acted aggressively, then he is the culprit), whereas the method of agreement designates the cause to generalities across different conditions (e.g. if the sun goes up every time the cock crows, then the cock caused it). Research has documented that the method of difference is preferentially applied for making causal attributions, while the joint application of the methods of difference and agreement is preferred in making dispositional attributions (Hilton, Smith, & Kim, 1995; Van Overwalle, 1997). The operation of both methods was later codified as the principle of *covariation* in social psychology (cf. Kelley, 1967) and *contingency* in learning theory. Basically, these principles state that, for a condition to be indicated as a cause of an effect, the condition and the effect should be either always present together or absent together.

However, not all conditions that covary with an effect are designated a causal status, because less relevant conditions are often discounted. According to Kelley (1971) who introduced this principle in attribution theory, "the role of a given cause in producing a given effect is discounted if other plausible causes are also present" (p.8). A similar principle is also known in associative learning models and termed *blocking* (Rescorla & Wagner, 1972; see also Van Overwalle & Van Rooy, 1998). Although Kelley originally meant the discounting principle to describe competition between alternative explanations based on prior knowledge and minimal causal information (see Chapter 5 and Morris & Larrick, 1995), associative learning theory and later social research focused primarily on the dynamic context of discounting during causal induction, that is, when novel causally relevant information is received and processed (see Hansen & Hall, 1985; Kruglanski, Schwartz, Maides, & Hamel, 1978; Rosenfield & Stephan, 1977; Van Overwalle & Van Rooy, 1998, 2001b; Wells & Ronis, 1982). It is evident that when minimal information is provided, other processes, such as prior knowledge or normative beliefs about what an average person might do in a similar situation, may come into play more strongly. In this chapter, the term discounting is broadly used to encompass all sorts of causal competition, including the application of prior knowledge as well as the learning of novel causal relations. As is elaborated in more detail in the General Discussion, the present connectionist approach—although mainly focused on the learning component— can actually incorporate also the application of prior causal knowledge structures.

The starting point of my analysis is that inferring causal judgments by means of the principles of covariation and discounting can be understood and modeled from a connectionist perspective (see also Van Overwalle, 1998). General-purpose connectionist models possess information-processing characteristics that make them ideally suited to model causal attribution and learning, and hence provide a unique vantage point for analyzing the conditions under which discounting fails and the fundamental attribution bias emerges. For instance, connectionist systems have no need for a central executive, so that they are ideally suited to studying the fundamental attribution bias, which is presumably driven by implicit and automatic mechanisms without explicit awareness of their origin or presence. In addition, connectionist systems may elucidate the idea that the fundamental attribution bias is naturally embedded in general learning processes that are otherwise quite adaptive in human learning and development.

This chapter is organized as follows: I present a series of simulations, using the same network architecture applied to a number of important causes of the fundamental attribution bias. I will not review the voluminous literature on the fundamental attribution bias, but rather build on the excellent reviews of Gilbert and Malone (1995) and McClure (1998) to illustrate how connectionist principles can be used to shed light on the processes underlying this bias. Based on the simulations, a comparison to other computational theories of causal attribution and discounting will be made, pointing out basic differences and limitations of earlier approaches, which are also relevant outside the scope of the fundamental attribution bias. Finally, I discuss the limitations of the proposed connectionist approach and discuss areas where further theoretical developments are under way or are needed.

Throughout this chapter, I use the same basic network model—namely, the linear recurrent autoassociator developed by McClelland and Rumelhart (1986, 1988) using the error-driven delta learning algorithm for adjusting the connection weights (see Equations 3.3, 3.4, and 3.8, p.38, p.40). The acquisition and competition properties of the delta learning algorithm shape the connections between multiple causes and effects (see Chapter 3). Essentially, these properties describe different ways in which a growing number of observations affect connections in the network. The acquisition property describes how the cause → effect connections grow stronger as a function of a growing sample size, and so enables it to develop stronger causal estimates when more evidence is available. The competition property describes how stronger cause → effect connections inhibit the development of weaker cause → effect connections. This latter property drives the phenomenon of discounting. Thus, one of the most interesting characteristics of the error-driven delta learning algorithm is that discounting is a natural emergent property of it. No special features or mechanisms have to be built in the model to obtain this effect, as it derives spontaneously from the learning algorithm's goal to predict the external environment as accurately and diagnostically as possible.

For all simulations, the learning rate that determines the speed of learning was set to 0.25. All connection weights were initialized at starting values randomly chosen between −.20 and .20 to allow some variation in the data so that we could conduct some statistical tests on the results of the simulations. In order to generalize across a range of presentation orders and starting values, each network was run for 100 different random orders and starting values, thus simulating 100 different "participants". Unless otherwise stated, most of the effects reported are relatively robust to changes in parameters and stimulus distributions. Consequently, for simplicity of presentation, a smaller number of trials were used in some of the simulations than is typically the case in actual experiments.

WHEN DISCOUNTING FAILS: CAUSES OF THE FUNDAMENTAL ATTRIBUTION ERROR

Given that competition is a natural emergent property of the delta learning algorithm, how is it possible that situational constraints are ignored so that discounting of the actor is insufficient? To understand this, it is important to realize that competition depends on a subtle balance between stronger and weaker causal factors. If this balance is disturbed by some extraneous factors, then discounting will not operate normally. Although previous theorists considered "the correspondence bias to be something of a misnomer inasmuch as several different psychological mechanisms can give rise to the same general effect" (Gilbert & Malone, 1995, p.24), I demonstrate that a common connectionist network can underlie the attribution bias, although different factors may interfere with the balance in discounting. By pointing out a common ground, I attempt to bring unity in the diversity of factors contributing to the bias and suggest potential additional sources of the bias.

In this overview, I concentrate on four distinct causes: (1) lack of perceptual attention and encoding to situational constraints; (2) lack of integration of situational constraints; (3) perceived strength of the effect; and (4) correspondent motives that determine dispositional attributions. The first three causes can be subsumed under the heading of perceptual and attentional factors, while the latter cause deals with processing factors. All these causes are listed in Table 6.1, together with a brief description of the connectionist mechanism that may be responsible for it. Each of these causes is illustrated with a simulation on the basis of a well-known experiment from the social cognition literature.

Simulation 1: Lack of attention to situational constraints

To avoid the fundamental attribution error, the cognitive system must be aware that the situation plays a causal role in the actor's outcomes and behaviors. This may fail because we do not pay sufficient attention to this information, so that it is not encoded. Typically, we do not take in all the information that arrives at our senses, but rather make a selection in function of our current goals and desires, and the salient features in the environment. This filtering-out of irrelevant stimuli in favor of important stimuli obviously has adaptive and survival functions, but may result in unbalancing the normal operation of causal learning and discounting.

A crucial consequence of filtering-out less salient or relevant information is that observers do not realize the causal role of the situation on the actor's behaviors or outcomes. Lack of attention and encoding has been put forward as one of the main causes of insufficient discounting by several reviewers (Gilbert & Malone, 1995; McClure, 1998). There are many reasons why attention to the situation is suffering. For instance, the observer may simply not see the situation in which the actor behaves. This is often the case in everyday

Table 6.1 Overview of the simulated sources of the fundamental attribution bias and their connectionist explanation

Less discounting due to	*Simulated findings*	*Connectionist explanation*	
1. Lack of attention to (situational) constraints	When a person is not attended to, its causal impact is weaker than a person that is the focus of attention	Less attention to (situational) information leads to less activation and hence to s*lower learning* of that information	
2. Incomplete processing of information	When cognitive resources are limited, there is less discounting by situational information	Less attention to causal information leads to less activation and *slower learning* overall, resulting in *more learning error* and less competition	
3. Increased strength of the effect	When the effect is strong, there is less discounting by situational information	Increasing the effect leads to *more learning error* and hence to less competition	
4. Correspondent motives	Less discounting by situational information when evaluative implications of perceived motives coincide with effect	Correspondent implications of actor's *motives counterbalance* discounting by situational constraints	

In the figures, the top unit represents the effect and the bottom units the target cause (person), the alternative cause (situation), and the inferred motive, respectively.

social life, because many situational constraints reflect social norms or threats imposed during earlier social learning, so that the pressures working on the actor's behavior are removed from the current situation. In general, we either do not see or do not know about the external pressures that impinge on the actor.

The role of (visual) attention was clearly demonstrated in a seminal experiment by Taylor and Fiske (1975, Experiment 1). In this experiment, two people (actually confederates) had a conversation with each other in which different mundane topics were addressed. A number of observers were seated around the two conversants, so that some observers saw only one conversant, while other observers saw both. After the conversation, the observers rated the extent to which the conversant was viewed as the causal agent in the situation (how much he or she set the tone of the conversation, determined the kind of information exchanged and caused the partner to behave the way as he did). As can be seen in Figure 6.1, observers facing both conversants viewed them as equally important in causal terms, while observers facing one conversant saw this person as more causally responsible than the unseen partner, thus revealing lack of discounting of the focal person.

Simulation

Such lack of attention and encoding to situational information can be easily simulated in a recurrent network. A common assumption in connectionist modeling is that the degree of external activation reflects the attention given to and degree of processing of that stimulus (O'Reilly & Munakata, 2000). Research on the neurological underpinnings of attention suggests that task-specific attention and voluntary control is most likely modulated by supervisory executive centers in the prefrontal neocortex, which in turn determine

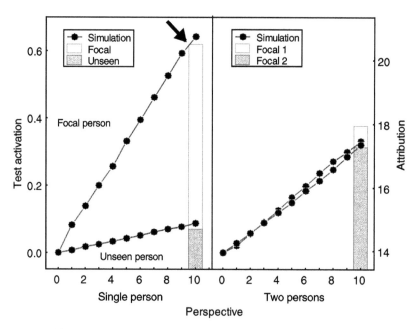

Figure 6.1 Simulation 1: Insufficient attention. Test activation in function of external activation directed to a single person or two persons. Simulation based on the design of Taylor and Fiske (1975, Experiment 1) and observed data. Cov, Covariation. The arrow depicts the data revealing insufficient discounting of the focal person. The data are from Table 1 in "Point of view and perceptions of causality" by S. E. Taylor & S. T. Fiske, 1975, *Journal of Personality and Social Psychology, 32*, 441. Copyright 1975 by the American Psychological Association.

the activation in the relevant cortical regions in the brain (LaBerge, 1997, 2000; Posner, 1992). By changing the external activation levels in a connectionist model, changes in the balance between causes should emerge, resulting in lack of appropriate discounting under some circumstances.

I simulated a hypothetical learning history reflecting these attentional factors as they played a role in the experiment by Taylor and Fiske (1975, Experiment 1). As can be seen in Table 6.2, the network involved two causes (the two conversants) connected to the effect (initiating a topic). I assume that each conversant initiated five topics (resulting in five learning trials each). Crucially, when facing both confederates, external activation was equally divided between the two persons (each .50), while when facing only one confederate, external activation was mainly given to this focal person (activation = .75) while less activation was given the other person (activation = .25). An equal activation level will produce the same learning rate for (the causal weights of) the two conversants, while a higher or lower activation level will result in faster or slower learning rate of the focal and other conversant respectively.

As can be seen in Figure 6.1 (left panel), learning was fastest for the conversant who attracted most attention, and slowest for the conversant who attracted the least attention. This resulted in a fundamental attribution bias in favor of the focal conversant to the detriment of the unseen partner, $t(99) = 43.95$, $p < .001$. In contrast, on the right panel, it can be seen that learning was very similar when both conversants were attended to. This resulted in appropriate discounting of the causal contribution of both conversants so that their causal contributions did not differ, $t(99) = 0.79$, *ns*.

Table 6.2 Simulation 1: Insufficient attention (simulation history based on the design of Taylor & Fiske, 1975, Experiment 1)

Condition and trial frequency	Causes		Effect
	Target person	*Other person*	*Initiate*
Experimental phase			
Focusing on target person			
#5	0.75		0.75
#5		0.25	0.25
Focusing on both persons			
#5	0.50		0.50
#5		0.50	0.50
Test			
Target person	1		?
Other person		1	?

Cell entries denote external unit activation and empty cells denote 0 activation.

Initiate, initiate conversation topics; #, number of times the trial is repeated; ?, resulting test activations (without external activations). The order of the trials within conditions was randomized.

Taken together, the simulation reproduced the empirical data of Taylor and Fiske (1975), which is also depicted on Figure 6.1.

Simulation 2: Incomplete processing of information

A common assumption in many textbook treatments of the fundamental attribution error is that people initially make a trait inference that corresponds with the behavior. This correspondent inference serves as an anchor for adjustments that take account of other situational factors. Gilbert and collaborators (Gilbert, Pelham, & Krull, 1988; Gilbert & Osborne, 1989; Gilbert & Malone, 1995) proposed that anchoring of a trait is an automatic process, whereas adjustment requires more cognitive control and effort. This adjustment process is therefore more easily disrupted by limited cognitive resources, so that it can often lead to insufficient adjustment or discounting. Note that this explanation presumes that information is processed in two distinct steps: anchoring and adjustment. This contrasts with a connectionist approach, where information encoding and weight adjustment typically occurs in parallel. Thus, while disruptions or limited resources can certainly cause incomplete processing of information, given non-selective attention, a connectionist approach would predict a global lack of adjustments to all information rather than of one particular set of information (e.g. situation) during one specific moment in the process (e.g. anchoring).

In a now classic experiment, Gilbert et al. (1988) demonstrated how disruption of processing information may reduce discounting by situational information. Participants observed a silent video showing a woman behaving anxiously while discussing various topics. For some participants, the topic involved mundane issues such as fashion trends, while for the others, the topic involved anxiety-provoking issues, such as her sexual fantasies. Under normal viewing circumstances, there was no bias in that the participants refrained from rating the woman as dispositionally anxious when she discussed anxiety-provoking topics. However, when given a secondary task, which limited available cognitive resources, they failed to take into account the situational circumstances and rated the woman as equally anxious given both conversation topics (see Figure 6.2, p.131).

Simulation

The experiment by Gilbert et al. (1988) can be easily simulated in a recurrent network consisting of two causes (the person and the topic) connected to the effect (behaving anxiously). The learning history is briefly depicted in Table 6.3. First, a pre-experimental learning history is provided, which reflects prior social learning indicating that we often behave anxiously when discussing intimate topics while we typically do not behave anxiously when conversing about mundane topics. Ten trials were chosen to approach asymptote. Next, the five critical topics discussed during the video in the original

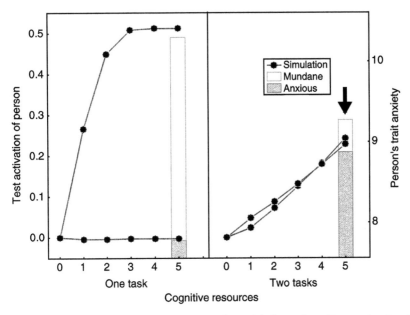

Figure 6.2 Simulation 2: Incomplete processing of information. Test activation in function of cognitive resources. Simulation based on the design of Gilbert, Pelham, & Krull (1988, Experiment 1) and observed data. The arrow depicts the data revealing insufficient discounting of the person in the anxious condition. The data are from Table 2 in "On cognitive busyness: When person perceivers meet persons perceived" by D. T. Gilbert, B. W. Pelham, & D. S. Krull, 1988, *Journal of Personality and Social Psychology*, *54*, 735. Copyright 1988 by the American Psychological Association.

experiment were taken as the number of trials run in the simulation. The connections developed earlier during the pre-experimental trials serve as additional input to these experimental trials. Of course, this is somewhat simplified from reality in that prior knowledge structures are not always directly available in memory, but need to be reactivated by contextual cues to be applicable. The simulation assumes that this reactivation of prior knowledge is the default in most cases.

The simulation results of the person are shown in Figure 6.2. As can be seen in the left panel, given a mundane topic and an anxious behavior, the causal weights of the person quickly reached asymptote at a level of 0.5 (as also the causal weight of the topic did, both summing to +1). In contrast, given an anxiety-provoking topic, the causal weight of the person was totally blocked at 0 because the weight of the topic (closely approaching +1) already predicted her anxious behavior. The difference between the two topics was reliable, $t(198) = 54.44$, $p < .001$. Now consider what happened when all causal input was activated only to a 0.15 level instead of the default +1 to simulated disruption of normal information intake. The simulation results

Table 6.3 Simulation 2: Incomplete processing (simulation history based on the design of Gilbert et al., 1988, Experiment 1)

	Causes		Effect
Condition and trial frequency	*Person*	*Topic*	*Anxious*
Pre-experimental phase			
Mundane topic			
#10		1	
Anxious topic			
#10		1	1
Experimental phase			
#5	1[a]	1[a]	1
Test			
Person's trait anxiety	1		?

Cell entries denote external unit activation and empty cells denote 0 activation.

Anxious, behaving anxiously; #, number of times the trial is repeated; ?, resulting test activations (without external activations). To reflect the common knowledge that most people typically behave anxiously when talking about anxiety-provoking topics while they do not given mundane topics, the pre-experimental learning history preceded all conditions. The pre-experimental phase was followed by the experimental phase.

[a] Activation set at 0.15 under two task conditions to reflect limited cognitive resources.

are shown in the right panel. Because the topic does not sufficiently predict the behavior given this low activation, the connection weight of the person now gains substantial strength given both topics, resulting in lack of discounting of the person and no reliable difference between topics, $t(198) = .87$, *ns*.

It is important to note that this result is obtained without assuming a sequential process in which the judgment is first anchored on the trait, and then insufficiently adjusted for the situation due to limited processing resources as assumed by Gilbert et al. (1988). Instead, the present simulation strongly suggests that limited resources may affect trait attributions in parallel. Thus, insufficient resources limit the application of the situation in explaining the effect, and so directly lead to stronger person attributions.

Simulation 3: Increased strength of the effect

Another factor that leads to the fundamental attribution error is when the strength of the effect exceeds norms or expectations (Gawronski, 2003; Jones, Worchel, Goethals, & Grumet, 1971; Miller, Ashton, & Mishal, 1990). Like an imbalance in causal inputs, a crucial consequence of an unusual strong effect is that typical causes do not suffice in explaining the actor's behavior, making it is less likely that observers will discount a causal candidate. On the contrary, when the effect is unusually weak, it is more likely that one or more of the causal candidates will be discounted. There are several reasons why observers may have flawed expectations about the effect. Observers may have unrealistic expectations of the power of the actor or the situation in provoking the effect. Or they may have realistic expectations but nevertheless occasionally encounter an extremely weak or strong outcome that exceeds expectations.

A nice illustration of the impact of differential effect strength was given by Miller et al. (1990, Experiment 5). In a replication of the well-known essay experiment by Jones and Harris (1967), participants read an essay on the legalization of abortion. This essay was either pro- or anti-abortion, and was described as having been written either by the choice of the writer, or under the assignment of a pro- or anti-abortion direction given by the experimenter. Time after time, research has revealed that observers underestimate the situational pressures under which the essay is written and typically attribute a pro- or anti-abortion attitude not only under choice, but also under experimental assignment (although to a somewhat lesser degree). Thus, participants seem to believe that the essay "leaks" the true attitude of the writer. Of prime interest is the manipulation of the perceived essay strength by Miller et al. (1990), who provided another essay on abortion immediately prior to the target essay. This prior essay was either much stronger or weaker. On the basis of a contrast effect, a stronger prior essay should lead to the inference that the target essay was quite weak, whereas a weaker prior essay should lead to the inference that the target essay was quite strong. As can be seen in Figure 6.3, the middle panel (*no prior essay → normal target essay*) illustrates a replication of the typical fundamental attribution bias when the strength of the target essay was perceived as moderate (i.e. a pro- or anti-abortion essay led to different attitude inferences even under assignment). More importantly, the left panel (*weak prior essay → strong target essay*) shows an increased bias when the target essay was perceived as strong, while the right panel (*strong prior essay → weak target essay*) shows that the contribution of the author was fully and appropriately discounted when the target essay was perceived as weak (i.e. a pro- or anti-abortion essay led to identical attitude inferences under assignment).

Simulation

One of the earliest mechanisms to explain the lack of discounting given an extreme outcome was put forward by Kelley (1971) in terms of a multiple necessary schema that implies that two causes are needed to explain an effect. However, in his review, McClure (1998) concluded that in contrast to normal or weak outcomes, extremely strong outcomes are either explained by a single extreme cause or by a conjunction of causes. He therefore proposed a matching principle, which implies that the combined strength of the causes should match the strength of the outcome. However, this matching principle is merely a description of empirical findings without revealing the underlying cognitive processes. In contrast, the present recurrent network can easily simulate "matching" by changing the external activation of the effect to a

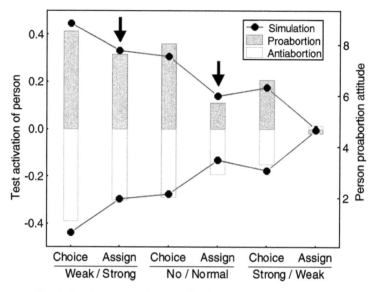

Figure 6.3 Simulation 3: Increased strength of the effect. Test activation in function
of the perceived strength of the prior/current essay. Simulation based on
the design of Miller, Ashton, & Mishal (1990, Experiment 5) and observed
data. Appropriate discounting is revealed by values close to zero, and the
arrows depict insufficient discounting of the person. The data are from
Figure 3 in "Beliefs concerning the features of constrained behavior: A
basis for the fundamental attribution error" by A. G. Miller, W. Ashton, &
M. Mishal, 1990, *Journal of Personality and Social Psychology, 59*, 646.
Copyright 1990 by the American Psychological Association. Adapted with
permission of the author.

higher or lower level for an extremely strong or weak outcome respectively.
According to the delta learning algorithm, when the external activation of
the effect is increased, so will be the learning error in predicting the effect and
this will result in less discounting. In contrast, when the external activation
is decreased, this will result in a smaller learning error, leading to more
discounting.

Table 6.4 depicts a learning history that replicates the essential aspects of
Miller et al.'s (1990) experiment. The network involves four causes (the
author, the instructions and two essays) connected to the effect (writing the
essay). Like the previous simulation, a pre-experimental learning history is
provided, which simulates prior social learning that we typically obey instructions. For instance, we built-up knowledge from our school experiences that
we write essays according to the instructions of teachers. As in the previous
simulation, 10 trials are chosen to approach asymptote. Then, a prior essay is
provided, which can be weak (activation 0), normal (activation +1 or −1), or
strong (activation +1.5 or −1.5). Each essay is assumed to consist of two
major arguments (or two trials). A positive activation indicates that the essay

Table 6.4 Simulation 3: Increased strength of effect (simulation history based on the design of Miller et al., 1990, Experiment 5)

Condition and trial frequency	Causes				Effect
	Person	Instruction	Prior essay	Target essay	Writing
Pre-experimental phase					
#10	1				1
#10	−1				−1
Prior pro(anti)abortion essay[a]					
Weak					
#2			1		0 (0)
Normal					
#2			1		1 (−1)
Strong					
#2			1		1.5 (−1.5)
Target pro(anti)abortion essay[a]					
Choice					
#2	1		=[b]	1	1 (−1)
Assign					
#2	1	0.25 (−0.25)	=[b]	1	1 (−1)
Test					
Person's attitude	1				?

Cell entries denote external unit activation and empty cells denote 0 activation.

Writing, writing pro-abortion arguments; #, number of times the trial is repeated; ?, resulting test activations (without external activations). The order of the trials within conditions was randomized. To reflect the common knowledge that most people typically follow instructions, the pre-experimental learning history preceded all conditions. Next, each prior pro-abortion essays (weak, normal or strong) was followed by a pro-abortion target essay (choice or assign), and likewise for the antiabortion essays.

[a] Between parentheses is the activation for the antiabortion condition. [b] Half of the activation (or 0.50) from the prior essay was spread to the target essay to reflect priming of prior essay.

is pro-abortion, while a negative activation indicates that the essay is anti-abortion. Finally, a target essay is provided with similar characteristics as the prior essay, but now all activation levels are at the default level (+1). Moreover, during the encoding of the target essay, it is assumed that the instructions are less salient and therefore attended to only weakly (activation. 25; see also Simulation 1).[1] The equal sign indicates that part of the activation of the prior essay spills over to the target essay. By virtue of the competition property, this reproduces the contrast effect on the target essay. Compared to

---

1 Indeed, research has demonstrated that when assign instructions are made more salient, as when participants transcribe assays written by someone else, the fundamental attribution bias disappeared (Ajzen, Dalto, & Blyth, 1979; Snyder & Jones, 1974).

a normal essay, a strong prior essay competes with the target essay akin to discounting, while a weak prior essay lead to a stronger target essay akin to augmentation (see also Chapter 8 for a simulation of this contrast effect).

Figure 6.3 shows that these different strengths of the effect lead to more or less discounting, as found by Miller et al. (1990). As can be seen by comparing the pro- and anti-abortion topic in the assign condition, a strong target essay (Figure 6.3, left panel) shows a strong fundamental attribution bias, $t(198) = 49.49$, $p < .001$, a normal target essay (middle panel) shows a moderate fundamental attribution bias, $t(198) = 18.86$, $p < .001$, while a weak target essay (right panel) shows a complete abolishment of the fundamental attribution bias, $t(198) < 0.29$, *ns*.

Simulation 4: Correspondent implications of perceived motives

So far, we have tacitly assumed that causal and dispositional attributions are very much alike and basically depend on the causal relation or covariation between the actor and the effect. However, recent findings challenge this view. While the fundamental attribution error is very prone to disruptions and limitations in cognitive resources, as we have seen in Simulation 3, this is not always the case for causal attributions. In a recent study, Van Overwalle (2006) provided short sentences involving forward blocking (similar to Simulation 2) and then asked his participants to rate either the causal contribution of the target actor or the correspondent dispositional trait of the actor. As we saw earlier, under normal processing conditions, there was more attributional discounting of the target actor given a strong as opposed to a weak alternative actor. This result held for both causal and dispositional formats. Surprisingly, however, when encoding of these sentences was made more difficult, discounting was robust for causal attributions but failed for dispositional ratings. In a similar vein, Taylor and Fiske (1975) reported less or more discounting when the conversation partner was made invisible as opposed to the focus of attention respectively (see Simulation 1), but they failed to replicate these findings for dispositional ratings.

What might be the cause of this differential result? First, as noted earlier, prior research has documented that the method of difference is preferentially applied for making causal attributions, while the joint application of the methods of difference and agreement is preferred in making dispositional attributions (Hilton et al., 1995; Van Overwalle, 1997). Thus, it takes more generalizations across people or situations to infer a disposition. Under difficult or unusual processing circumstances, observers might therefore be especially hesitant about drawing conclusions on a person's disposition on the basis of the given information, leading to the ironic effect that their ratings in effect become more biased. However, there is little research on this issue so that this explanation remains hypothetical.

Second, and perhaps more importantly, in making a dispositional impression about a person, besides causality, people may take into account other inferences in the process. Recently, Reeder and collaborators (Reeder, Kumar, Hesson-McInnis, & Trafimow, 2002; Reeder, Vonk, Ronk, Ham, & Lawrence, 2004) proposed a *multiple inference model* suggesting that, in addition to causal inferences, observers routinely infer much more about the actor, such as his or her motives for engaging in a given behavior and its social implications. Although it is widely acknowledged that perceivers spontaneously take note of an actor's goals or intentions (e.g. Fein, 1996; Hassin, Aarts, & Ferguson, 2005; Heider, 1958; Malle, 1999; Read & Miller, 1993), Reeder et al.'s important insight is that these inferences help to shape the impression formation process. As Reeder (2001) argued, "consider that Balzac, an unrepentant spendthrift, wrote many of his works under financial duress . . . Yet the presence of (external) financial pressure would hardly preclude our attributing a variety of traits to the writer, including a genius for prose. It makes the most sense to assume that Balzac's writing required both financial incentive and genius" (p.34). As another example, when an actor engages in helpful or harmful behavior, we may infer not only to what extent situational pressures are responsible for this, but also which reasons or motives may have compelled the actor and how these motives are socially valued. By taking this information into account, Reeder argued, we may end up with a completely different impression about the person. Thus, when a person intentionally, rather than accidentally, treats women less favorably then men we infer that the actor is prejudiced and discriminatory. The importance of intent in identification of an actor's behavior can also be seen within the law (e.g. manslaughter or discrimination; see Swim, Scott, Sechrist, Campbell, & Stangor, 2003).

To illustrate the multiple inference perspective, consider the following video shown in Reeder et al.'s (2004) research. The video depicted a student named Sara, who helped a professor to stack a large pile of books and journals on a cart. Prior to this helping incident, another one of two videos was shown, which made it clear either that Sara was under no particular situational constraints (choice)—that part of her student job assignment was to help professors moving books (assign), or that she had an ulterior motive for helping the professor as this might increase her chances of getting an award (Fein, 1996; Fein, Hilton, & Miller., 1990). The results across several experiments demonstrated that Sara was seen as less helpful in the ulterior motive situation, whereas she was seen as very helpful in the other two conditions. This reveals appropriate discounting of the person due to situational factors in the ulterior motive situation only, but not in the assign situation (see also Figure 6.4, p.138). What might have been the reason for this unexpected result? Although the participants estimated the situational causality as being high in the assign and ulterior motive situation, the assign situation was also perceived as revealing more obedience and lack of self-interest. These (positive) motives led to increased helpfulness ratings of Sara up to the same degree as in the choice situation. Thus, Reeder et al. (2004, p. 536) concluded that "causal attributions . . . were less predictive of dispositional inferences of helpfulness than were inferences about motive".

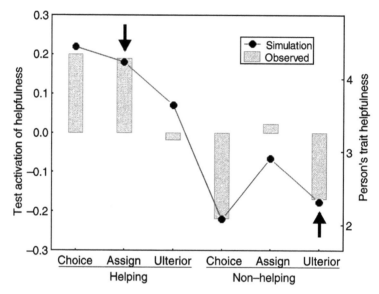

Figure 6.4 Simulation 4: Correspondent motives. Test activation in function of (non-) helping and situational constraints. Simulation based on the design of Reeder, Vonk, Ronk, Ham, & Lawrence (2004, Experiment 3) and observed data. Appropriate discounting is revealed by values close to zero, and the arrows depict insufficient discounting of the person. The data are from Table 6 in "Dispositional attribution: Multiple inferences about motive-related goals" by G. D. Reeder, R. Vonk, M. J. Ronk, J. Ham, & M. Lawrence, 2004, *Journal of Personality and Social Psychology*, *86*, 541. Copyright 2004 by the American Psychological Association.

Now consider the opposite situation, in which Sara does not provide help to the professor under situational conditions of choice, assign (it was her explicit job assignment not to help professors), or an ulterior motive (chances for the award were higher if she did not help). Now the results revealed that discounting did not occur under ulterior motives but that it did occur under the assign condition. Although the participants again rated the situational causality as being high for both the assign and ulterior motive situation, further analysis indicated that the ulterior motive situation led to fewer inferences of low obedience and high selfishness. These (positive) motives may have in turn led to more helpfulness dispositions. Thus, according to Reeder et al. (2004, p.31), only "to the extent that perceivers infer a high level of obedience, they . . . infer a relatively high level of helping as well".

An important implication of Reeder et al.'s (2004) findings is that they challenge general causality-based models of dispositional inference, such as those of Kelley (1971), Gilbert and Malone (1995) and McClure (1998), in that perceivers apparently fail to apply Kelley's discounting principle. But how are inferences about motives integrated with causal inferences about traits? Reeder et al. (2002, 2004) proposed that an inferred motive tends to be evaluated either positively (or justified) or negatively (or unjustified), and that these evaluative reactions are reconciled with the dispositional inferences. Thus, person inferences are based on the evaluative consistency of inferred motives and traits. To the extent that the motive is perceived positively, inferences about the moral character of the person are positive as well. Of course, this invites the question of how inferences about motives are integrated with inferences about dispositions?

Simulation

A connectionist network seems ideally suited to the parallel integration of consistent and inconsistent information about causality and motives in an overall evaluative judgment. To do this, I simply extended the earlier networks focusing exclusively on causality with inferences about motives and their evaluative meaning. However, the coding of the behaviors is somewhat different from the earlier simulations, in that the opposite endpoints of a dimensions (helpful versus non-helpful; pro- versus asocial) were coded by two units, rather than one unit. This was done to illustrate the ambiguities driving the fundamental attribution bias more clearly (as we will see shortly). As can be seen in Table 6.5, this extended network consists of three causes (the actor, the motive to obey, and the motive of self-interest or gain) and four effects (helping or not, being pro- or asocial). Note that motives are here responses to situational constraints and that, for simplicity of the simulation, these situational constraints were not coded explicitly. The table shows a learning history replicating the essence of the experimental conditions of Reeder et al. (2004, Experiment 3). I assumed two trials for processing the information in the videos.

As can be seen in Figure 6.4, in general, this simulation history was capable of replicating the empirical findings. Note that discounting of the person is revealed here by values close to zero. There was less discounting of helping behavior when this was part of job assignment than when there was an ulterior motive, $t(198) = 14.74$, $p < .001$. In contrast, non-helping behavior was much less discounted when there was an ulterior motive than as part of job assignment, $t(198) = 15.17$, $p < .001$.[2] It is important to note that lack of discounting (when an external explanation was available) was obtained by coding some motives as correspondent with the behavior, as opposed to other situations which were more ambiguous, involving both pro- and asocial elements (see Table 6.5). Thus, the assign situation in the helping simulation was unambiguously coded as prosocial in correspondence with the behavior,

---

2 Although the conditions with less discounting showed some reliable difference with the choice situation, these differences were much less significant, $ts(198) = 5.71–6.24$, $p < .001$. Moreover, in the simplified simulation with only the person and pro- and antisocial evaluations, these differences were unreliable, $ts(198) = 1.56–1.68$, *ns*.

Table 6.5 Simulation 4: Ambiguous evaluative content (simulation history based on the design of Reeder et al., 2004, Experiment 3)

Condition and trial frequency	Causes			Effects			
		Motives		Behavior		Evaluation	
	Person	To obey	To gain	Help	No help	Prosocial	Asocial
Experimental condition: helping							
Choice							
#2	1			1		1	
Assign							
#2	1	1		1		1	
Ulterior motive[a]							
#2	1		1	1		1	1
Experimental condition: non-helping							
Choice							
#2	1				1		1
Assign[b]							
#2	1	1			1	1	1
Ulterior motive							
#2	1		1		1		1
Test							
Person's helpfulness	1			?	–?	?	–?

Cell entries denote external unit activation and empty cells denote 0 activation.

Motives, motives in response to situational constraints; to gain, motive for self-gain or selfishness; #, number of times the trial is repeated; ?, resulting test activations (without external activations) averaged per row; the minus sign indicates that the test activation is subtracted before averaging. The signs for the test activations are reversed for testing non-helping.

[a] The motive for self-gain results in the additional activation of an asocial evaluation.
[b] The motive to obey results in the additional activation of a prosocial evaluation.

resulting in lack of discounting. In contrast, the ulterior motive situation was coded as ambiguous, containing both prosocial (the professor was helped) and asocial (it was for the wrong reason) elements and resulting in low helpfulness. Likewise, for the non-helping simulation, the ulterior motive situation contained only asocial elements in correspondence with the behavior, and therefore led to lack of discounting. In contrast, the assign situation was ambiguous because it contained elements that were prosocial (obedience to job instructions) and asocial (the professor was not helped), and so resulted in higher helpfulness. Indeed, simulations with a simpler architecture, without motives and behaviors but only pro- and asocial evaluations reached very similar results. Additional simulations also revealed a good fit between the simulation and the observed ratings of the person's motives of obedience and selfishness, and, more importantly, with ratings of the causal influence of the situation.

OTHER CONNECTIONIST MODELS OF ATTRIBUTION

Is the recurrent model, together with similar models using the delta learning algorithm, the only approach that can integrate all sources of the fundamental attribution bias discussed in this chapter? Perhaps there are other connectionist models in the literature that are capable of doing this equally well or even better? (For a discussion of the failures of algebraic models, see Chapter 4.) Before drawing some final conclusions about the strength and limitations of the current framework, I first briefly describe some other relevant connectionist models of causal and dispositional inference, and compare them with the current model. Given the pervasive nature of the fundamental attribution bias, the comparisons may reveal important implications for theories of attribution in general.

Constraint satisfaction network

Read and collaborators (Read & Marcus-Newhall, 1993; Read & Miller, 1993) and Kunda and Thagard (1996) proposed an alternative connectionist approach of causal and dispositional inferences embedded in a constraint satisfaction network, based on the underlying assumption that "in explaining social interactions, people often have to choose among several alternative explanations. How do they make this choice? We suggest that . . . people . . . find the explanation that best fits or is the most coherent with the events to be explained" (Read & Marcus-Newhall, 1993, p.429). This reasoning process can be implemented in a parallel constraint satisfaction network based on Thagard's (1992) ECHO model. Like the recurrent model, a parallel constraint satisfaction network encodes different aspects of social information, including the person and the specific causes that are responsible for the effect. Input leads to activation of a number of units representing these causes and effects. This activation is then propagated through all related concepts and this is iterated until the activation converges on the best compromise among the constraints imposed by the positive and negative links between the units. The cause that receives the highest activation is then chosen as the best explanation, followed by other causes with less activation. Discounting can be simulated in the model by assuming that alternative explanations are contradictory. That is, they have negative links and hence sent negative activation to each other so that they reduce each other's activation (Read & Miller, 1993, p.534ff.).

   An important difference with the recurrent network is that these models do not possess a learning algorithm. Hence, the connections in a constraint satisfaction model are not learned but simply hand-set by the theorist. This restriction has important psychological consequences in that it assumes that humans cannot learn from their previous judgments. For instance, imagine that you encounter a novel person at a friend's party, and that you judge that person quite attractive and easy going. If you encounter that person again a few months later, the constraint satisfaction model would assume that you have forgotten your judgment about him or her completely, because the links between that person and your trait evaluations have not been updated. Only when you are able to remember the earlier party situation might activation again flow between the relevant units, and this might again result in a positive inference. This is, of course, not very plausible as a model of dispositional inference because we often judge people or objects without remembering the exact situation in which we encountered them previously. There is abundant evidence in the social cognition literature that perceivers develop all sorts of judgments online (Anderson, 1981; Chaiken, 1980; Hastie & Park, 1986; Petty & Cacioppo, 1986), without relying on their memory.

Another important limitation of the constraint satisfaction model is that discounting is predicted only when the link between the alternative causes is negative, so that they exclude each other. As admitted by Read and Montoya (1999), "one problem with our earlier account of discounting is that we had to impose a post hoc negative or inhibitory link" (p.740). This assumption is incorrect, as recent research has documented that discounting occurs when causes are unrelated or even positively related (Van Overwalle & Timmermans, 2005).

Tensor product model

Kashima and collaborators (Kashima & Kerekes, 1994; Kashima, Woolcock, & Kashima, 2000) proposed a connectionist model of person and group impression formation that they called the tensor product model. Like the present recurrent model, it encodes the person and other social constraints in memory as connections between sets of units reflecting these different aspects, and which are updated during encoding. However, a crucial difference lies in the learning algorithm, which is the Hebbian algorithm. A major characteristic of the Hebbian algorithm is that the learning process is not bounded or normalized because it simply keeps on accumulating the weights from previous learning, forcing them beyond -1 and $+1$. In the tensor product model, normalizing takes place only during judgment; for instance, by retrieving appropriate low-end and high-end anchors to calibrate the current judgment. Although research has revealed that people can shift their standards of judgment as they think of members of different social groups (e.g. an assertive person is judged "very assertive" as a women but only "mildly assertive" as a man; Biernat & Manis, 1994), it seems quite plausible that, for most mundane actions, people have a fair idea of the social or idiosyncratic norms of these behaviors. As put forward by Gilbert and Malone (1995) in their analysis of the processing steps involved in discounting, "observers bring to this recognition a general set of beliefs about how people typically behave in such situations" (p.25). Hence, the idea underlying the delta learning algorithm that learning and judging is bounded by a check with reality seems quite plausible. Moreover, the delta learning algorithm can explain small shifts in judgment standards due to the context, also known as contrast effects (see Chapter 8 and Van Overwalle & Labiouse, 2004).

An important consequence of non-normalized Hebbian learning is that learning is not error driven, but that it simply accumulates the weights from previous learning. Thus, activation is not limited by external activation at each learning trial, and neither is weight adjustment. As a consequence, competition and discounting are not natural emergent properties of the Hebbian learning rule. Another limitation of the model is that, as the authors admitted themselves, the model "cannot do away with a control mechanism [to explain] ... the individuation process involved in stereotype change and group differentiation" (p.935). In the present recurrent model, such a supervisory system is not needed.

ALTERNATIVE CODING AND PROCESSING IN THE RECURRENT MODEL

In contrast to the alternative models discussed so far, the simulations with the recurrent model replicated the empirical data reasonably well. However, it is possible that this fit is due to some procedural choices of the simulations rather than to conceptual validity. To verify that these simulations are robust and are not invalidated by changes in the chosen model specifications, I tested a distributed versus the localist encoding of concepts, and a non-linear version of the recurrent network.

Distributed coding

In the present simulations, we used a localist or symbolic representation of concepts, that is, each unit represented a concrete concept. In contrast, in a distributed encoding, a concept is represented by a *pattern* of activation across an array of units, none of which reflects a symbolic concept but rather some subsymbolic micro-feature of it (Thorpe, 1995; and see Chapter 7). Distributed coding usually implies an overlap of the concepts' representations (i.e. an overlap of pattern activations coding for different concepts). I used a localist encoding scheme to facilitate the presentation of the sources underlying the fundamental attribution bias. However, a localist encoding is far from realistic because, unlike a distributed coding, it implies that each concept is stored in a single processing unit and, except for explicit differing levels of activation, is always perceived in the same manner without noise. In social cognition in particular, where none of the concepts like situational norms, motives, and traits can actually be observed, this material might be more realistically represented by a distributed encoding scheme, where information is embedded in a pattern of noisy activations that the recurrent network must abstract from these patterns, just as real participants must do.

Given the advantages of distributed coding, is it possible to replicate the present localist simulations with a distributed representation?

I reran all simulations with a distributed encoding scheme in which each concept was represented by five units that each reflects some micro-feature of the concept (see Table 6.6, below, for details of the simulations). Because all activations receive some noise, this creates an overlap between concepts and also reflects the imperfect conditions of perception. As can be seen, all distributed simulations attained a good fit to the data and, in all cases, the relevant pattern of results from the localist simulations was reproduced. These findings suggest that the underlying principles and mechanisms put forward as being responsible for the fundamental attribution bias can be obtained not only in the more contrived context of a localist encoding, but also in a more realistic context of a distributed encoding.

Non-linear recurrent model

In the simulations, I used a simple *linear* updating activation function and a *single internal updating* cycle (for collecting the internal activation from related units). However, other researchers typically used a *non-linear* updating algorithm with multiple internal cycles (e.g. McClelland & Rumelhart, 1986; and see Chapters 5 and 7). In simulations of other issues, such as the formation of semantic concepts, multiple internal cycles are useful for performing "clean-up" in the network so that the weights between, for instance, a perceptual and conceptual level of representation are eventually forced to settle into representations that have a pre-established conceptual meaning (McLeod, Plunkett, & Rolls, 1998). However, the present linear and single updating scheme was sufficient for reproducing the fundamental attribution bias. To see whether a non-linear activation specification would improve on

Table 6.6 Fit of the simulations, including alternative encoding and models

Causes of the fundamental attribution bias	Original simulation	Distributed representation	Non-linear recurrent
1. Lack of attention to (situational) constraints	.99	.98	.99
2. Incomplete processing of information	.99	.99	.93
3. Increased strength of the effect	.99	.99	.96
4. Correspondent motives	.95	.97	.97

Cell entries are correlations between mean simulated values (averaged across randomizations) and empirical data. All specifications were similar to the original simulations, except for the following: For the distributed encoding, each concept was represented by five units and an activation pattern drawn from a normal distribution with M = activation of the original simulation and SD = .20 (10 such random patterns were run and averaged) and additional noise at each trial drawn from a normal distribution with M = 0 and SD = .20, and with learning rate = .05 and starting weights = 0. For the non-linear autoassociative model, the parameters were: Estr = Istr = Decay = .15 and internal cycles = 9 with learning rate = 1.00.

these results, I reran all the simulations with a non-linear activation function and nine internal cycles (10 cycles in total), which is identical to Read and Montoya (1999; see also McClelland & Rumelhart, 1988, pp.168–169).

As can be seen from Table 6.6, the results were very similar to the simulations reported earlier, and the non-linear simulations did not improve the fit. This suggests that the present linear activation update algorithm with a single internal cycle is sufficient for simulating many phenomena in discounting. In fact, too many internal cycles might even reduce discounting. The reason is that the non-linear updating algorithm forces the activations automatically to the +1 and −1 default levels. Hence, if two causes are activated together and overpredict an effect, then the overly high output activation of the effect tends to restore to the default +1 ceiling level. This reduces discounting of the cause → effect connections.

Summary

Many alternative computational models lack the fundamental properties of automatic learning (weight adjustment) and discounting in explaining causal judgment processes. The present recurrent approach (and similar approaches using the delta learning algorithm) seem to be the only ones that can simulate all sources of the bias adequately, without important changes in the model. Moreover, the recurrent network is quite robust against changes in coding and activation updating. In summary, the present model seems to be better equipped to deal with a number of important issues in causal attribution. However, this does not deny the merits of earlier alternative models. In particular, associative learning models (e.g. Rescorla & Wagner, 1972) have great historical and conceptual value, as they were the first to point out that simple, online adjustment processes could explain most learning of causal relationships and the discounting of alternative explanations. In the context of social cognition, the constraint satisfaction models (Read & Marcus-Newhall, 1993; Read & Miller, 1993) were the first pioneering attempts to show social psychologists how connectionist ideas could be fruitfully applied in this domain. Perhaps some of these models would be better suited for other issues or simulations for which they were originally designed, such as, for example, reasoning and judgment during explicit causal deduction.

GENERAL DISCUSSION

The simulations in this chapter demonstrate that a recurrent connectionist model can account for a number of sources of the fundamental attribution bias under diverse circumstances. Unlike previous reviews of the bias, the present approach offers a more integrated view on how differences in encoding, attention, and internal processing may affect the outcome of the attribution process, by describing how old and novel knowledge structures are accumulated through the development of connections between causes and effects. These moment-by-moment increments distinguish connectionist models from previous algebraic approaches that can only describe the attribution process at asymptote, that is, after a great deal of information is taken in (Cheng & Novick, 1990; Försterling, 1989, 1992; Hewstone & Jaspars, 1987; Hilton & Slugoski, 1986; Kelley, 1967). It also distinguishes the present approach from associationist perspectives, which used static spreading activation networks with non-adjustable links to present the logical relationships or constraints between causes and effects, rather than their covariation or learning history (Kunda & Thagard, 1996; Read & Marcus-Newhall, 1993; Read & Miller, 1993; Shultz & Lepper, 1996). The reason for this advantage over these earlier models, as well as other connectionist models like the tensor product network (Kashima & Kerekes, 1994; Kashima et al., 2000), is its computational power. The delta learning algorithm applied in the recurrent model has a number of emergent properties that are responsible for simulating the causes of the fundamental attribution bias.

The acquisition property accounted for sample size differences in the bias. Whenever there was a reduction in attention, this resulted in less learning and so in weaker cause $\rightarrow$ effect connection strengths and hence in less discounting (see Simulations 1 and 2). Far more important is the competition property, as this is the kernel of all the discounting effects that were simulated. My emphasis on this property distinguishes the present approach from other implementations of the autoassociator (McClelland & Rumelhart, 1988; see Chapter 7), although it shows some parallels with the approach to attribution proposed by Read and Montoya (1999; see also Chapter 5). However, these authors have a somewhat different view on discounting. They distinguish the present approach, in which competition results from the *learning* of causal connections, from competition resulting from activation spreading alone, which apparently should reflect *reasoning* or the use of already learned causal explanations and preexisting knowledge schemata (cf. Kelley, 1967). As they put it, induction deals "with competition for weight strength in the learning of new causal relationships", whereas reasoning deals "with competition for activation in the use of already learned causal relationships" (p.740). This reasoning perspective comes from schema theory and static activation spreading networks, unlike the present induction approach, which has its roots in associative learning theory and dynamic network models.

I do not believe that the two phenomena of learning and reasoning are fundamentally different. Except in the case of amnesia, the brain is constantly updating novel information, extracting statistical regularities from it, and adding these to previous knowledge traces. It is difficult to defend a view where the cognitive system would suddenly change its mode of processing from one issue to the other. One of the advantages of connectionist modeling is that recent information (external activation) and older knowledge (connection weights) are seamlessly integrated in a dynamic network, without the need to postulate different processes. The spreading of activation is part and parcel of the recurrent processing, and I demonstrated that increasing the activation spreading cycles did not change much of the outcome of the present simulations (see Table 6.6). So why would there be a need to argue for completely different processes, one concerned with the initial acquisition of information and the other with its later use in spreading activation? It seems more advantageous to concentrate on the different aspects of the recurrent model—activation spreading and learning—rather than to argue for entirely different processes.

To use an example from Read and Montoya (1999), suppose one is told that a person gets an A in an extremely easy exam. Evidently, one uses pre-existing causal knowledge that the person contributed little to the exam outcome. We agree with Read and Montoya that the perceiver is not learning for the first time that someone who can overcome an easy barrier has contributed much to it. However, I would argue, the perceiver is learning something about the target person. After retrieving and applying prior knowledge (in the sense that I used prior knowledge in the pre-experimental simulations of the effect of instructions or conversation topics and applied it on experimental procedures; see Simulations 2 and 3) in addition to the current input, the perceiver has learned that the person might not need to be very smart to pass the exam. These are the things that a recurrent system learns, and it seems intuitively plausible to assume that our brain does the same.

Perhaps one could argue that causal reasoning reflects explicit processes outside the realm of connectionist networks. There is widespread agreement among connectionist modelers that many outcomes of the implicit connectionist process may become accessible to consciousness (how would we otherwise be able to communicate our causal estimates?), which involves symbolic and serial processes, and that these explicit processes may again feed in the implicit associative system. However, to argue that all causal reasoning retrieved from prior knowledge would have to go through such an elaborate and explicit stage seems intuitively implausible and unnecessary.

In fact, connectionist models paint a different picture of information processing than many earlier models in cognition. They describe the ability of humans to dynamically adjust associations between concepts (traits, causes, attitudes, behaviors . . .) in a variety of settings (e.g. social, personal). In particular, they assume that automatic and local learning algorithms update these associations, requiring little conscious effort or awareness and without the necessary control of a supervisory device such a central executive. Hence, the connectionist approach explains how we are able to form quick impressions of social agents effortlessly in the rush of everyday life (Bargh, 1996). This is in line with research on stereotyping, which shows that prejudiced responses often occur on implicit measures over which participants have limited conscious control (Greenwald & Banaji, 1995; Whitney, Davis, & Waring, 1994).

It is important to emphasize that causal learning is not inherently biased. Many earlier theories of cognition suggested that, to cope with the strong demands of the situation, human perceivers resort to biased processes such as heuristics (Gilbert & Malone, 1995; Tversky & Kahneman, 1974) to shortcut effort-demanding judgments. In the present framework, these shortcuts do not impact on the processing of information but rather reflect selective attention given to some pieces of information (attention to situational factors, correspondent motives, etc.) due to instructions and motivational factors that direct the perceiver's attention toward or away from some particular information. Thus, contrary to earlier models, the input to the system is processed in an essentially unbiased manner. For reasons of evolutionary survival, humans should be capable of detecting at least simple causal relationships between features in their situation (Wasserman, Elek, Chatlosh, & Baker, 1993). Moreover, the processes that lead to the fundamental attribution bias are basically parallel in nature (Trope & Gaunt, 2000), contrary to some earlier views on the serial process in dispositional attribution (Gilbert & Malone, 1995).

Directions for future research

The present simulations of the fundamental attribution bias offered either a novel interpretation of old wisdom and evidence (see Simulations 1, 2, and 3) or novel predictions that were supported by initial evidence. Reeder et al. (2004) demonstrated that correspondent motives matter just as much as correspondent traits in the fundamental attribution bias. They found that when a behavior is unambiguously seen as driven by a correspondent motive, then there will be lack of discounting, even in the clear presence and recognition of situational pressures. These results are difficult to reconcile with pure causality-based theories of the fundamental attribution bias (Gilbert & Malone, 1995; Kelley, 1967; Trope, 1986). Future research should focus on the question of whether ulterior motives are inferred spontaneously from someone's behavior, and how widespread their impact is on dispositional inferences. In addition, research might discover additional factors that contribute to dispositional inferences, such as the greater use of the method of agreement or generalizations in behavior (Hilton et al., 1995; Van Overwalle, 1997, 2004), or the time perspective of the information, as initial evidence seems to suggest that short-term information has less impact on dispositional inferences under uncertain processing circumstances (Van Overwalle, 2006).

By bringing together a diversity of causes of the fundamental attribution bias in a single framework, the connectionist approach can contribute to a more parsimonious theory of biases in judgments in several ways. First, simply putting these findings into a common model, promotes looking at possible further parallels between these different sources of the fundamental attribution bias, as well as with other biases. For instance, Van Rooy et al. (2003; see also Chapter 9) described how several group biases, such as illusory correlation, accentuation, and subtyping, might result from processing in a recurrent system. Of more relevance is that actor-observer differences, or the fact that actors are less vulnerable to the fundamental attribution bias than observers (Watson, 1982), can be explained in much the same manner as the fundamental attribution bias. Some factors (incomplete processing of information, increased strength of the effect; see Simulations 2 and 3) would result in similar lack of discounting when an actor makes the attribution instead of an observer. However, in some cases, different outcomes are to be expected. When an actor makes the attribution, it is expected that relatively less attention will be focused on the person in favor of the situation, leading to less bias (see Storms, 1973, for empirical evidence). In contrast, because actors have privileged access to their own motives and desires, one would expect more bias when correspondent motives play a role. No evidence is yet available on these contradictory predictions.

Second, Van Overwalle and collaborators (Van Overwalle & Labiouse, 2004; Van Overwalle & Siebler, 2005; Van Rooy et al., 2003; see Chapters 8, 9, and 11) have demonstrated that this same recurrent approach was also able to account for many phenomena in social cognition, including person and group impression, assimilation, generalization and contrast, causal attribution, and attitude formation (see also Chapters 5 and 10). These authors also reported that the recurrent model with delta learning algorithm integrates earlier algebraic theories of impression formation (Anderson, 1981) and attitude formation (Ajzen, 1991). In addition, our recurrent network parallels basic associative learning principles applied in a growing tradition of studies using associationist theories to human learning (for reviews, see Shanks, 1995; Van Overwalle & Van Rooy, 1998). The revival of associative learning models is largely due to the development of models using similar error-correcting learning mechanisms such as the delta learning algorithm, which has been used widely in the connectionist literature (McClelland & Rumelhart, 1986). In sum, the present connectionist approach places biases in the wider perspective of the larger field of learning and cognition.

Limitations

Although the connectionist framework can potentially provide a parsimonious account of biases in diverse judgments, it is evident that this is not the only valid approach to modeling social cognitive phenomena. A limitation of some simulations that depended on changes in attention was that they were simulated by changes in external activation that were hand set. Research on the neurological substrate of attention shows that voluntary control and attention is most likely to be determined by supervisory executive centers in the prefrontal cortex (LaBerge, 1997, 2000; Posner, 1992). In past modeling, there have been attempts in which an attention module directly impacts on the relevant parts of the network through direct and fixed links (e.g. Cohen, Dunbar, & McClelland, 1990), but this is, in fact, conceptually not much different from simple hand-coding a higher activation level. More recent attempts to model these changes in higher-level voluntary control and attention processes are underway in more advanced connectionist models (e.g. O'Reilly & Munakata, 2000, pp.305–312, 379–410). The basic idea of this approach is that activation plays a major role in maintaining and switching attention (through dopamine-based modulation), resulting in greater accessibility or activation of the internal representations. Because such central executive "subnetworks" are beyond the scope of the present chapter, we simply hand-set activation to a lower or higher level to simulate selective attention.

Perhaps a more important limitation of connectionist networks in general is a lack of integration of motivation and emotionality. For instance, with the learning algorithms that focus exclusively on accuracy of predicting (delta learning algorithm) or co-occurrence of input (Hebbian algorithm), it is impossible to account for motivation-based attribution biases, such as the hedonic or ethnocentric bias, that is, the tendency to explain the behavior of oneself or one's group, respectively, in more favorable terms than others. How can such algorithms simulate the pervasive drive to provide oneself and one's group with a more shiny view? How can such models explain why we eschew negative feedback about ourselves? These are non-cognitive sources of biases that current connectionist models cannot explain. To model such biases, it seems necessary to incorporate in these models an advantage of avoiding negative feedback about the organism itself, and of actively exploring positive information, within the wider background of evolutionary fitness that such information-processing strategies might have. In sum, when considering the broader domain of non-cognitive biases, we quickly face the limits of existing computational models, including connectionist network. It appears that one of the next steps in model development is the inclusion of "hot" topics of social cognitive thinking.

SIMULATION EXERCISES

In these exercises, you explore the recurrent simulations described in this chapter. You are expected to have some experience with the FIT program, for instance, by having completed some of the exercises in Chapter 3 and 4. The manual of the program is available in the Appendix at the end of the book.

Exercise 1: Lack attention of to situational constraints

Choose menu **File | Open Project**, search for *Taylor+Fiske75.ft2* in folder *Chapter 6*, and click the **Open** button. Alternatively, you can press the 🖪 speed button. This project file contains the necessary set-up for the simulation of the Taylor and Fiske (1975) experiment.

Specifying trials

Click the **Trial** tab to open the Trial Grid, which defines the Trial Categories. The two top rows show two input units representing the causes and one output unit representing the behavior (i.e. initiating the conversation), as also listed in Table 6.2. In the second row, you can define a name for the units, either by double clicking, or by choosing the **Data | Edit Column Names** menu. The names *Target, Other* and *Initiate* are already chosen for you:

- The Trial Category *$1* is used for the first condition (focusing on the target person), while Trial Category *$2* is used for the second condition (focusing on both persons). As can be seen in Table 6.2, in Learning Category *$1*, when focusing on the target person, the activation is predominantly directed to the actor (0.75) while the other person is relatively neglected (activation = 0.25). In contrast, in Learning Category *$2*, when focusing on both persons, the activation is equally divided between both persons as each person gets activation 0.50.
- Test Category *$50* measures each person's contribution to the conversation by activating each person's unit and reading off the resulting activation on the behavioral unit.

Specifying sessions

Click the **Session** tab to open the Session Grid and to specify the ordering of the Learning and Test Trial Categories. As you can see, this is straightforward. One Learning Category is followed by one Test Category for each condition. What is more particular is that Combined Learning and Test Categories (e.g. *1+50*) were used. A combined *1+50* Category allows after each trial of Learning Category $1 to test all trials of Test Category $50. Thus, after each learning trial you can test the progress of the connection weights. This goes on until all the learning trials of Learning Category $1 are processed. This setup allows us to graph the incremental acquisition of the connection weights for the target and other person (see below). You enter "*1+50*" by selecting the entry "edit . . ." in the drop-down list, or by right clicking the cell. The simulation values of the Combined Categories have no observed counterpart, hence * is entered in the **DV1** and **DV2** columns. After the combined Category, Category *$50* is tested again, now with corresponding observed values.

Specifying the simulation parameters

Choose the **Simulation | Parameters** menu, or press the ✸ speed button. In the top panel, four drop-down list boxes list the major options. In the **Model** drop-down list box, the *Linear Recurrent* model developed by McClelland and Rumelhart (1988) is chosen. If not, select that model now. Leave the other boxes at *standard* (**External Coding**), *none* (**External Noise**) or *mean* (**Response**).

Now click the **General** tab. Specify in **Session** that you want to run session *1*, and select the button *yes* in **Graph Simulated Values** (automatically, the **Log Simulated Values** will also turn to *yes*). In addition, set **Randomize Order for All Learning Trials** to *yes*, and specify *100* runs. Leave the categories to which this applies to *1–49*. Set all other parameters to *no*.

Now click the **Model** tab. Enter a learning rate of *0.25*, as in the chapter. Leave the other parameters blank, or set them to *auto* or *no*.

Finally click the **Weights & Activation** tab. Set the **Starting Weights** to *0*, and set the **Random Starting Weights** to **add** $\pm$ *0.20*.

Running the Simulation

To run the simulation as specified above, choose the **Simulation | Run Simulation** menu, or press the ♣ speed button. If you want to follow the simulation step-by-step, choose the **Simulation | Parameters** menu, press the **General** tab, and set **View Details** to *View*. Alternatively, you can hit the 🐾 speed button for a display of the network or the ⌀ speed button for a tabular display.

After the simulation is finished, the **Graph** tab will open automatically (because you requested a graph). Make the following selections:

- **filter**: (*none*).
- **X-Axis**: *Count* (the running count of each trial which allows you to plot the simulation values tested after each trial).
- **X-Axis Labels**: (*none*).
- **Y-Axis Line(s)**: select all simulated and observed **DVs**.

The variable names preceded by a ~ sign denote the simulated values. Check the **List Stats** and **Regress** boxes. Note that, unlike all other simulations in this book, the simulated values were not regressed onto the observed human values, but rather the other way around. To do so, click the **Options** button, and in the **Regress Options**, select the radio button *From Observed Means to Simulated Means*. This allows you to report on the left Y-axis the simulated activation values, and on the right Y-axis the observed human data (as in the text). After hitting the **Graph Log** button, you will see a graph of the simulation results.

From Count 1–10, you see the incremental increase of strength for the target and the other person in the Target Condition, and Count 11 repeats the last test (together with observed values). From Count 12–21, you see the incremental increase in the Both Condition, and count 22 repeats the last test.

For the numerical results, press the **Log** tab. To test the difference between the Target and Other Conditions, you need within-participants tests. Such tests are not provided by FIT, and so you need to export the logged data into a statistical package. Hit the **Log** tab if you have not yet done so. Then select the **File | Export** menu and export the data to **Excel** or **Statistica**. If you now run paired *t*-tests in a statistical package, you will end up with similar values as in the text.

Questions

1. Run the other models that were reported in this chapter: the distributed and non-linear models, as specified in Table 6.6. For the Non-linear auto-associative model, the parameters were: Estr = Istr = Decay = .15 and internal cycles = 9 with learning rate = 1.00. To enter these parameters, choose the **Simulation | Parameters** menu or press the ❀ speed button. Then do the following:

    *   Select in the **Model** option box (top panel) the *non-linear recurrent* model
    *   Then hit the **Model** tab, and set the **lrate** to *1*, **estr, istr**, and **decay** to *.15*, and the total number of (internal and external) **cycles** to *10*

2. For the distributed encoding, each concept was represented by five units and an activation pattern drawn from a Normal distribution with M = activation of the original simulation and SD = .20 (ten such random patterns were run and averaged) and additional noise at each trial drawn from a Normal distribution with M = 0 and SD = .20, and with learning rate = .05 and starting weights = 0.

    To enter these parameters, choose the **Simulation | Parameters** menu or press the ❀ speed button. Then do the following:

    *   Select in the **External Coding** box (top panel) the option *Normal Distributed Pattern (M = activation, SD = 0.2)*.
    *   The **Distributed Coding & Noise** tab will automatically open, and there you select *5* **Micro-Features per Unit**.
    *   To have ten of such distributed patterns over the 100 random runs, set **Reshuffle the Distributed Coding each Run** to *10*.
    *   You then add **random noise**. In the **External Noise (while learning)** option box (top panel) select from the drop-down list *Add Normal (M = 0, SD = 0.20)*.
    *   Then hit the **Model** tab, and set the **lrate** to *0.05*.

3. It is possibile to do a between-participants *t*-test for this simulation. To do this, open the Trial Grid by clicking the **Trial** tab. Copy *Test Category $50* and paste it underneath (enter first a new empty row), and split it in two novel Test Categories, *$51* and *$52*, consisting of a single trial for the Target and Other Person, respectively. Open the Session Grid and change the set-up as indicated in Figure 6.5. Note that there is a single **DV1** now distributed between conditions *1* to *4*, so that all differences between simulated values can be tested. Of course, the results are not

Trials	IVLabel		IV2	DV1	C
			Condition	Target	
1+50	Focusing on Target Person		0	ˣ	
51	Focusing on Target Person - Target		1	20.50	
52	Focusing on Target Person - Other		2	13.77	
reset					
2+50	Focusing on Both Persons		0	ˣ	
51	Focusing on Both Persons - Target		3	17.51	
52	Focusing on Both Persons - Other		4	16.75	

Figure 6.5 Exercise 1: Session Grid for a between-participants *t*-test of the simulation.

exactly the same as for the within-participants *t*-test. If you want to make sure that this run is based on exactly the same data as above, use the random seed that was obtained earlier from the **Listing** tab. You can change the **Random Seed** by clicking the **General** tab from the **Simulation | Parameters** menu. This set-up can also be found in the file *Taylor+Fiske75_conditions.ft2*.

Exercise 2: Incomplete processing of information

We now discuss the other simulations of this chapter. Given that you have had some experience with Exercise 1, you will get only a brief overview of the major changes in each Simulation. You can explore for yourself the questions listed in Exercise 1. For this exercise, choose menu **File | Open Project** (or press the 🖼 speed button), search for *Gilbert88_1.ft2* in folder *Chapter 6*, and click the **Open** button.

As you can see in the Trial Grid, Category $1 and $2 are actually identical, but you will specify that Category $2 receives only 0.15 of the default activation to simulate strongly reduced attention due to the additional load imposed. To do this, open the **Parameter** dialog panel (via the **Simulation | Parameters** menu or the ⚙ speed button):

- Click the **Model** tab. Select *0.25* for the **lrate**, and more importantly, enter *0.15* for the **alpha_1** parameter. This parameter reduces the activation on the units that are specified in Trial Category *$–1*.
- Next, hit the **Weights & Activation** tab, and specify *2* for the **Learning $** in the **Alpha_1 and 2 Coding** option. This indicates that the alpha coding is applied for Learning Category $2 only.

Exercise 3: Increased strength of the effect

For this exercise, choose menu **File | Open Project** (or press the 🖼 speed button), search for *Miller90_5.ft2* in folder *Chapter 6*, and click the **Open** button. To select an appropriate activation level under the Assign conditions, similar changes as in the previous simulation are applied. Open the **Parameter** dialog panel (via the **Simulation | Parameters** menu or the 🌐 speed button):

- Click the **Model** tab. Enter *0.25* for the **alpha_1** parameter.
- Next, hit the **Weights & Activation** tab, and specify *3–4* for the **Learning $** in the **Alpha_1 and 2 Coding** option.
- All other options are similar to the previous simulation.

Exercise 4: Correspondent implications of perceived motives

For this exercise, choose menu **File | Open Project** (or press the 🖼 speed button), search for *Reeder2004_3.ft2* in folder *Chapter 6*, and click the **Open** button. All options are similar to the previous simulations, but note in the Test Categories that not only the traits themselves are used for measuring the resulting activation (i.e. *?*), but also the pro- or antisocial aspects of it.

Part 3

Person and group impression formation

7 Knowledge acquisition, accessibility, and use in person perception and stereotyping: Simulation with a recurrent connectionist network*

Eliot R. Smith and Jamie DeCoster

Connectionist models contrast in many ways with the symbolic models that have traditionally been applied within social psychology. In this article, the authors apply an autoassociative connectionist model originally developed by J. L. McClelland and D. E. Rumelhart (1986) to reproduce several well-replicated and theoretically important phenomena related to person perception and stereotyping. These phenomena are exemplar-based inference, group-based stereotyping, the simultaneous application of several stereotypes to generate emergent characteristics, and the effects of recency and frequency of prior exposures on accessibility (the probability of a representation's use). Although many of these phenomena are explained by current theories in social psychology, the simulation contributes to parsimony and theoretical integration by showing that a single, very simple mechanism can generate them all. The model also predicts a new phenomenon-rapid recovery of accessibility after it has declined to zero.

In recent years, and particularly following the publication of the influential two-volume work by McClelland, Rumelhart, and their colleagues (McClelland, Rumelhart, & the PDP Research Group, 1986; Rumelhart, McClelland, & the PDP Research Group, 1986), parallel distributed processing or connectionist models have had a strong and growing influence in many areas of cognitive psychology. Connectionist models have been developed for phenomena ranging from low-level visual and auditory perception to higher-level processes such as language processing, categorization, schema use, memory, and decision making. Many of these higher-level processes are also prominent in theoretical accounts of social psychological phenomena, such as person perception and stereotyping. In this article we argue that connectionist models can shed new light on important social psychological phenomena, as they have on various areas of non-social cognition.

* Adapted from *Journal of Personality and Social Psychology*, *74*, 21–35. Copyright 1998 by the American Psychological Association. Reprinted with permission of the publisher.

A RECURRENT CONNECTIONIST MODEL OF LEARNING AND MEMORY USE

The connectionist model applied in this article is a recurrent network, developed by McClelland and Rumelhart (1986). In recurrent networks, flows of activation set up by the presentation of an input pattern may show various forms of dynamic behavior, including periodic oscillation, chaotic behavior, or—the behavior typical of the McClelland and Rumelhart network—settling to a fixed final state.

In this network, the equations governing activation flow and learning produce particularly useful forms of behavior, which can be conceptualized as pattern learning and retrieval. As it processes a number of input patterns, the network in effect learns about relationships among activation values of different units in the inputs it sees. The network can then use those learned expectations to fill in values in patterns that it encounters later. Obviously, if input patterns were structureless and random, without any constraints or predictability across the pattern elements, there would be no useful relationships for the network to extract. However, if the input has structure, the network can learn it. Certainly, social information typically has structure that can be exploited in this way; for example, people who are warm are also usually friendly and smiling. After learning, if a new input contains part but not all of a known pattern, flows of activation within the network will reconstruct the remaining portions of the pattern. We could say that the network has learned expectations about regularities in its inputs and can use that knowledge—in addition to the actual input pattern—to make inferences.

We propose that this type of connectionist network may account for certain phenomena within social psychology, particularly those involved in preconscious conceptual interpretation. In many current theories in social cognition this is termed *schematic processing*. The inputs to this module may come either from relatively unprocessed sensory inputs or from other modules that perform prior processing (see McClelland & Rumelhart, 1986, p.174). The pattern's output by this module, presumably after much additional processing in other modules, help constitute the individual's conscious experience. A module of this sort needs to be supplemented in several ways to form a complete theory of the human social-cognitive system; we return to this point later in the article. This model is intended only as an account of the learning and processing mechanisms that underlie preconscious schematic processes. This still includes many diverse phenomena, including schema learning and application, schema combination, and accessibility. In recent years, social cognition theorists have heavily emphasized automatic and preconscious processes of the sort that we intend this model to capture (see Banaji & Greenwald, 1994; Bargh, 1994; Higgins, 1996).

TARGET PHENOMENA FOR THE SIMULATIONS

Computer simulations can be conducted in two different ways. For one, the investigator can select a single crucial experiment or several closely related experiments, usually incorporating many conditions, and try to simulate the empirical data patterns in precise quantitative detail. An example appears in McClelland and Rumelhart (1986, pp.200–204). This approach can be valuable if a single experiment exists that captures (perhaps in different conditions) all the processes of interest to the model and if the limitations on generality that are inherent to any single study or research paradigm are accepted.

We take the alternative approach: We select robust and well-replicated data patterns from literature and use the simulation to reproduce qualitatively these findings (as in Smith, 1991). McClelland and Rumelhart (1986, pp.194–199) also took this approach as part of their original investigation of the properties of this network. This approach has the advantage of generality: If successful, it means that the simulation captures what are consensually regarded as major themes in the empirical literature rather than the specific quantitative results of a single experiment. In addition, no one study (to our knowledge) adequately represents all of the processes we want to simulate, particularly the learning as well as the use of social knowledge structures.

To support our claims about the major data patterns in the literature, formal meta-analyses would be desirable in principle. However, conducting several meta-analyses would carry the reader far beyond the scope of this article. Our intent is to focus on relatively uncontroversial generalizations that are widely represented in textbooks and reviews (Fiske & Taylor, 1991; Wyer & Srull, 1994). In the following descriptions and throughout this article, we often use the term *trait* for brevity, but the model applies equally to personality traits, typical behaviors, physical characteristics, and other types of characteristics that are part of person impressions (Carlston, 1994). We target the following phenomena:

1. People can learn the idiosyncratic characteristics of a specific well-known person; they can apply this knowledge to make inferences about unobserved traits of a new exemplar (Andersen & Cole, 1990; Lewicki, 1985).
2. People can learn a group stereotype or specific pattern of traits from exposure to members of a group; they can apply this knowledge to make inferences about unobserved traits of a new exemplar of the group (Hamilton & Sherman, 1994).
3. People can simultaneously learn multiple knowledge structures; they can apply them in combination to infer new, emergent characteristics of a new exemplar that combines features of several existing categories (Hastie, Schroeder, & Weber, 1990; Kunda, Miller, & Claire, 1990).

4. Recently or frequently encountered patterns will have a bigger impact on future inferences; this is the principle of accessibility (Higgins, 1996).

Our goal in this article is to demonstrate that a single (and simple) mechanism can reproduce all of these findings. Each of these has an existing explanation in the literature—but the explanations are all distinct. Bringing the phenomena under a common theoretical umbrella not only increases parsimony but also yields a deeper understanding of these findings as seemingly distinct outcroppings of a common set of underlying processes. Later in the article we also demonstrate that the same model makes intriguing new predictions as well as reproducing known findings.

OVERVIEW OF AUTOASSOCIATIVE MODEL

Distributed representations

The model we apply here, an autoassociative memory, is a type of connectionist network that can learn to reconstruct information about a number of distinct stimuli. The network uses distributed representations, in which each stimulus is encoded as a pattern of activation across a common set of units (Thorpe, 1995; Touretzky, 1995). In a distributed representation, a stimulus or concept is identified with a pattern of activation across all of the units. Consequently, units are not specifically associated with particular stimuli or concepts. They are not assumed to have any meaningful semantic interpretation. However, we do assume that semantically similar concepts are represented by similar patterns of activation across the units (Clark, 1993).

Models using local representations (one unit per concept or proposition) can reproduce some social psychological phenomena (Read & Marcus-Newhall, 1993). However, we see several advantages of models being distributed over local representations. Generalization of learning across similar concepts is a direct consequence of distributed representations. As we discuss later, learning occurs at the unit level rather than at the level of meaningful stimuli or concepts. Because similar concepts are assumed to have similar representations, learning something about one concept will influence how the network processes related concepts. It is also much easier to incorporate new concepts into a network that uses distributed representations than into one that uses localized representations. In a localist network, each concept must be represented by its own unit. This means that the network itself must grow larger each time it encounters a new concept, and difficult decisions must occasionally be made as to when an input represents an instance of an existing concept versus when a new unit must be created. In a distributed network, on the other hand, the model represents every possible concept on the same units. Novel concepts induce new patterns of activity across the network, but the network's structure stays the same. More thorough discussions of distributed representations may be found in Hinton, McClelland, and Rumelhart (1986), van Gelder (1991), and Thorpe (1995).

Learning and processing in autoassociative networks

Autoassociative networks operate by processing input information in a way that depends on their past learning. Through training, an autoassociator learns predictive relationships among features of the inputs, and it uses this knowledge (represented in the connection weights) as it processes new stimuli. For example, a trained autoassociator exposed to an incomplete version of a stimulus pattern that it has previously processed will use what it has learned to fill in missing information. This process can be viewed as a type of assimilation: Past experiences affect processing of the current input cues, to the extent that they are similar to those cues.

Consider as an example an autoassociative network designed to store information about people. Let us say that the network observes patterns of activation representing several people, each of whom is perceived as hostile and narrow minded. That is, the overall patterns representing these individuals each include subpatterns representing the concepts of hostility and narrow mindedness. The network will alter its connection strengths to represent these observed relationships. If a new input pattern representing a hostile person is now encountered, the pattern of units corresponding to "narrow minded" will likely be activated as well, representing an inference.

Once the learning process has modified the connections in this way, an autoassociator can combine input information with information derived from past experiences. If a stimulus is somehow incongruent with its past training, a trained autoassociator will modify the output pattern so that it better matches its prior experiences. For example, assume that the person network described earlier is trained on a number of descriptions of hostile, narrow-minded individuals. If the network is then given a pattern representing a person who is hostile but with no information about other attributes, it will use its knowledge to fill in a pattern representing the inference that the person is also narrow minded. In addition, if the network receives a pattern indicating a person who is hostile and broad minded, it may report (depending on the details of the current stimulus and its learning history) either that the person is not hostile or that he or she is likely narrow minded rather than broad minded. This occurs because the internal flows of activation within the network, as well as the external inputs, affect the final activation pattern. Thus, the network can use its experience to correct for possible perceptual errors as well as to fill in unobserved details.

The network carries out these functions without constructing or storing discrete representations of specific types of expected stimuli (Rumelhart, Smolensky, McClelland, & Hinton, 1986). All representations are stored together in the connection weights in the network, and all representations simultaneously influence the processing of new inputs (for all processing depends on those same weights). These assumptions contrast with those of traditional models, in which general processes construct, search for, retrieve, and use discretely stored representations (see Smith, 1998).

In summary, autoassociative networks possess many of the features we believe are part of human memory. Autoassociators provide for memory storage and retrieval, they can learn simply by observing examples, they automatically generalize their knowledge across similar experiences, they store information by using a finite amount of resources, and they use distributed representations.

GENERAL SIMULATION APPROACH

We designed our simulations to capture the conceptual features of the empirical phenomena as much as possible. Research participants enter a typical person memory experiment with a store of background knowledge (such as group stereotypes). In the experiment itself, they may be exposed to some social stimuli and then report their memory or judgments concerning those stimuli. Therefore, for each simulated topic we built a set of stimulus patterns to represent: (1) the participant's pre-experimental knowledge as well as any learning that takes place in the experiment; and (2) the test stimuli used to elicit memory reports or social judgments. We had an autoassociative network learn the patterns (1) and then presented the test stimuli (2) and recorded the network's output for each. The specific characteristics of each stimulus set were chosen to reproduce conceptually the experiences of the human participants in the experimental paradigm we were trying to simulate, as discussed later for each simulated topic. Note that we do not model background knowledge directly, but the process of learning it. That is, we do not start with the assumption that people enter a situation possessing specific knowledge structures with specific levels of accessibility, but we assume that those knowledge structures stem from a history of past exposure to and use of specific stimuli.

In real life, people cannot neatly define those that they meet as possessing specific quantities of individual traits or other characteristics. Situational variables, as well as our internal states, can influence the way we perceive others. Our perceptions, therefore, vary with the presence or absence of these factors. If we wish to generalize from our model to human behavior we should show that the model reproduces known data patterns not only when stimuli are clear and error free but also when variability is included in the stimuli. We therefore added some element of noise, quantitative random variation, to all of our stimulus patterns. The inclusion of random variation means that we cannot run the simulation program a single time and declare that its output represents the prediction of the model. To make confident statements about the model's predictions we must average over the results of several independent simulation runs, each with a new set of stimuli that satisfies the constraints for the experiment but has new random values added. The simulation output from each such stimulus set corresponds conceptually to the responses of an individual research participant in a standard experiment. Correspondingly, we applied standard statistical techniques, such as *t* tests and correlations, to analyze the simulation results for assurance that the patterns we report go beyond chance fluctuations.

Simulation 1: Exemplar-based inference

Inferences concerning a target person can be based on the perceived characteristics of a specific well-known individual (Smith & Zárate, 1992). Research by Andersen and her colleagues (e.g. Andersen & Cole, 1990) and by Lewicki (1985) has shown that exemplar-based knowledge can affect inferences about newly encountered persons who resemble the known exemplars in some way.

Method

We used the autoassociative model discussed in McClelland and Rumelhart (1986) for all our simulations (see also Figure 3.1, p.33 for a generic autoassociator). The simulated network has 40 interconnected units. The number 40 was an arbitrary choice, mainly reflecting the limits of our available computational resources. In keeping with the fundamental representational assumption of distributed connectionist models, a person, social group, or other social object is represented by a pattern of activation across these units. The global parameter that determines how fast the network learns was fixed at a value of .01 in our simulation runs; the global parameters that set the rates of excitation (i.e. *istr* and *extr*) and decay were fixed at .15 (see McClelland & Rumelhart, 1988, p.182). The network is allowed to propagate its activation for 50 processing cycles, which in our simulations is enough to develop a stable interpretation of the input.

We simulated 10 subjects and exposed each to 1,200 patterns. (Here, and in the other simulations we report, this total number of patterns is an arbitrary choice.) One thousand were used to represent general background knowledge about people and had all of their pattern values drawn from a normal distribution with a mean of zero and a standard deviation of .5 (henceforth to be written as $N[xx, yy]$ to indicate a normal distribution with mean *xx* and standard deviation *yy*).[1] The other 200 patterns were copies of a single exemplar, in which the values were randomly drawn from an $N[0, .5]$ distribution. These copies of the exemplar were presented without variation. The presentation order of these 1,200 patterns was determined randomly for

---

1 This random generation produces some input values that fall outside of the range from −1 to +1. Though the activation level of each unit is constrained by the equations given earlier to lie within that range, the input values are not so constrained.

each subject. We presented the background patterns (not just the copies of the specific exemplar) because it would not be very exciting or interesting if a network that had encountered nothing but copies of the single exemplar was found to be able to reproduce that pattern as its output.

We tested the network's memory for the exemplar by presenting it with an incomplete version of the exemplar—representing a new individual who resembles the known exemplar. This test pattern had 35 of the original exemplar's values. We then correlated the values instantiated by the network's output on the 5 non-presented characteristics with the corresponding values from the original exemplar. Again, the decision to present 35 of 40 input pattern elements and look at the network's output on the other 5 was arbitrary.

Results

The mean correlation between the instantiated values and the original exemplar characteristics was .828. This was a significant correlation, $t(9) = 26.37$, $p < .0001$.

Discussion

This simulation shows that the network can learn a pattern from multiple presentations. Through the learning process, the connections between units come to hold information about the specific repeatedly encountered exemplar. When a new input pattern is similar to the learned one, the network uses its stored knowledge to fill in unobserved parts of the pattern. Conceptually, this process resembles exemplar-based inference in person perception (e.g. Andersen & Cole, 1990).

Simulation 2: Group-based stereotyping

A stereotype is defined as a representation of attributes associated with a particular group membership, learned through experience with individual group members or from social learning. The stereotype affects inferences about new group members. Stereotyping research (see Hamilton & Sherman, 1994) has typically examined stereotype content and representation, as well as the processes involved in the application of stereotypes in person perception. Our simulation broadens the focus to include the process by which a stereotype is learned, as well as representation and use.

In common with other exemplar-based models of stereotype acquisition (e.g. Smith & Zárate, 1992), we assume that stereotypes form when perceivers encounter a number of group members possessing specific characteristics that are perceived to differ from "the average person". These encounters, of course, need not reflect everyday interactions with real people but can stem from portrayals of group members in the media or in stories, jokes, or descriptions provided by others. Thus, this model (like other exemplar models of stereotyping) is not committed to a "grain-of-truth" theory about the origin of stereotypes (although it is certainly consistent with that viewpoint). Nor does an exemplar model necessarily predict that people will lack stereotypes about groups they have never personally encountered. Biased and stereotypic media portrayals, or social learning from others, can allow the individual to construct mental representations of group members that are predominantly consistent with cultural stereotypes.

Method

We simulated 10 subjects and exposed each to 1,200 patterns. One thousand were used to represent general background knowledge about people and had all of their characteristics distributed $N[0, .5]$. The remaining 200 were constructed to represent some members of a particular group who have distinctive subpatterns, including positive mean values on 6 particular units and negative values on 6 other units. (As before, the use of 6 characteristics was arbitrary.) These 200 patterns had 6 characteristics distributed $N[.5, .5]$, 6 characteristics distributed $N[-.5, .5]$, and the remaining 28 characteristics distributed $N[0, .5]$. The presentation order of all 1,200 patterns was determined randomly for each subject. Note that we do not include a single attribute representing group membership *per se*, but we assume that parts of the distributed pattern represent attributes (such as aspects of physical appearance) that are cues to group membership, whereas other parts represent characteristics (such as traits) that are perceived to be correlated with group membership.

After exposure to these patterns, we tested the network's use of the stereotype by presenting it with an incomplete version of the stereotype pattern, containing just 7 of the 12 relevant units (with the other 33 units set to zero) to see if it would infer the group-typical values for the 5 missing units.

Results

The activation values across the five non-presented units were correlated with the known-group average values (either .5 or −.5 for each characteristic). The value of this correlation, averaged across the 10 simulated subjects, was .647, which is reliably different from zero, $t(9) = 10.54$, $p < .0001$. Thus, the network filled in group-typical values for a new individual who had some features that defined him or her as a member of the stereotyped group.

Discussion

This simulation shows that the network learning rule, which extracts information from input patterns and represents it as patterns of connection weights, can reproduce stereotyping effects. Non-zero connections among units included in subpatterns representing the group-typical attributes give rise to inferences about new group members. The difference between this simulation and the previous one (exemplar-based inference) is that in this case the average or typical pattern was abstracted from many group members, which incorporated some variability; whereas in the previous case the pattern was learned from multiple presentations of an unchanged exemplar.

McClelland and Rumelhart (1986) provided similar demonstrations, showing that a network of the sort simulated here can simultaneously extract several prototype patterns from the presentation of noisy exemplars and then reproduce the prototypes from appropriate new inputs. In fact, they showed that a single network can even learn a general pattern (corresponding to "dog") from exposure to multiple randomly varied dog exemplars, plus a specific exemplar ("Fido") that is repeatedly presented. Then exposure to a new dog pattern (i.e. the dog prototype plus new random variation) gives rise to the dog pattern in the network's output—in effect, the network says "that's another dog". However, presentation of the Fido pattern, perhaps with a small amount of noise added, produces Fido and not just dog on the output. Fido is not just another dog but is represented as a specific individual, even though a new pattern with equal similarity to the dog prototype is simply classified as a dog.

Thus, the McClelland and Rumelhart (1986) network has previously been shown to have the general abilities on which our first two simulations rely. However, in the context of the processing of social information, these two simulations have a highly significant implication: A common mechanism can account for the seemingly disparate phenomena of exemplar-based inference and group stereotyping. Existing theories in social cognition generally postulate that these rest on fundamentally different representational formats and processes, such as abstract group-trait associations for stereotypes, and more concrete and complex "personalized" representations for specific individuals. Existing theories also face difficult questions such as when to use each type of knowledge representation or which type has priority when they conflict (Kunda & Thagard, 1996; Smith & Zárate, 1992). In contrast, the current model is parsimonious: These simulations show that a common mechanism can reproduce both types of effects. This is because the learning rule can abstract general regularities and ignore random variation while also preserving specific details about oft-encountered patterns. Theorists do not have to choose between exemplar and abstractionist mechanisms, for a single mechanism can both extract general regularities from variable presentations and record the specifics of an oft-encountered individual stimulus pattern. Other connectionist theorists have similarly emphasized the benefits of a single mechanism that can handle behaviors that seem on the surface to involve separate processes using "rules" and "exceptions" (e.g. Seidenberg, 1993).

Simulation 3: Emergent attributes from combining knowledge structures

Current theories of impression formation (e.g. Brewer, 1988; Fiske & Neuberg, 1990; Wyer & Srull, 1989) claim that under normal or default processing conditions, perceivers search for a single schema, stereotype, or other knowledge structure in memory that fits available information about a target person. The schema is then used to direct the search for further information, to make inferences, and to derive affective and evaluative responses. Only special motives push people to go beyond schema-driven processing to personalize or individuate the target by focusing on specific attributes. Recent research demonstrates, however, that people are able to use many sources of knowledge in parallel (Kunda & Thagard, 1996). They can even combine two or more schemata or stereotypes in creative ways, often producing emergent characteristics not present in the input or in any pattern that directly matches the input. For example, a Harvard-educated carpenter might be assumed to be "non-materialistic", an attribute that is not highly salient in either the Harvard or the carpenter stereotypes (Asch & Zukier, 1984; Hastie et al., 1990; Kunda, Miller, & Claire, 1990). Such emergent attributes are difficult to explain from the perspective of a schema theory in which the preferred mode of processing is to fit a single schema to each input. Can the connectionist network model account for such findings?

Method

The design of the stereotypes used in this simulation may be thought of as follows. Three stereotypes, each including three characteristics, are learned by the network:

- Stereotype 1: ABC
- Stereotype 2: DEF
- Stereotype 3: CFG

Now consider how the stimulus pattern ABDE will be processed. A model that applies only a single knowledge structure to interpret new input would activate Stereotype 1 and infer characteristic C, or else activate Stereotype 2 and infer F. Perhaps a more flexible model might activate both of these stereotypes and infer both C and F. With our model, however, we wanted to test whether the network would be able to draw on all of its knowledge—including Stereotype 3, which has no overlap with the stimulus input—to infer characteristic G as well. In other words, Stereotype 1 permits an inferential link between characteristics A and B in the input and C, Stereotype 2 permits an inference of F from D and E, and Stereotype 3 permits an inference of G from C and F. Note that the three stereotypes are not applied in a sequential fashion; all are represented in the same set of interunit connections, so all simultaneously affect the processing of the new input stimulus.

To implement this design, we simulated 10 subjects and exposed each to 1,600 patterns in a random order. One thousand formed a general background and had all of their characteristics distributed $N[0, .5]$. Two hundred patterns represented each of the three stereotypes. A distributed representation was used, with each of the abstract attributes (the letters in the descriptions of the previous paragraph) represented by a subpattern of positive and negative activation levels across a given set of three units. Thus, the "prototype" pattern for each stereotype had nine units with values of $+.5$ or $-.5$ (corresponding to the three letters), as well as 31 units with zero values. The two hundred patterns actually presented to the network were constructed by adding random noise with a standard deviation of .5 to each unit of this prototype. As in the abstract specification indicated earlier, the characteristics of the first two stereotypes did not overlap, but the pattern for the third stereotype shared parts with each of the first two stereotypes (the subpatterns corresponding to C and F) and also had a unique subpattern (corresponding to G).

Results

The network was tested with a stimulus including the subpatterns corresponding to ABDE (with other units set to zero). We examined the network's output for the unique subpattern corresponding to G of the third stereotype. The three units in this pattern were significantly different from zero in the correct directions ($-$, $-$, $+$; see Table 7.1). In other words, the network activated the specific subpattern corresponding to attribute G.

Discussion

First, this simulation shows that more than one pattern can simultaneously be represented in the network and used to make inferences. In contrast, the two earlier simulations only required the storage of a single pattern. The information in all three stereotypes is maintained in distributed form in the connection weights (van Gelder, 1991) rather than being represented in

Table 7.1 Network outputs on units corresponding to novel attribute G

| Unit | r | | $t(9)$ | p |
	M	SD		
1	$-.202$	.167	-3.83	.004
2	$-.112$	.144	-2.47	.036
3	.183	.134	4.30	.002

discrete, independently retrievable parcels or chunks as assumed in current symbolic theories.

Second, the results show that the network successfully inferred from the input pattern that the subpattern corresponding to G should be present. The specific units involved in this subpattern do not appear in the input stimulus or in Stereotypes 1 or 2. Thus, the network must have activated the first two stored patterns (stereotypes) to infer characteristics C and F for the given input and must also have used the third stereotype to activate these three units corresponding to G. However, this description does not imply that processing is sequential (i.e. first activate Stereotypes 1 and 2 and then Stereotype 3), for all stored knowledge (encoded in the connection weights) actually affects processing simultaneously.

In terms of our example, the performance demonstrated by this network could yield the emergent attribute of non-materialistic for the Harvard-carpenter stereotype combination. Say Stereotype 1 represents the Harvard stereotype, with attribute C meaning something like "qualified for a high-paying occupation". Stereotype 2 represents carpenter, with attribute F representing "low paid". Stereotype 3 could represent a general-knowledge structure stating that if a person is qualified for a high-paying occupation (C) and is low paid (F), it might be because he or she is non-materialistic (G). As this simulation shows, activation of the first two stereotypes by other cues besides C and F may result in the activation of G through the simultaneous use of all three of these knowledge structures. Of course, the combination of multiple knowledge structures can be a complex and creative process involving extensive thought (Asch & Zukier, 1984; Smith, Osherson, Rips, & Keane, 1988), and such processes are not incorporated in our simulations. These results suggest, however, that it is also possible for novel attributes to emerge from conceptual combination through a relatively simple process of memory retrieval and reconstruction, as implemented in an autoassociative network memory.

Recently, several theorists have advanced parallel-constraint-satisfaction models in various domains in social psychology (Kunda & Thagard, 1996; Read & Marcus-Newhall, 1993; Shultz & Lepper, 1996). Like the current simulation, these models are able simultaneously to apply multiple stored knowledge structures to generate inferences, rather than selecting a single schema to guide processing. However, they differ from our model in one key respect: All of these models rely on localist (non-distributed) representations in which a node represents a belief or proposition, and connections between nodes represent their relations of consistency or inconsistency. Each of these models uses a structure of nodes and links set up by the theorist for a particular problem. Many decisions must be made: which nodes (propositions) to include as relevant in a problem representation at all, what initial activation levels (belief strengths) to give the nodes, and what sign and weight to give each link. When the proper representations are hand coded in this way, flows of activation in the network according to the models' rules perform parallel constraint satisfaction and yield the desired inferences.

In contrast, the model described here (as is typical of models using distributed rather than local representations) learns, from a series of input stimuli, the representations on which it bases inferences. Our simulations are not free of theoretical assumptions, of course: The specific structure and sequence of the input patterns presented to the network embody our assumptions about regularities in the social environment that are available to be learned by the network. We believe that our model nevertheless has three advantages over localist parallel-constraint-satisfaction models (leaving aside any issues of the neural plausibility of distributed representations): (1) Ours represents a more complete model, covering the construction as well as the use of representations. In contrast, models that require hand coding of their representations deal only with the use of knowledge and leave open questions as to how the representations that are assumed to underlie a given inference can be produced in the first place. (2) Assumptions about the nature and sequence of input stimuli seem more transparent and easier to justify, compared with assumptions about the N starting activation levels and N^2 link strengths in a localist model. (3) Finally, assumptions about the nature of stimulus inputs give rise to testable hypotheses, which could be confirmed in studies of the inputs that people naturally receive or in experimental studies that vary stimulus inputs and test their consequences for memory and judgment. In contrast, assumptions about activations and links of localist nodes are not directly testable in any independent way, other than by through their effects on the system's overall output.

Simulation 4: Accessibility from recency and frequency

Not all learned knowledge structures (such as concepts, exemplars, or schemata) have equal effects on the interpretation of a new input. Structures that have been processed frequently or recently generally have larger effects. This property is termed accessibility (Higgins, 1996). In social cognition, this theoretical conception has been applied to an exceptionally wide range of issues. Priming studies (e.g. Higgins, Rholes, & Jones, 1977) demonstrate that recent exposures to a concept in an irrelevant context can influence the way people interpret later information. Studies of chronic accessibility (e.g. Bargh, Lombardi, & Higgins, 1988) show that people who have used a particular concept frequently in the past are more likely to use it to interpret ambiguously concept-related input information. This simulation is intended to determine whether the connectionist network can not only store and retrieve patterns (as shown by the previous simulations) but also maintain representations of patterns with varying levels of accessibility, qualitatively matching the effects of recent and frequent exposure demonstrated by social psychological research.

Method

We simulated 50 subjects per condition for this topic. (The larger number of subjects was due to our desire to find statistically reliable results for all of our conditions, even those not particularly conducive to memory.) Each simulated subject was exposed to a set of patterns, in which the exact composition differed to form four conditions. Each set of patterns included multiple copies of a particular exemplar, interspersed among a larger number of background patterns. The value of each characteristic in the exemplar was independently drawn from an $N[0, .5]$ distribution. The same exemplar was used in all simulations and was presented without variation. The general background patterns had all of their characteristics drawn from an $N[0, .5]$ distribution. The number and order of presentation varied across conditions (Table 7.2).

As Table 7.2 shows, recency was manipulated by presenting the exemplar patterns either followed by 300 additional random patterns or at the end of the stimulus sequence. Frequency was manipulated by presenting either 30 or 150 copies of the exemplar. We tested each network's memory for the exemplar by presenting it with an incomplete version of the exemplar (containing 35 features) and then correlating the network's output on the remaining 5 characteristics with the original exemplar pattern.

Results

The mean r-to-z transformed correlations are presented in Table 7.3; the transformation is used because comparisons among conditions (not simply a mean difference from zero) are important in this simulation. The t tests in Table 7.3 are separate comparisons of each condition's mean against a mean of zero, the expected value if no instances of the specific exemplar had ever been encountered.

Table 7.2 Design of stimulus presentation sequences for four conditions of recency by frequency

Condition	Description	Sequence of presentations
1	Neither recent nor frequent	300 background patterns, 30 copies of exemplar, 300 background patterns
2	Recent and not frequent	600 background patterns, 30 copies of exemplar
3	Frequent and not recent	300 background patterns, 150 copies of exemplar, 300 background patterns
4	Recent and frequent	600 background patterns, 150 copies of exemplar

Table 7.3 Accessibility values predicted by network for four conditions of recency by frequency

Condition	Mean r-to-z transformation	t(49)	p
1 (Not recent and not frequent)	.157	1.84	.07
2 (Recent)	.452	5.46	.0001
3 (Frequent)	.527	5.71	.0001
4 (Recent and frequent)	1.90	33.53	.0001

Discussion

All four conditions yielded results in the predicted direction, although, as expected, the effect in the not-recent-and-not-frequent condition was small (marginally significant with 50 simulated subjects). The more important results involve comparisons among conditions on the basis of t tests on the r-to-z-transformed correlations. All comparisons discussed here were significant at $p < .05$. Recency had a clear and strong effect on the magnitude of accessibility, demonstrated by the significant comparisons of Condition 2 versus Condition 1 (effect of recency with only 30 exposures), $t(98) = 2.48$, and also Condition 4 versus Condition 3 (recency with 150 exposures), $t(98) = 12.63$.

Frequency also had an effect, which was similar in size: compare Condition 3 versus Condition 1 (effect of 150 vs. 30 non-recent exposures), $t(98) = 2.94$, and Condition 4 versus Condition 2 (effect of 150 vs. 30 recent exposures), $t(98) = 14.40$. One cannot conclude that the model generally predicts that frequency and recency effects will be comparable in size, for the specific effect sizes depend, of course, on such arbitrary details as the numbers chosen to instantiate the various conditions (e.g. 150 vs. 30 exposures; exposures followed by 0 or 300 more random patterns). In general, the simulation results show that the model qualitatively matches patterns of accessibility found with human subjects: recency and frequency both increase accessibility. The connectionist network is able not only to store multiple representations but to maintain them at appropriately varying levels of accessibility, depending on the specific history of stimulus exposures.

In this model, accessibility is not explained as some extra property (such as position in a storage bin or charge on a storage battery) added on to discrete representational entities. In fact, this model does not have any discrete representations in the first place. The relative accessibilities of all the patterns known to the network, in the sense of their respective potentials for activation, are an emergent property determined by the entire set of connection weights.[2]

---

2 Accessibility has nothing to do with the decay term in the activation equation; decay of activations takes place over short time periods and is independent of the long-lasting changes in the connection weights produced by learning, which are responsible for accessibility.

The weights influence the rapidity and precision with which a pattern appears on the network outputs as activation flows, given a related set of input cues. Processing a given pattern changes the weights (through the learning rule) in the direction of making that pattern and similar ones a bit easier to activate. Simultaneously, processing an unrelated pattern makes the original pattern a bit harder to activate because from its perspective random noise is being added to the weights. In this way, the connectionist framework uses an extremely simple and general mechanism to reproduce qualitatively the known aspects of accessibility effects.

Simulation 5: New prediction of rapid recovery of accessibility after decay

In the autoassociative model, the current level of accessibility depends on the current values of the connection weights: Specifically, it depends on how well the weights allow flows of activation to reconstruct the entire target pattern, given a subset of the pattern as input. Changes in accessibility due to exposure to new patterns, however, depend on the learning rule and the way the connection weights are altered by newly processed stimuli. Thus, a dissociation between current performance and change due to learning can be predicted. Specifically, two different sets of connection weights may have the same level of accessibility but still change in different ways when the learning rule is applied to new input stimuli.

To visualize how this can occur, think of a particular network (i.e. a specific set of connection weight values) as corresponding to a point on a flat surface. Neighboring points on the surface correspond to very similar networks (formed by very small changes in the connection weights).[3] Each of these networks has a particular value of accessibility for the specific target pattern, which one could measure by feeding in the partial version of the target pattern as input and comparing the network's output to the target. Now consider this accessibility value as defining a vertical distance above the flat plane for each possible network. Areas in which the weights produce relatively good accessibility would correspond to high peaks or plateaus of the resulting "landscape", whereas areas with low levels of accessibility would produce "valleys". A one-dimensional version of this picture is shown as Figure 7.1. Note, for example, that the network corresponding to Point B does a good job of reconstructing the target pattern from partial inputs (it has a high value of accessibility).

In a picture like this, the operation of the learning rule can easily be visualized: Starting with a set of weights corresponding to a specific spot on the

---

3   This surface (in actuality, a space with as many dimensions as there are connection weights in the network) is technically called a *weight space* (see Churchland & Sejnowski, 1992, Chapter 3).

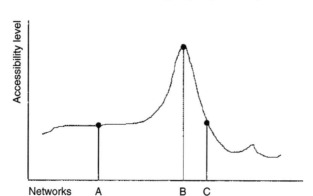

Figure 7.1 Schematic illustration of accessibility of a target pattern for a range of networks, each corresponding to a specific set of connection weight values. The learning process, by changing connection weights, moves a network along the horizontal axis of this diagram, resulting in changes in the target pattern's accessibility.

landscape, learning after exposure to an instance of the target pattern changes the weights slightly in a way that moves uphill-toward increased accessibility of the target pattern. In contrast, learning after exposure to a random input pattern moves that current point in a random direction, possibly uphill and possibly downhill.

Now, as Figure 7.1 illustrates, two points (like A and C) may have the same current accessibility level (i.e. the same height in the landscape) but may change in very different ways with further learning. For example, Point A is on a fairly flat portion of the landscape, so many learning trials are required to get very far upward (accessibility will increase only slowly with learning). In contrast, another point at the same level (Point C) may lie on a steep slope, so just a few learning trials will result in a large gain in height (accessibility). Thus, the connectionist model predicts that a dissociation may exist between the current accessibility level and the change in accessibility with further stimulus exposures (for a related prediction, see Hinton & Sejnowski, 1986).

A concrete test of this prediction may be conducted as follows. Assume that a person is frequently exposed to instances of a specific stimulus concept intermixed with other, irrelevant stimuli. The accessibility of this stimulus should steadily rise, probably with diminishing returns after a while. Then assume that the person is exposed only to unrelated, random stimuli until the accessibility of the target pattern declines to zero (i.e. there is no longer any detectable tendency to generate the completion of that particular pattern when given a partial version of it as input). Now, if the person again begins to encounter that pattern, accessibility should rise again at a faster rate than it did the first time. The reason is that in the initial state, with random connection weights, the network is on average in a flat portion of the landscape, like Point A in Figure 7.1; accessibility will increase at a relatively slow rate. After accessibility has grown to a high level (e.g. Point B), the decay process (learning many unrelated patterns) effectively adds random numbers to the weights. This will reduce accessibility, eventually to the same level as at first—but it will leave the state of the network at a point like C: near a high peak (the high-accessibility region reached after the initial learning). Thus, further learning can more quickly return the network to a high level of accessibility.

Method

We simulated 100 subjects. First, the network was given 500 random patterns as an initial background (for clarity, we begin counting patterns after this point). Then the network was exposed to 100 learning trials in blocks of 20. Each block consisted of 10 copies of a single pattern (chosen with all units drawn from an $N[0, .5]$ distribution) intermixed with 10 random patterns. After each block (i.e. after 0, 20, 40, 60, 80, and 100 patterns), the accessibility of the target pattern was tested in the usual way. We presented an incomplete version of the pattern (containing the pattern's specific values on 35 of the 40 input units), with learning turned off so that the test had no effect on the connection weights. We measured the network's output on the remaining 5 units and correlated these values with the values of the target pattern. Finally, the correlation was transformed with the *r*-to-*z* transformation.

Following the presentation of these 100 patterns, 500 random patterns with no copies of the target stimulus were presented to the network. Accessibility was again tested at this point (i.e. after Pattern 600) to verify that it had returned to zero. Finally, two more blocks like the initial ones (again including the target pattern) were presented, and accessibility was tested after Patterns 620 and 640. The question is whether the increase in accessibility after the decay proceeds at the same rate or more quickly than the increase at the initial trials.

Results

The results are shown in Figure 7.2. Clearly, the increase in accessibility is much faster after the decay, even though at Trial 600 accessibility was close to zero (virtually identical to the accessibility before training). Paired *t* tests show that the accessibility level was greater at Trial 620 than at Trial 20, $t(99) = 9.49$, $p < .0001$, and also greater at Trial 640 than at Trial 40, $t(99) = 38.83$, $p < .0001$. To quantify the greater rate of increase, note in Figure 7.2 that attaining an accessibility level corresponding to a z of 0.5 required approximately 40 trials initially but fewer than 20 after the decay. Accessibility of 1.0 was attained with just under 80 trials initially but with well under 40 after decay. The rate of increase is at least twice what it was initially.

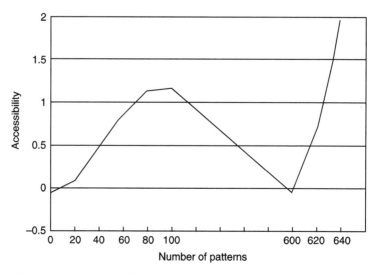

Figure 7.2 Graph of accessibility of the target pattern as the network is trained on a number of patterns. Patterns 1–100 and patterns 601–640 were half-and-half mixtures of random patterns and instances of the target pattern; patterns 101–600 were random patterns.

Discussion

The network shows rapid recovery of accessibility after a period of decay caused by non-use of a target pattern. This constitutes a significant new prediction made by our connectionist model, which has not yet been empirically tested. However, similar empirical findings are well known with dependent variables other than accessibility. For example, explicit memory measures such as recall and recognition generally show savings in relearning; that is, relearning after forgetting proceeds much more quickly than original learning of the same material (Carlston & Skowronski, 1994; Ebbinghaus, 1885/1964). Still, this pattern needs to be demonstrated experimentally with an accessibility dependent measure. If empirically validated, rapid recovery of accessibility after decay would have important theoretical and practical implications.

In theoretical terms, it constitutes a prediction uniquely generated by this connectionist model and not shared by current theories of accessibility (Higgins, 1996; Wyer & Srull, 1989). These theories treat accessibility as a unitary property. This means that if the level of accessibility is the same under two different conditions (as it is at Trial 0 and Trial 600 in Figure 7.2), then changes in accessibility due to further stimulus exposure would be predicted to be the same as well. In contrast, as outlined earlier, the connectionist model can predict a dissociation between two aspects of accessibility: its current level and its change in response to new stimulus input.

This predicted pattern, if found in experimental work, has important practical as well as theoretical implications. Often, people do not wish particular knowledge structures to be accessible. Such structures might include racial and ethnic stereotypes, thoughts about past events tied to feelings of guilt or sadness, and the like. Current theoretical models of accessibility predict that if one can somehow refrain from activating such knowledge structures for long enough, their accessibility would diminish and eventually approach zero. Even though avoiding the thoughts might be difficult in practical terms (Wegner, 1994), if it can be done then current models promise a lasting decrease in accessibility. Our model paints a less optimistic picture. Even after non-use leads to a decline to zero accessibility, a few new encounters with the knowledge structure are predicted to pop accessibility right back to (and even above) its previous level. Thus, if this prediction of the model holds true, it suggests the need for remedies other than the simple decline in accessibility over time (such as the intentional build-up of the accessibility of competing knowledge structures).

GENERAL DISCUSSION AND CONCLUSIONS

Summary and implications

In summary, the results of these simulations are as follows: The connectionist model can reproduce effects of a frequently encountered exemplar on inferences, effects of a group stereotype learned from varying group exemplars, and effects of recency and frequency on accessibility. Traditional theories in social cognition also explain all of these phenomena. However, to do so, they use at least three distinct types of mechanism: (1) a schematic abstraction process that summarizes specific observations to produce generic schemata or group prototypes and uses them to make inferences; (2) an exemplar storage and retrieval process; and (3) a special-purpose mechanism attached to each distinct representation (e.g. each schema and exemplar) to track its current level of accessibility. This autoassociative connectionist network is able to simulate all of these phenomena by using only a single mechanism.

The same mechanism also produces effects that current social psychological models do not generally consider: (1) simultaneous use of multiple learned representations (rather than just one) to make inferences; and (2) rapid recovery of accessibility after a period of decay. The first of these has already been empirically documented, whereas the second is a novel prediction that awaits confirmation by using accessibility dependent measures (although, as "savings in relearning", the pattern is well-known with memory dependent variables).

As well as its consistency with several known phenomena and its intriguing new prediction, the new connectionist model offers additional advantages. Its account of the learning of representations such as stereotypes from exposure to specific group members is more precise and explicit than current accounts in social cognition, which tend to neglect learning altogether. The connectionist model also avoids difficult questions that tend to remain unanswered in current models, such as the question of when to stop storing individual exemplars and engage a summary or abstraction process instead, and whether to use a group stereotype or a well-known exemplar as a basis for inferences.

McClelland and Rumelhart (1986, pp.195–205) demonstrated that the same network is also able to reproduce details of several findings in the memory literature, such as repetition priming effects, effects of familiarity on response latency, and effects of exemplar exposures on perceptual identification performance. Thus, the model serves the purpose of theoretical integration, offering a single account for diverse findings that have typically been attributed to separate mechanisms. In comparison to current social cognition models, such as Wyer and Srull (1989), it also offers a considerable advantage in precision and simplicity. Parsimony and precision, as well as integrative potential, which may allow fruitful investigations of conceptual parallels among phenomena previously viewed as unrelated, are important criteria for evaluation of any theory. Finally, as reviewed by Smith (1996, pp.901–903), connectionist models hold much promise in accounting for phenomena like context sensitivity of concepts; multidirectional causation among cognitions like attitudes, beliefs, and goals; and cognition-motivation interactions. For all of these reasons, the type of connectionist model used here would appear to deserve further exploration by social psychologists.

Limitations

Besides its strengths, this particular connectionist model has some limitations. As McClelland and Rumelhart (1986) pointed out, the model can learn a set of patterns perfectly only if the external input to each unit can be predicted perfectly by a linear combination of the activations of all other units, across the entire set of input patterns. Although this is a relatively stringent constraint, several points can be made about it. First, perfect reproduction of learned patterns is not an appropriate goal for a network intended as a model of human memory performance. People cannot remember perfectly; they blend separate memories and display interference from related knowledge even when they are trying to retrieve a specific memory exactly. For example, they may remember only the general characteristics of a group rather than the detailed features of each individual exemplar. In fact, we argue that a memory model that predicted perfect performance under realistic circumstances would be ill-suited as a model of human memory.

In addition, modifications to the model can overcome this linearity constraint on pattern learning. Preprocessing of the inputs by other networks can help: If the input features presented to the network are not derived independently from sensory inputs or other sources, but reflect context-sensitive encodings of more basic features, the constraint can be bypassed. Also, the incorporation of so-called hidden units—units without direct connections to the network's inputs or outputs—allows the network to develop its own representations of meaningful features. Without hidden units the network is limited to a fixed set of features (corresponding to the network's inputs) out of which to construct distributed representations. However, hidden units allow the development of features that are flexible and sensitive to the patterning of the inputs in a particular stimulus set. This represents another way to overcome the original model's linearity constraint (McClelland & Rumelhart, 1986).

A second limitation of the model proposed here is that it can learn only from frequent repetition of stimulus patterns. A single presentation of a pattern would have little effect on the network's weights. Yet people are evidently capable of one-trial learning. In response to such observations, several theorists (e.g. McClelland, McNaughton, & O'Reilly, 1995; see Schacter & Tulving, 1994) have recently proposed connectionist models involving multiple components, with one network (comparable to the network simulated here) that learns slowly to abstract the statistical structure of the environment (e.g. the central tendency of varying individual group members or the details of a frequently encountered stimulus). Another network using a different learning rule is responsible for rapid learning, focusing particularly on novel and unexpected information, and constructs the episodic memories that are available to consciousness. Independent evidence (both behavioral and neuropsychological in nature) is consistent with this type of distinction between two memory systems, mediated, respectively, by the neocortex and by hippocampal structures in the brain. As McClelland et al. (1995) argued, such a multiple-network architecture can avoid the problems of "catastrophic interference" that have been documented when a single network is subjected to changing task demands. New information can be maintained in a separate fast-learning system and is then gradually and non-destructively integrated into the slow-learning system over time.

Most social psychological theories (in fact, most symbolic models of cognition in general) assume, in contrast, that all knowledge and beliefs are represented in a single memory system. One implication of this assumption is that the beliefs people can consciously access and verbally report are the same ones that guide their preconscious interpretation of their experiences and reconstruction of their explicit memories. This assumption now seems highly questionable (McClelland et al., 1995; Schacter & Tulving, 1994). Within social psychology there is evidence, for example, that "intuitive" emotional reactions or racial prejudices may be quite independent of verbally reportable knowledge and consciously held beliefs (Devine, 1989; Kirkpatrick & Epstein, 1992). Further tests of the assumption within social psychology may be spurred by the derivation of distinctive predictions regarding separate memory systems in a connectionist framework.

In fact, some key findings within social psychology may be related to the existence of two separate memory systems. In addition to differences in learning speed and conscious accessibility, the two systems are postulated to differ in the type of information to which they attend (see McClelland et al., 1995). Schematic learning is chiefly concerned with regularities, so it records primarily what is typical and expected. In contrast, episodic memories should record the details of events that are novel and interesting: In other words, this system should attend more to the unexpected and unpredicted. Social psychological studies (e.g. Hastie & Kumar, 1979) show that people attend to and recall mostly expectancy-inconsistent information when forming a new impression but that they mostly attend to expectation-consistent information when working with a well-formed and solid expectation (Higgins & Bargh, 1987). This empirical distinction may be a reflection of more basic differences between two underlying memory systems: one that is consciously accessible, learns quickly, and emphasizes novelty; and one (modeled in this article) that operates preconsciously, slowly accumulates information, and emphasizes regularities. An implication of this suggestion is that researchers would not expect this particular network to be able to simulate such findings as the recall advantage of expectation-inconsistent over expectation-consistent information (Hastie & Kumar, 1979) or contrast effects due to correction following priming (Martin, Seta, & Crelia, 1990). This is because both of these effects appear to depend on effortful conscious processing, which is not incorporated in our current simulation (Kunda & Thagard, 1996, described a similar limitation of their model).[4]

Despite these limitations, the model does reproduce several key phenomena, as described earlier. Autoassociative connectionist networks can be implemented in many ways, and we assume that most of the general properties of this model are probably common to autoassociators in general rather than specific to the details of the McClelland and Rumelhart (1986) model. For this reason, in this article we have focused on demonstrating the model's multiple implications for such phenomena as stereotype learning and use, accessibility, and conceptual combination. We have not yet endeavored to extend this network with additional components (e.g. a fast-learning episodic memory system or a system for consciously controlled processing) to build toward a complete model of human social cognition. In fact, although others prefer such a modeling strategy (e.g. Wyer & Srull, 1989), we are skeptical of it as an initial approach. In a large and complex model with dozens of assumptions and distinct processing mechanisms, it is often far from clear which parts of the model are responsible for any given prediction and therefore which should be modified when a prediction fails. Our approach in this article has been to demonstrate properties of a single, simple mechanism (an autoassociative network) to make the case that implications of connectionist models for social psychology should be more fully investigated. Only as a later

---

4   For a different approach on these issues, see Chapter 8.

step—after the scope of both the successes and failures of predictions developed from this mechanism have become clearer—does it seem wise to modify the network's assumptions or add additional mechanisms to correct the failures.

Conclusion

To date, the development of connectionist models within psychology has been conducted largely by cognitive and developmental psychologists concerned with learning, memory, language processing and development, and so on. We hope that social psychologists will begin to take part in this development so that they can assess how well the phenomena that are studied (including social stereotyping, accessibility, evaluations, attitudes, etc.) fit within the connectionist framework. Potentially, social psychologists may help shape connectionist theories to incorporate their insights that cognition is deeply and intrinsically social, depends on social interaction and social influence, and results in motivated behavior in social contexts. These insights will represent important contributions to the future development of connectionist theory.

SIMULATION EXERCISES

You can now explore the recurrent simulations described in the article. However, rather than using the non-linear model variant and parameters from Smith and DeCoster (1998), as in the previous exercises (see Chapter 5) you will again use the simpler linear variant. There are two reasons for this. First, the linear recurrent model is more in line with the other simulations that you will explore in this book and is closer to the feedforward model discussed in the introductory chapters. Second, and perhaps more important, many properties of the non-linear recurrent model (the non-linear updating of the activation by spreading the activation through the network over multiple cycles) are not necessary to make the simulations work. Hence, for the present simulations, you will focus on the essential properties of the linear autoassociator rather than bother with those that are superfluous.

You are expected to have some experience of the FIT program, perhaps by having completed some of the exercises in Chapter 3 and 4. The manual of the program is available in the Appendix at the end of the book.

Exercise 1: Simulation of exemplar-bases inference

Choose menu **File | Open Project**, search for *Smith+DeCoster98_1.ft2* in folder *Chapter 7*, and click the **Open** button. Alternatively, you can press the ☞ speed button. Note that some of the specifications in this simulation are rather unusual and complex because the representation uses distributed patterns and because there are no empirical data with which to compare the simulated values. Rather, you explore pattern completion, that is, you are going to compare the activation pattern of a missing input with the activation generated by the other units of the network.

Specifying trials

Click the **Trial** tab to open the Trial Grid, which defines the Trial Categories. The two top rows show seven input units and one output unit representing the information about the individual exemplar and his or her traits (e.g. narrow-minded, aggressive). As you will see later, each *localist* unit will in fact be "blown up" to five *distributed* units. This is also indicated in the second row where, for clarity's sake, each unit's name gets the range that is applied in the distributed version. You can change these names either by double clicking, or by choosing the **Data | Edit Column Names** menu. In Figure 7.3, you see the names and input data that have been given in this project.

There is only a single Learning Trial Category *$1*. As you can see, it contains 1,000 trials of background patterns and 200 trials of the same exemplar. As you will see later, additional noise will be applied to the background, but not to the exemplar. To do this, you use a little trick here. In the distributed parameters, you will specify that all cells with a zero activation get additional noise, while no noise is applied to the non-zero cells. Therefore, the background gets exactly 0 as value, while the exemplar gets small values close to 0 (+.01 or −.01).

Testing patterns never get additional noise. The activation patterns that are specified in the cells of the Test Categories are exact copies of the Learning Category, except for the explicitly missing cells (zero activation) or for reading off the resulting activation (? activation). As you are going to extend each localist unit with five distributed units, you need to repeat each test 5 times. Test Category *$50* directly activates the missing part of the total pattern (distributed units *36–40*) and this activation will then be compared with the activation generated by the network after priming an incomplete pattern (distributed units *1–35*) in Test Category *$51*. This is further specified in the Session. Note that the program will issue a warning that no "?" is specified in Test Category *$50*, but you can simply ignore this for this exercise.

Trial		Session		Listing		Log		Graph			
7:1	#	i1	i2	i3	i4	i5	i6	i7	o1	**Comments**	
		1-5	6-10	11-15	16-20	21-25	26-30	31-35	36-40		
1	$1	Learning of Background and Person Exemplar									
2	1000	0	0	0	0	0	0	0	0	Background with noise	
3	200	.01	-.01	.01	-.01	.01	-.01	.01	-.01	Exemplar without noise / variation	
4	$50	Test the missing pattern									
5	5	0	0	0	0	0	0	0	-.01		
6	$51	Test the incomplete pattern									
7	5	.01	-.01	.01	-.01	.01	-.01	.01	?		

Figure 7.3 Exercise 1: Names and input data in the trial grid.

Specifying sessions

Click the **Session** tab to open the Session Grid and to specify the ordering of the Learning and Test Trial Categories. As you can see, Learning Category *$1* is followed by the *$50* and *$51* Test Categories. Each of these Test Categories is given a different number (*0* to *1*) in **IV2**. The resulting test activation from the five distributed units is linked to five DVs, from **DV1** to **DV5**. They are labeled to conform their distributed position from *36* to *40*.

The manner by which the values are put in the DVs allows you to examine pattern completion. First, the missing part of a pattern is measured in Test Category $50. This activation will then be compared against the internal activation generated by the network after activating the input units representing the non-missing part of the pattern (Test Category $51). Specifically:

- Test Category $50: To indicate that you simply take the external activation of the missing pattern as baseline, you set in **DV1** to **DV5** the *equal sign =*. This tells the program that it should take the external activation of each output unit as **observed data value** for the next test categories marked with * as value (until there is a *reset*).
- Test Category $51: This computes the activation generated by the incomplete pattern of distributed units 1–35 and reads this off at the distributed units 36–40 as indicated by ? As there are no observed values here, you put asterisks.

Specifying the simulation parameters

Choose the **Simulation | Parameters** menu, or press the 🏵 speed button. The most important options and parameters for this simulation are shown in Figure 7.4.

Model		External Noise (while Learning)	
51 : Linear Auto-associator (McClelland and Rumelhart, 1988)	∨	45 : Add Normal (M=0, SD=0.50)	
External Coding		Response	
15 : Normal Distributed Pattern (M=activation, SD=0.5)	∨	12 : Paired (nth Target<>0 -> nth Observed)	

General	Model	Weights & Activation	Distributed Coding & Noise	Robustness	Interaction

Distributed Coding at Learning & Test Trials

Noise

Noise at Learning Trials

of (Micro-) Features per Unit 5 ⬍

In learning $ 1 - 49

☐ Also on Zero External Activation

Noise on Zero External Activation

☐ Link (Micro-) Features of Same Unit

○ No   ○ Also   ◉ Only

Figure 7.4 Exercise 1: Options and parameters for the simulation.

In the top panel, four option boxes (with a drop-down list) provide the major options:

- In the **Model** option box, the *Linear Recurrent* model developed by McClelland and Rumelhart (1988) is chosen. If not, select that model now.
- In the **External Coding** option box, *Normal Distributed Pattern (M = activation, SD = 0.5)* is selected. If not, select that option now. This option indicates that you are now using a distributed representation for the background and exemplar, with an activation pattern for each unit randomly selected from a Normal Distribution with mean = the activation indicated in the cells of the Trial Grid, and standard deviation = 0.5. Note that this pattern is used until completion of the simulation runs (unless you specify otherwise by the **Reshuffle** option).
- In the **External Noise (while Learning)** option box, select *Add Normal (M = 0, SD = 0.5)*. This is used to add random noise to the background, using again a Normal Distribution now with mean = 0 and standard deviation = 0.5. (The mean is logically 0 because otherwise you would add a fixed value to the external activation.)
- In the **Response** option box, select *Paired (nth Output → nth Observed)*. This makes sure that the five resulting activations at the output layer (i.e. distributed output units 36–40) are each paired with one DV (**DV1** to **DV5**). Thus, distributed unit 36 is compared with **DV1**, unit 37 with **DV2** and so on.

Now Click the **Distributed Coding and Noise** tab:

- Here you can specify that each localist unit will be extended or "blown up" to a pattern of distributed activations across five subfeatures or units. Simply enter *5* in **the # of (Micro-)Features per Unit** field. Each localist unit is now converted to five units with an activation pattern as specified above by the **External Coding** option box. This is all that is needed to turn a localist representation into a distributed representation if the exact content of the distributed representation does not matter and can be randomly chosen.
- The **Also on Zero Activation** check box must **not** be marked. This makes sure that the background gets no random distributed activation pattern as used for the exemplar. Thus, the distributed activation for the background is just a flat zero. However, as you will see shortly, our little trick is to produce noise on the background that changes every trial.
- In addition, specify that the noise in the Learning Trials applies to all Learning Categories *1–49*.
- Importantly, you should now indicate that the noise is applied only to units with **Zero External Activation** (as specified in the Trial Grid). This is our little trick to produce noise on the background that differs at every

learning trial, but not on the exemplar itself (by using small non-zero values for the exemplar).

- Leave the other parameters blank, or set them to *no*.

Now you enter the parameters in the other tabs, as you have done in the other simulations. Click first the **General** tab. Specify in **Session** that you want to run session *1*, and select the button *yes* in **Graph Simulated Values** (automatically, the **Log Simulated Values** will also turn to *yes*). In addition, set **Randomize Order for All Learning Trials** to *yes* and specify *10* runs to simulate 10 participants as specified by Smith and DeCoster (1998). Leave the categories to which this applies to at *1–49*. Set all other parameters to *no*. Finally, click the **Model** tab. Enter a learning rate of *0.01* as in the article. Leave the other parameters blank, or set them to *auto* or *no*.

Running the simulation

To run the simulation as specified above, choose the **Simulation | Run Simulation** menu or press the ⚒ speed button. If you want to follow the simulation step by step, choose the **Simulation | Parameters** menu, press the **General** tab, and set **View Details** to *View*. Alternatively, you can hit the ⚒ speed button for a display of the network or the ⚒ speed button for a tabular display.

After the simulation is finished, the **Graph** tab will open automatically (because you requested a graph). Make the following selections:

- **filter**: *Test*, and enter values **From *1* To *1***. This enables us to take only the internal activation values generated by Test Category $51 that reflect pattern completion, and to filter out the baseline or "observed" values taken from Test Category $50.
- **X-Axis**: # ½ *DV*. This allows the model to compare each of the **observed DVs** with the **simulated DVs**, rather than the different conditions within each DV as is usually the case. As the **observed DVs** make up half of all **DVs**, you select # ½ *DV*.
- **X-Axis Labels**: *IVLabel*.
- **Y-Axis Line(s)**: select all simulated and observed **DVs**. The variable names preceded by a ~-sign denote the simulated values.

Then select **Regress** to make sure that you can directly compare the patterns of the "observed" and simulated values. In addition, you can also select **List Stats**. After hitting the **Graph Log** button, you will see a graph of the simulation results. It is perfectly normal that the points in the graph are not connected by lines, because each point refers to a different DV. For the numerical results (means and correlations) press the **Listing** tab.

Although the recurrent variant and testing procedure you used differ from those used by Smith and DeCoster (1998), the obtained internal activation is very close to the original activation of the missing input. In the Listing Sheet, you can see that the correlation between simulated and "observed" means of the original simulation of the exercises is very high, $r = 1.000$ (5, $p < 0.001$) and much higher than the correlation reported by Smith and DeCoster (1998).

Questions

1. You can check that the background gets no exemplar activation by selecting *none* in the **External Noise (while Learning)** option box. To see the input activation, select the menu **Simulation | View Network** or press the 🏃 speed button before starting the simulation. Then press the **Input** tab. To begin the simulation, press the **Start Run** button or the 🏃 speed button. To move between successive trials, press the **Next Trial** button. To move quickly between learning and testing, press the **Next Category** button.

2. Alternatively, you can check that only the background gets noise by selecting *Distributed pattern without noise* in the **External Coding** option box. Again, select the menu **Simulation | View Network** or press the 🏃 speed button. Then press the **Input** tab.

3. You can experiment with the non-linear model that was used by Smith and DeCoster (1998). Choose the **Simulation | Parameters** menu or press the ⚙ speed button, and select the *non-linear recurrent* model in the **Model** option box. Enter the model parameters as indicated in the text (**istr** = *0.15*; **estr** = *0.15*, **decay** = *0.15*, and **#cycles** = *50*). To run the simulations, choose the **Simulation | Run Simulation** menu or press the 🏃 speed button. Do you see any difference with the previous simulation? Probably not, which suggests that the properties of the linear autoassociator are sufficient to produce the emergent property of pattern completion.

4. You can explore other models. For instance, in principle, the feedforward model is not capable of performing pattern completion, although it is in the current simulation. Do you know why?

5. You can also explore whether it is really necessary to have 200 presentations of the exemplar. Can you obtain sufficient pattern completion with 20, 5 or 2 exemplar trials? Does the model matter if you use less exemplars?

Exercise 2–5: Other simulations

Choose menu **File | Open Project**, search for *Smith+DeCoster98_x.ft2* (where *x* stands for the number of the simulation) in folder *Chapter 7*, and click the **Open** button. Alternatively, you can press the 📖 speed button. You can explore the same questions as for Simulation 1. The simulations are set up in the same manner as above, with the following exceptions:

- Simulation 2: This tests only six (instead of seven in the text) relevant units to see if the network infers the group-typical values for the six (instead of five) missing units.
- Simulation 4: Only 20 "participants" or random simulation runs were used, and the number of presentations of the exemplar was reduced to 2 and 10 (instead of 30 and 150 in the text) to obtain results that were less "neat" so that some differences between conditions 1 to 4 could be observed. Note that each of these conditions should be tested separately, by filtering-out the relevant condition. Thus, in the **filter** box, **click** *Test*, and enter values **From** *1* **To** *1* for condition 1 (not recent and not frequent) and then request the graph, enter values **From** *2* **To** *2* for condition 2 (recent), and so on.
- Simulation 5: Only 20 "participants" or random simulation runs were used and, for the reasons given in Simulation 4, the number of presentations of the exemplar was reduced to 1 (instead of 10 in the text; the number of trials of the random exemplar remained at 10) while the number of presentations for the background was slightly increased to 530 (instead of 500). Again, note that each of the conditions should be tested separately, by filtering out the relevant condition.

You will notice that the pattern of results reported by Smith and DeCoster (1998) is difficult to replicate. Returning to an (almost) zero correlation after adding massive background noise (up to Trial 600 in Figure 7.2) was not always easy to accomplish. Moreover, when it was accomplished by adding more background noise trials, return to high levels of accessibility (as in Trial 640 in Figure 7.2) was not always guaranteed. Similar difficulties were faced even with the non-linear network used by Smith and DeCoster (1998).

8 A recurrent connectionist model of person impression formation*

Frank Van Overwalle &
Christophe Labiouse

Major findings in impression formation are reviewed and modeled from a con-
nectionist perspective. The findings are in the areas of primacy and recency in
impression formation, asymmetric diagnosticity of ability- and morality-related
traits, increased recall for trait-inconsistent information, assimilation and con-
trast in priming, and discounting of trait inferences by situational information.
The majority of these phenomena are illustrated with well-known experiments
and simulated with an autoassociative network architecture with linear activation
update using the delta learning algorithm for adjusting the connection weights.
All of the simulations successfully reproduced the empirical findings. Moreover,
the proposed model is shown to be consistent with earlier algebraic models of
impression formation (Anderson, 1981; Busemeyer, 1991; Hogarth & Einhorn,
1992). The discussion centers on how our model compares to other connec-
tionist approaches to impression formation and how it may contribute to a more
parsimonious and unified theory of person perception.

Getting to know others socially often involves inferences about characteristics and traits of individuals. This is crucial to social reasoning, as it
allows one to go beyond the specific behavior of the individual and to generalize to similar events in the future and to similar people. How do we make
trait inferences from observing an individual's behavior? How is this information processed and stored in memory? The purpose of this article is to
attempt to gain insight into this process by taking a computational modeling
perspective—in particular, a connectionist approach—to these questions.

In the recent past, the dominant view on the impression-formation process
in social psychology was that people are intuitive statisticians who extract
behavioral information by applying some kind of a rule to them. Many of
these models rely on an algebraic function to transform social information
into abstract traits. Models of this type include the weighted averaging model
of Anderson (1981), the step-by-step belief-adjustment model of Hogarth

---

* Adapted from *Personality and Social Psychology Review, 8, 28–61.* Copyright 2004 by
  Lawrence Erlbaum Associates. Reprinted with permission of the publisher.

and Einhorn (1992) and the serial averaging strategy of Busemeyer (1991). Although supported by an impressive amount of empirical research, the most popular model, developed by Anderson (1981), was criticized on the grounds that it lacked psychological plausibility because it seems unlikely that people would perform all the necessary weighting and averaging calculation in their minds to arrive at an impression. For this reason, many researchers abandoned algebraic models altogether.

The main purpose of this article is to revive computational modeling of impression formation by adopting a connectionist framework to describe the perceivers' internal computations. This framework is loosely patterned after how the brain works—neurons spreading activation to other neurons and developing synaptic connections with each other—to develop computational models of human thinking. Earlier attempts of applying the brain metaphor in social psychology used neuron-like representation and activation spreading as its major principles (Hamilton, Katz, & Leirer, 1980; Hastie & Kumar, 1979), but did not provide any computational formalization of these ideas. However, the ever-increasing success of connectionist models in cognitive psychology that provide more precise computational implementations has led a number of authors to turn to these models in an attempt to develop connectionist models of diverse social psychological phenomena, including causal attribution (see Chapter 5; also Van Overwalle, 1998), cognitive dissonance (Shultz & Lepper, 1996; and see Chapter 12), and group impression formation and change (Kashima, Woolcock, & Kashima, 2000; and see Chapter 9).

Connectionist models have also been developed in the area of impression formation. Kunda and Thagard (1996) developed a parallel-constraint-satisfaction model that described how social stereotypes and individuating information constrained each individual's meaning and jointly influenced their impression formation. However, this model was static, lacking a learning mechanism by which novel impressions or stereotypes of groups and individuals could be developed and stored in memory. This shortcoming was addressed in the tensor product model of impression formation (Kashima & Kerekes, 1994), from which emerged various results in primacy and recency effects. In addition to this model, the recurrent model by Smith and DeCoster (1998; see Chapter 7) describes how perceivers may use past knowledge of individuals or groups to make inferences on unobserved or novel characteristics about them. Both models incorporate a learning algorithm that allows the integration of old and novel information and the subsequent storage of the resulting impression in memory. The goal of this article is to extend the work of Smith and DeCoster (1998) by highlighting how the recurrent model can explain many additional phenomena in impression-formation research. In so doing, we hope to contribute to the theoretical integration of the connectionist approach to impression formation. We also formulate "postdictions" that have been confirmed by past research and, importantly, novel predictions that have been subsequently confirmed by recent research.

Many mainstream processes and findings on impression formation can be explained within a connectionist framework and, in many cases, explained better than by the algebraic or activation-spreading models developed in the past. In this article, we present a series of simulations, using the same network architecture applied to a number of significantly different phenomena. These phenomena involve primacy and recency in impression formation; the asymmetric impact of ability-related versus morality-related behaviors; memory advantages for inconsistencies, assimilation, and contrasts in priming; and the effect of situational constraints on trait inferences.

Our review of empirical phenomena in the field is not meant to be exhaustive, but is rather designed to illustrate how connectionist principles can be used to shed light on the processes underlying impression formation. Although the emphasis of this article is on the use of a particular connectionist model to explain a wide variety of phenomena in social cognition, previous applications of connectionist modeling to social psychology (Kashima & Kerekes, 1994; Kunda & Thagard, 1996; see also Chapter 7) are also mentioned. In addition, we compare and contrast our model with a number of different models. Finally, we discuss the limitations of the proposed connectionist approach and point to areas where further theoretical developments are under way or are needed.

A RECURRENT MODEL

Throughout this article, we use the same basic network model—namely, the recurrent linear autoassociator (see Chapter 3) developed by McClelland and Rumelhart (1985; for an introductory text see also McClelland & Rumelhart, 1988, pp.161 ff.; McLeod, Plunkett, & Rolls, 1998, pp.72ff.). This model is already familiar to a number of social psychologists studying person and group impression (Queller & Smith, 2002; Smith & DeCoster, 1998; Van Rooy et al., 2003, see also Chapters 7–10), causal attribution (see Chapter 5) and attitude formation (see Chapter 11). We decided to apply a single basic model to emphasize the theoretical similarities that underlie a broad variety of processes in person impression. In particular, we chose this model because it is capable of reproducing a wider range of phenomena than other connectionist models, such as feedforward networks (e.g. Van Overwalle, 1998; see also Chapter 12), parallel-constraint-satisfaction models (e.g. Kunda & Thagard, 1996) or tensor product models (e.g. Kashima & Kerekes, 1994; Kashima et al., 2000).

We believe that one of the strengths of our approach is that—despite the great flexibility of connectionist models, which is sometimes seen as rendering them theoretically empty because, as models of human cognition, they are *too* powerful—we actually make little use of that flexibility here. As we demonstrate shortly, the parameters of our model are not varied at will to fit each different situation. Rather, only the learning rate and the assumed sequence of learning inputs vary from problem to problem. This makes the network directly testable because, at least in principle, assumptions about sequence of input information and speed of learning (e.g. depth of encoding) can be tested empirically. This stands in sharp contrast to parallel-constraint-satisfaction models, in which the key assumptions are not about potentially observable inputs but about unobservable internal structure, such as connection weights that are set by hand by the researchers but are not directly testable.

In the linear version of activation spreading in the autoassociator that we use here, the final activation at each cycle is the linear sum of the external and internal input. In non-linear versions used by other social-psychology researchers (see Chapters 5 and 7), the final activation is determined by a non-linear combination of external and internal input (typically, a sigmoid function). During our simulations, however, we found that the linear version with a single internal updating cycle often reproduced the observed data slightly better, for reasons that we will discuss later. Therefore, we used the linear variant of the autoassociator with a single internal updating cycle (see Equation 3.8, p.40). Weight changes in the network were accomplished by an error-reducing learning mechanism known as the *delta learning algorithm* (McClelland & Rumelhart, 1988; see Equations 3.3 and 3.4, p.38).

BASIC EMERGENT CONNECTIONIST PRINCIPLES

Before moving on to the social phenomena of interest, a brief discussion of the basic principles or mechanisms that drive many of our simulations is needed. These principles are emergent properties of the delta learning algorithm and include acquisition, competition, and diffusion. Some of these principles have already been documented in prior social connectionist work (Van Overwalle, 1998; Van Overwalle & Van Rooy, 1998, 2001a, 2001b; see also Chapter 9). However, because they are essential for understanding our examples, and because they differentiate the autoassociator from other connectionist models, we will describe the implications of these principles for impression formation first.

Acquisition property and sample size effect

The acquisition property of the delta learning algorithm predicts that the more information that is received about the joint presence of an actor (or stimulus) and a trait category, the stronger their connection weight will become. This results in a pattern of increasing weights as more information is processed, that is, a sample size effect (see Chapter 3). Most earlier algebraic models of impression formation also predict this gradual increase of the strength of judgments (Anderson, 1981; Busemeyer, 1991; Hogarth & Einhorn, 1992). It can be demonstrated that the delta learning algorithm converges to Anderson's (1981) weighted averaging model (see the Annexe at the end of this chapter). That is, the delta learning algorithm predicts that in the initial phases of learning, a person's impression gradually becomes stronger, as if the information is *summed* (e.g. Betsch, Plessner, Schwieren, & Gütig, 2001) but, after more information, the impression is characterized as a *weighted average* of the information.

In addition, it is easy to show that other algebraic models (Busemeyer, 1991; Hogarth & Einhorn, 1992) are mathematically identical to a simplified version of the delta learning algorithm applied in connectionist models, one that deals with only one cause at the time (for a proof, see Van Overwalle & Van Rooy, 2001a; Wasserman et al., 1996). Because these models can be considered to be special cases of the more general delta learning algorithm, only with less computational power, we will ignore them for the most part in the remainder of this article. Note that parallel-constraint-satisfaction models (Kunda & Thagard, 1996; Read & Marcus-Newhall, 1993; Shultz & Lepper, 1996) do not posses a learning algorithm and are therefore not able to make the sample size prediction.

Competition property and discounting

Another essential property of the delta learning algorithm is that it gives rise to competition between connections. This competition favors the more predictive or diagnostic features (see Chapter 3). A typical example of competition is the phenomenon of discounting in causal attribution. When one cause acquires a strong causal weight, perceivers tend to ignore alternative causes (Hansen & Hall, 1985; Kruglanski, Schwartz, Maides, & Hamel, 1978; Rosenfield & Stephan, 1977; Van Overwalle & Van Rooy, 1998, 2001b; Wells & Ronis, 1982). In impression formation, information on the situational context in which a behavior occurred often (but not always) leads to discounting of trait inferences to the actor (Gilbert & Malone, 1995; Trope & Gaunt, 2000). In contrast, another well-known connectionist learning algorithm, the Hebbian algorithm, used in the tensor product model of Kashima and Kerekes (1994) does not possess this property and is therefore not able to make straightforward discounting predictions.

Diffusion property and memory for inconsistent information

Still another property of the delta learning algorithm is responsible for the weakening of connections when a single trait node is connected to many behavior nodes that are only occasionally activated (see Chapter 3). This property is introduced to explain enhanced recall for inconsistent as compared to consistent behavioral information in impression formation (Hastie & Kumar, 1979). Enhanced recall for inconsistent behavior has, traditionally, been explained in terms of a spreading-activation model of memory where inconsistent information is more deeply processed so that it develops stronger lateral connections with other behavior nodes (Hastie & Kumar, 1979).

Other researchers have argued that enhanced memory for unique information is due to a fan effect, in which a given amount of activation is divided between the connections fanning out to other nodes. The more numerous the connections, the less activation each one gets (Anderson, 1976). However, the diffusion property is a fundamentally different mechanism. While fan-out causes a division of activation, diffusion involves the division of weights. In the associative learning and connectionist literature, this is a novel property that—to our knowledge—was not detected or mentioned earlier.

OVERVIEW OF THE SIMULATIONS

Simulated phenomena

We applied the three emergent connectionist processing principles to a number of classic findings in the social cognition literature. For explanatory purposes, we replicated a well-known experiment that illustrates a particular phenomenon. Table 8.1 lists the topics of the simulations to be reported, the relevant empirical data that we attempted to replicate, and the major underlying processing principle responsible for producing the data in the simulation. Although not all relevant data in impression formation can be addressed in a single paper, we are confident that we have included some of the most relevant phenomena in the current literature.

Essentially the same methodology was used throughout the simulations. The particular conditions and trial orders of the focused experiments were reproduced as faithfully as possible, although sometimes minor changes were introduced to simplify things (e.g. fewer trials than in the actual experiments). For each simulation, the autoassociative network was run 50 times (i.e. simulating 50 "participants") with a randomized or fixed trial order (as in the real experiment), and the results were then averaged over the 50 runs.

Architecture of the network

The concepts of interest in the simulations, such as actors, traits, and behaviors, are each represented by a single node. This is a localist encoding, whereby each node reflects a "symbolic" concept. In contrast, in a distributed encoding, as used by Kashima and Kerekes (1994) and Smith and DeCoster (1998; see Chapter 7), a concept is represented by a *pattern* of activation across an array of nodes, none of which reflects a symbolic concept but rather some subsymbolic micro-feature of it (Thorpe, 1995). We acknowledge that localist encoding lacks biological plausibility because it implies that each concept is stored in a single processing unit and, except for explicit differing levels of activation, is always perceived in the same manner by the network. However, this localist coding scheme was chosen as a simplifying assumption in our attempt to demonstrate the power of our model. At the end of this

Table 8.1 Overview of the simulated person impression topics and the underlying properties

Topic	Findings	Property
Person impression formation		
1. Online integration	More extreme judgments given more evidence on positive or negative features	*Acquisition* of actor-trait weights
2. Serial position weights	The last item in a series has most impact on trait inferences (recency). In addition:	
	• Recency attenuates after longer lists of items	*Competition:* Stronger context discounts impact of inconsistent item on trait
	• Primacy if only a final trait inference is given	*Acquisition* of trait → actor link sends inconsistent trait activation to actor and so reduces learning
Inferring behavior-correspondent traits		
3. Asymmetric cues	High ability and low morality behaviors are more diagnostic for an actor's traits than low ability and high morality	*Acquisition:* Skewed distribution of ability and morality behaviors
Recall of behavioral information		
4. Inconsistent behavior	Recall is better for trait-inconsistent behaviors	Less *diffusion* of infrequent trait → behavior links
Priming		
5. Assimilation and contrast	Priming with:	
	• a trait leads to assimilation of that trait	*Acquisition:* Additional trait activation is linked to the actor
	• an exemplar leads to contrast away from the implied trait	*Competition:* Exemplar → trait link competes with actor → trait link
Discounting by situational constraints		
6. Integration of situational information	Discounting of a trait given situational information, especially if this information is more salient or applicable	*Competition:* discounting of actor → trait link given a stronger situation → trait link
7. Discounting and sample size	Discounting of an actor's trait when there is more evidence on an alternative actor	*Acquisition* of alternative → trait link which leads to *competition* against target → trait link

paper, we show that when distributed representations are used they yield approximately the same results.

Representation of traits

We assume that behaviors or actors are naturally categorized by at least one of two opposing trait categories (i.e. represented by two nodes given localist encoding). For instance, someone's performance may be characterized as "stupid" or "intelligent". More fine-grained categorizations, such as different levels of intelligence, are also possible. However, perceivers in an experimental setting are sometimes forced to make one-dimensional judgments, for instance, when the experimental instructions call for participants to make ratings on a single intelligence or likeability scale. When such demands dominate the impression task—especially when participants have to give unidimensional ratings repeatedly—we assume that perceivers are likely to represent their judgment along a single integrative conceptual category (i.e. represented by a single node given localist encoding). This single unidimensional representation is used only in the first two simulations discussed shortly, but it is critical to reproduce some of the phenomena of interest.

How might such a novel unitary trait concept be represented in human memory? Research in neuropsychology has revealed that traces of novel episodic events or concepts are stored in the hippocampus; recently, connectionist modelers began to model these processes (e.g. O'Reilly & Munakata, 2000, pp.287–293; O'Reilly & Rudy, 2001). The basic idea is that novel information or concepts consist of a unique combination of existing features, and this configuration is temporarily stored in a hippocampal layer by representing each unique event or concept by an internal representation (e.g. a limited set of nodes) that is connected with its constituting features. However, because such a detailed network is beyond the scope of this article, in our simulations we simply added a single node to represent an integrative one-dimensional representation of a trait. To elucidate the most basic learning principles, we made use only of this integrative trait node and ignored the two opposing trait categories (i.e. represented by two nodes in a localist encoding). Although it is very likely that these opposing trait categories continued to play a role in learning because they seem most natural, adding them in the simulation did not meaningfully alter the results (if anything, it slightly improved the fit with the observed data).

Context nodes

In practically all simulations that involved a judgment about an actor, the target actor was accompanied by a general context or other comparison persons. This serves as a standard of comparison, to judge the level of a trait that an actor possesses. This is a crucial process in social cognition. Because there are no objective standards for judging people's behaviors and opinions, perceivers need another, social standard of comparison in their judgments. This idea was perhaps best elaborated in attribution theory (Kelley, 1967). An abundance of research has documented that attributions to an actor depend on low consensus, or the degree to which the behavior of the person differs from that of other comparison persons. If the behavior is similar, we do not make attributions to the person but rather to some external circumstances or context (Kelley, 1967; Van Overwalle, 1997). Other persons thus provide a standard of comparison, often internalized as norms for different target categories (e.g. sex, social groups). Comparisons can be made against general norms or specific comparison persons, depending on task instructions and the availability of specific individuals to compare with. In other words, including a context is necessary to determine whether the actor is responsible for his or her behavior, and is thus required for making trait inferences. Indicating how often a behavior occurs in general allows us to establish what the relevant social norms or standards are. How much the actor's behavior deviates from this norm is indicative of the actor's underlying trait.

What connectionist mechanism allows a context to serve as a standard of comparison in trait inferences? The underlying mechanism is the principle of competition. If the context develops a strong connection with a trait because it is paired equally (or more) often with a trait-implying behavior than with the actor, it tends to compete against the actor → trait connections, leading to weaker trait inferences. In contrast, when the context develops a weaker connection with the trait because it is less often paired with the behavior than with the actor, it cannot discount the actor → trait connection, leading to stronger trait inferences.

Competition by the context plays a role in all our simulations of trait judgments. We used a variety of contextual factors. In some experiments, the context was implicit (e.g. only trait adjectives described the person), so that we used a general context node without specifying in great detail what it represented. In these cases, the context might reflect a variety of aspects from task instructions to (unspecified) cues in the actor's behavioral environment (Simulations 1 and 2). In other experiments, the context was explicitly manipulated and was defined by specific actor exemplars with detailed meanings or behaviors, which we used in our Simulations 5, 6, and 7.

Activation and learning parameters

All parameters of the autoassociative model that influence the spreading of activation were kept fixed for all simulations (cf. Equation 3.8, p.40; McClelland & Rumelhart, 1988). In contrast, we did not impose a common learning rate for all the experiments simulated, because of the different contexts, measures, and procedures used in them. Rather, we selected a learning rate value (between .10 and .35) that provided the highest correlation with the observed data of each simulation, after examining all admissible parameter values (see Gluck & Bower, 1988a; Nosofsky, Kruschke, & McKinley, 1992).

Variations in the learning rate are assumed to arise from differences in attention to the task. These differences can originate from modulations in basic arousal and behavioral activation (e.g. sleep–wake cycle); responsiveness to novel, affect-laden, motivation-relevant, or otherwise salient stimuli; or responsiveness to task-specific attentional focus and voluntary control of exploring, scanning, and encoding information. Research on the neurological underpinnings of attention suggest that general arousal is driven by lower-level nuclei and pathways from the brainstem, whereas basic features of the stimuli are detected by the thalamus and related subcortical nuclei (e.g. amygdala, basal ganglia). In contrast, task-specific attention and voluntary control is most likely modulated by supervisory executive centers in the prefrontal neocortex (LaBerge, 1997, 2000; Posner, 1992). We felt that this wide range of sources of attention justified our allowing the learning rate to vary from simulation to simulation.

Further, in several simulations, variations in learning rate stem predominantly from conscious control over one's attentional focus. For instance, instructing participants to memorize behavioral details, or giving them an additional cognitive task (Simulations 4 and 7), causes them to turn their attention away from trait inferences. Some connectionist researchers have begun to model these higher-level voluntary control and attention processes (e.g. O'Reilly & Munakata, 2000, pp.305–312, 379–410). The basic idea of their approach is that activation plays a major role in maintaining and switching attention (through dopamine-based modulation), resulting in greater accessibility and impact of the internal representations. When information is actively maintained, it is immediately accessible to other parts of the system and constantly influences the activation of other representations. It is assumed that task instructions directly impact on the activation of internal representations.

Because such central executive "subnetworks" are beyond the scope of this article, to simulate reduced attention to the target task, we simply hand-set overall learning to a lower rate to reproduce the idea that encoding and learning was hampered and more shallow. For instance, when instructed to memorize behaviors or by giving participants a secondary task, we assumed that they would be less attentive to making trait inferences, so that the rate of development of trait-relevant connections is diminished. Although we could have manipulated the activation of the input nodes rather than the speed of learning to simulate reduced attention (which gives similar results), for reason of parsimony in the manipulation of parameters, we varied only the learning rate (for a similar approach, see Kinder & Shanks, 2001).

In some cases, apart from a general learning rate, the context node received a separate learning rate for all context → trait connections. Because, as noted earlier, the context was not always sharply defined in the experiments on which the simulations were based, it was unclear what constituted its representation. For instance, it might consist of fewer or more relevant features than other representations in the network, and this might lower or increase, respectively, the speed of learning about the context. Nor was it clear how much attention participants would pay to contextual features as compared to other information. Rather than making ad-hoc arbitrary assumptions about the content or encoding of contextual features, for reasons of consistency with our overall simulation approach, we estimated a separate learning rate for the context that fitted most closely with the observed data.

Varying the learning rate, as described previously, does not violate the locality principle of connectionism, which says that each connection weight should be able to be updated using locally available information from associated nodes. That is because the learning rate affects only the general speed of learning in the network, not how much and in which direction weight adaptation should occur, which is uniquely determined by local information according to the delta learning algorithm. Generally, the selected learning rates were quite robust. In other words, increasing or decreasing this parameter had little substantial effect on the simulations. Only when the original learning rate was already high ($\geq .25$) did increasing the rate further become problematic because the weights became too large and became unstable. Moreover, this would give too much impact to novel information and would result in a complete neglect of earlier information.

Dependent measures

At the end of each simulated experimental condition, to simulate the empirical dependent measures, test trials were run by prompting certain nodes of interest (i.e. turning on their activation), and the resulting output activation in other nodes was recorded. For instance, to test trait inferences, the actor node was turned on and the resulting activation of the trait node (without any additional external activation) was read off. Similar test procedures for the other dependent variables are explained and motivated in detail for each simulation.

Our predictions were verified by comparing the resulting test activations with observed experimental data. Given that the resulting activation values and experimental results are difficult to compare quantitatively, we examined only the general pattern of activations and projected them visually onto the observed data (i.e. we re-scaled the obtained test activations by linear regression with a positive slope). In addition, we report statistical tests between conditions of interest. All tests involved between-subjects analyses of variance (ANOVAs) or unpaired t tests, unless otherwise noted. These tests would be impossible in some simulations because a fixed order of trials prevents variability in the results. To avoid this and to add realism to our simulations, in all the localist encodings, we added to the default starting weights a random value ranging between -0.1 and $+0.1$.

IMPRESSION FORMATION

Most processes of impression formation can be thought of as categorization. That is, in making trait inferences on the basis of feature information or based on the behaviors of an actor, the social perceiver attempts to decide to which trait category the person belongs. The categorization of diverse information into meaningful trait concepts or categories that contain similar features, roles, or behaviors promotes cognitive economy and organization, thus enabling us to go beyond the given information and to plan our behavior and interaction with social agents accordingly.

In recent approaches, categorization is most often described in terms of either a prototype or an exemplar approach. According to the prototype approach, learners abstract a central tendency of each category and then classify instances according to their similarity to the category's central prototype (e.g. Rosch, 1978). In contrast, no such average or typical prototype is assumed in the exemplar approach, in which categorizing depends on the similarity of the given object to a sample of memory traces of category exemplars (Fiedler, 1996; Hintzmann, 1986; Medin & Schaffer, 1978; Nosofsky, 1986; Smith & Zárate, 1992). In this recurrent approach, as in most connectionist models, categorization is performed by prototype extraction, that is, by developing connections between the person and various trait prototypes. The stronger a person's connection with a particular trait category, the more the person is thought to be a member of that category and to possess that trait.

In the following simulations, we illustrate how a recurrent network can model impression formation without recourse to explicit arithmetical calculations, as assumed in algebraic models, with two experiments that grew out of Anderson's (1981) weighted averaging model. In these experiments, participants typically receive a series of trait adjectives or behavior descriptions about an actor and are requested to make overall trait or likability impressions of that person (e.g. Anderson, 1981; Asch, 1946; Kashima & Kerekes, 1994). We focus on representative findings from this research that reflect:

- how impressions are integrated online and grow stronger or weaker after participants are given information bearing on the positive (high) or negative (low) status of a trait.
- when initial or final pieces of information are weighted more heavily in making an impression.

In this experimental paradigm, judgments are requested along a single dimensional rating scale from the start of the experiment and at several intervals during the experiment, so that we assume a single trait representation (by a single trait node).

Simulation 1: Online integration

We first consider an experiment by Stewart (1965) in which an actor was des-cribed by four adjectives implying a high trait (e.g. "talkative") and were fol-lowed by four adjectives implying the opposite (or low) trait (e.g. "reticent"). Some participants received high trait information about an actor in the first half of the experiment and low trait information in the second half, whereas other participants received the reverse low–high order. In the continuous con-dition that we simulate here, after each adjective participants had to rate the actor on a likability scale that ranged from *highly unfavorable* to *highly favor-able*. In line with the predictions of Anderson's weighted averaging model, Stewart (1965) documented that when high trait information was given, the likability ratings went up, and when low trait information was given, likability went down (Figure 8.1). In addition, Stewart also documented a recency effect, that is, the later information had somewhat more impact on the final judgment than the earlier information, as can be seen from the cross-over to the right of the figure.

Simulation

Stewart's (1965) experiment was modeled using a network architecture con-sisting of an actor node connected to a trait node, and an additional context

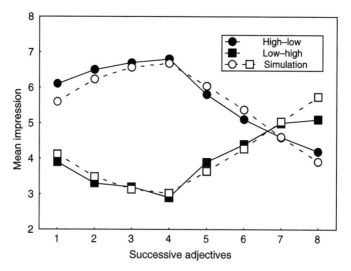

Figure 8.1 Online integration of trait-implying information: Observed data from Stewart (1965) and simulation results (general learning rate = .32, for con-text = .08). The human data are from Figure 1 in "Effect of continuous responding on the order effect in personality impression formation" by R. H. Stewart, 1965, *Journal of Personality and Social Psychology, 1*, 161–165. Copyright 1965 by the American Psychological Association. Adapted with permission.

node that reflects situational constraints (e.g. social and group norms) or other experimental context variables (e.g. instructions). This context node guarantees a smooth acquisition curve in agreement with Stewart's data and, without it, the acquisition pattern is more rigid.

What we want to demonstrate here is how the trait-implying information is applied to build up an impression of a specific actor by changing the weights linking the actor with the trait according to the acquisition principle. Therefore, the simulation starts from the assumption that the likability implied by the adjectives has already been learned and recruited from semantic and social knowledge. This assumption is elaborated in more detail in the next section (Simulation 3). Specifically, we assume here that adjectives associated with likeability are denoted by an activation value of +1 for the trait node, whereas adjectives associated with unlikability have an activation value of −1 (this is equivalent to Anderson's scale values).

Table 8.2 schematically depicts a list of the trials to simulate the information given in Stewart's (1965) experiment. When the actor is described by a positive (high) trait, the trait node is activated by a value of +1 and the connection weight is increased according to the acquisition principle of the delta learning algorithm. In contrast, when the actor is described by a negative (low) trait, the trait node is activated by a value of −1 and the weight is decreased according to the acquisition principle. After each adjective, the actor node in the network is prompted and the resulting activation of the trait node indicates what trait the actor conveys (see bottom "test" panel of the table).

Simulation results

The simulation using the recurrent network was run with 50 "participants" (i.e. 50 different simulation runs) and a fixed trial order. The results with

Table 8.2 Online integration of trait-implying information (Simulation 1)

	Actor	Context	Trait
Condition 1: High–low presentation order			
#4 High trait	1	1	+1
#4 Low trait	1	1	−1
Condition 2: Low–high presentation order			
#4 Low trait	1	1	−1
#4 High trait	1	1	+1
Test			
Trait of actor	1		?

Schematic representation of the experimental design of Stewart (1965); High, adjective implies trait; low, adjective implies opposite trait; Cell entries denote external activation and empty cells denote 0 activation; #, number of trials. The simulation was run separately for each condition.

learning rate 0.32 (0.08 for the context) are shown in Figure 8.1. Recall that the simulation data were rescaled by a linear regression to make them directly comparable to the observed data. As can be seen, there is a close fit between the simulation and the empirical data, which strongly suggests that online integration in impression formation is adequately captured by the acquisition principle of our recurrent connectionist model, much like Anderson's weighted averaging model. A repeated measures ANOVA showed that the differences between trial order were significant in both the high–low condition, $F(7, 343) = 3853.21$, $p < .001$, and the low–high condition, $F(7, 343) = 3344.23$, $p < .001$, and simple t tests confirmed that the differences between all adjacent trials in each condition were significant, $p < .001$.

Of particular interest is the cross-over at the end of training. The difference between the two conditions in the most recent trials was significant, $t(98) = 44.11$, $p < .001$. This reflects a recency effect where the most recently presented adjectives win over the adjectives presented earlier. It is interesting to note that increasing the learning rate would produce an even stronger recency effect, as it would force novel information to have more impact than older information. Together, the results suggest that the revision and adjustment of person impressions is an online acquisition process whereby novel information often "overwrites" older information previously stored in the connection weights.

Simulation 2: Serial position weights

As a second example, we considered research in which disconfirmatory information is given during a single, specific position in a series of trials. By comparing the effect of disconfirmatory with confirmatory information at the same position in the trial series (denoted as *serial position*), one can estimate the weight each trait takes at a given position (Anderson, 1979; Anderson & Farkas, 1973; Busemeyer & Myung, 1988; Dreben, Fiske, & Hastie, 1979; Kashima & Kerekes, 1994). Early disconfirmatory trait information might be important in crystallizing an impression (primacy effect), whereas late information might be influential because it sheds new light on traits presented earlier (recency effect).

The bulk of research suggests that when participants give their trait ratings continuously after each adjective is presented, item weights are relatively equal in all but the last position, at which point they rise sharply. This reflects a recency effect that was also observed in the previous simulation. However, it is important to note that this recency effect attenuates after more trait information is given and processed. That is, after being given only a few pieces of trait-implying information, disconfirmatory information has a stronger recency effect than when given a lot of trait-implying information. It is as if increasing the amount of confirmatory information shields the perceiver from the disconfirmatory information. In contrast, when trait ratings are given only once after the whole series of information is presented, then primacy is more likely (for reviews, see Hogarth & Einhorn, 1992; Kashima & Kerekes, 1994).

In a typical experiment by Dreben et al. (1979), participants read about several actors, each described by four behaviors that implied the same high (H) or low (L) extreme of a trait (e.g. HHHH, HHHL, HHLH, . . ., LLLL). In the continuous condition, the participants were requested to make a likability rating about the actor after each behavioral description on a scale with endpoints labeled *most likable* to *least likable*. In the final condition, this rating was made after all behavioral descriptions of an actor were presented. Serial position was measured by comparing the judgments of each item list with another list that had the same set of high or low items except for one opposite item (i.e. with a behavior conveying the opposite trait). This inconsistent item was positioned at the first, second, third, or last position of the series so as to provide a means of measuring the weight of the item in the first, second, third, or fourth position of the list. For instance, if we present behavioral items implying the same (high or low) trait by the same characteristic x, y, or z, then the weight of serial position 1 is measured by the mean difference in the ratings between all item lists Hxyz and Lxyz. Similarly, the weight of serial position 4 is measured by the mean difference between all item lists xyzH and xyzL. The results were as expected (Figure 8.2). When given concurrent ratings, a recency effect appeared that became weaker at the end of the list, as indicated by the dotted line depicting attenuation of recency. Conversely, after a single final rating, a primacy effect was observed.

Simulation

To simulate the experiment of Dreben et al. (1979), we used the same recurrent architecture as before. The learning history is listed schematically in Table 8.3, which depicts only the fourth serial position; the other serial positions were simulated by changing the order of the inconsistent trial in the item lists. The likability rating was simulated by priming the actor node and reading off the activation of the likability node after presentation of each trial. The serial position weight was measured just as in the original experiment, by calculating the mean difference of the resulting likability activations between items lists that differed only on a single trait.

Simulation results

The recurrent simulation was run with 50 "participants" and a fixed order of trials. The results with learning rate .25 (and .025 for the context) are shown in the top panel of Figure 8.2. The recurrent network was clearly able to reproduce the predicted recency effects (indicated by the solid lines). For each likability rating, *t* tests confirmed that the weights were significantly higher at the last position than at previous positions, $ts(98) = 2.37\text{--}12.21$, $p < .05$. More important, there was also attenuation of recency, as a one-way ANOVA

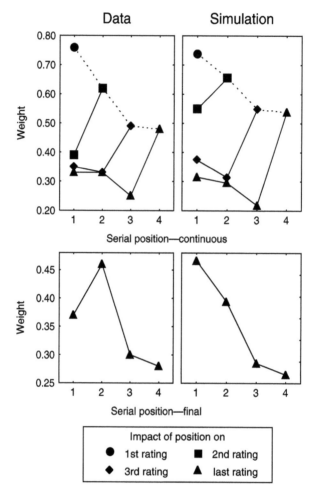

Figure 8.2 Serial position weight: Observed weight curves from Dreben, Fiske, and Hastie (1979; left panels) and simulation (right panels) of attenuation of recency given continuous responding (top; general learning rate = .25, for context = .025) and primacy given final responding (bottom; general learning rate = .25, for context = .00). The human data are from Figure 1 in "The independence of evaluative and item information: Impression and recall order effects in behavior-based impression formation" by E. K. Dreben, S. T. Fiske & R. Hastie, 1979, *Journal of Personality and Social Psychology, 37*, 1758–1768. Copyright 1979 by the American Psychological Association. Adapted with permission.

showed that the weights at the last serial position (indicated by the dotted line) decreased significantly from ratings given at the beginning(first) to the end (fourth) of the item list, $F(3, 196) = 9.26, p < .001$.

As we saw in the previous simulation, recency is a natural consequence of acquisition in a connectionist network, because later information tends to

Table 8.3 Serial position weights (Simulation 2)

	Actor	Context	Trait
Item list			
#3 High or low	1	1	+1 or −1
#1 High[a]	1	1	+1
Item list with opposite trait			
#3 High or low (same as above)	1	1	+1 or −1
#1 Low[a]	1	1	−1
Test			
Trait of actor	1		?

Schematic representation of the experimental design of Dreben, Fiske, and Hastie (1979); High, behavior implies high extreme of a trait; Low, behavior implies opposite extreme of trait; Cell entries denote external activation and empty cells denote 0 activation; Initial weights were set at .05 (for distributed coding .02); #, number of trials. The simulation was run separately for each item list.

[a] This trial is presented at position 1, 2, 3, or 4 of the series (here it is shown at position 4), and the resulting test activation averaged across all target trait lists and across all opposite trait lists are subtracted from each other to measure the serial position weight.

overwrite earlier information stored in the connection weights. The more crucial question is how the network attained *attenuation* of recency. Here context plays a crucial role. Because the context is always paired with the implied trait, the context → trait weight becomes increasingly stronger given more information, and hence competes more strongly against the person → trait weight. Thus, when inconsistent items are provided later in a series, they tend to be discounted more by the increasing (confirmatory) impact of the context. Stated somewhat differently, a robust impression that is the consequence of earlier information in the same context makes the perceiver more resistant to changing his or her impression in the face of one disconfirmatory item. This explanation differs from Anderson's reasoning based on a distinction between item-specific and abstract aspects of impression formation (Anderson & Farkas, 1973; Dreben et al., 1979), but is similar to the tensor product simulation by Kashima and Kerekes (1994) in its emphasis on the role of the judgmental context.

Let us now turn to the primacy effects that are typically revealed when impression judgments are given at the end of the series of trials rather than continuously (Anderson, 1979; Hogarth & Einhorn, 1992). Perhaps the simplest way to obtain a basic primacy effect is by reducing the learning rate of the context node to zero, or by ignoring the context altogether (i.e. by setting the external context activation to zero). The bottom panel of Figure 8.2 shows the results of the simulation when the learning rate is set to zero. A one-way ANOVA showed that the differences between trial orders were significant, $F(3,196) = 29.32, p < .001$.

How did recency disappear by reducing the learning rate or external activation of the context? An analysis of the simulation suggests the following explanation. After a few trials, the person node and the trait node develop strong connections with each other in both directions (cf. the acquisition principle). When a disconfirmatory trial is presented, the negative (or disconfirmatory) activation of the trait node spreads to the person node and reduces the net activation of the person node. (This does not happen when a context is present, because that context sends positive activation to the actor node so that a reduction of net activation in the person node is prevented.) The same logic applies to the trait node. The positive external activation of the person node spreads to the trait node and reduces the negativity of the trait activation. As a consequence of the reduced net activation of the person and trait nodes, there is little adjustment of the person → trait connection. In other words, in the recent trials, the opposing external activations of the person and the trait tend to cancel each other out, resulting in little learning and no recency. This reduction is stronger at later trials when the person and the trait have developed stronger connections. Note that this mutual cancellation is only possible if a single integrative trait node rather than two independent opposite traits is assumed, otherwise this primacy effect would not happen.

A more direct way to simulate primacy is for the actor node to have a higher learning rate at the beginning of the item list, and for this to then gradually decrease. This explanation shares with Anderson's (1981) attention decrement hypothesis the notion that the most attention is paid to and the most uptake of information occurs during the earliest trials, thus allowing little impact of information presented later. Such a procedure was followed in the tensor product simulation of primacy by Kashima and Kerekes (1994). However, because this forces a primacy effect to occur rather than having it emerge from underlying processing mechanisms, it leaves open the question of the origin of a decrement in attention.

In sum, based on our connectionist simulations, we can explain the different effects of continuous and final judgments by differences in learning or encoding of the context. We assume that when perceivers are made more accountable of their impression by requesting judgments continuously, information uptake and processing becomes more careful, taking into account more of the contextual cues in the actor's situation or experimental set-up. This might be less the case when a trait judgment is requested only once, resulting in more negligence of the context and hence primacy rather than recency.

Discussion and further research

Our recurrent model reproduced both recency and primacy effects. Although Kashima (Kashima & Kerekes, 1994; see also Busemeyer & Myung, 1988) pointed out that attenuation of recency could not be simulated with a feedforward network (which is correct) or even with a recurrent network (Kashima et al., 2000), we have demonstrated here that, on the contrary, it can easily be reproduced with a recurrent connectionist model. The tensor product model proposed by Kashima and Kerekes (1994) was also able to replicate these effects but required additional assumptions, such as a changing context after each judgment, to obtain attenuation of recency. This was not needed in our model, as the presence of the context was sufficient.

We suggest that encoding contextual cues in the presence of the actor allows later information to have more impact (recency), whereas ignoring the context is responsible for building up an impression very quickly (primacy). Furthermore, we suggest that attenuation of recency was due to a growing discounting of inconsistent information by the context. There is some support for our hypothesis that recency is driven by greater attention to the information (including the context). This comes from research demonstrating that conditions that induce increased accuracy or motivation result in more recency as opposed to primacy. A series of studies by Kruglanski (Freund, Kruglanski, & Shpitzajzen, 1985; Heaton & Kruglanski, 1991; Kruglanski & Freund, 1983) documented that conditions that promote accurate judgments reduce primacy. Similarly, Gannon, Skowronski, and Betz (1994) observed that depressives who are more motivated to process information show enhanced recency.

Future research might be able to provide additional support for the predictions of the recurrent network. According to our network, giving more attention to the context to explain the actor's behavior should increase recency as opposed to primacy. Moreover, the more constant the context is, the more the attenuation of recency might be expected because an unchanging contextual core increases its strength and hence tends to discount more inconsistent information.[1]

INFERRING TRAITS FROM CORRESPONDENT BEHAVIOR

In the previous simulations, we ignored the issue of how information on behaviors or features of an actor is used to make a trait judgment. We simply assumed that the implied trait or evaluative meaning that these behaviors and features carry was directly applied to the actor. Although this simplification might characterize the most important aspects of person-impression processes, there are two questions that remain unanswered. First, are all behaviors equally diagnostic for traits, that is, are some behaviors applied

---

1   Dreben et al. (1979) reported also serial position effects on recall. Regardless of the response conditions (continuous or final), they found primacy of the first two items and recency of the last item. Recall of behavioral information can be simulated by extending the present network (including the original opposite traits) with nodes that reflect unique behavioral information (see also Simulation 4). This approach was able to reproduce the reported primacy effect, but not the recency effect.

more readily than others in making a trait inference? Second, can this process of inferring associations between behaviors and traits be modeled by a recurrent network? In the next simulation, we attempt to address these questions.

Simulation 3: Asymmetry in inferences of ability and morality

A remarkable finding in the research on dispositional inferences is that the diagnosticity of a particular behavior varies according to the content of the inference domain. In the domain of ability, for example, because perceivers typically expect that a high level of performance could have been attained only by someone with a disposition of high ability, an actor's high level of performance should prompt an inference of high ability. In contrast, a low level of performance should create greater uncertainty for the perceiver as it may indicate both low and high ability, as even someone with high ability may occasionally fail. This pattern is completely reversed for inferences of morality. Because perceivers expect that a low level of moral conduct could have been attained only by someone with a disposition of low morality, an actor's immoral act should prompt an inference of low morality. In contrast, a high level of moral conduct could indicate both low and high morality, because even immoral persons behave morally most of the time. These behavior–trait expectations lead to an asymmetry in the diagnosticity of ability- and morality-related behaviors. High performance is more diagnostic for inferences of ability, whereas low moral conduct is more diagnostic for inference of morality. Moreover, extreme behaviors are generally seen as more diagnostic of people who have extreme traits, whereas moderate behaviors may be characteristic of both extreme and moderated traits (Lupfer, Weeks, & Dupuis, 2000; Reeder, 1997; Reeder & Fulks, 1980; Reeder & Spores, 1983; Skowronski & Carlston, 1987; Wojciszke, Brycz, & Borkenau, 1993; for reviews see Reeder & Brewer, 1979; Skowronski & Carlston, 1989).

Where do these asymmetric behavior–trait expectations come from? One of the explanations that has received considerable empirical support is the cue-diagnosticity interpretation of Skowronski and Carlston (1989). In line with our perspective, these authors assume that behavioral cues are used to assign an actor to one or more trait categories. Behaviors that strongly suggest one trait category (e.g. dishonest) over alternative categories (e.g. honest) are said to be more diagnostic. The asymmetry is assumed to come from differential associations with ability and morality trait categories. According to Skowronski and Carlston (1989), extremely immoral actors may rob banks but they may also help an old woman to cross the street. However, moral actors may lie about their age but will never rob banks. In contrast, in the ability domain, an outstanding high-jumper will sometimes clear 7 feet and sometimes fail to do so. On the other hand, a poor high-jumper will probably never clear 7 feet. Thus, immoral behaviors are more often associated with immorality than moral behaviors are associated with morality, whereas competent behaviors are more often associated with high ability than incompetent behaviors are associated with low ability.

One possible interpretation of the cue-diagnosticity notion might result from the semantic meaning of ability and morality traits. This argument relies on the semantics of high or low ability and morality to infer what behaviors are most likely. However, this leaves unanswered the question of how this semantic knowledge was learned in the first place. From a developmental perspective, it seems more likely that when toddlers learn to correct a semantic error, such as, an overgeneralization (e.g. calling all male adults "Daddy"), they do so not because they were explicitly told the correct meaning but rather because they experienced first-hand the circumstances under which children call someone "Daddy". Therefore, a more interesting interpretation is that the asymmetric strength of the behavior–trait associations is due to the asymmetric distribution of prior relevant observations in the morality and ability domain. These observations might be direct or indirect (e.g. when other people relate their own experiences or observations), and may only later become incorporated in the meaning of ability and morality traits.

The aim of the next simulation is to demonstrate that a skewed distribution during prior learning may lead to differential diagnosticity, as revealed in a study by Skowronski and Carlston (1987, Experiment 1). In this study, participants were provided with descriptions of positive and negative behaviors reflecting five different levels of intelligence and morality. Examples of extreme morality behaviors were robbing a store (low) and returning a lost wallet (high); examples of extreme ability behaviors were failing most exams (low) and teaching at university (high). For each behavior, participants were asked to estimate to what extent "would a (trait) person ever [behavior]?" (Skowronski & Carlston, 1987, p.691), with possible traits including dishonest, honest, intelligent, and stupid.

Simulation

A possible (simplified) learning history that may reflect participant's acquisition of prior relevant knowledge on behavior–trait occurrences is illustrated in Table 8.4, which lists five levels of ability and morality behavioral features together with the implied high or low traits. Extreme behaviors are characterized by a configuration of extreme to neutral features, moderate behaviors by a configuration of moderate and neutral features, and neutral behaviors by a configuration of only neutral features. Thus, for instance, extremely competent behavior does not involve only neutral features, such as writing up your research, or moderate features, such as having your article accepted, but also extreme features like publishing the article in a top journal (see first row in the table). In contrast, moderate and neutral competent behaviors involve only lower-level features (see rows 2 and 3).

To be realistic, because extreme behaviors are less likely than moderate behaviors, we began by setting the frequencies of the extreme trait-consistent

Table 8.4 Asymmetry in ability and morality trait inferences (Simulation 3)

	Behavioral features										Traits			
	A++	A+	A0	A-	A—	M++	M+	M0	M-	M—	A+	A-	M+	M-
High ability trait														
#6	1	1	1								1			
#7		1	1								1			
#6		1									1			
#5		1	1								1			
#4		1	1	1							1			
Low ability trait														
#0	1	1	1									1		
#3		1	1									1		
#4		1										1		
#5		1	1									1		
#4		1	1	1								1		
High morality trait														
#6						1	1	1					1	
#7							1	1					1	
#6							1						1	
#3							1	1					1	
#0							1	1	1				1	
Low morality trait														
#2						1	1	1						1
#3							1	1						1
#4							1							1
#5							1	1						1
#4							1	1	1					1
Test														
Trait A+			?	?	?						1			
Trait A-	?	?	?									1		
Trait M+								?	?	?			1	
Trait M-						?	?	?						1

Schematic representation of the experimental design of Skowronski and Carlston (1987, Experiment 1), A, ability; M, morality; ++, extremely positive; +, positive; 0, neutral; –, negative; —, extremely negative. Cell entries denote external activation and empty cells denote 0 activation; #, number of trials. All learning trials were presented in an order randomized for each run.

behaviors equal to those of the neutral behaviors. In addition, to reflect the common finding that perceivers typically hold positive expectations about people, we also assumed that the behaviors for high ability and high morality traits were more frequent (i.e. 6, 7, 6, 5, 4, from high to low) than those for the low traits (i.e. 4, 5, 4, 3, 2 from low to high). The realism of this learning history is reflected in the fact that the overall distribution reveals many more neutral than moderate or extreme features in people's behavior, and many more moderate than extreme features.

The asymmetric distribution during learning is revealed by the fact that an actor with high ability will most often perform well to very well, but will sometimes perform moderately or even occasionally very poorly. For instance, a top researcher will most often publish in top journals, but occasionally in lower ranked journals as well. In contrast, an actor with low ability will most often perform poorly or sometimes moderately, but never extremely well. In the table, non-diagnostic behaviors were introduced by setting the frequencies much lower: For extreme behaviors, the frequencies were set to zero; for moderate behaviors, the frequencies were set to 3. In the morality domain, this asymmetry is reversed. Apart from this, the simulation was quite robust for changes in the non-zero frequencies of Table 8.4, such as setting the non-zero frequencies to other smooth distributions or even setting them all equal.

Trait-inconsistent behaviors were considered to be most diagnostic by Skowronski and Carlston (1987) and therefore constituted the most important test of their cue-diagnosticity hypothesis. As an example of trait-inconsistent behavior, participants were asked whether an honest person would ever engage in an immoral behavior. As can be seen in the bottom panel of Table 8.4, these ratings were simulated by prompting the trait and then reading off the output activation of the inconsistent behavior. The reverse direction of testing that would make theoretically more sense would involve asking for the trait implied by the behavior (but was not used in the experiment). This would be simulated by prompting the behavior and testing for the output activation of the trait, and this procedure worked equally well in the simulation.

Simulation results

The learning-history and testing prompts depicted in Table 8.4 were run for 50 participants, each with a different random trial order. Figure 8.3 shows the results with a learning rate of .10. As can be seen, the simulation results clearly conform to the empirical data obtained by Skowronski and Carlston (1987) and the predicted interaction is significant, $F(1,196) = 79.98$, $p < .001$. Inconsistent low performance is more probably given high ability than high performance is given low ability, $t(98) = 8.42$, $p < .001$. Conversely, an inconsistent high moral behavior is more probably given low morality than low moral conduct is given high morality, $t(98) = 4.18$, $p < .001$.

The underlying connectionist principle that produces these results is low acquisition of the behaviors low in diagnosticity. Recall that testing occurred for trait-inconsistent behaviors. Because high performance behaviors never occurred with low ability, low ability is not a good predictor of (inconsistent) high performance. In contrast, because both high and low performance behaviors occur with high ability, high ability is a relatively good predictor of (inconsistent) low performance. The reasoning is analogous for morality behaviors, and for the reverse connections from behaviors to traits. Simply put, the network does not learn things that it was never taught.

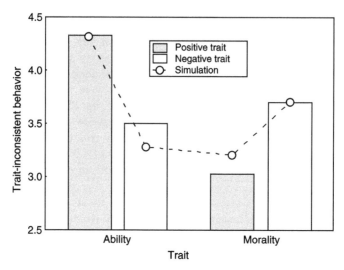

Figure 8.3 Asymmetric cues of ability and morality: Observed data from Skowronski and Carlston (1987, Experiment 1) and simulation results (learning rate = .10). The human data are from Figure 1 in "Social judgment and social memory: The role of cue diagnosticity in negativity, positivity and extremity biases" by J. J. Skowronski & D. E. Carlston, 1987, *Journal of Personality and Social Psychology, 52*, 689–699. Copyright 1987 by the American Psychological Association. Adapted with permission.

Extensions and further research

The same learning history also reproduced Skowronski and Carlston's (1987) straightforward prediction and finding that trait ratings are higher for moderately inconsistent behaviors than for extremely inconsistent behaviors. This was tested in a simulation by comparing the resulting output activation of extreme positive or negative behaviors (as shown by "?" in the bottom panel of Table 8.4) by the resulting output activation of moderate behaviors (not shown).

With respect to trait-consistent behaviors, Skowronski and Carlston (1987) reported that there were no diagnosticity effects, although earlier work indicates that typical behaviors are usually very diagnostic of the implied trait (e.g. Anderson, 1981; Cantor & Mischel, 1977). Consistent with these latter findings, our model does predict diagnostic effects for trait-consistent behaviors, in the same direction as trait-inconsistent behavior. Thus, high performance is predicted to be more diagnostic of high ability than is low performance of low ability; and low moral conduct is more diagnostic of low morality than is high moral conduct of high morality.

Another issue is how prior learning about the different levels and diagnosticity of ability and morality behaviors (as simulated previously) can be used to make a trait inference about a particular actor. Our assumption is that this prior learning on behavior–trait associations is stored in semantic memory, and that novel behavioral information automatically spreads to the implied trait. There is considerable evidence to demonstrate that traits are automatically and immediately inferred upon reading behavioral information (for a review, see Uleman, 1999). This activated trait is then paired with the actor, resulting in the acquisition of a connection between the actor and the implied trait. Skowronski and Carlston (1987) investigated this process in a second experiment. Participants read information about actors engaging in five different levels of ability- or morality-related behaviors, and then judged how intelligent or moral each actor was. As one might expect, the results documented a linear decrease in trait inferences when going from extremely high to extremely low levels of the behaviors. Our recurrent model can easily reproduce this linear relation using the same learning history from Table 8.4, extended with an actor node.

In the simulations that follow, we do not further implement explicitly the prior learning of behavior–trait association, but rather assume—as before—that the implied trait is automatically activated from semantic memory. This allows us to focus on other person-impression phenomena of interest.

MEMORY FOR BEHAVIORAL INFORMATION

When we learn about others from our own observations, we infer traits from the behaviors that are associated with them. In addition to the question of how we make these inferences as addressed in the previous section, it is also important to understand how these behavioral observations are stored in memory. An intriguing finding is that inconsistent or unexpected behavioral information about an actor is often better recalled than information that is consistent with the dominant trait expectation (for a review see Stangor & McMillan, 1992). Thus, we better recall a hooligan helping an old woman cross the street than a nurse performing the same act.

Hastie (1980; Hastie & Kumar, 1979) reasoned that the inconsistent information requires an extra cognitive effort to explain and to make sense of the inconsistency, and is therefore elaborated more deeply. This leads to extra links between the inconsistent information and other locations in memory, and, thereby, to better recall. Hastie (1980) supported this interpretation by research indicating that inconsistent information leads to more causal elaborations of the behavioral sentences. However, these sentence elaborations were explicitly requested from the participants after the initial phase of impression formation was over. It is thus not clear whether they were generated spontaneously during initial encoding or constructed only after the request (cf. Nisbett & Wilson, 1977). Moreover, recent research questioned the assumption that inconsistent behaviors are more strongly associated with other behavioral information about the actor, because support for this assumption was based on flawed measures of associative strength (Skowronski & Gannon, 2000; Skowronski & Welbourne, 1997). It was, therefore, concluded that "associative linkages may not provide the only mechanism, and may not even provide the primary mechanism, for incongruency effects in recall" (Skowronski & Gannon, 2000, p.17).

Simulation 4: Higher recall for inconsistent information

Can our connectionist principles account for the enhanced memory of inconsistent information without recourse to explicit elaborative processes or associations between behaviors? Yes, and to illustrate this, we simulate a well-known experiment by Hamilton et al. (1980, Experiment 3). Participants read information concerning several fictional actors. For each actor, they read a list of ten consistent and one inconsistent behavioral descriptions about that actor, after which they had to recall as many behavioral sentences as possible. The consistent descriptions conveyed common, everyday behavior (e.g. read the newspaper, cleaned up the house), whereas the inconsistent description included violent behavior (e.g. lost his temper and hit a neighbor, insulted his secretary without provocation). Half of the participants were instructed to form an impression of the actor and the other half were told to memorize the behavioral information. After a distracter task, the participants were asked "to list as many of the behavior descriptions as they could remember" (p.1053). The recall data (Figure 8.4) documented that under impression-formation instructions, participants were more likely to recall inconsistent items, whereas this difference disappeared under memory instructions.

Simulation

To understand enhanced memory for inconsistent behavioral information, consider a network architecture with an actor node connected to two opposing trait nodes. One trait node reflects a "neutral" trait as conveyed by the descriptions of everyday (non-violent) behavior, whereas the other trait reflects a "violent" trait implied by the inconsistent violent behavior. In addition, the behavioral descriptions were represented each by a separate node that reflects the particular behavioral exemplar. In sum, each description is represented by two nodes that reflect the categorical trait implied by the behavior as well as the individual behavioral exemplar. Table 8.5 provides a schematic description of Hamilton et al.'s (1980) experiment with ten consistent behaviors and one inconsistent behavior.

As can be seen in the table, each behavior was activated together with the associated trait and the actor node. As predicted by the diffusion principle, however, many of the consistent behaviors are not activated when the consistent trait is present, resulting in a negative learning error for these behaviors and weaker trait → behavior connections. Thus, the more behaviors confirm

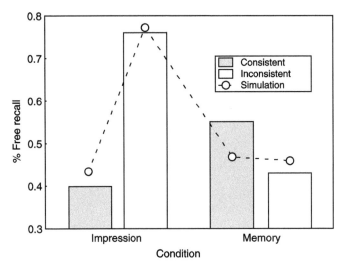

Figure 8.4 Recall of inconsistent behavioral information after impression formation and memory instructions: Observed data from Hamilton, Katz, and Leirer (1980, Experiment 3) and simulation results (learning rate given impression instructions = .27, given memorizing instructions = .027). The human data are taken from Table 2 in "Cognitive representation of personality impressions: Organizational processes in first impression formation" by D. L. Hamilton, L. B. Katz & V. O. Leirer, 1980, *Journal of Personality and Social Psychology, 39,* 1050–1063. Copyright 1980 by the American Psychological Association.

the consistent trait, the less indicative each behavior becomes for that trait. Because there are more consistent behaviors than inconsistent behaviors, diffusion is particularly strong for consistent behavior. As a result, the trait → behavior connections are weaker for consistent as opposed to inconsistent behavior. It is important to note that because the actor is always active together with the traits, the learning error that causes increased diffusion for consistent behaviors impacts not only on the trait → behavior connections but also on the actor → behavior connections.

In contrast, in the memorizing condition, perceivers are less motivated to form a unified trait impression of the actor. As discussed earlier, we assumed that this would result in a much shallower encoding of actor and trait information, which was simulated by setting the learning rate to 10% of its original value. As a result, all connection weights between the actor or trait and the behaviors would sharply decrease.

To simulate recall of the behavioral episodes, we activated the actor node and read off the resulting activation at each behavioral episode (see bottom panel of Table 8.5). This priming procedure assumes that the actor is most strongly available in memory and used as a cue to recall the behaviors. The resulting activation reflects the probability that any of the behavioral

Table 8.5 Memory for inconsistent information (Simulation 4)

		Traits		Behaviors				
	Actor	Neutral	Violent	Consistent				Inconsistent
Item list								
#1 Consistent	1	1		1				
#1 Consistent	1	1			1			
...								
#1 Consistent	1	1				1		
#1 Consistent	1	1					1	
#1 Inconsistent	1		1					1
Test								
Recall								
Consistent	1			?	? .. ?	?		
Inconsistent	1							?
Unbiased (and biased) recognition[a]								
Consistent	?	0 (?)		1[b]	1[b] .. 1[b]	1[b]		
Inconsistent	?	0 (?)						1

Schematic representation of the experimental design of Hamilton, Katz, and Leirer (1980, Experiment 3). There were 10 consistent items overall. Although the inconsistent item was given at specific positions in the series, a random order is simulated here (like in most similar studies). Cell entries denote external activation and empty cells denote 0 activation; #, number of trials. All learning trials were presented in an order randomized for each run. The learning rate was reduced to 10 % under memorizing instructions.

[a] Between parentheses is the coding for recognition biased in the direction of consistent traits.
[b] Only one exemplar node was activated (with value +1) at a time, and the resulting output activation of all of them was averaged.

exemplars would be recalled. Because research suggests that participants may use also the actor's traits as cue (e.g. Hamilton, Driscoll, & Worth, 1989), we also ran the simulations with traits as additional primes to retrieve the behavioral information, together with the actor prime. These simulations gave very similar results.

Simulation results

Figure 8.4 shows the results of the recurrent simulation with 50 participants each receiving a different random trial order. The learning rate under impression instructions was .27 and, as mentioned earlier, under memorizing conditions it was set to 10% of this value (or .027) to reflect shallower encoding. The expected interaction was significant, $F(1,196) = 5.72, p < .05$. As can be seen, the simulation replicated the basic finding that inconsistent information was better recalled than consistent information under impression-formation instructions, $t(98) = 2.33, p < .05$. However, under memorizing instructions this difference disappeared, $t < 1$. The diffusion principle suggests that higher recall of inconsistent behavioral information is primarily due to relatively stronger trait → behavior and actor → behavior links of unique or infrequent behavioral information. Thus, this connectionist account emphasizes the direct connections from a particular person or trait to behavioral exemplars. This account is consistent with Skowronski's (Skowronski & Gannon, 2000; Skowronski & Welbourne, 1997) argument that associations between behaviors are not responsible for better recall of inconsistent behaviors, in contrast to earlier suggestions by Hastie (1980) and Srull (1981).

Extensions and further research

This network model makes a number of additional "postdictions" (i.e. a "prediction" of something that was already known independently). The model predicts better recall for items at the end of a list than at the beginning of a list, because diffusion impacts more on earlier information than later information. This has been confirmed by research (Srull, Lichtenstein, & Rothbart, 1985, Experiments 5 and 6). In addition, the model predicts less recall advantage when the number of inconsistent items increases, because this results in more diffusion of the inconsistent items. This prediction has also been confirmed (Hastie & Kumar, 1979, Experiment 3; Srull, 1981, Experiments 1–3; Srull et al., 1985, Experiment 3). However, research has shown that a recall advantage remains even when the number of consistent and inconsistent items is equal, and inconsistency is manipulated by providing advanced trait expectations about the actor (Hastie & Kumar, 1979, Experiment 3). The model also predicts this result if an advanced learning phase is inserted in which the actor is first paired with the consistent trait.

Support for Hastie's (1980) alternative suggestion of effortful generation of elaborations came from studies that found decreased recall for inconsistent behaviors when mental resources were limited by reducing answering time, by making the task more complex, or by adding distracter tasks (Bargh & Thein, 1985; Hamilton et al., 1989; Macrae, Hewstone, & Griffiths, 1993; Stangor & Duan, 1991). However, these results can easily be simulated with our connectionist network by simply assuming that load decreased the encoding of the behavioral episodes or even all information (e.g. by reducing the learning rate to 10% of its original value). This suggests that poorer encoding of conceptual information, rather than less inconsistency reduction and elaboration might have been responsible for the reduced recall of inconsistent information (for a similar view, see Pandelaere & Hoorens, 2002). Again, there seems to be no need to postulate explicit elaborations to explain higher recall of inconsistent behavior.

Other conditions under which less cognitive effort is spent on the impression-formation task, and that typically reveal no enhanced memory for inconsistent recall, can be explained in a similar manner. For instance, when an impression or stereotype is formed of a group of individuals rather than a single individual, there seems to be enhanced memory for stereotype-consistent behaviors (for a review, see Fyock & Stangor, 1994). This can be simulated by assuming a decreased learning rate, based on the idea that perceivers do not expect the same level of evaluative consistency in a group of people and are therefore less willing to invest cognitive effort in encoding an overall coherent impression. This results in a loss of enhanced memory of inconsistent behaviors, and to the extent that the dominant stereotype biases retrieval when in doubt, a stereotype-consistency memory effect is observed.

This network can also simulate recognition measures, when participants are presented with behaviors and asked to assign each of them to the correct actor. Hence, in contrast to recall measures, recognition is simulated by testing the opposite behavior → actor direction. Typically, recognition is biased in the direction of consistent information presumably because consistent traits guide recognition when the perceiver relies on guessing rather than on genuine memory traces (for a review see Stangor & McMillan, 1992). This can be replicated by a recognition test that is biased by detecting more easily behaviors congruent with the consistent trait (see "?" for the consistent "neutral" trait in the bottom panel of Table 8.5). However, if this bias is removed in the simulation (by setting the activation to zero for all consistent and inconsistent traits), then inconsistent behaviors are again better recognized than consistent behaviors, in line with research showing that improved recognition sensitivity measures reveal better memory for inconsistent behavior (see Stangor & McMillan, 1992). It is important to note that, unlike recall, improved recognition of inconsistent behaviors is based on the competition between trait → actor and behavior → actor connections. When consistent behaviors are presented, the trait that they reflect becomes more strongly associated with the actor. This strong trait → actor connection competes against the weaker behavior → actor connections, so that these latter connections are discounted (see also Chapter 9).

Overall, it appears that the proposed model is broadly consistent with a relatively large spectrum of research findings. This suggests that the diffusion principle provides an interesting alternative hypothesis explaining increased recall for inconsistent information. Moreover, the competition property might play an additional role in the enhanced memory of inconsistent information when recognition measures are used.

ASSIMILATION AND CONTRAST

An important feature of recurrent models is their capacity to generalize. A trained network exposed to an incomplete pattern of information fills in the missing information on the basis of the complete pattern learned previously. This property was convincingly demonstrated by Smith and DeCoster (1998, Simulations 1 and 2) who used a recurrent network very similar to this one. This generalization process can be seen as a type of assimilation in that past experiences influence how we perceive and interpret novel information that is similar or closely related to it. For instance, when seeing a photograph of Hitler, we might immediately complete this image with activated memories on his aggressive wars, mass annihilation of Jews, and so on. There is abundant evidence showing that accessible knowledge like traits, stereotypes, moods, emotions, and attitudes is likely to result in the generalization to unobserved features.

Perhaps a more intriguing and unique property of a recurrent network is the creation of new emergent attributes by combining parts of existing attributes (see Smith & DeCoster, 1998, Simulation 3). Traditional theories of categorization assume that people use a single schema, stereotype, or knowledge structure to make inferences about a target person or a group. Even if multiple schemas are relevant, each of them is independently activated and applied. However, people can combine many sources of knowledge to construct new emergent properties to describe subtypes or subgroups of people. For instance, a militant feminist who is also a bank teller may become subtyped as a feminist bank teller with specific idiosyncratic attributes that are not those traditionally associated either with the militant feminist or the bank teller representations (Asch & Zukier, 1984; see also Chapter 7). Previous connectionist models, such as constraint satisfaction models (Kunda & Thagard, 1996), were unable to model this process.

Simulation 5: Assimilation with traits, contrast with exemplars

The abundance of assimilation effects in social cognition research may result in the idea that filling in unobserved characteristics is the default or most natural process. Thus, when primed with "violent", we judge a nondescript or ambiguous target person as more hostile, and when primed with "friendly" we judge that same target as less hostile. However, under some circumstances, the opposite effect may occur. Sometimes primed features may lead to contrast rather than assimilation.

For instance, when primed with the exemplar "Gandhi", people may judge a target person as relatively more hostile, whereas primed with "Hitler", they may judge the same target as relatively less hostile. Under these conditions, the exemplars Gandhi and Hitler serve as an anchor against which the target is judged, and so lead to contrast effects. In sum, contextually (or chronically) primed information may not only serve as an interpretation frame that leads to assimilation in impression formation, but also as a comparison standard that leads to contrast.

What produces assimilation or contrast? According to Stapel, Koomen, and van der Pligt (1997), trait concepts are more likely to serve to interpret an ambiguous person description (assimilation), because traits carry with them only conceptual meaning. On the other hand, exemplars—if sufficiently extreme—will be used as a comparison standard (contrast) because both the exemplar and the target are persons that can be compared to each other.

An experiment by Stapel et al. (1997, Experiment 3) confirmed this pro-position. Participants were asked to form an impression of an ambiguous friendly or hostile actor. Before they were exposed to the description of the target, they were primed with traits (e.g. violent or nice) or with names of extreme exemplars (e.g. Hitler or Gandhi). Finally, they indicated their impression of the target by scoring five trait dimensions that implied either a high or low degree of hostility. A composite scale of these trait ratings demonstrated assimilation in the trait-priming condition but contrast in the exemplar-priming condition (Figure 8.5).

Simulation

A recurrent network can simulate this combination of assimilation and contrast. As listed in Table 8.6, the network first builds up background knowledge about extreme exemplars like Gandhi and Hitler by linking them with friendly and hostile traits, respectively. The essential idea of the simulation is that during priming, the primed stimulus and the target description are temporarily activated together. This is represented by programming two learning trials. The first trial represents the priming condition and the second trial the description of the ambiguous target whereby the activation from the previous priming trial is left as the starting activation in addition to

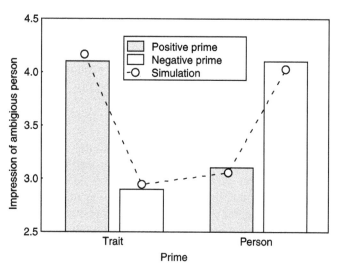

Figure 8.5 Assimilation and contrast effects after priming with a trait or person: Observed data from Stapel, Koomen, and van der Pligt (1997, Experiment 3) and simulation results (learning rate = .15). The human data are taken from Table 3 in "Categories of category accessibility: The impact of trait concept versus exemplar priming on person judgments" by D. A. Stapel, W. Koomen, & J. van der Pligt, 1997, *Journal of Experimental Social Psychology, 33*, 47–76. Copyright 1997 by Academic Press.

Table 8.6 Assimilation and contrast (Simulation 5)

	Actors			Traits	
	Target	Gandhi	Hitler	Friendly	Hostile
Prior learning history					
#10 Gandhi		1		1	
#10 Hitler			1		1
Condition 1: Priming Gandhi exemplar					
#1 Gandhi		1			
#1 Target description	1	$=^a$			
Condition 2: Priming Hitler exemplar					
#1 Hitler			1		
#1 Target description	1		$=^a$		
Condition 3: Priming friendly trait					
#1 Friendly				1	
#1 Target description	1			$=^a$	
Condition 4: Priming hostile trait					
#1 Hostile					1
#1 Target description	1				$=^a$
Test					
Trait of target	1			?	–?

Schematic representation of prior knowledge acquisition and experimental design of Stapel, Koomen, and van der Pligt (1997, Experiment 3); Cell entries denote external activation and empty cells denote 0 activation; #, number of trials. All trials during the prior learning history were presented in an order randomized for each run. The simulation was run separately for each condition.

[a] Activation from previous trial is left as starting activation for current trial.

the external activation of the actor (see Table 8.6). We tested the impression of the target by prompting the target node and reading off the activation of the friendly node and the (reversed) activation of the hostility node.

Simulation results

Figure 8.5 depicts the results for 50 participants run in different random orders with a learning rate of .15. As can be seen, the simulation replicated the empirical findings reported in the study of Stapel et al. (1997). The predicted interaction was significant, $F(1,196) = 797.33$, $p < .001$. There was assimilation of the trait prime, as the rating of the ambiguous actor was higher after priming with a positive as opposed to negative trait, $t(98) = 22.59$, $p < .001$. Conversely, there was contrast away from the exemplar prime, as the rating was lower after priming with a positive as opposed to negative prime, $t(98) = 17.42$, $p < .001$.

How was this result obtained? When a trait concept is primed, this activation spills over when the actor is presented, leading to stronger actor → trait connections through the principle of acquisition. As judging the actor's trait involves testing these actor → trait connections, this leads to the usual assimilation of the trait impression. In contrast, when an exemplar such as Hitler is primed, competition arises between this primed exemplar and the target exemplar in their connection to the hostile trait. Thus, competition arises between the (stronger) Hitler → trait connection and the target → trait connection, leading to discounting of the target → trait connection or a contrast effect.

Extensions and further research

This network makes an interesting prediction with respect to the impact of the extremity of exemplar and trait primes. According to the competition principle, extreme exemplars that serve as a comparison standard should cause more overestimation in the network and thus lead to stronger contrast. Similarly, as one might expect from the generalization (acquisition) property, extreme trait primes should lead to more assimilation. This prediction was supported by a recent study by Moskowitz and Skurnik (1999). In two experiments, they found that moderate exemplars (e.g. Kissinger) led to less contrast than extreme exemplars (e.g. Hitler), and that moderate trait primes led to less assimilation than extreme primes. This was produced in our simulations by replacing our friendly Gandhi exemplar (from Stapel et al., 1997) by a moderately hostile Kissinger exemplar (as used by Moskowitz & Skurnik, 1999) linked with a moderate hostility trait (i.e. with activation .10) to obtain a moderate exemplar; and priming the hostility trait by an activation of only .10 to simulate a moderate trait.

Interestingly, this latter simulation was also able to reproduce the additional finding of Moskowitz and Skurnik (1999) that cognitive interference (i.e. increasing task load or interrupting the current task) minimized the effects of trait assimilation but left the effects of exemplar contrasts relatively untouched. This was done by simulating decreased resources during priming by a decreased (10% of the original) learning rate. This eliminated assimilation effects, but preserved the contrast effects, as found by Moskowitz and Skurnik (1999, Experiments 3 and 4).

DISCOUNTING BY SITUATIONAL CONSTRAINTS

Most of the simulations that we have discussed so far rely on experimental paradigms in which trait-relevant information is provided about an actor in the form of traits or short behavior descriptions, and participants are to assume that this information is applicable to this person. As discussed earlier, however, social perceivers are much more sophisticated, and often realize whether they should either utilize or disregard such information. When there are situational constraints that may have provoked the actor's behavior, or when there are many others behaving in similar ways, perceivers tend to discount the behavioral information and are less likely to make a correspondent trait inference (Gilbert & Malone, 1995; Gilbert, Pelham, & Krull, 1988; Trope, 1986, Trope & Gaunt, 2000).

The operation of this discounting process should be most evident when situational constraints are explicitly manipulated in the experiment. In the following simulations, we discuss such experimental paradigms in which complex behavioral scenarios about an actor are provided, including information about the situation, so that the perceiver must decide whether the actor was the cause of the behavior before a correspondent trait inference can be made. Discounting by the context or situation involves the competition property as we discussed before. This principle has already been demonstrated on mere causal attributions using a connectionist network with the delta learning algorithm (see Chapter 5; and Van Overwalle, 1998) but not yet on trait inferences. The aim of the next section is to extent this approach also to trait inferences, to verify whether the underlying principles in causal attribution are generalizable to traits, and to motivate further the use of context nodes as applied in the earlier simulations.

Simulation 6: Situational correction or integration?

One of the current debates in the literature on trait attributions concerns the process by which behavior-correspondent trait inferences are discounted given situational demands. In so-called "correction" theories, it is assumed that perceivers first automatically attribute the behavior to the correspondent trait and then discount the trait inference on the basis of situational information in a separate resource-dependent stage (Gilbert & Malone, 1995; Gilbert et al. 1988). In contrast, integration theories assume that situational information is used as an integral part of drawing trait inferences from behavior, whereby the weighting of the contribution of person and environmental factors "involves an iterative or even simultaneous evaluation of the various hypotheses before reaching a conclusion" (Trope & Gaunt, 2000, p.353, see also Trope, 1986). It is evident that the connectionist perspective is more in line with the latter perspective because network models typically allow many processes to occur in parallel without the need of separate and sequential process stages.

To demonstrate that discounting in trait inferences can be explained in part by parallel processing in a connectionist network, we focus on the work by Trope and Gaunt (2000). Trope and Gaunt replicated the well-known finding that situational information is often underutilized to discount trait inferences, especially under conditions of cognitive load. This finding has often been taken by correction theorists as evidence that the effortful correction stage was interrupted by the cognitive load manipulation (Gilbert & Malone, 1995). However, Trope and Gaunt argued that situational information might be underutilized because it is often less salient or applicable for the actor, and that this, rather than effortful correction, might explain why cognitive load often disrupts discounting. To support their view, they made situational information more cognitively salient, active, or applicable, and found that, under these circumstances, situational information was used to discount trait inferences even under cognitive load (Trope & Gaunt, 2000).

In one of their experiments, Trope and Gaunt (2000, Experiment 3) provided a description of a teaching assistant who used strict criteria in grading an exam. Information about situational demands varied according to condition. In one condition, no demand was provided; in a general demand condition, participants were told that there was a university-wide requirement to use strict criteria in grading exams; and in a specific demand condition, participants were told that the professor of the exam gave specific instructions for the assistant to use strict criteria. Finally, the participants were asked to infer how strict the assistant was on a 13-point rating scale ranging from 1 (*not a strict person at all*) to 13 (*a very strict person*). In the cognitive load condition, the participants were asked to recall an eight-digit number during the task. The results showed that under no load conditions, discounting was applied. That is, the teaching assistant received less strict ratings given both general and specific demands. More crucially, in line with their integration prediction, Trope and Gaunt also documented that discounting was applied even under cognitive load when the demand was specific and directly applicable, but not when it was general and less applicable (see also Figure 8.6,

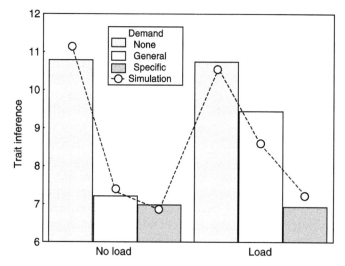

Figure 8.6 Integration of situational information: Observed data from Trope and Gaunt (2000, Experiment 3) and simulation results (learning rate given no load = .33; given load = .18). The human data are taken from Table 3 in "Processing alternative explanations of behavior: Correction or integration?" by Y. Trope & R. Gaunt, 2000, *Journal of Personality and Social Psychology, 79*, 344–354. Copyright 2000 by the American Psychological Association.

below). This demonstrates that discounting could not have been applied in a second effortful correction stage, as the cognitive load should have prevented any discounting in this stage. In the next simulation, we demonstrate that a recurrent approach can explain these findings, by replicating Trope and Gaunt's experiment.

Simulation

Table 8.7 provides a schematic description of the learning history reflecting Trope and Gaunt's (2000) Experiment 3. As can be seen, the difference between specific and general demands was implemented in the prior learning history that participants brought with them. This learning history assumed that teaching assistants are typically strict in their grading, just like professors, although professors have more experience (i.e. more learning trials). In contrast, general academic instructions are less often followed (i.e. stricter grading was used most of the time, but sometimes lenient grading was

Table 8.7 Integration of situational information (Simulation 6)

	Actors			Traits	
	Teaching assistant	University administration	Professor	Strict	Lenient
Prior learning history					
#5 Teaching assistant	1			1	
#10 Professor			1	1	
#8 University administration		1		1	
#2 University administration		1			1
Condition 1: No demand					
#2 No Demand	1			1	
Condition 2: General demand					
#2 University administration	1	1		1	
Condition 3: Specific demand					
#2 Professor	1		1	1	
Test					
Trait of teaching assistant	1			?	–?

Schematic representation of prior knowledge acquisition and experimental design of Trope and Gaunt (2000, Experiment 1). Cell entries denote external activation and empty cells denote 0 activation; #, number of trials. All trials during the prior learning history were presented in an order randomized for each run. The simulation was run separately for each condition. In the load condition, the learning rate was reduced to 50% in conditions 1 to 3.

applied as well). As a consequence, a specific demand by the professor should lead to stronger actor → trait connections than a general demand by the academic authority. (Different trial frequencies lead to similar simulation results as long as they preserve a similar proportion of strict versus lenient.)

The three demand conditions were then simulated in separate simulation runs in which we assumed two trials per condition. Cognitive load was simulated by reducing the learning rate in the three demand conditions to 50% of its original value. Unlike some of the previous simulations, we assumed more trials and less reduction of learning rate because information consisted not of a simple trait adjective or trait-implying behavior, but rather of more elaborated behavioral scenarios that presumably take somewhat longer and more attention to process. Finally, trait inferences were measured as before, by probing the actor node and reading off the trait nodes.

Simulation results

The simulation was run with 50 participants for each condition, with different random orders for each participant. The learning rate was .33 under no load conditions and 50% of this default under load conditions or .18. The results, depicted in Figure 8.6, demonstrate that the recurrent network largely replicated the findings of Trope and Gaunt (2000). The predicted interaction between demand and cognitive load reached significance, $F(2,294) = 4.08$, $p < .05$. More importantly, as predicted, specificity of demands had a differential effect under cognitive load than under no load. Although all demand conditions produced discounting, $t(98) = 4.78$ to 9.74, $p < .001$, under no load, general and specific demands did not differ from each other, $t(98) < 1$, *ns*. In contrast, under load, general demands produced less discounted inferences than specific demands did, $t(98) = 3.03$, $p < .01$.

How was discounting achieved in the simulation? This was due to the principle of competition. Recall that a strong actor → trait connection by the professor or administration was built up in the prior learning history. When these actors (i.e. their demands) are present, their strong connection competes against the assistant's actor → trait connection. Consequently, the assistant → trait connection is not increased further, reflecting discounting in comparison with a condition without any demand. Thus, it is important to realize that in this approach, when perceivers are aware of the situational demands, they never make a trait inference that is later reduced, as the two-stage model of Gilbert and Malone (1995) would predict. Rather, from the beginning of the parallel connectionist computation, the actor's trait inference is effectively discounted by the situational demand.

How was the crucial difference in discounting of general demands (by the administration) under no and high load achieved in the simulation? This is quite straightforward. Because of the increased processing (that is, higher learning rate) in the no-load condition, competition was applied more strongly, so that even the softer general demand led to a blocking of correspondent trait inferences in the no load condition. This was less so in the load condition, where there was a lower learning rate and thus less competition. These same principles used in our simulation also allowed replicating the results of the other experiments by Trope and Gaunt (2000).

Simulation 7: Discounting and sample size

An important assumption in the previous simulation was that stronger or more salient competing situational factors prevent the building up of trait inferences about the actor. This assumption is built on the combination of the principles of acquisition (to develop strong situation → trait connections during prior learning) and of competition (to induce discounting of the actor → trait connections). But is there more direct evidence for this assumption?

The combination of the principles of acquisition and competition provides an interesting test case to distinguish our approach from previous algebraic models of attribution (Cheng & Novick, 1992; Försterling, 1992) and impression formation (Anderson, 1981; Hogarth & Einhorn, 1992). These models would not predict that the increased frequency by an alternative actor or situational factors alone results in a greater discounting of a target actor (Van Overwalle & Van Rooy, 2001b). Alternative connectionist models also fail to make this prediction: The tensor product model by Kashima and Kerekes (1994) because it does not possess the competition property, and the constraint satisfaction model by Kunda and Thagard (1996) because of the lack of the acquisition property.

To test this prediction, Van Overwalle (2006) combined differences in sample size with discounting. In particular, trait inferences were increased by increasing the frequency of an actor's behaviors, and this was expected to induce greater discounting of the trait inferences of a target actor. Participants read several stories each describing a *competing* actor who engaged in a particular behavior (e.g. "Stephan solved one or five questions during a quiz"). The competing actor engaged in this behavior only one time (i.e. small size condition) or five times (large size condition). Next, regardless of condition, participants read five descriptions in which the competing actor engaged in the same behavior together with a novel target actor (e.g. "Stephan and Walter worked together to solve another five questions"). After receiving this information, they had to rate the traits of the two actors. In our example, they had to rate how intelligent each contestant was on an 11-point scale ranging from 1 (*not at all intelligent*) to 10 (*very intelligent*; Van Overwalle, 2006). Consistent with our connectionist prediction, but contrary to earlier models, the results revealed that a greater frequency (i.e. sample size) of the competing actor led not only to higher inferences of the implied trait to the competing actor, but also to significantly greater discounting of these trait inferences for the novel target actor (Figure 8.7). In other words, when Stephan solves more questions he is seen as more intelligent, whereas Walter is seen as less intelligent. These results for trait inferences

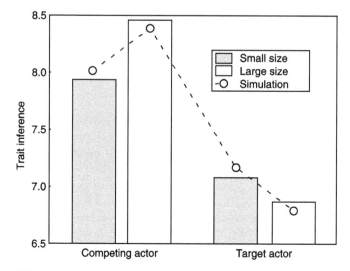

Figure 8.7 Discounting and sample size: Observed data from Van Overwalle (2006) and simulation results (general learning rate = .08, for competing actor = .13).

replicated similar findings for mere causal attributions following the same combined manipulation of sample size and competition (Van Overwalle & Van Rooy, 2001a).

Simulation

Table 8.8 shows the design of the simulation for this experiment (Van Overwalle, 2006). Because only one type of behavior was described in each of the stories, only a single trait node was provided (i.e. there was no behavior implying the opposite trait). As can be seen, the competing actor first engaged in a trait-implying behavior alone, and then together with the target actor. The crucial difference between conditions is sample size, or the number of times (one or five) the competing actor engaged in the behavior alone.

Simulation results

The simulation was run with 50 participants and trial order was fixed. Each sample size condition was run in a separate simulation. Figure 8.7 depicts the results for a learning rate of .08 (and .13 for the competing actor). As can be seen, the simulation replicated the empirical data. An ANOVA with Sample Size as between-subjects factor and Rating (target vs. competing actor) as repeated measures indicated that the predicted interaction was significant, $F(1,196) = 95.38$, $p < .001$. Given a greater sample size, the simulation reveals stronger trait inferences of the competing actor, $t(98) = 6.63$, $p < .001$, and simultaneously weaker trait inferences of the target actor, $t(98) = 6.60$,

Table 8.8 Discounting in function of sample size of the competing actor (Simulation 7)

	Actors		
	Competing	Target	Trait (e.g. intelligent)
Condition 1: Small sample size			
#1 Competing actor	1		1
#5 Target and Competing actor	1	1	1
Condition 2: Large sample size			
#5 Competing actor	1		1
#5 Target and competing actor	1	1	1
Test			
Competing actor	1		?
Target actor		1	?

Schematic representation of the experimental design of Van Overwalle (2006). Cell entries denote external activation and empty cells denote 0 activation; #, number of trials. The simulation was run separately for each condition.

$p < .001$. Thus, the simulation supports the unique prediction of the connectionist approach that the more often other people perform the same behavior, the less likely perceivers believe that the target actor possesses the correspondent trait. Note that when the order of the trials is randomized rather then blocked per condition (as it was in the simulation), the network still predicts discounting, although to a lesser degree because the influence of the competing actor is built up in later trials and thus has less impact.[2]

Extensions and further research

As noted above, the competition principle illustrated here can be extended to explain the influence of covariation information (Kelley, 1967) on trait inferences. When only a few people engage in behaviors similar to the actor (i.e. low consensus), we tend to make stronger person attributions and correspondent trait inferences than if a lot of people engage in similar behaviors (i.e. high consensus). Alternatively, if the actor engages in the behavior only under specific circumstances (i.e. high distinctiveness), we tend to make more entity attributions and hence less correspondent trait inferences than when the actor behaves similarly under many different circumstances (i.e. low distinctiveness). Van Overwalle (1997, 2003) showed that the joint manipulation of these two covariation methods leads to trait ratings very similar to those obtained by Stewart (1965, see also Figure 8.1) where only simple trait

---

2 To simulate that both actors work independently rather than together on the quiz, one would have to assume that each of them is linked to a different behavior or outcome, each leading to the same intelligent trait. As such, no competition would arise and no discounting would be predicted.

descriptions of a single target were provided. These results could be simulated by a similar learning history as depicted for Simulation 1.

FIT TO DATA AND MODEL COMPARISONS

The simulations that we have reported all replicate empirical data and theoretical predictions reasonably well. However, it is possible that this fit is due to some procedural choices of the simulations rather than a more general conceptual validity. The aim of this section is to demonstrate that changes in these choices generally do not invalidate our simulations. To this end, we explore a number of issues, including the localist versus distributed encoding of concepts, and the specific recurrent network used. In addition, we also discuss how the recurrent approach compares to other connectionist network models. We do not discuss the algebraic models of Busemeyer (1991) and Hogarth and Einhorn (1992) as they are, in fact, simplified versions of the delta learning algorithm applied in connectionist models. We address each issue in turn.

Distributed coding

The first issue is whether the nodes in the autoassociative architecture encode localist or distributed features. As mentioned earlier, localist features reflect "symbolic" pieces of information, that is, each node represents a concrete concept. In contrast, in a distributed encoding, a concept is represented by a *pattern* of activation across an array of nodes, none of which reflects a symbolic concept but rather some subsymbolic micro-feature of it (Thorpe, 1995). We used a localist encoding scheme to facilitate the understanding of the processing mechanisms underlying connectionism. However, localist encoding is far from biologically and psychologically realistic because it implies that each concept is stored in a single processing unit and, except for differing levels of activation, is always perceived in the same manner. Unlike such a localist encoding scheme, a distributed activation pattern allows for noisy or incomplete inputs to receive a fair amount of activation from similar inputs seen earlier (see Chapter 7) and to sustain partial damage. Given the advantages of distributed coding, is it possible to replicate our localist simulations with a distributed representation?

To address this question, we reran all simulations with a distributed encoding scheme in which each concept (e.g. trait, behavior, situation) was represented by a pattern of activation along five nodes instead of a single node. All simulations were run with 50 participants and each set of 10 participants received a different random pattern of activation for each concept to ensure that the simulation results generalized across activation patterns. For each participant and trial, random activation (i.e. noise) was added to this activation to simulate the imperfect conditions of perceptual encoding (see Table 8.9 for details). The fit with the observed data was measured by calculating the correlation between the observed and simulated means. These correlations are merely indicative, as the number of means (four or more) is too few to obtain reliable differences between correlations. By way of comparison, the correlation of the original localist simulations is also given.

As can be seen, all distributed simulations attained a good fit to data. In all cases, the pattern of results from the original localist simulations was reproduced. This suggests that the underlying principles and mechanisms that we put forth as being responsible for the major simulation results can be obtained not only in the more contrived context of a localist encoding, but also in a more realistic context of a distributed encoding.

Feedforward model

In our discussion of the three properties of the delta learning algorithm, typically one direction of the connections was responsible for replicating the phenomena. Specifically, we focused on the connections as they were oriented from input (involving most often actors and behaviors) to output (involving trait categories) except for the diffusion property in Simulation 5, where this order was reversed. To illustrate that these input $\rightarrow$ trait connections are of primary theoretical importance, we reran the simulations with a feedforward pattern associator (McClelland & Rumelhart, 1988) that consists only of feedforward connections from input to trait (see also the arrangement of nodes from left to right in Tables 8.2 to 8.9).

Table 8.9 Fit and robustness of the simulations, including alternative encoding and models

No. and topic	Original simulation	Distributed	Feedforward	Non-linear recurrent
1 On-line integration	.98	.95	.97	.96
2a Weight—continuous	.94	.89	.85[x]	.81
2b Weight—final	.71	.72	< 0[x]	< 0[a,x]
3 Asymmetric cues	.96	.91	.91	.89
4 Inconsistent behavior	.96	.96	.92	.82
5 Assimilation and contrast	.99	1.00	.99	1.00
6 Situational integration	.97	.96	.93[x]	.96[a]
7 Discounting and size	.99	.99	.99	.99

Cell entries are correlations between mean simulated values (averaged across randomizations) and empirical data. For the distributed encoding, we ran 50 "participants" and each concept was represented by five nodes and an activation pattern drawn from a normal distribution with $M =$ activation of the original simulation and $SD = .20$ (five such random patterns for 10 "participants" were run and averaged) and additional noise at each trial drawn from a normal distribution with $M = 0$ and $SD = .20$. For the non-linear autoassociative model, the parameters were: $E = I = Decay = .15$ and *internal cycles* = 9 (McClelland & Rumelhart, 1988). For all alternative models, we searched for the best-fitting learning parameter.

[a] Number of internal cycles = 4; [x] predicted pattern was not reproduced.

As can be seen in Table 8.9, for most simulations, a feedforward architecture did almost as well as the original simulations. One major exception was the simulation of recency and primacy effects in serial position weights (Simulation 2). As noted earlier, the feedforward network is unable to replicate the critical finding of attenuation of recency in continuous judgments and robust primacy in final judgments. In addition, in Simulation 6 there was an unexpected difference between the general and specific demand conditions given no load, although, as predicted, overall discounting was stronger in these two conditions than given high load. This confirms that for the majority of phenomena in person perception, one direction of the connections in the network was most crucial. This does not deny the fact that the additional lateral or backward connections play a role, although only a smaller one.

Non-linear recurrent model

We also claimed earlier that a recurrent model with a *linear* updating activation algorithm and a *single internal updating* cycle (for collecting the internal activation from related nodes) was sufficient for reproducing the social phenomena of interest. This contrasts with other social researchers who used a non-linear activation updating algorithm and many more internal cycles (see Chapters 5 and 7). Are these model features necessary or even preferably? To answer this question, we ran all our simulations with a non-linear activation algorithm and 10 (i.e. one external and nine internal) cycles.

As can be seen from Table 8.9, although the non-linear model yielded an adequate fit, most simulations did not improve substantially compared to the original simulations. In the simulation on integration of situational information (Simulation 6), the number of internal cycles had to be reduced from nine to four to obtain meaningful results. The reason is that the non-linear updating easily attenuates the competition property because it drives activations that are too high (beyond +1) back to the default ceiling level of +1, and so prevents overestimation and competition. By taking fewer internal cycles, this attenuation of competition is sometimes prevented. However, in the simulation on serial position weights (Simulation 2b), reducing the number of internal cycles to four or even one was not enough to obtain a primacy effect. The reason is similar, as the non-linear updating drives the reciprocal reduction of activation by actor and trait given disconfirmatory items (which slowed down learning and caused primacy) back to normal +1 ceiling levels. Taken together, this suggests that the linear activation update algorithm with a single internal cycle is sufficient for simulating many phenomena in impression formation.[3] This should not come as a surprise. In recurrent simulations

---

3   The simulation results by Smith and DeCoster (1998, Simulations 1–3) could also be obtained with linear updating of activation.

of other issues, such as the formation of semantic concepts, multiple internal cycles were useful to perform "clean-up" in the network, so that after activating a perceptual input (e.g. hearing the word "cat"), the activations of the associated semantic concept were forced to eventually settle into "attractor" representations that had pre-established conceptual meaning (e.g. McLeod et al., 1998, pp.145–148). Such a distinction between perceptual and conceptual levels was not made here and, as a result, multiple internal cycles had no real function.

The parallel-constraint-satisfaction model

We can be brief about the parallel-constraint-satisfaction network model developed by Kunda and Thagard (1996). This model lacks a learning algorithm and therefore has no acquisition property and is incapable of replicating any of the simulations we presented. We cannot see how this model could be amended, unless by major alterations that would definitely change the model drastically.

The tensor product model

The tensor product model is an important alternative connectionist approach to person and group impression formation and change (Kashima & Kerekes, 1994; Kashima et al., 2000). A major difference to our recurrent model is that the tensor product model uses a Hebbian learning algorithm. This type of learning has the significant disadvantage that it does not imply the competition property. Hence, social phenomena explained by this property, such as contrast, situational correction, and discounting (Simulations 5 to 7), can presumably not be simulated with this model, at least not without additional assumptions. In addition, to simulate attenuation of recency in impression formation, this model requires the ad-hoc assumption of different context presentations before and after a judgment (Kashima & Kerekes, 1994). This assumption was not required with our simulations (see Simulation 2). For all other phenomena that we simulated, it appears to us that the tensor-product model might simulate most of them, although we are not sure about the diffusion property (Simulation 4). Of course, we do not have any idea as to how close the tensor product model might fit the data, and whether it might do so equally well as the recurrent model.

GENERAL DISCUSSION

In this article, we have presented an overview of a number of major findings in impression formation and have shown how they might be accounted for within a connectionist framework. This connectionist perspective offers a novel view on how information can be encoded, how it might be structured and activated, and how it can be retrieved and used for social judgment. This view differs from earlier theories in impression formation, which relied on metaphors such as algebraic arithmetic (Anderson, 1981; Busemeyer, 1991; Hogarth & Einhorn, 1992), phase-like integration of information (Gilbert, 1989), or spreading-activation and constraint-satisfaction networks with fixed weights (Kunda & Thagard, 1996; Read & Marcus-Newhall, 1993; Shultz & Lepper, 1996). The problem is that these various metaphors give a rather inflexible, incomplete, and fragmentary account of person perception mechanisms.

In contrast, the connectionist approach proposed in this article, although relying on the same general autoassociative architecture and processing algorithm, has been used in such a way as to be applicable to a wide-ranging number of phenomena in impression formation. Moreover, we have shown that this model provides an alternative interpretation of earlier algebraic models (Anderson, 1981; Busemeyer, 1991; Hogarth & Einhorn, 1992). In addition, this model can also account for the learning of social knowledge structures. This involves not only the episodic relation between actors and their traits and behaviors (Hamilton et al., 1980), but also the more permanent semantic knowledge that relates behaviors to traits (Skowronski & Carlston, 1987, 1989). Hence, this approach could potentially be used to investigate the development among infants and children of the structures underlying social knowledge.

A basic assumption in our simulations of the development of semantic trait meaning is that traits are seen as prototypes, in which strong associations between certain cues (behaviors) and categories (traits) are built from more frequent exposure to behavior–trait pairings. This assumption might seem questionable, because behaviors or attributes that are highly prototypical of trait categories are also very rare, and may never even have been encountered before. After all, how often do we have exposure to someone who behaves extraordinarily honestly or dishonestly? Hence, one might argue that these extreme or idealized trait prototypes are not simply retrieved from memory when making a judgment but are instead constructed as needed. However, in contrast to this idea, research has demonstrated that extraordinary features not seen previously are judged more atypical and are categorized less quickly than extraordinary features seen earlier (Nosofsky, 1991). Thus, some limited exposure to extraordinary instances is important in making extreme trait inferences, otherwise people may be tempted to classify extraordinary exemplars to different categories, such as, for instance, UFOs or heroes, to which normal exemplars do not belong. Moreover, note that in our simulations (e.g. Simulation 3), an extreme trait inference was not viewed solely as stemming from higher behavioral frequency (in fact, the frequencies were set equal to neutral behaviors), but also as involving behaviors with a wider-ranging configuration of features. Thus, not only feature frequency but also the configuration of many features (some of which are typical and others that are extreme) was sufficient to induce extreme trait inferences.

We have focused to a large extent on the model as a learning device, that is, as a mechanism for associating patterns that reflect social concepts by means of very elementary learning processes. One major advantage of a connectionist perspective is that complex social reasoning and learning can be accomplished by putting together an array of simple, interconnected elements that greatly enhance the network's computational power, and by incrementally adjusting the weights of the connections with the delta learning algorithm. We have demonstrated that this learning algorithm gives rise to a number of novel properties, among them the acquisition property that accounts for sample size effects, the competition property that accounts for discounting, and the diffusion principle that accounts for higher recall of inconsistent information. These properties can explain most of our simulations of social judgment and behavior. In contrast, introductory textbooks on the autoassociator (e.g. McClelland & Rumelhart, 1988; McLeod et al., 1998) emphasize other capacities of the autoassociator, including its content-addressable memory, its ability to do pattern completion (see Chapter 7), and its fault and noise tolerance.

Implications

What are the implications of this work for theories of impression formation? The key contribution of this article is that a wide range of phenomena was simulated with the same overall network model (differing only in the learning rate parameter and the learning history), suggesting that these phenomena are based, at least during early processing, on the same fundamental information-processing principles. Providing a common framework for these different phenomena will hopefully generate further research and extend to new areas of social psychology usually seen as too different to be brought under a single theoretical heading. In addition, not only can this model account for prior empirical data, it can also generate new hypotheses that can be tested in a classical experimental setting. We briefly discuss some potential questions and research issues that emerge from this model.

Knowledge acquisition

To what extent is the learning history assumed in our simulations correct? What mechanisms and architectural considerations are necessary to preserve the network's knowledge base? How does prior (trait) knowledge interact with novel (behavioral) information? One of the suggestions made earlier is that semantic behavior–trait associations stored in semantic memory are applied spontaneously when novel behavioral information is received. This suggestion is in line with the bulk of research on spontaneous trait inferences (see Uleman, 1999). Perhaps answers to these questions could also be obtained by laboratory replications of the assumed learning histories, which should reveal an equivalence with the prior knowledge of participants and similar effects on trait inferences as we have reviewed here.

Automatic versus conscious reasoning

Our approach does not make a clear and explicit distinction between automatic and conscious processing, or between implicit and explicit processing.
Quite often, setting learning rate to a lower or higher (default) level made it
possible, to simulate this distinction, suggesting that automatic and conscious
processing is, perhaps in part, a matter of slow or shallow versus fast and
deep learning of information. This differential level of learning gives rise to
a differential emphasis on, for example, prior information versus novel
information, and may result in different judgments. Some researchers (e.g.
Smith & DeCoster, 2000) have proposed a distinction between two processing
modes: a slow-learning (connectionist) pattern-completion mode and a more
effortful (symbolic) mode that involves explicit symbolically represented rules
and inferences. Other theorists have suggested, in line with our approach, that
such sharp distinction is not necessary and that many social judgments—
although differing in content—may share the same underlying process (e.g.
Chun, Spiegel, & Kruglanski, 2002). Within the framework of a single connectionist network, differences between shallow and deep learning are possible
by assuming that "explicit, conscious knowledge . . . involves higher quality
memory traces than implicit knowledge" (Cleeremans & Jiménez, 2002,
p.21). This approach has also been taken to simulate differences between
heuristic and central processes in attitude change (see Chapter 11) and
between implicit and explicit reasoning (Kinder & Shanks, 2001).

Heuristics

Although heuristics are typically viewed as rules-of-thumb that short-cut
logical thinking and often result in biased judgments (Kahneman, Slovic, &
Tversky, 1982), we would like to argue that they actually provide a window
to see how the brain—as a connectionist device—works. For example, the
availability heuristic, invoked to explain why many judgments are biased by
information about facts and arguments recently or frequently available in
memory, can also be viewed from a connectionist framework as information
that is recently primed or activated and that is spread automatically to other
related concepts, influencing judgments about them (as we have seen in the
assimilation simulation). Of course, this does not exclude the possibility that
subjective experiences that may go together with activating memory traces,
such as the ease to recall a given number of exemplars, may additionally
influence how people utilize that activated information in further judgments
(Schwarz et al., 1991). In addition, the representativeness heuristic that has
been invoked to explain why categorization is often guided by a resemblance
between concepts rather than by statistical base rates, may in fact reflect
the strength of the connections between a category and its members (as
demonstrated in the simulation on the asymmetry of ability- and morality-
related behavior). Finally, the anchoring and adjustment heuristic, originally

proposed to explain why judgments are often biased toward an initial anchor, can be simply taken as a property of the delta learning algorithm, in which weight adjustments are often stronger initially (i.e. during anchoring) because of the greater error in the network, whereas later adjustments become increasingly smaller because the error is reduced. This approach might also explain insufficient adjustments in later phases of learning as due to decreased cognitive effort during integration of situational information.

Limitations and future directions

Given the breadth of impression formation, we inevitably were not able to include many other interesting findings and phenomena. Perhaps the most interesting area omitted involves group processes. Connectionist modeling may well help to explain how group identity is created, how perceptions of group homogeneity are changed, how accentuation of correlated features is enhanced, and how illusory correlation and unrealistic negative stereotypes of minority groups are developed. These questions are addressed in Van Rooy et al. (2003; see also Chapter 9), using the same model as ours. These applications merely reflect our current thinking and will almost certainly be replaced by improved models in the future. We believe, however, that the *essence* of the approach proposed here will survive.

Although we have attempted to show that a connectionist framework can potentially provide a parsimonious account of a number of disparate phenomena in impression formation, we are not suggesting that this is the only valid means of modeling social cognitive phenomena. On the contrary, we defend a multiple-view position in which connectionism would play a key role but would coexist alongside other viewpoints. We think that strict neurological reductionism is untenable, especially in personality and social psychology, where it is difficult to see how one could develop a connectionist model of such high-level abstract concepts as "need for closure", "prejudice", "close relationships", "motivation", and the like. These limitations suggest a number of possible directions for extending the connectionist approach. First, a critical improvement to our recurrent network might be the inclusion of hidden layers (McClelland & Rumelhart, 1988, pp.121–126), possibly with coarse coding of nodes (e.g. O'Reilly & Rudy, 2001) or exemplar nodes (e.g. Kruschke & Johansen, 1999) that may potentially increase its power and capacity, for instance, to process non-linear interactions.

Second, a more modular architecture will almost certainly be necessary to produce a better fit of the model to empirical data. For example, one severe limitation of most connectionist models is known as "catastrophic interference" (McCloskey & Cohen, 1989; Ratcliff, 1990, see French, 1999 for a review), which is the tendency of neural networks to forget, abruptly and completely, previously learned information in the presence of new input. Although catastrophic interference has been observed when perceivers process novel information (see Simulation 1), it is untenable for a realistic model of long-term social cognitive processes, whereby prior knowledge—such as stereotypes—is often resistant to change in the presence of new information. In response to such observations, it has been suggested that, to overcome this problem, the brain developed a dual hippocampal–neocortical memory system in which new (mainly episodic) information is processed in the hippocampus and old (mainly semantic) information is stored and consolidated in the neocortex (McClelland, McNaughton, & O'Reilly, 1995; Smith & DeCoster, 2000). Various modelers (Ans & Rousset, 1997; French, 1997) have proposed modular connectionist architectures mimicking this dual-memory system with one subsystem dedicated to the rapid learning of unexpected and novel information and the building of episodic memory traces and the other subsystem responsible for slow incremental learning of statistical regularities of the environment and gradual consolidation of information learned in the first subsystem. There is considerable evidence for the modular nature of the brain, in particular for the complementary learning roles of hippocampal and neocortical structures (McClelland et al., 1995), the predominant role of the amygdala in social judgment and perception of emotions (Adolphs, Tranel & Damasio, 1998), and so forth. A dual-memory representation raises the intriguing possibility that, for a limited period of time, old trait knowledge as well as novel trait inferences may coexist in memory. It strikes us that the next step in connectionist modeling of social cognition will involve the exploration of connectionist architectures built from separate but complementary systems.

Third, as a special case of modularization, it will ultimately be necessary to incorporate factors such as attention, consciousness, and motivation, which are important in social perception, into an improved model. For the time being, attentional aspects of human information processing are not part of the dynamics of our network (variations were simply hand coded as differences in learning), which focuses almost exclusively on learning and pattern association. However, there are recent developments that provide insights in how an attentional switching mechanism might be implemented. O'Reilly and Munakata (2000) suggested a network model of attention and motivation based on the idea that a specialized module residing in the prefrontal cortex would be capable of active maintenance of rapidly updateable activation, which would enable this module to provide a sustained, top-down biasing influence over processing elsewhere in the system. These actively maintained frontal cortex representations could guide behavior and judgment according to goals, motivation, and other types of internal constraints.

Conclusion

Connectionist modeling of person impression formation fits seamlessly into a multilevel integrative analyses of human behavior (Cacioppo et al., 2000). Given that cognition is intrinsically social, connectionism will ultimately have to begin to incorporate social constraints into its models. On the other hand, social psychology will need to be more attentive to the biological underpinnings of social behavior. Social and biological approaches to cognition can therefore be seen as complementary endeavors, with the common goal of achieving a clearer and deeper understanding of human behavior. We hope that connectionist accounts of social cognition will provide the common ground for this exploration.

ANNEXE

Anderson's averaging rule and the delta learning algorithm

This annexe demonstrates that the delta learning algorithm converges at asymptote to Anderson's (1981) averaging rule under two conditions. First, learning must have reached asymptote (i.e. after sufficient trials), and, second, the relative weights in Anderson's (1981) model can be represented by the relative frequencies of person–trait pairings. Anderson's (1981) averaging rule of impression formation expresses a rating about a person as:

$$rating = \Sigma \, \omega_i \, s_i / \Sigma \, \omega_i \qquad (8.1)$$

where ω_i represents the weights and s_i the scale values of the trait.

This proof uses the same logic as Chapman and Robbins (1990) in their demonstration that the delta learning algorithm converges to the probabilistic expression of covariation. In line with the conventional representation of covariation information, person impression information can be represented in a contingency table with two cells. Cell A represents all cases where the actor is ascribed a focal trait; Cell B represents all cases where the actor is ascribed the opposite trait. For simplicity, I use only two trait categories, although this proof can easily be extended to more categories.

In a recurrent connectionist architecture with localist encoding as used in the text, the target person j and the trait categories i are each represented by a node, which are connected by adjustable weights w_{ij}. When the target person is present, its corresponding node receives external activation, and this activation is spread to each trait node. We assume that the overall activation received at the trait nodes i (or internal activation) after priming the person node, reflects the impression on the person.

According to the delta learning algorithm (see Equations 3.3 and 3.4, p.38), the weights w_{ij} are adjusted proportional to the error between the actual trait category (represented by its external activation *ext*) and the trait category as predicted by the network (represented by its internal activation *int*). If we substitute in Equation 3.3 *ext* by Anderson's scale values (s_1 for the focal trait, and s_2 for the opposite trait) and if we take in Equation 3.4 the default activation for a_i (which is 1), then the following equations can be constructed for the two cells in the contingency table:

For the A cell: $\Delta w_i = \varepsilon \, (s_1 - int)$ (8.2)

For the B cell: $\Delta w_i = \varepsilon \, (s_2 - int)$ (8.3)

The change in overall impression is the sum of Equations 8.2 and 8.3, weighted for the corresponding frequencies a and b, in the two cells, or:

$$\Delta w_i = a \, [\varepsilon \, (s_1 - int)] + b \, [\varepsilon \, (s_2 - int)] \tag{8.4}$$

These adjustments will continue until asymptote, that is, until the error between actual and expected category is zero. This implies that at asymptote, the changes will become zero, or $\Delta w_i = 0$. Consequently, Equation 8.4 becomes:

$$0 = a \, [\varepsilon \, (s_1 - int)] + b \, [\varepsilon \, (s_2 - int)]$$
$$= a \, [s_1 - int] + b \, [s_2 - int]$$
$$= [a * s_1 + b * s_2] - [a + b] * int$$

so that:

$$int = [a * s_1 + b * s_2]/[a + b]$$

Because the internal activation of the trait nodes reflects the trait impression on the person, this can be rewritten in Anderson's terms as:

$$impression = \Sigma f_i \, s_i / \Sigma f_i \tag{8.5}$$

where f represents frequencies with which a person and the traits co-occur. As can be seen, Equation 8.5 has the same format as Equation 8.1. This demonstrates that the delta learning algorithm predicts a weighted averaging function at asymptote for making overall impression judgments, where Anderson's weights ω are determined by the frequencies by which person and traits are presented together.

SIMULATION EXERCISES

These exercises enable you to explore the recurrent simulations of the text, and you can experiment yourself by simulating other models or variants of the experiments chosen in the text. You are expected to have some experience with the FIT program, perhaps by having completed some of the exercises in Chapter 3 and 4, which explain the working of the program in somewhat more detail. The manual of the program is available in the Appendix at the end of the book.

Exercise 1: Online integration

Choose menu **File | Open Project** or press the 📖 speed button. Browse for *Stewart65.ft2* in folder *Chapter 8*, and click the **Open** button.

Specifying trials

Click the **Trial** tab to open the Trial Grid, which defines the Trial Categories. The top rows show two input units and one output unit representing the information about the actor and the context, together with a single trait. (You can change the names given to the units in the second row either by double clicking, or by choosing the **Data | Edit Column Names** menu). The following Trial Categories are specified:

- Learning Trial Category $1 depicts the learning of a single *High Trait*, while Learning Trial Category $2 depicts the learning of a single *Low Trait*.
- Throughout the simulations of this chapter, you will modify the learning rate of the context using the alpha_1 parameter. To indicate that you apply this parameter on the context unit, you specify in Learning Category $–1 value *1* for the context unit, and you set the other units to zero or leave them blank.
- For measuring the trait, in this and all remaining simulations, you prime the actor and observe how much the relevant trait units are activated (see "*?*" in Test Category $50).

You can see that all these specifications (except Category $–1) closely resemble Table 8.2, which depicts the learning history, as is also the case for the other simulations. (Making such a copy is easily done by using menu **File | Export | Trial Data Grid to Excel**, and then copying the table in Excel to Word.)

Specifying sessions

Click the **Session** tab to open and specify the ordering of the Learning and Test Trial Categories. Note that the automatic IVLabels were not used, but rather overwritten by the trial number.

- As you can see for the High-Low condition (with the observed data specified in **DV1**), Learning Category $1 (*High Trait*) is followed by Test Category $50, and this is repeated four times, after which Learning Category $2 (*Low Trait*) is followed by Test Category $50 four times.
- After *reset*ting the program, this is repeated for the Low-High Condition (see also **DV2**), but now the order of the Learning Categories $1 and $2 is reversed.

Specifying the simulation parameters

Choose the **Simulation | Parameters** menu, or press the ⊕ speed button. In the top panel, four drop-down list boxes list the major options. Note that the model to be simulated is the *Linear Autoassociator* developed by McClelland and Rumelhart (1988). Leave all the other option boxes on their default values. The following parameters need to be set by opening (clicking) the different tabs:

- **General** tab.
    Specify in **Session** that you want to run session *1* and select button *yes* in **Graph Simulated Values** (automatically, the **Log Simulated Values** will also turn to *yes*). Set **Randomize Order for All Learning Trials** to *yes*, and specify 50 runs. Leave the categories to which this applies to *1–49*. Set all other parameters to *no*.
- **Model** tab.
    Set the **learning rate** = 0.35 (This applies to all the units except the Context) and **alpha_1** = 0.24 (This applies only to the Context, as noted previously). Hence, the learning rate for the context becomes 0.35 × 0.24 = 0.08, as noted in Table 8.2. Leave all other parameters open, or set them to *auto* or *no*.
- **Weights and Activation** tab.
    Because the program starts with weight values randomly chosen between −.10 and +.10 to have some random noise in the simulated data that allow meaningful statistical tests, you set **Starting Weights** to *0* and **Random Starting Weights** *Add ± 0.10*.
    More importantly, because the alpha_1 activation parameter has to impact on the learning rate only (and not on the activation of the units as well), you need to set the **Alpa_1 & 2 determines . . .** parameter to *Lrate Only*. Although the program output will act as if the activation was changed (when you follow the simulation step by step after pressing the ⊗ or ⟲ speed button), this parameter makes sure that only the learning rate is actually affected.

Running the Simulation

To run the simulation as specified above, choose the **Simulation | Run Simulation** menu, or press the ⚒ speed button. If you want to follow the simulation step by step, choose the **Simulation | View Network** menu. Alternatively, hit the ⊗ speed button.
    After the simulation is finished, the **Graph** tab will open automatically (because you requested a graph). Make the following selections:

- **filter**: (*none*).
- **X-Axis**: *Condition* (the label specified for **IV2**).

- **X-Axis Labels**: *Trial* (the label specified for **IVLabel**).
- **Y-Axis Line(s)**: select all simulated and observed **DVs**.

The variable names preceded by a ~ sign denote the simulated values as obtained by Test Trial Category $50. Proceed now as follows:

- Check the **Regress** check box, so that the simulated values are projected onto the observed values (this can be altered by opening the **Graph Options** and choosing another option on the bottom right).
- Check the **List Stats** check box so that you get additional statistical analyses. Note, however, that the analyses in the text are repeated measures ANOVAs whereas the Listing Sheet reports between-subject ANOVAs (you can see this by the differences in the degrees of freedom).
- Hit the **Graph Log** button. You will see a graph of the simulation results, as they appear in Figure 8.1. (The means of the graph were exported by hitting the graph's **Options** button, the **Data** tab, and finally the **Export Graph Means to Excel** button; alternatively, you can use menu **File | Export | Graph Option Grid to Excel**.)
- For the numerical results, press the **Listing** tab.

Questions

1. You can experiment a little bit with the model parameters of the simulation. For instance, you can search yourself for the best fitting model parameters. Choose the **Simulation | Parameters** menu or press the ⊕ speed button, and press the **Model** tab. Enter as **learning rate**: 0.00 > 0.50 (in the **left box** and **right box**, respectively) and as **alpha_1**: 0.00 > 2.00 (in the **left box** and **right box**, respectively).

   The program will automatically search for the best-fitting parameters (turn **automatic search** *on* and turn **logging** *off* as requested by the program). You will probably end up with pretty much the same parameters as used above. However, these best parameters and the correlation may differ slightly. This is because the random order and the random noise of the starting weights is different for each run. You can select the same random order at each run by selecting a fixed value for **Random Seed**.

   Now choose the **Simulation | Run Best Fit and Graph** menu or press the ⊑ speed button. The program will automatically enter the best-fitting model parameters of the last run, will run the simulation once again, and will finally make a graph. You can inspect the results from the Graph Sheet that opens automatically.

2. What would happen if you did not alter the learning rate of the context but simply assumed that less activation (due to decreased attention) is given to the context? To pursue this question, choose the **Simulation | Parameters** menu, or press the ⊕ speed button, and click the **Weights and Activation** tab. Because the alpha_1 activation parameters need to

impact on the activation instead of learning rate, set the **Alpha_1 & 2 determine . . .** parameter back to *Activation*. To select a novel set of best-fitting parameters, press the **Model** tab. Enter as **learning rate**: 0.00 > 0.50 (in the **left box** and **right box**, respectively) and as **alpha_1**: 0.00 > 2.00 (in the **left box** and **right box**, respectively). After searching, choose the **Simulation | Run Best Fit and Graph** menu or press the ⊑ speed button. As you will see, the same pattern of results will appear (with different best fitting parameters). This attests to the robustness of the simulation.

3. You can also explore other models. Choose the **Simulation | Parameters** menu or press the ⊕ speed button, and select another model in the **Model** option box. For instance, you might select the *feedforward* or *non-linear recurrent* model as indicated in Table 8.9. For the non-linear model, specify **istr = estr = decay** = *0.15*. Choose or search for the other parameters as indicated in the table (you should now be able to do this by yourself). Alternatively, you can specify a distributed representation as indicated in Table 8.9. You practiced distributed representations in Chapter 7, so you can look up the exercises of that chapter to see how this works.

4. You can test whether a dual-dimensional (or dual-unit) representation for the trait will also do. Hence, in the Trial Grid, add a negative trait unit, and switch all *–1* trait values to zero, and turn them into a *+1* value in the negative trait node as illustrate below. Add *–?* in the test Category. The result looks like in Figure 8.8. Search for the best-fitting parameters (as illustrated in Question 1), and you will most likely obtain results that are largely similar. This again attests to the robustness of the simulation.

Exercise 2: Serial position weights

In this and all subsequent simulations, you use the same basic approach. Hence, in the next exercises, we concentrate on the specific issues and prob-

2:2	#	i1	i2	o1	o2
		Actor	Context	Trait+	Trait-
1	$1	High Trait			
2		1	1	1	
3	$2	Low Trait			
4		1	1		1
5	$-1	Learning Rate			
6			1		
7	$50	Test			
8		1		?	-?

Figure 8.8 Exercise 1: Dual-unit representation in the trial grid.

lems of the simulation and do not repeat the general instructions because these can be found in Exercise 1. Turning now to this exercise, choose menu **File | Open Project** or press the ☚ speed button, browse for *Dreben79.ft2* in folder *Chapter 8*, and click the **Open** button. For the final ratings, browse for *Dreben79-Final.ft2* in folder *Chapter 8*.

Specifying trials and session

The manner in which the position weights are calculated requires some clarification. Take for instance, the position weights of rating 2. A list of two items with a description of a person with a high (H) or low (L) trait can have the following four trait combinations:

- HH
- LH
- HL
- LL

The trial specifications in the Trial Grid that reflect these four combinations are shown in Figure 8.9. To obtain the weight of the first item or position, you need to take H*x* (where *x* means a low or high trait, or HH and HL) and subtract from this L*x* (LH and LL). Similarly, to obtain the weight of the second item or position, you need to take *x*H (HH and LH) and subtract from this *x*L (HL and LL).

To obtain the first, positive part of the subtraction you take Test Category $50, which tests for the *presence* of the trait (indicated by *?*); to obtain the second, negative part of the subtraction you use Test Category $51, which tests for the *absence* of the trait (indicated by –*?*). Hence, by combining the

2:1	#	i1	i2	o1
		Actor	Context	Trait
5	$21			
6		1	1	1
7		1	1	1
8	$22			
9		1	1	-1
10		1	1	1
11	$23			
12		1	1	1
13		1	1	-1
14	$24			
15		1	1	-1
16		1	1	-1

Figure 8.9 Exercise 2: Different low and high trait combinations in the trial grid.

relevant learning and test categories, you obtain the required subtractions. Thus, for instance, to obtain the weight of the first item or position, you take Hx (or Categories $21 and $23 each followed by Test Category $50) and L$x$ (or Categories $22 and $24 each followed by Test Category $51). That is exactly what you see in the Session Grid shown in Figure 8.10 (although in a different order). Note that all the obtained simulated values are averaged in the Graph (you take that option by default in the **Response** option box), so that you automatically obtain the serial position weights after pressing the **Graph** button.

Questions

Experiment with Questions 1–4 in Exercise 1. Of specific interest is that a simulation with a feedforward network cannot replicate attenuation of the recency effect. Try this now.

Exercise 3: Asymmetry in ability and morality inferences

Choose menu **File | Open Project** or press the 📄 speed button, browse for *Skowronski+Carlston87_1.ft2* in folder *Chapter 8*, and click the **Open** button. Make sure that you select the first Experiment (indicated by "*_1*"), not the second one.

Questions

Explore Questions 1–3 in Exercise 1 in this and the following exercises. More interesting for this simulation is that you can also explore some particular issues raised in the *Extensions and further research* section of the text (p.214).

1 : 4	#	Trials	IVLabel	DV1	DV2
			Serial Position	Rating 1	Rating 2
8		21			
9		50	1		.39
10		reset			
11		22			
12		51	1		.39
13		reset			
14		23			
15		50	1		.39
16		reset			
17		24			
18		51	1		.39

Figure 8.10 Exercise 2: Serial positions in the session grid.

1. As you can see, you can test for extreme versus moderate inconsistent behaviors by running Session Category $3.
2. You can also test for consistent behaviors by running Session Category $2.
3. How are trait implications of behaviors associated with a particular actor? In the previous and subsequent simulations, we assume that the traits associated with behaviors are automatically retrieved and activated during learning. However, it is clear that people must learn to associate behaviors with particular traits (this is precisely the topic of this exercise). Hence, the fundamental question is, how can people apply these behavior-trait associations when judging the trait of some particular target person? This is investigated in Skowronski and Carlston's (1987) Experiment 2, and the simulation can be found in *Skowronski+Carlston87_2.ft2* in folder *Chapter 8*. In a first learning phase (Category $1), the trait inferences from behaviors are learned. In the next phase and for each condition (Categories $2-6), a particular behavior in the first trial is activated and results in the internal activation of the implied trait units, and this activation then carries over to the next trial (denoted by a = sign; see also Simulation 5) where it is associated with the actor. This is shown in Figure 8.11. Make sure that you use no randomization in these trial categories (in the **Parameters | General** menu, limit the application of **Randomize Order** to Category 1, or use **Randomize per Block** and indicate that you randomize per 2 trials).

Exercise 4: Memory for behavioral information

Choose menu **File | Open Project** or press the ☀ speed button, browse for *Hamilton+Katz+Leirer80_3.ft2* in folder *Chapter 8*, and click the **Open** button. For this simulation, note that Learning Categories $1-3 was copied into Learning Categories $11-13 to specify learning under memorizing instructions. For Categories $11-13, the learning rate is only 10% of the original one (see **Weights and Activation** tab).

Questions

As well as Questions 1–3 in Exercise 1, you can explore some particular issues raised in the *Extensions and further research* section of the text (p.219):

5 : 3	#	i1	i2	i3	i4	i5	o1	o2	o3
		M++	M+	M0	M-	M--	Actor	Trait M+	Trait M-
15	$2								
16		1	1	1					
17							1	=	=

Figure 8.11 Exercise 3: Associating trait implications of behaviors with a particular actor in the trial grid.

1. To test the "postdiction" that the memory advantage of inconsistent items will disappear with more inconsistent items, choose menu **File | Open Project** and select *Hastie+Kumar79.ft2* in *Chapter 8*. As you can see, in each Learning Category a test is performed for increasingly less consistent and increasingly more inconsistent items (as indicated by the first and second number, respectively), and you will observe after running the simulation that the memory advantage of inconsistent items diminishes.

2. You can also test for recognition by using *Test Categories $60* and *$61* instead of *$50-51*, and running only the first two conditions. You will notice that there is a bias in favor of consistent information. If you remove the *?* for the *Neutral Trait* (which reflects the idea that people expect the neutral trait to be present), the bias will disappear.

Exercise 5: Assimilation and contrast

Choose menu **File | Open Project** or press the ☞ speed button, browse for *Stapel97_3.ft2* in folder *Chapter 8*, and click the **Open** button.

Questions

As well as Questions 1–3 in Exercise 1, you can again explore some issues raised in the *Extensions and further research* section, p.224 of the text. For instance, to test the "postdiction" that moderate exemplars lead to less contrast, whereas moderate traits lead to less assimilation, choose menu **File | Open Project** and select *Moskowitz+Skurnik99_4.ft2* in *Chapter 8*. As you can see, these postdictions were confirmed for the exemplars, but the difference in assimilation between moderate and extreme traits was not reliable (note that it was not very clear-cut in the real data also).

Exercise 6: Situational correction or integration?

Choose menu **File | Open Project** or press the ☞ speed button, browse for *Trope+Gaunt00_3.ft2* in folder *Chapter 8*, and click the **Open** button.

Questions

As well as Questions 1–3 in Exercise 1, you can try to replicate the other experiments by Trope and Gaunt (2000).

Exercise 7: Discounting and sample size

Choose menu **File | Open Project** or press the ☞ speed button, browse for *VanOverwalle01_1.ft2* in folder *Chapter 8*, and click the **Open** button. (Note that the learning rates of the target and competing actors were accidentally switched in the original article, and are now corrected in the text.)

Questions

As well as Questions 1–3 in Exercise 1, you can explore the parallel between impression formation and dispositional attribution discussed in the *Extensions and further research* section, p.231. To simulate dispositional attributions, choose menu **File | Open Project** and select *VanOverwalle03.ft2* in Chapter 8.

9   A recurrent connectionist model of group biases*

*Dirk Van Rooy, Frank Van Overwalle,
Tim Vanhoomissen, Christophe Labiouse
and Robert French*

Major biases and stereotypes in group judgments are reviewed and modeled from a recurrent connectionist perspective. These biases are in the areas of group impression formation (illusory correlation), group differentiation (accentuation), stereotype change (dispersed versus concentrated distribution of inconsistent information), and group homogeneity. All these phenomena are illustrated with well-known experiments, and simulated with an autoassociative network architecture with linear activation update and delta learning algorithm for adjusting the connection weights. All the biases were successfully reproduced in the simulations. The discussion centers on how the particular simulation specifications compare to other models of group biases and how they may be used to develop novel hypotheses for testing the connectionist modeling approach and, more generally, for improving theorizing in the field of social biases and stereotype change.

> Petite, attractive, intelligent, WSF, 30, fond of music, theatre, books, travel, seeks warm, affectionate, fun-loving man to share life's pleasures with view to lasting relationship. Send photograph. Please no biochemists. (Personal ad, *New York Review of Books*, cited in Barrow, 1992, p.2)

The ability to learn about groups and their characteristics is crucial to the way people make sense of their social world. Nevertheless, quite a number of studies have indicated that people can have great trouble learning associations between groups and their attributes and often perceive associations that do not exist. It is generally assumed that these shortcomings or biases are partly responsible for group stereotyping and minority discrimination. Among the most prominent of these group biases are illusory correlation—the perception of a correlation between a group and some characteristics that do not exist (Hamilton & Gifford, 1976; Hamilton & Rose, 1980), accentuation—making a distinction between groups beyond actual differences (Eiser, 1971;

* Adapted from *Psychological Review, 110*, 536–563. Copyright 2003 by the American Psychological Association. Reprinted with permission of the publisher.

Tajfel & Wilkes, 1963), subtyping—the rejection of stereotype-inconsistent information concentrated in a few group members (Hewstone, 1994), and outgroup homogeneity—the perception of outgroups as more homogeneous and stereotypical than the ingroup (Linville, Fisher, & Salovey, 1989; Messick & Mackie, 1989).

It is crucial to psychologists to understand how these biases are created and how they can be eliminated (Hewstone, 1994). However, many empirical reports on the occurrence of group biases were explained by appeals to what often appear to be rather ad-hoc hypotheses and assumptions. Moreover, the field of group perception, which includes such domains as person perception, impression formation, attribution, and attitudes (Hamilton & Sherman, 1989), has developed largely independently from other important areas in cognition at large, and social cognition in particular. There have been some recent attempts, however, to provide a common theory of group judgments and shortcomings under the heading of exemplar-based models (Fiedler, 1996; Smith, 1991) or a tensor product connectionist network (Kashima, Woolcock, & Kashima, 2000). The goal of the present paper is to build further on these initial proposals and to present a connectionist model that—potentially—can explain a wider range of group biases than these earlier attempts. Moreover, the proposed model has already been applied fruitfully to other areas in memory and cognition (for a classic example, see McClelland & Rumelhart, 1986, p.170), including the domain of social cognition (Read & Montoya, 1999; Smith & DeCoster, 1998; Van Overwalle & Jordens, 2002; Van Overwalle & Labiouse, 2004; Van Overwalle & Siebler, 2005; see also Chapters 5–12), where it has been applied to encompass and integrate earlier algebraic models of impression formation (Anderson, 1981), causal attribution (Cheng & Novick, 1992), and attitude formation (Ajzen, 1991).

Our basic claim is that a connectionist account of group biases does not require special processing of information as many theories in social cognition posit (e.g. Hamilton & Gifford, 1976; Hastie, 1980). Rather, general information-processing characteristics captured in general-purpose connectionist models lead to these biases. For instance, connectionist systems have no central executive, so that biases in information processes are, in principle, due to implicit and automatic mechanisms without explicit conscious reasoning. In addition, the ability to learn incrementally puts connectionist models in agreement with developmental and evolutionary pressures. This implies that group biases emerge from general processes that are otherwise quite adaptive.

This article is organized as follows: First, we present the proposed connectionist model. Second, we describe a series of simulations of a number of important biases in group judgments, including illusory correlation, accentuation, stereotype change, and homogeneity. Our review of empirical phenomena in the field is not meant to be exhaustive, but is rather designed to illustrate how connectionist principles can be used to shed light on the processes underlying group judgments. Although the emphasis of the present article is on the use of a particular connectionist model to explain a wide variety of group biases, previous applications of connectionist modeling to social psychology (e.g. see Chapters 5, 7, and 12) are also mentioned and compared to the present approach. Finally, we discuss the limitations of the proposed connectionist approach and discuss areas where further theoretical developments are under way or are needed. Ultimately, what we would like to accomplish in this paper is to create a greater awareness that connectionist principles could potentially underlie diverse shortcomings in group judgments, as a natural consequence of the basic processing mechanisms in these adaptive cognitive systems.

A RECURRENT IMPLEMENTATION OF GROUP BIASES: ILLUSORY CORRELATION

Throughout this paper, we use the same basic network model—namely, the recurrent autoassociator developed by McClelland and Rumelhart (1986, 1988) using the delta learning algorithm for changing the weights of the connections (see Chapter 3). We decided to apply a single basic model to emphasize the theoretical similarities that underlie group biases with a great variety of other processes in cognition. To provide some background to our specific implementation of group biases, we illustrate its major characteristics with the phenomenon of illusory correlation. Illusory correlation occurs when perceivers erroneously see a relation between categories that are actually independent. For instance, minorities or outgroups are often stereotyped with bad characteristics, although these characteristics sometimes occur in equal proportions in the ingroup. The earliest demonstration of illusory correlation in a group context comes from a study by Hamilton and Gifford (1976). Participants read about members of two groups A and B that engaged in the same ratio of desirable to undesirable behaviors (9 : 4), but twice as many behaviors referred to members of group A than to members of group B. Although there was no objective correlation between group membership and desirability of behavior, participants showed greater liking for the majority group A than for the minority group B. In sum, the typical finding in illusory correlation research is *decreased evaluation* for minority group B, together with *increased memory* for undesirable group B behavior (for reviews, see Hamilton & Sherman, 1989; Mullen & Johnson, 1990).

To account for these two distinct effects in illusory correlation, we introduce a recurrent connectionist model that permits encoding and retrieval of two types of information. One type of information concerns some salient regularity or attribute about the group (such as desirability) and is assumed to underlie the evaluative (i.e. likeability) judgments in illusory correlation. The other type of information involves specific episodic knowledge about the behavioral items and is assumed to account for the memory effects.

We have chosen a "localist" encoding scheme, that is, each piece of information (or concept) is represented by a single node. Figure 9.1 shows how the two groups, A and B, are each represented by a *group node* and how the implied attribute (i.e. desirable or undesirable) is represented by two separate *attribute nodes*. Two separate unitary attribute nodes were taken rather than a bipolar attribute node (with positive and negative activation to represent desirable and undesirable stimuli respectively) because our evaluations about groups are not represented as a single point on a one-dimensional construct but are probably more mixed and complex, including both positive and negative instances of the attribute (Wittenbrink, Judd, & Park, 2001). To explain memory for specific statements presented, we also include *episodic nodes* that reflect the specific (i.e. behavioral) information contained in the statements. Episodic memory refers to information about particular events that have been experienced (Tulving, 1972). The important advantage of episodic nodes is that they preserve information about discrete events in the network. In sum, we assume that the unique meaning of each behavioral statement in an illusory correlation experiment is encoded at two levels: Its evaluative meaning ("the behavior is good") and its unique episodic meaning ("helps an old lady across the street"). By representing different aspects (or features) of each piece of information over two nodes, evaluative and episodic, this model in fact uses a semi-localist encoding scheme.

It is instructive to note that although, in principle, in an autoassociative network all interconnections between all nodes play a role, to understand the present simulations, the reader should focus mainly on the connections between different sets of nodes (e.g. between attribute nodes, episodic nodes, and group nodes) that are of most relevance for explaining group biases,

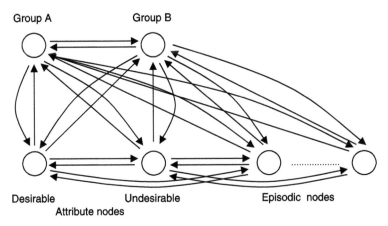

Figure 9.1 Recurrent network for simulations of group bias with two group nodes representing groups A and B, two attribute nodes representing the desirability and undesirability of the behavior and several episodic nodes each representing the unique meaning of one behavioral statement. (Note that not all lateral connections between nodes at the same layer are drawn to avoid cluttering the figure, but all are working during the simulations.)

whereas the lateral interconnections linking the same sets of nodes are less relevant (contrary to spreading activation models of impression formation; Hastie & Kumar, 1979). The connections between episodic nodes and group nodes (in both directions) are collectively termed *episodic connections*, while the connections between evaluative attribute nodes and the group nodes (in both directions) are termed *evaluative connections*.

The delta learning algorithm gives rise to a number of emergent properties that are used to explain all the effects associated with group biases. Below, we describe two of the most important properties and illustrate their effect on the illusory correlation bias.

Acquisition property and sensitivity to sample size

According to the delta learning algorithm, the more an attribute such as an (un)desirable behavior is presented with information on group membership, the stronger the connection between the corresponding (un)desirability attribute node and group node becomes. This illustrates an important property of the delta learning algorithm, namely that as more confirmatory information is received, the connections gradually grow in strength. We call this the *acquisition property* (see Chapter 3). Thus, in the beginning phases of learning (before asymptote is reached), the connection weights reflect the amount of evidence, that is, the network is sensitive to sample size.

How does the acquisition property explain illusory correlation? The mechanism is straightforward. Because of the larger sample size in the majority group A, its evaluative connections are stronger at the end of learning than the corresponding connections for the minority group B. Thus, both the connections with desirability and undesirability are stronger for group A than for group B. As a result, the relative proportion of desirable versus undesirable information is more clearly encoded in the evaluative connections of the network for majority group A than for minority group B, resulting in a more favorable impression overall for the majority group A. In addition, this also means that the mental representation of the majority group A, in contrast to the minority group B, will consist of well-established connections between group membership and (un)desirability of behavior, so that the perceiver can form a relatively correct impression of the majority group. It is important to note, however, that when both groups become larger, the relative advantage of the majority group A is lost as the evaluative connections of both groups will reach their asymptote. However, this is not typical of illusory correlation experiments, where the number of statements is most often less than 20 for each group.

Figure 9.2 depicts a simulated example of this process. We focus here on the connections from the group nodes to the desirability and undesirability nodes. We simulated the presentation of desirable and undesirable statements on the groups by activating, for each statement, the respective desirability nodes and group nodes. After each statement, we tested the strength of the evaluative

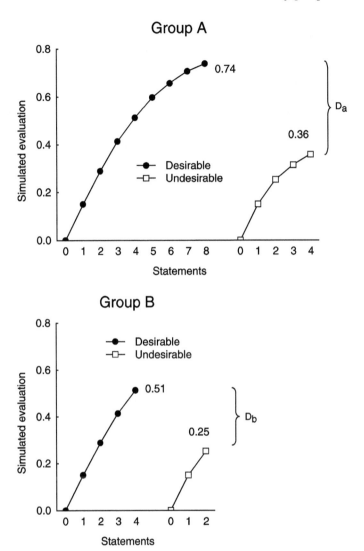

Figure 9.2 Simulated evaluative strength ($D_{a,b}$ = Difference between desirable and undesirable evaluation for group A and B, respectively) in an illusory correlation design in which two desirable and one undesirable behavior(s) were presented alternately to the network.

connections by cuing each group node and measuring how much of the activation was spread to the desirability nodes. As can be seen, the strength of the evaluative connections increases as a function of the growing number of statements. The top half of the figure shows this for majority group A, the bottom half for minority group B. Every time a statement is presented (for instance "John helps an old lady across the street"), the simulated evaluation increases. Although the increase with each statement is equal for both groups, the larger amount of statements (larger sample size) for group A results in stronger connections and a larger difference between desirable and undesirable evaluations for the majority group A than for the minority group B ($D_a > D_b$ in the figure). As a minor point, note that the evaluations after four trials in Figure 9.2 differ between groups A (.36) and B (.25) because the lateral connections between the nodes also differ in number between groups (these curves would have been exactly similar if lateral connections were omitted such as in feedforward network models, discussed later).

Competition property and discounting

To explain enhanced memory for negative behaviors and for minority behaviors, we now turn to the episodic nodes that reflect memory during illusory correlation. We propose that a memory advantage for these infrequent behaviors in recognition measures, where episodic nodes presumably serve as retrieval cue to remember the group, may in part be produced by what has been termed the *competition property* of the delta learning algorithm (see Chapter 3). The term "competition" stems from the associative learning literature on animal conditioning and causality judgments where it is also known as blocking (Rescorla & Wagner, 1972; Shanks, 1995) and should not be confused with other usages in the connectionist literature such as competitive networks (McClelland & Rumelhart, 1988).

How does the competition property explain enhanced memory in illusory correlation? The basic mechanism behind competition is that only a limited amount of connection strength is available during learning. In illusory correlation, this limitation is a function of the external activation of a group node (limited to +1 in the present case to reflect group membership) and of the internal activation received from other evaluative and episodic nodes, and affects the connections from the evaluative and episodic nodes to the group nodes (see upward arrows in Figure 9.1). Because the delta learning algorithm seeks to match internal with external activations, the internal activation received from the evaluative and episodic nodes (and hence also their connection weights) cannot grow out of bounds, as their sum is limited by the upper value of the external activation of the group node. Stated differently, given an upper external activation of +1 of a group node, the internal activation sent by episodic and evaluative nodes to that group node is limited. To the extent that the sum of this internal activation approaches or exceeds the upper bound, these nodes have to compete for connection weights and the growth of their connections is blocked or reduced. A consequence of this is that strong attribute → group connections contribute much more in approaching or exceeding the upper limit than weaker attribute → group connections, and so tend to discount or block the further growth of the episodic → group connections more.

To take the acquisition example of Figure 9.2, the connection weight from the desirable node to group A at the end of learning is 0.74, and hence leaves only 0.26 activation available before the upper bound of the external activation (+1) of the group node is exceeded. Conversely, the same weight for group B is only 0.51, and there is thus much more room (0.49) for increasing the weights of the desirability and other nodes. Thus, because of the stronger attribute → group connections of group A, the episodic-→ group connections of this group are much more discounted, resulting in reduced memory for behavioral episodes. In contrast, because of the weaker attribute → group connections of group B, the episodic → group connections of this group are less discounted, so that they can gain more connection weight resulting in enhanced memory. By the same mechanism, because the desirable → group connections are larger than the undesirable → group connections, the episodic → group connections of positive behaviors are weaker than those of the negative behaviors, resulting in an increased memory for negative behavior. In sum, the competition property generates a memory advantage, not for paired distinctive stimuli like the distinctiveness account would predict, but separately for undesirable and minority behaviors because of their infrequency.[1]

Summary

The acquisition and competition properties of the delta learning algorithm shape the connections between group nodes, attribute nodes, and episodic nodes as information is provided about the groups. Essentially, these properties describe different ways in which a growing number of observations affect connections in the network. The acquisition property describes how the attribute connections grow stronger as a function of a growing sample size, and so enables a preponderance of desirable behaviors in the majority group much faster than in the minority group. As a consequence, no paired distinctive stimuli are necessary to produce the illusion correlation effect. This implication has received empirical support from recent studies (Shavitt, Sanbonmatsu, Smittipatana, & Posavac, 1999; Van Rooy, 2001) that have showed that the effect is obtained without any negative behavioral information on the minority group, contrary to the distinctiveness hypothesis. The competition property describes how stronger attribute → group connections inhibit the development of weaker episodic → group connections. This latter property plays a role in the memory advantage for infrequent behaviors.

---

1 Because this is a recurrent network, competition may in principle work also on the (downward) connections from the group to the attribute and episodic nodes. For instance, strong group → attribute connections may hamper the development of episodic → attribute connections. However, these latter connections do not play a direct role in our testing procedures. Other sources of competition that involve episodic connections are less likely, because these connections are relatively weak and thus may have little influence.

OTHER RELEVANT THEORIES

Before applying our recurrent implementation to several group biases of interest, we will first briefly compare the recurrent approach with the two most relevant models that have been proposed in the recent past to explain group biases such as the illusory correlation effect.

Exemplar models

Perhaps the most well-known theoretical approach to explain group biases was inspired by recent exemplar models of memory (Fiedler, 1996; Nosofsky, 1986; Smith, 1991; Smith & Zárate, 1992). According to exemplar models, perceivers store single exemplars of behaviors in memory. To make a judgment about a target stimulus (e.g. a group), perceivers form a composite estimate of activated memory traces of the stored exemplars that are highly similar to the target stimulus. Thus, group judgments are based on specific exemplars that are retrieved from memory and aggregated. In the exemplar models of Smith (1991) and Fiedler (1996; Fiedler, Kemmelmeier, & Freytag, 1999) that provide the most detailed accounts of social judgments, this aggregation is based on a simple or weighted linear summation. Such an aggregation process will cancel out unsystematic perceptual or encoding errors between the exemplars and will reinforce systematic variance. An important consequence is that less error variance is left in the aggregate, the larger the number of observations. This is important, because as less error variance is left, then perceptions of the group become more accurate, alleviating the tendency to make biased judgments. Hence, exemplar theories essentially explain many group biases by information loss or insufficient evidence, and predict that increasing the encoding of actual group information can alleviate judgmental shortcomings. Like the present recurrent network, they are thus sensitive to sample size differences.

One major difference with our recurrent approach is that, in exemplar models, information about behavioral episodes and their trait or evaluative implication is solely encoded at the exemplar level, while (aggregated) attributes are computed at retrieval. In addition, because the evaluative attributes are computed from the exemplars, it is predicted that there should be a positive correlation between judgment and memory, that is, lower liking for minority group B should result in lower recall for the behavior exemplars also (Fiedler, Russer, & Gramm, 1993). This stands in contrast to illusory correlation research that shows increased memory for group B exemplars (for recent evidence, see Hamilton, Dugan, & Trollier, 1985; McConnell, Sherman, & Hamilton, 1994; Stroessner, Hamilton, & Mackie, 1992). This observed discrepancy between judgment (decrease) and memory (increase) was overcome in the implementation of our recurrent network by encoding both types of exemplar and attribute information, and by the competition property of the delta learning algorithm. Such a competition mechanism does not exist for exemplar-based models. Another difference is that our model does not require random noise in the encoding of the information to explain group biases, because the delta learning algorithm is an acquisition device that in itself is sensitive to sample size differences.

Tensor product model

Kashima et al. (2000) proposed a connectionist model of group impression formation and change that they called the tensor product model. This encodes different aspects of social information, including the person, the group to whom he or she belongs, as well as the specific action or character-istics he or she expresses. Like our model, it assumes that this information is encoded in memory as connections between sets of nodes reflecting these different aspects. Thus, aggregation of episodic information takes place during encoding rather than during retrieval, through the strengthening of the connections between nodes. The Hebbian learning algorithm, which involves a weighted linear summation of information, determines weight adjustments.

One of the most important differences with our recurrent model is that the tensor product model does not say anything about recall of specific behavioral information. In principle, all episodic information is immediately aggregated in the connections and then lost after activation fades away. Moreover, all connections between two nodes are symmetric; while they can differ in the recurrent model depending on the direction in which the activation is spread between the nodes.

Another difference is that the Hebbian algorithm applied in the tensor product model is not bounded or normalized as it simply keeps on accumulat-ing the weights from previous learning, forcing them beyond −1 and +1. Normalizing takes place only during judgment, for instance, by retrieving appropriate low-end and high-end anchors to calibrate the current judgment. Although research has revealed that people shift their standards of judgment as they think of members of different social groups (e.g. an assertive person is judged "very assertive" as a women but only "mildly assertive" as a man; Biernat & Manis, 1994), this does not necessarily imply that anchors are used during retrieval only. Perhaps anchors are also used during encoding. For instance, group stereotypes and norms may act as a context against which novel information about members is assessed. This latter anchoring process is outside the scope of the model (although the delta learning algorithm can address this through the competition property; for more details, see Chapter 11). Perhaps the most important limitation of non-normalized learning in the tensor product model is that it does not allow limiting activation at each learning trial, so that competition cannot take place. As a consequence, the discrepancy between information loss and increased memory cannot be accounted for.

OVERVIEW OF THE SIMULATIONS

The following sections describe a connectionist simulation of several biases in group judgments. An overview of these simulations is given in Table 9.1, together with the major connectionist property that drives the bias.

Model parameters

For all simulations, we used the linear autoassociative recurrent network described above, with parameters for decay and excitation (for internal and external input) all set to 1, and with one internal activation cycle. Node activation was determined by the linear sum of all external and internal activation received after one internal cycle through the network (see Equation 3.8, p.40). This effectively means that neither activation decay nor multiple cycles of activation updating plays any role in the simulations. The learning rate that determines the speed by which the weights of the connections are allowed to change was set to 0.15. To generalize across a range of presentation orders, each network was run for 50 different random orders, thus simulating 50 different "participants". All connection weights were initialized at starting values of zero. Unless otherwise stated, most of the effects are relatively robust to changes in parameters and stimulus distributions. Consequently, for simplicity of presentation, a smaller number of trials were used in some of the simulations than is typically the case in actual experiments.

Testing the network

To test the judgments, categorizations, and memory arising from the network, we measured how much some concepts in memory are able to activate other concepts. Thus, we simply activated node x and looked at the resulting internal activation of node y. For instance, to measure the attributes associated with a group, the group node that serves as a cue is primed by turning on its external activation to 1. This activation then spreads to related nodes in proportion to the weights of their connection, and the resulting internal activation (or output activation) is then measured (i.e. read off) from the attribute nodes. To simplify, one might think of this procedure as testing the strength of the connection between nodes x and y, because the lateral connections between the same types of nodes quite often (but not always) play only a minor role.

We used the same basic cue and measurement nodes throughout all the simulations. Unless stated otherwise, for central tendency measures of the group (e.g. liking, frequency estimates), the group nodes were turned on and the differential output activation of the attribute nodes was read off. For instance, the resulting activation of the undesirable attribute was subtracted from the resulting activation of the desirable attribute to obtain an overall

Table 9.1 Overview of the simulated group biases and the property creating the bias

Bias	Findings	Property
Group impression formation		
1. Size-based illusory correlation	• A minority group is seen as more negative despite the fact that the proportion of positive and negative items is identical to a majority group	*Acquisition*: greater sample size of opposite attributes in majority group
	• Better memory (assignment latencies) for items from a minority category	*Competition*: greater sample size of attributes in majority group discounts episodic weights
2. Expectancy-based illusory correlation	More stereotyped judgments despite the lack of an actual correlation	Prior *acquisition* of greater sample size of stereotypical attributes in group carries over to present acquisition
Group differentiation		
3. Accentuation	• Perceived differences in attributes are pronounced if group membership is correlated with attribute	*Acquisition*: greater sample size of correlated attribute
	• Better memory (of foils) in uncorrelated condition	*Competition*: greater sample size of attributes in correlated condition discounts episodic weights
Changing group impressions		
4. Stereotype change	Group stereotype changes more if stereotype-inconsistent information is dispersed across many members rather than concentrated in a few	*Competition*: greater discounting of inconsistent attribute concentrated in a few members
Group variability		
5. Group homogeneity	Outgroup is seen as more homogenous; however ingroup is seen as more homogenous when it is a minority	*Acquisition*: greater sample size of ingroup attribute, unless ingroup is minority

likeability estimate. For central tendency measures of exemplars (e.g. attitude position of statements, typicality of members), we used exemplar nodes as cues instead of group nodes. Recognition in the assignment task was simulated by first activating each episodic node and reading off the resulting activation of the group node. Finally, for measures of variance, the same cues and measurement nodes were used as for the central tendency measure of the group, but the resulting activation of the two opposing attribute nodes was summed instead of subtracted. For more details, we refer to each of the simulations and associated tables (where measurement nodes are denoted by "?").

All the results of the simulations are presented together with observed means from an illustrative experiment. Like many authors in the associative learning domain (e.g. Nosofsky, Kruschke, & McKinley, 1992; Shanks, 1991), we assume that the relationship between the activation resulting from such a test and the judgments by participants is monotonic. Hence, given that we are mainly interested in patterns of the simulated values, the simulated means per condition are estimated to fit as closely to the human data using linear regression (i.e. we linearly regressed all simulation means onto all human means and use that regression to compute human-like values for the simulation). This procedure also enables us to demonstrate visually the fit of the simulations.

GROUP IMPRESSIONS

How do perceivers develop a stereotyped impression of a group? Of the many processes that can contribute to a biased group perception, we focus on illusory correlation as a consequence of sample size differences (as introduced earlier) and as a consequence of prior expectancies (to be discussed later).

As noted earlier, size-based illusory correlation refers to the tendency to perceive minority groups as more negative than majority groups, despite an equal preponderance of desirable behaviors in the two groups (Hamilton & Gifford, 1976). This finding has been replicated under different conditions and is very robust (see, for an overview, Hamilton & Sherman, 1989). An important reason for the popularity of this concept lies in its practical implications. The study of the illusion can give us an insight into the processes underlying the formation of social stereotypes and negative attitudes towards minorities in society.

An experiment that shows many of the typical findings in illusory correlation research conducted by McConnell et al. (1994, Experiment 2) is used here to illustrate our simulation of the bias. Before proceeding to the simulation, we first discuss the most important empirical measures of the illusion and previous rival explanations.

Evaluative judgments

The majority of illusory correlation studies used the same set of measures that were originally introduced by Hamilton and Gifford (1976) and that were also used by McConnell et al. (1994). As noted earlier, in many studies these measures showed an evaluative bias in favor of the majority group.

- *Likability ratings*: McConnell et al. (1994, p.416) asked their participant to rate "how much they thought they would like members of Group A and Group B" on a 10-point scale ranging from "strong disliking" to "strong liking", and found that group A was liked most.
- *Frequency estimates*: For each group, participants were asked "to estimate how many of [the behaviors] were undesirable" (p.416). The number of undesirable behaviors performed by minority group B members was overestimated relative to the number of undesirable behaviors performed by majority group A members.
- *Group assignment*: Participants were given each behavior without group assignment and then had to indicate "whether a member of Group A or Group B performed the action" (p.416). It was found that disproportionately more undesirable behaviors were attributed to the minority group B than to the majority group A.

Process measures

The previous measures record the extent of the illusion but reveal little about the underlying encoding and memory processes that may be responsible for it. To explore these processes in more depth, researchers introduced additional process measures. Although the results obtained with these measures are less robust than those obtained with the traditional evaluative measures, they avoid guessing strategies that may cloud memory measures. The following results have been reported:

- *Free recall*: Participants were instructed "to write down as many of the behaviors as they could recall" (McConnell et al., 1994, p.416) without receiving any cue about behavior or group. It was found that they remembered disproportionately more undesirable behaviors of minority group B than any other condition. This may imply better encoding and memory of these undesirable minority B behaviors.
- *Assignment latencies*: In this process measure, the latencies in the group assignment task (see above) are recorded. McConnell et al. (1994) found that participants are fastest in assigning undesirable behaviors to the minority group B (but see Klauer & Meiser, 2000). As this effect in group latencies shows the same pattern as the free recall data, it was again interpreted as a result of better encoding and memory of these behaviors.

Prior theoretical accounts

What are the theoretical explanations provided for this pervasive bias? The first account of illusory correlation proposed by Hamilton and Gifford (1976) was inspired by Chapman's (1967) original explanation that centered on the distinctiveness or salience of stimuli that form a minority. Hamilton and Gifford (1976) argued that the co-occurrence of two infrequent events, that is, undesirable behaviors from a minority group, are particularly attention getting and distinct, and therefore received more extensive encoding, which in turn leads to greater accessibility in memory. Because undesirable behaviors are in a minority in typical illusory correlation experiments, they become especially salient and memorable in the minority group B. This memory advantage of undesirable group B behaviors was assumed to be the key factor causing the negative group impressions of the minority group B. This distinctiveness-based explanation has gained quite a lot of empirical support (for extensive reviews, see Hamilton & Sherman, 1989; Mullen & Johnson, 1990), which was corroborated by recent studies in which higher recall for distinct undesirable minority group was documented (Hamilton, et al., 1985; McConnell et al., 1994; Stroessner et al., 1992). Despite the popularity and empirical support of the distinctiveness account, however, alternative approaches to illusory correlation have been put forward.

According to exemplar models of Smith (1991) and Fiedler (1996), aggregation of more information reduces unsystematic error and so leads to perceptions that are more accurate. As a consequence, for majority group A, which contains a large number of behaviors, the difference between desirable and undesirable behaviors is more accurately perceived than for minority group B, where there are fewer behaviors. Based on these differences, exemplar models predict an illusory correlation bias, that is, more favorable liking of the majority group. Unlike the distinctiveness account, these models posit that unequal frequencies are responsible for the effect, not selective memory. Similarly, the tensor product model (Kashima et al., 2000) proposes that the encoding and aggregation of unequal frequencies by means of the Hebbian learning algorithm drives the illusion. Thus, Kashima et al. (2000) emphasize encoding rather than retrieval as the basis of the illusion. However, the increased recall for infrequent and undesirable behaviors noted earlier (Hamilton, et al., 1985; Klauer & Meiser, 2000; McConnell et al., 1994; Stroessner et al., 1992) is currently problematic for both the exemplar and tensor product account, as they do not address this memory advantage.

To resolve the discrepancy between increased evaluation and decreased memory, alternative models that emphasize a dual-retrieval process in which likeability and frequency estimates depend on the spontaneous availability or ease of retrieval of the episodic items, while free recall depends on an exhaustive search guided by the number and direction of the links between episodic nodes, have been put forward (e.g. Garcia-Marques & Hamilton, 1996).

However, such models are strongly limited by the fact that they do not account for the development of group impressions.

Simulation 1: Size-based illusory correlation

Like the tensor product model, our connectionist account also assumes that illusory correlation is created by differences in sample sizes that affect encoding rather than by memory retrieval differences between behaviors. Because of the acquisition property of the delta learning algorithm, the prevalence of desirable (relative to undesirable) behavior is more clearly encoded in the evaluative connections for the majority group, so that perceivers have a more positive impression of the majority group compared to the minority group. In addition, increased memory for undesirable minority behaviors is driven by the competition property of the delta algorithm as described earlier.

Table 9.2 represents a simplified simulated learning history of a typical illusory correlation experiment as conducted by McConnell et al. (1994, Experiment 2). Each line in the top panel of Table 9.2 represents a pattern of external activation at a trial that corresponds to a statement presented to a participant. The first two cells represent the group label present in each statement, the next two cells denote the valence of the statement, and the last cells represent episodic nodes reflecting the behavioral information presented.

In the simulation, to measure the traditional evaluative judgments on the groups (i.e. likability ratings, frequency estimations, and group assignments), the group nodes were turned on and the resulting activation of the evaluative nodes was read off (denoted by "?", see bottom panel of Table 9.2). As noted earlier, no additional external activation was provided to the evaluative nodes (or any other "measurement" node) because null activation is a neutral resting activation state that allows an unbiased assessment of the evaluative activation generated directly or indirectly by the group nodes. In particular, we tested the resulting differential activation from the desirable and undesirable node. Although it is also possible that the evaluative nodes are first primed and that this activation then travels to the group nodes, this has little effect on the network's predictions. The reason is that the sample size effect that drives the illusion is largely symmetric over opposing directions of the evaluative connections.

As discussed earlier, episodic memory can be measured by a group assignment task, preferably by measuring latencies that avoid contamination by guessing strategies or response biases that are driven by evaluative memory. In a group assignment task, behaviors are presented and participants have to indicate as fast as possible by which group member they were performed. To reflect this measure, each episodic node from different sets of behaviors (A+, A–, B+, B–) was activated one at a time (see bottom panel of Table 9.2). This episodic activation spreads to the group nodes and so determines response times. This testing procedure is based on the assumption that awareness of group membership depends on the crossing of a minimal activation

Table 9.2 Size-based illusory correlation: Learning history (based on McConnell et al., 1994, Experiment 2)

	Group		Desirability		Episodic behaviors[a]			
Trial frequency	*A*	*B*	*+*	*−*	*A+*	*A−*	*B+*	*B−*
Experimental phase								
Group A+ #8	1		1		1			
Group A− #4	1			1		1		
Group B+ #4		1	1				1	
Group B− #2		1		1				1
Test phase								
Evaluation of A	1		?	−?				
Evaluation of B		1	?	−?				
Assignment latencies of A	?				1			
	?					1		
Assignment latencies of B		?					1	
		?						1

Cell entries denote external activation and empty cells denote 0 activation. #, Number of times the trial is repeated; +, desirable; −, undesirable; ?, resulting test activations (without external activations) averaged across each row. The order of the experimental trials was randomized.

[a] Each type of behavior is shown in a separate column that involves multiple episodic nodes of which a different one is turned on (activation +1) per trial (e.g. in the 1st trial the 1st episodic node is activated, in the 2nd trial the 2nd node and so on).

threshold (Cleeremans & Jiménez, 2002). By assuming that the time to spread the activation through the network is proportional to the strength of the connection weights, stronger episodic→group connections will lead to higher group activations and faster crossing of the awareness threshold for group membership.[2]

2 An alternative procedure is based on the assumption that awareness depends on convergence of activation into a stable "attractor" state for the group node (Cleeremans & Jiménez, 2002). The time needed to settle in such an attractor state can be simulated by recording the number of activation updating cycles before an attractor is reached (McLeod, Plunkett, & Rolls, 1998). As one might expect, this yielded very similar results. However, in keeping with our general simulation methodology in which multiple cycles are avoided, and because we are not specifically interested in response times but rather more broadly in any measure of episodic memory, we do not report this more elaborated procedure.

Results

The 18 "statements" succinctly listed in Table 9.2 were processed by the network for 50 "participants" with different random orders. Figure 9.3 depicts the mean test activation for all simulated dependent measures, together with the observed likeability and reaction time data from McConnell et al. (1994, Experiment 2). The top panel of the figure shows the results of the

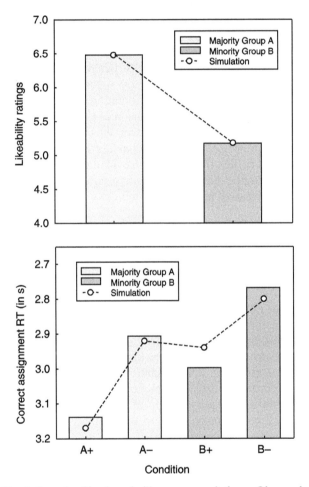

Figure 9.3 Simulation 1: Size-based illusory correlation. Observed data from McConnell, Sherman, and Hamilton (1994, Experiment 2) and simulation results. (Note that in the bottom panel, the scale is reversed so that higher values reflect better memory and, consequently, faster latencies.) The human data are from Tables 4 and 5 in "Illusory correlation in the perception of groups: An extension of the distinctiveness-based account" by A. R. McConnell, S. J. Sherman, & D. L. Hamilton, 1994, *Journal of Personality and Social Psychology*, *67*, 414–429. Copyright 1994 by the American Psychological Association. Adapted with permission.

simulation of the evaluative measures, together with the likeability ratings from McConnell et al. (1994, Experiment 2). The simulation shows that the majority group A received higher evaluative activations than the minority group B, $F(1, 49) = 39.05$, $p < .001$, mirroring the same pattern of the observed data (the perfect fit is exceptional and simply due to the rescaling of the test activation of the network to the observed data that consists here only of two data points).

The bottom panel depicts the results of the memory simulation together with the observed assignment latencies of McConnell et al. (1994, Experiment 2). Although the observed differences between B+ and B– are somewhat underestimated, as predicted, the competition property resulted in stronger episodic connections for minority behaviors, $F(1, 49) = 425.44$, $p < .001$, and undesirable behaviors, $F(1, 49) = 264.28$, $p < .001$. These two main effects indicate that it is not the combination of negative and minority behaviors (i.e. B–) that might drive the illusion as the distinctiveness account would predict, but rather two independent effects of increased memory stemming from two minority categories (behaviors from group B and negative behaviors). As noted earlier, these results also distinguish the present network from alternative exemplar-based and tensor product models, which cannot account for the increased memory for minority groups and undesirable behaviors.

Simulation 2: Expectancy-based illusory correlation

Although the differential sample size paradigm of Hamilton and Gifford (1976) represents a very dramatic demonstration of illusory correlation despite the lack of an actual relationship, very often, group stereotypes are created as a consequence of existing relationships between attributes and a group. Once such group conceptions are formed, however, these beliefs will bias judgments based on newly acquired information, even if that new information does not contain an actual relationship. Thus, already-established stereotypes may produce illusory correlations through the expectations that are associated with a group. This type of illusory correlation is therefore termed expectancy based, in contrast to the Hamilton and Gifford (1976) paradigm, which we refer to as size based.

In an illustration of this expectancy-based illusory correlation, Hamilton and Rose (1980, Experiment 1) presented their participants with a series of statements, each of which described a person as a member of an occupational group such as accountants and doctors. In addition, each member was described by two trait-implying adjectives, some of which were stereotypically associated with the group while others were not. For instance, the traits *perfectionist* and *serious* were stereotypical of accountants, and the traits *wealthy* and *attractive* were stereotypical of doctors. All these trait adjectives were presented in descriptions of all occupational groups, so that there was no relationship between occupational group and any particular attribute.

Moreover, there were always two members associated with each set of two adjectives, so that sample size was kept constant. Nevertheless, when asked to indicate "how many times each of these adjectives described each occupational group" (p.835), participants overestimated the frequency of traits that were stereotypical of a group. For instance, they estimated the frequency of perfectionist and serious accountants to be on average 2.7 (while the actual number was 2). In contrast, the frequency of doctors having these traits was estimated to be 2 (which was the actual number).

This finding cannot be explained by differences in sample size in the information set. Apparently, pre-existing expectancies about these occupational groups had biased the frequency estimates of co-occurrence. Subsequent studies have replicated these findings (Kim & Baron, 1988; Slusher & Anderson, 1987; Spears, Eiser, & van der Pligt, 1987).

Several explanations have been put forward to account for expectancy-based illusory correlation, including facilitated encoding of stereotypical traits or biases at retrieval. We propose a connectionist explanation that builds on the suggestion by Hamilton and Rose (1980) that "an associative basis for an illusory correlation would exist whenever one's previous experiences had resulted in a perceived relationship between two stimulus variables. The perceiver would then have an expectation that the two variables are related" (p.833). Specifically, we assume that the bias results from previous experiences with co-occurences of stereotypical traits with an occupational group, and so creates pre-existing stereotypical beliefs that are encoded in stronger weights connecting the stereotypical traits with the group. Consequently, when novel information is presented, the new weight changes resulting from this information are "added" on these prior weights, leading to a stereotypical weight advantage. These stronger weights for stereotypical traits produce the illusory correlation. More generally, the integration of old and new information in a connectionist model by adding weight changes, explains how expectancy-driven biases are created.

We used the same model architecture as depicted in Figure 9.1 for size-based illusory correlation, with the exception that trait nodes replace the desirability nodes. However, the present simulation is driven by another property of the delta learning algorithm—the modification of weights derived from old and new information. Specifically, during a pre-experimental phase, the model builds up an association or expectancy about typical traits of each occupational group by presenting five trials in which stereotypical traits co-occur with their occupational group (without any episodic information on specific trait adjectives, as this information is most probably lost by the time the experiment starts). Next, the experimental phase presents information that is either consistent or inconsistent with the stereotype (two trials each), leading to a zero correlation overall. At the end of learning, to simulate frequency estimates that reflect "how many times each of these adjectives described each occupational group" (p.835), each group is primed and the resulting activation of each trait node is read off (the reverse direction of testing from trait to group nodes works equally well). Because we simulated single traits (without the presence of an opposing trait), simulation of the frequency measure was tested by the resulting activation of a single trait only (instead of the usual differential activation).

Results

Like the previous simulation, the network processed all "trait adjectives" for 50 "participants" with different random orders. The mean test activations for the simulated frequency estimates are depicted in Figure 9.4, together with the observed means for two occupational groups from the first experiment of Hamilton and Rose (1980). As can be seen, the simulation replicates the basic finding that stereotypical traits are overestimated in frequency in comparison with non-stereotypical traits. A within-subjects ANOVA revealed that, like in the original study of Hamilton and Rose (1980), the interaction between Group (accountants versus doctors) and Typicality (typical of accountant versus doctor) reached significance, $F(1, 49) = 5554.86, p < .001$.

GROUP DIFFERENTIATION

Several biases and stereotypes in group judgments such as illusory correlation emerge from categorizing people or objects in different groups. A factor that

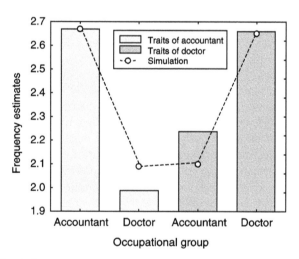

Figure 9.4 Simulation 2: Expectancy-based illusory correlation. Observed data from Hamilton and Rose (1980, Experiment 1) and simulation results. The human data are from Table 1 in "Illusory correlation and the maintenance of stereotypic beliefs" by D. L. Hamilton & T. L. Rose, 1980, *Journal of Personality and Social Psychology, 39*, 832–845. Copyright 1980 by the American Psychological Association. Adapted with permission.

exacerbates the creation of stereotypes is accentuation, or the tendency to exaggerate differences on a feature that determines group categories (Tajfel, 1969). For instance, differences between skin colors are exaggerated between blacks and whites, but are seen as more similar among people belonging to the same racial group. In a classic study, Tajfel and Wilkes (1963) reported that when short and long lines were systematically associated with different categories, the perceived difference between the short and the long lines became more pronounced while similarities of the items within each category were increased (but see Corneille, Klein, Lambert, & Judd, 2002). Such accentuation leads to less individuation and hence more stereotypical beliefs about social categories.

Early theories remained vague about the psychological process underlying the accentuation effect. For instance, Tajfel and Wilkes (1963) suggested that the main drive behind the effect is a desire to maximize predictability. Cognitive explanations have also been offered: Exemplar theories (Fiedler, 1996; Krueger & Clement, 1994) assume that in a correlated condition, attention to the group label of an exemplar leads to the recruitment from memory of more exemplars from the same group, which are then aggregated into a composite evaluation that gives more weight to exemplars of the same group than from other groups. This increases the perceived similarity within groups and difference between groups. The tensor product model (Kashima et al., 2000) proposes a similar account. Because of the correlation between exemplars and the category, all exemplars of the same category share a common group label, and so become more similar to each other and more different from other groups. In sum, both the exemplar and tensor product model offer an account of the accentuation effect in terms of the sample size of the group category.

Like the exemplar and tensor product theories, our recurrent network also offers a sample size account. The idea is that accentuation is produced by the group → attribute connections. Because a correlated condition implies a greater sample size of the co-occurrence of a group and attribute nodes, based on the acquisition property, stronger group → attribute connections will develop. For example, if eight pro-gay articles are all correlated with one newspaper, strong associations will develop between the newspaper source and this attitude position. In contrast, when four pro-gay articles are correlated with one newspaper and another four to another newspaper, the connections of each of the newspaper sources with the attitude position will be much weaker.

For the group → attribute connections to have any effect on judgment, we assume that when perceivers judge an exemplar, not only the episodic trace but also the newspaper source is activated to some degree. As noted earlier, this assumption was also made by previous exemplar and tensor product theories. Moreover, recent findings corroborate the idea that accentuation is more likely to emerge when the task is sufficiently complex, suggesting that, especially under such conditions, participants additionally rely on categorical (i.e. source) information (Corneille et al., 2002; Lambert, Klein, & Azzi, 2002). Because of the stronger group → attribute connections in the correlated condition, this leads to accentuation of differences with the other group that would not occur if group labels were not correlated. For example, because the connection between a newspaper source and the pro-gay attitude in the correlated condition is stronger, activating this newspaper node will result in higher activation of the pro-gay attitude node (and almost no effect on the anti-gay node, as this newspaper was obviously not correlated with anti-gay articles), leading to increased pro-gay ratings or accentuation. In contrast, because this connection is weaker in the uncorrelated condition, activating the newspaper node will result in relatively weaker activation on the pro-gay attitude node, leading to fewer pro-gay ratings and loss of accentuation. The reasoning is similar for anti-gay articles and the anti-gay attitude node.

Novel prediction and initial empirical support

The present account makes a novel prediction that earlier exemplar models (Fiedler, 1996) or the tensor product model (Kashima et al., 2000) do not make. Given that the effect of acquisition is largely symmetric over the evaluative connections, not only the group → attribute connections should be weaker in the uncorrelated condition than in the correlated condition as described above, but also the attribute → group connections. By the competition property, this should lead to less discounting of the episodic → group connections (just as it was the case for minority groups in illusory correlation). Hence, our recurrent model predicts that the episodic → group connections should be stronger in the uncorrelated than in the correlated condition, leading to better recognition (assignment of source labels).

To verify this prediction, Vanhoomissen, De Haan, and Van Overwalle (2001) explored the effect of classification on accentuation of attitudes. Participants were presented with statements reflecting favorable versus unfavorable attitudes towards homosexuality, which came ostensibly from two newspapers (cf. Eiser, 1971). In an correlated condition, the favorable statements were consistently attributed to one paper and the unfavorable statements to another paper. In an uncorrelated condition, statements were attributed equally often to each newspaper. After reading the statements, the participants were requested to rate all the statements on an 11-point scale ranging from *very negative* to *very positive*. In line with the accentuation prediction, the difference between favorable and unfavorable statements was accentuated in the correlated condition as compared to the uncorrelated condition.

In addition, a newspaper assignment task was included. Participants read the original statements as well as novel distracter statements (foils) that contained the same material but differed in their evaluative meaning (i.e. switched from favorable to unfavorable and vice versa), and had to indicate from which newspaper the statements came or whether it was not presented earlier. The rationale behind the foils was that this would allow unconfounding episodic memory from guessing on the basis of evaluative memory. If the participants were (mis)led by the evaluative meaning of the statements, we would find worsened recognition performance on the foils, in that they would not be sufficiently rejected. However, if the participants were led by their episodic memory of the statements, they should show improved recognition performance on the foils, that is, they should reject them more often.

Our novel recurrent prediction for the recognition task was better (episodic) memory of the foils in the uncorrelated condition than in the correlated condition. Consistent with this prediction, in the recognition task, participants more often rejected distracter foils in the uncorrelated condition than in the correlated condition. This suggests that, compared to the correlated condition, these participants were less often misguided by the evaluative implication of the foils and used their episodic memory for making correct recognition judgments. Conversely, as one would expect, participants in the correlated condition more often accepted the original items, indicating again that they were (in this condition) correctly guided by the evaluative implication of these statements.

Simulation 3: Accentuation

A recurrent implementation of Vanhoomissen et al.'s (2001) accentuation and assignment findings is given in Table 9.3. We used the same semi-localist encoding of attribute (attitudes) and episodic (articles) information as before. Again, we simulated 50 "participants" with different random orders. To measure accentuation, participants were requested to give an estimate of the attitude position of each stimulus (e.g. how pro- or anti-gay each statement was). Hence, in the network, we tested for accentuation by cuing each episodic node representing an article as well as its associated newspaper node. (To unconfound source from favorability across the two correlation conditions, we activated only four favorable and four unfavorable articles, which came from the same newspaper in the two correlation conditions.) The degree to which this activation spreads to the attitude nodes determines the perceived attitude strength of the articles (see bottom panel in Table 9.3). The best fit with the observed data from Vanhoomissen et al. (2001) was obtained when the newspaper nodes were activated for only .15 rather than the default value [suggesting that belongingness to the newspaper was recruited from memory not to its full degree; the same .15 activation value provided the best fit in simulations in a similar study by Eiser (1971)].

In addition, we measured rejection of the foils in the newspaper assignment task. We assumed that this rejection would follow as a function of the conflicting group activations associated with: (1) the behavior described in the foils; and (2) the reversed attitude positions. Therefore, we first tested

Table 9.3 Accentuation: Learning history for correlated and uncorrelated conditions (based on Vanhoomissen et al., 2001)

Trial frequency	Newspaper A	B	Attitude +	−	Statements in Articles[a, b] A+(A+)	A+(B+)	B−(A−)	B−(B−)
Correlated (uncorrelated) condition								
Favorable articles[a]								
#4	1 (1)	0 (0)	1		1			
#4	1 (0)	0 (1)	1			1		
Unfavorable articles								
#4	0 (1)	1 (0)		1			1	
#4	0 (0)	1 (1)		1				1
Test phase								
Attitude position on favorable articles from A and unfavorable articles from B								
	.15		?	−?	1			
		.15	?	−?				1
Recognition memory on favorable articles from A and unfavorable articles from B								
	?		1	1				
		?	1					1

Cell entries denote external activation and empty cells denote 0 activation. #, Number of times the trial is repeated; +, favorable; −, unfavorable to a given attitude position; ?, resulting test activations (without external activations) averaged across each row. The order of the learning trials was randomized.

[a] Between parentheses are the episodic node types and activations for the uncorrelated condition.

[b] Each type of statement is shown in a separate column that involves multiple episodic nodes of which a different one is turned on (activation +1) per trial

recognition of the foils, by measuring how participants "falsely" recognized the foils as belonging to the original group. Specifically, we activated the foils by priming each episodic statement together with the reversed attitude position, and read off the resulting activation from the newspaper group nodes (see last two rows in the bottom panel of Table 9.3). Next, we measured the conflict with the group activation arising from the reversed attitude position. To accomplish this, we did the same test as before except that we primed only the reversed attitude positions and then subtracted the resulting group activation from that obtained for the foils. This difference score reflects the experienced conflict arising from episodic and reversed attitude information. The greater the conflict, the more likely the foil is recognized and rejected.

Results

Figure 9.5 shows the simulation results of 50 randomized "participants". As can be seen on the top panel of the figure, the simulation demonstrates a clear accentuation effect in that the perceived attitude positions were more extreme in the correlated condition compared to the uncorrelated condition, and the expected interaction was significant, $F(1, 98) = 121.46$, $p < .001$. In addition, the bottom panel shows that our novel memory prediction was also

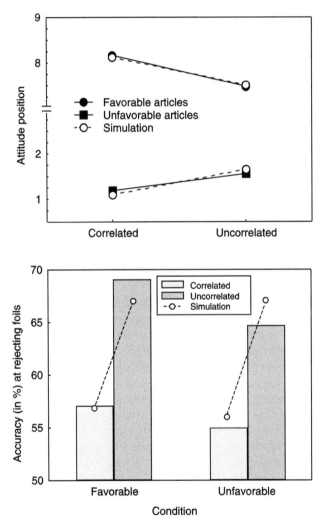

Figure 9.5 Simulation 3: Accentuation. Observed data from Vanhoomissen et al. (2001) and simulation results in function of a correlated or uncorrelated condition.

supported as episodic memory was higher in the uncorrelated condition than in the correlated condition, $F(1, 98) = 438.83$, $p < .001$.

This demonstrates that our recurrent network can model accentuation and the associated effect of enhanced memory for uncorrelated attributes. We argue that the network's ability to reproduce the accentuation effect is due to sample size sensitivity of the acquisition property, while enhanced recognition (i.e. assignment) is due to the competition property. Other theories, such as the exemplar-based model of Fiedler (1996) and the tensor product model by Kashima et al. (2000), make the same accentuation prediction but are silent with respect to enhanced recognition.

STEREOTYPE CHANGE

So far, we have seen how cognitive processes in humans—as modeled by a recurrent network—may shape distorted impressions about groups. The important question then is how might we be able to get rid of these biased impressions? Three tactics for providing stereotype-inconsistent information have been proposed in the literature to counter biased group perceptions (Weber & Crocker, 1983; for an overview, see Hewstone, 1994). First, according to the conversion model, extreme group members have an especially strong impact on perceptions of a group as a whole, so that disconfirming behavior of these members is especially likely to change group stereotypes. However, this model has received little empirical support. More evidence was found for the book-keeping model, which predicts a gradual modification of stereotypes by the additive influence of each piece of disconfirming information. Thus, for instance, more frequent disconfirming information will elicit more changes (Weber & Crocker, 1983). This prediction is in line with the recurrent model, as the acquisition property also predicts that more evidence leads to more extreme judgments (see also, for example, the sample size effects on illusory correlation and accentuation, discussed earlier).

Second, the subtyping model has perhaps inspired the most promising tactic. This model predicts that extreme group members are subtyped into subcategories and separated from the rest of the group. This insulates the group from dissenting members, so that the content of the existing group stereotype is preserved. Hence, contrary to the conversion model, this model predicts that the best tactic to change group stereotypes is to distribute disconfirming information among as many group members as possible, so as to avoid subtyping of extreme disconfirmers. Empirical evidence has generally supported this prediction (Hewstone, Macrae, Griffiths, & Milne, 1994; Johnston & Hewstone, 1992; Weber & Crocker, 1983).

For instance, Johnston and Hewstone (1992, Experiment 1) provided stereotype-inconsistent information on occupational groups that was either dispersed across many members or concentrated within a few members. When participants were asked how characteristic several stereotype-consistent and inconsistent traits were of the group in general, they showed a strong increase of stereotype-inconsistent traits in the dispersed condition. Frequency estimates of each type of information showed the same pattern, that is, higher estimates of inconsistent information in the dispersed condition. When asked to rate the typicality of the confirmers and disconfirmers in each group, it was found that the disconfirmers were seen as much less typical in the concentrated condition. This suggests that, as predicted by the subtyping model, disconfirmers were probably subcategorized more in the concentrated condition than in the dispersed condition.

Third, might the recurrent model reproduce these changes? It can, by simulating subtyping through the property of competition. We again assume a semi-localist representation in which not only the trait description is encoded in a stereotype-consistent or inconsistent node, but also the person to whom the trait is attributed. When stereotype-inconsistent information is concentrated in a few members, this implies that, after repeated presentation, the exemplar nodes representing these disconfirming members develop their own strong connection with the inconsistent node. (This is less the case for confirming members, because their exemplar → consistent connections are blocked by the strong group → consistent connection.) These strong exemplar → inconsistent connections compete with the group → inconsistent connections, resulting in a discounting of this latter connection. Psychologically, this leads to a decreased impact of inconsistent information on the group as a whole. In addition, because the disconfirming exemplar nodes develop stronger connections with the inconsistent node, as noted above, this results in a greater impact of the few disconfirming members on inconsistency ratings, resulting in these members being recognized as more inconsistent compared to the majority (i.e. subtyping).

In contrast, when the stereotype-inconsistent information is dispersed across members, these exemplar nodes do not develop strong connections with the inconsistent node, so that no competition arises with the connections linking the group with the inconsistent traits. Hence, no discounting of the inconsistent information occurs and no subtyping appears. In sum, the connection linking the group with the inconsistent node is more discounted by disconfirming members in the concentrated condition than in the dispersed condition, leading to a conservation of stereotypical perceptions of the group as a whole. In addition, the stronger connections of disconfirming members with the inconsistent node in the concentrated condition results in more subtyping of disconfirming members away from the rest of the group.

Simulation 4: Dispersed versus concentrated stereotype-inconsistent information

Table 9.4 lists a recurrent implementation of Johnston and Hewstone's study (1992, Experiment 1). As can be seen, the network architecture consists of a group node, two trait nodes reflecting stereotype-consistent and

Table 9.4 Dispersed or concentrated stereotype-inconsistent information: Learning history (Johnston & Hewstone, 1992, Experiment 1)

Trial frequency	Group	Traits		Specific group members[a]		
		Consistent	Inconsistent	Confirmer	Mixed	Disconfirmer
Pre-experimental phase						
#10	1	1				
Concentrated						
Consistent						
#4	1	1		1		
#8	1	1			1	
Inconsistent						
#12	1		1			1
Dispersed						
Consistent						
#6	1	1		1		
#4	1	1			1	
#2	1	1				1
Inconsistent						
#8	1		1		1	
#4	1		1			1
Test phase						
Consistent and inconsistent trait ratings of group						
	1	?				
	1		?			
Typicality of confirmers / disconfirmers						
		?	−?	1		
		?	−?			1

Cell entries denote external activation and empty cells denote 0 activation. #, Number of times the trial is repeated; ?, resulting test activations (without external activations) averaged across each row. The order of the learning trials was randomized within each condition.

[a] There were two group members who always confirmed the stereotype, two who always disconfirmed the stereotype, and four who showed mixed traits. Each member type is shown in a separate column that involves multiple nodes of which a different one is turned on (activation +1) per one to six trials (see footnote 2).

stereotype-inconsistent traits, and several exemplar nodes reflecting individual members. The representation of stereotype-consistent and stereotype-inconsistent traits as two unitary nodes is similar to the representation in the illusory correlation network (Simulation 1) of behaviors in desirable and undesirable nodes. In contrast to the earlier simulations, however, the exemplar nodes only represent members, and not their behaviors (which were not simulated). To provide the network with prior expectancies on stereotypical beliefs of the group, we provided 10 trials of stereotypical traits in a pre-experimental phase. Next, in the concentrated condition, all inconsistent information was concentrated in the disconfirming group members, whereas in the dispersed condition, inconsistent information appeared in all members except the confirmers. The overall amount of inconsistent information was identical (i.e. 12) in the two conditions.

Again, we simulated "50 participants" with different random orders. To measure stereotypical beliefs, participants are typically requested to rate to what extent some stereotype-consistent and inconsistent traits describe the group (Johnston & Hewstone, 1992; Johnston, Hewstone, Pendry, & Frankish, 1994; Weber & Crocker, 1983). In the network, this was tested by cuing the group node and reading off the resulting activation on the consistent or inconsistent node. We assume that frequency estimates are based on a similar testing procedure (see also illusory correlation, discussed earlier). To measure subtyping, Park, Wolsko, and Judd (2001) demonstrated that one of the more valid measures was to request the perceived typicality of confirming and disconfirming group members. In the network, this was tested by activating the two members that were either confirmers or disconfirmers in both conditions, and reading off the resulting trait activation (bottom panel in Table 9.4).

Results

Figure 9.6 shows the simulation results of 50 randomized "participants" on the trait ratings (top panel) and the typicality ratings (bottom panel). As can be seen in the top panel, the simulation demonstrates no considerable difference for consistent traits and, more importantly, a substantial effect of discounting of inconsistent traits in the concentrated condition as opposed to the dispersed condition. That is, the inconsistencies were less strongly associated with the group in the concentrated condition than in the dispersed condition, as in Johnston and Hewstone's (1992) study. A between-subjects ANOVA confirmed that the difference between the two conditions was significant for inconsistent traits, $F(1, 98) = 26.29$, $p < .001$, but not for the consistent traits, $F(1, 98) < 1$, *ns*. In addition, the bottom panel shows lower typicality ratings for disconfirmers in the concentrated than in the dispersed condition (and, as one would expect, almost no differences for confirmers). Again, this difference was significant, $F(1, 98) = 1572.17$, $p < .001$. This suggests that disconfirmers in the concentrated condition are more easily subtyped away from the overall group stereotype.

This simulation demonstrates that a recurrent network can model subtyping. The network's ability to reproduce this effect is due to the property of competition, which allows discounting of inconsistent information concentrated in a few disconfirmers. To be precise, disconfirmers are not discounted, but rather their implications for the whole group are. Other theories, such as the exemplar-based model by Fiedler (1996) and the tensor product model by Kashima et al. (2000), do not posses this property and hence cannot make this prediction except by adding auxiliary assumptions. For instance, Kashima

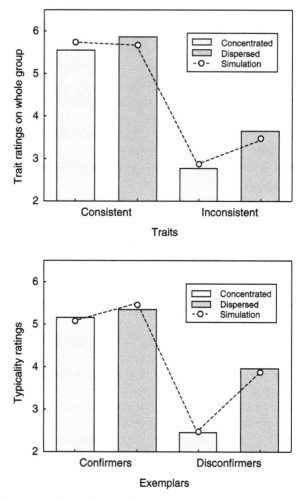

Figure 9.6 Simulation 4: Dispersed versus concentrated stereotype-inconsistent information. Observed data from Johnston and Hewstone (1992, Experiment 1) and simulation results. The human data are from Table 3 in "Cognitive models of stereotype change: (3) Subtyping and the perceived typicality of disconfirming group members" by L. Johnston & M. Hewstone, 1992, *Journal of Experimental Social Psychology, 28,* 360–386. Copyright 1992 by Academic Press. Adapted with permission.

et al. (2000) assumed that the amount of stereotype change is mediated by the extent to which inconsistent group members are individuated away from the group's resting state (p.931), a process that was added to the model to incorporate individuation in social judgments. In the recurrent model, such additional individuation process was not necessary because the results came out naturally from the competition property of the delta algorithm.

Very recently, Queller and Smith (2002; see also Chapter 10) proposed another recurrent connectionist model to model subtyping processes. Although many specifications and parameters of their model differ from our network (i.e. distributed representation, symmetric weights, contrastive Hebbian learning algorithm), the basic architecture and processing mechanisms are very similar. However, a more important difference is that Queller and Smith (2002) focused on the distribution of counterstereotypic information among behaviors rather than persons. That is, their simulations do not reflect whether discrepancies are concentrated among a few members or dispersed among most, but instead reflect a difference between moderate and extreme disconfirming members, differing only in the number of counterstereotypic behaviors. This variation adequately reflects their own experiment with human subjects (Experiment 3; see also Weber & Crocker, 1983, Experiment 2), and certainly has merit because it points to other mechanisms underlying subtyping.

Based on their simulations, Queller and Smith (2002) concluded that earlier explanations of subtyping are not important. However, it is invalid to generalize these conclusions to the more typical case of subtyping when inconsistencies are concentrated within a few members. Instead, as we claimed earlier, our simulations confirm that, in order to change stereotypes of a group, it is essential that discrepant members are still seen as a member of the group, so that the link between group membership and counterstereotypic attributes is not weakened. It is interesting to note that in spite of these differences, our network can reproduce Queller and Smith's (2002) simulation showing that subtyping is reduced when counterstereotypic information is presented throughout with stereotypic information (e.g. when learning about a novel unknown group), instead of after an initial stereotypic phase (e.g. when unlearning stereotypes of a known group for which one has already developed strong stereotypes).

Moderating factors

The present network can simulate other findings in the literature that examined the effects of several moderating variables on subtyping:

- *Sample size*: Weber and Crocker (1983, Experiments 1 and 2) reported more stereotype change in the dispersed condition when more inconsistent information was provided. The model explains this finding by sample-size differences. A growing sample size leads to more inconsistency information being incorporated in the group schema for the dispersed condition, but being discounted and subtyped in the concentrated condition. This can be simulated in the network by increasing the number of inconsistent trials (e.g. by doubling their frequency).
- *Individual members*: Gurwitz and Dodge (1977) reported that, in contrast to group judgments, estimates of individual members were seen as less

stereotypical in the concentrated than in the dispersed condition. However, Weber and Crocker (1983) did not replicate this finding as they found the same pattern of results for individual members as for the whole group. In line with their finding, our simulation also predicts the same overall pattern for individual group members as for group judgments (by placing 1s on the member nodes instead of on the group node; see the first two lines in the bottom panel of Table 9.4).

- *Expectancy*: Johnston et al. (1994, Experiment 3) documented more stereotypical ratings when stereotypical beliefs about groups were made explicit (high expectancy) than when they were not made explicit (low expectancy). In addition, in what may appear a ceiling effect, she also found less change when expectancy was high rather than low. To reproduce Johnston et al.'s (1994) findings, low expectancy can be simulated in the recurrent network by reducing the pre-experimental trials (e.g. 2) in comparison with the high expectancy condition (e.g. 10).

PERCEIVED GROUP VARIABILITY

Thus far, we have discussed how categorization between groups may distort how we perceive the central tendency of a group attribute (e.g. likeability, attitude, stereotype). However, the perceived homogeneity or variability of people is also strongly affected by group categorization. On the basis of available evidence, Dijksterhuis and van Knippenberg (1999) concluded that "variability judgments are quite accurate (in the sense that they reflect the actual stimulus variation quite well) and are being updated continuously" (p.529). This is consistent with a connectionist approach in which group characteristics such as variability are updated online. The concept of group variability is important, because high variability implies inconsistencies in the relationship between a group and some attribute, and this may help to dilute or change undesired group stereotypes. However, in contrast to Dijksterhuis and van Knippenberg's (1999) claim, research has also documented a number of shortcomings and biases in perceived group variability. Before we turn to these biases, we first briefly discuss how variability is measured in prior research and modeled in our network.

Simulation of group variability

A crucial question is how group variability is measured. Research addressing this issue has used a plethora of measures. Park and Judd (1990) analyzed these different measures and found that two independent constructs account for perceived variability. The first construct can be conceived as the dispersion of group members around the mean of one attribute, while the second construct reflects the degree to which the group as a whole is seen stereotypically. We focus here on the first construct, involving measures of perceived dispersion. Park and Judd (1990) reported that the *perceived range* measure was the most valid of group variability. Other measures inspired by an exemplar approach (Linville et al., 1989) known as "perceived variability", "probability of differentiation", or direct ratings of perceived similarity seemed less valid.

In a recurrent network, variability can be simulated by an approximation of the range measure. In this measure, participants are given a bipolar rating scale spanning the low to high ends of the attribute and asked to indicate where the most extreme (opposite) members would fall (Simon & Brown, 1987). To answer this question, we suggest that participants consider the group and estimate to what extent this group implicates each opposing attribute. This is simulated during testing by priming the group node and reading off the resulting activation on the attribute nodes, just like in a central tendency measure. However, to measure the distance or range between the attributes, these two resulting activations are then summed, rather than subtracted as in a central tendency measure. (The reverse direction of testing by which first the two opposing attributes are primed and then the activation of the group node is read off gives very similar results.)[3]

We chose the implementation of the range measure for several reasons. First, it is the most valid measure of group variability (Park & Judd, 1990) and it reflects actual judgments by participants (of range) rather than experimenter-based calculations (of variance). Second, it is cognitively least demanding because it makes use of information that is already available in memory under the form of group → attribute connections, and is thus more likely recruited spontaneously when judging group variability. Third, it is consistent with the finding (Park & Hastie, 1987) that estimates of variance are constructed and stored online rather than from retrieved exemplars, as the group → attribute connections on which our range measure is based are developed during learning (using the acquisition property).

To illustrate our implementation of variability as range measure, we simulated an exemplary case. In this simulation, we wanted to demonstrate that variability is sensitive to sample size. Therefore, variability was created by taking, for each block of four trials, three group members that possessed the high end of an attribute and only one member that possessed the low end. According to the incremental acquisition property of the delta learning algorithm, given its greater sample size, asymptote should be reached more quickly for the high end of the attribute than for the low end. To demonstrate this, we measured the results separately for the high and low extreme of the

---

3   Alternatively, in line with an exemplar approach (Linville et al., 1989), one can also activate all group members and read off the resulting attribute activation. This alternative gives very similar results, because the number of members who typify an attribute act as proxy for the strength of the group node with that attribute. Hence, the more members there are, the stronger the group → attribute connection is, resulting in very similar outcomes.

attribute. A direct measure of variability can be obtained by summing the two extremes of the attribute.

The results are depicted in Figure 9.7. As expected, the central tendency of the high extreme of the attribute approached asymptote much more quickly than the low extreme. This is due to sample size differences, as there are three times more members placed on the high extreme than on the low extreme. However, as more information is provided, the high and low extremes are more spread apart, resulting in more variability. This illustration suggests that the variability measure is susceptible to sample size. That is, when little information is available on group members, the variability of the group is perceived as low. The more information is available, the more the group is seen as heterogeneous until a maximum variability is attained that depends on the spread between the central tendencies of both extremes.

Simulation 5: Outgroup and ingroup homogeneity

In group perception, there is a pervasive tendency to perceive an outgroup as less variable than an ingroup, a bias known as the outgroup homogeneity effect (Linville et al., 1989; Messick & Mackie, 1989). Research revealed that outgroup homogeneity is related to the fact that perceivers are more familiar with the ingroup and therefore form a more differentiated impression on the ingroup compared to an outgroup (Linville et al., 1989). This explanation is also supported by the finding that ingroup heterogeneity is larger for real and enduring groups where everyone knows each other very well, than for

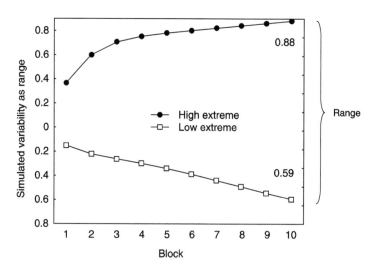

Figure 9.7 Simulation of group variability in function of the high and low extreme of an attribute. The high attribute is shown on the top half, the low attribute on the bottom half. The activation of the low attribute is reverse scored to visualize that variability is measured by range, i.e. the sum of the values obtained for the two opposite attributes.

artificial and laboratory-created groups (Mullen & Hu, 1989). In line with this explanation, many researchers provided an exemplar-based account of this effect (Fiedler, 1996, Fiedler et al., 1999; Hamilton & Trollier, 1986; Linville & Fisher, 1993; Linville et al., 1989; Park & Judd, 1990). Because perceivers have a richer knowledge base of the ingroup, they tend to recruit more exemplar information from memory about the ingroup than the outgroup, leading to more differentiated ingroup judgments.

Our connectionist approach makes a similar prediction as the exemplar approach. Because of the more extensive contact with one's ingroup, perceivers sample more information on the ingroup, leading to more differentiated views of the ingroup. However, contrary to exemplar theories, the connectionist approach assumes that the effect of sample size occurs at encoding rather than retrieval.

Clear support for the sample size account of outgroup homogeneity comes from the finding that the bias can be reversed when the ingroup is not a majority. Under these conditions, the variability of the ingroup is perceived as much smaller than that of the outgroup (Simon & Brown, 1987; Simon & Pettigrew, 1990; Simon & Hamilton, 1994; see for an overview Mullen & Hu, 1989). In a well-known experiment by Simon and Brown (1987, Experiment 1), children were arbitrarily assigned to one of two groups (blue or green) depending on their capacity to correctly categorize blue or green colors. Then they were given information on the number of children in each group, indicating that the ingroup was a minority, a majority, or equal in number to the outgroup. Finally, they were asked to estimate the two scale values that would bracket the values of all individuals in each group (i.e. range measure) in their ability to perceive blue and green colors. The results demonstrated that ingroup variability was highest when the ingroup was not a minority (either a majority or equal), and outgroup variability was highest when the ingroup was a minority. This finding was reproduced in the next simulation.

A simplified simulation of the Simon and Brown's (1987, Experiment 1) experiment is listed in Table 9.5. The network consists of an ingroup and an outgroup node, two nodes reflecting the high and low extremes of the attribute (e.g. good or bad in perceiving blue) and several episodic nodes. As can be seen, some variability in the group was introduced by varying the degree to which members had one of the attributes, that is, by varying the attribute node activation between 0 and +1, including intermediate values of 0.5 and 0.8. Importantly, to reflect our assumption that perceivers typically have more information on the ingroup than on the outgroup, the ingroup was described by eight behaviors and the outgroup by four behaviors. In contrast, to simulate ingroup homogeneity due to the ingroup being a minority, we simply reversed the group labels so that the ingroup had four behaviors and the outgroup eight behaviors (not shown). Perceived group range was tested by activating the group node and reading off the (summed) activation of the high and low attributes, as explained earlier.

Table 9.5 Outgroup and ingroup homogeneity: Learning history (based on Simon & Brown, 1987, Experiment 1)

Trial frequency	Group		Attribute		
	Ingroup	*Outgroup*	*High*	*Low*	*Episodic behaviors[a]*
Experimental phase					
Ingroup (outgroup)[b]					
#2 (1)	1 (0)	0 (1)	1.0	0	1
#2 (1)	1 (0)	0 (1)	0.8	0	1
#2 (1)	1 (0)	0 (1)	0.5	0.5	1
#2 (1)	1 (0)	0 (1)	0	0.8	1
Test phase					
Variability as range					
	1		?	?	
		1	?	?	

Cell entries denote external activation and empty cells denote 0 activation. #, Number of times the trial is repeated; ?, resulting test activation (without external activation). The order of the experimental trials was randomized.
[a] Each behavior involves multiple episodic nodes of which a different one is turned on (activation +1) per trial.
[b] Between parentheses are the trial frequencies and activations for the outgroup.

Results

The network was run with 50 "participants" with a different random order. As can be seen in Figure 9.8, the simulation produced a larger variability for the ingroup compared to the outgroup when more information on the ingroup is available (non-minority), thus successfully replicating the outgroup homogeneity effect. In contrast, when the ingroup was a minority, the effect was reversed just as in Simon and Brown (1987, Experiment 1). An ANOVA with Ingroup Size as a between-subjects factor and Group (ingroup versus outgroup) as a within-subjects factor confirmed that the interaction was significant, $F(1, 98) = 2110.31$, $p < .001$.

FIT AND MODEL COMPARISONS

A summary of the simulations that we have reported together with the major property responsible for generating the group biases can be found in Table 9.1. All simulations replicated the empirical data reasonably well. This can also be verified in Table 9.6, where the correlations between simulated and observed data are listed. However, it is possible that this fit is due to some procedural choices of the simulations rather than conceptual validity. To demonstrate that changes in these choices generally do not invalidate our

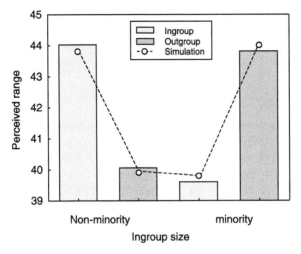

Figure 9.8 Simulation 5: Simulation of ingroup–outgroup homogeneity in function of (non-) minority status of ingroup. Observed data from Simon and Brown (1987) and simulation results. The human data are from the top panel of Figure 1 in "Perceived homogeneity in minority-majority contexts" by B. Simon & R. J. Brown, 1987, *Journal of Personality and Social Psychology, 53,* 703–711. Copyright 1987 by the American Psychological Association. Adapted with permission.

Table 9.6 Fit of the simulations, including alternative encoding and models

No.	Bias	Empirical Measure	Original Simulation	Distributed	Feedforward	Non-linear Recurrent
1.	Size-based illusory correlation	Likeability[a]	1.00	1.00	1.00	1.00
		Assignment RT	.94	.88	.88	$<0^x$
2.	Expectancy-based illusory correlation	Frequency	.97	.95	.97	.96
3.	Accentuation	Attitude	1.00	1.00	$.76^x$	.96
		Memory (foils)	.95	.99	.95	$<0^x$
4.	Stereotype change	Trait	.99	.99	.95	.98
		Typicality	1.00	1.00	$<0^x$	1.00
5.	Group homogeneity	Range	1.00	1.00	1.00	1.00

Cell entries are correlations between mean simulated values (averaged across randomizations) and empirical data. For the distributed encoding, each concept was represented by five nodes and an activation pattern drawn from a normal distribution with M = activation of the original simulation and SD = .20 (five such random patterns were run and averaged) and additional noise at each trial drawn from a normal distribution with $M = 0$ and SD = .20, and with learning rate = .03 (except .05 for simulation 1). For the non-linear autoassociative model, the parameters were: $E = I = Decay$ = .15 and internal *cycles* = 9 (McClelland & Rumelhart, 1988) with learning rate = .20.

[a] The correlations in this row are trivial as only two data points are compared and thus necessarily yield only +1 or −1; the correlations in the other rows each involve four data points.

[x] Predicted pattern was not reproduced.

simulations, we explore a number of issues, including the localist versus distributed encoding of concepts, and the specific recurrent network used versus a feedforward network. In addition, we will also briefly discuss major differences with other relevant models.

Distributed coding

The first issue is whether the nodes in the autoassociative architecture encode localist or distributed features. Localist features reflect "symbolic" pieces of information, that is, each node represents a concrete concept. In contrast, in a distributed encoding, a concept is represented by a *pattern* of activation across an array of nodes, none of which reflects a symbolic concept but rather some subsymbolic micro-feature of it (Thorpe, 1995). Moreover, distributed coding usually implies an overlap of the concepts' representations (i.e. an overlap of pattern activations coding for different concepts). Although we used a localist encoding scheme to facilitate our introduction to the most important connectionist processing mechanisms underlying group biases, we admit that localist encoding is far from realistic. Unlike distributed coding, it implies that each concept is stored in a single processing unit and, except for explicit differing levels of activation, is always perceived in the same manner without noise. This may limit the model's capacity to simulate properties like pattern completion, generalization, and graceful degradation.

For instance, in the semi-localist encoding of our simulations, the implied attributes in the statements were directly coded as given, such as whether the behavior was desirable or undesirable, whether the attitude was favorable or unfavorable, and so on. However, participants were not literally told that the statements had these attributes. Therefore, this material is more realistically represented by a distributed encoding scheme, where attribute information is embedded in a pattern of noisy activations that the recurrent network must abstract from these patterns, just like real participants must do. Given the advantages of distributed coding, is it possible to replicate our localist simulations with a distributed representation?

To address this question, we ran all simulations with a distributed encoding scheme in which each concept was represented by five nodes that each reflects some micro-feature of the concept. We maintained the same level of overlap between concepts that was already introduced in the semi-localist encoding, that is, the overlap consisted of the attribute nodes shared by the exemplars. Although it would perhaps be more realistic to add even more overlap between concepts, this was not done here because that would require ad-hoc assumptions on how much additional differential pairwise overlap there should be between different concepts. We also added random noise to the activation of theses nodes to simulate the imperfect conditions of perception (see Table 9.6 for details). All simulations were run with 50 "participants" with different distributed representations and random noise for each participant. As can be seen, all distributed simulations attained a good fit to the data and, in all cases, the relevant pattern of results from the localist simulations was reproduced. These findings suggest that the underlying principles and mechanisms that we put forward as being responsible for the major simulation results can be obtained to the same degree not only in the more contrived context of a localist encoding, but also in a more realistic context of a distributed encoding.

Feedforward model

We claimed earlier that the connections between attributes, exemplars, and group nodes were presumably most responsible for replicating the phenomena of interest. This claim can be partly tested by using a feedforward network model in which only the feedforward connections from attributes and exemplars to the group play a role (i.e. the upward connections in Figure 9.1). However, this leaves out the important lateral connections between attribute and episodic nodes, such as the ones involved in the attitude ratings of accentuation (between attitude positions and exemplary statements; Simulation 3) and the typicality ratings of stereotype change (between traits and specific group members; Simulation 4). Thus, except for these two latter cases, we expect a feedforward network to do about equally well as the autoassociative network. To explore this, we ran all simulations with a feedforward pattern associator (McClelland & Rumelhart, 1988) that consists only of feedforward connections (with additional backward spreading of activation from the group node during testing if necessary; see Van Overwalle, 1998). As can be seen in Table 9.6, for all simulations except those mentioned above, a feedforward architecture did almost equally well as the original simulations. This confirms that feedforward connections are crucial to reproduce many phenomena in group bias. Nevertheless, it is necessary to incorporate lateral connections of a recurrent network to explain all findings of interest.

Non-linear recurrent model

We also claimed earlier that a recurrent model with a *linear* updating activation function and a *single internal updating* cycle (for collecting the internal activation from related nodes) was sufficient for reproducing the group biases. This contrasts with other researchers who used a non-linear activation updating function and more internal cycles (McClelland & Rumelhart, 1986; see also Chapters 5 and 7). Cycling in a recurrent network has some advantages. For instance, it would allow measuring response latencies in an alternative manner by the number of cycles needed to converge on a stable response. (Recall that we simply assumed that the strength of the connection is proportional to the time to spread the activation.) Are such activation specifications necessary? To answer this question, we ran all our simulations with a non-linear activation function and nine internal cycles (or 10 cycles in total).[4] Our model specifications were identical to those of Read and Montoya (1999; see also McClelland & Rumelhart, 1988, pp.168–169).

As can be seen from Table 9.6, although the non-linear model yielded an adequate fit, most simulations did not substantially improve on the fit compared to the original simulations. This suggests that the present linear activation update algorithm with a single internal cycle is sufficient for simulating many phenomena in group judgments. This should not come as a surprise. In recurrent simulations of other issues, such as the formation of semantic concepts, multiple internal cycles were useful to perform "clean-up" in the network so that the weights between, for instance, a perceptual and conceptual level of representation were forced to eventually settle into representations that had pre-established conceptual meaning (McLeod, Plunkett, & Rolls, 1998). Such a distinction between perceptual and conceptual levels was not made here, and, as a result, multiple internal cycles seem unnecessary. Nevertheless, non-linear recurrent activation made it possible to simulate accentuation without providing external activation to the source nodes. Whether doing away with this external activation might better reflect real psychological processes is unclear, because research has shown that accentuation does not always occur, and that it depends on reliance to source categories when the task is ambiguous (Corneille et al., 2002; Lambert et al., 2002).

Perhaps more importantly, the non-linear activation algorithm tends to abolish the effects of competition in the memory and latency measures (Simulations 1 and 3). The reason for this is that the non-linear updating algorithm forces the activations automatically to the +1 and −1 default levels. Hence, if two features are activated together and overpredict a category, then the overly high output activation of the category tends to restore activation to the normal +1 ceiling level. This reduces discounting of the connections with the features.

Exemplar and tensor product models

As mentioned above, there are a number of differences between the present recurrent network and the exemplar (Fiedler, 1996; Fiedler et al., 1999; Smith, 1991) and tensor product (Kashima et al., 2000) models. These differences allow the recurrent model to explain more biases in a more parsimonious manner with less assumptions.[5] We discuss these differences in function of the properties that create the biases in the recurrent model:

---

4 To make sure that the non-linear activation adjustments settled on a stable state, we also conducted simulations with 49 internal cycles (or 50 cycles in total). The results were very similar.

5 The recurrent model was also able to reproduce attenuation of recency and response dependency in serial position weights, as documented by Kashima et al. (2000). More generally, the delta learning algorithm on which the recurrent model was built is well designed to handle most basic forms of category learning (e.g. Estes et al., 1989; Gluck & Bower, 1988a). However, because of space limitations, these issues and simulations are not discussed further.

Acquisition

The exemplar (Fiedler, 1996; Smith, 1991) and tensor product (Kashima et al., 2000) models explain many group biases by aggregation over samples of different sizes, as does our connectionist approach. Consequently, these models can explain biases such as illusory correlation, accentuation, and group homogeneity (Simulations 1, 3, and 5). However, in exemplar models, sample-size differences appear only when noise in perception and encoding is assumed; this assumption is unnecessary in our and Kashima et al.'s (2000) connectionist approach. The reason is that aggregation in a connectionist network is performed during encoding by a learning algorithm that is in itself sensitive to sample size. However, these differences are minor because noise and information loss seem quite plausible from a neuropsychological perspective (and were used in our distributed simulations).

Competition

Perhaps the most important limitation of exemplar and tensor product models is that the competition property is absent. The reason for this is that aggregation in these models is unbounded and has no asymptote. Multiple inputs do not compete against each other for weight but add to the aggregated output in equal amounts. Although these models often use some sort of a normalization function that limits the overall activation (Fiedler et al., 1999, p.12; Kashima et al., 2000, p.918), as we understand it, this function has a global effect that does not cause competition between the summed activation received from multiple inputs like in the delta error-reducing algorithm. Consequently, these models cannot explain enhanced memory for minority behaviors (in illusory correlation) or for uncorrelated conditions (in accentuation), or the effect of dispersed versus concentrated distribution in stereotype change (Simulations 1, 3, and 4). These biases were not discussed in the exemplar models of Fiedler (1996; Fiedler et al., 1999) and Smith (1991; Smith & Zárate, 1992). We see no immediate remedy for the lack of competition in exemplar models. In the tensor product model, these biases were explained by individuation processes that require additional elaboration and controlled processing. As stated by Kashima et al. (2000), "the individuation process involved in stereotype change and group differentiation was explained in terms of the construction of a person representation. Some mechanism is needed to control ... the construction process for a person representation" (p.935). In contrast, our model assumes that these effects are a natural consequence of the competition property of the delta learning algorithm without any need for a control mechanism. The tensor product model can avoid such controlled processes by adopting an error-reducing learning algorithm such as the delta learning algorithm.

Group variation

With the exception of Fiedler et al. (1999), previous approaches mostly modeled the central tendency of the attribute (e.g. liking) in group perception, and did not address variability in stereotyping. Fiedler et al. (1999, p.15) measured variability by cuing memory with a gradually degraded pattern of activation reflecting the ideal attribute features, to instantiate the different scale points spanning the high to low ends of the attribute. In our approach, group variation was based on the range measure and modeled by adding the aggregates of the two opposite attributes of the groups (rather than differentiating between them as in central tendency measures). Both approaches are able to model ingroup–outgroup homogeneity (Simulation 5). However, our approach seems preferable because it appears simpler and more direct by using existing memory traces and because it is based on the more reliable range measure (Park & Judd, 1990).

Summary

In summary, the present model seems to be better equipped to deal with a number of important issues in group judgments. However, this does not deny the merits of earlier alternative models. In particular, Fiedler's (1996) exemplar model has great historical and conceptual value, as it was the first to point out that simple aggregation processes could explain most basic effects of group biases. It was also an important inspiration in developing our connectionist network model. In addition, these models, and particularly the tensor product model (Kashima et al., 2000), could be more adequate on other issues or simulations for which they were originally designed.

GENERAL DISCUSSION

The simulations in this article illustrate that a recurrent connectionist model is able to account for biases and shortcomings in judgments about groups under diverse conditions. The perspective presented here offers a novel view on how perceivers process social information, by describing how knowledge structures are learned through the development of associations between social concepts. This clearly distinguishes it from earlier associationist approaches that used static networks (with non-adjustable links) to represent logical relationships or constraints between concepts (Kunda & Thagard, 1996; Read & Marcus-Newhall, 1993; Read & Miller, 1998; Shultz & Lepper, 1996). An important advantage of the dynamic and adaptive nature of the present recurrent network compared to these previous models, as well as other connectionist models like the tensor product model (Kashima et al., 2000), is its computational power. This power comes from the delta learning algorithm, which generates a number of important emergent properties responsible for a wide range of group biases (see Table 9.1).

The acquisition property accounted for sample size effects in (the evaluative bias of) illusory correlation, accentuation of group differences, and group homogeneity. The competition property accounted for decreased accessibility and lower recall of frequent events in illusory correlation and correlated exemplars in accentuation, and the greater discounting of inconsistent information concentrated in a few group members. Our emphasis on these sometimes-neglected properties of the delta learning algorithm distinguished the present approach from other implementations of the autoassociator (McClelland & Rumelhart, 1988; see also Chapter 7) that used properties related to distributed representation (e.g. pattern completion, generalization) to explore cognition. It is also different from other distributed connectionist models of group processes (Kashima et al., 2000) that use the Hebbian learning rule that is unable to reproduce the competition property.

We also presented unique predictions by the recurrent model on illusory correlation and accentuation. Some of these predictions have already received some initial evidence. In a series of experiments, Van Rooy (2001) demonstrated that the typical illusory correlation in likability ratings and other measures of group evaluation are exacerbated given an increasingly smaller sample size and, more importantly, that this effect occurs even in the absence of undesirable minority behaviors (see also Shavitt et al., 1999). This poses clear problems for competing models of illusory correlation, such as the distinctiveness account, that situate the origin of illusory correlation at an enhanced memory of these infrequent undesirable behaviors (Hamilton & Gifford, 1976; McConnell et al., 1994). Other novel findings have demonstrated that memory is enhanced for undesirable behaviors (Van Rooy, 2001) as well as for behaviors that are uncorrelated with a group attribute (Vanhoomissen et al., 2001). These results are problematic for exemplar-based approaches (Fiedler 1991, 1996; Fiedler et al., 1993, 1999; Smith, 1991) that claim that impaired—rather than increased—information aggregation of rare events is the key factor of illusory correlation and other group biases.

By bringing together biases from traditionally different fields of group research, the presented connectionist approach can contribute to a more parsimonious theory of biases in judgments in several ways. First, simply integrating these findings in this manner invites a search for possible further parallels between them. Second, a connectionist approach makes predictions at a more precise level of detail than these previous approaches. Third, Van Overwalle and colleagues (see Chapters 8 and 11)—using the same network model—demonstrated that this approach was also able to account for many phenomena in social cognition, including categorization, person impression, assimilation, generalization and contrast, causal attribution, and attitude formation (see also Chapters 5 and 7). These authors also reported that the recurrent model, with the delta learning algorithm, integrates earlier algebraic theories of impression formation (Anderson, 1981), causal attribution (Cheng & Novick, 1992), and attitude formation (Ajzen, 1991). In addition, our recurrent network parallels basic associative learning principles applied in a growing tradition of studies using associationist theories to human learning (for reviews, see Shanks, 1995; Van Overwalle & Van Rooy, 1998). The revival of associative learning models is largely due to the development of models using error-correcting learning mechanisms such as the delta learning algorithm, which has been used widely in the connectionist literature (McClelland & Rumelhart, 1986). In sum, the present connectionist approach places group biases in the wider perspective of the larger field of learning and cognition.

Connectionist models paint a different picture of information processing than that described by many earlier models in cognition. They describe the ability of humans to dynamically adjust associations between concepts (groups, attitudes, behaviors ...) in a variety of settings (e.g. social, personal). In particular, they assume that automatic and local updating algorithms update these associations, requiring little conscious effort or awareness and without the necessary control of a supervisory device, such a central executive. Hence, the connectionist approach provides an answer as to how we are able to form quick impressions of social agents effortlessly in the rush of everyday life (Bargh, 1996). This is in line with research on stereotyping that shows that prejudiced responses often occur on implicit measures over which participants have limited conscious control (Greenwald & Banaji, 1995; Whitney, Davis, & Waring, 1994). This distinguishes the present recurrent approach also from the tensor product model of Kashima et al. (2000) that, as the authors admitted themselves, "cannot do away with a control mechanism [to explain] ... the individuation process involved in stereotype change and group differentiation" (p.935). In our model, it is assumed that some control could occur, for instance, at the time the information is integrated to produce an explicit answer or judgment.

In addition, it is important to stress that the connectionist learning process on groups is not inherently biased. Many earlier theories of cognition suggested that to cope with the strong demands of the environment, human perceivers resort to biased processes, including heuristics (Tversky & Kahneman, 1974), selective attention (Hamilton, 1981), and over-generalizations (Tajfel & Wilkes, 1963). In contrast, within the current framework, this learning process is seen as essentially unbiased. For reasons of evolutionary survival, humans should be capable of detecting at least simple relationships between features in their environment (Wasserman, Elek, Chatlosh, & Baker, 1993). Biases arise mainly because of lack or abundance of evidence (e.g. sample-size effect), competition between different types of (evaluative versus episodic) information, or instructions and motivational factors that direct the perceiver's attention toward or away from some particular information.

Limitations and directions for future research

While we believe we have shown that a connectionist framework can potentially provide a parsimonious account of a number of disparate phenomena in group judgment, we are not suggesting that this is the only valid means of modeling cognitive phenomena. On the contrary, we defend a multiple-view position in which connectionism would play a key role but would coexist alongside other viewpoints. We think that a strict neurological reductionism is untenable, especially in personality and social psychology, where it is difficult to see how one could develop a connectionist model of high-level abstract concepts such as existing personality differences, motivation, love, and violence, which obviously remain far beyond the current scope of connectionist modeling.

The strong overlap in the basic architecture and learning algorithm of the present recurrent model of group biases with similar models of social cognition in general (Read & Montoya, 1999; Smith & DeCoster, 1998; Van Overwalle & Labiouse, 2004; Van Overwalle & Siebler, 2005; see also Chapters 5–12) opens a lot of interesting avenues for future research. One such topic might be the differences between group and person perception, which is now attracting increasing interest (e.g. Hamilton & Sherman, 1994; Welbourne, 1999). Within the recurrent framework, group and person perception are based on the same learning process, during which perceivers form online connections between features (traits, characteristics) and targets (individuals, groups). We suggest that differences between group and person perception arise because information concerning individuals (or groups perceived as highly entitative) directs attention to general attributes in the information that might reveal the presence of a trait, while less entitative groups invite less to search for such consistencies (Hamilton & Sherman, 1994; Wyer & Srull, 1989). This increased attention can be implemented in the model by higher activation levels. Because of the raised activation of general regularities, such as evaluative meaning and social categories, the recurrent model predicts greater speed of learning of general attribute information and, as a consequence, more discounting of episodic traces. This might result, respectively, in weaker illusory correlations for individuals than for groups, but in worse memory for specific episodes related to individuals than to groups.

Our model can be applied very flexibly to accommodate other relevant findings. Differential attention to some aspects of social information at the expense of other aspects may be relevant for other moderating factors of illusory correlation. For instance, decreased activation and a resulting decrease of learning may explain loss of illusory correlation under increased or incongruent mood (Mackie et al., 1989; Kim & Baron, 1988; Stroessner et al., 1992) or when one's attitude position is already consistent with a majority (Spears, van der Pligt, & Eiser, 1985). Conversely, increased activation may explain increases in perceived variability of a group, such as when low-status members set themselves apart from a group (Doosje, Ellemers, &

Spears, 1995). However, as noted earlier, the mechanism that produces attentional differences is not modeled in the present network, and presumably requires the inclusion of additional modules in the network dealing with controlled processes. Even without additional activation assumptions, our model can produce other biases such as Simpson's paradox (Fiedler, Walther, Freytag, & Stryczek, 2002; Meiser & Hewstone, 2002).

Another direction for future research might be an integration of research on group stereotype change and attitude change. Typically, these two research topics have been conducted almost independently. Group research has typically emphasized immutable characteristics, like race and gender, or artificial categorizations, like groups A and B. In contrast, attitude research often focuses on thematic issues that unite or divide people in real-life groups. A considerable amount of research has been inspired by dual-process models of attitude formation (Chaiken, 1980; Petty & Cacioppo, 1986), which describe how the content of arguments, as well as other contextual information, can help to change people's attitudes. This research, however, has often neglected the robust finding in group stereotype research that inconsistent information received from a few group members is less effective in changing stereotypical beliefs than that same information received from many (Weber & Crocker, 1983). The present recurrent model was capable of modeling both processes of distributed inconsistent information (see Simulation 4) as well as attitude change (see Chapter 11). Perhaps, by taking a similar integrative approach, social research might become more successful in changing people's stereotypes and attitudes with respect to devalued minority groups in society.

SIMULATION EXERCISES

These exercises enable you to explore the recurrent simulations on group biases. You are expected to have some experience with the FIT program, perhaps by having completed some of the introductory exercises in Chapter 3 and 4. The manual of the program is available in the Appendix at the end of this book.

Because the original simulations were run in an earlier version of the FIT program, the published simulations could not be recovered for these exercises. Hence, the statistical means and analyses reported in the **Listing** tab may differ slightly from those in the published articles. In addition, a within-participants analysis of variance (ANOVA) was originally used, whereas the FIT program offers only a between-participants ANOVA. This was done by exporting the logged data to a statistical package. If you use Statistica, you can export the logged data through the menu **File | Export | Log Data Grid To Statistica**. If you use another statistical package, you can export to Excel by first clicking the **Log** tab and then choosing the menu **File | Export | Log Data Grid To Excel**.

Exercise 1: Demonstrating size-based illusory correlation

Choose menu **File | Open Project** or press the 📖 speed button. Browse for *IllusoryCorrelation_demo.ft2* in folder *Chapter 9*, and click the **Open** button.

Specifying trials

Click the **Trial** tab to open the Trial Grid. The top rows show 22 units comprising of 2 desirability units ("+" denotes desirable and "–" denotes undesirable), 18 behavioral statement units and 2 group units. The specific status as input or output is of no importance in a recurrent model (but is useful for a feedforward network). You can change the names given to the units in the second row either by double clicking, or by choosing the **Data | Edit Column Names** menu.

Each Trial Category specifies a single trial which comprises a behavioral statement. Specifically, each trial has the activation turned on (= set to 1) of a single desirability unit, a single statement unit, and a single group unit. As can be seen from top to bottom, there are 8 desirable (positive) and 4 undesirable (negative) behaviors by group A members, and 4 desirable and 2 undesirable behaviors by group B members. This reflects a typical illusory correlation design, where the ratio of desirable and undesirable behaviors is equivalent across groups.

For measuring group evaluation, in this and all other simulations, you prime the group and then observe how much the desirability units are activated (see "*?*" in Test Categories *$51–54*).

Specifying sessions

Click on the **Session** tab to open the Session Grid. You will see two orders in which two desirable behaviors were alternated with one undesirable behavior. In the first order, the simulation begins with two desirable behaviors; in the second order, it begins with a desirable and then an undesirable behavior. Each set of behavioral statements about a group is separated by *reset*, to start learning from scratch for each group. As you can see, each behavioral statement is followed by a test category. A desirable statement of Group A is followed by Test Category *$51*, an undesirable statement of Group A is followed by Test Category *$52*, and similarly for Group B.

The desirable and undesirable statements of each group are logged by different **DV**s (or columns) as can be seen by the * in the columns. This is done so to obtain different lines in the graph for each of the groups and desirable vs. undesirable behaviors. A * is used because no observed or hypothesized values for the **DV**s exist, so that a * merely functions as a place holder.

Specifying the simulation parameters

Choose the **Simulation | Parameters** menu, or press the ⊕ speed button. In the top panel, four drop-down list boxes list the major options. Note that the model to be simulated is the *Linear autoassociator* developed by McClelland and Rumelhart (1988). Leave all the other option boxes to their default values. The following parameters need to be set by opening (clicking) the different tabs.

- **General** tab.
   Specify in **Session** that you want to run session *1*, and select in **Graph Simulated Values** the button *yes* (automatically, the **Log Simulated Values** will turn to *yes* also). Set all other parameters to *no*.
- **Model** tab.
   Set the **learning rate** = 0.15. Leave all other parameters open, or set them to *auto* or *no*.

Running the simulation

Choose the **Simulation | Run Simulation** menu, or press the ⚖ speed button. If you want to follow the simulation step by step, choose the **Simulation | View Network** menu. Alternatively, hit the ⊯ speed button first.

   After the simulation is finished, the **Graph** tab will open automatically (because you requested a graph). You will see a graph of the simulation results, as they also appear in Figure 9.2. If the graph does not show properly, make the following selections:

- **filter**: (*none*).
- **X-Axis**: *Trial* (the label specified for **IV2**).
- **X-Axis Labels**: *TrialLabels* (the label specified for **IVLabel**).
- **Y-Axis Line(s)**: select all four simulated **DVs** but none of the observed **DVs** (as these latter are empty). The variable names preceded by a ~ sign denote the simulated values.
- Set the lower part of the Y-axis to 0 (as in Figure 9.2) by hitting the **Options** button, and specifying the value *0* for the **Left Axis Scaling** in the **From** box.

Now hit the **Graph Log** button again (if you changed some of the options above) and you will see the graph as it appears in Figure 9.2. If you want to use your favorite graphics program, you can export the means of the graph by hitting the graph's **Options** button, the **Data** tab, and finally the **Export Graph Means to Excel** button (alternatively, you can use menu **File | Export | Graph Option Grid to Excel**).

   If you are interested in the numerical results and the parameters that you used for the simulation, press the **Listing** tab.

Questions

1. You can experiment a little with the model parameters of the simulation. For instance, you can choose a higher learning rate parameter. Select the **Simulation | Parameters** menu or press the ❀ speed button, and press the **Model** tab. Enter **learning rate** = 0.30. As you will see, the illusory correlation will disappear, as the difference between desirable and undesirable evaluations is now almost identical for the two groups. The reason is that the weights of the desirable behaviors in group A increase much more slowly at the end (as they approach asymptote), so that the difference between desirable and undesirable behaviors becomes less apparent.

2. What would happen if you selected another model? Choose the **Simulation | Parameters** menu or press the ❀ speed button and select another model in the **Model** option box. For instance, you might select the *feedforward* or *non-linear recurrent* model, as indicated in Table 9.6. For the feedforward model, keep the input and output units as they are. For the non-linear model, specify **istr = estr = decay** = *0.15*. Does the illusion also appear for these models when the learning rate is set to .15, and does it also disappear when the learning rate is increased to .30? Try this for yourself.

3. Alternatively, you can specify a distributed representation. You practiced distributed representations in Chapter 7, so you can look up the exercises of that chapter to see how to do this.

Exercise 2: Size-based illusory correlation

Choose menu **File | Open Project** or press the 🖘 speed button, browse for *McConnell94_2.ft2* in folder *Chapter 9*, and click the **Open** button.

Specifying trials and session

This simulation is very similar to the previous one, with the exception that all statements are now given in a single Trial Category in a random order. This greatly simplifies the set up of the **Trial** and **Session sheets**.

As you can see at the bottom of the **Trial sheet**, to obtain measures of likeability, each group was primed and the differential activation of the desirability units was measured (see Test Categories *$50–51*). That is, the difference between desirable and undesirable units was taken (as indicated by *?* and *-?* respectively). This reflects how people, when asked about a particular group, typically indicate their likeability on a scale with two extremes (with positive and negative anchors).

In contrast, in a group assignment task, a behavioral statement is given and the task is to indicate as quickly as possible from which group the member's behavior came. To obtain a measure of response time during this task, you activate statements of a particular set of behaviors (e.g. A+, A−, B+, and B−) and measure how much they activated the group unit. By activating all statements at once, you immediately get an average of the amount of activation that is generated for the appropriate group. The amount of activation is divided by the number of units activated, so that the total activation in each Test Category equals 1. Note that the activation measured was inversed (as indicated by -? in Test Categories *$55–58*) because the observed RT is inversely related to the strength of memory. Indeed, the graph that you will obtain is the reverse of Figure 9.3 in the article.

To randomize the statements, choose the **Simulation | Parameters** menu, or press the ❀ speed button. After clinking the **General** tab, specify in **Randomize Order of All Learning Trials** *yes* with *50* runs, and set the learning trials to the default Categories *1–49* (although 1 might have been enough). Leave all other parameters as in the previous simulation.

Running the simulation

To run the simulation, choose the **Simulation | Run Simulation** menu, or press the ❀ speed button. If you want to follow the simulation step by step, choose the **Simulation | View Network** menu. Alternatively, hit the ❀ speed button.

After the simulation, you will see a graph of the simulation results as they also appear in Figure 9.3. To obtain the top panel of Figure 9.3 with the likeability ratings, do the following before hitting the **Graph** button:

- **filter**: *Condition*, and select **Between values** *1* to *2*.
- **X-Axis**: *Condition*.
- **X-Axis Labels**: *IVLabel*.
- **Y-Axis Line(s)**: select *~Likeability* and *Likeability*.

To obtain the bottom panel of Figure 9.3 (reversed) with the RTs, change the following before hitting the **Graph** button:

- **filter**: *condition*, and select **Between values** *3* to *6*.
- **Y-Axis Line(s)**: select *~RT* and *RT*.

If you are interested in the numerical results and the parameters that you used for the simulation, press the **Listing** tab.

Questions

Experiment with Questions 1–3 in Exercise 1.

4. Of specific interest is that the article (see footnote 2) specifies an alternative way of simulating response time (RT), by measuring the time (i.e. number of cycles) to stabilize the activations in an "attractor state". You

can try this alternative. First, omit the minus sign before the ? in the Test Categories *$55–58*, because now the time to settle in an attractor state goes in the same direction as the observed RT. Choose the **Simulation | Parameters** menu, or press the 🐌 speed button. In the **Response** option box, select *MSS activation change < .001*. This means that the test activations are allowed to cycle unbounded until they converge, that is, until the difference between the mean sum of squares (MSS) of the current activations and the MMS of the prior activation update is less than .001. You can experiment with other convergence values and other learning rate parameters. Notice that not all convergence criteria will results in the observed results. This is most probably due to the fact that they are either too crude (large convergence criterion), or in the case of a small convergence criterion, because the maximum number of 100 cycles is reached.

Exercise 3: Expectancy-based illusory correlation

Choose menu **File | Open Project** or press the 📖 speed button, browse for *Hamilton+Rose80_1.ft2* in folder *Chapter 9*, and click the **Open** button. Of importance here is that Learning Category $9 is added to learn the associations between stereotypical traits and each occupational group. Specific traits are left out in this learning phase, because they are not important. We assume here that during the actual learning of specific traits of a target person (in Learning Category *$1*), perceivers will automatically infer whether or not they are typical (although this learning is not modeled). The results of the simulation are shown in Figure 9.4.

Questions

Explore Questions 1–3 in Exercise 1.

4. As another exercise: Can you model the prior learning of associations of occupations and specific traits rather than global typicality? How would you test whether or not their frequencies are overestimated in an occupational group? Think a minute about this before you read on.

    One possible solution is that you hide the "typical trait" units i1 and i2 in the Trial Grid, and instead use the specific traits in units i3–i6 for learning the prior stereotypical associations in Learning Phase *$1* and for measuring their activation in Test Categories *$51–54*. This is shown in Figure 9.9.

Exercise 4: Accentuation

Choose menu **File | Open Project** or press the 📖 speed button, browse for *Vanhoomissen2001.ft2* in folder *Chapter 9*, and click the **Open** button. To

#	i3 Perfectionist	i4 Timid	i5 Thoughtful	i6 Wealthy	o1 Accountant	o2 Doctor
$9	Prior Learning to built expectancies					
5	1	1			1	
5			1	1		1
$1	statements					
	1				1	
		1			1	
			1			1
				1		1
	1					1
		1				1
			1		1	
				1	1	
$51	Acc - Acc stereotypes					
	?	?			1	
$52	Doc - Acc stereotypes					
	?	?				1
$53	Acc - Doc stereotypes					
			?	?	1	
$54	Doc - Doc stereotypes					
			?	?		1

Figure 9.9 Exercise 4: Modeling prior learning of associations between occupations and specific traits in the trial grid. Note the dark bands on top to indicate the hidden columns of the "typical trait" units i1 and i2.

obtain the same graph as the top panel in Figure 9.5 (attitude position), make the following selections before hitting the **Graph** button:

- **filter**: *Category*, and select **Between values** *50* to *50*.
- **X-Axis**: *Condition*.
- **X-Axis Labels**: *IVLabel*.
- **Y-Axis Line(s)**: select all.

To obtain the bottom panel of Figure 9.5 (accuracy in rejecting the foils), change the following choice before hitting the **Graph** button:

- **filter**: *Category*, and select **Between values** *51* to *52*.

Questions

Explore Questions 1–3 in Exercise 1.

Exercise 5: Subtyping

Choose menu **File | Open Project** or press the ☞ speed button, browse for *Johnston+Hewstone92_1.ft2* in folder *Chapter 9*, and click the **Open** button. To obtain the same graph as the top panel in Figure 9.6 (trait ratings on whole group), do the following before hitting the **Graph** button:

- **filter**: *Condition*, and select **Between values** *1* to *4*.
- **X-Axis**: *Condition*.
- **X-Axis Labels**: *IVLabel*.
- **Y-Axis Line(s)**: select all.

To obtain the bottom panel of Figure 9.6 (typicality ratings), change the following choice before hitting the **Graph** button:

- **filter**: *Condition*, and select **Between values** *5* to *8*.

Questions

Explore Questions 1–3 in Exercise 1. Alternatively, you can explore the issues raised in the *Moderating Factors* section in the text, p.283. We focus here on conditions *1–4* in the graph and Test Categories *$51–52*.

4. Test the prediction that a growing sample size leads to more stereotype change in the dispersed condition (i.e. more inconsistent and fewer consistent trait ratings), by doubling the frequency of the inconsistent trials. This should increase the amount of inconsistency accumulated by the network, and hence more change. Compare the graph before and after you made the change.
5. Test the prediction that individual's patterns are similar to the group pattern by omitting the priming of the group units and priming the individual members instead (you might use 0.125 instead of 1, as suggested in the text to obtain an overall priming of 1). Compare the graph before and after you made the change. As you will see, this prediction is correct for inconsistent traits, but less so for the consistent traits (that did not show significant differences in the original study by Johnston & Hewstone, 1992).
6. Test the prediction that lower expectancies lead to less stereotypical ratings of the group, by reducing the number of pre-experimental trials to 2 (instead of 10). Compare the graph before and after you made the change.

Exercise 6: Variability

Choose menu **File | Open Project** or press the speed button, and open *Variability_demo.ft2* in folder *Chapter 9* for a demonstration of range as a variability measure (see also Figure 9.7) or open *Simon+Brown87_1.ft2* for a demonstration of group homogeneity in function of the minority status of the ingroup (see also Figure 9.8).

Questions

Explore Questions 1–3 in Exercise 1.

10 Subtyping versus bookkeeping in stereotype learning and change: Connectionist simulations and empirical findings*

Sarah Queller and Eliot R. Smith

A distributed connectionist network can account for both bookkeeping (Rothbart, 1981) and subtyping (Brewer, Dull, & Lui, 1981; Taylor, 1981) effects. The finding traditionally regarded as demonstrating subtyping is that exposure to moderate (compared with extreme) disconfirmers leads to subsequent ratings of the group that are less stereotypic. Despite learning that is incremental and analogous to bookkeeping, the simulations replicate this finding and suggest that the "subtyping" pattern of results will be drastically reduced if disconfirmers are encountered before the stereotype is well-established. This novel prediction holds with human participants and offers a tantalizing suggestion: Although moderate disconfirmers may produce more stereotype change, stereotype development might be discouraged by exposure to either extreme or moderate disconfirmers.

Negative stereotypes about social groups (defined by race, gender, religion, occupation, or other characteristics) frequently go hand in hand with prejudiced feelings and overt discrimination against members of those groups, ranging from mild social sanctions up through pogroms, campaigns of "ethnic cleansing", and genocide. The interlinked issues of stereotyping, prejudice, and discrimination thus constitute major social problems, and social scientists have been active in searching for remedies. A natural assumption embodied in many suggested remedies is that negative stereotypes will weaken and change when people encounter positive (or, more generally, stereotype-inconsistent) information about members of the stereotyped group. If firsthand experience or reliable reports indicate that group stereotypes are incorrect or at least are not universally applicable, it makes sense that the stereotypes should be weakened or ultimately even set aside.

Unfortunately, anecdotal reports and everyday experience, as well as the accumulated results of much social psychological research, suggest that this happy outcome is rare. One White woman from Chicago, for example, was

---

*   Adapted from *Journal of Personality and Social Psychology, 82*, 300–313. Copyright 2002 by the American Psychological Association. Reprinted with permission of the publisher.

quoted in a newspaper report as saying that she thought most blacks were violent and criminally inclined (Wilkerson, 1992). At the same time, she emphasized that the few black people she knew personally were "lovely people". How could this woman maintain her general stereotype in the face of disconfirming evidence from personal encounters? More generally, how and when will stereotypes change in response to stereotype-inconsistent information?

MODELS OF STEREOTYPE CHANGE

In an influential volume on stereotyping (Hamilton, 1981), researchers out-lined three possible mechanisms of stereotype change that might occur following exposure to stereotype-disconfirming information. The bookkeep-ing model (Rothbart, 1981) assumes that the perceiver essentially tallies up confirming versus disconfirming information and modifies the stereotype accordingly, in a data-driven fashion. If the stereotype starts out fairly extreme, then each bit of disconfirming information will have some moderat-ing impact. As such information is increasingly encountered, the stereotype will gradually and incrementally change to become less extreme.

The conversion model (Rothbart, 1981) holds that no change whatever occurs until a threshold amount of disconfirming information has been encountered. Once the threshold is reached, the perceiver is assumed to critically reevaluate the stereotype and decide that it is incorrect. The picture is of no change for a time, followed by sudden and catastrophic change. This contrasts with the gradual and incremental change postulated by the bookkeeping model.

Finally, the subtyping model (Brewer et al., 1981; Taylor, 1981) holds that the treatment of disconfirming information depends on the structure of that information. Individuals who are highly counterstereotypic are actu-ally grouped into a new subtype that is mentally segregated from the rest of the group. As such, their attributes do not affect the perceiver's representa-tion of the group as a whole. Only individuals who are slightly to moderately counterstereotypic will have an influence on the group stereotype.

Research evidence to date has generally been interpreted as supporting the bookkeeping and subtyping models. No studies to our knowledge have directly claimed support for the hypothesized conversion process, although some researchers (e.g. Weber & Crocker, 1983) have interpreted Gurwitz and Dodge (1977) as supporting the conversion model.

Bookkeeping processes are consistent with the observation that when people are exposed to information about a group, the overall balance of positive versus negative information is generally reflected in the positive versus negative nature of the resulting stereotype (Weber & Crocker, 1983).

However, a number of studies have obtained evidence supporting subtyping processes. In the paradigm used in these studies, typically the same set of information (e.g. 12 stereotypic plus 12 counterstereotypic plus 24 stereotype-irrelevant behaviors) is divided up in different ways. The information may be arranged to create a small number of strongly disconfirming person descriptions (along with some stereotype-consistent descriptions), a condition termed *concentrated*. Alternatively, the same information may be used to construct a larger number of only mildly disconfirming descriptions, creating a condition termed *dispersed*. Studies following this general paradigm find that the resulting stereotype change is typically less under concentrated than under dispersed conditions (Johnston & Hewstone, 1992; Weber & Crocker, 1983). The smaller stereotype change in the concentrated condition is attributed to subtyping processes; perceivers are assumed to regard the extreme disconfirmers as not real group members, and so their characteristics have little impact on the stereotype.

It is worth noting that Weber and Crocker (1983) found evidence of bookkeeping in a study in which the primary finding was one of subtyping. In this study, moderately disconfirming group members produced more stereotype change than did extremely disconfirming members, supporting the subtyping model of stereotype change. However, a bookkeeping model was also supported by the finding that both moderately and extremely disconfirming group members led to less stereotypic ratings as compared with a condition in which no disconfirming group members were presented.

DISTINGUISHING UNDERLYING MECHANISMS FROM OVERT JUDGMENTS

Since the initial formulation of the three alternative models of stereotype change, it has been assumed that the underlying processes described by the models map in a relatively direct and transparent fashion onto research participants' overt judgments. For example, the bookkeeping model states that a perceiver would incrementally alter the internal mental representation of the group as each item of information was encountered. Correspondingly, as the relative amount of counterstereotypic information increased, overt judgments about the group would show a gradual decrease in stereotypicality. However, in more complex and arguably more realistic models of mental representation and process, underlying structures do not necessarily map in a simple, direct, and linear fashion onto observable responses. We illustrate this point with connectionist models.

When connectionist memories are used to model the processes underlying stereotyping, the learning rules mean that at the level of underlying structures, connectionist models are, in essence, bookkeeping models. That is, in these models all learning proceeds by gradual, incremental changes of the connection weights after each stimulus is presented. This statement applies equally to initial learning of a stereotype for a group and to stereotype "change", which in these models is just more learning. In a simple connectionist memory there is no underlying mechanism that goes back and re-evaluates prior assumptions after a threshold amount of disconfirming information has been seen (i.e. conversion). Nor is there any complex attributional processing that judges some group members as too inconsistent to be "real" members (i.e. subtyping). There are only incremental weight changes following each stimulus.

Importantly, however, the overt responses of connectionist models may not resemble the patterns expected from a bookkeeping approach. Elman and colleagues (1996) provide a dramatic illustration of this fact, although in a realm far removed from stereotype learning and change. They constructed a network using the so-called simple recurrent network architecture, which took a sequence of 0s and 1s as input. After each input digit, the network was supposed to output a 0 if the total number of 1s seen so far was even or a 1 if the total number of 1s in the input so far was odd. For example, for the input 1 1 0 1 0 the correct output would be 1 0 0 1 1 (odd, even, even, odd, odd). The network was trained on many short sequences of two-to-five symbols in length. Training used typical connectionist rules, which produced slight alterations in the connection weights after each training pattern. After varying amounts of training, the network's performance was tested with a long string of one hundred 1s, for which the correct output is 1 0 1 0 1 0, and so forth.

After 15,000 training inputs (these networks learn slowly!) the network was able to produce the correct output for the first four symbols of the test string. An observer assessing the network's performance would say that it had not yet mastered the task even for the sequence lengths (up to five) that it had seen in training. After some additional training—17,999 inputs—the network displayed correct performance for the first 13 symbols on the test. The observer would note that the network had learned to generalize somewhat beyond the range of sequence lengths seen in training. However, it clearly had not "learned the general rule" distinguishing odd from even, because performance fell off to chance levels after length 13. Elman et al. (1996, p. 234) describe what happened next:

> At least, this is the state of affairs after 17,999 training cycles. What is remarkable is the change that occurs on the very next training cycle. After one additional input, the network's performance changes dramatically. The network now is able to discriminate odd from even [for the entire sequence of 100 input symbols]. The magnitude of the output is not as great for longer sequences, so we might imagine that the network is not fully certain of its answer. But the answer is clearly correct and in fact can be produced for sequence[s] of indefinite length. Subsequent training simply makes the outputs more robust.

The network, from the perspective of an outside observer, appears suddenly to have induced the general rule. Correct performance that can be maintained for indefinite strings of inputs, far beyond the lengths seen in training, would seem to be a signature of the use of an abstractly formulated rule—seemingly an entirely different underlying process from the limited generalization observed just one trial earlier. Elman and his colleagues (1996) go on to give a technical explanation of how gradual, incremental weight changes are able to produce such a discontinuity in observed performance. We do not need this technical discussion here, however, to see the crucial point: With connectionist models, changes in overt performance (i.e. the network's outputs for specific test patterns presented as input) need not correspond qualitatively to changes in underlying mechanisms (i.e. the nature of the connection weight changes that drive performance). As this example illustrates, observed performance that involves "conversion-like" sudden and qualitative shifts can be generated by a bookkeeping process of gradual, incremental change within the network itself.

Examples like this one motivated the work we present in this article. We conducted a number of simulations to determine the implications of connectionist memory models for stereotype change—following up on the prior demonstration that a connectionist memory could learn and use a stereotype (see Chapter 7). Specifically, we wished to determine whether a single set of connectionist assumptions could account for not only the bookkeeping-like properties found with some aspects of stereotype change (Weber & Crocker, 1983) but also the subtyping behavior found in a number of studies (Hewstone, Macrae, Griffiths, & Milne, 1994; Johnston & Hewstone, 1992; Weber & Crocker, 1983). These simulations ultimately generated a new prediction, which we describe at the end of Study 2A, that had not previously been tested in studies with human participants. The article concludes by presenting a successful empirical test of this new hypothesis.

DESCRIPTION OF THE NETWORK USED IN SIMULATIONS

The network we used was a 40-unit fully recurrent, distributed network using the constraint satisfaction module from the PDP++ simulation software.[1] Each of the 40 units was connected to its 39 counterparts by weighted connections. At the beginning of the simulation, the weights were set to randomly determined moderate values. Thus, the network started out with no pre-existing knowledge. After an input pattern consisting of 40 different activation values was applied to the 40 units, activation flowed across the weighted connections until a stable state of activation was reached (see Chapter 3).

A contrastive Hebbian learning rule was used to adjust the weights after each stimulus presentation (Movellan & McClelland, 1993). This rule

---

1   The PDP++ software is available for free at the following web address: http://www.cnbc.cmu.edu/PDP++/ (Software copyright © 1995 Randall C. O'Reilly, Chadley K. Dawson, James L. McClelland, and Carnegie Mellon University).

includes both Hebbian and error-driven components. Thus, after each input is presented, the weight between any pair of units is adjusted as a function of the error between the output and the desired output, as well as the concurrent activation of the pair of units. Specifically, weight change was a function of the difference between the product of the actual output activations on two units and the product of the desired (or input) activations on the two units. When this discrepancy was large the weight was adjusted more, and when it was small the weight was adjusted less.

Thus, small, incremental weight changes were made after each stimulus pattern was presented as input. Because learning in this type of network is slow and the network learns many different input patterns, the network can only learn a pattern well if it is presented many times. Alternatively, the network can learn a particular type of pattern well (e.g. a stereotype of a group) if it has seen many instances of that type (e.g. many group members that are random variations on a common stereotype pattern).

Study 1: Bookkeeping simulation

Because the network described here learns via incremental weight changes, it would not be surprising if this network performed in a manner consistent with the bookkeeping model of stereotype change. To test this empirically, we ran a simulation similar to that of Smith and DeCoster (1998; see Chapter 7) to which we added some stereotype-inconsistent stimuli and varied the number of stereotype-inconsistent group members presented. If the bookkeeping model of stereotype change holds for this network, the stereotypicality of the output in response to a test stimulus should decrease as the number of stereotype-inconsistent stimuli increases.

Method

Procedure

We set-up the simulation program to present a series of training stimuli as inputs to the network. Each stimulus consisted of 40 activation values applied to the 40 units in the network. Following the presentation of each stimulus, the connection weights were changed according to the contrastive Hebbian learning rule with a learning rate of 0.01.[2]

After the whole training set had been presented, a test stimulus was provided as input. The test stimulus consisted of a partial pattern with some activation values missing (i.e. set to the null activation value of zero). We

---

2   The following network parameters were set at the default values provided by the PDP++ constraint satisfaction program: learning rate = 0.01, momentum = 0, and decay = 0. See the Annexe for more detail on the technical aspects of the simulation.

tested the stereotypicality of the output of the network by looking at the activation values on the units with missing inputs and comparing them with stereotypic activation values. This test is analogous to presenting experimental participants with a novel person about whom they know only group membership and seeing if they will infer that the person possesses the group's stereotypic characteristics.

In total, 10 simulated subjects were run in each of two conditions for a total of 20 simulation runs. Each simulated subject learned about stimuli generated from a different randomly constructed group prototype. The two conditions differed in the ratio of counterstereotypic to stereotypic stimuli presented.

Training stimuli and manipulation

We first trained the network on the stereotype by presenting a mixture of stereotypic stimuli and background stimuli. People obviously have more knowledge stored in memory than just the information presented about the experimental group. In addition, it would not be terribly interesting if the network could learn about the group in the absence of any information not relevant to the group. For these two reasons, background stimuli were included in the training set. Following Smith and DeCoster (1998; see Chapter 7), we designed the stereotypic stimuli to have a set of activation values that were characteristic of stereotyped group members and not characteristic of the background stimuli. Specifically, the prototypical activation values for group-member stimuli were defined for each simulated subject as a randomly determined set of 1 or –1 values on units 1 through 21 and null inputs (zeroes) on units 22–40 (Table 10.1). Each stereotypic stimulus for that simulation was then generated by adding normally distributed random noise ($s = 0.2$) to these prototypical values. In contrast, the prototypical activation values for background individuals consisted of null inputs (zeroes) for all 40 units. The activation values for the background stimuli were created by the addition of normally distributed random noise ($s = 0.2$) to these zero activation values.

After we trained the network on the stereotype by presenting a randomly ordered set of 150 stereotypic and 150 background stimuli, the network began a second phase of training that included counterstereotypic stimuli.[3] We generated each of the counterstereotypic stimuli by first creating a normally distributed random deviation ($s = 0.2$) from each of the 40 prototypical group-member activation values and then reversing the valence on units 13–21 (which were stereotypical units prior to the valence reversal). We

---

3 Pretesting indicated that presentation of a combination of 150 stereotypic group-member stimuli and 150 background stimuli was sufficient for learning to reach asymptote (i.e. minimal additional learning occurred with greater than 300 stimuli).

Table 10.1 Prototypes of stimuli presented during stimulation of study 1

Training phase	1	2	3	4	5	6	7	8	9	10	11	12	13	14	15	16	17	18	19	20	21	22	23	...	39	40
1st																										
300 (Background)	0	0	0	0	0	0	0	0	0	0	0	0	0	0	0	0	0	0	0	0	0	0	0	...	0	0
300 (Stereotypic)	S	S	S	S	S	S	S	S	S	S	S	S	S	S	S	S	S	S	S	S	S	0	0	...	0	0
2nd: 45 conditions																										
270 (Background)	0	0	0	0	0	0	0	0	0	0	0	0	0	0	0	0	0	0	0	0	0	0	0	...	0	0
45 (Counterstereotypic)	S	S	S	S	S	S	S	S	S	S	S	S	C	C	C	C	C	C	C	C	C	0	0	...	0	0
90 (Stereotypic)	S	S	S	S	S	S	S	S	S	S	S	S	S	S	S	S	S	S	S	S	S	S	0	...	0	0
2nd: 15 conditions																										
270 (Background)	0	0	0	0	0	0	0	0	0	0	0	0	0	0	0	0	0	0	0	0	0	0	0	...	0	0
15 (Counterstereotypic)	S	S	S	S	S	S	S	S	S	S	S	C	C	C	C	C	C	C	C	C	C	0	0	...	0	0
120 (Stereotypic)	S	S	S	S	S	S	S	S	S	S	S	S	S	S	S	S	S	S	S	S	S	S	S	...	0	0

All stimuli were normally distributed random deviations of prototypical values ($s = 0.2$). Stimuli were presented in random order within each learning phase. S designates a 1 or −1 activation value in accordance with the prototypical stereotype for a given simulated subject. C designates a counterstereotypic activation value that is the opposite valence of the stereotypic value.

arbitrarily selected units 1–12 and maintained stereotypic values (with noise added) on these units for both stereotypic and counterstereotypic stimuli. By doing so, the network always had some cue indicating which stimuli were group members and which were background stimuli. Maintaining units 1–12 at stereotypic values is loosely analogous to telling experimental participants that all of the people they will read about are group members. For example, a participant told that all the people are lawyers knows that even those that do not behave in concert with the lawyer stereotype are still lawyers.

The bookkeeping model predicts that an increased number of counterstereotypic stimuli should produce more stereotype change. To test this, we included 15 counterstereotypic stimuli in the second-phase stimuli of one condition and 45 counterstereotypic stimuli in the second-phase stimuli of the other condition. More specifically, the 15 condition included 15 counterstereotypic, 120 stereotypic, and 135 background stimuli, whereas the 45 condition consisted of 45 counterstereotypic, 90 stereotypic, and 135 background stimuli. Thus the total number of stimuli presented was held constant, but the ratio of counterstereotypic to stereotypic stimuli was either low (15 : 120) or high (45 : 90). Order of presentation in the second learning phase was randomized. In summary, the network first learned about 150 stereotypic and 150 background stimuli and then subsequently learned about an additional 270 stimuli that included either 15 or 45 counterstereotypic stimuli.

Test stimulus and dependent measure

The test stimulus consisted of prototypical stereotypic values on units 1–12, null inputs on units 13–21 that had experienced counterstereotypic values during training, and null inputs on units 22–40. Using units 13–21, we computed a stereotype discrepancy score by first squaring the difference between each unit's output and the prototypical stereotypic value for that unit and then summing these squared differences across the nine units. The stereotype discrepancy score thus provides a measure of the extent to which the network filled in missing values with stereotypic information. A smaller stereotype discrepancy score is indicative of more stereotypic output, and a larger stereotype discrepancy score is indicative of less stereotypic output.

Results and discussion

The stereotype discrepancy score for each simulated subject comparing the output activation to the prototypical group-member values on the test units (units 13–21) was submitted to a one-way analysis of variance (ANOVA). One might ask why we are presenting ANOVA as a means of describing predictions from our network model. That is, why would we run multiple simulated subjects and statistically analyze their results? On the face of it, this procedure may seem strange, as an arbitrarily large number of simulated subjects could be run, making statistical significance levels, in a sense, arbitrary. There is, however, a fundamental reason for this procedure. We need to ensure that the network's predictions are not constrained to a single set of stimuli and a single set of starting weights. Running multiple simulations with different stimuli and different starting weights will produce a distribution of different outputs. We wish to make statements about the model's predictions in general (e.g. that the model predicts that condition X will have a greater discrepancy between output and stereotypic values than condition Y). Hence, we must perform statistical tests to see whether the condition difference that we wish to interpret is reliable, given the variation across individual runs (simulated subjects). The rationale for performing such tests is therefore identical to the rationale for using statistics on results from human participants. Ideally, we would run an infinite number of simulated subjects and we could say with absolute certainty what the model predicts in our different conditions. Failing infinite sampling, enough simulated subjects should be run to ensure that all meaningful comparisons have good-enough significance levels that one can be confident that they do not arise simply through chance fluctuations. (Of course, ideally, one would also run enough human participants in all studies to reach this same level of confidence. However, unlike simulated subjects, human participants are expensive, and so, as is well known, many studies actually have low statistical power.)

The ANOVA indicated that stereotype discrepancy scores were larger for the condition in which 45 counterstereotypic group members were presented ($M = 3.54$, $s = 0.72$) than for the condition in which 15 counterstereotypic group members were presented ($M = 1.71$, $s = 0.20$), $F(1, 18) = 60.85$, $p = .0001$. This result is consistent with the bookkeeping model of stereotype change because it indicates that the output becomes less stereotypic as more counterstereotypic group members are encountered. This is not a surprising finding, however, as the incremental, trial-by-trial learning mechanism used in this type of network operates in line with a bookkeeping model.

Study 2A: Subtyping simulation

Although the recurrent network's ability to generate output consistent with the bookkeeping model of stereotype change was expected, it is less clear whether the network can account for subtyping. Recall that subtyping is argued to occur when strongly stereotype-disconfirming group members become regarded as a special type of group member with the result that they have less impact in bringing about stereotype change than do mildly or moderately disconfirming group members. The finding of less stereotype change in response to strongly disconfirming group members than in response to moderately disconfirming group members (holding the total amount of stereotypic and counterstereotypic information constant) has been reported repeatedly (e.g. Hewstone et al., 1994; Johnston & Hewstone, 1992; Weber &

Crocker, 1983). A simulation that is similar to the experimental paradigm used in these studies is straightforward.

We modeled the simulation stimuli after Johnston and Hewstone's (1992) stimuli. In their study, they had participants read about eight students who were majoring in physics. Pretesting showed that the participants held an initial stereotype of physics majors. Each of the eight physics majors was described by six behaviors he had (allegedly) performed. In all, the 48 behavior statements included 12 that were stereotypic, 12 that were counter-stereotypic, and 24 that were stereotype irrelevant. To create conditions of concentrated versus dispersed counterstereotypic information, Johnston and Hewstone manipulated which behaviors were attributed to each group member. In the concentrated condition, two of the group members were described as each performing six counterstereotypic behaviors. The remaining behaviors were attributed to the other six group members so that each of these six members was described by two stereotypic and four stereotype-irrelevant behaviors. Thus, in the concentrated condition, each of the stereotype-discrepant group members was strongly disconfirming. In the dispersed condition, each of four stereotype-discrepant group members was described by three counterstereotypic, one stereotypic, and two stereotype-irrelevant behaviors. The remaining two group members each were described by two stereotypic and four stereotype-irrelevant behaviors. Thus, in the dispersed condition, each stereotype-discrepant group member was only moderately disconfirming.

In our simulation, the network and procedure for training the network were identical to those described in Study 1 with the exception of the training stimuli. As in Study 1, the network was first trained on stereotypic and background stimuli. After this training, the network could be said to have an established stereotype just as human participants might have when they begin an experiment and are told they will learn about some physics majors. The stimuli in the second training phase were modified to create the concentrated and dispersed conditions. A finding that the network produces less stereotypic output in the dispersed condition than in the concentrated condition would suggest that the network can produce output that parallels the subtyping results.

Although all of the concentrated/dispersed studies we are aware of attempt to change pre-existing stereotypes, an equally interesting question involves how stereotypes are learned in the first place. This bias toward studying stereotype change may stem, at least in part, from the fact that the memory models researchers have relied on in social psychology primarily deal with the ways people use their representation at a given point in time (for exceptions, see Park, 1986; Sherman, 1996). In contrast, the network we used has the learning process explicitly built into the model. It makes sense to see if the subtyping phenomenon operates in the same way in a condition in which an established stereotype is challenged versus in a condition in which the counterstereotypic information is encountered throughout the process of learning about the group. Learning about groups in the context of an environment that includes stereotype-discrepant group members should be quite relevant in our society because exposure to members of other groups may be very different from one generation to the next and from one neighborhood to the next.

To study this issue, we expanded the scope of our simulation to include conditions in which the counterstereotypical group members were learned about throughout the learning process instead of only after the stereotype had been well established. Thus, the design for the Study 2A simulation was a 2 (information distribution: concentrated vs. dispersed) × 2 (learning order: post-stereotype vs. throughout learning) between-subjects design. Less stereotypic output in the dispersed condition than in the concentrated condition—at least in the case in which counterstereotypic information is encountered after stereotype learning—would be consistent with the findings from human studies on subtyping.

Method

Procedure

The procedure was identical to that of Study 1 with the exception of the stimuli that were presented. Again, 10 simulated subjects were run in each of the four conditions for a total of 40 simulation runs.

Training stimuli and manipulations

The generation of prototypical group-member stimuli and prototypical background stimuli was identical to that used in Study 1. We describe the poststereotype learning conditions first. The 45 condition of Study 1 was used as the poststereotype learning/concentrated condition in Study 2. Recall that, in this condition, the network learned the stereotype by training on 150 stereotypic and 150 background stimuli prior to encountering any counterstereotypic stimuli. In the second learning phase, 135 background stimuli and 135 group-member stimuli were presented. Of the 135 group-member stimuli, 45 were counterstereotypic and each of these was counterstereotypic on nine units (units 13–21). The remaining 90 group-member stimuli were stereotypic.

Table 10.2 shows how the stimuli were changed to create the poststereotype learning/dispersed condition. The first learning phase again presented 150 stereotypic and 150 background stimuli. In the second learning phase, 135 background stimuli and 135 group-member stimuli were presented. Among the total set of 135 group-member stimuli, each of the units from 13 to 21 flipped to a counterstereotypic value 45 times, maintaining a constant amount of stereotype-disconfirming evidence across conditions. However, instead of all nine units flipping valence to counterstereotypic values at once, only three

Table 10.2 Prototypes of stimuli presented during study 2

Training phase	1	2	3	4	5	6	7	8	9	10	11	12	13	14	15	16	17	18	19	20	21	22	23	...	39	40
1st																										
300 (Background)	0	0	0	0	0	0	0	0	0	0	0	0	0	0	0	0	0	0	0	0	0	0	0	...	0	0
300 (Stereotypic)	S	S	S	S	S	S	S	S	S	S	S	S	S	S	S	S	S	S	S	S	S	0	0	...	0	0
2nd: Concentrated condition																										
135 (Background)	0	0	0	0	0	0	0	0	0	0	0	0	0	0	0	0	0	0	0	0	0	0	0	...	0	0
45 (Counterstereotypic)	S	S	S	S	S	S	S	S	S	S	S	C	C	C	C	C	C	C	C	C	C	0	0	...	0	0
90 (Stereotypic)	S	S	S	S	S	S	S	S	S	S	S	S	S	S	S	S	S	S	S	S	S	0	0	...	0	0
2nd: Dispersed condition																										
135 (Background)	0	0	0	0	0	0	0	0	0	0	0	0	0	0	0	0	0	0	0	0	0	0	0	...	0	0
45 (Counterstereotypic)	S	S	S	S	S	S	S	S	S	S	S	S	S	C	C	S	S	S	S	S	S	0	0	...	0	0
45 (Counterstereotypic)	S	S	S	S	S	S	S	S	S	C	S	S	C	S	S	C	C	S	S	S	S	0	0	...	0	0
45 (Counterstereotypic)	S	S	S	S	S	S	S	S	S	S	S	S	S	S	S	S	S	S	C	C	C	0	0	...	0	0

All stimuli were normally distributed random deviations of prototypical values ($s = 0.2$). In the poststereotype conditions, stimuli were presented in random order within each learning phase. In the throughout learning conditions the order of presentation was randomized throughout the stimulation (rather than only within each of the learning phases). S designates a 1 or −1 activation value in accordance with the prototypical stereotype for a given simulated subject. C designates a counterstereotypic activation value that is the opposite valence of the stereotypic value.

units flipped at any given time. Thus, instead of 45 strongly disconfirming group-member stimuli being presented, 135 moderately disconfirming group-member stimuli were presented.

The two throughout learning conditions were created by taking the same stimuli used in each of the poststereotype learning conditions and fully randomizing the order of presentation. That is, to create the throughout/concentrated condition, we presented all 570 stimuli from the poststereotype/concentrated condition in random order. To create the throughout/dispersed condition, we presented all 570 stimuli from the poststereotype/dispersed condition in random order. Thus, in the throughout condition there were no separate stages of training and the very first stimulus encountered by the network could have been a counterstereotypic one.

Test stimulus and dependent measure

The test stimulus was the same as that used in Study 1 with stereotypic activation values applied as inputs to units 1–12, null activation values applied as inputs to units 13–21, and stereotype discrepancy scores computed over units 13–21 for each simulated subject.

Results and discussion

The stereotype discrepancy score for each simulated subject comparing the outputs to the prototypical group-member values on units 13–21 were submitted to a two-way ANOVA. (Remember that because we had a distribution of outputs and we could not run infinite simulated subjects, we used ANOVA to make sure any predictions based on our simulation are very unlikely to be due to sampling error.) The main effect for learning order was significant, $F(1, 36) = 85$, $p = .0001$, indicating that the output was less stereotypic (i.e. the sum squared error was larger) in the poststereotype learning condition than in the throughout learning condition. The main effect for information distribution was also significant, $F(1, 36) = 43$, $p = .0001$, indicating that the output was less stereotypic in the dispersed condition than in the concentrated condition. Both of these main effects were qualified by a significant interaction, $F(1, 36) = 15$, $p = .0005$ (Figure 10.1). In the poststereotype learning condition, the output was less stereotypic (i.e. the stereotype discrepancy score was larger) for the dispersed condition ($M = 4.74$, $s = 0.40$) than for the concentrated condition ($M = 3.20$, $s = 0.73$). In the throughout learning condition, however, this difference was drastically reduced (dispersed condition $M = 2.81$, $s = 0.25$; concentrated condition $M = 2.40$, $s = 0.37$).

The finding in the poststereotype condition is consistent with the results of the subtyping studies. These studies typically produce more stereotype change in response to moderately discrepant group members than in response to highly discrepant group members. Note that the poststereotype learning

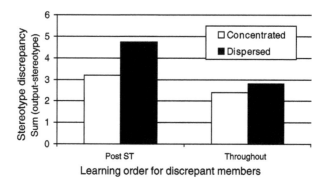

Figure 10.1 Simulated stereotype (ST) discrepancy as a function of information distribution (concentrated vs. dispersed) and order of learning about discrepant group members (poststereotype learning vs. throughout learning).

condition best mimics the conditions of the human studies: In both cases, a stereotype is well established before the experimental counterstereotypic information is encountered. Thus the simulation shows that a simple, incremental learning system such as our recurrent network can account for the pattern of results usually considered to point to subtyping. The attenuation of the traditional subtyping finding in the throughout condition generates a novel prediction that humans may show a much-reduced subtyping effect if the discrepant group members are presented before the stereotype of the group has become well established. Under these conditions, moderate and extreme disconfirmers may have similar impact in reducing stereotyping.

Before turning to an investigation of this novel prediction for human subjects, we address the following question: Why did the network perform as it did?

Study 2B: What has the network learned?

One interesting finding from Study 2A was that the simulation replicated the traditional subtyping finding using a simple, incremental learning strategy. How can this be? Recall that the weight values change over the course of learning for a given simulated subject, from the random starting values (which average 0.00) toward the final weight values that affect the test performance after learning is complete. Thus, to answer this question, we turn to an analysis of how the final connection weights vary as a function of experimental condition. The analysis should also reveal why the traditional subtyping result is attenuated when the stereotype-discrepant members are encountered throughout learning. Our goal here is it to get an intuitive understanding of why the network behaved as it did.

There are 780 weights in a fully interconnected recurrent network with 40 units (i.e. $[(40)(40) - 40]/2 = 780$). However, given our training stimuli, there are only a few different types of connections. We focused our efforts on evaluating three types of connections:[4]

1. ***ST–CST connections***: ST units (units 1–12) remained stereotypic for all group-member stimuli throughout training. CST units (units 13–21) were stereotypic for most of the group-member stimuli, but flipped to counterstereotypic values for approximately one-third of the group-member stimuli. Recall that the stereotypicality of the network's output was tested by applying stereotypic inputs on the ST units and null inputs on the CST units and then recording the values that were output on the CST units. Thus, the stronger the ST–CST connection weights, the better the network generates the stereotypic values on units 13–21 in the test, when given just the group-label attributes on units 1–12 as input (i.e. those attributes that remained stereotypic for all group-member stimuli).

2. ***CST$_a$–CST$_a$ connections***: Recall that in the dispersed conditions, there were three different types of mildly discrepant group-member stimuli, each created by flipping only three of the nine CST units to counterstereotypic values. The CST$_a$–CST$_a$ connections link two units, each of which is from the same set of three, as indicated by the common subscripts. That is, this is a connection between two units that flipped to counterstereotypic values on the same trials. In the concentrated conditions, all nine CST units flipped to counterstereotypic values on the same trials, so all pairs of CST units act as CST$_a$–CST$_a$ connections. In general, the stronger the CST$_a$–CST$_a$ connection weights, the better the stereotypic pattern hangs together across units 13–21.

3. ***CST$_a$–CST$_b$ connections***: In the dispersed conditions, the CST$_a$–CST$_b$ connections link two units, each of which is from a different set of three, as indicated by the different subscripts. That is, this is a connection between two units that both flipped to counterstereotypic values during training, but never on the same trial. In the concentrated conditions, all nine CST units flipped to counterstereotypic values on the same trials, so there is no distinction between a CST$_a$ unit and a CST$_b$ unit. Said another way, in the concentrated conditions, CST$_a$–CST$_a$ connections are the same as CST$_a$–CST$_b$ connections. In general, the stronger the CST$_a$–CST$_b$ connection weights, the better the stereotypic pattern hangs together across units 13–21.

The design of Study 2B was the same as that of Study 2A, a 2 (information distribution: concentrated vs. dispersed) × 2 (learning order: post-stereotype vs. throughout learning) design. As in Study 2A, 10 simulated subjects were run in each of the four experimental conditions. However, instead of logging activation values only once after presenting all 570 training

---

4   ST–ST connections were also analyzed, but revealed no differences between conditions.

trials and a test stimulus, we logged activation values after each stimulus was presented throughout the course of learning. From the activation values and the target values on each trial, we computed the final weight value (using the learning rule described in the Annexe at the end of the chapter).

Method

Procedure

The procedure was identical to that of Study 2A with one exception: We logged activation values after each of the 570 training stimuli was presented rather than logging activation after presentation of a final test stimulus.

Training stimuli

The training stimuli were generated in a manner similar to that used in Study 2A. However, we used a group-member prototype that consisted of a series of 1 values on units 1–21 and 0 values on units 22–40. In generating stimuli from this prototype, we did not add noise to units 1–21 as we did in Study 2A. We did add normally distributed random noise to units 22–40 ($s = 0.2$.) Using group-member stimuli that included activation values equal to 1 with no added noise allowed us to more easily track patterns of coactivation between units.

Background stimuli were generated as they were in Study 2A. The background prototype had zero activation values on all 40 units and normally distributed noise ($s = 0.2$) was added to each input to generate the stimuli. As mentioned above, stimuli were generated for 10 subjects in each of the four conditions.

Dependent measure

The dependent variables in Study 2B were the weights on connections between various types of units. After each training stimulus, the weight-change values were computed by plugging the target and output activation values into the learning rule. The final connection weight was simply computed as the cumulative weight change over the course of the 570 learning trials.

Results

For each simulated subject, the final weight values were averaged over nine randomly selected connections of each type (nine ST–CST, nine CST_a–CST_a, and nine CST_a–CST_b.) These average final weight values for the 40 simulated subjects (10 per condition) were submitted to a 2 (information distribution: concentrated vs. dispersed) × 2 (learning order: post-stereotype vs. throughout learning) ANOVA. A separate analysis was done for each of the three connection types.

ST–CST connections

The ANOVA for the ST–CST connection weights indicated a significant main effect such that the dispersed condition produced stronger positive connections ($M = 0.28$, $SD = 0.06$) than did the concentrated condition ($M = 0.18$, $SD = 0.07$), $F(1, 36) = 26.45$, $p < .0001$. These weight values would suggest that the test output in the dispersed conditions should be more stereotypic than the test output in the concentrated conditions. This was clearly not the case in the Study 2A simulation. In fact, the opposite main effect was found in Study 2A. Thus, the increased positive ST–CST weight learning in the dispersed conditions clearly does not drive the Study 2A results. We turn to analyses of the other types of connections for an explanation of the network's behavior in Study 2A.

CST_a–CST_a connections

The ANOVA for the CST_a–CST_a connection weights indicated significant main effects for both information distribution, $F(1, 36) = 87.94$, $p < .0001$, and order of learning, $F(1, 36) = 6.77$, $p = .013$, that were qualified by a significant interaction, $F(1, 36) = 9.25$, $p = .004$. Generally, the weights in the dispersed condition were more strongly positive than those in the concentrated condition, but this difference was larger in the throughout-learning condition than in the post-stereotype-learning condition (throughout: dispersed $M = 1.15$, $SD = 0.14$ and concentrated $M = 0.68$, $SD = 0.10$; post-stereotype: dispersed $M = 0.94$, $SD = 0.14$ and concentrated $M = 0.70$, $SD = 0.08$). This finding suggests that the output should be more stereotypic in the dispersed condition than in the concentrated condition and that this difference should be more pronounced when the network encounters the counterstereotypic group members throughout learning. The interaction on the CST_a–CST_a weights runs counter to the findings of Study 2A. In Study 2A, the output was more stereotypic for concentrated conditions than for dispersed conditions, especially when the network encountered counterstereotypic group members after the stereotype was established. Although the CST_a–CST_a weights produce a statistically significant interaction, this interaction certainly does not explain the Study 2A results. In fact, the pattern of CST_a–CST_a weights by experimental condition must be compensated for by other weight changes to produce the Study 2A results.

CST_a–CST_b connections

As expected on the basis of finding no explanation of the Study 2A results in our analyses of ST–CST and CST_a–CST_a connections, the ANOVA for the

$CST_a–CST_b$ connection weights produced an interaction that can, in fact, explain the Study 2A results. The $CST_a–CST_b$ ANOVA produced a significant main effect for information distribution, $F(1, 36) = 805.36$, $p < .0001$. The weights are rather strongly positive in the concentrated condition ($M = 0.68$, $SD = 0.085$) but are weakly negative in the dispersed condition ($M = –0.068$, $SD = 0.102$). The findings of strong positive $CST_a–CST_b$ weights in the concentrated condition and mildly negative $CST_a–CST_b$ weights in the dispersed condition are not surprising given that the CST_a and CST_b activation values always positively covaried for stimuli in the concentrated condition but covaried both positively and negatively for stimuli in the dispersed condition. The $CST_a–CST_b$ connection weights are consistent with the main effect found in Study 2A that the concentrated condition produces more stereotypic output and the dispersed condition produces less stereotypic output overall. Note also that this effect is much larger than the opposite main effect mentioned above for ST–CST and $CST_a–CST_b$ connection weights.

The main effect for final $CST_a–CST_b$ weight values was qualified by a significant interaction, $F(1, 36) = 10.92$, $p = .0022$. The interaction is also consistent with the output of the network in Study 2A. As would be expected given the output values in Study 2A, the difference between the final weight values for the concentrated versus dispersed conditions in the post-stereotype condition was larger than the same difference in the throughout condition (post-stereotype: concentrated $M = 0.70$, $SD = 0.07$; dispersed $M = –0.13$, $SD = 0.11$ vs. throughout: concentrated $M = 0.65$, $SD = 0.10$; dispersed $M = –0.01$, $SD = 0.05$).

Discussion

What limits stereotype change in the simulation is quite different from the mechanism proposed by most researchers. The conceptual focus in most current thinking about stereotypes is on the associations between group membership and stereotypic attributes (e.g. Devine, 1989). This focus is also maintained by researchers studying stereotype change, who argue that discrepant group members must keep their group membership salient if their discrepant attributes are to have any impact in producing stereotype change (Brown, Vivian, & Hewstone, 1999; Rothbart & John, 1985; Van Oudenhoven, Groenewoud, & Hewstone, 1996). According to this argument, the key is to make sure a discrepant individual is still seen as a member of the group, so that for the perceiver, the link between group membership and counterstereotypic attributes is strengthened.

Keeping the salience of group membership high for stereotype-disconfirming group members is analogous to boosting the ST–CST weights in our network. However, as Study 2B shows, the ST–CST weights are not responsible for the subtyping-like behavior of the network in Study 2A—that is, its tendency to produce more stereotypic patterns after concentrated rather than dispersed disconfirming information. In fact, somewhat stronger

ST–CST weights were found in the dispersed than in the concentrated condition. We can conclude that this mechanism involving the connections between group membership and stereotypic attributes, despite the attention it has received in the literature, cannot account for our results.

Fortunately, our analyses in Study 2B suggest two other potential mechanisms, involving the degree of cohesion between counterstereotypic attributes. The CST_a–CST_a and CST_a–CST_b connections show different patterns. The CST_a–CST_a weights are more positive in dispersed than in concentrated conditions, suggesting that the cohesion of attributes that are simultaneously counterstereotypic is better maintained in dispersed conditions. This should lead to more stereotypical judgments in the dispersed conditions. Obviously, this is the opposite of what we found in the overall results of our network (Study 2A). The countervailing effect is observed with the CST_a–CST_b connections, which show the exact same pattern as our overall results: a main effect with weights stronger in the concentrated than dispersed condition, and an interaction such that this difference is greater in the poststereotype condition. In other words, with regard to counterstereotypic attributes that are not part of the same set (i.e. not simultaneously counterstereotypic in the dispersed stimuli), the concentrated condition maintains their cohesion better than the dispersed condition. This means that in the test phase those attributes receive support through flows of activation from other attributes as well as from the group label itself.

For an illustration of this mechanism, suppose that stereotypic physics majors are smart and introverted. Counterstereotypic physics majors in a concentrated condition are then stupid and extroverted. Our simulations suggest that the strong covariation between intelligence and introversion in this condition limits stereotype change. When the physics-major group label is encountered, activation flows from the label to both the stereotypic attributes—and in addition activation flows bidirectionally between those attributes. The result is strong, mutually reinforcing activation of the entire stereotypic configuration. In a dispersed condition, on the other hand, some counterstereotypic physics majors are stupid (but introverted) whereas other counterstereotypic physics majors are extroverted (but smart), lowering the covariation between the traits intelligent and introverted. This can effectively weaken the stereotype. Although encountering the group label will still activate both of the stereotypic traits, the reduced strength of the connections between those traits will diminish the overall activation of the whole stereotypic pattern.

Note that this finding can be explained without recourse to typical assumptions about the covariation and therefore the strength of the connections between the group label and the stereotypic attributes differing between concentrated and dispersed conditions. In other words, the mechanism at work in our simulation is quite different from that typically assumed: that the salience of group membership is stronger for moderate disconfirmers than for extreme disconfirmers, with greater salience leading to greater change in the group-label—stereotype association. It is possible that in human perceivers, as well as in our simulation, associations among stereotypic attributes rather than group-membership salience drives the decrease in stereotype change in response to highly atypical group members. Alternatively (and more likely), both mechanisms may play a role.

Although their effect was overshadowed by the opposing effect of the CST_a–CST_b connections in our simulation, the findings for the CST_a–CST_a connections suggest yet a third potential mechanism relevant to stereotype change. The CST_a–CST_a connections were stronger for dispersed than for concentrated stimulus patterns. This suggests that encountering physics majors who are intelligent, introverted, and stylish (the latter attribute being counterstereotypic) might strengthen the stereotypic associations between intelligence and introversion to a greater extent than would encountering purely stereotypic physics majors. Under conditions different from those studied here, it might be possible for this mechanism to produce stronger stereotypicality in a dispersed condition than in a concentrated condition. We leave this possibility to future research.

For now, having established how the network produced a subtyping effect, we turn to a test of the novel hypothesis that the subtyping effect may be diminished in human perceivers when the discrepant group members are encountered throughout learning.

Study 3: Novel groups and subtyping

Study 3 tests the novel prediction suggested by the Study 2A simulation. Essentially, we replicated the design of Study 2 but we tailored the stimuli to a manageable number of behavioral statements that was more in line with the quantity of information provided in prior tests of the subtyping hypothesis with humans.

This investigation goes beyond previous studies of subtyping and stereotype change in two ways. First, we introduced participants to a novel group for which the participants did not have a pre-existing stereotype. In contrast, other studies of subtyping have investigated differences in stereotype change in the context of a well-established stereotype (e.g. physics majors).[5] Thus,

---

5   Maurer, Park, and Rothbart (1995) came close to presenting group members without a pre-established stereotype. However, in their Study 1, the stereotypic attributes were presented to the participants in summary form at the beginning of the experiment, thus going at least part way toward "establishing" the stereotype. In addition, trait ratings for the target group in the Maurer et al. study (Big Brothers) taken at Indiana University for participants presented with only the group label were significantly different from midpoint for three of five characteristics used in this study, suggesting students do have a preexisting stereotype for this group. Maurer et al.'s Study 2 used a gay activist group and, although the instantiations of the stereotype varied, the stereotype was nonetheless one that was pre-existing and was not created from scratch during the course of the lab session.

Study 3 tested whether having a newly established expectation that is based on repeated encounters with individual group-member behaviors is sufficient to create the subtyping pattern of results. The second and more important way in which this study goes beyond previous work is that it tests the prediction that the typical subtyping finding should be drastically reduced when the discrepant group members are learned about throughout the learning process.

In summary, then, we predicted that when people learn about disconfirming group members after an initial exposure to only stereotypic information, they should make less stereotypic ratings in response to the moderately discrepant group members (dispersed) than in response to the highly discrepant group members (concentrated). However, when the discrepant members are learned about throughout the process of learning about the group, people should produce stereotypic ratings in response to the highly discrepant group members (concentrated) that are more similar to those produced in response to moderately discrepant group members (dispersed). A finding that supports these hypotheses would suggest that different strategies might be effective in situations in which one is attempting to challenge existing stereotypes versus in situations in which people are first forming their stereotypes.

Method

Participants and design

Participants were 100 undergraduates at Purdue University who participated in the experiment in exchange for partial course credit. The experiment was a 2 (information distribution: concentrated vs. dispersed) × 2 (learning order: post-stereotype vs. throughout) design with both manipulations created by rearranging the stimulus presentation while maintaining a constant set of behavioral information across conditions.

Procedure

Participants recorded demographic information (e.g. race, gender) that was not part of the present experiment (and they were told as much). Each was then placed in a separate cubicle at a computer terminal. Instructions, stimuli, and dependent measures were all delivered on the computer. Participants were simply told they would read about some members of an unnamed group and that their task was to form an impression of the group on the basis of what they learned about the group members.

Computer instructions then informed them that each screen would describe one member of the group and that after they had read about each one, they could press the space bar to read about the next one. Each screen presented three descriptive behaviors attributed to one of the group members as described in the *Training stimuli* section below. Each group-member description was presented for a minimum of 5 *s* to avoid: (1) participants ignoring the stimuli and just pressing the space bar; and (2) inadvertent key presses.

After the last group member was presented, the computer described the trait-rating task. Participants were instructed to rate the group on several different traits. They pressed a number key corresponding to their response for each of the trait words. The experimenter then verbally debriefed, thanked, and excused the participants.

Training stimuli

The stimuli were analogous to those presented in the Study 2 simulation. However, we introduced fewer stimuli in this study than we did in the simulations. This allowed us to avoid overloading our participants and to maintain a stronger parallel with previous studies on subtyping. In addition, we did not introduce non-member stimuli (background individuals) to our human participants because, unlike the networks, our participants already had a lifetime of experience with a variety of people. Finally, to parallel previous studies on subtyping, we simply told participants that all of the people they would be learning about belonged to the same group. This differs from the simulations. In the simulations, each individual stimulus had some stereotypic activation values (units 1–12) that provided the network with a cue to group membership.

We created 30 descriptions of people from behaviors relevant to friendliness, intelligence, and adventurousness. We chose behaviors that were rated as neutral on two of the traits and either above or below the neutral point on the third trait. Each group member was described by three behaviors, with each behavior reflecting one of the three trait dimensions. As the majority of the behaviors involved being friendly, intelligent, and adventurous, we assumed that participants would form stereotypes that would reflect these traits (Sherman, 1996).

Each stereotypic group member was described by one friendly, one intelligent, and one adventurous behavior. Each moderately disconfirming group member was described by two stereotypic behaviors and one counterstereotypic behavior. That is, a moderately discrepant group member was described by either an unfriendly or an unintelligent or an unadventurous behavior and was stereotypic in terms of the behaviors on the other two trait dimensions. Each extremely disconfirming group member was described by one unfriendly, one unintelligent, and one unadventurous behavior.

The ratio of stereotypic to counterstereotypic information was 4 : 1 with 24 stereotypic behaviors and 6 counterstereotypic behaviors on each of the three trait dimensions. In the concentrated conditions, 6 of the 30 group members were discrepant from the rest of the group on all three trait dimensions. In the dispersed conditions, 18 of the 30 group members were discrepant from the rest of the group, but each on only one trait dimension. Again, we held the total amount of confirming and disconfirming evidence constant (24 stereotypical and 6 counterstereotypical behaviors on each trait dimension).

Previous research indicates that 12 group members should be sufficient to establish expectations about the group (Sherman, 1996.) Thus, in the poststereotype condition, participants did not read about discrepant group members until they had first read descriptions of at least 12 stereotypical group members. Following these first 12 stereotypical group members, the remaining 18 group members were presented, including the 6 extremely discrepant group members in the concentrated condition or the 18 moderately discrepant group members in the dispersed condition. Behaviors of the appropriate type for each stimulus were selected randomly for each participant. In addition, the order of presentation of the different stimulus types was randomized with the following constraints: The first 12 had to be stereotypic, and of the remaining 18, either 2 extremely disconfirming (and 4 stereotypic) group members were presented in each block of six presentations or 6 moderately disconfirming group members (2 of each type) were presented in each block of six presentations.

To create the conditions in which the discrepant group members were presented throughout the learning sequence, we simply altered the order of presentation. In the concentrated condition, one extremely discrepant group member was presented in each block of five group members. For the dispersed condition, one moderately discrepant group member of each type was presented in each block of five group members. Behaviors of the appropriate type were again selected randomly, and the order of presentation was randomized within the blocks of five group members.

Dependent measures

The dependent measures were simply ratings of the group on nine trait scales. Participants rated how much each trait described the group on a scale of 1 (*not at all*) to 7 (*very much*). Three of the traits reflected the trait of friendliness (friendly, sociable, nice), three reflected adventurousness (adventurous, daring, courageous), and three reflected honesty (honest, trustworthy, upstanding). The first six traits allowed us to test the hypotheses that encountering stereotype-discrepant information has differential effects on the extent to which the challenged traits are rated as descriptive of the group. The last three traits allowed us to see if similar effects would arise for a trait that was not stereotypical, but that was the same valence as the stereotypical traits (i.e. whether participants would display evaluative generalization). The trait ratings were presented in a different random order for each participant.

Results and discussion

To remain consistent with the dependent variable used in the simulation, we calculated discrepancy from stereotypic values. That is, we calculated participants' deviations from the most stereotypic rating for each trait rating (i.e. each rating was subtracted from 7). The deviation scores for the three friendly traits and the three adventurous traits were averaged together for each participant. These average discrepancy scores were submitted to a 2 (information distribution) × 2 (learning order) between-subjects ANOVA that indicated a significant interaction, $F(1, 97) = 5.62$, $p = .02$. Figure 10.2 shows the pattern of means for the stereotype-discrepancy scores.

When stereotypical group members are presented initially and stereotype-discrepant group members are encountered only later, the subtyping effect is obtained. That is, moderately disconfirming group members led to less stereotypic perceptions than did extremely disconfirming group members (moderate $M = 1.73$, $SD = 0.78$; extreme $M = 1.40$, $SD = 0.64$). Recall that the simulation predicted that this effect would be drastically reduced if the discrepant group members were encountered throughout learning. The results indicate that, for human participants, the finding traditionally viewed as reflecting subtyping is at least attenuated (and in this study actually reversed) when disconfirming group members are encountered throughout the learning process (moderate $M = 1.63$, $SD = 0.73$; extreme $M = 2.02$, $SD = 0.87$).

To see if this pattern extended to trait dimensions that were not stereotypic but were similar in valence to the stereotypic traits, we took the average discrepancy score of the three honesty-related ratings and submitted them to a 2 (information distribution) × 2 (learning order) ANOVA. The results indicated that neither of the main effects nor the interaction reached statistical levels of significance (moderate post-stereotype $M = 1.81$, $SD = 0.83$; extreme post-stereotype $M = 1.68$, $SD = 0.78$; moderate throughout $M = 1.91$, $SD = 0.94$; extreme throughout $M = 1.98$, $SD = 0.81$). At a minimum, this suggests that the effects are not present with the same strength as they are for the stereotypic traits. A stronger interpretation would be that these effects

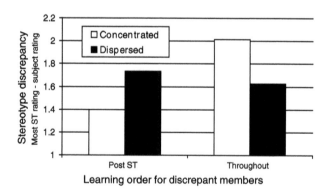

Figure 10.2 Stereotype (ST) discrepancy for human participants' stereotype-relevant trait ratings as a function of information distribution (concentrated vs. dispersed) and order of learning about discrepant group members (poststereotype learning vs. throughout learning).

do not extend to nonstereotypic traits of the same valence. However, the latter claim cannot be fully substantiated at the levels of power associated with this experiment.

GENERAL DISCUSSION

The current set of studies suggests that approaching stereotype learning and change from the perspective of connectionist models of memory can be illuminating. First, we explained that our recurrent network, like all standard connectionist models, operates as an incremental learner. This type of learning is well aligned with the bookkeeping model of stereotype change. In fact, in Study 1 a simulation including either 15 or 45 stereotype disconfirmers suggested that the network does, indeed, simulate the bookkeeping aspects of stereotype change. That is, the output of the network gets increasingly less stereotypic as the number of counterstereotypical stimuli presented increases.

Not surprisingly, the network's incremental learning operations were able to simulate gradual, incremental change. The next step was to see if the network could produce output consistent with typical subtyping results. That is, if we held the total complement of information provided constant, would the network produce less stereotypic output in response to moderately disconfirming group members than in response to extremely disconfirming members? The simulation in Study 2A clearly showed that the answer to this question was "yes" when conditions approximated those used in the concentrated/dispersed paradigm. Thus, when the network was allowed to first develop its stereotype, its subsequent encounters with moderately disconfirming group members led it to produce less stereotypic output than when the subsequent encounters were with extremely disconfirming group members.

This finding alone is rather fascinating. With no suggestion of attributional or attentional processes that would allow a perceiver to cast an extreme disconfirmer as a special type of group member, the network nonetheless produces output that parallels the responses from subtyping studies. This finding suggests that the subtyping effects found in the dispersed/concentrated paradigm may be the result of a process of incremental learning. This argument achieves parsimony, in that both the bookkeeping and subtyping effects on stereotype change can be accounted for by the same operations.

We acknowledge that Yzerbyt, Coull, and Rocher's (1999) finding that cognitive load diminishes subtyping suggests an alternate, more effortful, mechanism for dismissing disconfirmers. We do not claim that incremental effects fully account for all dismissals of disconfirmers. Rather we claim that incremental effects contribute to the subtyping effect, at least as studied in conditions such as the concentrated/dispersed paradigm in which attributes covary differently in different conditions. Yzerbyt et al. (1999; see also Kunda & Oleson, 1995) did not use a concentrated/dispersed paradigm and, in fact, studied only one to three targets, so these experiments would not necessarily provide covariance information and would not necessarily be expected to be subject to the mechanism we propose here.

Study 2B went on to reveal exactly how the incremental learning produced a subtyping-like result. The key to the effect displayed in the simulation is not a change in group–attribute associations as has been proposed by some researchers. Instead, it is the attribute–attribute associations that are altered by exposure to moderate disconfirmers. Specifically, associations between stereotypic attributes that are challenged by some group members and not by others are weakened, producing a weakened propensity to combine these attributes into the complete stereotype pattern. Although increasing group–attribute associations for highly atypical group members might provide some payoff in an effort to diminish stereotyping, it will not attack an underlying mechanism of weakened attribute–attribute associations.[6]

The simulation approach thus replicated bookkeeping and subtyping effects and suggested an alternate mechanism for subtyping effects. The contribution of the simulation work does not stop here, however. Because recurrent network memories are dynamic and explicitly specify learning (and change), thinking about stereotyping from a recurrent memory perspective led to our interest in the effects of extreme and moderate disconfirmers that are encountered throughout learning. When we simulated this condition, we found that the difference in the impact of moderate and extreme disconfirmers was attenuated when the disconfirmers were presented throughout learning, before a stereotype had been well established. Whereas moderate disconfirmers are more effective in bringing about change in an already-learned stereotype than are extreme disconfirmers, the simulation suggested moderate and extreme disconfirmers would be more similar in their ability to weaken stereotypes when they were encountered throughout learning.

Of course, a simulation is just that, a simulation. We had to go further to see if the novel prediction made by the simulation held with human participants. As Study 3 shows, the novel prediction received support. That is, the interaction effect in the human participants' data parallels that of the simulation. More specifically, the model was correct in predicting that learning about disconfirmers throughout learning would reduce the advantage that moderately atypical group members have over highly atypical group members in their ability to retard stereotypic responding. However, the model did not go as far as to predict the crossover interaction.

What might account for this unexpected crossover in the human data? First, recognize that the difference in the non-crossover interaction of the simulation (see Figure 10.1) and the crossover interaction of the human data (see Figure 10.2) can be accounted for by a shift in the main effect for concentrated versus dispersed information. (If you simply add 1 to the

---

6   For a different account, see Chapter 9, Simulation 4.

concentrated conditions in the simulation, you get a crossover pattern similar to the one exhibited in the human data.) Relative to the predicted interaction, such a change in the main effect is of less conceptual interest, and it could stem from several sources. Remember that our network models a slow learning, long-term type of memory. In contrast, in our human study we cannot divorce the effects of slow learning processes from those of fast learning processes (e.g. McClelland, McNaughton, & O'Reilly, 1995; Smith & DeCoster, 2000). Rather, in humans, the fast and slow learning systems work in concert. In the fast learning system, unusual events tend to have greater impact on memory than typical events do (e.g. Hastie & Kumar, 1979). Arguably, the extreme disconfirmers (concentrated condition) might seem particularly unusual to human perceivers. Contributions from the fast learning system in humans might explain the difference between the non-crossover interaction of the simulation and the crossover interaction of the human data. Further research attempting to dissociate slow and fast learning in humans might help clarify the contributions of each to stereotype development and change.

Consider also that humans are not blank slates when they walk into the laboratory. Unlike the network, they have substantially more information in memory than that pertaining to the experimental stimuli and some arbitrary background set of individuals. Given this, and the fact that the network is solely a slow learning system, it is remarkable that the model was able to predict an interaction that bore out in the human data. Again, in both the simulation and the human data, moderate disconfirmers had relatively less advantage over extreme disconfirmers in producing stereotype change when the atypical group members were encountered throughout learning.

This set of findings is interesting in both an applied sense and a modeling sense. The applied sense admittedly goes beyond our current data. Our results suggest, however, that changing an adult's well-established stereotype may be best accomplished through encounters with large numbers of moderate disconfirmers. In contrast, given the same overall body of evidence regarding the stereotyped group, changing the stereotype being developed by a child may be accomplished equally or even more effectively through encounters with relatively fewer extreme disconfirmers. In more general terms, moderate disconfirmers may bring about more stereotype change but extreme and moderate disconfirmers may be similarly effective at retarding the development of stereotypes.

The interest from a modeling perspective is threefold. First, we provide an alternative explanation for a set of findings that are currently explained by subtyping mechanisms. Second, simulations with the recurrent network allowed us to make a novel prediction that was then established as being supported (or oversupported!) with humans. The existence of this new prediction falsifies the sometimes-expressed view that connectionist models are nothing but sophisticated data-fitting tools, able to capture any existing findings but not to make predictions that go beyond current data. And finally, this perspective offers parsimony. The simple incremental learning mechanism of our recurrent network can account for three apparently quite different types of stereotyping phenomena: (1) change that corresponds to bookkeeping; (2) enhanced change for dispersed over concentrated information if the stereotype is established; and (3) similar stereotyping for concentrated and dispersed information if the stereotype is not well established.

In closing, as suggested by Elman et al.'s (1996) simulation of conversion-like behavior in a recurrent network, the present studies also confirm that the overt responses of recurrent networks do not necessarily resemble the patterns one might expect based on the underlying bookkeeping-like mechanism of learning. We feel that these networks, with their dynamic nature, hold prom-ise for increasing our understanding of stereotype change. They might also encourage social-psychological researchers to increase their focus on stereo-type development, an area that has been relatively neglected. We are far from understanding the intricacies of prejudice, and the model discussed here deals only with cognition while remaining mute on the motivational aspects of stereotyping and prejudice. Nonetheless, we suggest that the success of the recurrent model described here warrants its consideration as a useful tool as we continue to slowly progress toward an understanding of why those "lovely people" fail to sufficiently affect our assessments of the groups from which they hail.

ANNEXE

Details of simulation

The simulation used the cs++ program of PDP++, with the cs_det.def defaults (appropriate for a deterministic network). This annexe can be better understood when read in conjunction with the PDP++ user manual found at ftp://cnbc.cmu.edu/pub/pdp++/old_v1/docs/pdp++-user-manual-1.2.ps.gz, especially Chapter 16.

Network and connections

The network consists of a single module with 40 units. Bidirectional connec-tions were present between each pair of units. As such, the network operates as a pattern-recognition system. Inputs are applied and the network learns to replicate those inputs on the units after settling. The same 40 units thus act as both inputs and as outputs.

Units

The standard sigmoid unit specification was used with activation limits of .98 and −.98.

Settling and learning

The training teaches the network to replicate patterns of activation that occurred during training. That is, the network does pattern recognition (with inherent generalization to similar patterns). When input activations are applied to the units, the network flows activation across connections (using the current set of connection weights), repeatedly updating activations on each unit in each time step until the network "settles" on the output values. The learning rule is then applied to encourage better recognition of that stimulus on future presentation. Specifically, we used contrastive Hebbian learning (Movellan & McClelland, 1993). This learning rule updates connection weights after each stimulus presentation by subtracting two simple Hebbian terms. The minus phase is the state of the network when it settles after application of an input pattern of activation. That is, inputs are applied to the 40 units, and activation propagates across connections repeatedly over multiple time steps until the network settles. Unit activations are synchronous. The network is considered settled into a final state when no activation change is greater than 0.01 from one time step to the next. The settling process used parameters cyclemax 1000, step 0.2. After settling, all 40 activation values are recorded as the "minus" activation values, a_i^- for all units i.

The plus phase is the state when both inputs and outputs are presented to the network. For a single-layer network such as ours, this is the same as clamping the units' activation values to the desired (or input) values, a_i^+ for all units i. The contrastive Hebbian learning (CHL) algorithm updates connection weights in proportion to the difference of the coproduct of the activation values in the plus and minus phases: $\Delta w_{ij} = l(a_i^+ a_j^+ - a_i^- a_j^-)$, where i is the receiving unit and j is the sending unit across the connection between unit i and unit j. The *a* symbols refer to final activation values (after settling) of units i and j in the plus and minus phases. The learning rate, *l*, was 0.01. Our simulations used parameters soft-then-hard-clamp, clamp gain1. The weights were constrained to be symmetric and in all other respects used PDP++'s standard constraint satisfaction connection specification.

You can think of the CHL rule as having two component parts. First, changing weights in proportion to the product of plus-phase (or desired) activation values is the basic Hebbian learning rule. This change strengthens connections between units that are coactive in the input patterns (which are the desired output patterns) and weakens connections between units that are opposite in activation for the input patterns. Second, subtracting the product of the minus-phase activation for each pair of units can be seen as anti-Hebbian learning: It discourages the network from taking these patterns of activation in the future. With both of these components happening simultaneously, the CHL rule essentially tells the network, "Don't go into the pattern into which you settle naturally (minus phase). Instead go to the pattern I tell you to go to (plus phase)."

If the network performs perfectly in the minus phase (in which inputs are applied and the network settles freely), the network perfectly replicates its own inputs as outputs. In this case, the minus-phase activations equal the plus-phase activations, and the two terms in the CHL equation cancel out so that no further weight change occurs.

Learning procedure

Learning proceeded until all stimuli in a simulation had been presented one time. Note that our numbers of stimuli were chosen so that learning had reached asymptote by the end of training with a set of 150 stereotypic group-member stimuli plus 150 background individuals. Specifics about the stimuli are described in the *Method* sections of the simulation studies presented in this article.

SIMULATION EXERCISES

You can now explore the simulations described in the article. Unlike the original article, the exercises do not use the contrastive Hebbian learning algorithm (as this is currently unavailable in FIT), but rather the conventional delta learning algorithm. To reproduce the results obtained by Queller and Smith (2002), however, you have to use the non-linear recurrent network variant and some particular parameters settings. This restriction may indicate that their simulations are less robust against some changes in the network parameters. For all other aspects, these simulations are very much similar to the exercises from Chapter 7. You are expected to have some experience with the FIT program, perhaps because you have completed some of the exercises in Chapter 7.

Exercise 1: Bookkeeping simulation 1

Choose menu **File | Open Project**, search for *Queller+Smith02_1.ft2* in folder *Chapter 10*, and click the **Open** button. Alternatively, you can press the 📂 speed button.

Specifying trials

Click the **Trial** tab to open the Trial Grid. The two top rows show 13 input units representing the information or characteristics of a group, of an individual group member, and other unspecified traits or characteristics. As you will see later, each *localist* unit will be "blown up" to three *distributed* units. This is also indicated in the second row, where each unit's name gets the range that is applied in the distributed version. You can change these names either by double clicking, or by choosing the **Data | Edit Column Names** menu.

There is a single Learning Trial Category *$1* for learning a stereotypical group member (embedded in some background noise). It contains 150 trials of background patterns, and 150 trials of the same member exemplar. Additional random noise is applied to the background and the non-specified characteristics of the exemplar. Technically, you do this by adding only noise when the external activation is 0 (see more about it shortly). Next is the Learning Trial Category for either 15 or 45 counterstereotypic exemplars in Category *$2* and *$3* respectively. The counterstereotypic characteristics are obtained by reversing the 1 and −1 values from the stereotypical member units *13–21* (while the characteristics from group units *1–12* are not changed).

Testing patterns never get additional noise. To test the degree to which the member units deviate from the stereotype after exposure to a counterstereotypic exemplar, Queller and Smith (2002) "computed a stereotype-discrepancy score by first squaring the difference between each unit's output and the prototypical stereotypic value for that unit and then summing these squared differences across the nine units" (p.304). You do something very similar. After learning about the background and stereotypical exemplar (Category $1), you test the stereotypical pattern by priming the group units and then reading off the member units. Next, you do the same after exposure to the counterstereotypic member (Category $2 or $3). I will specify below how a squared difference score between these two results is computed in the Session Grid.

Specifying sessions

Click the **Session** tab to open the Session Grid and to specify the ordering of the Learning and Test Trial Categories. As you can see, Learning Category *$1* is followed by Test Category *$50*, and then condition 15 or 45 is again followed by Test Category *$50*. Each of these Test Categories is given a different number (*0* to *2*) in **IV2**. The difference score is computed in **DV1**. To indicate that you want the absolute differences score between the first and second Test Category *$50*, you enter a *double minus sign* − − in the **DV1** column for the first test. The obtained resulting activations for the second test will be subtracted from those of the first test, using the formula:

new simulated value at 2nd test =

$$\sqrt{[(\text{simulated value at 2nd test}) -- (\text{simulated value at 1st test})]^2}$$

where the *simulated value at the 1st test* is obtained from the − − cell. (More details can be found in the help file in the section on **Special DV Data Values**).

Specifying the simulation parameters

Choose the **Simulation | Parameters** menu, or press the ❀ speed button.
  In the top panel, four drop-down list boxes list the major options:

- In the **Model** option box, the *Non-linear Recurrent* model developed by McClelland and Rumelhart (1988) is chosen. If not, select that model now.
- In the **External Coding** option box, *Normal Distributed Pattern (M = activation, SD = 0.2)* is selected. If not, select that option now. This option indicates that you are now using a distributed representation for the exemplar, with a fixed activation pattern for each unit randomly selected from a normal distribution with mean the activation indicated in the cells and standard deviation 0.2.
- In the **External Noise (while Learning)** option box, select *Add Normal (M = 0, SD = 0.2)*. This is used to add random noise to the background, using a similar Normal Distribution with mean = 0 and standard deviation = 0.2.
- In the **Response** option box, select the standard option *Mean*.

Now Click the **Distributed Coding and Noise** tab. Among other things, we will make sure that the noisy pattern of the exemplar remains fixed during all runs, while the noise for the background and unspecified characteristics of the exemplar change after each trial.

- First, you specify that each localist unit will be extended or "blown up" to a pattern of distributed activations across three subfeatures or units. Simply enter *3* in the **# of (Micro-) Features per Unit** field.
- The **Also on Zero Activation** Check Box must **not** be marked. This makes sure that the background (and unspecified other characteristics) get no fixed activation pattern throughout the whole simulation run, in contrast to the exemplar that gets a fixed activation pattern (because its external activation in the cell differs from zero).
- In addition, specify that the noise in the Learning Trials applies to all Learning Categories *1–49*.
- Importantly, you should now indicate that the noise is applied *only* to units with **Zero External Activation** (as specified in the Trial Grid). Hence, noise is produced only for the background and unspecified characteristics.
- Leave the other parameters blank, or set them to *No*.

Now you enter the parameters in the other tabs. Click first the **General** tab. Specify in **Session** that you want to run session *1*, and select in **Graph Simulated Values** the button *yes* (automatically, the **Log Simulated Values** will turn to *yes* also). In addition, set **Randomize Order for All Learning Trials** to *yes*, and specify *10* runs to simulate 10 participants as specified by Queller and Smith (2002). Leave the categories to which this applies to *1–49*. Set all other parameters to *no*. Finally, click the **Model** tab. Enter a **learning rate** of *0.01* as in the article, and *0.15* for **estr** and **istr**, *0.75* for **decay**, and *10* **cycles**. Leave the other parameters blank, or set them to *auto* or *no*.

Running the simulation

To run the simulation as specified above, choose the **Simulation | Run Simulation** menu, or press the ⚙ speed button. If you want to follow the simulation step by step, choose the **Simulation | Parameters** menu, press the **General** tab, and set **View Details** to *View*. Alternatively, you can hit the ⚙ speed button for a display of the network or the ⚙ speed button for a tabular display.

After the simulation is finished, the **Graph** tab will open automatically (because you requested a graph). Make the following selections:

- **filter**: *Condition*, and enter values **From** *1* **To** *4*. This enables us to take only the internal activation values generated by Test Category $50 that reflect the difference score of interest, and to filter out the baseline values taken from the first Test Category $50.
- **X-Axis**: *Condition*.
- **X-Axis Labels**: *IVLabel*.
- **Y-Axis Line(s)**: select only the simulated **DV**. The variable name (*difference*) is preceded by a ~ sign to denote that this is a simulated value.

Then select **List Stats**. After hitting the **Graph Log** button, you will see a graph of the simulation results.

For the numerical results (means and statistics) press the **Listing** tab. Although you used another recurrent variant and a different learning algorithm, you can see that this simulation also results in a significant difference between conditions 15 and 45. This is revealed by the results of the **Unpaired *t*-test** and the **Between-subjects ANOVA**.

Questions

1. It is unclear from the article whether Queller and Smith (2002) used exactly the same exemplar in each condition (as in Chapter 7) or whether they used different exemplars at each trial. In the simulation described above, the same exemplar pattern was chosen throughout the whole simulation run. However, there are alternatives:

   - You can specify a different distributed pattern for each exemplar for each trial within a simulation run. To do so, omit the noise in the distributed coding (by selecting the **Parameter** tab and selecting in the **External Coding** option box the entry *Normal distributed pattern without noise*). Then, select the **Distributed Coding and Noise** tab and choose the radio button *also* for the **Noise on Zero Activation** option. This provides different random noise for each trial on zero and non-zero activation inputs.

- Alternatively, you can use a different exemplar for each run. To do so, choose the **Distributed Coding and Noise** tab and enter *1* Run for the option **Reshuffle the Distributed Coding each Run**.

2. You can experiment a little bit with the parameters of the non-linear model. Choose the **Simulation | Parameters** menu or press the ✿ speed button, and enter different model parameters in the **Model** tab. Alternatively, you can choose the linear model. After running the simulation, do you note any difference with the previous simulation? You will probably note that serious deviations from some of the original parameter values results in non-significant differences between the 15 and 45 conditions. Can you explain this?

3. You can also explore whether there is really a need to have 200 presentations of the exemplar. Can you have sufficient stereotypic exemplar formation with 20, 5, or 2 exemplar trials?

Exercise 2: Subtyping simulation 2A

Choose menu **File | Open Project**, search for *Queller+Smith02_2a.ft2* in folder *Chapter 10*, and click the **Open** button. Alternatively, you can press the 🖼 speed button. All specifications are identical to the previous exercise, except for the following changes noted below.

Click the **Trial** tab to open the Trial Grid. As you can see, Categories *$3* and *$4* reflect the post-stereotype learning conditions after prior learning of stereotypical member exemplars (Category *$1*), while Categories *$13* and *$14* reflect the throughout condition where Category *$1* is an integral part of the Learning Categories (instead of coming prior to them). In each category, the counterstereotypical member is either completely the reverse of the stereotypical pattern (see concentrated condition), or is partly reversed in only one unit (or three distributed units; see dispersed condition). Note that a "fake" Learning Category *$9* (with 1 trial consisting of zero activations) was used before the first Testing Category in the throughout condition. This is needed because at least one (empty) Learning Trial is needed before any Test Trial (otherwise an error will appear).

Click the **Session** tab to open the Session Grid and verify how these changes are implemented here.

In column **DV1**, the human data from the experiment conducted by Queller and Smith (2002) are provided. After running the simulation, *t*-tests reveal that there is a significant difference between the concentrated and dispersed condition for the post-stereotype learning condition, $t(18) = 9.00$,

$p < .001$, but not for the throughout condition. This was also the case in the simulation of Queller and Smith (2002). Our simulation also reveals a non-significant positive correlation of 0.68 between the human data and the simulation.

Questions

You can explore the same questions as in the previous exercise.

Exercise 3: Subtyping simulation 2B

Choose menu **File | Open Project**, search for *Queller+Smith02_2b.ft2* in folder *Chapter 10*, and click the **Open** button. Alternatively, you can press the 🖘 speed button. Again, all specifications are identical to the previous exercise, except for the following noted below.

Unlike Queller and Smith (2002) we retain the noise in all patterns to be as close as possible to Simulation 2A. The only difference concerns the test trials. The procedure used here is broadly similar to Queller and Smith (2002). However, instead of measuring each change in connection weights during learning (as they did), you measure the final connection weight after the training has ended. You test the stereotypical → counterstereotypical (ST–CST) connections of the group and the members, respectively, and the counterstereotypical$_a$ → counterstereotypical$_b$ (CST$_a$–CTS$_b$) connections within the members. You are not going to test the counterstereotypical$_a$ → counterstereotypical$_a$ (CST$_a$–CTS$_a$) connections within the members because, to do so, you would have to abandon the automatic distributed representation and implement a distributed representation entirely by yourself to test the connections within each set of reversed (counterstereotypical) activations. (However, you can attempt to do this as an extra exercise.)

After running the simulation, the ANOVA and t-tests reveal for the CST$_a$–CTS$_b$ connections a significant difference between the concentrated and dispersed condition for the post-stereotype learning condition, $t(58) = 40.56$, $p < .001$, indicating more stereotype discrepancy for the dispersed condition, and also for the throughout condition although to a lesser extent, $t(58) = 24.28$, $p < .001$. This was also the case in the simulation of Queller and Smith (2002), and this pattern explains the Simulation 2A results. Moreover, you also find for the ST–CTS connections a significant difference between the concentrated and dispersed condition for the post-stereotype learning condition, $t(18) = 21.00$, $p < .001$, but not for the throughout condition, $t(18) = 1.23$, *ns*. Although this pattern was not revealed in Queller and Smith (2002), it may additionally explain the Simulation 2A results. Indeed, the means indicate that the ST–CTS connections (which reflect the stereotypicality of the member exemplar) are stronger for the concentrated condition than for the dispersed condition given post-stereotype learning, and hence may explain why the divergence from the stereotypical pattern was smaller in the concentrated condition than in the dispersed condition (as revealed in Simulation 2A).

Questions

1. Explore the questions in Exercise 2.
2. What was an alternative explanation for the differential results of dispersed versus concentrated counterstereotypical exemplars by Van Rooy et al. (2003; see Chapter 9)? Is this incompatible with the present explanation? Why?
3. You can test the counterstereotypical$_a$ → counterstereotypical$_a$ (CST$_a$–CTS$_a$) connections within the members. To do so, you have to implement a distributed representation unit by unit without the use of the automatic distributed representation option. What are the results? Do they conform to the simulation findings of Queller and Smith (2002)?

Part 4
Attitudes

11 A connectionist model of attitude formation and change*

Frank Van Overwalle and
Frank Siebler

This paper discusses a recurrent connectionist network, simulating empirical phenomena usually explained by current dual-process approaches of attitudes, thereby focusing on the processing mechanisms that may underlie both central and peripheral routes of persuasion. Major findings in attitude formation and change involving both processing modes are reviewed and modeled from a connectionist perspective. We use an autoassociative network architecture with a linear activation update and the delta learning algorithm for adjusting the connection weights. The network is applied to well-known experiments involving deliberative attitude formation as well as the use of heuristics of length, consensus, expertise and mood. All these empirical phenomena are successfully reproduced in the simulations. Moreover, the proposed model is shown to be consistent with algebraic models of attitude formation (Fishbein & Ajzen, 1975). The discussion centers on how the proposed network model may be used to unite and formalize current ideas and hypotheses on the processes underlying attitude acquisition, and how it can be deployed to develop novel hypotheses in the attitude domain.

Evaluations of our environment are a ubiquitous aspect of human life. Attitudes pervade our thinking because they provide valenced summaries of the favorable and unfavorable objects and organisms, and so serve as a behavioral guide to approach or avoid them. Without such a spontaneous guidance by our evaluations, survival in a complex and, sometimes, threatening world would be impossible.

Social psychologists have made substantial progress in the understanding of attitudes. Most definitions proposed in the literature point to the notion that an attitude involves the categorization of an object along an evaluative dimension. In an extensive overview of theorizing and research, Eagly and Chaiken (1993, p.1) defined an attitude as "a psychological tendency that is expressed by evaluating a particular entity with some degree of favor or

* Adapted from *Personality and Social Psychology Review, 2005, 9,* 231–274. Copyright 2005 by Lawrence Erlbaum Associates. Reprinted with permission of the publisher.

disfavor". Attitudes are stored in memory where they persist over time, and from where they "become active automatically on the mere presence or mention of the object in the environment" (Bargh, Chaiken, Govender, & Pratto, 1992, p.893). After being activated, they provide a ready aid for interaction while at the same time freeing the person from deliberative processes. Furthermore, they aid in a coherent interpretation of the environment by biasing our preferences in a congruent manner (Schuette & Fazio, 1995).

How do attitudes reside in memory? Perhaps the most prominent view is that attitudes are stored in memory in the form of object–evaluation associations. As Fazio (1990, p.81) noted:

> An attitude is viewed as an association in memory between a given object and one's evaluation of that object. This definition implies that the strength of an attitude, like any construct based on associative learning, can vary. That is, the strength of the association between the object and the evaluation can vary. It is this associative strength that is postulated to determine the chronic accessibility of the attitude and, hence, the likelihood that the attitude will be activated automatically when the individual encounters the attitude object.

Empirical tests of this view of attitudes as object–evaluation associations have yielded confirming results. For instance, participants who had been induced to express their attitudes repeatedly, which should strengthen the object–evaluation association, have been found to respond relatively quickly to direct inquiries about their attitudes (for an overview, see Fazio, 1990). However, attitudes are more than evaluations. As stated by Chaiken, Duckworth, and Darke (1999), "attitudes are represented in memory not only as mere object–evaluation linkages (e.g. Fazio, 1990), but also in a more complex, structural form wherein cognitive, affective and behavioral associations also appear as object–association linkages . . . When such linkages are many . . ., or when such linkages are evaluatively consistent . . ., attitudes are stronger and thus manifest greater persistence, resistance to change and predictability over behavior" (p.121).

Until now, however, there has been little theoretical advancement in our understanding of the storage and strengthening of attitude object associations in human memory. We concur with Eiser, Fazio, and colleagues (2003) that "attitude theorists . . . have tended to make relatively little use of paradigms developed in other areas of learning research. . . . The time is ripe for a renewed analysis of the learning processes underlying the acquisition of attitudes" (pp.1221–1222). In particular, we present a recurrent connectionist model (McClelland & Rumelhart, 1985) that describes how attitude associations are developed, strengthened, and maintained in memory. Connectionist approaches have enjoyed an increasing interest in psychology during the last decade and in particular in social psychology, because they offer a new perspective on diverse social psychological phenomena, including person impression formation (Smith & DeCoster, 1998; Van Overwalle & Labiouse, 2004), causal attribution (Read & Montoya, 1999; Van Overwalle, 1998), group biases (Kashima, Woolcock, & Kashima, 2000; Queller & Smith, 2002; Van Rooy, Van Overwalle, Vanhoomissen, Labiouse, & French, 2003), and many other social judgments (for a review, see Read & Miller, 1998; see also Chapters 5–12).

There are several important characteristics that make connectionist approaches superior to earlier attitude models (for an accessible introduction to connectionist networks, see McLeod, Plunkett, & Rolls, 1998). First, a key difference is that the connectionist architecture and processing mechanisms are based on analogies with properties of the human brain. This allows a view of the mind as an adaptive learning mechanism that develops accurate mental representations of the world. Learning is modeled as a process of online adaptation of existing knowledge to novel information provided by the environment. Specifically, the network changes the weights of the connections with the attitude object so as to better represent the accumulated history of co-occurrences between objects and their attributes and evaluations. Most traditional algebraic and associative models in social psychology (for an overview, see Fishbein & Ajzen, 1975), in contrast, are incapable of learning. In many algebraic models, attitudes are not stored somewhere in memory so that, in principle, they need to be reconstructed from their constituent components (i.e. attributes) every time an attitude is accessed (but see Anderson, 1971). Earlier associative models, proposed in social psychology, can only spread activation along associations but provide no mechanism to update the weights of these associations. This lack of a learning mechanism in earlier models is a significant restriction. In connectionist models, retrieval and judgment is also reconstructive in the sense that activation spreading along the object–valence association is needed to reactivate the evaluation associated with the attitude. However, this involves dramatically less computational steps than retrieving all constituent attributes and their evaluations, and computing some sort of algebraic integration of it (Fishbein & Ajzen, 1975). The present approach is consistent with the idea that strong attitudes are stored in object–valence associations that are easily accessible, whereas weak attitudes are stored in weaker associations and are therefore more susceptible to salient temporary information and context effects. Interestingly, the ability to learn incrementally puts connectionist models in broad agreement with developmental and evolutionary constraints.

Second, connectionist models assume that the development of internal representations and the processing of these representations are done in parallel by simple and highly interconnected units, contrary to traditional models where the processing is inherently sequential. As a result, these systems do not need a central executive, which eliminates the requirement of central and deliberative processing of attitude information. Although many attitude theories assume that simple object associations are learned implicitly through conditioning (e.g. Fishbein & Ajzen, 1975) or heuristic processing (e.g. Chaiken, 1987; Petty

& Cacioppo, 1981, 1986), the process by which the different evaluative reactions to a stimulus are integrated in an overall attitude is often left vague and couched in verbal terms only. At most, the outcome of this integration is described in an algebraic formula, without specifying the underlying mental mechanism. Given that a supervisory executive is superfluous in a connectionist approach, this suggests that much of the information processing in attitude formation is often implicit and automatic, without recourse to explicit conscious reasoning. This does not, of course, preclude people to be aware of the outcome of these preconscious processes. In addition, based on the principle that activation in a network spreads automatically to related concepts and so influences their processing, connectionist models exhibit emergent properties such as pattern completion and generalization (for a review, see Smith, 1996), which are potentially useful mechanisms for an account of the biasing effect of attitudes on the interpretation of the environment.

A CONNECTIONIST ACCOUNT OF ATTITUDE PROCESSES

The main goal of this article is to take current attitude models couched either in verbal descriptions, such as dual-process models (e.g. Chaiken, 1987; Petty & Cacioppo, 1981, 1986), or in computational formulations, such as algebraic models (e.g. Fishbein & Ajzen, 1975) as starting points, and to develop a connectionist model that is consistent with these earlier theories. This endeavor may have significant benefits. First, it may provide a stronger fundament to these earlier theories because it provides a lower-level description for some of their major theoretical postulates. By providing a more formal description of these underlying processes, it may perhaps weed out some confusion about the nature of attitude formation. For example, a connectionist approach might underscore the growing realization among social psychologists that many processes in social cognition, and attitude formation in particular, are implicit and non-conscious. The model is capable, among other things, to specify which aspects of information integration might be largely outside awareness, and how attitude heuristics (Chaiken, 1987) have an impact on an attitude.

Second, it may provide a theoretical framework that enables us to integrate various theoretical positions that have until now resided somewhat alongside each other. By doing so, it may potentially explain a larger set of empirical data than earlier formal theories of attitude formation (e.g. Fishbein & Ajzen, 1975). In fact, many of the assumptions in our connectionist model are drawn from previous attitude theories. Below, we highlight the main sources of inspiration of the proposed connectionist model, and explain very briefly how these notions are implemented in the model.

The model defines attitudes primarily as object–evaluation associations (Fazio, 1990) and adopts additional cognitive and behavioral components of attitudes (Katz & Stotland, 1959; Rosenberg & Hovland, 1960) as elements that shape the object–evaluation association. In line with Fazio (1990), the model predicts that when people encounter a novel attitude object, they develop object–evaluation associations in memory in accordance with the information that is currently accessible. When people are confronted again with the object, their stored evaluation comes to mind automatically and guides behavior and thoughts. Consistent with Anderson's (1971) information integration theory, the attitude is further updated, if warranted, by the novel information that is provided. In so doing, the connectionist mechanisms specifying the underlying information processes ends up making the same formal predictions as the algebraic model of Fishbein and Ajzen (1975). These connectionist updating mechanisms are almost identical to earlier formal theories of classical conditioning (Rescorla & Wagner, 1972), which have been quite popular in attitude research (Olson & Fazio, 2001; Staats & Staats, 1958).

In addition, in line with dual-process models of attitude (Chaiken, 1987; Chen & Chaiken, 1999; Petty & Cacioppo, 1981, 1986; Petty & Wegener, 1999), the connectionist model draws on the notion of elaboration likelihood (Petty & Cacioppo, 1981, 1986) or depth of processing in assuming that sources of information may vary in strength as well as in the depth by which they are considered, and thus receive little or substantial weight. This leads to variation in the strength of the attitudes as well as to different modes of processing which are the cornerstone of dual-process models. Essentially, dual-process models conceive two routes by which people use accessible information to change their attitudes. When capacity and motivation are relatively high, people are assumed to carefully consider and weight the available information (central or systematic route). When capacity or motivation are low, people process the information more shallowly and rely on simple heuristics or peripheral cues that give rise, automatically, to stored decision rules such as "experts can be trusted", "majority opinion is correct", and "long messages are valid messages" (peripheral or heuristic route; see Chaiken, 1987; Chen & Chaiken, 1999; Petty & Cacioppo, 1981, 1986; Petty & Wegener, 1999).[1] In the connectionist model, the notion of elaboration likelihood or depth of processing is simulated by changing a single parameter in the network, the general activation (i.e. attention) to persuasive information, which is assumed to be generally lower under peripheral than under central processing. Although our connectionist network is based on a single form of knowledge representation, acquisition, and processing, this single parametric change, together with the inclusion of prior learning of heuristic knowledge

---

1   In this article, we use the broad terms *central* and *peripheral* (Petty & Cacioppo, 1981, 1986; Petty & Wegener, 1999) to denote the two routes of processing in general, and we reserve the term *heuristic* (Chaiken, 1987; Chen & Chaiken, 1999) for cases where persuasive heuristics are clearly involved in the peripheral process. While central and systematic are almost synonymous concepts, peripheral is a broader term that includes not only heuristics but also conditioning and other implicit processes.

structures, allows simulating these major differences between the processing modes.

This article is organized as follows: After briefly presenting the proposed connectionist model, we describe a series of simulations, using the same network architecture applied to a number of significantly different phenomena, including central and heuristic processing in attitude formation. We decided to apply this model to emphasize the theoretical similarities that underlie attitude formation and change with a great variety of other processes in social cognition. Previous models of attitudes are reviewed and compared with the present approach. Finally, we discuss the limitations of the proposed connectionist model and discuss areas where further theoretical developments are under way or are needed.

A RECURRENT MODEL

For all simulations reported in this paper, we use the same basic network model—namely, the linear recurrent autoassociator developed by McClelland and Rumelhart (1985). To update the connection weights in the network, we used the delta learning algorithm (see Equations 3.3, 3.4, and 3.8, pp.38–40). It is interesting to note that the delta learning algorithm is formally identical to the Rescorla-Wagner (1972) model of associative conditioning (see Van Overwalle & Van Rooy, 1998, pp.149–151, for mathematical details). Early attitude theories around 1950 assumed that attitudes are developed through conditional learning and that affective experiences determine the attitude or evaluative response (Olson & Fazio, 2001; Staats & Staats, 1958). According to classical conditioning theory, an attitude is an evaluative response (conditioned response) established by the temporal association of a stimulus (unconditioned stimulus) eliciting an affective reaction with the judgmental target or attitude object (conditioned stimulus). For instance, in one of their first experiments, Staats and Staats (1958) presented Swedish or Dutch names paired with words having a positive (e.g. pretty) or negative value (e.g. failure). They reported a positive attitude towards names associated with positive words and a negative attitude towards names associated with negative words (see also Zanna, Kiesler, & Pilkonis, 1970).

Hence, by using the delta learning algorithm, the present connectionist model incorporates these earlier conditioning models. This is consistent with the dual-process model of Petty and colleagues (Petty & Cacioppo, 1981, 1986; Petty & Wegener, 1999), although they did not include conditioning processes in their theorizing at such a formal level of analysis as in the present connectionist approach. Hence, an important advantage of our connectionist model using the delta learning algorithm is that conditioning is an intrinsic part of it, based on the same learning principles. In the next section, we further describe how these learning principles work.

A RECURRENT IMPLEMENTATION OF
ATTITUDE FORMATION

To provide some background to our specific implementation of attitude formation, we illustrate its major characteristics with an example that represents processing persuasive information via the central route as outlined in the theory of reasoned action by Fishbein and Ajzen (1975; see also Ajzen, 1991; Ajzen & Madden, 1986).

According to this model, an attitude is a function of:

- the expectation or belief that the behavior will lead to a certain consequence or outcome (e.g. using a car is a fast and dry mode of transportation, but also causes air pollution), and
- the person's evaluation of these outcomes (e.g. fast and dry is good, pollution is bad).

According to Fishbein and Ajzen (1975), multiplying the expectancy and value components associated with each outcome and summing these products determines an attitude (see the Annexe, p.411). Many social psychologists have interpreted this summed multiplication as indicating that the integration of this information typically occurs in a conscious, rational and deliberative manner. For example, Fazio (1990, p.89) stated that "the Ajzen and Fishbein model is clearly based upon deliberative processing". Furthermore, he argued, "deliberative processing is characterized by considerable cognitive work. It involves the scrutiny of available information and an analysis of positive and negative attributes, of costs and benefits. The specific attributes of the attitude object and the potential consequences of engaging in a particular course of action may be considered and weighted" (pp.88–89).

However, this characterization is not in line with more current views. Although attitude researchers agree that people may pay attention to available information, they do not assume that the process involving the integration of this information is necessarily open to introspection, nor that this process needs to be repeated once attitudes have been established. As Ajzen (2002) claimed, "the theory of planned behavior does not propose that individuals review their behavioral, normative, and control beliefs prior to every enactment of a frequently performed behavior. Instead, attitudes and intentions—once formed and well-established—are assumed to be activated automatically and to guide behavior without the necessity of conscious supervision" (p.108). Research confirmed that preferences are automatically activated on the mere presence or mention of the attitude object without explicit instruction or environmental cues to evaluate the object (Bargh et al., 1992; Fazio, 1990; Fazio, Sanbonmatsu, Powell, & Kardes, 1986) and that they facilitate decision-making (Fazio & Powell, 1997) and attitude-consistent behavior (Fazio, 1990). Nevertheless, current researchers have focused on the indicators and outcomes of attitude processes, leaving unspecified the underlying implicit mechanisms involved in these outcomes. Although these mechanisms were intuitively seen as non-symbolic and non-conscious, they were presumably not spelled out because researchers lacked the necessary theoretical framework to articulate this process.

Fortunately, connectionism may provide a more appropriate theoretical framework for these implicit processes. As we will argue, it requires only a conscious encoding of attributes or persuasive arguments, while the integration of this information and resulting evaluations can occur implicitly by means of connectionist learning principles. We demonstrate this with the example of a car as a transport vehicle.

Representing expectations and values

Figure 11.1 depicts a recurrent architecture of someone's attitude towards cars as a means of transportation. It serves as an illustration of how Fishbein and Ajzen's (1975) expectancy-value theory is implemented by a connectionist framework. As can be seen, the car is the focal attitude object linked by modifiable connection weights to various cognitive and evaluative outcomes. The cognitive attitude component—the belief that the use of a car will result in certain outcomes—can be represented as expectations linking the car with likely outcomes or attributes, such as how fast and how polluting a car will be, and how dry the trip will be. The likelihood of these outcomes

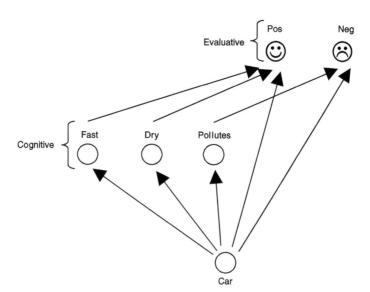

Figure 11.1 Network architecture with 1 attitude object (car) connected to three cognitive nodes (fast, dry, and pollutes) and two valence nodes. All nodes are interconnected to all other nodes, but for a clear understanding of the major mechanisms underlying attitude formation, only the most important (feedforward) connections are shown.

is expressed in the weight of the car → attribute connections, acquired during prior observations. These observations are based on one's own direct experiences as well as on indirect communication or observational modeling (i.e. persuasive messages via the media, witnessing other people's experiences); although indirect information might potentially have less impact. Specifically, as determined by the delta learning algorithm, the more often a particular consequence or a specific attribute of the attitude object is observed, the stronger the relevant object → attribute connection weight becomes. Conversely, the less often a particular consequence is observed, the weaker this weight will be. Psychologically, this is reflected in an increased or decreased expectation or perceived likelihood that this outcome will occur.

The evaluative attitude component can be represented by affective or evaluative responses to the cognitive attributes, such as how much the person likes or dislikes using a fast, dry, and polluting car, again acquired during prior experiences. Thus, in line with Ajzen (1991, p.191), we assume that the outcomes linked with a behavior or attitude object are "valued positively or negatively". As can be seen, the evaluative responses are represented by two separate unipolar valence nodes, one reflecting a positive evaluation and the other a negative evaluation. We assume that positive and negative evaluations are represented by two separate affective systems because recent neurological evidence suggests that the "neurocognitive system for positive affective associations ... serves different functions and can be described without references to neurocognitive systems for negative affect" (Ochsner & Lieberman, 2001, p.727; see also Canli, Desmond, Zhao, Glover, & Gabrieli, 1998; Ito & Cacioppo, 2001; Lane et al., 1997). These evaluations are expressed in the connections from the cognitive outcomes, or attributes, to the evaluative reactions, and are acquired and modified during direct or indirect experiences on the basis of the delta algorithm. Specifically, the more often an evaluation is experienced as a consequence of an attribute, the stronger the relevant attribute → valence connection weight becomes.

In line with Fazio (1990), we suggest that a person's attitude is reflected in the connection between a given object and one's evaluation of that object. Specifically, we define an attitude as the activation of the valence nodes after the attitude object (i.e. car) was activated. This spreading mechanism implements Fazio's (1990) idea that the role of attitudes depends on the extent that "encountering the attitude object [will] automatically activate the evaluation from memory" (pp.93–94). In this definition, an attitude depends solely on the connections between objects and evaluations that are accessible in memory at the time of judgment. Outcomes reflecting cognitions related to the attitude object (e.g. fast, dry, and polluting attributes) can be computed in the network and "retrieved" later, but they are actually not taken into account for constructing an attitude. This is consistent with the dominant view in the attitude literature that takes attitudes primarily as evaluative responses.

Integrating expectations and values: The attitude

How are the cognitive and evaluative components integrated to create a novel attitude? The core idea of the expectancy-value model is that any object is associated with an evaluation, so that when some objects form a (first-order) connection with an evaluation, these connections mediate the formation of second-order connections and this is repeated for higher-order connections. Thus, what we have called attribute → valence connections in the previous section are basically also object → valence connections. From this perspective, the attribute → valence (e.g. fast → positive) connections are first-order connections that mediate the formation of second-order object → valence (e.g. car → positive) connections. This will, of course, go on recursively so that these newly formed object → valence connections mediate the formation of still further higher-order connections. This expectancy-value logic has been adopted in the implementation of our connectionist framework and has several consequences.

One implication is that the evaluative reactions to some attributes are learned relatively early in human life (first-order), while other are learned relatively late (second-order). We presume that what is learned relatively early are evaluative responses to attributes such as dry, fast, and polluting, because these are consequences of direct experiences as well as responses to substantive arguments. These arguments often rely on simple persuasive phrases such as "improved", "better", "advantageous", "do's and don'ts", and so on, that children and adolescents are repeatedly exposed to in advertisements, school and family. In contrast, people are continuously faced with new objects—products and social agents—so that these are unfamiliar and their constituent attributes are learned only much later. Consequently, for the model depicted in Figure 11.1, we assume that the attribute → valence connections are typically developed early and constitute first-order connections, whereas the object → attribute connections are developed relatively later.

Now comes the integration of cognitive and evaluative components (see Figure 11.1). In the connectionist model we implemented two activation-spreading cycles, so that activation sent out by the attitude object to the attributes (along the object → attribute connections), is further spread to the evaluative reactions (along the attribute → valence connections). These connections were shaped during earlier learning, as explained above, and may be further updated given novel information. However, what is most crucial is that this activation spreading leads to the co-activation of the attitude object and valence nodes, resulting in the development of novel second-order connections from the object to the evaluative responses. These second-order object → valence connections reflect the formation of a novel attitude.

It is interesting to note that our definition of an attitude is mathematically very close to the multiplicative function of expectations and values in Fishbein and Ajzen's (1975) theory of reasoned action. To see this, replace "expectations" in their model by object → attribute connection weights, and "values" by attribute → valence connection weights. If the activation from the attitude object is turned on, it spreads to the valence nodes in proportion to the combined weight of these two connections. Mathematically, this is accomplished by multiplying these connections weights, which is very similar to Fishbein and Ajzen's proposed algorithm (see the Annexe for a formal proof).

A second implication of the recursive expectancy-value mechanism is that we augmented the standard recurrent approach with additional features to enable the network to generate and use evaluative reactions in the formation of higher-order connections. In particular, after a standard network has learned the attribute → valence connections, it is not capable of using these first-order connections to generate these same evaluative reactions again by means of spreading of activation. The reason for this is that, in the absence of an explicit coding of the valenced outcome, the network recognizes the internal activation spread to the valence nodes as mere internal predictions by the system. This causes a decrease in the existing connections (e.g. the delta learning algorithm interprets the absence of an explicit evaluation at a valence node while receiving high internal activation, as an error of over-estimation, to which it reacts by reducing the connection weight). One way of overcoming this limitation of standard recurrent networks is by coding the evaluations generated by automatic spreading of internal activation as genuine or external input (denoted by "i" to represent "internal input", see Table 11.2, p.363). However, this does not yet allow second-order learning as there is no error in the learning algorithm because the internal and external activation match. To allow the development of second-order connections, we created error by "boosting" these external activations beyond the internal activation. Specifically, we forced them to approach the extremes of −1 and +1, using a standard non-linear updating algorithm with ten internal cycles and decay = .15. In effect, these two mechanisms give the valence nodes a special status, as compared to all other nodes. This can be seen as a limitation of the current implementation. On the other hand, with evaluation being a ubiquitous aspect of everyday life, people may actually have learned to use their evaluative responses in a somewhat different way to other information (for a similar argument, see De Houwer, Thomas, & Baeyens, 2001). If so, then our connectionist implementation would model a psychological tendency to rely particularly strongly on one's evaluation as a basis for judgment and learning.

Developing expectations and values

Before moving on, we illustrate how connection weights with attribute nodes (or expectations) and with valence node (or values) are developed through experiences with the attitude object. We illustrate this with a small simulation example. To make the understanding of this example as easy as possible, the reader should focus mainly on the most important upward connections drawn in Figure 11.1, although all interconnections between all nodes play a role in an autoassociative network.

In general, according to the delta learning algorithm, the more often an attitude object is experienced with the same pleasant or unpleasant evaluations, the stronger the connection between the corresponding (un)favorable valence nodes and the attitude object node becomes. This illustrates an important property of the delta learning algorithm, namely that as more confirmatory information is received, the connections gradually grow in strength. We call this the *acquisition property* (see Chapter 3). The sensitivity to sample size has been documented in past conditioning research on attitude change (e.g. Berkowitz & Knurek, 1969; Staats & Staats, 1958; for a review see Petty & Cacioppo, 1981). It has been found that the more often an initially neutral cue (i.e. conditioned stimulus) is paired with another stimulus that strongly evokes an evaluative response (i.e. unconditioned stimulus), the stronger the cue–value association becomes, resulting in more vigorous evaluative or affective responses when the cue is present.

Figure 11.2 depicts an idealized example of the acquisition process in attitude formation. Consider first the simplest case in which a person experiences once each cognitive consequence, or attribute, of car driving. First, activation is spread to the attribute of pollution (e.g. the person realizes that cars pollute the air). This activation is then spread to the unfavorable valence node where it generates a negative evaluative reaction (e.g. the person feels uncomfortable about using a polluting car). For simplicity, let's assume that the unfavorable node is activated to its maximum value of +1, while the favorable node remains inactive. The concurrent activation of the car and the unfavorable reaction, leads to an increase of the connection between these two nodes. With a learning rate of .20, the connection weight increases to .20 (see bottom half of Figure 11.2A). Similarly, following the same mechanism as described above, for each of the two positive consequences (i.e. fast and dry), the favorable valence node is activated (e.g. the person feels good about this), resulting in an increase of the connection between the car and the favorable evaluation. Because this increase occurs two times, the resulting weight is .36 given the same learning rate (see top half of Figure 11.2A). Taken together, the weights of the favorable evaluations exceed those of the unfavorable evaluations. When testing for the attitude response, that is, after activating the car attitude object, this results in a stronger activation of the favorable node than the unfavorable node or a differential activation of .16, leading to a positive attitude in favor of car driving.

In general, however, an attitude depends not only on the direction of the evaluative responses for each of the cognitive outcomes, as illustrated in the preceding example, but also on the perceived likelihood of these consequences. As noted earlier, the perceived likelihood is represented in the connection weights of the attitude object and the cognitive consequences, or attributes. Each of these weights, as well as the weights of the attitude object with the evaluative responses, increases as a consequence of the number of

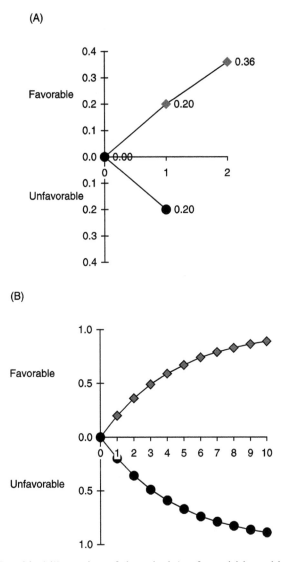

Figure 11.2. Graphical illustration of the principle of acquisition with learning rate 0.20. The Y-axis represents the weight of the connection linking the attitude object node with the favorable and unfavorable valence nodes. (A) Weights after two favorable and one unfavorable experience(s). (B) Favorable and unfavorable weights growing to asymptote after multiple experiences.

experiences with each outcome. For example, if we would repeat the favorable information of the previous example, this would result in an increase of connection weight (see Figure 11.2B, top). After many positive experiences, the acquisition property of the delta learning algorithm dictates that the weight of the favorable valence node becomes much stronger than that of the unfavorable node, resulting in an overall positive attitude in favor of car driving. Conversely, imagine that the unfavorable consequences of pollution are experienced more often because of recent media coverage. By the property of acquisition of the delta learning algorithm, this should lead to an increase of the connection weights with the unfavorable valence node, as illustrated in Figure 11.2B (bottom).

It is important to note that according to the delta learning algorithm, when getting closer to the external environment, the learning error shrinks and learning slows down resulting in a negatively accelerating learning curve. Thus, acquisition is fast and steep at the beginning, but then gradually gets slower and flat towards an asymptote (+1 or −1 in this example, see Figure 11.2B). Stated more generally, during the first phases of learning, the connection weights reflect the amount of evidence, that is, the network is sensitive to sample size. However, the error decreases as more information is processed in the network, so that, after some time, learning reaches asymptote and the weight of the connections reflects the average of the favorable versus unfavorable evidence.

In sum, the delta learning algorithm shapes the connections between attitude object nodes with the cognitive and evaluative responses. The acquisition property describes how the connections from the attitude object grow stronger in function of a growing sample size, and so result in the preponderance of favorable or unfavorable evaluations in proportion to the number of experiences with each of these consequences.

GENERAL METHODOLOGY OF THE SIMULATIONS

We basically used the same methodology throughout all simulations. We applied the connectionist processing principles, including the property of acquisition and sample size, to a number of classic findings in the attitude literature. For explanatory purposes, most often, we replicated a well-known representative experiment that illustrates a particular phenomenon, although we also simulated a theoretical prediction. Table 11.1 lists the topics of the simulations we report shortly, the relevant empirical study or theory that we attempted to replicate, as well as the major underlying processing principle responsible for reproducing the data. Although not all relevant data in the vast attitude literature can be addressed in a single paper, we are confident that we have included some of the most relevant phenomena in the current literature of dual-process models.

We first describe the successive learning phases in the simulations, the general parameters of the model, how cognitions and evaluations were coded, and how often they were presented to the network; we end with how attitudes and attribute-relevant thoughts were measured.

Table 11.1 Overview of the simulations

No.	Topic	Empirical evidence/ theoretical prediction	Major processing principle
1.	Reasoned action	Fishbein & Ajzen, 1975	Acquisition of valued information
2.	Length heuristic	Petty & Cacioppo, 1984	Prior acquisition of few vs. many values
3.	Consensus heuristic	Maheswaran & Chaiken, 1991, Experiment 1	Prior acquisition of few vs. many values
4.	Expertise heuristic	Chaiken & Maheswaran, 1994	Prior acquisition of high (expert) vs. low (non-expert) values
5.	Mood heuristic	Petty et al., 1993, Experiment 2	Prior acquisition of high (positive mood) vs. mixed (neutral mood) values
6.	Ease of retrieval	Tormala, Petty & Briñol, 2002, Experiment 2	Competition with valences acquired earlier

Learning phases

In all simulations, we assumed that participants brought with them learning experiences taking place before the experiment. We argued before that evaluative responses to attributes and outcomes typically develop early. This was simulated by inserting a prior valence learning phase, during which the connections between the object's attributes and their evaluations were developed. When appropriate, we also inserted a prior heuristic learning phase during which connections were established between attitude objects and the heuristic cues of the environment in which they were generated. These two prior learning phases are based on earlier direct experiences or observations of similar situations, or on indirect experiences through communication or observation of others' experiences. Thus, the connection weights established during these pre-experimental phases reflect the beliefs and evaluations that participants bring with them into the experimental situation.

We then simulated specific experiments. The particular conditions and trial orders of the focused experiments were reproduced as faithfully as possible, although minor changes were introduced to simplify the presentation (e.g. fewer trials or arguments than in the actual experiments). Nevertheless, the major results hold across a wide range of stimulus distributions.

Model parameters

For all simulations, we used the linear autoassociative recurrent network described above, with parameters for decay and excitation (for internal and external activation) all set to 1, and with two internal activation cycles. This means that activation is propagated to neighboring nodes and cycled twice through the system, so that nodes linked via one or two connections receive activation from an external source. The activation of a node is computed as the linear sum of all internal and external activations received by this node (McClelland & Rumelhart, 1988; McLeod et al., 1998). Assuming that the major experiments to be simulated used very similar stimulus materials, measures, and procedures, the general learning rate that determines the speed by which the weights of the connections are allowed to change was set to 0.35. This learning rate was chosen because it accommodated all simulations to be reported, although any value between .33 and .37 typically yielded the same general pattern. All connection weights were initialized at zero. In order to ensure that prior learning would not overshadow the learning of the experimental information, external activation during prior learning was set to 0.5 or −0.5 instead of the standard level of +1 or −1, whereas learning during the experimental phase was set to the standard level.

Trial frequencies

For simulating prior valance learning, in all simulations, we first ran a number of trials in which positive and negative attributes, or strong and weak arguments, were paired with the favorable and unfavorable valence nodes, respectively. The rationale for this is that strong arguments elicit primarily favorable evaluations about the attitude object, while weak arguments elicit primarily unfavorable evaluations (see Petty & Cacioppo, 1984, p.73). The number of trials for each attribute or argument was set to 15, to ensure that the connection weights approached asymptote. For simulating prior heuristic learning, we first ran a number of pre-experimental trials that varied between 1 and 12 (to be discussed later). These pre-experimental phases and one condition in the experimental phase were run till completion by going once through all trials. In order to generalize across a range of presentation orders, each network run was repeated for 50 different random orders, thus simulating 50 different "participants". Because of the random ordering of trials, the results for each run (or "participant") were somewhat different, reflecting the variable conditions of human perception in the actual experiments.

Given that a critical experimental manipulation usually lasts about 1 minute (the time to read the information), it seemed reasonable to assume that participants would think at least once about each piece of information and that this would generate their evaluations about it. This was implemented by using one trial for each attribute presented in the experimental condition. It is important to note that the frequencies in the experimental phase were intentionally kept low for two reasons. First, it seemed to us that individuals do not exert extreme effort in thinking about attributes or in interpreting substantive arguments, so that a single trial for each attribute or argument seemed appropriate. Second, a limited number of trials avoids the destruction of the connection weights learned previously, a result that is known as catastrophic interference (French, 1997; McCloskey & Cohen, 1989). It is implausible that a novel piece of information would totally reverse long-term background knowledge, and this indeed never occurred in the simulations (see more on this later).

Measuring attitudes and relevant thoughts

At the end of each simulated experimental condition, test trials were run in which certain nodes of interest were turned on and the resulting activation in other nodes was recorded to evaluate our predictions or to compare with observed experimental data. For measuring the attitude, we turned on the attitude object and recorded the resulting activation at the favorable and unfavorable valence nodes. The unfavorable activation was subtracted from the favorable activation to arrive at an overall attitude measure. For measuring attribute-relevant thoughts, we also activated the attitude object and recorded not only the differential activation of the valence nodes, but also the activation of the nodes reflecting the attributes or arguments presented. Hence, this measure reflects a combination of valences and thoughts about the object's attributes, which seems most appropriate to measure valenced thought, or the degree of positively versus negatively valenced thinking. This will be explained in more detail for each simulation. These obtained test activations were averaged across all "participants" and then projected onto the observed data using linear regression (with intercept and a positive slope) to visually demonstrate the fit between the simulations and experimental data. The reason is that only the pattern of test activations is of interest, not the exact values.

CENTRAL PROCESSING

Dual-process models of persuasive communication assume that, given sufficient motivation and capacity, an audience will process incoming arguments extensively via the central or systematic route of persuasion. Perhaps the most influential model of attitude formation that describes this sort of deliberative weighting of all salient alternatives and consequences is the theory of reasoned action of Fishbein and Ajzen (1975; see also Ajzen, 1991; Ajzen & Madden, 1986). As noted earlier, according to this theory, an attitude is a function of the expectation that the behavior will lead to certain consequences or outcomes (e.g. a car is fast and dry, but also pollutes the air), and the person's evaluation of these outcomes (e.g. fast and dry is good, pollution is bad). The attitude is the outcome of this weighting process, and is computed by multiplying the expectancy and value components associated with each outcome and summing up these products. This formula of attitude formation has received considerable empirical support in many studies (see Ajzen, 1991; Ajzen & Madden, 1986; Fishbein & Ajzen, 1975), although it has been found that other factors besides attitudes may also exert an influence on behavior. However, a limitation of the theory is that it remained vague about the underlying integration process.

Current views on the attitude process assume that many aspects of deliberative attitude formation and change through the central route to persuasion are implicit. For instance, Chen and Chaiken (1999) claimed that "although perceivers are clearly aware when they are systematically processing information, they are by no means necessarily aware of the precise form of this processing or of the factors that may influence it" (p.86). Our connectionist model is consistent with this position and assumes that perceivers must be minimally aware only of the information provided at the time of encoding. In contrast, the generation of evaluative reactions to this information and the integration of these evaluations depend on automatic spreading of activation and weight updating, which proceed at an automatic and implicit level as we have seen earlier.

Recent evidence supports this view (e.g. Betsch, Plessner, Schwieren, & Gütig, 2001; Lieberman, Ochsner, Gilbert, & Schacter, 2001; Olson & Fazio, 2001). A very convincing neuropsychological study by Lieberman et al. (2001) documented that amnesic patients could form and change their attitudes for various pictures at different moments in time, despite a severe impairment in their ability consciously to remember the pictures they had encountered earlier, in contrast to control participants, who were able to recollect their earlier preferences. Thus, although the amnesic patients might have been aware of the pictures at the time of exposure, and probably also of their preferences for some pictures, the online evaluative integration over time of these preferences occurred largely outside awareness.

Simulation 1: Central processing of expectations and valences

We demonstrate the integration of persuasive information using the central route by mimicking the predictions of the theory of reasoned action (Fishbein & Ajzen, 1975). As assumed by Ajzen (1988), this integration will follow "reasonably from the beliefs people hold about the object of the attitude" so that "we learn to like objects we believe have largely desirable characteristics, and we form unfavorable attitudes toward objects we associate with mostly undesirable characteristics" (p.32). To illustrate this "reasoned" integration of persuasive information, we extend the car example used in the introduction with other transportation modes such as public buses or bicycles. Table 11.2 lists a simplified simulated learning history of this example.

Simulation

Each line in the top panel of Table 11.2 represents a pattern of external activation at a trial that corresponds to either a direct personal encounter or an indirect persuasive statement. The first three cells of each line represent the attitude object presented in each trial. The next three cells reflect the

Table 11.2 Learning experiences during reasoned behavior (Simulation 1)

	Objects			Attributes			Valence	
	Car	*Bicycle*	*Bus*	*Fast*	*Dry*	*Pollutes*	☺	☹
Prior valence learning								
#15				+			+	
#15					+		+	
#15						+		+
Car								
#1	1			1			i	i
#1	1				1		i	i
#1	1					1	i	i
Bicycle								
#1		1		1			i	i
#2		1			−1		i	i
Bus								
#2			1	−1			i	i
#1			1		1		i	i
#2			1			1	i	i
Test								
Attitude toward car	1						?	−?
Attitude toward bicycle		1					?	−?
Attitude toward bus			1				?	−?

Schematic version of learning experiences in attitude formation along Fishbein and Ajzen (1975). ☺, favorable; ☹, unfavorable; #, frequency of trial; cell entries denote external activation and empty cells denote 0 activation; +, external activation of 0.5; i, internal activation (generated mainly by the attributes) is taken as external activation. Each of the transportation means was trained separately, and was always preceded by the prior valence learning phase and followed by the test phase. Trial order was randomized in each phase and condition.

attributes paired with an attitude object. The last two cells denote the evaluation of these attributes, which is either favorable or unfavorable. As can be seen, each node was turned on (activation level of +1, 0.5, −0.5 or −1) or turned off (activation level 0).

As argued earlier, the likelihood variable in the Fishbein and Ajzen (1975) formula is determined by the frequency that an attitude object is paired with an attribute, and the evaluation variable is determined by the degree of satisfaction or dissatisfaction experienced when that attribute is present. We further assumed that learning the attribute → valence connections occurs relatively early while the object → attribute connections develop relatively late. Therefore, in the simulation history, first a prior learning phase is inserted during which valences are developed, and then the main learning phase in which the attributes of each transportation vehicles are learned.

These learning phases not only determine the weight of the object → attribute and attribute → valence connections, they also shape the object →

valence connections that reflect the attitude. Thus, an attitude is stored in the network in the connections from each attitude object with the favorable and unfavorable evaluations. Consequently, testing or measuring an attitude in the network is accomplished by activating the attitude object and reading off the resulting activation of the favorable and unfavorable valence nodes (denoted by ? in the bottom panel of Table 11.2). In particular, we tested the differential activation of the favorable and unfavorable nodes.

We compared the predictions of the recurrent network model with those of the theory of reasoned action, using the summed multiplicative equation outlined earlier (Fishbein & Ajzen, 1975; see also the Annexe). For computing this equation, we used the trial frequencies as estimate of the likelihood of outcomes; we used a value of $+1$ for favorable attributes and a value of -1 for unfavorable attributes. Assuming that higher frequencies lead to stronger beliefs, we took the raw trial frequencies rather than proportions or probabilities. Hence, the predictions reflect the relative attitude towards each object; and the pattern is identical if taken proportional to the total number of trials.

Results

The "statements" listed in Table 11.2 were processed by the network for 50 "participants" with different random orders. In Figure 11.3, the simulated values (broken lines) are compared with the predictions from the theory of reasoned action (striped bars). As can be seen, the simulated and predicted data match almost perfectly. Furthermore, an ANOVA on the simulated

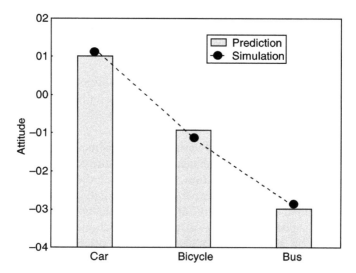

Figure 11.3 Attitude formation: Predicted data from Fishbein and Ajzen (1975) and simulation results. Theoretically predicted data are denoted by bars, simulated values by broken lines.

attitude revealed that the main effect of transportation modes was significant, $F(2,147) = 53.72$, $p < .0001$, and further t-tests indicated that all transportation modes differed significantly from each other, $t(98) = 3.67–10.85$, $ps < .001$.

It is important to note that as soon as the external activation was turned on for the attitude objects and their attributes during the main learning phase, all the remaining mechanisms were implicit as they involved only activation spreading and weight updating. Thus, this simulation presents a formal mechanism that explicates that perceivers need only be aware of the information provided (i.e. the attitude object and its attributes, either perceived directly or communicated through persuasive arguments) and that the rest of deliberative attitude processing may proceed outside awareness.

HEURISTIC PROCESSING

Although people may prefer to systematically scrutinize all relevant information for forming an opinion about an important issue (Gollwitzer, 1990), in many cases attitudes are created or changed in a more shallow or heuristic manner. This distinction is crucial to dual-process models like the elaboration likelihood model (Petty & Cacioppo, 1981, 1986; Petty & Wegener, 1999) and the heuristic-systematic model (Chaiken, 1980, 1987; Chen & Chaiken, 1999). According to these dual-process models, when motivation or capacity for systematic scrutiny of information is low, such as when the issue is of low personal relevance or when time is limited, people use a heuristic processing strategy. Heuristic processing implies that people form or change their attitudes by using situational cues that automatically give rise to stored decision rules such as "experts can be trusted", "majority opinion is correct", and "long messages are valid messages".

The nature of heuristics

What are heuristics and how do they work? According to Chaiken, Liberman, and Eagly (1989, p.213), "rules or heuristics that define heuristic processing are learned knowledge structures . . . perceivers sometimes use heuristics in a highly deliberate, self-conscious fashion, but at other times they may use heuristics more spontaneously, with relatively little awareness of having done so". They argued that heuristics are abstracted on the basis of past experiences and observations or via direct instruction form socializing agents. Consequently, they can vary in their strength or perceived reliability, depending on the statistical relationship between situational cues and agreement with messages during prior learning. As Chaiken et al. (1989, p.218) put it, "a person whose past experience with likable and unlikable persons has yielded many confirmations and few disconfirmations of the liking-agreement rule, should perceive a stronger association between the concept of liking and

interpersonal agreement than a person whose experience has yielded pro-
portionally more disconfirmations". Heuristics will only exert an impact
on the attitude to the extent that they are reliable and available in memory,
and to the extent that the situation provides cues that can be processed
heuristically.

However, except for the notion that heuristics are knowledge structures
reactivated from memory before they can take effect, as far as we know, dual-
process theories did not spell out in much detail how these heuristics are
applied and integrated into an attitude judgment. Heuristic processing in
the attitude literature is often equated with inferential rules, schemas, and
procedural knowledge. Hence, one interpretation is that heuristics consist
of well-learned abstracted rules like "I agree with people I like" that are
"applied" in some way or another on the current attitude. Another interpretation is that heuristics consist of summarized past knowledge people have
about similar situations and the statistical relation between situational cues
and agreement with messages. This latter interpretation does not involve
the development of abstract, rule-based knowledge and is compatible with
a connectionist perspective (see also Smith & DeCoster, 2000; Strack &
Deutsch, 2004).

Indeed, numerous simulations in connectionist research have suggested
that sensitivity to an abstract rule need not involve the acquisition of a
corresponding abstract rule, and that a single connectionist network is
quite capable of processing both rule-abiding and rule-deviating behaviors
and judgments (cf. Pacton, Perruchet, Fayol, & Cleeremans, 2001). Many
instances of seemingly rule-like behavior need not necessarily depend on
explicit rule knowledge, and instead may be based on the processing of exemplars and subsymbolic properties of connectionist models (McLeod et al.,
1998). A very well-known example is the Rumelhart and McClelland (1986)
model of the acquisition of the past tense morphology. In this model, not
only are regular verbs processed in just the same way as exceptions, but
neither are learned through anything like processes of abstract rule acquisition. In the domain of social cognition, Smith and DeCoster (1998; see
Chapter 7) demonstrated that a connectionist network can learn a schema
from exposure to exemplars of a category (e.g. learn a stereotype about a
social group from exposure to its members) and apply this knowledge to
make inferences about unobserved attributes of the category.

Heuristics as learned connections

Our core idea on heuristics is that they consist of summarized exemplar
knowledge, embedded in connection weights reflecting past co-occurrences of
heuristic cues and attitude agreement. Hence, there is no storage of explicit
abstracted or symbolic rules (Smith & DeCoster, 2000). In an early phase,
when heuristic learning occurs, the communicated message establishes a
cue → valence connection such as, for instance, between a likeable source and

attitude agreement (Chaiken et al., 1989). This heuristic learning phase can result in different heuristic "rules" by associations of the valences with different cues such as message length, consensus, and expertise, and by variations in the association frequencies or valences. In a later application phase, whatever heuristics that is operative at the time, it directs the system at reusing the heuristic knowledge on the basis of the cue → valence connection, with little input from the object → attribute → valence connections (used in central processing). We believe that the preferential use of one of these connections or "routes" depends on differences in attention to either heuristic cue information or substantive arguments (i.e. attributes). We assume that these differences in attentional focus (and thus of heuristic versus central processing) is governed by the same factors of motivation and capacity that determine elaboration likelihood as proposed by dual-models of attitude (Chen & Chaiken, 1999; Petty & Wegener, 1999).

Let us first elaborate on the prior heuristic learning phase. Our perspective on heuristic learning posits that heuristic knowledge is principally built from earlier persuasive messages in which some arguments drive the valences in a positive or negative direction (e.g. strong arguments producing a favorable valence, weak arguments generating an unfavorable valence). What results from this learning process is an association between the heuristic cue and the valence. The specific arguments in this process are of no further substance and are easily forgotten later, because they typically differ between situations and so become a random noise that drops out. Thus, what is stored in memory is a direct association between a cue such as message source and attitude agreement or disagreement (without arguments), that reflects the statistical relationship during prior learning of messages varying in source expertise and acceptance of opinions. For instance, many confirmations that experts' strong arguments in favor of a certain position leads to attitude agreement will create a strong connection between trustworthy pro-arguing sources and positive valences. Conversely, one can also develop source knowledge indicating that trustworthy experts arguing against a certain position most often leads to attitude disagreement. (For ease of presentation, however, we tacitly assume a favoring expert in most examples.) People can also abstract the functional realm of application of a heuristic cue. For instance, an "expert" source is defined as trustworthy only in a limited range of domains. Thus, a doctor is an expert in diagnosing diseases but not in advising how to enjoy rock-and-roll.

Second, once this cue → valence connection is formed, it resides in memory so that any heuristic processing of novel messages that contains information about the cue (e.g. source) will not start from scratch but instead starts from a non-zero connection. This non-zero connection facilitates all further activation spreading and learning on similar issues. For example, an expert's message will be received favorably if processed heuristically because the only thing that matters is the reactivation of the valence associated with the expert cue. This is how our model conceives the spontaneous application of heuristics, without depending on symbolic abstraction of rules. Of course, it is possible that under some circumstances, "people can reflect on their own past experiences and summarize them, perhaps in the form of a symbolically represented rule" (Smith & DeCoster, 2000, p.116). In this case, perceivers consciously decide "whether it is appropriate to use activated mental constructs as guides to judgment" (Chen & Chaiken, 1999, p.83). In sum, we typically see heuristics as implicit knowledge based on past exemplars, although they may sometimes be abstracted as symbolic rules. As we argue later, this view may have important consequences on how heuristics influence attitude formation.

Simulating heuristic learning

In the simulations, we implemented heuristic processing in two steps. First, we assumed that alongside attributes of an attitude, the system also stores old experiences with heuristic cues (Figure 11.4). Specifically, as shown on the right side of Figure 11.4, we programmed a pre-experimental heuristic learning phase in which cue → valence connections were built up (via arguments that shape the valence, but which are of no further importance and therefore not shown). Second, after this heuristic learning phase, a novel attitude is developed under heuristic processing by a *generalization* of the cue's valence to the attitude object. With generalization we mean that the prior cue → valence connection creates a similar object → valence connection, during the co-occurrence of the cue and the attitude object. This object → valence connection stands on its own. For instance, although the sheer number of favorable reviews in the media shaped our high respect for an artist and created a cue → valence link, because of this generalization to the artist himself we may be able to report later that we evaluated this artist very highly but do not remember that is was because of a great number of flattering reviews.

The fact that the attitude is directly based on an object → valence link, without strong supporting links to attributes or environmental cues, may explain why attitudes formed by the heuristic route are not very enduring. As soon as a novel generalization is established between the attitude object and another situational cue (or new links with substantive arguments under central processing), this changes the earlier object → valence link. For instance, if a friendly art expert tells us that she read negative reviews, we might change our mind about this artist more quickly than if we had developed our own arguments under central processing.

We also explored an alternative process in which heuristic processing is not based on a direct generalization of the cue's valence to the attitude object, but rather on an indirect generalization through an object → cue → valence link. This alternative implies that the reactivation of the cue is a crucial mediator in attitude activation. To take our previous artist example, we would be able to report later that the reason why we evaluated this artist very highly was the

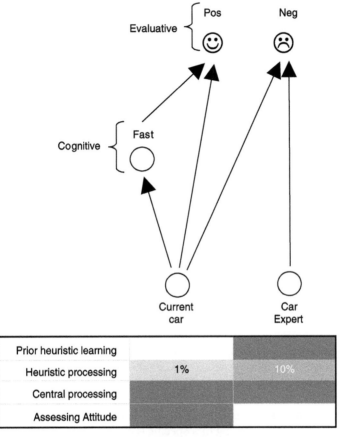

Figure 11.4 Network architecture with one attitude object (current car) and a heuristic cue (car expert). The example illustrates prior learning when the expert is negatively disposed toward cars. For a clear understanding of the major mechanisms underlying heuristic processing, only one attribute is listed and only the most important connections are shown. The table at the bottom reflects the activation of the network involved in different phases of learning and testing; a lighter shade of gray reflects less activation than the default (activation level indicated by %).

great number of flattering reviews (without remembering the content of it). This approach converges on very similar simulation results. However, because it seems to us that most people tend to forget the heuristic cue under which they developed their attitude, this alternative seemed less intuitively plausible and is therefore not reported. However, future research should establish convincingly that none of the heuristic cues is remembered at a later stage, or only very little of it.

Returning to the heuristic learning phase, how often need heuristic events be repeated before the statistical relationship between the cue and message acceptance is stored in memory? For instance, if a perceiver agrees with a message that was advocated by a trustworthy source, how many times should this event (and the opposite event involving an untrustworthy source and disagreement) be repeated before a strong connection is established with the valence nodes? Obviously, perceivers need to be exposed to multiple events or episodes before the heuristic cue is summarized and its application automated. Moreover, there is a growing realization that memory for specific episodic events and the extraction of more generalized statistical knowledge resides in different memory systems in the brain (the hippocampus and neocortex respectively; see McClelland, McNaughton, & O'Reilly, 1995; Smith & DeCoster, 2000). Prior knowledge—such as schemas and stereotypes—is often built up slowly and is often resistant to change in the presence of new contradictory information. Various modelers have proposed modular connectionist architectures mimicking this dual-memory system with one subsystem dedicated to the rapid learning of unexpected and novel information and the building of episodic memory traces and another subsystem responsible for slow incremental learning of statistical regularities of the environment and gradual consolidation of information learned in the first subsystem (Ans & Rousset, 1997, 2000; French, 1997, 1999; McClelland et al., 1995). Efforts to improve these models are still under way.

Therefore, a full-blown dual-memory system is beyond the scope of the present article. However, all these approaches agree that learning in semantic memory is much slower than in episodic memory. Based on this central idea, in the present simulations we used a single system in which the heuristic episodes were repeated 10 times with a learning rate that was only 10% of the learning rate of the other material. This implementation conserves the basic tenet that learning of statistical regularities embedded in earlier messages is much slower than the learning of a specific (i.e. current) message.

Heuristic versus central processing: Differences in attention

As noted earlier, to explain the difference between heuristic and central modes of processing, we borrow the elaboration likelihood assumption from dual-process models (Petty & Wegener, 1999). This implies that "central-route attitude changes are those that are based on relatively extensive and effortful information-processing activity, aimed at scrutinizing and uncovering the central merits of the issue or advocacy. Peripheral-route attitude changes are based on a variety of attitude change processes that typically require less cognitive effort" (p.42). Thus, during central processing, people assess the relevance and favorability of the persuasive arguments, which requires a lot of mental effort and attention, whereas during heuristic processing, due to lack of cognitive resources or motivation, current persuasive arguments are less well attended to. Because of the shallower encoding of novel persuasive arguments during heuristic processing, they will have less effect on the final attitude than prior heuristic knowledge, so that heuristic knowledge will prevail. In contrast, during central processing, the persuasive arguments are more carefully attended to and scrutinized, so that they largely override prior knowledge and dominate the final attitude.

These differences in attentional focus put our approach in large agreement with dual-process models. Heuristic and central processing differ both quantitatively and qualitatively (Petty & Wegener, 1999). They differ quantitatively because they presume differences in elaboration likelihood of information that is learned by the same fundamental delta algorithm, whether it was learned previously or currently. However, they also differ qualitatively because the information base underlying previous heuristic learning and current central processing differs completely.

Simulating differences in attention

We have already seen how the model implements the different learning histories of heuristic and central processing (the qualitative difference). How do we simulate differences in elaboration likelihood (the quantitative difference)? We propose that the degree of elaboration essentially depends on differences in attention to earlier versus recent information, and that this determines what type of information will have the most impact on attitude formation. Specifically, we argue that, under heuristic processing, there is a general reduction in attention so that it becomes negligible for novel arguments but remains influential for the cue. This remaining attention for the cue allows the generalization of the cue's valence to the attitude. In connectionist models, variation in attention is typically implemented by differences in external activation.

Research has demonstrated that differences in attention can originate from modulations in basic arousal and behavioral activation (e.g. the sleep–wake cycle), responsiveness to salient stimuli, or to task-specific attentional focus and voluntary control of exploring, scanning, and encoding information. Research on the neurological underpinnings of attention suggest that general arousal is driven by lower-level nuclei and pathways from the brainstem, while basic features of the stimuli are detected by the thalamus and related subcortical nuclei (e.g. amygdala, basal ganglia). In contrast, task-specific attention and voluntary control is most likely modulated by supervisory executive centers in the prefrontal neocortex (LaBerge, 1997, 2000; Posner, 1992). Variations in elaboration likelihood stem mainly from such conscious control over one's attentional focus. Some connectionist researchers have attempted to model these higher-level voluntary attention processes (e.g. O'Reilly & Munakata, 2000, pp.305–312, 379–410). The basic idea of their approach is that motivation or task instructions maintain activation in the frontal areas of the brain (through dopamine-based modulation), and that this "attentional" activation spreads to other internal representation in the brain where it results in greater accessibility and activation of other internal representations.

In line with the basic ideas of O'Reilly and Munakata's (2000) model, but somewhat more simplified, we incorporated a general attentional module in our model that served as gateway to all other areas of our network and that modulated the activation of the nodes in some areas. By varying the attention level in this general attentional module during heuristic processing, all activation levels in some areas were changed to the same degree (see also the bottom scheme in Figure 11.4). Of course, this is again a simplification of real life. It may well be that, during heuristic processing, some members of the audience evaluate some arguments with high motivation and attention, and then stop when they realize that it is of little personal relevance. This could be built into the simulations. On average, however, all arguments will be processed less extensively, and therefore we kept the simpler simulation procedure. Note that changes in the activation level do not violate the locality principle of connectionism, which says that each connection weight should be updated using only locally available information from associated nodes. That is because the activation level only affects the general speed of learning, not how much and in which direction weight adaptation should occur, which is uniquely determined by local information according to the delta learning algorithm.

In the next simulations, we implemented four heuristic "rules" of length, consensus, expertise, and mood, which were largely based on this assumption, although there were some essential differences between each heuristic which prompted us to consider each of them separately. We are focusing here on the effects of heuristics given low and high elaboration conditions, and do not address how the heuristics themselves can sometimes determine the extent of thinking (see the section on Quantitative and qualitative processing differences, p.393).

Simulation 2: Length heuristic

We begin the demonstration of our connectionist approach to heuristic reasoning with the length heuristic. In empirical research, lengthy messages are typically manipulated by providing more arguments or by repeating the same arguments in different words with more detail (Haugtvedt, Schumann, Schneier, & Warren, 1994; Petty & Cacioppo, 1984; Schumann, Petty, & Clemons, 1990; Wood, Kallgren, & Preisler, 1985). According to the principle of acquisition, greater sample size of arguments should result in stronger effects on attitude judgments. Thus, the more often an argument that an attitude object possesses a positive or negative attribute is repeated, the stronger the object → valence connection grows.

Sometimes, people are misled by the apparent length of a message even if it does not include more persuasive arguments, but only contains cosmetic alterations such as the use of larger fonts and margins (Wood et al., 1985) or minor rewording (Haugtvedt et al., 1994; but see Schumann et al., 1990). This seems to suggest that superficial characteristics of a message can sometimes influence processing, rather than the arguments themselves. A connectionist framework can account for this effect by assuming that such superficial characteristics of length are often correlated with actual differences in message length, and so may influence attitudes also.

Key experiment

Petty and Cacioppo (1984) provided a well-known demonstration of the length heuristic. Participants read about a committee that would advise a change in academic examination policy. Involvement in the issue was manipulated by telling participants that the recommendations would be initiated the following year (high involvement) or after 10 years (low involvement). Next, participants read either three or nine arguments in favor of the proposed changes that were all strong or weak. As can be seen in Figure 11.5 (top panel), under low involvement, the number of arguments had a strong impact, suggesting that the length heuristic was applied. In contrast, under high involvement, the quality of the arguments had a greater impact so that nine strong arguments led to more attitude change than three strong arguments, and similarly, that nine weak arguments led to less attitude change than three weak arguments.

It is important to note that the length heuristic in the Petty and Cacioppo (1984) study revealed only more agreement with the advocated position, although in principle the length heuristic might result in less agreement if weak or unconvincing arguments had been considered. This seems to suggest that, under heuristic processing, perceivers primarily reactivate knowledge indicating that lengthy arguments were strong and convincing. This may perhaps reflect statistical regularities in perceivers' past experiences, in that among all naturally encountered messages in the past, the longer ones might usually have been the more convincing ones. This idea is reproduced in the simulations by using only strong arguments in the prior heuristic learning phase, and this assumption is crucial in simulating the results from the experimental data.

Dual-process models assume that the cognitive responses while receiving a persuasive message are crucial mediators in forming an attitude. The greater the proportion of favorable responses, and the smaller the proportion of unfavorable responses elicited by a message, the greater is the attitude change in the direction advocated. To measure these cognitive responses, Petty and Cacioppo (1984) gave their participants a thought-listing task in which they had to "try to remember the thoughts that crossed your mind while you were reading the material" (p.74). The results of this thought-listing task, taking into account the favorable or unfavorable valence of the thoughts, are depicted in Figure 11.5 (bottom panel). Under conditions of high involvement, they show a similar pattern of increased agreement with the message given more arguments, but under conditions of low involvement, they reveal little explicit thinking. These results are consistent with the dual-process

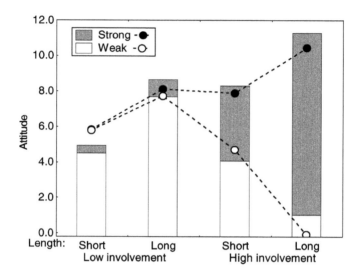

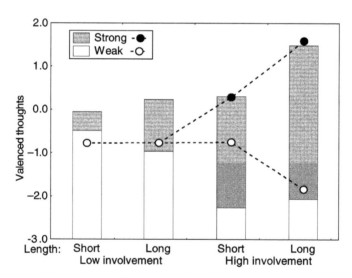

Figure 11.5 Length heuristic: Observed data from Petty and Cacioppo (1984) and simulation results of attitudes (top panel) and valenced thoughts (bottom panel). Human data are denoted by bars, simulated values by broken lines. The human data are from Table 1 in "The effects of involvement on responses to argument quantity and quality: Central and peripheral routes to persuasion" by R. E., Petty & J. T. Cacioppo, 1984, *Journal of Personality and Social Psychology, 46,* 75. Copyright 1984 by the American Psychological Association.

model's hypothesis that valenced attribute-relevant thoughts mediate attitude change given central processing, but that heuristic processing elicits little thought about the attitude-related arguments.

Based on these findings, Petty and Cacioppo (1984) concluded that the number of arguments in a message leads to agreement with a message by serving as a simple heuristic cue when personal involvement was low, while it increases issue-relevant thinking when personal involvement was high.

Simulation

Table 11.3 represents a simplified simulated learning history of the experiment by Petty and Cacioppo (1984). As can be seen, the network consists of a current attitude object (exam) and a contextual cue (message length), and of six strong and six weak arguments and two (favorable and unfavorable)

Table 11.3 Learning experiences and the length heuristic (Simulation 2)

	Object and cue		Arguments[a]						Valence	
	Exam	Length	Str1	Str2	Str3	Wk1	Wk2	Wk3	☺	☻
#10 Prior heuristic learning: Short *(long)* strong message										
#1 *(4)*	+		+						+	
#1 *(4)*	+			+					+	
#1 *(4)*	+				+				+	
Short strong *(weak)* message										
#1	1	1	1(0)			0(1)			i	i
Long strong *(weak)* message										
#1	1	1	1(0)			0(1)			i	i
#1	1	1		1(0)			0(1)		i	i
#1	1	1			1(0)			0(1)	i	i
Test										
Attitude toward exam	1								?	–?
Valenced thoughts	1		?	?	?	?	?	?	6?	–6?

Simplified version of the experimental design by Petty and Cacioppo (1984). Str, strong; Wk, weak; ☺, favorable; ☻, unfavorable; #, frequency of trial or condition; cell entries denote external activation and empty cells denote 0 activation; +, external activation of 0.5; i, internal activation (generated mainly by the arguments) is taken as external activation. Each experimental condition was run separately, and always preceded by a prior valence learning phase (not shown) and prior heuristic learning phase, followed by the test phase. Trial order was randomized in each phase and condition. During prior valence learning (not shown), all strong and weak argument nodes were paired with the favorable or unfavorable valence nodes, respectively, for 15 trials (see also Simulation 1). During prior heuristic learning, each condition was repeated 10 times with 10 % of the default learning rate. During heuristic processing of the experimental phase, activation was reduced to 10% for the cue and to 1% for the arguments during acquisition of novel information and testing of attribute-relevant thoughts.

[a] The arguments during prior learning are completely different from those in the experimental and test conditions, but are shown in the same columns to conserve space. The arguments during prior heuristic learning serve to drive the cue's valence into a positive or negative direction, but are of no further importance.

valences, each represented by a node. The table lists three strong and weak arguments during prior heuristic learning, and three strong and weak arguments during the experimental phase. Note, however, that these arguments are totally different between the two phases, but listed in the same columns to conserve space. As in the first simulation, each line or trial in the top panel of Table 11.3 corresponds to an argument presented to participants. Because this is the first of four simulations on heuristic processing, we describe it in somewhat more detail.

First, during the prior valence learning phase, argument quality was paired with the valences. This aspect of the simulation is not listed in the table, but is similar to the previous simulation (see top panel of Table 11.2). Specifically, all six strong arguments and all six weak arguments were paired 15 times with favorable or unfavorable valences, respectively. The rationale for this pairing is that, in most empirical studies, strong arguments are represented by descriptions of attributes that are predominantly superior to alternative attitude objects, while weak arguments are represented by predominantly inferior attributes. Consequently, strong arguments elicit primarily favorable thoughts and evaluations about the attitude object, and weak arguments elicit primarily unfavorable thoughts and evaluations (see Petty & Cacioppo, 1984, p.73). Note that this implementation ignores the fact that arguments may be sensitive to the context or attitude for which they are used (e.g. "improved colors" are crucial for a TV screen but irrelevant for a answering machine; see also Barden, Maddux, Petty, & Brewer, 2004). This sensitivity could be built in by incorporating a more distributed representation in which the arguments are bound with an attitudinal context or category (by so-called configural nodes), and so develop weak or strong connections with the valence nodes depending on the attitudinal context (see also the section Alternative implementations).

Second, the acquisition of the length heuristic was simulated during the prior heuristic learning phase. In particular, to reflect prior learning of short messages, a single trial was presented for each of the three strong arguments, while to reflect prior learning of long messages, four trials were presented for each argument, or three versus twelve arguments overall (we used these frequencies in most of subsequent simulations). Recall that we used different subsets of arguments for prior learning versus the experimental phase. To simplify the simulation, during prior learning, we repeated the arguments from the prior-learning subset. This is admissible because the specific arguments themselves do not matter and serve only to activate a positive valence, and so increase the connection from the length cue to the positive valence node. As noted earlier, given that research indicates that the length heuristic typically increases endorsement of a message (while in principle it might also decrease endorsement if the audience assumes a weak or unconvincing argumentation), we assumed here that lengthy messages are retrieved mainly from strong and convincing arguments, leading to a link with positive valence. To simulate the idea that multiple heuristic experiences are necessary to detect statistical regularities and consolidate them in long-term memory, the entire heuristic episode of this phase was repeated 10 times with a learning rate that was only 10% of the learning rate for the other material.

Next, during the experimental phase, the simulation ran through each experimental condition that consisted of a simplified replication of Petty and Cacioppo's (1984) experiment. In one condition, the attitude object (the exam) was paired with strong arguments, which elicited favorable evaluations, while in the other condition the attitude object was paired with weak arguments, which elicited unfavorable evaluations. To represent short versus long messages, the simulation was run through either one or three arguments, which reflects the same proportion of arguments as in Petty and Cacioppo's (1984) empirical study. During the high-involvement conditions, central processing was reproduced by setting the activation levels of all nodes in the experimental phase to standard levels. During low involvement, heuristic processing was implemented by setting the activation levels of the heuristic cue to one-tenth of these standard levels (= .10), while activation for the arguments was reduced even further one-tenth (= .01). Other activation values are also possible, but increasing the activation much above the levels described here may result in an indirect generalization of the cue's valence rather than a direct generalization, as discussed earlier.

Finally, in the test phase, measuring the attitude was accomplished in the same manner as the previous simulation (see bottom panel of Table 11.3). We additionally measured post-message attribute-relevant thoughts, taking in to account their favorable or unfavorable valence. Like our measures of attitude, this involves activating the attitude object node and then reading off the activation of the valence nodes and, additionally, the activation of the cognitive nodes representing the arguments. Specifically, as shown in the last line of Table 11.3, the activation of the attitude object node was turned on and the activation of the arguments and valence nodes was measured and then averaged. To balance the output activation of the arguments and valences, the activation of the valences was multiplied by the number of arguments before all output activations were averaged. (In the present network model, this procedure is analogous to testing each argument and its associated evaluative activation one after the other, and then averaging the results.) During heuristic processing, all testing activation levels of the attribute-relevant thoughts (including those indicated by?) were reduced to 1% of the standard activation level (in the same manner as for the activation of the arguments in the Experimental phase).

Results

The "statements" of each condition listed in Table 11.3 were processed by the network for 50 "participants" in each condition with different random orders for each phase. Figure 11.5 depicts the mean test activation for all simulated attitude measures (top panel) and thought measures (bottom panel), projected on top of the empirical data from Petty and Cacioppo (1984). As can be seen, the simulation matched the attitude data reasonably well. Under low involvement, the length heuristic had the strongest impact on the simulated attitude, while under high involvement, the quality and number of the arguments had a greater impact. As can be seen, under high involvement, the simulation reproduced a significant increase and decrease of attitude given more strong or weak arguments, respectively. The thought data were also replicated, although to a somewhat lesser degree. Under low involvement there were few simulated thoughts, and under high involvement thought favorability revealed the same general pattern as the simulated attitudes.

These observations were verified with an ANOVA with three between-subjects factors: Involvement (low and high), Quality of Arguments (strong and weak) and Number of Arguments (few and many). The analysis on the simulated attitudes revealed the expected three-way interaction, $F(1,392) = 1225.20$, $p < .0001$. Two interactions were of special interest and were also observed in the empirical data (Petty & Cacioppo, 1984). First, there was a significant interaction between Involvement and Number of Arguments, $F(1,392) = 1043.71$, $p < .0001$. As expected, increasing the number of arguments produced significantly more agreement under low involvement, $t(396) = 5.33$, $p < .0001$, and less so under high involvement, $t(396) = 2.81$, $p < .01$. Second, there was a significant interaction between Involvement and Quality of Arguments, $F(1,392) = 4385.29$, $p < .0001$. As predicted, strong arguments produced significantly more agreement than did weak arguments under high involvement, $t(396) = 29.60$, $p < .0001$, but not under low involvement, $t < 1$, *ns*.

The same ANOVA applied to the valenced thoughts revealed the predicted interaction between Involvement and Quality of Arguments, $F(1,392) = 4526.89$, $p < .0001$. Strong arguments generated significantly more thoughts that were consistent with the valence of the arguments than did weak arguments under high involvement, $t(396) = 34.51$, $p < .0001$, but not under low involvement, $t < 1$.

Simulation 3: Consensus heuristic

Let us now turn to the consensus heuristic. Dual-process research has documented that, under heuristic processing, a higher consensus or majority endorsement of a message implies correctness of that message (Axsom, Yates, & Chaiken, 1987; Darke et al., 1998; Erb, Bohner, Schmälzle, & Rank, 1998; Maheswaran & Chaiken, 1991). This consensus heuristic works in very similar ways as the length heuristic. Instead of the sheer number of arguments, here it is the number of people endorsing the arguments that is crucial. In both cases, however, the arguments are more often repeated and therefore influence our attitudes more strongly. Thus, past encounters with many people providing strong arguments in favor of an attitude position led to links of high consensus with positive valence. Conversely, past encounters with many people providing weak arguments in favor of an attitude position (or strong arguments counter to that position) led to links of low consensus with nega-tive valence. In sum, high consensus builds a link with a positive valence, while low consensus builds a link with negative valence. In a connectionist framework, this prior consensus knowledge is "retrieved" under heuristic pro-cessing and dominates attitude formation because little attention is given the novel information, whereas under central processing, the novel information is fully attended to and tends to overwrite the effects of prior consensus beliefs.

Key experiment

We explore our connectionist approach to the consensus heuristic by simulat-ing a prominent study by Maheswaran and Chaiken (1991, Experiment 1). Participants read about a fictitious "XT–100" telephone answering machine. Involvement in the issue was manipulated by telling the participants that their reactions would be used to decide whether to distribute the product in their own State (high involvement) or in another State (low involvement). Next, participants read the results of an ostensible marketing test which revealed that either 81% (high consensus) or less than 3% (low consensus) of the consumers were extremely satisfied with the product. Finally, they read a message that described the answering machine as mainly superior to compet-ing brands (strong arguments) or mainly inferior (weak arguments). As can be seen in Figure 11.6 (top panel), the results confirmed the dual-process predictions. Under low involvement, the proportion of satisfied customers had a strong impact suggesting that the consensus heuristic was applied. The smaller the proportion of satisfied customers indicating satisfaction with the product, the smaller the agreement was with the message and the greater the proportion, the higher the agreement. In contrast, under high involve-ment, the quality of the arguments had a greater impact so that strong arguments led to more attitude change than weak arguments.

What about the cognitive responses mediating attitude formation? Unfortunately, Maheswaran and Chaiken (1991) reported only the amount of thoughts without their valence, so that Figure 11.6 (bottom panel) pres-ents non-valenced thoughts. They suggested that, apart from the influence of the consensus heuristic, incongruency between the majority position and the novel arguments would result in increased central processing by undermining perceiver's confidence in their heuristic-based judgments (see also Erb et al., 1998; Mackie, 1987). This is indeed what they found. As can be seen in Figure 11.6, the amount of non-valenced thinking under heuristic processing reveals the expected interaction between congruency and consensus. There was little thinking under low involvement when there was congruency between consensus information and persuasive arguments. In contrast, when there was incongruency, the amount of thinking under low involvement was equally high as under high involvement. However, these results are theor-etically less informative as they do not reveal to what extent valenced thoughts mediated attitude change, although Maheswaran and Chaiken

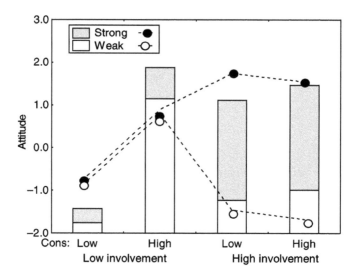

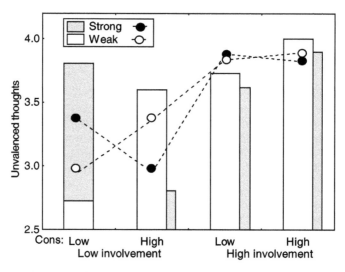

Figure 11.6 Consensus heuristic: Observed data from Maheswaran and Chaiken (1991, Experiment 1) and simulation results of attitudes (top panel) and unvalenced thoughts (bottom panel). Human data are denoted by bars, simulated values by broken lines. The human data are from Table 1 in "Promoting systematic processing in low-motivation settings: Effect of incongruent information on processing and judgment" by D. Maheswaran & S. Chaiken, 1991, *Journal of Personality and Social Psychology*, *61*, 18. Copyright 1991 by the American Psychological Association.

(1991) reported regression analyses revealing a positive relationship which was stronger under high than low involvement.

Although valenced thoughts were not available, we found it interesting to see whether we could simulate non-valenced thinking instead. To do so, we had to incorporate Maheswaran and Chaiken's (1991) finding that there is increased thinking given incongruency. We presume that the incongruency in the stimulus material alerted the attentional control system so that more activation was devoted to it. Specifically, we implemented the same test procedure as in the previous simulation for the thought-listing task (i.e. with only one-third of the default attention during heuristic processing), with the exception that—in line with Maheswaran and Chaiken (1991)—attention was back at the default level during recall of incongruent thoughts.

Simulation

Table 11.4 represents a schematic learning history of our simulation of the experiment by Maheswaran and Chaiken (1991, Experiment 1). The rationale

Table 11.4 Learning experiences and the consensus heuristic (Simulation 3)

	Object and cue		Arguments[a]							Valence	
	XT–100	Consensus	Str1	Str2	Str3	Wk1	Wk2	Wk3	☺	☻
#10 Prior heuristic learning: High (*low*) consensus											
#4		+	+(0)			0(+)			i	i
#4		+		+(0)			0(+)		i	i
#4		+			+(0)			0(+)	i	i
Strong (*weak*) message											
#1	1	1	1(0)			0(1)			i	i
#1	1	1		1(0)			0(1)		i	i
#1	1	1			1(0)			0(1)	i	i
Test											
Attitude toward XT–100	1								?	–?
Non-valenced thoughts	1		?	?	?	?	?	?	6?	6?

Simplified version of the experimental design by Maheswaran & Chaiken (1991, exp. 1). Str, strong; Wk, weak; ☺, favorable; ☻, unfavorable; #, frequency of trial or condition; cell entries denote external activation and empty cells denote 0 activation; +, external activation of 0.5; i, internal activation (generated mainly by the arguments) is taken as external activation. Each experimental condition was run separately, and always preceded by a prior valence learning phase (not shown) and prior heuristic learning phase, followed by the test phase. Trial order was randomized in each phase and condition. During prior valence learning (not shown), all strong and weak argument nodes were paired with the favorable or unfavorable valence nodes, respectively, for 15 trials (see also Simulation 1). During prior heuristic learning, each condition was repeated 10 times with 10% of the default learning rate. During heuristic processing of the experimental phase, activation was reduced to 10% for the cue and to 1% for the arguments during acquisition of novel information and testing of attribute-relevant thoughts.

[a] The arguments during prior learning are completely different from those in the experimental and test conditions, but are shown in the same columns to conserve space. The arguments during prior heuristic learning serve to drive the cue's valence into a positive or negative direction, but are of no further importance.

is similar as in the simulation of the length heuristic. During the prior heuristic learning phase, to reflect low consensus, four trials were presented for each unfavorable argument, while four trials were presented of favorable arguments to reflect high consensus. These trial frequencies reflect an arbitrary number of other people who expressed their opinions on the issue, and were chosen to represent a simple learning history of extreme low consensus (all perceivers disagree) and high consensus (all perceivers agree). As before, this whole phase was repeated 10 times with a learning rate reduced to 10% to mimic consolidation of heuristic information in long-term memory.

Next, the network ran through the experimental phase. Each argument was presented once, and their quality—strong versus weak—differed according to condition. During the low-involvement conditions, heuristic processing was simulated by setting the activation of the cue to 10% of the default and to 1% for the arguments, while during high-involvement conditions, central processing was implemented by setting the standard activation levels.

Measuring the attitude and post-message valenced thoughts was accomplished in the same manner as the previous simulation (see bottom panel of Table 11.4). We additionally measured non-valenced thought by reading off the total amount of favorable and unfavorable evaluation, instead of the differential activation of the favorable and unfavorable evaluation, using the activation levels as indicated above. That is, when there was incongruency between the information implied by the consensus information and the novel arguments, we assumed that the activation levels were restored to the standard levels while measuring these thought (but not when the learning phases were running).

Results

The information listed in Table 11.4 was processed by the network for 50 "participants" in each condition with different random orders. Figure 11.6 depicts the mean test activation for all simulated attitude measures (top panel) and thought measures (bottom panel) on top of the empirical data of Maheswaran and Chaiken (1991). It can be seen that the simulation closely matched the attitude data. Under low involvement, level of consensus had the strongest impact on the simulated attitude, while under high involvement, the quality of the arguments had a greater impact. The simulation also replicated the observed data on the non-valenced attribute-relevant thoughts. Fewer thoughts were found under congruent conditions of low involvement, while the largest number of thoughts was observed under incongruent conditions as well as under high involvement.

These observations were tested with an ANOVA with three between-subjects factors, Involvement (low and high), Quality of Arguments (strong and weak) and Consensus (low and high). The analysis on the simulated attitudes revealed two predicted interactions that were also observed in the empirical data (Maheswaran & Chaiken, 1991). First, there was a significant interaction between Involvement and Consensus, $F(1,392) = 2096.25$, $p < .0001$. As expected, increasing the consensus produced significantly more agreement under low involvement, $t(396) = 9.51$, $p < .0001$, but not under high involvement, $t(396) = 1.27$, *ns*. Second, there was a significant interaction between Involvement and Quality of Arguments, $F(1,392) = 6419.85$, $p < .0001$. As predicted, strong arguments produced significantly more agreement than did weak arguments under high involvement, $t(396) = 38.46$, $p < .0001$, but not under low involvement, $t(396) = 1.46$, *ns*.

We applied the same ANOVA on the simulated valenced thoughts, that is, the thoughts including their valence (not in Figure 11.6). The analysis revealed the predicted interaction between Involvement and Quality of Arguments, $F(1,392) = 9956.85$, $p < .0001$. Strong arguments generated significantly more positive thoughts than weak arguments primarily under high involvement, $t(396) = 68.14$, $p < .0001$, and less so under low involvement, $t(396) = 15.05$, $p < .0001$. In addition, an analysis on the non-valenced thoughts revealed (see Figure 11.6), consistent with Maheswaran and Chaiken's (1991) congruency hypothesis, a significant interaction between Consensus and Quality of Arguments under low involvement, $F(1, 392) = 606.19$, $p < .0001$. Congruency between consensus and argument quality led to less non-valenced thoughts than incongruency, $t(396) = 6.14$, $p < .0001$.

Simulation 4: Expertise heuristic

Another heuristic cue often explored in the context of dual-process approaches is the expertise heuristic, which says that "experts can be trusted". Again, this heuristic can be viewed as another instance of the acquisition property of the delta learning algorithm, by assuming that the arguments and thoughts compiled from highly regarded experts are more favorable than those compiled from non-experts. This is consistent with the assumption by Bohner, Ruder, and Erb (2002) that source expertise may lead people to form different expectations about message strength. This can be simulated by a prior heuristic learning phase in which experts or trusted sources are seen as using stronger arguments that elicit more favorable valences than non-experts or untrustworthy sources.

Several studies revealed different effects of heuristic and central processing given different levels of source credibility, in line with predictions of dual-process models. It was found that source credibility determined attitudes under heuristic processing, but not under central processing where argument quality was of major importance (Chaiken & Maheswaran, 1994; Petty, Cacioppo, & Goldman, 1981; Ratneshwar & Chaiken, 1991). Similar results have also been reported for likeable or famous sources (Chaiken, 1980; Petty, Cacioppo, & Schumann, 1983) because such communicators are seen as more expert and trustworthy (Chaiken, 1980; Chaiken & Eagly, 1983).

Key experiment

One of the studies by Chaiken and Maheswaran (1994) is particularly important because it also demonstrated that central and heuristic processing modes are not mutually exclusive. For instance, when the arguments are too ambiguous to form an opinion by extensive processing alone, heuristic cues may additionally help to form an opinion by biasing the selection and interpretation of ambiguous information. This interaction between central and heuristic processing, referred to as the bias hypothesis (Chaiken et al., 1989; Chen & Chaiken, 1999), was investigated by Chaiken and Maheswaran (1994), who presented a message about a fictitious "XT–100" answering machine in which different attributes were described. Involvement was manipulated in the typical manner by telling the respondents that their opinion about the answering machine would have little bearing on the manufacturer's decision to distribute the product in another State (low involvement) or would count heavily on the decision to distribute the product in their own State (high involvement). Expertise was manipulated by taking this information ostensibly from a highly regarded magazine specializing in scientific testing of new products (high expertise) or in a promotional pamphlet prepared by sales personnel (low expertise). The message described the answering machine as superior to competing brands on all important attributes (strong arguments), inferior on all important attributes (weak arguments), or superior on some attributes while inferior on others (ambiguous arguments).

As can be seen in Figure 11.7 (top panel), consistent with the predictions of Maheswaran and Chaiken (1991), source credibility was the only determinant of people's attitude under low involvement. In contrast, under high involvement, argument quality was the main determining factor, except when the message was ambiguous and source credibility alone influenced the attitude. As might be expected, the valenced thoughts reflected a similar pattern under high involvement, and little thought under low involvement (see Figure 11.7, bottom panel).

Simulation

We simulated the biasing nature of heuristic cues on central processing as investigated by Chaiken and Maheswaran (1994). Table 11.5 presents a simplified learning history, with a similar network architecture and history as before, except for the elements detailed next.

In the prior heuristic phase, knowledge about expertise is built up by several experiences of good and bad argumentation by expert and non-expert sources, respectively. As in the earlier simulations, three arguments were each presented in four trials (or 12 arguments overall), so that strong connections from the expert source to the favorable or unfavorable valences were established for expert and non-expert sources respectively. This whole

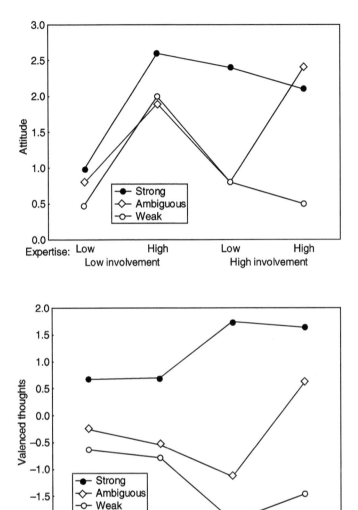

Figure 11.7 Expertise heuristic: Observed attitude data (top panel) and observed valenced thoughts (bottom panel) from Chaiken and Maheswaran (1994). The human data are from Figure 1 and Table 2 respectively in "Heuristic processing can bias systematic processing: Effects of source credibility, argument ambiguity, and task importance on attitude judgment" by S. Chaiken & D. Maheswaran, 1994, *Journal of Personality and Social Psychology*, *66*, 466. Copyright 1994 by the American Psychological Association. Adapted with permission.

Table 11.5 Learning experiences and the expertise heuristic (Simulation 4)

	Object and cue		Arguments[a]						Valence	
	XT–100	Source	Str1	Str2	Str3	Wk1	Wk2	Wk3	☺	☹
#10 Prior heuristic learning: High (*low*) expertise										
#4		+	+(*0*)			0(+)			i	i
#4		+		+(*0*)			0(+)		i	i
#4		+			+(*0*)			0(+)	i	i
Strong (*weak*) message										
#1	1	1	1(*0*)			0(*1*)			i	i
#1	1	1		1(*0*)			0(*1*)		i	i
#1	1	1			1(*0*)			0(*1*)	i	i
Ambiguous message										
#1	1	1	1						i	i
#1	1	1			1				i	i
Test										
Attitude toward XT–100	1								?	–?
Valenced Thoughts	1		?	?	?	?	?	?	6?	–6?

Simplified version of the experimental design by Chaiken and Maheswaran (1994). Str, strong; Wk, weak; ☺ favorable; ☹, unfavorable; #, frequency of trial or condition; cell entries denote external activation and empty cells denote 0 activation; +, external activation of 0.5; i, internal activation (generated mainly by the arguments) is taken as external activation. Each experimental condition was run separately, and always preceded by a prior valence learning phase (not shown) and prior heuristic learning phase, followed by the test phase. Trial order was randomized in each phase and condition. During prior valence learning (not shown), all strong and weak argument nodes were paired with the favorable or unfavorable valence nodes, respectively, for 15 trials (see also Simulation 1). During prior heuristic learning, each condition was repeated 10 times with 10% of the default learning rate. During heuristic processing of the experimental phase, activation was reduced to 10% for the cue and to 1% for the arguments during acquisition of novel information and testing of attribute-relevant thoughts.

[a] The arguments during prior learning are completely different from those in the experimental and test conditions, but are shown in the same columns to conserve space. The arguments during prior heuristic learning serve to drive the cue's valence into a positive or negative direction, but are of no further importance.

phase was repeated 10 times with a learning rate reduced to 10% of the standard rate.

During the experimental phase, we ran one of three message types involving strong, weak, and ambiguous arguments. As before, strong messages were represented by three strong arguments associated with a favorable evaluation, while weak messages were represented by three weak arguments associated with an unfavorable evaluation. In addition, ambiguous messages were represented by one strong and one weak argument. This reflects—in a simplified manner—the quality and direction of the arguments in Chaiken and Maheswaran's (1994) empirical study. Simulating heuristic versus central processing and measuring the attitude and post-message valenced thoughts was accomplished in the same manner as in the previous simulation (see also note of Table 11.5).

Results

The "statements" in each condition listed in Table 11.5 were processed by the network for 50 "participants" in each condition with different random orders. Figure 11.8 depicts the mean test activation for all simulated attitude measures (top panel) and thought measures (bottom panel). When comparing with the empirical results of Chaiken and Maheswaran (1994; see Figure 11.7), it can be seen that the simulation closely matched the attitude

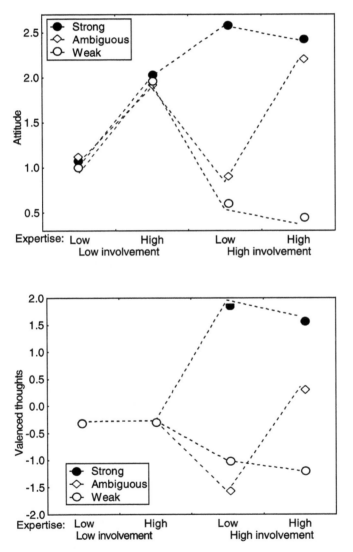

Figure 11.8 Expertise heuristic: Simulation results of attitudes (top panel) and valenced thoughts (bottom panel) from the simulation of the Chaiken and Maheswaran (1994) study.

data. Source credibility strongly determined the simulated attitudes under low involvement while, under high involvement, argument quality was the main determining factor, except when the message was ambiguous and source credibility alone influenced the attitude. The thought data were also replicated, although to a somewhat lesser degree. There were few simulated thoughts under low involvement, and under high involvement, the thoughts revealed the same pattern as the simulated attitudes.

These observations were verified with an ANOVA with three between-subjects factors, Involvement (low and high), Quality of Arguments (strong, ambiguous and weak) and Expertise (low and high). The analysis on the simulated attitudes revealed the expected three-way interaction, $F(2,588) = 105.48$, $p < .0001$. Two interactions were of special interest and were also observed in the empirical data (Chaiken & Maheswaran, 1994). First, there was a significant interaction between Involvement and Expertise, $F(1,588) = 118.97$, $p < .0001$. As expected, increasing the expertise produced significantly more agreement under low involvement, $t(596) = 11.16, p < .0001$, and much less so under high involvement, $t(596) = 4.07, p < .0001$. Second, there was a significant interaction between Involvement and Quality of Arguments, $F(2,588) = 438.26, p < .0001$. As predicted, strong arguments produced significantly more agreement than did weak arguments under high involvement, $t(594) = 26.44$, $p < .0001$, but not under low involvement, $t < 1$, *ns*. More importantly, as predicted by the bias hypothesis, when the arguments were ambiguous, higher expertise produced more agreement, $t(594) = 13.27, p < .0001$.

The same ANOVA applied on the valenced thoughts revealed the predicted interaction between Involvement and Quality of Arguments, $F(2,588) = 520.74, p < .0001$. Strong arguments generated significantly more thoughts that were consistent with the valence of the arguments than did weak arguments under high involvement, $t(594) = 32.85, p < .0001$, but not under low involvement, $t < 1$, *ns*. Again, as predicted by the bias hypothesis, when the arguments were ambiguous, high expertise elicited more favorable thoughts about the message than low expertise, $t(594) = 7.96, p < .0001$.

Simulation 5: Mood heuristic

Dual-process research has revealed that mood also operates like a heuristic, and that it also influences central processing (e.g. Petty, Schumann, Richman, & Strathman, 1993; for discussion, see Schwarz, Bless, & Bohner, 1991). Our connectionist approach to the heuristic impact of mood on cognition shares many similarities with affect priming theories (e.g. Bower, 1981) and affect-as-information theories (e.g. Schwarz & Clore, 1983) that instigated a lot of research on mood-congruent judgments (for an overview, see Forgas, 2001). According to affect priming theory (Bower, 1981; Isen, 1984), mood biases occur through mood-congruent attention, encoding, and retrieval of information involved in judgmental processes. These biases were explained by the mechanism of activation spreading in an associative memory network. This is obviously consistent with the present connectionist approach that assumes the same mechanism of automatic activation spreading. According to affect-as-information theory (Schwarz, 1990; Schwarz & Clore, 1983), affect has an informational value because people ask themselves "How do I feel about it?" when they evaluate persons or objects. More importantly, this theory posits that mood biases occur when people attribute (erroneously) the source of their affect to the attitude object.

In the present simulations, we take this former mood activation-spreading approach to simulate the impact of the mood heuristic. This assumes that, unlike the previous heuristic simulations, mood has a direct effect on valence without the aid of arguments. Thus, we learn that a positive mood is favorable and a neutral mood is a mixture of favorable and unfavorable valences. However, if we take the latter misattribution approach, which assumes that perceivers often erroneously associate their feelings with the quality of the arguments or attributes of an attitude object, we obtain similar simulation results. This alternative presupposes that perceivers attribute their positive mood during heuristic processing to high-quality attributes and arguments, which elicit a positive valence, whereas they interpret their neutral or negative mood to the low-quality attributes and arguments, which elicit a negative valence. In other words, mood acts like if it is equivalent to a piece of positive or negative information[2].

Key experiment

In a prominent study by Petty et al. (1993, Experiment 2), the effects of mood on attitude formation were investigated under low and high personal involvement. After a positive or neutral mood induction, participants were exposed to a persuasive communication concerning a fictitious "Maestro" pen. Involvement was manipulated by telling the participants that the Maestro pen would be marketed soon in their community and that they had to make a selection between several brands of writing implements (high involvement), or they were told that the marketing would take place in other cities and that they had to make a selection between several brands of instant coffee (low involvement). Quality of argumentation was manipulated in this study, but had no significant effects on attitudes (see Petty et al, 1993, for details[3]). This factor will therefore not be further discussed here. As can be seen in Figure 11.9 (top panel), positive mood produced more positive attitudes in agreement with the persuasive message under both low and high

---

2 Research has shown that people can discount their current mood as a source of information when made aware of it (e.g. Sinclair, Mark, & Clore, 1994). Such strategic use of mood is not modeled in the present simulation.

3 For their first study, Petty et al. (1993) reported a similar problem in that "it was possible . . . to interpret the weak arguments in a positive light" (p.10).

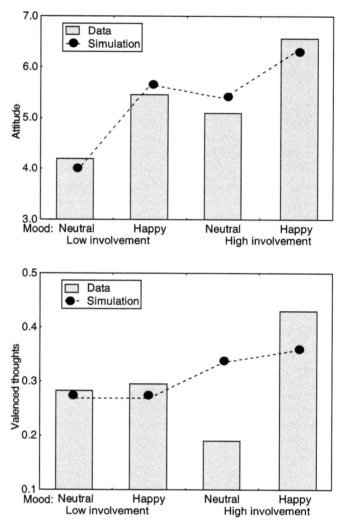

Figure 11.9 Mood heuristic: Observed data from Petty et al. (1993, Experiment 2) and simulation results of attitudes (top panel) and valenced thoughts (bottom panel). Human data are denoted by bars, simulated values by broken lines. The human data are from Figure 3 in "Positive mood and persuasion: Different roles for affect under high- and low-elaboration conditions" by R. E. Petty, D. W. Schumann, S. A. Richman & A. J. Strathman, 1993, *Journal of Personality and Social Psychology*, *64*, 16. Copyright 1993 by the American Psychological Association. Adapted with permission.

involvement, whereas positive mood influenced the positivity of thoughts only under high involvement (bottom panel).

Simulation

We simulated the effects of mood as explored by Petty et al. (1993, Experiment 2). Table 11.6 presents a schematic learning history that is similar to earlier simulations of heuristic processing, except for the following elements. As mentioned previously, because quality of arguments had no effect, to simplify the simulation, we simulated only strong arguments. In the prior heuristic phase, we assume that positive mood generates favorable evaluations, while neutral mood generates favorable and unfavorable evaluations.

Results

The "statements" listed in Table 11.6 were processed by the network for 50 "participants" with different random orders. Figure 11.9 depicts the mean test activation for all simulated attitude measures (top panel) and thought

Table 11.6 Learning experiences and the mood heuristic (Simulation 5)

	Object and cue		Arguments			Valence	
	Pen	Mood	Str1	Str2	Str3	☺	☹
#10 Prior heuristic learning: Positive (*neutral*) mood							
#4		+				1	0(*1*)
#4		+				1	0(*1*)
#4		+				1	0(*1*)
Strong message							
#1	1	1	1			i	i
#1	1	1		1		i	i
#1	1	1			1	i	i
Test							
Attitude toward pen	1					?	–?
Valenced thoughts	1		?	?	?	3?	–3?

Simplified version of the experimental design by Petty, Schumann, Richman, and Strathman (1993, Experiment 2). Str, strong; Wk, weak; ☺, favorable; ☹, unfavorable; #, frequency of trial or condition; cell entries denote external activation and empty cells denote 0 activation; +, external activation of 0.5; i, internal activation (generated mainly by the arguments) is taken as external activation. Each experimental condition was run separately, and always preceded by a prior valence learning phase (not shown) and prior heuristic learning phase, followed by the test phase. Trial order was randomized in each phase and condition. During prior valence learning (not shown), all strong and weak argument nodes were paired with the favorable or unfavorable valence nodes, respectively, for 15 trials (see also Simulation 1). During prior heuristic learning, each condition was repeated 10 times with 10% of the default learning rate. During heuristic processing of the experimental phase, activation was reduced to 10% for the cue and to 1% for the arguments during acquisition of novel information and testing of attribute-relevant thoughts.

measures (bottom panel) on top of the empirical data of Petty et al. (1993). As can be seen, the simulation closely matched the attitude data. Positive mood increased the simulated attitude under both low and high involvement. The valenced thoughts were also replicated, although to a somewhat lesser degree. There were few simulated thoughts under low involvement; under high involvement, the thoughts revealed the same pattern as the simulated attitudes.

These observations were verified with an ANOVA with two between-subjects factors, Involvement (low and high) and Mood (neutral and happy). The analysis on the simulated attitudes revealed a main effect of Mood, $F(1,196) = 2666.88$, $p < .0001$, indicating that a happy mood produced significantly more agreement. There was also an expected main effect of Involvement, $F(1,196) = 1702.67$, $p < .0001$, indicating that high involvement (in the processing of strong arguments) led to more agreement with the message than low involvement.

The analysis on the valenced thoughts revealed the predicted interaction between Mood and Involvement, $F(1,196) = 213.17$, $p < .0001$. A happy mood generated significantly more positive thoughts than did a neutral mood under high involvement, $t(196) = 20.96$, $p < .0001$, but not under low involvement, $t < 1$, ns.

IMPLICATIONS AND EXTENSIONS

All simulations in the preceding sections successfully reproduced the observed attitude and thought data from the empirical studies that tested a dual-process approach to attitude formation and change (Chaiken, 1987; Chen & Chaiken, 1999; Petty & Cacioppo, 1981, 1986; Petty & Wegener, 1999). Providing a formal account of the most important psychological processes in attitude formation by a unitary connectionist framework is an important achievement in its own right, because it organizes existing research and also because earlier attempts (e.g. Fishbein & Ajzen, 1975) articulated only fragments of these processes (e.g. central processes) at a mere input–output or computational level (cf. Marr, 1982). Perhaps more crucially, it allows making some tentative hypotheses about the nature of these under-lying processes. To the extent that other comprehensive formalizations are lacking, it gives more weight to the present hypotheses than to alternative hypotheses that are not supported by a connectionist approach. In addition, it points to similarities with other connectionist models of social cognition (see Chapters 8 and 9), which may suggest ways in which attitude research can be extended to similar phenomena uncovered in these areas. Although we have touched on some of these issues already, we first recapitulate some implications of the present model and then discuss empirical and theoretical extensions.

Implications for the underlying psychological mechanisms

Quantitative and qualitative processing differences

Perhaps, the most central idea of this article was that the delta learning algorithm may provide a common underlying psychological mechanism responsible for different routes or modes of processing at a surface level of perceivers' intuition and awareness. We assumed that heuristic and central processes are based on different information bases (prior knowledge versus novel information, respectively) that are developed and applied somewhat differently (generalized cue knowledge versus second-order object → valence connections) rather than involving radically different processing systems or brain structures. In this manner, we were able to account for qualitative differences in persuasion that attitude researchers have uncovered (Petty & Wegener, 1999). However, the network was endowed with sufficient flexibility through a supervisory attentional system that funneled activation to one of these information bases, so that it could also account not only for these qualitative differences, but also for quantitative differences in elaboration likelihood (Petty & Wegener, 1999). One implication of this flexibility is that it also allows the network to consider heuristic cues as an information basis for deliberative scrutiny, if attention is sufficiently large (see also Chen & Chaiken, 1999). For example, several studies have documented that, under moderate elaboration, expertise can determine the extent of thinking (e.g. Heesacker, Petty, & Cacioppo, 1983) as can mood (e.g. Mackie & Worth, 1989; Schwarz, Bless, & Bohner, 1991). In general, the supervisory attention module in our model can account for switching of strategies, although the executive processes that implement such changes in attention are not yet part of the model.

Nevertheless, another sense of qualitative difference is not captured in our model. Some authors have argued that central processing involves the effortful analysis of logical links via the use of propositional reasoning (e.g. Smith & DeCoster, 2000; Strack & Deutsch, 2004). Needless to say, propositional or symbolic processing is not part of our model. We only assume that once the essence of the arguments (e.g. the attributes) are symbolically understood (which is sometimes very easy when simple persuasive appeals are used such as "better", etc.), then our model proposes that their associated valences are retrieved automatically from memory and combined into a novel attitude. Thus, our model cannot fully accommodate all aspects of central processing, as it leaves propositional understanding and reasoning on the coherence and relevance of the arguments to a higher-level symbolic subsystem of the brain.

Valenced thoughts mediate attitude formation

We simulated the typical finding in dual-process research, borrowed from the cognitive response approach (Greenwald, 1968), that the quality and valence of the object's attributes as expressed in thought-listing measures, determine attitude change under effortful or central processing. Although some authors claimed that attribute-relevant thoughts may just represent an alternate dependent measure of persuasion (Miller & Colman, 1981), in our connectionist model, the attitudes depended entirely on the favorable or unfavorable evaluations generated by the object's attributes and, without these, no object → valence connections would be established. Thus, consistent with the dual-process approach, our formalization points out that the evaluations generated by attribute-relevant thoughts (as later revealed in a thought-listing task) greatly impact on attitude formation under central processing.

Implicit integration of valences

Our simulations also suggest that, after the object's attributes have been symbolically analyzed during central processing (see above), the subsequent integration of evaluations into a single attitude estimate can occur largely outside awareness. This is because the delta learning algorithm, which implements this integration, does not need a central supervisory unit to control this process, as all changes involve low-level modifications in object → valence connection strength. As discussed earlier, this is consistent with recent theorizing in attitude models (e.g. Ajzen, 2002; Chen & Chaiken, 1999) and findings documenting that the processes underlying attitude formation and change are largely non-symbolic and non-conscious (Betsch et al., 2001; Betsch, Plessner, & Schallies, 2004; Lieberman et al., 2001; Olson & Fazio, 2001). It puts the present approach also closer to lower-level processes like (subliminal) conditioning (e.g. Dijksterhuis, 2004; Riketta & Dauenheimer, 2003) and mere exposure effects, which do not require conscious attention either.

Recent neural imaging research suggests that distinct subsystems are responsible for the controlled integration of valenced information versus the automatic conditioning and activation of valences (located in the medial prefrontal cortex versus amygdala respectively, cf. Cunningham, Johnson, Gatenby, Gore, & Banaji, 2003). It would be interesting to see how the results of these imaging studies would extend to a typical persuasive paradigm, although neural techniques may not allow revealing in a clear-cut manner the distinction made here between controlled information access and automatic evaluative integration.

Heuristics are not abstracted rules

As noted earlier, at least two possible interpretations of heuristics were not clearly distinguished in dual-process attitude theories (e.g. Chaiken et al., 1989). One interpretation is that heuristics are knowledge structures consisting of abstracted inferential rules that are activated from memory and applied as tools for cognitive work. Another interpretation, consistent with our connectionist approach, sees heuristics as exemplar-based summarized

experiences that reflect people's implicit knowledge about the statistical relation between situational cues and agreement with messages. These summarized exemplars reside in cue → valence connections, which are automatically
integrated into novel information merely on perceiving or thinking about the
cue. This is in line with an increasing number of connectionist simulations
in other domains of psychology, illustrating that many rule-like behaviors
are not necessarily driven by abstract inferential rules and can be more par-
simoniously explained by subsymbolic properties of connectionist models
(e.g. McLeod et al., 1998; Pacton et al., 2001; Rumelhart & McClelland,
1986; Smith & DeCoster, 2000).

Initial evidence of heuristics as exemplar based

If it is indeed true that persuasion heuristics in people's minds reflect summarized exemplar knowledge rather than explicit inferential rules, this may
have testable implications. For instance, our approach predicts that, under
peripheral processing, one can induce the application of heuristics by priming
relevant exemplars more so than by priming explicit heuristic rules.

Take, for instance, the consensus heuristic. According to an inferential rule
approach, priming an abstract consensus rule like "I agree often with the
majority" should lead to stronger attitude agreement under heuristic processing. The effect of priming heuristic rules has been investigated. Chaiken (1987)
reported on two unpublished studies in which the consensus and length rule
were made more accessible by priming. During an ostensibly unrelated
experiment, eight sentences were provided that conveyed the gist of the rule
(pp.27–29). However, overall, there were no significant attitude effects and
only participants who were low in Need For Cognition (i.e. who tend to avoid
extensive thinking and elaboration; Cacioppo & Petty, 1982) were somewhat influenced by the primed rule. Chaiken (1987) admitted that none of
these results "yielded statistically robust effects favoring our [rule] priming
hypotheses" (p.29).

Our connectionist or exemplar-based approach makes a different prediction. Instead of rules, priming many versus few exemplars of relevant
people should lead to stronger attitude agreement. Recent studies from our
laboratory have confirmed this prediction. In one study (Van Duynslaeger,
Timmermans, & Van Overwalle, 2006, Experiment 1) that manipulated the
consensus heuristic, 292 freshmen read five weak or strong arguments about
a topic, ostensibly given by "some student associations", and were then asked
to provide their opinion about it. To induce heuristic processing, the topic
was of little concern to the freshmen because it involved research in non-
university higher education. Before heuristic processing, they were primed
with either exemplars or a rule indicating low or high consensus. Specifically,
in the exemplar-priming condition, the freshmen were primed with one or
eight exemplar sources (i.e. different students from different student associations featuring in an article on the renovation of the university restaurant).

In the rule-priming condition, they were primed one or five times with the consensus rule (i.e. "I always agree with the opinion of the majority"), using the repeated expression procedure of Powell and Fazio (1984) that is typically applied to manipulate the activation of attitudes.

The results (Figure 11.10, top panel) were largely consistent with our predictions. An ANOVA revealed the predicted interaction between type and degree of priming, $F(1, 284) = 4.95$, $p < .05$. After priming more exemplars, the participants changed their attitudes more, $F(1, 141) = 3.42$, $p < .05$

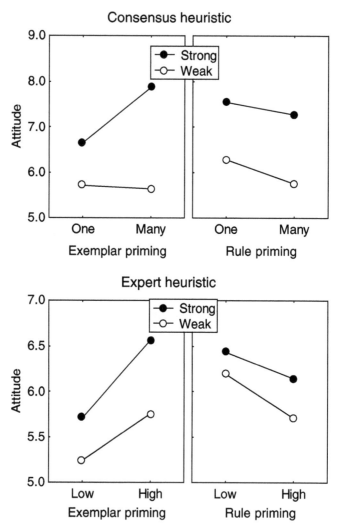

Figure 11.10 Heuristic use as a function of exemplars or rules priming: Observed data on the consensus and expert heuristic from Van Duynslaeger, Timmermans, and Van Overwalle (2006, Experiments 1 and 2).

(one-tailed), whereas after priming the consensus rule, there was no change, $F < 2$. However, one aspect of the results was unexpected. The exemplar priming was effective only for strong arguments, $t(141) = 2.76$, $p < .01$, but not for weak arguments, $t < 1$. Although this raises the possibility that attitude change was due to more systematic processing of the arguments or of the heuristic cues, a correlational analysis with the thought data ruled out this explanation. Perhaps, the stronger quality of the arguments induced a minimal amount of cognitive attention that was necessary for the exemplars to have impact.

In another study (Van Duynslaeger et al., 2006, Experiment 2) that manipulated the expert heuristic, 160 students from higher education school read the same five weak or strong arguments, ostensibly given by an unspecified "famous Flemish person". Before this, they were primed with either well-known exemplars varying in expertise on scientific issues (i.e. an astronaut versus a reality-show celebrity), or they were primed with the expert rule (i.e. "I often agree with the opinion of a trustworthy expert") using the repeated expression procedure. The results (Figure 11.10, bottom panel) were again in agreement with our predictions. An ANOVA revealed the predicted interaction between type and degree of priming, $F(1, 152) = 4.54$, $p < .05$. After priming the expert exemplar, the participants changed their attitudes more than after priming the non-expert exemplar, $F(1, 79) = 3.85$, $p < .05$ (one-tailed), whereas priming the expert rule did not have any effect, $F < 2$. Again, exemplar priming was more effective for strong arguments, $t(76) = 1.72$, $p < .05$ (one-tailed), than for weak arguments, $t < 1.1$. Taken together, consistent with our prediction, priming heuristics had only an effect if it involved exemplars and not symbolic rules.

Extensions from simulations in other domains

One of the major goals of this article was to demonstrate that attitude formation processes, like many other processes in social cognition, can be interpreted in a connectionist framework. Besides its theoretical interest as a step in the construction of a unifying theory of social thinking, it may also introduce novel cross-domain predictions that have been rarely tested in attitude research. Below, we would like to suggest a number of such cross-domain findings that may perhaps lay the ground for more hypotheses and research in the future.

Attitude ambivalence

Sometimes, people experience a great deal of conflict and ambivalence underlying the attitude (e.g. Kaplan, 1972; for a review, see Priester & Petty, 1996). Ambivalence in one's attitudes may have important consequences. It may result in decreased attitude accessibility (Bargh et al., 1992) and less attitudinal confidence and persistence (Jonas, Diehl, & Brömer, 1997; MacDonald

& Zanna, 1998). According to Kaplan (1972), ambivalence is determined in part by the sum of positive and negative attitude components. Thus, as more opposing beliefs are considered, the person would experience more ambivalence. Hence, in connectionist terms, the most simple and direct manner to measure ambivalence is by taking—instead of the differential activation of the favorable and unfavorable valences for measuring the attitude—their summed activation. This measure provides an indication of the spread or range between the two opposing valences, and is akin to a connectionist measure of people's estimates of the heterogeneity of group attributes recently proposed by Van Rooy et al. (2003; see Chapter 9). Using this measure, it is possible to "postdict" the finding of Priester and Petty (1996, Experiments 2 and 3) that ambivalence is a function of the number of deviant or conflicting pieces of information that is negatively accelerating. That is, as more conflicting information contributes to the ambivalence, its contribution becomes increasingly smaller. This is precisely what the emergent acquisition property of the delta algorithm would predict.

Increased memory for inconsistent arguments

Simulations with a recurrent network using the delta learning algorithm in the domain of person perception (see Chapter 8) replicated the intriguing finding that inconsistent or unexpected behavioral information about an actor is often better recalled than information that is consistent with the dominant trait expectation (for a review, see Stangor & McMillan, 1992). Earlier theorizing explained this finding in terms of deeper processing of inconsistent information, which results in more dense associations with the inconsistent behavior (Hastie, 1980). However, Van Overwalle and Labiouse (2004) proposed a novel emergent connectionist property of *diffusion* to explain this finding in terms of weakened memory for consistent behavioral information. This same emergent property may operate for attitudes, and may likewise result in weaker memory for majority and consistent arguments as opposed to minority and inconsistent arguments. In addition, this emergent property predicts that the recall advantage should: (1) increase for arguments at the end of a list; (2) decrease when the number of inconsistent arguments increases; but (3) should remain high even when the number of consistent and inconsistent arguments is equal and inconsistency is manipulated by inducing a prior attitude.

Subtyping of deviant sources

Another finding in group processes that was simulated in a recurrent network by Van Rooy et al. (2003; see Chapter 9) is subtyping. Members of a group with extreme positions on an issue are typically subtyped into subcategories and separated from the rest of the group, more so than members with moderate deviating positions. This insulates the group from dissenting members, so that the content of the existing group stereotype is preserved. Van Rooy et al. (2003) explained this phenomenon by the delta learning algorithm's emergent property of *competition*, which predicts that the more information is concentrated in a few members, the more it must compete against the group stereotype and is discounted (see also Chapter 3). This emergent property may also apply in attitude formation. Hence, we predict that extreme deviant positions on issues that are defended by a few sources are more easily discounted than mildly deviant positions supported by many sources. Consequently, the best tactic to change attitudes is to distribute disconfirming information among as many sources as possible, so as to avoid subtyping of extreme deviant sources.

Contrast effect in ease of retrieval

The present approach can be extended to other heuristic effects, such as the ease of retrieval effect under central processing conditions (Tormala, Petty, & Briñol, 2002). The ease of retrieval effect refers to the phenomenon that when people are asked to come up with arguments for a given attitude position, they are more in favor of the communication if they had to generate only a few arguments, and less in favor if they had to generate a high number of arguments (see also Wänke & Bless, 2000; Wänke, Bless, & Biller, 1996; Wänke, Bohner, & Jurkowitsch, 1997). People thus reveal a contrast away from the requested number of arguments (e.g. less in favor if more arguments are requested). This effect can be simulated based on the idea that the requested number of arguments serves as a standard of comparison. Recently, Van Overwalle and Labiouse (2004; see Chapter 8) proposed a connectionist account for contrast effects in person perception through the presence or priming of exemplary others who serve as a standard of comparison. They documented that this contrast effect may be due to the emergent property of competition against a standard, and this idea might be extended to the attitude domain. To understand how this might work, we describe a simulation of the ease of retrieval effect in somewhat more detail below.

Simulation 6: Ease of retrieval effect

Key experiment

Tormala et al. (2002, Experiment 2) asked their participants to read a persuasive communication concerning a new exam policy and to generate either two or ten favorable arguments in response. They found that, under central processing, participants were more in favor of the communication if they had to generate only two arguments, and they were less in favor if they had to generate ten arguments. However, under peripheral processing, the opposite pattern was found. Presumably, participants did not consider the material thoroughly but were rather influenced by the sheer number of the arguments required and generated. Tormala et al. (2002) explained these results by arguing that subjective confidence influences judgments. The easier it is to generate a list of arguments (because a low number is required), the more confidence an individual has in them. The more difficult it is to generate a list of arguments (because a high number is required), the less confidence an individual has in them. Confidence in one's thoughts is especially important under central processing, when people's motivation and ability to process the information is relatively high, and less so under peripheral processing.

The previous explanations of the ease of retrieval effect rely on meta-cognitive processes, that is, the subjective sense of ease or difficulty of generating arguments, or confidence. These processes are not part of our model. Therefore, we suggest an alternative connectionist explanation of Tormala et al.'s (2002) findings that does not involve meta-cognitive processes, and where these subjective feelings are merely an epiphenomenon of an underlying connectionist mechanism.

To understand our approach, it is important to realize that participants in this type of research typically retrieve fewer arguments than the requested high number, and are thus forced to generate novel arguments (e.g. Wänke et al., 1996). We argue that these novel arguments are less convincing because the difficulty in generating them "will be attributed some qualitative aspect of the information" (Wänke & Bless, 2000, p.158) or, alternatively, because they are mostly redundant with respect to the already retrieved arguments. For instance, after retrieving "good health" as a reason for doing sport, people might construe "on doctor's advice" as a novel argument that actually only rephrases the original one. Although observers read novel arguments as equally convincing in isolation (Wänke et al., 1996), participants themselves find them less "compelling" (Wänke & Bless, 2000), less "strong" (Haddock, 2000; but see Haddock, Rothman, & Schwarz, 1996), and have less "confidence" in them (Tormala et al., 2002). There is also research demonstrating that the ease of retrieval effect is found regardless of whether the requested arguments are actually listed or not (Wänke et al., 1997), suggesting that participants have the intuition that they only rephrase or use less compelling arguments. Because the exact reason for the reduced convincingness is not known, future research may explore in more depth the source of it, and whether argument overlap plays a significant role (e.g. by assessing the perceived redundancy of newly construed arguments). Anyway, in the simulation, we implemented our interpretation in terms of reduced perceived quality by ignoring additional constructed (but less convincing) arguments, thus keeping the same amount of spontaneously retrieved arguments in all conditions.

We suggest that the required number of arguments may act like a situational length cue. Under peripheral processing, this promotes the operation of the length heuristic, and so dominates attitude formation in much the same way as in Simulation 2. However, under central processing, the reverse effect of ease of retrieval is due to a contrast effect of the heuristic length cue against one's own spontaneously retrieved number of arguments. In line with

Van Overwalle and Labiouse (2004, Simulation 5) analysis of contrast effect in person impression formation, this latter effect relies on the emergent connectionist property of competition. This property arises when multiple factors compete in predicting or causing an outcome, and produces a lowering of the connection weights, similar to discounting in causal attribution (Kelley, 1971) and blocking in the conditioning literature (Rescorla & Wagner, 1972; see also Chapter 3).

In the simulations, the competition effect ensues most strongly under central processing, because the novel information receives full activation so that it may compete more against prior knowledge. Specifically, when a high number of arguments is requested, competition will ensue between the strong cue $\rightarrow$ valence connection and the object $\rightarrow$ valence connection, resulting in discounting of the latter connection. This mechanism produces a contrastive effect away from the advocated position in the communication (i.e. ease of retrieval effect). In contrast, when a low number of arguments is requested, little competition will ensue between the weak cue $\rightarrow$ valence connection and the object $\rightarrow$ valence connection, and so the attitude will be relatively favorable.

Simulation

Table 11.7 represents a simplified simulated learning history of Tormala et al. (2002; Experiment 2). The prior valence and prior heuristic learning phases were identical to Simulation 2 of the length heuristic. A request of a low versus high number of arguments was simulated in a prior heuristic learning phase by simulating one or six arguments, which is roughly equivalent to the number of arguments used by Tormala et al. (2002). Next, the experimental phase replicated the generation of arguments. In this line of research, the two requested numbers are selected by the experimenter such that they are smaller and larger, respectively, than the number of arguments that people would retrieve spontaneously (see, e.g. Wänke et al., 1996). Accordingly, we choose two arguments.

Results

The "statements" of each condition listed in Table 11.7 were processed by the network for 50 "participants" in each condition with different random orders. Figure 11.11 depicts the mean test activation for all simulated attitude measures, projected on top of the empirical data from Tormala et al. (2002). As can be seen, the simulation closely matched the attitude data. An ANOVA with Involvement (low and high) and Number of Requested Arguments (low and high) as between-subjects factors, revealed that the expected interaction was significant, $F(1, 396) = 308.13$, $p < .0001$. As Tormala et al. (2002) did not report subjective ease of retrieval, we were not able to assess their role in this simulation.

Table 11.7 Learning experiences and ease of retrieval effect (Simulation 6)

	Object and cue		Arguments[a]			Valence	
	Exam	Length	Str1	Str2	Str3	☺	☹
#10 Prior heuristic learning: Short *(long)* strong Message							
#0 (2)		+	+			i	i
#1 (2)		+		+		i	i
#0 (2)		+			+	i	i
Strong message							
#1	1	1	1			i	i
#0	1	1		1		i	i
#1	1	1			1	i	i
Test							
Attitude toward exam	1					?	–?

Simplified version of the experimental design by Tormala, Petty, and Briñol (2002, Experiment 2). Exam, exam policy; Str, strong; ☺, favorable; ☺, unfavorable; #, frequency of trial or condition; cell entries denote external activation and empty cells denote 0 activation; +, external activation of 0.5; i, internal activation (generated mainly by the arguments) is taken as external activation. Each experimental condition was run separately, and always preceded by a prior valence learning phase (not shown) and prior heuristic learning phase, followed by the test phase. Trial order was randomized in each phase and condition. During prior valence learning (not shown), all strong argument nodes were paired with the favorable valence nodes, respectively, for 15 trials (see also Simulation 1). During prior heuristic learning, each condition was repeated 10 times with 10% of the default learning rate. During heuristic processing of the experimental phase, activation was reduced to 10% for the cue and to 1% for the arguments during acquisition of novel information and testing of attribute-relevant thoughts.

[a] The arguments during prior learning are completely different from those in the experimental and test conditions, but are shown in the same columns to conserve space. The arguments during prior heuristic learning serve to drive the cue's valence into a positive or negative direction, but are of no further importance.

MODEL COMPARISONS

What have other recent approaches in the literature besides dual-process models to tell about attitude formation, and how do they compare with the present approach? In addition, how robust are the present simulations with respect to other possible connectionist implementations? We begin with the last issue, and then turn to a comparison with alternative models.

Alternative implementations of the simulations

The simulations that we have reported all replicate the empirical data or theoretical predictions reasonably well. However, it is possible that this fit is due to some procedural choices of the simulations rather than conceptual validity. To explore whether our simulations are robust to changes in implementational choices, we applied a number of alternative encodings and processing parameters. First, we compared the present localist coding with a

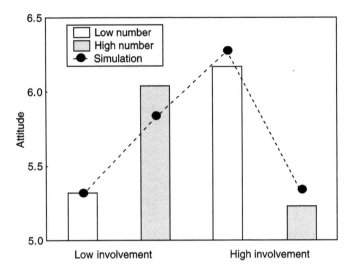

Figure 11.11 Ease of retrieval effect: Observed data from Tormala et al. (2002, Experiment 2) and simulation results. Human data are denoted by bars, simulated values by broken lines. The human data are from Figure 1 in "Ease of retrieval effect in persuasion: A self-validation analysis" by Z. L., Tormala, R. E., Petty & P., Briñol, 2002, *Personality and Social Psychology Bulletin, 28,* 1705–1707. Copyright 2002 by the Society for Personality and Social Psychology. Adapted with permission.

distributed coding to add more realism to the simulations. In a distributed coding, each concept or object is represented by a set of nodes, instead of one node as in localist encoding. The advantage is that these nodes reflect sub-symbolic features that we are not always aware of but that nevertheless may influence our attitudes and that may also include the context in which the attitude is typically applied. As a first attempt toward such a more realistic implementation, each concept was represented by a distributed pattern of activation across four nodes, drawn from a normal distribution with mean as indicated in the learning histories and standard deviation .10. In addition, in all prior learning phases, random noise drawn from a normal distribution with mean 0 and standard deviation .10 was added to these activations to reflect the variation in past experiences. Second, we compared the present dual encoding of favorable versus unfavorable evaluations with a unitary valence encoding in which unfavorable evaluations are represented by nega-tive activation levels (instead of positive activation levels of an unfavorable valence). Third, instead of the present linear updating activation algorithm with two internal cycles, we used a non-linear activation updating algorithm as used by other social researchers (see Chapters 5 and 7). Note that apart from these alterations, all alternative implementations used the same simulation specifications, unless noted otherwise in Table 11.8.

Table 11.8 lists the correlations between the simulated values and the

Table 11.8 Fit and robustness of the simulations, including alternative encoding and models

No. and topic	Dependent measure	Original simulation	Distributed coding	Unitary valence	Non-linear recurrent
1. Central	Attitude	1.00*	.99*	.88	.99*[a]
2. Length	Attitude	.96*	.94*	.97*	.90*[a]
	Thoughts	.80*	.76*	.54	.75*[a]
3. Consensus	Attitude	.88*	.85*	.91*	.71*[a]
	Thoughts	.84*	.62*	.21	.56*[a]
4. Expertise	Attitude	.94*	.73*[b]	.89*	.70*
	Thoughts	.88*	.84*[b]	.74*	.86*
5. Mood	Attitude	.97*	.92*	.78	< 0
	Thoughts	.45	.69	.49	.79
6. Retrieval	Attitude	.95*	.92*	.92*	.82*
Means	Attitude	.95	.89	.89	.65
	Thoughts	.74	.73	.50	.74

Cell entries are correlations between mean simulated values (averaged across randomizations) and empirical data or theoretical predictions. The learning rate parameter for the distributed coding was the best fitting value between .01 and .05. The parameters for the non-linear recurrent model were similar to the linear model, except that decay = .77 (McClelland & Rumelhart, 1988).
[a] Decay = .70; [b]the biasing effect of the heuristic on ambiguous information was not reproduced.
* *p* < .05 (one-tailed).

observed or theoretical data from the original as well as from each of the alternative implementations. As can be seen from the mean correlations (see last two bottom rows), although some of the alternative implementations are adequate, the present simulations are often superior. First, the distributed coding is adequate for all simulations, except that the biasing effect of the expert heuristic on ambiguous information (Simulation 4) was not replicated. This finding is puzzling and we have no clear answer for it. Second, the unitary valence coding generally leads to a weaker fit with the data (especially for thoughts), presumably because a single valence node does not allow for a neutral or ambivalent evaluation that dual valence nodes can support (by coding the valences as both low or both high respectively). Finally, a non-linear recurrent model (with parameter values very close to the linear model) provides the weakest fit with the data. Overall, the results suggest that the present specifications are preferable to a unitary valence coding scheme and a non-linear activation update algorithm, while the results of the distributed coding were equivalent, with one exception. Of course, other implementations of the learning history and the network architecture that we did not explore, are also conceivable.

Siebler's parallel constraint satisfaction network

Recently, Siebler (2002) proposed a connectionist parallel-constraint-satisfaction model (McClelland & Rumelhart, 1988; McLeod et al., 1998) with a single connectionist mechanism to account for dual processing routes in attitude formation and change (Kunda & Thagard, 1996; see also Read & Marcus-Newhall, 1993; Shultz & Lepper, 1996; Spellman & Holyoak, 1992; Thagard, 1989). Siebler's constraint satisfaction model involves the simultaneous satisfaction of multiple, sometimes conflicting constraints on an individual's cognitions, including the *attitude* itself, positive and negative *heuristic cues*, weak and strong *arguments* and favorable and unfavorable *cognitive responses*. The model architecture assumes that cues are associated with attitudes in a relatively direct manner, whereas arguments are associated with attitudes more indirectly, via cognitive responses. These connections impose constraints that are soft rather than hard, so that they are desirable, but not essential to satisfy.

Although Siebler (2002) reports excellent fits with the empirical data of two experiments manipulating source expertise (Petty, Cacioppo, & Goldman, 1981; Chaiken & Maheswaran, 1994), the constraint satisfaction network has a number of shortcomings. First, the constraint satisfaction network has no learning mechanism. The process of developing the connections in the network is not modeled. As a result, the model is *non-adaptive*, as the connections have to be hand set by the experimenter and do not develop automatically from prior or current learning. Second, the constraint satisfaction network limits attitude formation and change to temporary changes of activation in the network, driven by satisfying all constraints present. Hence, the network reflects only a short-lived mental state of attitude that occurs only when all relevant prior beliefs, heuristic cues and persuasive arguments are activated (consciously or subconsciously) in the individual's mind. However, this is contradicted by a variety of empirical research showing that there is no substantial correlation between argument recall and attitude. Instead, it is now well established that most attitudes are formed online, while novel information is encoded and processed. To allow such online adjustment, a learning algorithm is essential.

Van Overwalle and Jordens' feedforward network of cognitive dissonance

Our attitudes are not only driven by immediate evaluations of attitude objects but sometimes also by reactions to our own behaviors, especially when these behaviors go against our initial preferences. This dilemma has been investigated under the heading of cognitive dissonance (Festinger, 1957). For instance, when induced to write an essay that runs counter to one's initial attitude (e.g. a student defending stricter exam criteria), an individual will tend to reduce dissonance by changing his or her attitude in the direction of the position taken in the essay. This tendency is stronger when alternative explanatory factors or justifications, such as high payment or social pressure, are absent. In contrast, when such external demands provide sufficient justification for engaging in the dissonant behavior, then dissonance reduction does not occur (e.g. Cooper & Fazio, 1984; Linder, Cooper, & Jones, 1967).

Van Overwalle and Jordens (2002) provided a feedforward model of this cognitive dissonance process. Their network involves the same types of concepts and connections as in the present recurrent model, with the important addition of a connection between the attitude object and behaviors performed by the person. The rationale was that individuals attempt not only to understand their evaluations but also attempt to justify their discrepant behavior. Both outcomes influence their attitudes. When alternative causal explanations for the discrepant behavior are absent, only the attitude object is sufficiently connected to these novel outcomes, resulting in the psychological realization that the object is liked more than initially thought. This results in attitude change. Conversely, when sufficient external explanations are available, their connections may sufficiently explain the outcomes, resulting in discounting and little attitude change. The mechanism responsible for this latter process in the network model of Van Overwalle and Jordens (2002) is the emergent property of competition.

This connectionist implementation of cognitive dissonance is largely consistent with the present network. First, in persuasive communication, little effect derives from one's behaviors, so that this factor could be safely ignored here. Second, because feedforward networks are more limited than recurrent models in the type of connections and the flow of activation, Van Overwalle and Jordens' (2002) feedforward network can be subsumed in the present, more general, recurrent model. They reported that their feedforward simulations of cognitive dissonance could easily be "upgraded" with very similar results to a recurrent architecture. Third, Van Overwalle and Jordens (2002) hand-coded all valences as +1, whereas in the present model they were indirectly "coded" by the recurrent activation accumulated through the object's attributes. In this respect, again, the recurrent model is more general than theirs. This leads to the conclusion that the present recurrent model perhaps encompasses a large range of earlier findings and models in the attitude literature, including attitude change due to cognitive dissonance (Festinger, 1957; see also Van Overwalle & Jordens, 2002).

Eiser et al.'s back-propagation network

Recently, Eiser, Fazio, and colleagues (2003) developed a connectionist model of attitude acquisition that differed from the previous connectionist models in that it assumes a more active role for the perceiver. Thus, not only was passive exposure modeled, but also active exploration of the environment. It was assumed that through such active learning people will choose to engage in activities that they find enjoyable, and avoid unpleasant activities as much as possible. Consequently, perceivers are much less accurate at identifying enjoyable versus unpleasant objects, resulting in an asymmetry in the appreciation of objects. In particular, unfamiliar objects are often seen as more negative than positive. Eiser et al. (2003) reported empirical support for this prediction, and also replicated these results with a multi-layer feedforward model with the generalized delta (or backpropagation) learning algorithm. The main advantages of their model are: (1) a hidden layer, which facilitates generalization from one situation to another; and (2) a behavioral output component, which makes active exploration in a virtual environment possible. However, a limitation is that the Eiser et al. (2003) model does not include nodes to represent the objects' attributes. Even after incorporating these, it remains to be seen to what extent this model is capable of replicating the empirical findings that were covered in this article. The present recurrent model does not incorporate a behavioral exploration process and hence does not expect differential learning of positive and negative attitudes, something that in any case was not reported in the persuasive literature discussed so far.

Kruglanski's unimodel

Kruglanski and Thompson (1999) questioned the assumption of dual-process theories that attitude change is attainable via two qualitatively distinct routes, and instead argued that these routes are functionally equivalent and differ only to the extent that they involve cognitive effort in decoding simple versus complex persuasive information. They proposed a unimodel that adopts a more abstract level of analysis in which the two persuasion modes are viewed as special cases of the same underlying process. Specifically, heuristic rules that are derived from prior beliefs and schemata stored in memory, as well as explicit thoughtful elaboration of persuasive arguments, rest on the same type of propositional if–then reasoning leading from evidence to a conclusion. For instance, heuristics are represented by an if–then propositional logic such as, "if an opinion is offered by an expert, then it is valid" (p.90), and central processing is also represented by if–then reasoning such as, "if something contributes to the thinning of the ozone layer, then it should be prohibited" (p.90). Thus, Kruglanski and Thompson (1999) concluded, "rule-based reasoning is common to both persuasion modes" (p.104). In a series of experiments, Kruglanski and Thompson (1999) demonstrated that if the heuristic information (e.g. on the expertise of the source) is sufficiently complex, then such "heuristic" information might also require central processing before it has any impact. Conversely, if the "central" arguments are sufficiently brief and simple, they can have an impact under peripheral processing.

Our connectionist network is in agreement with the unimodel in its claim that there is a single core mechanism underlying both central and peripheral routes of persuasion, and that both perspectives see the degree of elaboration as the main quantitative difference between the two processing routes. Although both models were developed independently from each other, they are remarkably similar in these respects. However, there are some noteworthy differences. First, there is a radically different view on the underlying mental processes responsible for attitude formation. Instead of the unimodel's explicit, symbolic, and sequential if–then reasoning logic of evidence, we proposed a lower-level connectionist mechanism, with a parallel, subsymbolic and implicit processing of this information, ultimately leading to an explicit attitude belief. As noted earlier, we believe that this perspective is more in agreement with neurological evidence on the working of the brain, and with recent findings showing that attitudes can be formed with little awareness of the integration process (Betsch et al., 2001; Lieberman et al., 2001). Second, our model proposes qualitative differences between processing modes, in that heuristic and central processes are based on different information bases (prior knowledge versus novel information respectively) that are developed and applied differently (generalized cue knowledge embedded in cue → valence connections versus second-order object → valence knowledge), whereas the unimodel treats these as similar and built from the same if–then propositional logic.

Betsch et al.'s value-account model

Recently, Betsch, Plessner, and Schallies (2004) put forward a value account model, which assumes that aggregation of preferences into a summary evaluation, or value account, is—by default—implicit and automatic. Only when provided with sufficient motivation and capacity do perceivers develop an aggregated attitude through explicit deliberation and weighting of specific information or episodes. This is consistent with most recent views on attitude processes, including ours. More importantly, based on a large series of experiments (e.g. Betsch et al., 2001), Betsch and colleagues suggested that implicit aggregation is guided by a summation principle, whereas explicit aggregation follows an averaging principle. Similarly, in evaluative conditioning research, De Houwer et al. (2001) argued that a summation pattern (based on a simple Hebbian learning algorithm) might be more typical of implicit preference learning, whereas an averaging pattern (by the delta learning algorithm) is more typical of explicit signal learning. How can these findings be reconciled with our model?

Recall that the delta learning algorithm predicts a negatively accelerating learning curve. In the beginning of learning, the learning error is still large, so that each novel input results in substantial weights adjustments that are added to each other, reflecting a *summation* of the favorable and unfavorable valences. However, towards asymptote, the error is much reduced (i.e. people reached an overall evaluative estimate based on the evidence given), so that novel evidence results in less weight adjustments, reflecting an *averaging* of prior and novel valences (see the Annexe to this chapter). Hence, the different patterns of integration can be accommodated in the present model by making the same assumption as we did for heuristic reasoning, that is, by taking the assumption that implicit learning is slower or shallower than explicit learning. Applied in the present context, this suggests that during implicit learning, the delta learning algorithm is still in its early "summation" phases, while explicit learning is faster, so that delta learning enters its later "averaging" phase much more quickly. An interesting implication of this assumption is that implicit learning should attain an averaging phase after extended time in which more information is presented.

Wilson et al.'s model of dual attitudes

An intriguing challenge to the present approach was recently posed by the dual-attitude model of Wilson, Lindsey, and Schooler (2000). According to these authors, people may hold in memory different explicit and implicit attitudes toward the same attitude object. When such dual attitudes exist, the implicit attitude is activated automatically, whereas the explicit attitude requires more capacity and motivation to retrieve. The implicit attitude changes more slowly like old habits, whereas the explicit attitude changes relatively easily. Most attitude researchers agree that this distinction exists, but there is disagreement as to what may cause it.

In some cases, different outcomes from explicit and implicit measures may be due to the fact that each measure focuses on different aspects of the same attitude object in memory. In terms of the present model, it would reflect testing the network by priming the subfeatures of the same attitude object with a different distributed activation pattern.[4] In other cases, it seems evident that the explicit attitude reflects some sort of suppression of illegitimate or unwanted thoughts, such as when people remove racial attitudes in explicit measures, but disclose their implicit racial stereotypes when measured implicitly (e.g. under time constraints). Another example is when people realize that the information received earlier was incorrect, but still hold in memory the (incorrect) association between the object and their negative evaluations, a phenomenon known as evaluative perseverance (Wilson et al., 2000). The present model is unable to account for this dissociation because we did not model episodic (recent) and semantic (old) memory as separate memory structures, but simply as different learning phases in time.

As noted earlier, several authors have made proposals for a dual memory system of the brain that may explain the dissociation between old and recent memories (French, 1997; McClelland, McNaughton, & O'Reilly, 1995; Smith & DeCoster, 2000). One subsystem would be dedicated to the rapid learning of unexpected and novel information and the building of episodic memory traces (e.g. the main experimental phase in our simulations). However, not

---

4 In addition to differences between implicit and explicit attitudes, people sometimes report different explicit attitudes depending on what information was activated before, what subset of data they attended to or retrieved from memory, what standard of comparison was salient and so on (e.g. Wilson & Hodges, 1992). Our approach can accommodate many (but not all) of these results as reflecting the impact of a person's recent, pre-message learning history, through priming or attentional focus.

only the learning but also the decay of episodic traces is relatively fast in this subsystem. Hence, episodic memory lasts only a few days. In contrast, the other subsystem would be responsible for slow incremental learning of statistical regularities of the environment and gradual consolidation of information learned in the first subsystem, resulting in stable and more last- ing semantic memory traces (e.g. the prior learning phases of our simula- tions). Because this latter subsystem has more permanent memory traces, novel information has relatively little effect so that the older attitudes often persist over time. The process of consolidation of recent memory into lasting memory could start a few minutes after receiving the novel information and last for several days. Consistent with this idea, Schooler (1990; cited in Wilson et al., 2000) reported that explicit attitude change resulted in a substantial dissociation between implicit and explicit attitude measures immediately afterwards, but that 48 hours later this difference gradually began to wear off.

GENERAL CONCLUSIONS

This article introduced a novel connectionist framework of attitudes that pro- vides an integrative account of many earlier perspectives of attitude formation, change, and use. The proposed model rests on the shoulders of pioneering work that was incorporated in its architecture and processing mechanisms. The model's architecture adopted the three-component view on attitudes as consisting of beliefs, evaluations and behavioral tendencies (Katz & Stotland, 1959; Rosenberg & Hovland, 1960) and also implemented the basic idea from spreading activation networks that attitudes consist of object–evaluation associations in memory (Fazio, 1990). The model's learning algorithm was based on older work on associative learning processes (Rescorla & Wagner, 1972) and classical conditioning of attitudes (Olson & Fazio, 2001; Staats & Staats, 1958), and was shown to incorporate algebraic approaches to attitude formation (Fishbein & Ajzen, 1975). Of most importance was that the present model was capable to simulate heuristic and central processing as proposed in earlier dual-process models (Chaiken, 1987; Petty & Cacioppo, 1981, 1986; Petty & Wegener, 1999).

The proposed connectionist perspective offers a novel view on how infor- mation could be encoded in the brain, how it might be structured and acti- vated, and how it could be retrieved and used for attitude judgments. One major advantage of a connectionist perspective is that it incorporates a learn- ing algorithm that allows the model to associate patterns that reflect social concepts and evaluations by means of very elementary learning processes. Hence, complex social reasoning and learning can be accomplished by putt- ing together an array of simple interconnected elements, which greatly enhance the network's computational power without the need of a central executive or awareness of its processing mechanisms. In addition, connectionist models have other capacities that we did not address, such as its content-addressable memory, its ability to do pattern completion, and its noise tolerance (for more on these issues, see McClelland & Rumelhart, 1988; McLeod et al., 1998; Smith, 1996).

Given the extensive breadth of attitude research, we inevitably were not able to include many other interesting findings and phenomena, which have now been simulated by similar connectionist models, such as cognitive dissonance (Van Overwalle & Jordens, 2002), and impression formation about persons or groups (Kashima et al., 2000; Queller & Smith, 2002; Smith & DeCoster, 1998; Van Overwalle & Labiouse, 2004; Van Rooy et al., 2003; see also Chapters 7–10). There are other obvious limitations of the present model: such as the lack of hidden or exemplar nodes (e.g. Kruschke & Johansen, 1999; McClelland & Rumelhart, 1988; McLeod et al., 1998; O'Reilly & Rudy, 2001), which limit its computational power; the lack of distinct episodic and semantic memory structures to overcome the problem of "catastrophic interference" (McCloskey & Cohen, 1989; Ratcliff, 1990); and the parallel existence of different implicit and explicit attitudes (Wilson et al., 2000).

Given the importance of attention and motivation in attitude formation and change, it will ultimately be necessary to incorporate these factors into an improved model. For the time being, we manipulated the overall attention by a supervisory activation module. However, other aspects of attention are not part of the dynamics of our network. For instance, salient situational factors such as heuristic cues can sometimes motivate people to scrutinize persuasive information more carefully. Credible and likeable sources, or majority positions, may motivate people to consider the message arguments more attentively, because these sources are more likely to provide correct or valuable information (Erb, Bohner, Schmälzle, & Rank, 1998; Heesacker, Petty, & Cacioppo, 1983; Mackie, 1987; Roskos-Ewoldsen, Bichsel, & Hoffman, 2002), whereas negative mood may signal that the message content is problematic (Mackie & Worth, 1989; Sinclair, Mark, & Clore, 1994; Wegener & Petty, 1996; Worth & Mackie, 1987; but see Bohner & Weinerth, 2001). It strikes us that the next step in connectionist modeling of attitudes and social cognition in general will involve exploring connectionist architectures built from separate but complementary systems, with more consideration for the interaction between different subsystems of the brain.

ANNEXE: FISHBEIN AND AJZEN'S (1975) MODEL AND THE DELTA LEARNING ALGORITHM

This annexe demonstrates that the delta learning algorithm converges at asymptote to the expectancy-value model of attitude formation by Fishbein and Ajzen (1975; Ajzen, 1991). According to this model, an attitude is formed by summing the multiplicative combination of (a) the strength of a salient belief that a behavior will produce a given outcome and (b) the subjective evaluation of this outcome, or (Ajzen, 1991, p.191):

$$attitude \approx \Sigma b_i e_i \qquad\qquad (11.1)$$

were b_i represents the strength of the belief and e_i the evaluation. Beliefs and evaluations are typically scored on 7-point scales. Although Fishbein and Ajzen (1975) suggest that the integration (of the multiplication of beliefs and evaluations) is a summative process, they acknowledge that evidence in favor of summation versus averaging is rather inconsistent and inconclusive (pp. 234–35). Moreover, to prevent their summative function to grow out of bounds, they restrict their formula to *salient* beliefs about an attitude object (typically not more than ten). Because of this implicit boundary assumption, and because there is "no rational a priori criterion we can use to decide how the belief and evaluation scales should be scored" (Ajzen, 1991, p.193), the preceding formula can be normalized by dividing it by the mean belief strengths, or:

$$attitude \approx \Sigma b_i e_i \,/\, \Sigma b_i \qquad\qquad (11.2)$$

This proof uses the same logic as Chapman and Robbins (1990) in their demonstration that the delta learning algorithm converges to the probabilistic expression of covariation. In line with the conventional representation of covariation information, attitude-relevant information can be represented in a contingency table with two cells. Cell a represents all cases where the attitude object is followed by a given (positive) evaluation, while cell b represents all cases where the same object is followed by the opposite (negative) evaluation. For simplicity, we use only an object with a single expectation or belief, although this proof can easily be extended to multiple beliefs.

In a recurrent connectionist architecture with localist encoding, the object j and the evaluation i are each represented by a node, which are connected by adjustable weights w_{ij}. We use a localist encoding to simplify the proof. When the object is present, its corresponding node receives external activation, and this activation is spread to both valence nodes. As defined in the text, we assume that the overall internal activation received at the valence nodes i after priming the object node j reflects the attitude.

According to the delta learning algorithm (see Equations 3.3 and 3.4, p.38), weights w_{ij} are adjusted proportional to the error between the actual evaluation (represented by its external activation *ext*) and the evaluation as predicted by the network (represented by its internal activation *int*). If we take the default activation for a_j (which is 1), then the following equations can be constructed for the two cells in the contingency table:

For cell a: $\Delta w_{ij} = \varepsilon(e_1 - int)$ $\qquad\qquad (11.3)$

For cell b: $\Delta w_{ij} = \varepsilon(e_2 - int)$ $\qquad\qquad (11.4)$

Note that e_1 reflects a positive evaluation and e_2 a negative evaluation. The change in overall attitude is the sum of Equations 11.3 and 11.4, weighted for the corresponding frequencies a and b, in the two cells, or:

$$\Delta w_{ij} = a[\varepsilon(e_1 - int)] + b[\varepsilon(e_2 - int)] \qquad (11.5)$$

These adjustments will continue until asymptote, that is, until the error between actual and expected evaluation is zero. This implies that at asymptote, the changes will become zero, or $\Delta w_{ij} = 0$. Consequently, Equation 11.5 becomes:

$$0 = a[\varepsilon(e_1 - int)] + b[\varepsilon(e_2 - int)]$$
$$= a[e_1 - int] + b[e_2 - int]$$
$$= [a * e_1 + b * e_2] - [a + b] \, int$$

so that:

$$int = [a * e_1 + b * e_2] / [a + b]$$

As noted above, the internal activation *int* received at the valence nodes after priming the object node reflects the attitude. Because e_1 was expressed in positive terms and e_2 in negative terms, the equation thus reflects the differential internal activation of the favorable and unfavorable valence nodes. Hence, the left side of the equation can simply be interpreted as the attitude. In addition, the right side of the equation can be rewritten in Fishbein and Ajzen's (1975) terms as:

$$attitude = \Sigma f_i e_i \, / \, \Sigma f_i \qquad (11.6)$$

where f represents the frequency that the attitude object leads to a given outcome and evaluation (which we assume determine the belief strength b). The equivalence between Equations 11.1 and 11.6 demonstrates that the delta learning algorithm predicts a (normalized) multiplicative function at asymptote for making attitude judgments, where the strength of the beliefs is determined by the frequencies by which the attitude object and evaluations co-occur.

Note that although the delta learning algorithm predicts an *averaging* multiplicative function after a large amount of input (i.e. at asymptote), in its beginning phase, the algorithm actually predicts an *additive* function. At the start of learning, every new piece of information results in relatively substantial weight adjustments because the error is still large. The more learning occurs, the greater the likelihood that the error decreases, so that novel information has less effect and is integrated with older information, resulting in a sort of averaging of earlier and recent novel input.

SIMULATION EXERCISES

These exercises explore the recurrent simulations of the text, and you can experiment yourself by simulating other models or variants of the experiments discussed in the text. You are expected to have had some experience with the FIT program, perhaps by completing some of the exercises in Chapter 3 and 4, which explain the working of the program in somewhat more detail. The manual of the FIT program is available in the Appendix at the end of the book.

Exercise 1: Central processing of expectations and valences

Choose menu **File | Open Project** or press the ☞ speed button. Browse for *ReasonedAction.ft2* in folder *Chapter 11*, and click the **Open** button.

Specifying trials

Click the **Trial** tab to open the Trial Grid. The top rows show three input units representing the three attitude objects (car, bicycle, and bus) and five output units representing the cognitive attributes (fast, dry, and polluting) and the valences (V+ and V–). (You can change the names of these units by double clicking the second row, or by choosing the **Data | Edit Column Names** menu). The following Trial Categories are specified:

- Learning Trial Category $7 depicts the prior valence learning phase, that is, the learning of the positive and negative valences associated with each of the three cognitive attributes. Thus, for instance, the system learns that driving fast and in dry circumstances is experienced as positive, while polluting is negative. You will note that the external activation was not set to the default, but to 0.5 for each unit in order to prevent the system to reach asymptotic connection weights which would dominate further learning too much.

    You can check for yourself that the connections are not too close to the asymptotic values of +1 and –1 by choosing the **Simulation | View Network** menu or by clicking once the ◯ speed button before running the simulation.
- Learning Trial Category $1 depicts the learning of the attributes associated with the car, as well as the valences associated with these attributes. Learning Trial Category $2 and $3 do the same for the bicycle and the bus.
- For measuring the attitude, in this and all remaining simulations, you prime the object and observe how much the valence units are activated. Of course, the positive valence unit is summed and the negative valence unit is subtracted (see "?" and "-?" in Test Categories *$51–53*).

You can see that all these specifications closely resemble Table 11.2, which depicts the learning history, as is also the case for the other simulations. (This was accomplished by exporting the Trial Grid using the menu **File | Export | Trial Data Grid to Excel**, and then copying the Excel file to Word.)

It is important to understand how the attributes are associated with the valences in the Learning Trial Categories $1–$3. For this, you use the Special Trial Value "i", which is termed **internal clamp**. This indicates that the *internal activation* is clamped and used as *external activation* by the system. In this manner, the activation (sent out from the cognitive attributes) received at the valence units is experienced as "real" by the system, rather than an internal signal that the system must match against an external goal. Thus, rather than imposing the valences externally by ourselves, we let the system generate these valences after it learned the attribute → valence connections in the Prior Valence Learning phase.

To allow the system to generate these internal clamps it needs to spread activation from the attributes to the valence units, and therefore at least three cycles are needed. Cycle 1 sets the external activation, cycle 2 spreads activation along the object → attribute connections, and cycle 3 spreads further activation along the attribute → valence connections. To set three cycles, select the **Simulation | Parameters** menu or the ✦ speed button, and hit the **Model** tab. You will find the model parameter #**Cycles**. In the simulation, the number of cycles is set to 3.

However, if you would only set the *internal activation* to the *external activation*, little learning would take place because there is no delta error when the internal and external activation match perfectly. To force the system to learn from the internal clamp, you need to drive these valences to their −1 or +1 asymptotes. In order to do this, choose the **Simulation | Parameters** menu or **hit** the ✦ speed button, and in the **Weights and Activation** tab you will find the entry **Cycle Internal Clamp**. In the simulation, the number of cycles for the internal clamp is set to 10. This means that the internal clamp goes through 10 cycles of a standard non-linear activation update algorithm with −1 and +1 as attractors. This is done according to the following formula (equivalent to Equation 3.9, p.40) with *decay* = 0.15; *int* = internal activation and *ext* = external activation:

if ($int > 0$)

then $ext = (1 - decay) * ext + int * (1 - ext)$

else $ext = (1 - decay) * ext + int * (ext + 1)$

Specifying sessions

Click the **Session** tab to open and specify the ordering of the Learning and Test Trial Categories. You can see that the learning for each attitude object is separated by a *reset* (in the **Trials** column) and given a different condition number (*1, 2*, and *3* in the **IV2** column). Each simulation begins with the prior valence learning phase, followed by the learning of the object's attributes, followed by a test of the object.

The values entered in the **DV1** column (that you attempt to replicate) are the values predicted by the theory of reasoned action using the summed multiplicative equation $\Sigma b_i e_i$ (see the Annexe), where b_i represents the strength of the belief and e_i the evaluation. For computing this equation, the trial frequencies in the Trial Categories were used as estimate of b_i, a value of +1 was used for favorable attributes, and a value of −1 for unfavorable attributes (see also text).

Specifying the simulation parameters

Choose the **Simulation | Parameters** menu, or press the ⊕ speed button. In the top panel, four drop-down list boxes list the major options. Note that the model to be simulated is the *Linear Auto-associator* developed by McClelland and Rumelhart (1988). Leave all the other option boxes to their default values. The following parameters need to be set by opening (clicking) the different tabs:

- **General** tab.
  Specify in **Session** that you want to run session *1*, and select in **Graph Simulated Values** the button *yes* (automatically, the **Log Simulated Values** will turn to *yes* also). Set **Randomize Order for All Learning Trials** to *yes*, and specify 50 runs. Leave the categories to which this applies to *1–49*. Set all other parameters to *no*.
- **Model** tab.
  Set the **learning rate** = 0.35 and **#cycles** = 3. Leave all other parameters open, or set them to *auto* or *no*.
- **Weights and Activation** tab.
  Because you want the internal clamp to move towards their asymptotic values of −1 and +1, as noted earlier, you set **Cycle Internal Clamp** to 10. This is sufficient to drive the internal activation close to −1 and +1. Leave all other parameters open, or set them to their default.

Running the simulation

To run the simulation as specified above, choose the **Simulation | Run Simulation** menu, or press the 🐜 speed button.

You will follow the simulation step by step in order to: (1) check that in the prior valence learning phase the connections did not reach asymptote; and to (2) observe how the internal clamp behaves. To do this, choose the **Simulation | View Network** menu. Alternatively, hit the 𝒫 speed button:

- In the **Simulations Details** window, click the **Start Run** button and then the **Next Category** Button. What you see now is the end of the prior valence learning phase. As you can see, none of the connections in the two bottom rows reaches an asymptotic value as intended. As you probably remember, this was done by setting the external activations to +0.5 instead of +1.

- Click the **Next Cycle** button twice. The button's name changes in **End Cycle A** and the hint (i.e. yellow text balloon that appears automatically after keeping the mouse for a second or so over the button) tells you that this cycle involves the setting of the external activation.
- Now click the **End Cycle A** button again. The button's name changes in **End Cycle B** and the yellow hint text tells you that this cycle involves the spreading of internal activation. You will notice that the valence units now have received some internal activation (see second top row).
- Click the **End Cycle B** button again. Now you see the effect of the internal clamp, as the valence units generate some external activation (see first top row). Note that this value is larger than the internal activation due to the cycling toward the attractors −1 and +1 after the internal activation was clamped. This external activation is then used as is, to let the system learn and change its connections weights. You can see this by clicking the **End Cycle B** button again, and observe the weight changes.
- You can repeat these last three steps to see how the simulation progresses. To end the simulation at once without viewing the details, hit the **Continue** or **Cancel View** button.

After the simulation is finished, the **Graph** tab will open automatically (because you requested a graph). Make the following selections:

- **filter**: (*none*).
- **X-Axis**: *Condition* (the label specified for **IV2**).
- **X-Axis Labels**: *IVLabel*.
- **Y-Axis Line(s)**: select all simulated and observed **DVs**.
- Check the **List Stats** check box so that you get additional statistical analyses.
- Check the **Regress** check box, so that the simulated values are projected onto the observed values (this can be altered by opening the **Graph Options** and choosing another option on the bottom right).
- Hit the **Graph Log** button. You will see a graph of the simulation results, as they also appear in Figure 11.1. (The means of the graph were exported by hitting the graph's **Options** button, the **Data** tab, and finally the **Export Graph Means to Excel** button; alternatively, you can use menu **File | Export | Graph Option Grid to Excel**.)

For the numerical results, press the **Listing** tab. The results of the ANOVA are also the ones reported in the text.

Questions

1. You can experiment somewhat with the model parameters of the simulation. For instance, you can search yourself for the best-fitting model parameters. Choose the **Simulation | Parameters** menu or press the ⊕ speed button, and press the **Model** tab. Enter as **learning rate**: 0.00 > 0.50 (in the **left box** and **right box** respectively).

    The program will automatically search for the best-fitting parameters (turn **automatic search** *on* and turn **logging** *off* as requested by the program). You will see that the program ends up with a much smaller learning rate. However, in the article 0.35 was chosen because this was the learning rate that was consistently appropriate for all simulations reported in the article. Hence, it is sometimes better to forego an ideal fit of a particular simulation in order to set a common learning rate that is more convincing to your audience because it points to the communalities between all simulations reported.

    Now choose the **Simulation | Run Best Fit and Graph** menu or press the ⊑ speed button. The program will automatically enter the best-fitting model parameters of the last run, will run the simulation once again, and will finally make a graph. You can inspect the results from the Graph Sheet that opens automatically.

2. You can also explore other models. Choose the **Simulation | Parameters** menu or press the ⊕ speed button, and select another model in the **Model** option box. For instance, you might select the *distributed* or *non-linear recurrent* model, as indicated in Table 11.8. For the distributed model, as indicated in the text, each concept was represented by a distributed pattern of activation across four units, drawn from a normal distribution with the external activation as means and standard deviation .10. In addition, in all prior learning phases, random noise drawn from a normal distribution with mean 0 and standard deviation .10 was added to these activations to reflect the variation in past experiences. You practiced distributed representations in Chapter 7, so you can look up the exercises in that chapter to see how to specify these implementational details. In addition, a learning rate was chosen that was the best-fitting value between .01 and .05 (use the procedure described above to find this best fitting parameter). For the non-linear recurrent model, the parameters were identical to the linear model, except that you need to specify **decay** = *0.70*.

3. You can test a unitary valence encoding as reported in Table 11.8. In a unitary valence coding, unfavorable evaluations are represented by negative activation levels instead of positive activation levels of an unfavorable valence. To obtain this, set in the *V+* column all numerical values of the *V–* column, but now with a negative sign before it. Actually, in this simulation this is only needed for the V– value in the third trial of Category $7. Once this is done, hide the *V–* column. You obtain a

following trial grid as shown in Figure 11.12. Now run the model. As you will see, with a sufficiently small learning rate, the model will closely fit the predicted values, indicating that in this case a unitary valence coding is equivalent. Table 11.8 demonstrates that this is the case for most attitude measures of the other simulations, but nòt for the other (valenced thought) measures introduced in these simulations.

Exercise 2: The length heuristic

We now discuss the simulation of the length heuristic. Because all heuristic simulations follow the same general principles and specifications, the length heuristic is chosen as our primary example, and it is up to you to run the simulations for the other heuristics with a little help in the next exercises. For the length heuristic, choose menu **File | Open Project** or press the ☞ speed button, browse for *Petty+Cacioppo84.ft2* in folder *Chapter 11*, and click the **Open** button.

In the heuristic simulations, you use the same basic approach as specified for central processing (see Exercise 1). In addition, to let the system learn heuristic "rules", it must have sufficient learning experiences with heuristic exemplars. This will be accomplished during additional prior heuristic learning phases.

Specifying trials

To allow heuristic learning, in the Trial Grid, you will see on the right of the attitude object "*exam*" several additional units: the heuristic cue "*length*" (column **i2**) and three strong and weak arguments (columns **i3** to **i8**).

Specifying sessions

The simulation basically proceeds as follows:

- First, in the prior valence learning phase (Category $7) that runs in all conditions, valences are associated with all the arguments.

3:5	#	i1	i2	i3	o1	o2	o3	o4	Comments
		Car	Bicycle	Bus	Fast	Dry	Pollutes	V+	
1	$7	Prior Valence Learning							
2	15				0.5			0.5	
3	15					0.5		0.5	
4	15						0.5	-0.5	
5	$1	Car							
6	1	1			1			i	
7	1	1				1		i	

Figure 11.12 Exercise 1: Unitary valence encoding in the trial grid.

- Second, in the prior heuristic learning phase, the system learns for the first three strong arguments that long messages lead to stronger cue → valence connections (weights around 1.00) than short messages (weights around 0.75). You can check these weights by clicking the **Simulation | View Network** menu or the $\wp$ speed button. Hit the **Next Category** button several times to reach the end of Category $8 or $9, and you will see the cue → valence weights in the bottom rows of the second column of the weight matrix.

  Perhaps you have noticed that the next three weak arguments are not used at all, because the length heuristic is used only as if people recall only strong messages (see also text). They are merely added here for consistency with the set-up of the other heuristic simulations. (If you hide these three columns, you will see that the simulation ends with pretty much the same results, although these are slight differences. This is due to the fact that these non-used arguments do acquire some internal activation when they are not hidden, and so contribute marginally to learning.)

- The prior heuristic learning phases are each repeated 10 times, with a learning rate that is 10 % of the overall learning rate of 0.35 (or 0.035) as indicated in the text. This is accomplished by choosing the **Simulation | Parameters** menu or pressing the ✤ speed button. After pressing the **Weights and Activation** tab, you can see that **alpha_1 and _2 Coding** is set to **LRate** (Learning Rate) **only** for the Trial Categories $8 and $9. In the **Model** tab, **alpha_1** is set to 0.1. These alpha_1 values are applied for all cells with a non-zero entry in Trial Category $-1. Taken together, these specifications tell the program that for Categories $8 and $9, it should decrease the learning rate to the alpha_1 value (or 10 %) during the weight updating of all units.

- Next, the system learns the message arguments under heuristic processing (Trial Categories $11–$14) or central processing (Trial Categories $1–$4). These categories are merely copies of each other, with the exception that the external input in the heuristic Categories $11–$14 is reduced to 10 % for the heuristic cue (or 0.1) and to 1 % for the arguments (or 0.01). Although this could have been coded with the **Weights and Activation** parameters like above, this parameter already uses a different option (**LRate only**) for Categories $8–$9. Hence, the reduced external activation was directly coded in the cells of the Trial Categories $11–$14.

- It is important to note that the arguments for the prior heuristic learning phase are not the same as those used for the learning of short and long messages during the simulation of the experiment. Hence, arguments are only instrumental in generating the cue → valence connections in the heuristic phase and the object → valence connections in the experimental phase, and need not to be identical in both phases.

- Finally, the attitudes are tested as well as the valenced thoughts. As you can see, to test the valenced thoughts, you take the same test as the attitude extended with ? for the argument units. To balance the contribution of cognitions and valences, the ? cells for the valence units are multiplied with the same amount as the number of arguments.

Questions

You can experiment with the same Exercises 1–3 as in the previous simulation. Of specific interest here are the following exercises:

4. You can explore the simulation of valenced thoughts using the **Simulation | View Network** menu or the 🔊 speed button
    Another interesting exercise is to explore the simulation of the indirect object → cue → valence connections reported briefly in the text. Indeed, this alternative heuristic processing is not based on a direct generalization of the cue's valence to the attitude object, but rather on an indirect generalization through an object → cue → valence link. This alternative implies that the reactivation of the cue is a crucial mediator in attitude activation.
    One way to run this simulation is to set all activation levels under heuristic processing to *.33*, except for the length cue where the activation is set to *1.5*. This is shown in Figure 11.13 for learning trials $11–$14 and test trial $51 (units **i3–i8** are hidden to conserve space). Alternatively, select the file *Petty+Cacioppo84_cue.ft2* where these codings have been applied already.

#	i1	i2	i9	i10	i11	i12	i13	i14	i15	i16
	Exam	Length	StrArq4	StrArq5	StrArg6	WkArq4	WkArq5	WkArq6	V+	V-
$11	Short and Strong									
	.33	1.5	.33						.33i	.33i
$12	Short and Weak									
	.33	1.5				.33			.33i	.33i
$13	Long and Strong									
	.33	1.5	.33						.33i	.33i
	.33	1.5		.33					.33i	.33i
	.33	1.5			.33				.33i	.33i
$14	Long and Weak									
	.33	1.5				.33			.33i	.33i
	.33	1.5					.33		.33i	.33i
	.33	1.5						.33	.33i	.33i
$-1										
	1	1	1	1	1	1	1	1	1	1
$51	Attitudes & Valenced Thoughts (peripheral)									
	1								?	-?
	.33		.33?	.33?	.33?	.33?	.33?	.33?	2?	-2?
$52	Attitudes & Valenced Thoughts (central)									
	1								?	-?
	1		?	?	?	?	?	?	6?	-6?

Figure 11.13 Exercise 2: Alternative heuristic process based on an indirect object → cue → valence link (Units **i3–i8** are hidden to minimize the figure and conserve space).

You can follow the simulation step by step to check the object → cue → valence links. To do this, choose the **Simulation | View Network** menu or hit the 🔎 speed button. In the **Simulation Details** window, click the **Start Run** button and hit the **Next Category** button several times. The object → cue → valence links can be most clearly seen after Learning Category $13 and $14 (hit the **Next Category** button about ten times). For instance, after Category $13, the *Exam → Length* weight is about .70 and the *Length → V+* weight is about .43 (see weight matrix in Figure 11.14). In contrast, the same weight matrix in the original simulation shows a negligible *Exam → Length* weight, and a direct *Exam → V+* weight of about .36.

Exercise 3: Other heuristics

Look again at the text to understand more about the particular assumptions of these heuristic simulations. The location of the simulation files is indicated below, as are the major differences with the previous simulation. You can explore the same issues and questions as in Exercise 2.

- For the consensus and expertise heuristics, open the files *Mahes+Chaiken91.ft2* and *Chaiken+Mahes94.ft2*, respectively (using the menu **File | Open Project** or the 📂 button). The logic of these simulations is pretty similar to those of the length heuristic.

				Exam	Length
				i1	i2
input (external activation)				0.33	1.50
net activation				0.79	2.06
				weights: from top to l
		input	net		
Exam	i1	0.33	0.79	0.00	0.12
Length	i2	1.50	2.06	0.70	0.00
StrArg1	i3	0.00	-0.02	0.03	-0.09
StrArg2	i4	0.00	-0.08	0.06	-0.09
StrArg3	i5	0.00	-0.06	0.01	-0.07
WkArg1	i6	0.00	0.00	0.00	0.00
WkArg2	i7	0.00	0.00	0.00	0.00
WkArg3	i8	0.00	0.00	0.00	0.00
StrArg4	i9	0.00	0.03	-0.11	-0.13
StrArg5	i10	0.00	0.27	-0.02	-0.15
StrArg6	i11	0.33	0.31	0.07	0.12
WkArg4	i12	0.00	0.00	0.00	0.00
WkArg5	i13	0.00	0.00	0.00	0.00
WkArg6	i14	0.00	0.00	0.00	0.00
V+	i15	0.17	0.16	0.03	0.43
V-	i16	0.00	0.00	0.00	0.00

Figure 11.14 Exercise 2: Weight matrix exploring the alternative heuristic process.

- For the mood heuristic, open the file *Petty+Shumann93_2.ft2*. As you can see, unlike the other heuristics, in Learning Categories $8 and $9, the mood heuristic is created not through the arguments, but by directly coding the valence units +1. (The first six arguments have no real function but were kept for consistency with the other simulations.)
- For the ease of retrieval heuristic, open the file *Tormala02_2.ft2*. You can see that only the strong arguments were used for this simulation.

Exercise 4: Ambivalence

The text discusses briefly the simulation of attitude ambivalence. Crucially, to measure ambivalence, instead of subtracting the negative valence from the positive valence (using a ? and -? Coding), these two valences are summed (using a ? and ? coding) so that this provides an indication of the spread of people's opinions. To explore this simulation, choose menu **File | Open Project** or press the 📂 speed button, and open *Priester+Petty96_2+3.ft2*.

Appendix

FIT2 for Connectionist and Algebraic Modeling

This manual provides some essential information on the working of the FIT program. Note that much more additional information of interest is available through the **Help** menu in the FIT program.

Getting Started
- Start from an Example
- Start from Scratch

Menus
- File Menu
- Edit Menu
- Data Menu
- Simulation Menu

Sheets

Windows
- Fit Results window
- Simulation Details window

Models
- Feedforward
- Linear Autoassociator
- Non-Linear Autoassociator

Simulation Options
- Model Options
- External Coding Options
- External Noise During Learning Options
- Response Options

Simulation Parameters
- General parameters
- Model parameters
- Weights and Activation parameters
- Distributed Coding and Noise parameters

GETTING STARTED

Double click the ▓ icon to start the FIT program.

If you are a novel user or if you downloaded an updated version, FIT will prompt you to **Verify** the correctness of its computations. You are strongly advised to first verify the program as requested by pressing **OK**, until you receive the message that the Test Examples ran accurately. Once this is done, you can be sure that the program will run normally.

It is important to note that FIT uses a **decimal point** '.' as the **Decimal Symbol**. In case your regional settings are different, FIT will nonetheless work only with the **decimal point.**

After FIT started up, you should see a set of menus and bars, as shown in the next figure.

- Below the menu, you see a row of speed buttons (i.e. the speed bar). Each button is equivalent to a commonly used task in the menu, and as such can speed up working with the program.
- Below the speed bar are five tabs. By clicking one of these tabs, you can open different sheets which contain the **Trial** grid, the **Session** grid, the **Listing** of results, the **Log** grid or the **Graph** environment.

FIT menu, speed bar and sheet tabs.

Now you can read a step-by-step introduction to the use of FIT. You can take either of the following possible ways to do this:

- **Start from an Example** (recommended for novice users).
- **Start from Scratch** (recommended only for experienced users).

Start from an example

There are a number of **Examples** that you can apply to get some feel of how the simulator works. You can open them by selecting the menu **Help | Open Example**.

The initial specifications of these examples are set so that you can see the architecture of the **Network** and go through the simulation step by step by clicking **Next Trial**. If you get tired of this and want to see the end result, simply click **Continue**.

This introduction walks you through Example1. In this example, you are going to explore how a cause, termed Cause A, acquires a stronger connection weight with its Effect after multiple cause-effect pairings. Open Example1 by selecting the menu **Help | Open Example1** (see the figure below).

Opening one of the Examples.

How to understand and set up Example1 is explained in four steps:

1. **How to Specify your Trial Data**
2. **How to Specify your Session**
3. **How to Specify your Simulation Parameters**
4. **Running the Simulation**

You are now ready to move to the first step in the Example:

1. How to specify your trial data

Click the **Trial** tab to open the Trial Grid, and then you will see the next figure. This grid defines the Trials, that is, the input to the simulation.

Trial		Session		Listing	Log	Graph
1 : 1	#	i1	o1	**Comments**		
		Cause A	Effect			
1	$1	Acquisition of A				
2	20	1	1			
3						
4	$2	Acquisition of A*				
5	8	1	1			
6	8	1				
7						
8	$50	Test of Causal Infl...				
9		1	?	Cause A		

Trial Grid of Example1.

Specify the input and output units of your network

The first row defines the architecture (input and output units) of the network. When moving from left to right, you can see the following entries:

1 : 1   This cell indicates here that there is 1 input unit and 1 output unit.
              You can switch between input and output units by double clicking this cell and define another number of input and output units (alternatively, you can choose the **Data | Specify Input/Output Units** menu). To add more units, use the menu **Data | Insert Column After**.

This column contains the **number of trials**, that is, how often this row (and its input) is repeated during the simulation.

i1   These column(s) contain the external activation levels for the **input units**. In this example there is only one input unit **i1**.

o1   These column(s) contain the external activation levels for the **output units**. In this example there is only one output unit **o1**.

Comments   This column provides free space to add your own comments.

In the second row, you can define your own name for the units, either by double clicking, or by choosing the **Data | Column Names** menu. As you can see, the names given to **i1** and **o1** are *Cause A* and *Effect*.

Specify trials containing external input

The aim of Example 1 is to simulate a block (or **Learning Category**) of 20 trials in which *Cause A* is paired with the *Effect*. And to test after each trial how strong the influence is of *Cause A* on the *Effect* (in a **Test Category**). This simulation will be detailed step-by-step.

    After that, you will see that there is another block (or **Learning Category**) of eight trials in which *Cause A* and the *Effect* are paired together, followed by another eight trials in which *Cause A* is present alone.

    After the first two (fixed) rows, you can see, on the next row, a **Trial Category** where number *$1* is specified to start a block of trials (i.e. rows in the grid). Each Trial Category is denoted by a $ sign, followed by a number. Apart from Trial Category *$1*, you can see other Categories *$2* and *$50*. All categories span the whole width of the Trial Grid.

    Important: Categories numbered *$1* to *$49* are restricted to **Learning Trials** during which weight updating occurs. Categories with number *$50* or more contain **Test Trials** during which no weight updating occurs.

    When moving from top to bottom, you can see the following **Categories**:

Learning Category $1   A description is added in the next column: *Acquisition of A*, but you can make a different one for your own. For your own convenience, make sure that it appropriately describes these trials as you will use this description later.

Going from left to right, the first row in this category defines **20 trials** where cause A and the effect are both activated to the default level of **1**. This means that cause A and the effect are always presented together, or paired together. This should lead to an increasing connection weight between cause A and the effect.

Learning Category $2   The description specifies *Acquisition of A°*, but you can fill in your own description.

Going from the first to the second row, you can see that after the first eight pairings of cause A with the effect, cause A is presented alone eight times (the activation of the effect is empty or zero). The specifications in the first row of this Category should lead to an increase of the connection weight between cause A and the effect, followed by a decrease in the second row.

Test Category $50   This provides a test of the causal strength of A. The causal strength of *cause A* is tested by prompting or priming cause A (see activation level *1*), and then reading off the resulting activation of the *effect* (as indicated by the *?-sign*). This is similar to asking yourself about cause A and then observe how much you spontaneously think about the effect (the ?-sign). The resulting activation will largely depend on the connection weight between cause A and the effect. For clarity, as multiple test trials are possible (although not in this example), the comment line provides space to label this test trial (*Cause A*).

Before you can run this network, you have to specify a session to indicate the order in which the Trial Categories are run. To do this, go now to the second step:

2. How to specify your session

Before you can run a simulation, you need to specify the ordering of the **Learning and Test Trial Categories**.

Click the **Session** tab to open the Session Grid. You will see the next figure. This grid defines the order in which the Trial Categories are run for the simulation. In Example1, there are two different sessions, but we cover only Session *$1* in detail.

Trial		Session		Listing	Log	Graph
1 : 1	#	Trials	IVLabel	DV1	**Comments**	
				Cause A		
1	$1	Acquisition of co-occurence of A and E				
2		1+50	Acquisition of A	×		
3						
4	$2	Acquisition of co-occurence of A* and E				
5		2+50	Acquisition of A*	×		

Session Grid of Example1.

Specify the independent and dependent variables in your simulation

The first row defines the set up of the simulations. When moving from left to right, you can see the following entries:

1 : 1   The information in this cell indicates that there is 1 **independent variable** or **IV** and 1 **dependent variable** or **DV**. The IVs are different conditions in your simulation, and the DVs are the different tests that you take (see **Test Trials** described in the Trial Grid).

You can switch between IVs and DVs by double clicking this cell (or, alternatively, you can choose the **Data | Specify IV/DV Variables** menu). To add more IVs or DVs, use the menu **Data | Insert Column After**.

This column contains the **number of trials**. (This number is multiplied with the number provided earlier in the # column of the Trial Grid.)

Trials   This column contains the Trial Categories that will be run.

IVLabel   This column contains the labels for the IVs, and will be used later for graphing your results.

IV2   These column(s) contain the Independent variables. In this example, there were no IVs, so this column does not exist.

DV1   These column(s) contain the Dependent variables. In this example, there is one DV, numbered **DV1**.

In the second row, like in the Trial Grid, you can define a name for the IVs and DVs, either by double clicking, or by the **Data | Column Names** menu. As you can see, the DV1 has been given the name *Cause A*. This label will be used throughout the simulation.

Specify the order of the simulation

As you can see, in the next rows, two sessions are specified. Lets walk through Session *$1*. Later, you can take a look at Session *$2* by yourself.

The trials in each session are simply selected by clicking in the **Trials column**, and selecting the appropriate Trial Category from the pop-up menu.

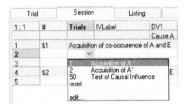

Selecting a Trial Category in Example1.

Your selection automatically fills the Trial Category number and its label, as you can see in the next figure. Thus, the **IVLabel** column provides a copy of the description of the Trial Categories (as given earlier in the Trial Grid).

Trial		Session		Listing		I
1 ; 1	#	Trials	IVLabel		DV1	
					Cause A	
1	$1	Acquisition of co-occurence of A and E				
2		1	Acquisition of A			

After selecting a Trial Category in Example1.

Usually, this is all you have to do.

Now, however, we use a special **combination of Learning and Test Categories**, so that we have to manually edit the Trial column. To do this, again click on the Trial column and select from the menu: "**edit . . .**" This can be seen below:

Trial		Session		Listing	
1 ; 1	#	Trials	IVLabel		DV1
					Cause A
1	$1	Acquisition of co-occurence of A and E			
2		1	Acquisition of A		
3		1	Acquisition of A		
4	$2	2	Acquisition of A*		E
5		50	Test of Causal Influence		
		reset			

Editing the Trials Column in Example1.

A dialog allows you to enter "*1+50*", so that now after each Learning Trial *$1* the Test Trail *$50* will be run. Now enter 20 in the # Column, and the system will repeat 20 times the execution of Categories *$1* and *$50*.

Specify the values of the dependent variables

In the **DV1** column you need to add the *-symbol. This symbol is needed for every Test Category specified in the Trials column (in this case *$50*) to tell the program **which DV will hold the test values**.

Tip: The *-symbol can be replaced by real data that you want to predict or fit with the program. If you provide actual values, the FIT program will automatically compute the correlations between the real and simulated values.

An alternative set-up

You can avoid combined Learning and Test Trials, but then you have to repeat the same information several times. For instance, you can first enter Learning Category *$1*, and then Test Category *$50*. Then you repeat this. (Do not forget to remove the *20* in the # column of the Trial Grid!) The result is shown below:

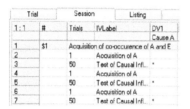

Alternative Trial specification of Example1.

You are now ready to set up the network and the input for your simulation. Go now to the third step:

3. How to specify your simulation parameters

Choose the **Simulation | Parameters** menu, or press the ⊕ speed button. This opens a window, the top panel is shown next:

The Options of Example1.

As you can see, there are four drop-down list boxes that list the major options. Leave them as they are, but note that the model to be used is the *Feedforward* model developed by McClelland and Rumelhart (1988).

General parameters

Now click the **General** tab. You will see the next panel:

Running the Simulation

Session
From 1   To 1

View Details / List All Results
◉ No   ○ View   ○ List All

Log Simulated Values
○ No   ◉ Yes   ○ Append

Graph Simulated Values
○ No   ◉ Yes

The General Parameters of Example1.

These are the **general parameters** for running the simulation. Leave all parameters at their default, except the following:

Session   Specifies which Session you want to run. You can choose session *1* or *2*.

Graph Simulated Values   Click the button *yes* (automatically, the **Log Simulated Values** will turn to *yes* also).

Model parameters

Now click the **Model** tab. You will see the next panel:

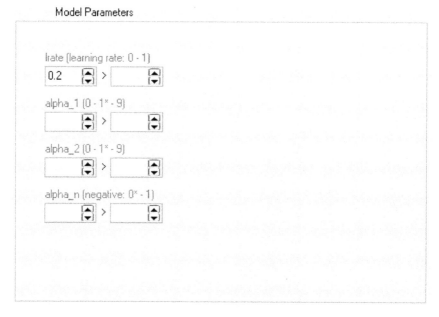

The Model Parameters of Example1.

These are the **model parameters** for running the simulation. Leave these parameters empty (i.e. at their default indicated by an *), except the following:

learning rate   Set this to 0.2 or any other parameter value you wish to test.

Go now to the last step:

4. Running the simulation

To run the simulation of the Example1 network, choose the **Simulation | Run Simulation** menu, or press the 🐜 speed button.

If you want to follow the simulation step-by-step, choose the **Simulation | Parameters** menu, and set **View Details** to *View*. Alternatively, you can hit the 🐜 speed button for a graphical display of the network with the activation levels and connections weights, or the 🔎 speed button for these numerical values in a table format.

After the simulation is finished, the **Graph** tab will open automatically (because you requested a graph). This is shown below:

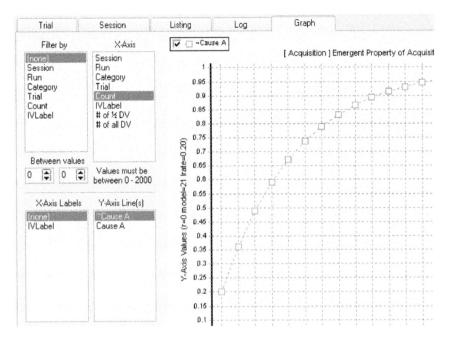

The graphical result of Example1.

As you can see, a number of selections are made already. It is best to keep these, so as to obtain in interpretable graph:

Filter   *(none)*.
X-Axis   *Count* (this is simply the running count of the trials).
X-Axis Labels *(none)*.
Y-Axis Line(s) *~Cause A*.
          The variable names preceded by a ~-sign denote the simulated values as obtained by the Test Trial Category $50, with their name as specified in the **DV** columns of the Session Grid.

You will see a graph of the simulation results as shown above on the right panel. By hitting the **Graph Log** button, you obtain the same graph again, or a different one if you ran a different simulation.
    For more information on:

• The results, including statistical analysis: press the **Listing** tab to open the **Listing Sheet**.
• The numerical simulation values per trial: press the **Log** tab to open the **Log data grid sheet**.

Start from scratch

You are going the hard way, and you want to specify your simulation completely by yourself. This is often quicker when you are an experienced user.

To do so, choose the menu **File | New**. A dialog opens:

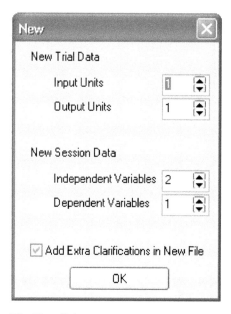

The New dialog.

As you can see, the dialog asks you to specify the number of:

- **Input** Units.
- **Output** Units.
- **Independent** Variables (do not forget that the **IVLabel** is the first IV).
- **Dependent** Variables.

MENUS

FIT menu.

The main menu gives access to the following operations:

- **File Menu**.
- **Edit Menu**.
- **Data Menu**.
- **Simulation Menu**.

File menu

Notice the distinction between an **active sheet**, which involves a single file as opposed to the **project**, which involved all sheets of the current simulation.

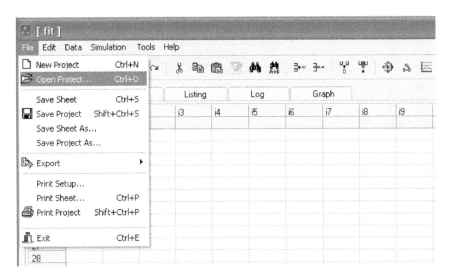

File menu.

New Project	Creates new trial and session data grids for a new simulation project.
Open Project	Opens all sheets of an existing simulation project. A simulation project has file extension ***.ft2**.
	If you want to open an individual sheet saved under another name (**Save As . . .**), then open the **auxiliary file** with that name and the appropriate extension.
	If you would encounter problems opening a *.ft2 project or if the file is damaged, it is possible to recover from the **backup file** indicated by a ~ in the file extension, or the **prior backup file** indicated by ~~ in the file extension. Delete or rename the *.ft2 file, remove the ~ from the backup file, and then try opening again.
Save Sheet	Saves the active sheet or parameters.
Save Project	Saves all sheets of an existing simulation project.

The whole project is saved into a file with extension *.ft2.

Warning: The program is aware of changes in a grid sheet as soon as you have left the cell in which you made these changes. If you make a single change but do not leave the cell, the program will not warn you to save this change. You can force saving any sheet by using **Save**.

Save Sheet As	Saves the active sheet under a new file name.
Save Project As	Saves all sheets of an existing simulation project under a new file name, and opens the new project.
Print Sheet	Prints the active sheet.
Print Project	Prints all sheets of the current simulation project, except the log data sheet.
Exit	Exits the program.

Edit menu

This menu is very similar to conventional spreadsheet or word processing programs.

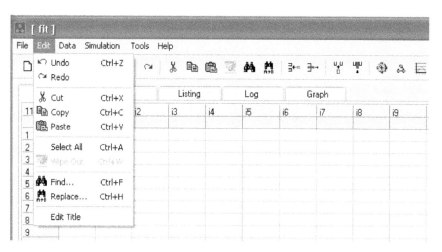

Edit menu.

Select one or multiple rows or columns by clicking **row** or **column headers**. Select multiple cells by using the **Shift + arrow keys**.

Undo	Undo last change(s). In a **grid sheet**, this affects only **cell editing**.
Redo	Redo last change(s). In a **grid sheet**, this affects only **cell editing**.
Cut	Cuts the selected character(s), grid cell(s) or graph.

Copy	Copies the selected character(s), grid cell(s) or graph.
Paste	Pastes the selected character(s), grid cell(s) or graph.
	Note: Existing rows and columns are overwritten.
Select All	Selects the whole content of the active sheet.
Wipe Out	Removes all but the last simulation run of the listing sheet.
Find	Searches for an entry in the active sheet. When a column is selected, find searches only this column. To search for empty cells, enter "".
	Note: when multiple columns or rows are selected, find starts at the **last row or column**.
Replace	Replaces an entry in the active sheet.
Edit Title	Makes a new project title or edits an existing project title. This title will appear in the print of all sheets.

Data Menu

This menu allows you to manipulate **rows or columns**.

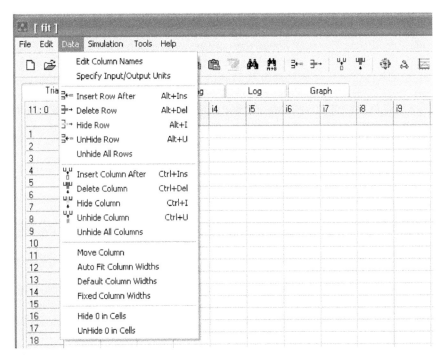

Data menu.

Edit Column Names	Allows you to provide your own names for all columns. This can also be accomplished for each column separately by **double clicking** the appropriate header cell where the name has to appear. **Note**: For the **DV columns** (see **Session Data Grid**), the program will suggest the names that you entered in the comments line of the test trials.
Specify In/Output Units	Allows you to change the number of input and output columns in the **trial data grid**. This can also be accomplished by double clicking the base cell (top left cell). You are not allowed to change the total amount of columns; use the **insert** and **delete** options (see below) for that.
Specify IV/DV Variables	Allows you to change the number of IV and DV columns in the **session data grid**. This can also be accomplished by double clicking the base cell (top left cell). You are not allowed to change the total amount of columns; use the **insert** and **delete** options (see below) for that.
Insert after	Creates a new row or column **after** the current one (below the current row or on the right of the current column).
Delete	Deletes the current row or column.
Hide	Hides the current row or column from view. The rows or columns on each side are marked by dark headers. Hiding might be convenient to temporarily try out novel trials or sessions, because **hidden data are not processed during the simulation**. Note that hidden data need to be unhidden or deleted permanently before saving them.
Unhide	Displays the hidden row or column by selecting the rows or columns on each side.
Unhide All	Displays all hidden rows or columns.
Move Column	Moves one column. You have to specify the column (by the name in the top row) after which the selected column will be moved.
Auto Fit Column Widths	Sets the smallest possible width for all columns.
Default Column Widths	Sets the default width for all columns.
Fixed Column Widths	Allows you to select a width for all columns. The highlighted width in the dialog is from the selected column.
Hide 0 in Cells	**Trial data grid:** Allows you to hide all **0** in the input or output units. Hidden or empty cells in the Trial data grid are interpreted as having an

external activation = 0 (unless the whole row is empty and therefore ignored).

UnHide 0 in Cells   **Trial data grid:** Allows you to unhide all **0** in the input or output units.

Fill Empty Cells   **Session data grid:** Allows you to fill empty cells with a * in the DV columns for test trials (with category number of 50 or above). This applies also to hidden columns.

Simulation menu

This menu controls the setting of simulation parameters and the running of the simulation.

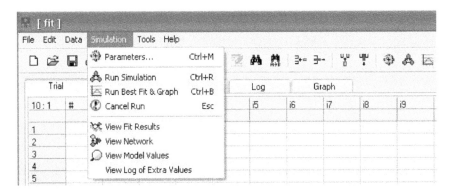

Simulation menu.

Parameters   Opens the parameter dialog.

Run Simulation   Starts the simulation specified by the Session parameter, using the parameters specified in the parameters dialog.

Run Best Fit & Graph Starts the simulation specified by the Session parameter, using the best-fitting model parameters of the previous run. After the simulation, the graph sheet is opened and the logged data are plotted.

View Fit Results   Opens the **Fit Results window** and shows you the basic simulation results while the simulation runs.

View Network   Opens the Simulation Details Window and shows a graphical display of the model's underlying Network architecture, with the weights and activations of all units in the network while the simulation runs.

View Model Values   Opens the Simulation Details Window and shows in a tabular format all Model Values including the

weights and activations of all units in the model
while the simulation runs.

View Log of Values   Opens the Simulation Details Window and allows
to Log Extra Values including the weights and
activations of all units in the model shown.

Cancel Run   Stops running the simulation.

SHEETS

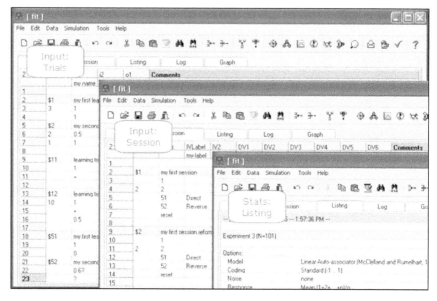

Various FIT sheets.

The sheets contain the data for running the simulations, and also give a text
and graphical output of the results:

- **Trial data grid sheet**.
- **Session data grid sheet**.
- **Listing sheet**.
- **Log data grid sheet**.
- **Graph sheet**.

Much of this is explained previously in the introductory example. Many more
additional information with special options and parameters is accessible
through the **Help** menu in the FIT program.

WINDOWS

Apart from the main window, several auxiliary windows provide additional information and help while the simulation is running:

- **FIT Results window**.
- **Simulation Details window**.

Other windows are also available, and provide ways to set or alter the **options** and **parameters** of the simulation.

FIT Results Window

When the simulation is running, you can follow the progress of the simulation in the **FIT Results Window**.

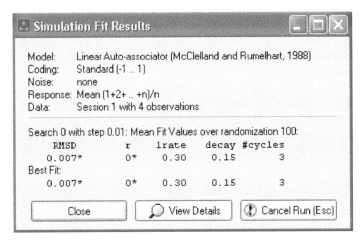

Fit results window.

This window echoes all the **options** and **model parameters** chosen for the simulation. In addition, it lists the results of the simulation and some additional **statistics**. The statistics are:

- **RMSD**: The Root Mean Squared Deviation between simulated and observed values in the case of a single simulation run; or the average RMSD across several simulation runs.
- **r**: The Pearson correlation between simulated and observed values in the case of a single simulation run; or the average correlation across several simulation runs.

Simulation Details Window

When the simulation is (about to be) running and you:

- turn **View option** on in the **Run Parameters** of the **Simulation | Parameters** menu
  or
- select the **Simulation | View Simulation Details** menu

then you can see the following information in the **Simulation Details Window** by clicking the appropriate tab:

- **Input**: Shows the external activation as input to the network of Learning and Test trials. Note that negative external input values appear with a minus sign on top.
- **Network**: Shows a graphical display of the model's underlying network architecture, with the weights and activations of all units (also directly accessible through the **Simulation | View Network** menu).
- **Model Values**: Shows the weights and activations of all units in the model in a tabular format (also directly accessible through the **Simulation | View Model Values** menu).
- **All Model Values**: Shows the weights and activations of all units in the model of all successive **next** button hits in a tabular format.
- **Log Extra Values**: Allows logging selected values that appear on the **Model values** window (also directly accessible through the **Simulation | View Log of Extra Values** menu).

View network

When you choose the **Simulation | View Network** menu, you can see a graphical display of the model's underlying network architecture, with the weights and activations of all units.

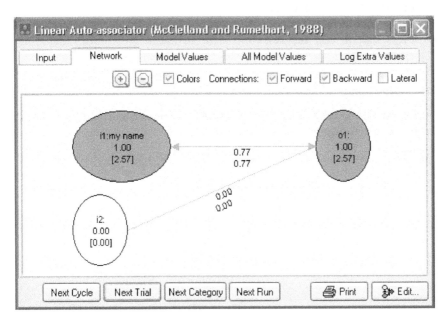

Network window.

The **input** for the unit is given on the second line in the unit; the **activation** of the unit is given on the third line between [ ] brackets.

The weight of the **forward connection** is given on the first line just below the arrow, while the weight of the **backward connection** is given on the second line. No weights are given for **lateral connections** as this would clutter the figure too much. You can edit, copy, save or export this network using the network editor by clicking the **Edit** button.

You can reposition the units at any moment. This gives the opportunity to place the units in a more visually attractive structure or hierarchy, or to better visualize the values of the connection weights (as they may sometimes overlap).

You have the following options (on top):

- Click the **Zoom In** or **Zoom Out** button to render the Network larger or smaller.
- Click **Colors** to provide a graded color from blue (−1.00) to light blue (−0.10) and from light red (+0.10) to red (+1.00).
- Depending on the type of model, you can select **forward, backward** and **lateral** connections.

You can follow the simulation step-by-step:

- Press the appropriate **Next** buttons to step through the simulation by each **Trial, Category** or **Run** (and additional possibilities depending on the model). All the results of your successive next hits are accumulated on the **All Model Values** tab.
- Press **Print** to print the network shown.
- Press **Edit** to edit the Network (with advanced possibilities including **exporting**).

View model values

When you choose the **Simulation | View Model Values** menu, you can see the weights and activations of all units in the model.

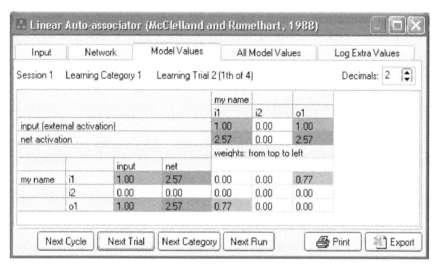

Model values window.

You have the following options (on top):

- Click **Auto Fit Columns** to provide the smallest possible width of all columns.
- Click **Color Values** to provide a graded color from blue (−1.00) to light blue (−0.10) and from light red (+0.10) to red (+1.00).
- You can also change the number of **Decimals**. This change will be effective on the next press on a **Next** button.

You can follow the simulation step-by-step:

- Press the appropriate **Next** buttons to step through the simulation by each **Trial, Category** or **Run** (and additional possibilities depending on the model). All the results of your successive **Next** hits are accumulated on the **All Model Values** tab.

- Press **Print** to print the values shown.
- Press **Export** to export the values to Microsoft Excel.

View log extra values

When you choose the **Simulation | View Log of Extra Values** menu, you can see the weights and activations of all units in the model, and select some so that their successive values are logged (see Log data grid sheet). The values that you select appear in green.

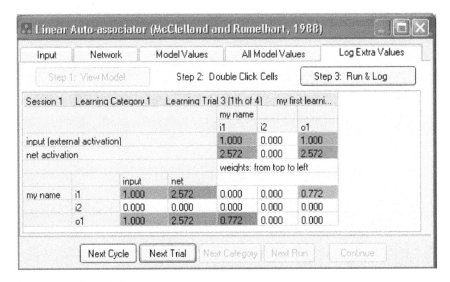

Log extra values window.

To select values for logging, go through the following steps (on top):

- **Step 1: View Model**: Gives you an overview of the model, with all weights at starting values.
- **Step 2: Double Click** the values (the cells) on the model's grid that you want to select for logging. Once selected, the values appear in green, and they also appear in the **Logging grid** on the right (not shown in the figure).
- **Step 3: Run & Log**: The model starts running with the logging of the extra values on. Be aware that logging of these extra values slows down the simulation considerably.

You can follow the simulation step-by-step:

- After Step 2, to get an idea of the values that are logged, you can press the appropriate **Next** buttons to step through the simulation.

Note: When pressing these **Next** buttons, nothing may be logged. To make sure that you log every trial, press **Cancel Run** and go through steps 1 and 3 above without interruption.

You have the following options (on top):

- By pressing the **Delete Row** button, you can remove some of the selected values.
- You can enter your own **Name** for logging (by default, the system takes the top column name and left-most row name of the grid).
- You can also change the number of **Decimals**. This change will be effective on the next press on a **Next** button or after clicking **Run & Log**.

You have the following options (at bottom):

- You can choose to log the extra values at **All trials** (that is, at all learning and test trials), or **Only at the test trials** (this latter option is to conform to standard logging). If you use the option **All trials**, make sure that you enter a value for the **IVs** for all Learning Categories in the Session Grid (in addition to the Test Categories) so that you can make an interpretable graph later on.

MODELS

This list is relevant only for the models described in the book. Many more model descriptions (e.g. **algebraic, associative** and **multi-agent** models) are available through the **Help** menu in the FIT program.

The following parameters are applicable to all models described below:

- **Learning algorithm:** All **connectionist** models use the **delta learning** algorithm only.
- **Starting Weights:** The default starting weights are zero for all models. See the menu **Simulation | Parameters | Weight and Activation Parameters** to change these initial weights.

Feedforward

In this network, all input units (denoted by i) are connected to all output units (denoted by o). Activation at the output units is the linear sum of the activation received from the input units. This model is labeled the **pattern associator** in McClelland and Rumelhart (1988).

This model has one parameter that can be accessed through the **Simulation | Parameters** menu and the **Model Parameters**. Consult the parameters also for additional (model-independent) parameters:

Learning Rate The learning rate parameter for the delta learning algorithm.

Linear Autoassociator

In this network, all units are connected with each other. Activation is updated at each cycle by linearly summing the internal and external input (see McClelland & Rumelhart, 1988).

This model has the following parameters that can be accessed through the **Simulation | Parameters** menu and the **Model Parameters**. Consult the parameters also for additional (model-independent) parameters:

Learning Rate	The learning rate parameter for the delta learning algorithm.
Estr	Scales the strength of the external input (input from outside the network).
Istr	Scales the strength of the internal input (input from other units in the network).
Decay	Decay rate parameter: The proportion by which the activation from the previous cycle decays before it is added to the novel state of the internal and external input.
#Cycles	The number of processing cycles in which the activation of the units is updated after combining the internal and external input.
Missing Threshold	Experimental parameter: Minimum activation level required to maintain internal input. Below this threshold, the activation is inversed to indicate that input activation is below expectations (see Van Overwalle & Timmermans, 2001).
#Varnt	Experimental parameter, do not use this.

Non-linear Autoassociator

In this network, all units are connected with each other. Activation is updated at each cycle by combining the internal and external input in such a manner that positive activation tends towards the +1 level after a number of cycles, while negative activation tends towards the −1 level. The parameters for this model are identical to the Linear Autoassociator, and can be accessed through the **Simulation | Parameters** menu and the **Model Parameters**.

SIMULATION OPTIONS

Through the **Simulation | Parameters** menu, the simulation **options** are available and can be seen on top of the **Parameter dialog**.

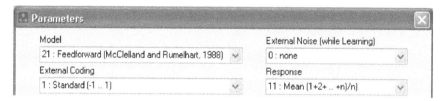

Simulation Options.

There are several kinds of major option on:

- **Models**
- **External coding**
- **External noise**
- **Response**

Models options

Through the **Simulation | Parameters** menu, the **model options** are available and can be seen on top of the **Parameter dialog**.

The model options allow you to select the appropriate **connectionist model** for your simulations. For a list and details of the available models, consult the Models section above.

External coding options

Through the **Simulation | Parameters** menu, the **external coding options** are available and can be seen on top of the **Parameter dialog**.

Normally, you use the **standard coding** of external values or activation which typically varies between −1 and +1. This external input reflects:

- a **localist** coding scheme if each unit reflects a single symbolic concept, or ·
- a **distributed** coding scheme if each unit reflects a subsymbolic feature of a concept.

There is also a more convenient way to specify a distributed coding scheme if the exact meaning of the subsymbolic features represented by each unit is of no importance. If that is the case, you can use the **distributed coding**, which will automatically replace each original unit by a fixed number of distributed units, and will automatically generate a **random pattern of activation** so that each of these distributed units has a somewhat different value or activation level throughout the simulation.

The following options for **Distributed Patterns** are available through a list box:

Uniform Random	This adds to the external activation (specified in the **Learning Trial Grid**) a uniform pattern of noise ranging between 0 and the activation specified (e.g. between 0 and 0.5 if the external activation in the unit is 0.5).
Normal Random	This adds to the external activation (specified in the **Learning Trial Grid**) a Normally distributed pattern of noise, with as mean the activation specified for the unit and a standard deviation chosen in the options (you can choose between SD = 0.01 to SD = 0.50).

No random pattern is applied for **zero activation** specified in the **Learning Trial Grid**, that is, these remain zero even when set to a distributed pattern, unless you specify otherwise in the **Distributed Coding and Noise Parameters**.

Specify the number of distributed features and other related parameters with the **Distributed Coding and Noise Parameters**.

The pattern of activation is determined randomly at the beginning of a simulation run, and remains fixed during the whole run, unless you choose to reshuffle the activation pattern after a fixed number of runs that you specify (see **Distributed Coding and Noise Parameters**). At each trial, you can also add random noise to these activation patterns (see **External Noise Options**).

External noise during learning options

Through the **Simulation | Parameters** menu, the **external noise options** are available and can be seen on top of the **Parameter dialog**.

These options allow you to specify how **random noise** is added to external activation **at each trial** during learning. This option is only available for distributed coding (however, if you would like to apply it also for localist coding, simply use distributed coding with a single distributed unit).

The following options are available through a list box:

Uniform Random	The distributed pattern of activation is randomly increased or decreased at each trial by random activation drawn from a uniform distribution ranging between a specified amount (you can choose between ±0.10 to ±0.50). For instance, if you choose ±0.20, random values are chosen between −0.20 and +0.20.
Normal Random	The distributed pattern of activation is randomly increased or decreased at each trial by random activation drawn from a normal distribution with

zero mean and specified standard deviation (you can choose between SD = 0.10 to SD = 0.50).

No noise is applied to "?" or test activations.

You can limit the Learning Categories to which the noise applies, and you can also specify how noise on zero activation is treated with the **Distributed Coding and Noise Parameters** (see below).

Response options

Through the **Simulation | Parameters** menu, the **response options** are available and can be seen on top of the **Parameter dialog**.

These options specify how the resulting test activation (e.g. as read off at the target or measurement unit denoted by ?) is converted into a response. Note that only the activation read off at the target **measurement** unit ? is used, and that these resulting activations are multiplied by the value preceding the ? mark (if there are any).

The following options are available through a list box:

Single Measurement Unit Only	Specify the rank order of the target that you want to read off. You need not specify a ? mark. Hence, this is typically used only for testing or "debugging" the simulation.
Combination of All Measurement Units	The activation of one of more units is activated (or "primed") and then the resulting activation in the ? measurement units is read off. This tests for the "memory" in the network, e.g. person impressions, attitudes:

- **Mean:** This is the typical option that combines the measured activation from different units in a single response. As noted above, by using multipliers before the ? mark, you can weight the contribution of each measurement unit in this overall response.
- **Paired:** This option is used to compare a series of ? measurement units with a series of observed data values, by pairing those units that occupy the same rank order in both series. Hence, you need as many test trials in the test category as observed data values. This option is especially useful to decompose a distributed encoding pattern which contains a series of units.

Convergence on Measurement Units	Takes the number of cycles needed to converge to a stable activation state during testing, and so reflects the time needed by the network to arrive at a stable state. That is, the difference between the mean sum of squares (MSS) of the current activations and the MMS of the prior activation update should be less than a specified value (you can choose between < 0.1 to < 0.0001). The maximum number of cycles is 100. This option is currently only available for the autoassociator.

SIMULATION PARAMETERS

Through the **Simulation | Parameters** menu, the simulation **parameters** can be accessed in the lower part of the **Parameter dialog**.

There are several kinds of parameters (additional parameters are explained through the **Help** menu in the FIT program):

- **General parameters, including:**
  — run parameters
  — randomize parameters.
- **Model parameters.**
- **Weights and activation parameters, including:**
  — weights parameters
  — activation parameters.
- **Distributed coding and noise parameters:**
  — distributed coding parameters
  — noise parameters.

General parameters

Through the **Simulation | Parameters** menu, the **general parameters** can be accessed by the **general** tab in the lower part of the **Parameter dialog**.

The different kinds of general parameter are:

- **Run parameters.**
- **Randomize parameters.**

Run parameters

These parameters control how the simulation is run. They can be accessed through the **Simulation | Parameters** menu and the **General** tab.

Running the Simulation

> Session
> From 1 [⇕] To [⇕]
>
> View Details / List All Results
> ○ No   ⊙ View   ○ List All
>
> Log Simulated Values
> ○ No   ⊙ Yes   ○ Append
>
> Graph Simulated Values
> ○ No   ⊙ Yes

Run parameters.

The following parameters are available:

Session	• **From**: The Session Category for analysis.
	• **To**: All Sessions in between.
View Details / List	• **No**: Nothing special is shown or listed.
All Results	• **View**: Show in a separate window details on each trial, category or run (is, in fact, an advanced selection of the **Simulation | View** menu).
	• **List All**: Write on the listing sheet all correlations of all runs in a search.
Log Simulated Values	• **No**: No logging in the log data grid (speeds up the searching of the best fit).
	• **Yes**: Log simulated and observed values of the Test Categories. For each session run, a new log grid is cleared and then filled with the log data.
	• **Append**: Same as yes, except that the grid is not cleared after each run, so that all logs are appended one after another. This allows you to

use different parameters for the same run and compare the end results later on (in a graph).

Graph Simulated Values • **No**: No graph is plotted of the logged data.
• **Yes**: A graph is plotted of the logged data.

Randomize parameters

These parameters control how the order of the trials is randomized. They can be accessed through the **Simulation | Parameters** menu and the **General** tab.

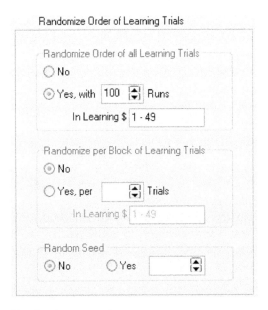

Randomize parameters.

The following parameters are available:

Randomize Order of All Learning Trials	• **No**: No Randomization. • **Yes**: Specifies how many times the simulation is run while: — the order of the **learning trials** is randomized for each run — the noise (if any) is randomized for each **learning trial** (see **Noise parameters**).
. . . In Learning $	Specify the Learning Categories for which the random ordering should apply when Randomization is set to **Yes**. You can specify this as: 1, 3–6, 8 etc . . . By default, this should be applied to all Categories $1 to $49.

If you want to apply random noise, but no random ordering of trials, then select here a non-existent trial category so that the random order is not applied on your learning trials.

Randomize per Block
of Learning Trials

- **No**: No Randomization.
- **Yes**: The random order of Learning Trials is applied on blocks of trials instead of each individual trial. Specify the number of Learning Trials to go in a block, and randomization will be performed between blocks. For instance, with a block of two trials, the random order of eight trials might be 3 4, 7 8, 1 2, 5 6. By default, the number of trials in each random block is one.

  Note: If the total number of Learning Trials in a Category is not divisible by the block, then the trailing/remaining trials are not randomized. FIT ignores empty trials.

. . . In Learning $

Specify the Learning Categories for which the blocked random ordering should apply when **Randomize Block of Trials** is set. You can specify this as: 1, 3–6, 8 etc . . . By default, this should be applied to all Categories $1 to $49.

Random Seed

- **No**: (recommended) No Random Seed.
- **Yes**: Randomization is initialized by the Seed specified. Use this option for an exact replication of random runs, distributed patterns and noise.

Model parameters

These parameters control how the model behaves. They can be accessed through the **Simulation | Parameters** menu and the **Model** tab.

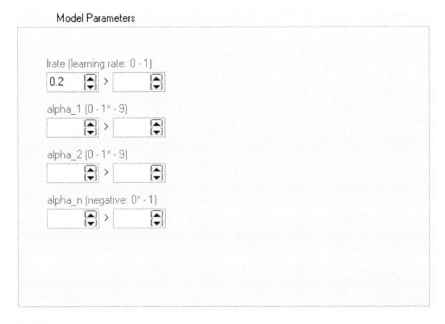

Model parameters.

The **model parameters depend on the model specified**, and their labeling and use is conform to standard use in the literature.

- If a **single parameter value** is given in the left box, this value is used in all simulations.
- If a **lowest and a highest value** of a parameter is given in a left and right box respectively, then FIT will search for a parameter value within the specified range that provides the best correlation with the observed data.
- Model Parameters are **typically specified in hundredths** (from 0.01 to 1.00 or higher), unless when the parameter label begins with a #, in which case an **integer number** is to be given. The spin button (which sets the parameter value higher or lower with a single click) automatically provides the appropriate scaling.

In addition to standard model parameters, there are some **special activation parameters** that can be used for several models. They affect the external activation of these units (as specified in the trial data, see **Trial Data Grid Sheet**).

These activation parameters can be viewed as a supervisory attentional system that serves as a gateway to other areas in the network and that modulate the activation of some nodes in these areas. Thus, it instantiates in a rough manner the supervisory executive centers in the prefrontal neocortex which modulate task-specific attention and voluntary control (LaBerge, 1997, 2000):

alpha_1   Proportion by which the **external activation of units is augmented**; the units involved are indicated in the first row of a special Learning Category $-1.

        You can use "1" to specify the units that should be augmented, but any value is acceptable (note that alpha_1 is multiplied with this value).

alpha_2   Same as for alpha_1; the units are indicated in the second row of Learning Category $-1.

alpha_n   Negative activation value for units with zero activation (see Van Hamme & Wasserman, 1994). Enter only the value, **not** the negative sign.

The **Activation parameters** in the **Simulation | Parameters | Weights & Activation** menu provide alternative ways on how the alpha_1 and alpha_2 for input units are effective. They allow influencing the **external activation** as described above, or **only the learning rate for input units**.

    In addition, there are also parameters that control the **searching of the best fitting** model parameters:

Search Step

- **Auto**: Automatic search of the best correlation between observed and simulated values, first in steps of 0.10 of the model parameters, then in steps of 0.05, and finally in steps of 0.01.
- **Step**: Search for the best correlation by stepping throughout all model parameters in steps as indicated (can be very time consuming).

Limit Simulation Values

- **No**: There are no limitations on the simulated values obtained.
- **Yes ±**: The simulated values must fall between the −limit and +limit to be eligible as Best Fit. A typical limit is 1.00 or 1.10.

Weights and activation parameters

These parameters control how the model behaves. They can be accessed through the **Simulation | Parameters** menu and the **Weights and Activation** tab.

    There are several kinds of these parameters:

- **Weights parameters.**
- **Activation parameters.**

Weights parameters

These parameters provide control on how the weights are treated. They can be accessed through the **Simulation | Parameters** menu and the **Weights and Activation** tab.

Weight parameters.

Starting Weights	• **Default**: As determined by the model (typically zero).
	• **Set to**: Provide your own starting values for all weights of the model (e.g. start with 0.10 instead of 0.00).
Random Starting Weights	(only available when **Starting Weights** are set to specific value):
	• **No**: No extra randomization is applied (except when random weight are applied by default in some models).
	• **Add ±**: Add a random value between – or + the value entered.

Activation parameters

These parameters provide further control on how alpha_1 and alpha_2 (see **Model Parameters**) are applied. They can be accessed through the **Simulation | Parameters** menu and the **Weights and Activation** tab.

Activation

Alpha_1 & 2 Coding (see Model parameters)

Determines...
○ Activation   ◉ LRate Only

In Learning $ 1 - 49

Multiply Clamped Activation
◉ No   ○ By ..

Cycle Internal Clamp
◉ No   ○ # of Cycles

Activation parameters.

Alpha_1 and 2 Coding (see Model Parameters)	**Determines . . .** • **Activation**: Typically, the alpha_1 and alpha_2 parameters for input units influence the external activation of these units (as given in the trial data grid). • **LRate Only**: The alpha_1 and alpha_2 parameters for **input units** influence the external activation only during weight adaptation and are not used while computing the learning error. As a result, they thus affect only the learning rate. If you want the **output units** to be treated the same, define them as input units (e.g. in recurrent models).
. . . In Learning $	Specify the Learning Categories for which the alpha_1 and alpha_2 coding applies. You can specify this as: 1, 3–6, 8 etc . . . By default, this should be applied to all Categories $1 to $49.

Note: Alpha_n is not affected by this parameter and is always applied.

Multiply Clamped Values	• **No**: Each clamped value (the activation from a previous trial row as indicated by a = in the **Learning Trials**) is multiplied by the default value 1. More information is available in the electronic help file using the **Help** menu.
	• **By**: Each clamped value is multiplied by the value given.
Cycle Internal Clamp	• **No**: Each internal clamped value (the internal activation received from other units in a trial row as indicated by a small "i" in the **Learning Trials**) is used as external activation (before weight adjustment). More information is available in the electronic help file using the **Help** menu.
	• **Cycle**: Each internal clamped value is used as external activation, and this external activation is then cycled a given number of times through a non-linear activation update algorithm with −1 and +1 as attractors (before weight adjustment). More information is available in the electronic help file using the **Help** menu.

Distributed coding and noise parameters

When you use a distributed coding scheme by automatically "upgrading" a localist coding (using the **External Coding options**, see **Simulation Options**), several parameters control how the distributed coding and additional noise is specified. They can be accessed through the **Simulation | Parameters** menu and the **Distributed Coding and Noise** tab.

There are several kinds of these parameters:

• **Distributed coding parameters.**
• **Noise parameters.**

Distributed coding parameters

These parameters provide further control on how distributed coding is applied.

Distributed Coding at Learning & Test Trials

of (Micro-) Features per Unit   [5] [↕]

[ ] Also on Zero External Activation

[✓] Link (Micro-) Features of Same Unit

Reshuffle Distributed Coding each Run
( ) No   (●) Each [10] [↕] th Run

Distributed coding parameters.

Number of Micro-Features per Unit	Determines the number of distributed features that replace a single localist unit.
Also on Zero Activation	If this option is checked, a distributed activation pattern is applied on all units with zero activation **also**, otherwise **no** distributed activation pattern is applied on these units.
Link Micro-Features of Same Unit	Links between units themselves are not allowed in an autoassociative network. It is recommended to leave this option **unchecked**, so that you apply a similar constraint among distributed features representing the same concept (i.e. localist unit).
Reshuffle Distributed Coding each Run	• **No**: The distributed pattern for the units remains identical through all simulation runs. • **Each .. th Run**: The distributed pattern will be reshuffled after the specified number of runs.

Noise parameters

These parameters provide further control on how noise is applied.

```
Noise
┌─────────────────────────────────────────────┐
│  ┌ Noise at Learning Trials ─────────────┐  │
│  │                                        │  │
│  │   In learning $  [ 1 - 1        ]      │  │
│  │                                        │  │
│  │                                        │  │
│  │      Noise on Zero External Activation │  │
│  │      ○ No     ○ Also    ⊙ Only         │  │
│  └────────────────────────────────────────┘  │
│                                               │
│  ┌ Response Noise (from Normal Distribution) ┐│
│  │  ⊙ No        ○ SD =    [      ⬍]          ││
│  └────────────────────────────────────────────┘│
└─────────────────────────────────────────────┘
```

Noise parameters.

Noise at learning trials

. . . In Learning $ Specify the Learning Categories for which the noise applies. You can specify this as: 1, 3–6, 8 etc . . . By default, this should be applied to all Categories $1 to $49.

Noise on Zero Activation • **No:** no noise is applied when the external activation is zero.
• **Also:** noise is also applied when the external activation is zero.
• **Only:** noise is applied only when the external activation is zero.

Response Noise   • **No**: No noise is applied on the response.
• **SD**: The response is increased or decreased at each trial by a random value drawn from a normal distribution with zero mean and the specified standard deviation. This can be useful to provide more realistic (i.e. noisy) outcomes of the simulation, so that statistical tests can be applied on the simulated data.

References

Abelson, R. P., & Lalljee, M. (1988). Knowledge structures and causal explanation. In D. Hilton (Ed.), *Contemporary science and natural explanation: Commonsense conceptions of causality* (pp. 175–203). London: Harvester Press.

Adolphs, R., & Damasio, A. (2001). The interaction of affect and cognition: A neurobiological perspective. In J. P. Forgas (Ed.), *Handbook of affect and social cognition* (pp. 27–49). Mahwah, NJ: Lawrence Erlbaum Associates, Inc.

Adolphs, R., Tranel, D., & Damasio, A. (1998). The human amygdala in social judgment. *Nature, 393*, 470–474.

Ajzen, I. (1988). *Attitudes, personality and behavior*. Homewood, IL: Dorsey Press.

Ajzen, I. (1991). The theory of planned behavior. *Organizational Behavior and Human Decision Processes, 50*, 179–211.

Ajzen, I. (2002). Residual effects of past on later behavior: Habituation and reasoned action perspectives. *Personality and Social Psychology Review, 6*, 107–122.

Ajzen, I., & Madden, T. J. (1986). Prediction of goal-directed behavior: Attitudes, intentions, and perceived behavioral control. *Journal of Experimental Social Psychology, 22*, 453–474.

Ajzen, I., Dalto, C. A., & Blyth, D. P. (1979). Consistency and bias in the attribution of attitudes. *Journal of Personality and Social Psychology, 37*, 1871–1876.

Allan, L. G. (1993). Human contingency judgments: Rule based or associative? *Psychological Bulletin, 114*, 435–448.

Allison, T., Puce, A., & McCarthy, G. (2000). Social perception from visual cues: Role of the STS region. *Trends in Cognitive Sciences, 4*, 267–278.

Andersen, S. M., & Cole, S. W. (1990). "Do I know you?": The role of significant others in general social perception. *Journal of Personality and Social Psychology, 59*, 384–399.

Anderson, J. R. (1976). *Language, memory and thought*. Hillsdale, NJ: Lawrence Erlbaum Associates, Inc.

Anderson, J. R., & Sheu, C-F. (1995). Causal inferences as perceptual judgments. *Memory and Cognition, 23*, 510–524.

Anderson, N. H. (1967). Averaging model analysis of set-size effects in impression formation. *Journal of Experimental Psychology, 75*, 158–165.

Anderson, N. H. (1971). Integration theory and attitude change. *Psychological Review, 78*, 171–206.

Anderson, N. H. (1979). Serial position curves in impression formation. *Journal of Experimental Psychology, 97*, 8–12.

Anderson, N. H. (1981). *Foundations of information integration theory*. New York: Academic Press.

Anderson, N. H., & Farkas, A. J. (1973). New light on order effect in attitude change. *Journal of Personality and Social Psychology, 28*, 88–93.

Ans, B., & Rousset, S. (1997). Avoiding catastrophic forgetting by coupling two reverberating neural networks. *Académie des Sciences de la Vie, 320*, 989–997.

Ans, B., & Rousset, S. (2000). Neural networks with a self-refreshing memory: Knowledge transfer in sequential learning tasks without catastrophic forgetting. *Connection Science, 12*, 1–19.

Asch, S. E. (1946). Forming impressions of personality. *Journal of Abnormal and Social Psychology, 41*, 258–290.

Asch, S. E., & Zukier, H. (1984). Thinking about persons. *Journal of Personality and Social Psychology, 46*, 1230–1240.

Axelrod, R. (1997). The dissemination of culture: A model with local convergence and global polarization. *Journal of Conflict Resolution, 41*, 203–226.

Axelrod, R., Riolo, R. L., & Cohen, M. D. (2002). Beyond geography: Cooperation with persistent links in the absence of clustered neighborhoods. *Personality and Social Psychology Review, 6*, 341–346.

Axsom, D., Yates, S., & Chaiken, S. (1987). Audience response as a heuristic cue in persuasion. *Journal of Personality and Social Psychology, 53*, 30–40.

Baker, A. G., Berbier, M. W., & Vallée-Tourangeau, F. (1989). Judgments of a 2×2 contingency table: Sequential processing and the learning curve. *Quarterly Journal of Experimental Psychology, 41B*, 65–97.

Baker, A. G., Mercier, P., Vallée-Tourangeau, F., Frank, R., & Pan, M. (1993). Selective associations and causality judgments: Presence of a strong causal factor may reduce judgments of a weaker one. *Journal of Experimental Psychology: Learning, Memory and Cognition, 19*, 414–432.

Baker, A. G., Murphy, R. A., & Vallée-Tourangeau, F. (1996). Associative and normative models of causal induction: Reacting to versus understanding cause. *The Psychology of Learning and Motivation, 34*, 1–46.

Banaji, M. R., & Greenwald, A. G. (1994). Implicit stereotyping and prejudice. In M. P. Zanna & J. M. Olson (Eds.), *The psychology of prejudice: The Ontario Symposium* (Vol. 7, pp. 55–76). Hillsdale, NJ: Lawrence Erlbaum Associates, Inc.

Barden, J., Maddux, W. W., Petty, R. E., & Brewer, M. B. (2004). Contextual moderation of racial bias: The impact of social roles on controlled and automatically activated attitudes. *Journal of Personality and Social Psychology, 87*, 5–22.

Bargh, J. A. (1994). The four horsemen of automaticity: Awareness, intention, efficiency, and control in social cognition. In R. S. Wyer & T. K. Srull (Eds.), *Handbook of social cognition* (2nd ed., Vol. 1, pp. 1–40). Hillsdale, NJ: Lawrence Erlbaum Associates, Inc.

Bargh, J. A. (1996). Automaticity in social psychology. In E. T. Higgins & A. W. Kruglanski (Eds.), *Social psychology: Handbook of basic principles*. (pp. 169–183). New York: Guilford Press.

Bargh, J. A., & Thein, R. D. (1985). Individual construct accessibility, person memory, and the recall–judgment link: The case of information overload. *Journal of Personality and Social Psychology, 49*, 1129–1146.

Bargh, J. A., Chaiken, S., Govender, R., & Pratto, F. (1992). The generality of the automatic attitude activation effect. *Journal of Personality and Social Psychology, 62*, 893–912.

Bargh, J. A., Lombardi, W. J., & Higgins, E. T. (1988). Automaticity of chronically accessible constructs in Person × Situation effects on person perception: It's just a matter of time. *Journal of Personality and Social Psychology*, *55*, 599–605.

Barr, D. J. (2004). Establishing conventional communication systems: Is common knowledge necessary? *Cognitive Science*, *28*, 937–962.

Barrow, J. D. (1992). *Pi in the sky: Counting, thinking and being.* Harmondsworth, UK: Penguin Books.

Berkowitz, L., & Knurek, D. A. (1969). Label-mediated hostility generalization. *Journal of Personality and Social Psychology*, *13*, 200–206.

Betsch, T., Plessner, H., & Schallies, E. (2004). The value-account model of attitude formation. In G. Haddock & G. R. Maio (Eds.), *Contemporary perspectives on the psychology of attitudes* (pp. 251–274). New York: Psychology Press.

Betsch, T., Plessner, H., Schwieren, C., & Gütig, R. (2001). I like it but I don't know why: A value-account approach to implicit attitude formation. *Personality and Social Psychology Bulletin*, *27*, 242–253.

Biernat, M., & Manis, M. (1994). Shifting standards and stereotype-based judgments. *Journal of Personality and Social Psychology*, *66*, 5–20.

Bohner, G., & Weinerth, T. (2001). Negative affect can increase or decrease message scrutiny: The affect interpretation hypothesis. *Personality and Social Psychology Bulletin*, *27*, 1417–1428.

Bohner, G., Ruder, M., & Erb, H.-P. (2002). When expertise backfires: Contrast and assimilation effects in persuasion. *British Journal of Social Psychology*, *41*, 495–519.

Bower, G. H. (1981). Emotional mood and memory. *American Psychologist*, *36*, 129–148.

Brewer, M. B. (1988). A dual process model of impression formation. In T. Srull & R. Wyer (Eds.), *Advances in social cognition* (Vol. 1, pp. 177–183). Hillsdale, NJ: Lawrence Erlbaum Associates, Inc.

Brewer, M. B., Dull, V., & Lui, L. (1981). Perceptions of the elderly: Stereotypes as prototypes. *Journal of Personality and Social Psychology*, *41*, 656–670.

Brown, R., Vivian, J., & Hewstone, M. (1999). Changing attitudes through intergroup contact: The effects of membership salience. *European Journal of Social Psychology*, *74*, 1–64.

Busemeyer, J. R. (1991). Intuitive statistical estimation. In N. Anderson (Ed.), *Contributions to information integration theory: Vol. 1. Cognition.* Hillsdale, NJ: Lawrence Erlbaum Associates, Inc.

Busemeyer, J. R., & Myung, I. J. (1988). A new method for investigating prototype learning. *Journal of Experimental Psychology: Learning, Memory, and Cognition*, *14*, 3–11.

Cacioppo, J. T., & Berntson, G. G. (2004). *Essays in social neuroscience.* Cambridge, MA: MIT Press.

Cacioppo, J. T., & Petty, R. E. (1982). The need for cognition. *Journal of Personality and Social Psychology*, *42*, 116–131.

Cacioppo, J. T., Berntson, G. G., Sheridan, J. F., & McClintock, M. K. (2000). Multilevel integrative analyses of human behavior: Social neuroscience and the complementing nature of social and biological approaches. *Psychological Bulletin*, *126*, 829–843.

Canli, T., Desmond, J. E., Zhao, Z., Glover, G., & Gabrieli, J. D. E. (1998). Hemispheric asymmetry for emotional stimuli detected with fMRI. *Neuroreport*, *9*, 3233–3239.

Cantor, N., & Mischel, W. (1977). Traits as prototypes: Effects on recognition memory. *Journal of Personality and Social Psychology, 35*, 38–48.

Carlston, D. E. (1994). Associated systems theory: A systematic approach to cognitive representations of persons. In R. S. Wyer & T. K. Srull (Eds.), *Advances in social cognition* (Vol. 7, pp. 1–78). Hillsdale, NJ: Lawrence Erlbaum Associates, Inc.

Carlston, D. E., & Skowronski, J. J. (1994). Savings in the relearning of trait information as evidence for spontaneous inference generation. *Journal of Personality and Social Psychology, 66*, 840–856.

Chaiken, S. (1980). Heuristic versus systematic information processing and the use of source versus message cues in persuasion. *Journal of Personality and Social Psychology, 39*, 752–766.

Chaiken, S. (1987). The heuristic model of persuasion. In M. P. Zanna, J. M. Olson, & C. P. Herman (Eds.), *Social influence: The Ontario Symposium* (Vol. 5, pp. 3–39). Hillsdale, NJ: Lawrence Erlbaum Associates Inc.

Chaiken, S., & Eagly, A. H. (1983). Communication modality as a determinant of persuasion: The role of communicator salience. *Journal of Personality and Social Psychology, 45*, 241–256.

Chaiken, S., & Maheswaran, D. (1994). Heuristic processing can bias systematic processing: Effects of source credibility, argument ambiguity, and task importance on attitude judgment. *Journal of Personality and Social Psychology, 66*, 460–473.

Chaiken, S., Duckworth, K. L., & Darke, P. (1999). When parsimony fails . . . *Psychological Inquiry, 10*, 118–123.

Chaiken, S., Liberman, A., & Eagly, A. H. (1989). Heuristic and systematic information processing within and beyond the persuasion context. In J. S. Uleman & J. A. Bargh (Eds.), *Unintended thought* (pp. 212–252). New York: Guilford Press.

Chapman, G. B. (1991). Trial order affects cue interaction in contingency judgment. *Journal of Experimental Psychology: Learning, Memory and Cognition, 17*, 837–854.

Chapman, G. B., & Robbins, S. J. (1990). Cue interaction in human contingency judgment. *Memory and Cognition, 18*, 537–545.

Chapman, L. J. (1967). Illusory correlation in observational report. *Journal of Verbal Learning and Verbal Behavior, 6*, 151–155.

Chen, S., & Chaiken, S. (1999). The heuristic-systematic model in its broader context. In S. Chaiken & Y. Trope (Eds.), *Dual-process theories in social psychology* (pp. 73–96). New York: Guilford Press.

Cheng, P. W. (1997). From covariation to causation: A causal power theory. *Psychological Review, 104*, 367–405.

Cheng, P. W., & Holyoak, K. J. (1995). Complex adaptive systems as intuitive statisticians: Causality, contingency, and prediction. In H. L. Roiblatt & J.-A. Meyer (Eds.), *Comparative approaches to cognitive science*. Cambridge, MA: MIT Press.

Cheng, P. W., & Novick, L. R. (1990). A probabilistic contrast model of causal induction. *Journal of Personality and Social Psychology, 58*, 545–567.

Cheng, P. W., & Novick, L. R. (1992). Covariation in natural causal induction. *Psychological Review, 99*, 365–382.

Chun, W. Y., Spiegel, S., & Kruglanski, A. W. (2002). Assimilative behavior identification can also be resource dependent: The unimodel perspective on personal-attribution phases. *Journal of Personality and Social Psychology, 83*, 542–555.

Churchland, P. S. (1986). Neurophilosophy: Toward a unified science of the mind/brain. Cambridge, MA: MIT Press.

Churchland, P. S., & Sejnowski, T. J. (1992). *The computational brain*. Cambridge, MA: MIT Press.

Clark, A. (1993). *Associative engines: Connectionism, concepts, and representational change*. Cambridge, MA: MIT Press.

Cleeremans, A., & Jiménez, L. (2002). Implicit learning and consciousness: A graded, dynamic perspective. In R. M. French & A. Cleeremans (Eds.), *Implicit learning and consciousness: An empirical, philosophical and computational consensus in the making* (pp. 1–40). Hove, UK: Psychology Press.

Cohen, J. D., Dunbar, K., & McCelland, J. L. (1990). On the control of automatic processes: A distributed processing account of the Stroop effect. *Psychological Review*, *97*, 332–361.

Cooper, J., & Fazio, R. H. (1984). A new look at dissonance theory. In L. Berkowitz (Ed.), *Advances in experimental social psychology* (Vol. 17, pp. 229–266). New York: Academic Press.

Corneille, O., Klein, O., Lambert, S., & Judd, C. M. (2002). Don't muddle up inches and centimeters: Evidence for the role of task complexity in obtaining intercategory accentuation effects with unidimensional estimates. *Psychological Sciences*, *13*, 380–383.

Couzin, I. D., Krause, J., Frank, N. R., & Levin, S. A. (2005). Effective leadership and decision-making in animal groups on the move. *Nature*, *433*, 513–516.

Cunningham, W. A., Johnson, M. K., Gatenby, J. C., Gore, J. C., & Banaji, M. R. (2003). Neural components of social evaluation. *Journal of Personality and Social Psychology*, *85*, 639–649.

Darke, P. R., Chaiken, S., Bohner, G., Einwiller, S., Erb, H-P., & Hazlewood, J. D. (1998). Accuracy motivation, consensus information, and the low of large numbers: Effects on attitude judgment in the absence of argumentation. *Personality and Social Psychology Bulletin*, *24*, 1205–1215.

De Houwer, K., Thomas, S., & Baeyens, F. (2001). Associative learning of likes and dislikes: A review of 25 years of research on human evaluative conditioning. *Psychological Bulletin*, *127*, 853–869.

Devine, P. G. (1989). Stereotypes and prejudice: Their automatic and controlled components. *Journal of Personality and Social Psychology*, *56*, 5–18.

Dickinson, A., & Burke, J. (1996). Within-compound associations mediate the retrospective revaluation of causality judgments. *Quarterly Journal of Experimental Psychology*, *49B*, 60–80.

Dijksterhuis, A. (2004). I like myself but I don't know why: Enhancing implicit self esteem by subliminal evaluative conditioning. *Journal of Personality and Social Psychology*, *86*, 345–355.

Dijksterhuis, A., & van Knippenberg, A. (1999). On the parameters of associative strength: Central tendency and variability as determinants of stereotype accessibility. *Personality and Social Psychology Bulletin*, *25*, 527–536.

Doosje, B., Ellemers, N., & Spears, R. (1995). Perceived ingroup variability as a function of group status and identification. *Journal of Social Experimental Psychology*, *31*, 410–436.

Dreben, E. K., Fiske, S. T., & Hastie, R. (1979). The independence of evaluative and item information: Impression and recall order effects in behavior-based impression formation. *Journal of Personality and Social Psychology*, *37*, 1758–1768.

Druian, P., & Omessi, E. (1984). *A knowledge structure theory of attribution*. Unpublished manuscript, Grinnell, IA: Grinnell College.

Eagly, A. H., & Chaiken, S. (1993). *The psychology of attitudes*. San Diego, CA: Harcourt Brace.

Easton, A., & Emery, N. J. (2005). *The cognitive neuroscience of social behavior*. New York: Psychology Press.

Ebbesen, E. B., & Bowers, R. J. (1974). Proportion of risky to conservative arguments in a group discussion and choice shifts. *Journal of Personality and Social Psychology*, *29*, 316–327.

Ebbinghaus, H. (1964). *Memory: A contribution to experimental psychology*. New York: Dover. (Original work published 1885.)

Eiser, J. R. (1971). Enhancement of contrast in the absolute judgment of attitude statements. *Journal of Personality and Social Psychology*, *17*, 1–10.

Eiser, J. R., Fazio, R. H., Stafford, T., & Prescott, T. J. (2003). Connectionist simulation of attitude learning: Asymmetries in the acquisition of positive and negative evaluations. *Personality and Social Psychology Bulletin*, *29*, 1221–1235.

Elman, J. L., Bates, E. A., Johnson, M. H., Karmiloff-Smith, A., Parisi, D., & Plunkett, K. (1996). *Rethinking innateness: A connectionist perspective on development*. Cambridge, MA: MIT Press.

Erb, H.-P., Bohner, G., Schmälzle, K., & Rank, S. (1998). Beyond conflict and discrepancy: Cognitive bias in minority and majority influence. *Personality and Social Psychology Bulletin*, *24*, 620–633.

Estes, W. K., Campbell, J. A., Hatsopoulos, N., & Hurwitz, J. B. (1989). Base-rate effects in category learning: A comparison of parallel network and memory storage-retrieval models. *Journal of Experimental Psychology, Learning, Memory and Cognition*, *15*, 556–571.

Fales, E., & Wasserman, E. A. (1992). Causal knowledge: What can psychology teach philosophers? *Journal of Mind and Behavior*, *13*, 1–28.

Fazio, R. H. (1990). Multiple processes by which attitudes guide behavior: The MODE model as an integrative framework. In M. P. Zanna (Ed.), *Advances in Experimental Social Psychology* (Vol. 13, pp. 75–109). San Diego, CA: Academic Press.

Fazio, R. H., & Powell, M. C. (1997). On the value of knowing one's likes and dislikes: Attitude accessibility, stress, and health in college. *Psychological Science*, *8*, 430–436.

Fazio, R. H., Eiser, J. R., & Shook, N. J. (2004). Attitude formation through exploration: Valence asymmetries. *Journal of Personality and Social Psychology*, *87*, 293–311.

Fazio, R. H., Sanbonmatsu, D. M., Powell, M. C., & Kardes, F. R. (1986). On the automatic activation of attitudes. *Journal of Personality and Social Psychology*, *50*, 229–238.

Fein, S. (1996). Effects of suspicion on attributional thinking and the correspondence bias. *Journal of Personality and Social Psychology*, *70*, 1164–1184.

Fein, S., Hilton, J. L., & Miller, D. T. (1990). Suspicion of ulterior motive and the correspondence bias. *Journal of Personality and Social Psychology*, *58*, 753–764.

Festinger, L. (1957). *A theory of cognitive dissonance*. Evanston, IL: Row, Peterson.

Fiedler, K. (1991). The tricky nature of skewed frequency tables: An information loss account of distinctiveness-based illusory correlations. *Journal of Personality and Social Psychology*, *60*, 24–36.

Fiedler, K. (1996). Explaining and simulating judgment biases as an aggregation phenomenon in probabilistic, multiple-cue environment. *Journal of Personality and Social Psychology*, *103*, 193–214.

Fiedler, K., Kemmelmeier, M., & Freytag, P. (1999). Explaining asymmetric intergroup judgments through differential aggregation: Computer simulations and some new evidence. *European Review of Social Psychology*, *10*, 1–40.

Fiedler, K., Russer, S., & Gramm, K. (1993). Illusory correlation and memory performance. *Journal of Experimental Social Psychology*, *29*, 111–136.

Fiedler, K., Walther, E., & Nickel, S. (1999). The auto-verification of social hypotheses: Stereotyping and the power of sample size. *Journal of Personality and Social Psychology*, *77*, 5–18.

Fiedler, K., Walther, E., Freytag, P., & Stryczek, E. (2002). Playing mating games in foreign cultures: A conceptual framework and an experimental paradigm for inductive trivariate inference. *Journal of Experimental Social Psychology*, *38*, 14–30.

Fishbein, M., & Ajzen, I. (1975). *Belief attitude, intention and behavior: An introduction to theory and research*. London: Addison-Wesley.

Fiske, S. T., & Neuberg, S. L. (1990). A continuum of impression formation, from category-based to individuating processes: Influences of information and motivation on attention and interpretation. In M. P. Zanna (Ed.), *Advances in experimental social psychology* (Vol. 23, pp. 1–74). New York: Academic Press.

Fiske, S. T., & Taylor, S. E. (1991). *Social cognition* (2nd ed.). New York: McGraw-Hill.

Forgas, J. P. (2001). *Handbook of affect and social cognition*. Mahwah, NJ: Lawrence Erlbaum Associates, Inc.

Försterling, F. (1989). Models of covariation and attribution: How do they relate to the analogy of analysis of variance? *Journal of Personality and Social Psychology*, *57*, 615–625.

Försterling, F. (1992). The Kelley model as an analysis of variance analogy: How far can it be taken? *Journal of Experimental Social Psychology*, *28*, 475–490.

French, R. (1997). Pseudo-recurrent connectionist networks: An approach to the "sensitivity–stability" dilemma. *Connection Science*, *9*, 353–379.

French, R. (1999). Catastrophic forgetting in neural networks. *Trends in Cognitive Sciences*, *3*, 128–135.

Freund, T., Kruglanski, A. W., & Shpitzajzen, A. (1985). The freezing and unfreezing of impressional primacy: Effects of the need for structure and the fear of invalidity. *Personality and Social Psychology Bulletin*, *11*, 479–487.

Frith, C. D., & Wolpert, D. M. (2004). *The neuroscience of social interaction: decoding, imitating, and influencing the actions of others*. Oxford: Oxford University Press.

Fyock, J., & Stangor, C. (1994). The role of memory biases in stereotype maintenance. *British Journal of Social Psychology*, *33*, 331–343.

Funder, D. C. (2001). The really, really fundamental attribution error. *Psychological Inquiry*, *12*, 21–23.

Gannon, K. M., Skowronski, J. J., & Betz, A. L. (1994). Depressive diligence in social information processing: Implications for order effects in impressions and for social memory. *Social Cognition*, *12*, 263–280.

Garcia-Marques, L., & Hamilton, D. L. (1996). Resolving the apparent discrepancy between the incongruency effect and the expectancy-based illusory correlation effect: The TRAP model. *Journal of Personality and Social Psychology*, *71*, 845–860.

Gärdenfors, P. (2000). *Conceptual spaces: The geometry of thought*. Cambridge, MA: MIT Press.

Gawronski, B. (2003). Implicational schemata and the correspondence bias: On the diagnostic value of situationally constrained behavior. *Journal of Personality and Social Psychology*, *84*, 1154–1171.

Gilbert, D. T. (1989). Thinking lightly about others: Automatic components of the social inference process. In J. S. Uleman & J. A. Bargh (Eds.), *Unintended thoughts: Limits of awareness, intention, and control* (pp. 189–211). New York: Guilford Press.

Gilbert, D. T., & Malone, P. S. (1995). The correspondence bias. *Psychological Review*, *117*, 21–38.

Gilbert, D. T., & Osborne, R. E. (1989). Thinking backward: Some curable and incurable consequences of cognitive busyness. *Journal of Personality and Social Psychology*, *57*, 940–949.

Gilbert, D. T., Pelham, B. W., & Krull, D. S. (1988). On cognitive busyness: When person perceivers meet persons perceived. *Journal of Personality and Social Psychology*, *54*, 733–740.

Gluck, M. A., & Bower, G. H. (1988a). From conditioning to category learning: An adaptive network model. *Journal of Experimental Psychology: General*, *117*, 227–247.

Gluck, M. A., & Bower, G. H. (1988b). Evaluating an adaptive network model of human learning. *Journal of Memory and Language*, *27*, 166–195.

Gollwitzer, P. M. (1990). Action phases and mind-sets. In E. T. Higgins and R. M. Sorrentino (Eds.), *Handbook of motivation and cognition: Foundations of social behavior* (Vol. 2, pp. 53–92). New York: Guilford Press.

Graham, S. (1999). Retrospective revaluation and inhibitory associations: Does perceptual learning modulate our perceptions of the contingencies between events? *Quarterly Journal of Experimental Psychology, 52B*, 159–185.

Greenwald, A. G. (1968). Cognitive learning, cognitive response to persuasion, and attitude change. In A. G. Greenwald, T. C. Brock, & T. M. Ostrom (Eds.), *Psychological foundations of attitudes* (pp.147–170). San Diego, CA: Academic Press.

Greenwald, A. G., & Banaji, M. R. (1995). Implicit social cognition: Attitudes, self-esteem and stereotypes. *Psychological Review*, *102*, 4–27.

Gurwitz, S. B., & Dodge, K. A. (1977). Effects of confirmations and disconfirmations on stereotype-based attributions. *Journal of Personality and Social Psychology*, *35*, 495–500.

Haddock, G. (2000). Subjective ease of retrieval and attitude-relevant judgments. In H. Bless & J. P. Forgas (Eds.), *The message within: The role of subjective experience in social cognition and behavior* (pp. 125–142). Philadelphia: Taylor & Francis.

Haddock, G., Rothman, A. J., & Schwarz, N. (1996). Are (some) reports of attitude strength context dependent? *Canadian Journal of Behavioral Science*, *28*, 313–316.

Hamilton, D. L. (Ed.). (1981). *Cognitive processes in stereotyping and intergroup behavior*. Hillsdale, NJ: Lawrence Erlbaum Associates, Inc.

Hamilton, D. L., & Gifford, R. K. (1976). Illusory correlation in interpersonal perception: A cognitive basis for stereotypic judgments. *Journal of Experimental Social Psychology*, *12*, 392–407.

Hamilton, D. L., & Rose, T. L. (1980). Illusory correlation and the maintenance of stereotypic beliefs. *Journal of Personality and Social Psychology*, *39*, 832–845.

Hamilton, D. L., & Sherman, J. W. (1989). Illusory correlations: Implications for stereotype theory and research. In D. Bar-Tal, C. F. Graumann, A. W. Kruglanski

& W. Stroebe (Eds.), *Stereotype and prejudice: Changing conceptions* (pp. 55–92). New York: Springer.

Hamilton, D. L., & Trollier, T. K. (1986). Stereotypes and stereotyping: An overview of the cognitive approach. In J. F. Dovidio & S. L. Gaertner (Eds.), *Prejudice, discrimination and racism* (pp. 63–127). London: Academic Press.

Hamilton, D. L., Driscoll, D. M., & Worth, L. T. (1989). Cognitive organization of impressions: Effects of incongruency in complex representations. *Journal of Personality and Social Psychology, 57*, 925–939.

Hamilton, D. L., Dugan, P. M., & Trollier, T. K. (1985). The formation of stereotypic beliefs: Further evidence for distinctiveness-based illusory correlation. *Journal of Personality and Social Psychology, 48*, 5–17.

Hamilton, D. L., Katz, L. B., & Leirer, V. (1980). Organizational processes in impression formation. In R. Hastie, T. M. Ostrom, E. B. Ebbesen, R. S. Vyer, D. L. Hamilton, & D. E. Carlston (Eds.), *Person memory* (pp. 121–153). Hillsdale, NJ: Lawrence Erlbaum Associates, Inc.

Hansen, R. D., & Hall, C. A. (1985). Discounting and augmenting facilitative and inhibitory forces: The winner takes all. *Journal of Personality and Social Psychology, 49*, 1482–1493.

Hassin, R., Aarts, H., & Ferguson, M. J. (2005). Automatic goal inferences. *Journal of Experimental Social Psychology, 41*, 129–140.

Hastie, R. (1980). Memory for behavioral information that confirms or contradicts a personality impression. In R. Hastie, T. M. Ostrom, E. B. Ebbesen, R. S. Wyer, D. L. Hamilton, & D. E. Carlston (Eds.), *Person memory: The cognitive basis of social perception* (pp. 155–177). Hillsdale, NJ: Lawrence Erlbaum Associates, Inc.

Hastie, R., & Kumar, P. A. (1979). Person memory: Personality traits as organizing principles in memory for behaviors. *Journal of Personality and Social Psychology, 37*, 25–38.

Hastie, R., Schroeder, C., & Weber, R. (1990). Creating complex social conjunction categories from simple categories. *Bulletin of the Psychonomic Society, 28*, 242–247.

Haugtvedt, C. P., Schumann, D. W., Schneier, W. L., & Warren, W. L. (1994). Advertising repetition and variation strategies: Implications for understanding attitude strength. *Journal of Consumer Research, 21*, 176–189.

Heaton, A. W., & Kruglanski, A. W. (1991). Person perception by introverts and extraverts under time pressure: Effects of need for closure. *Personality and Social Psychology Bulletin, 17*, 161–165.

Hebb, D. O. (1949). *The organization of behavior.* New York: Wiley.

Heesacker, M., Petty, R. E., & Caciopppo, J. T. (1983). Field dependence and attitude change: Source credibility can alter persuasion by affecting message-relevant thinking. *Journal of Personality, 51*, 653–666.

Heider, F. (1958). *The psychology of interpersonal relations.* New York: Wiley.

Hewstone, M. (1994). Revision and change of stereotypic beliefs: In search of the elusive subtyping model. *European Review of Social Psychology, 5*, 70–109.

Hewstone, M., & Jaspars, J. (1987). Covariation and causal attribution: A logical model of the intuitive analysis of variance. *Journal of Personality and Social Psychology, 53*, 663–673.

Hewstone, M., Macrae, C. N., Griffiths, R., & Milne, A. B. (1994). Cognitive models of stereotype change: V. Measurement, development, and consequences of subtyping. *Journal of Experimental Social Psychology, 30*, 505–526.

Higgins, E. T. (1996). Knowledge activation: Accessibility, applicability, and salience. In E. T. Higgins & A. W. Kruglanski (Eds.), *Social psychology: Handbook of basic principles* (pp. 133–168). New York: Guilford Press.

Higgins, E. T., & Bargh, J. A. (1987). Social cognition and social perception. *Annual Review of Psychology*, *38*, 369–426.

Higgins, E. T., Rholes, W. S., & Jones, C. R. (1977). Category accessibility and impression formation. *Journal of Experimental Social Psychology*, *13*, 141–154.

Hilton, D. J., & Slugoski, B. R. (1986). Knowledge-based causal attribution: The abnormal conditions focus model. *Psychological Review*, *93*, 75–88.

Hilton, D. J., Smith, R. H., & Kim, S. H. (1995). The process of causal explanation and dispositional attribution. *Journal of Personality and Social Psychology*, *68*, 377–387.

Hinton, G. E., & Sejnowski, T. J. (1986). Learning and relearning in Boltzmann machines. In D. E. Rumelhart, J. L. McClelland, & the PDP Research Group (Eds.), *Parallel distributed processing* (Vol. 1, pp. 282–317). Cambridge, MA: MIT Press.

Hinton, G. E., McClelland, J. L., & Rumelhart, D. E. (1986). Distributed representations. In D. E. Rumelhart, J. L. McClelland, & the PDP Research Group (Eds.), *Parallel distributed processing* (Vol. 1, pp. 77–109). Cambridge, MA: MIT Press.

Hintzmann, D. L. (1986). "Schema abstraction" in a multi-trace memory model. *Psychological Review*, *93*, 411–428.

Hogarth, R. M., & Einhorn, H. J. (1992). Order effects in belief updating: The belief-adjustment model. *Cognitive Psychology*, *24*, 1–55.

Houghton, G. (2005). Introduction to connectionist models in cognitive psychology: Basic structures, processes, and algorithms. In G. Houghton (Ed.), *Connectionist models in cognitive psychology* (pp. 1–41). Hove, UK: Psychology Press.

Hutchins, E. (1991). The social organization of distributed cognition. In L. Resnick, J. Levine, & S. Teasley (Eds.), *Perspectives on socially shared cognition* (pp. 283–307). Washington, DC: The American Psychological Association.

Hutchins, E., & Hazlehurst, B. (1995). How to invent a lexicon: The development of shared symbols in interaction. In G. N. Gilbert & R. Conte (Eds.), *Artificial societies: The computer simulation of social life* (pp. 157–189). London: UCL Press.

Isen, A. M. (1984). Towards understanding the role of affect in cognition. In R. S. Wyer, Jr. & T. K. Srull (Eds.), *Handbook of social cognition* (Vol. 3, pp. 179–236). Hillsdale, NJ: Lawrence Erlbaum Associates, Inc.

Ito, T. A., & Cacioppo, J. T. (2001). Affect and attitudes: A social neuroscience approach. In J. P. Forgas (Ed.), *Handbook of affect and social cognition* (pp. 50–74). Mahwah, NJ: Lawrence Erlbaum Associates, Inc.

Johnston, L., & Hewstone, M. (1992). Cognitive models of stereotype change: III. Subtyping and the perceived typicality of disconfirming group members. *Journal of Experimental Social Psychology*, *28*, 360–386.

Johnston, L., Hewstone, M., Pendry, L., & Frankish, C. (1994). Cognitive models of stereotype change: (4) Motivational and cognitive influences. *European Journal of Social Psychology*, *24*, 237–266.

Jonas, K., Diehl, M., & Brömer, P. (1997). Effects of attitudinal ambivalence on information processing and attitude-intention consistency. *Journal of Experimental Social Psychology*, *33*, 190–210.

Jones, E. E., & Davis, K. E. (1965). From acts to dispositions: The attribution process in person perception. In L. Berkowitz (Ed.), *Advances in experimental social psychology* (Vol. 2, pp. 219–266). New York: Academic Press.

Jones, E. E., & Harris, V. A. (1967). The attribution of attitudes. *Journal of Experimental Social Psychology*, *3*, 1–24.

Jones, E. E., Worchel, S., Goethals, G. R., & Grumet, J. F. (1971). Prior expectancy and behavioral extremity as determinants of attitude attribution. *Journal of Experimental Social Psychology*, *7*, 59–80.

Kahneman, D., Slovic, P., & Tversky, A. (1982). *Judgments under uncertainty: Heuristics and biases*. Cambridge: Cambridge University Press.

Kamin, L. J. (1969). Predictability, surprise, attention and conditioning. In B. A. Campbell & R. M. Church (Eds.), *Punishment and aversive behavior*. New York, Appleton Century Crofts.

Kaplan, K. J. (1972). On the ambivalence-indifference problem in attitude theory and measurement: A suggested modification of the semantic differential technique. *Psychological Review*, *77*, 361–372.

Kashima, Y., & Kerekes, A. R. Z. (1994). A distributed memory model of averaging phenomena in person impression formation. *Journal of Experimental Social Psychology*, *30*, 407–455.

Kashima, Y., Woolcock, J., & Kashima, E. S. (2000). Group impression as dynamic configurations: The tensor product model of group impression formation and change. *Psychological Review*, *107*, 914–942.

Katz, D., & Stotland, E. (1959). A preliminary statement to a theory of attitude structure and change. In S. Koch (Ed.), *Psychology: A study of a science* (Vol. 3, pp. 423–475). New York: McGraw-Hill.

Kelley, H. H. (1967). Attribution in social psychology. *Nebraska Symposium on Motivation*, *15*, 192–238.

Kelley, H. H. (1971). Attribution in social interaction. In E. E. Jones, D. E. Kanouse, H. H. Kelley, R. E. Nisbett, S. Valins & B. Weiner (Eds.), *Attribution: Perceiving the causes of behavior* (pp. 1–26). Morristown, NJ: General Learning Press.

Kelley, H. H. (1973). The processes of causal attribution. *American Psychologist*, *28*, 103–128.

Kim, H., & Baron, R. S. (1988). Exercise and the illusory correlation: Does arousal heighten stereotypic processing? *Journal of Experimental Social Psychology*, *24*, 27–40.

Kinder, A., & Shanks, D. R. (2001). Amnesia and the declarative/nondeclarative distinction: A recurrent network model of classification, recognition, and repetition priming. *Journal of Cognitive Neuroscience*, *13*, 648–669.

Kirkpatrick, L. A., & Epstein, S. (1992). Cognitive-experiential self theory and subjective probability: Further evidence for two conceptual systems. *Journal of Personality and Social Psychology*, *63*, 534–544.

Klauer, K. C., & Meiser, T. (2000). A source-monitoring analysis of illusory correlations. *Personality and Social Psychology Bulletin*, *26*, 1074–1093.

Krueger, J., & Clement, R. W. (1994). Memory-based judgments about multiple categories: A revision and extension of Tajfel's Accentuation Theory. *Journal of Personality and Social Psychology*, *67*, 35–47.

Kruglanski, A. W., & Freund, T. (1983). The freezing and unfreezing of lay inferences: Effects on impressional primacy, ethnic stereotyping, and numerical anchoring. *Journal of Experimental Social Psychology*, *19*, 448–468.

Kruglanski, A. W., & Thompson, E. P. (1999). Persuasion by a single route: A view from the unimodel. *Psychological Inquiry*, *10*, 83–109.

Kruglanski, A. W., Schwartz, S. M., Maides, S., & Hamel, I. Z. (1978). Covariation, discounting, and augmentation: Towards a clarification of attributional principles. *Journal of Personality*, *76*, 176–189.

Kruschke, J. K., & Johansen, M. K. (1999). A model of probabilistic category learning. *Journal of Experimental Psychology: Learning, Memory, and Cognition*, *25*, 1083–1119.

Kunda, Z., & Oleson, K. C. (1995). Maintaining stereotypes in the face of disconfirmation: Constructing grounds for subtyping deviants. *Journal of Personality and Social Psychology*, *68*, 565–579.

Kunda, Z., & Thagard, P. (1996). Forming impressions from stereotypes, traits, and behaviors: A parallel-constraint-satisfaction theory. *Psychological Review*, *103*, 284–308.

Kunda, Z., Miller, D. T., & Claire, T. (1990). Combining social concepts: The role of causal reasoning. *Cognitive Science*, *14*, 551–577.

LaBerge, D. (1997). Attention, awareness and the triangular circuit. *Consciousness and Cognition*, *6*, 149–181.

LaBerge, D. (2000). Networks of attention. In M. S. Gazzaniga (Ed.), *The new cognitive neuroscience* (pp. 711–724). Cambridge, MA: MIT Press.

Labiouse, C. (1999). *Utilisation et accessibilité de représentations distribuées dans la perception de personnes et la stéréotypisation: Simulations avec un réseau connexionniste*. Unpublished doctoral dissertation, Université de Liège, Belgium.

Lalljee, M., & Abelson, R. P. (1983). The organization of explanations. In M. Hewstone (Ed.), *Attribution theory: Social and functional extensions* (pp. 65–80). Oxford: Blackwell.

Lambert, S. B., Klein, O., & Azzi, A. (2002). *Revisiting Tajfel & Wilkes (1963): The joint influence of demand effects and uncertainty*. Paper presented at the Workshop on Social Psychology in Belgium, 18 January 2002. Brussels, Belgium: Royal Flemish Academy of Belgium for Sciences and Arts.

Lane, R. D., Reiman, E. M., Bradley, M. M., Lang, P. J., Ahern, G. L., Davidson, R. J., & Schwartz, G. E. (1997). Neuroanatomical correlates of pleasant and unpleasant emotion. *Neuropsychologia*, *35*, 1437–1444.

Lewicki, P. (1985). Nonconscious biasing effects of single instances of subsequent judgments. *Journal of Personality and Social Psychology*, *48*, 563–574.

Lieberman, M. D., Ochsner, K. N., Gilbert, D. T., & Schacter, D. L. (2001). Attitude change in amnesia and under cognitive load. *Psychological Science*, *12*, 135–140.

Linder, D. E., Cooper, J., & Jones, E. E. (1967). Decision freedom as a determinant of the role of incentive magnitude in attitude change. *Journal of Personality and Social Psychology*, *6*, 245–254.

Linville, P. W., & Fischer, G. W. (1993). Exemplar and abstraction models of perceived group variability and stereotypicality. *Social Cognition*, *11*, 92–125.

Linville, P. W., Fischer, G. W., & Salovey, P. (1989). Perceived distributions of the characteristics of in-group and out-group members: Empirical evidence and a computer simulation. *Journal of Personality and Social Psychology*, *57*, 165–188.

Lober, K., & Shanks, D. R. (2000). Causal induction based on causal power? Critique of Cheng (1997). *Psychological Review*, *107*, 195–212.

Lupfer, M. B., Weeks, M., & Dupuis, S. (2000). How pervasive is the negativity bias in judgments based on character appraisal? *Personality and Social Psychology Bulletin, 26*, 1353–1366.

MacDonald, T. K., & Zanna, M. P. (1998). Cross-validation ambivalence toward social groups: Can ambivalence affect intentions to hire feminists? *Personality and Social Psychology Bulletin, 24*, 427–441.

Mackie, D. M. (1987). Systematic and non-systematic processing of majority and minority persuasive communications. *Journal of Personality and Social Psychology, 53*, 41–52.

Mackie, D. M., & Worth, L. T. (1989). Processing deficits and the mediation of positive affect in persuasion. *Journal of Personality and Social Psychology, 57*, 27–40.

Mackie, D. M., Hamilton, D. L., Schroth, H. A., Carlisle, C. J., Gersho, B. F., Meneses, L. M., Nedler, B. F., & Reichel, L. D. (1989). The effects of induced mood on expectancy-based illusory correlations. *Journal of Experimental Social Psychology, 25*, 524–544.

Macrae, C. N., Hewstone, M., & Griffiths, R. J. (1993). Processing load and memory for stereotype-based information. *European Journal of Social Psychology, 23*, 77–87.

Maheswaran, D., & Chaiken, S. (1991). Promoting systematic processing in low-motivation settings: Effect of incongruent information on processing and judgment. *Journal of Personality and Social Psychology, 61*, 13–25.

Malle, B. F. (1999). How people explain behavior: A new theoretical framework. *Personality and Social Psychology Review, 3*, 21–43.

Manis, M., Dovalina, I., Avis, N. E., & Cardoze, S. (1980). Base rates can affect individual predictions. *Journal of Personality and Social Psychology, 38*, 231–248.

Marr, D. (1982). *Vision*. San Francisco, CA: Freeman.

Martin, L. L., Seta, J. J., & Crelia, R. A. (1990). Assimilation and contrast as a function of people's willingness and ability to expend effort in forming an impression. *Journal of Personality and Social Psychology, 59*, 38–49.

Maurer, K. L., Park, B., & Rothbart, M. (1995). Subtyping versus subgrouping processes in stereotype representation. *Journal of Personality and Social Psychology, 69*, 812–824.

McClelland, J. L., & Rumelhart, D. E. (1985). Distributed memory and the representation of general and specific information. *Journal of Experimental Psychology, 114*, 159–188.

McClelland, J. L., & Rumelhart, D. E. (1986). A distributed model of human learning and memory. In J. L. McClelland & D. E. Rumelhart (Eds.), *Parallel distributed processing: Explorations in the microstructure of cognition* (Vol. 2, pp. 170–215). Cambridge, MA: MIT Press.

McClelland, J. L., & Rumelhart, D. E. (1988). *Explorations in parallel distributed processing: A handbook of models, programs, and exercises*. Cambridge, MA: MIT Press/Bradford Books.

McClelland, J. L., McNaughton, B., & O'Reilly, R. (1995). Why there are complementary learning systems in the hippocampus and neocortex: Insights from the successes and the failures of connectionist models of learning and memory. *Psychological Review, 102*, 419–457.

McCloskey, M., & Cohen N. J. (1989). Catastrophic interference in connectionist networks: the sequential learning problem. *The Psychology of Learning and Motivation, 24*, 109–165.

McClure, J. (1998). Discounting causes of behavior: Are two reasons better than one? *Journal of Personality and Social Psychology, 74*, 7–20.

McConnell, A. R., Sherman, S. J., & Hamilton, D. L. (1994). Illusory correlation in the perception of groups: An extension of the distinctiveness-based account. *Journal of Personality and Social Psychology, 67*, 414–429.

McLeod, P., Plunkett, K., & Rolls, E. T. (1998). *Introduction to connectionist modeling of cognitive processes*. Oxford: Oxford University Press.

Medin, D. L., & Schaffer, M. M. (1978). Context theory of classification learning. *Psychological Review, 85*, 207–238.

Meiser, T., & Hewstone, M. (2002). *Cognitive processes in stereotype formation: Distinctiveness, statistical reasoning and parallel distributed memory*. Unpublished manuscript.

Messick, D. M., & Mackie, D. M. (1989). Intergroup relations. *Annual Review of Psychology, 40*, 45–81.

Milgram, S. (1963). Behavioral study of obedience. *Journal of Abnormal and Social Psychology, 67*, 371–378.

Mill, J. S. (1872/1973). *System of logic* (8th ed). In J. M. Robson (Ed.) Collected works of John Stuart Mill (Vols. 7 & 8). Toronto, Canada: University of Toronto Press.

Miller, A. G., Ashton, W., & Mishal, M. (1990). Beliefs concerning the features of constrained behavior: A basis for the fundamental attribution error. *Journal of Personality and Social Psychology, 59*, 635–650.

Miller, L. C., & Read, S. J. (1991). On the coherence of mental models of persons and relationships: A knowledge structure approach. In F. Fincham & G. J. O. Fletcher (Eds.), *Cognition in close relationships*. Hillsdale, NJ: Lawrence Erlbaum Associates, Inc.

Miller, N., & Colman, D. E. (1981). Methodological issue in analyzing the cognitive mediation of persuasion. In R. E. Petty, T. M. Ostrom, & T. C. Brock (Eds.), *Cognitive responses in persuasion* (pp. 105–125). Hillsdale, NJ: Lawrence Erlbaum Associates, Inc.

Miller, R. R., Barnet, R. C., & Grahame, N. J. (1995). Assessment of the Rescorla–Wagner model. *Psychological Bulletin, 117*, 363–386.

Morris, M. W., & Larrick, R. P. (1995). When one cause casts doubt on another: A normative analysis of discounting in causal attribution. *Psychological Review, 102*, 331–355.

Moskowitz, G. B., & Skurnik, I. W. (1999). Contrast effects as determined by the type of prime: Trait versus exemplar primes initiate processing strategies that differ in how accessible constructs are used. *Journal of Personality and Social Psychology, 76*, 911–927.

Movellan, J. R., & McClelland, J. L. (1993). Learning continuous probability distributions with symmetric diffusion networks. *Cognitive Science, 17*, 463–496.

Mullen, B., & Hu, L. (1989). Perceptions of ingroup and outgroup variability: A meta-analytic integration. *Basic and Applied Social Psychology, 10*, 233–252.

Mullen, B., & Johnson, C. (1990). Distinctiveness-based illusory correlations and stereotyping: A meta-analytic integration. *British Journal of Social Psychology, 29*, 11–28.

Nisbett, R. E., & Wilson, T. D. (1977). Telling more than we can know: Verbal reports on mental processes. *Psychological Review, 84*, 231–259.

Nisbett, R. E., Krantz, D. H., Jepson, C., & Kind, Z. (1983). The use of statistical heuristics in everyday inductive reasoning. *Psychological Review*, *90*, 339–363.

Nosofsky, R. M. (1986). Attention, similarity, and the identification-categorization relationship. *Journal of Experimental Psychology: General*, *115*, 39–57.

Nosofsky, R. M. (1991). Typicality in logically defined categories: Exemplar-similarity versus rule instantiation. *Memory and Cognition*, *19*, 131–150.

Nosofsky, R. M., Kruschke, J. K., & McKinley, S. C. (1992). Combining exemplar-based category representations and connectionist learning rules. *Journal of Experimental Psychology: Learning, Memory and Cognition*, *18*, 211–233.

Nowak, A., Szamrej, J., & Latané, B. (1990). From private attitude to public opinion: A dynamic theory of social impact. *Psychological Review*, *97*, 362–376.

Nowak, A., Vallacher, R. R., & Burnstein, E. (1998). Computational social psychology: A neural network approach to interpersonal dynamics. In Liebrand, W. B. G., Nowak, A., & Hegselmann, R. (Eds.), *Computer modeling of social processes* (pp. 97–125). London: Sage.

Ochsner, K. N., & Lieberman, M. D. (2001). The emergence of social cognitive neuroscience. *American Psychologist*, *56*, 717–734.

Olson, M. A., & Fazio, R. H. (2001). Implicit attitude formation through classical conditioning. *Psychological Science*, *12*, 413–417.

O'Reilly, R. C., & Munakata, Y. (2000). *Computational explorations in cognitive neuroscience: Understanding the mind by simulating the brain*. Cambridge, MA: MIT Press.

O'Reilly, R. C., & Rudy, J. W. (2001). Conjunctive representations in learning and memory: Principles of cortical and hippocampal function. *Psychological Review*, *108*, 311–345.

Orvis, B. R., Cunningham, J. D., & Kelley, H. H. (1975). A closer examination of causal inference: The role of consensus, distinction and consistency information. *Journal of Personality and Social Psychology*, *32*, 605–616.

Pacton, S., Perruchet, P., Fayol, M., & Cleeremans, A. (2001). Implicit learning out of the lab: The case of orthographic regularities. *Journal of Experimental Psychology: General*, *130*, 401–426.

Pandelaere, M., & Hoorens, V. (2002). *The role of behavior categorization in act frequency estimation processes*. Manuscript submitted for publication.

Park, B. (1986). A method for studying the development of impressions of real people. *Journal of Personality and Social Psychology*, *51*, 907–917.

Park, B., & Hastie, R. (1987). Perception of variability in category development: Instance- versus abstraction-based stereotypes. *Journal of Personality and Social Psychology*, *53*, 621–635.

Park, B., & Judd, C. M. (1990). Measures and models of perceived group variability. *Journal of Personality and Social Psychology*, *95*, 173–191.

Park, B., Wolsko, C., & Judd, C. M. (2001). Measurement of subtyping in stereotype change. *Journal of Experimental Social Psychology*, *37*, 325–332.

Pearce, J. M. (1994). Similarity and discrimination: A selective review and a connectionist model. *Psychological Review*, *101*, 587–607.

Pennington, N., & Hastie, R. (1986). Evidence evaluation in complex decision making. *Journal of Personality and Social Psychology*, *51*, 242–258.

Pennington, N., & Hastie, R. (1988). Explanation-based decision making: Effects of memory structure on judgment. *Journal of Experimental Psychology: Learning, Memory, and Cognition*, *14*, 521–533.

Pennington, N., & Hastie, R. (1992). Explaining the evidence: Tests of the story model for juror decision making. *Journal of Personality and Social Psychology*, *62*, 189–206.

Petty, R. E., & Cacioppo, J. T. (1981). *Attitudes and persuasion: Central and peripheral routes to attitude change*. New York: Springer.

Petty, R. E., & Cacioppo, J. T. (1984). The effects of involvement on responses to argument quantity and quality: Central and peripheral routes to persuasion. *Journal of Personality and Social Psychology*, *46*, 69–81.

Petty, R. E., & Cacioppo, J. T. (1986). The elaboration likelihood model of persuasion. In L. Berkowitz (Ed.), *Advances in experimental social psychology* (Vol. 19, pp. 123–205). San Diego, CA: Academic Press.

Petty, R. E., & Wegener, D. T. (1999). The elaboration likelihood model: Current status and controversies. In S. Chaiken & Y. Trope (Eds.), *Dual-process theories in social psychology* (pp. 41–72). New York: Guilford Press.

Petty, R. E., Cacioppo, J. T., & Goldman, R. (1981). Personal involvement as a determinant of argument-based persuasion. *Journal of Personality and Social Psychology*, *41*, 847–855.

Petty, R. E., Cacioppo, J. T., & Schumann, D. (1983). Central and peripheral routes to advertising effectiveness: The moderating role of involvement. *Journal of Consumer Research*, *10*, 135–147.

Petty, R. E., Schumann, D. W., Richman, S. A., & Strathman, A. J. (1993). Positive mood and persuasion: Different roles for affect under high- and low-elaboration conditions. *Journal of Personality and Social Psychology*, *64*, 5–20.

Phelps, E. A., O'Connor, K. J., Cunningham, W. A., Funayama, S., Gatenby, C., Gore, J. C., & Banaji, M. R. (2000). Performance on indirect measures of race evaluation predicts amygdala activation. *Journal of Cognitive Neuroscience*, *12*, 729–738.

Posner, M. I. (1992). Attention as a cognitive and neural system. *Current Directions in Psychological Science*, *1*, 11–14.

Powell, M. C., & Fazio, R. H. (1984). Attitude accessibility as a function of repeated attitudinal expression. *Personality and Social Psychology Bulletin*, *10*, 139–148.

Priester, J. R., & Petty, R. E. (1996). The gradual threshold model of ambivalence: Relating the positive and negative bases of attitudes to subjective ambivalence. *Journal of Personality and Social Psychology*, *71*, 431–449.

Queller, S., & Smith, E. (2002). Subtyping versus bookkeeping in stereotype learning and change: Connectionist simulations and empirical findings. *Journal of Personality and Social Psychology*, *82*, 300–313.

Ratcliff, R. (1990). Connectionist models of recognition memory: Constraints imposed by learning and forgetting functions. *Psychological Review*, *97*, 285–308.

Ratneshwar, S., & Chaiken, S. (1991). Comprehension's role in persuasion: The case of its moderating effect on the persuasive impact of source cues. *Journal of Consumer Research*, *18*, 52–62.

Read, S. J. (1987). Constructing causal scenarios: A knowledge structure approach to causal reasoning. *Journal of Personality and Social Psychology*, *52*, 288–302.

Read, S. J., & Marcus-Newhall, A. (1993). Explanatory coherence in social explanations: A parallel distributed processing account. *Journal of Personality and Social Psychology*, *65*, 429–447.

Read, S. J., & Miller, L. C. (1993). Rapist or "regular guy": Explanatory coherence in the construction of mental models of others. *Personality and Social Psychology Bulletin, 19*, 526–541.

Read, S. J., & Miller, L. C. (1998). On the dynamic construction of meaning: An interactive activation and competition model of social perception. In S. J. Read & L. C. Miller (Eds.), *Connectionist models of social reasoning and behavior* (pp. 27–68). Mahwah, NJ: Lawrence Erlbaum Associates, Inc.

Read, S. J., & Montoya, J. A. (1999). An autoassociative model of causal reasoning and causal learning: Reply to Van Overwalle's critique of Read and Marcus-Newhall (1993). *Journal of Personality and Social Psychology, 76*, 728–742.

Reeder, G. D. (1997). Dispositional inferences of ability: Content and process. *Journal of Experimental Social Psychology, 33*, 171–189.

Reeder, G. D. (2001). On perceiving multiple causes and inferring multiple internal attributes. *Psychological Inquiry, 12*, 34–36.

Reeder, G. D., & Brewer, M. B. (1979). A schematic model of dispositional attribution in interpersonal perception. *Psychological Review, 86*, 61–79.

Reeder, G. D., & Fulks, J. L. (1980). When actions speak louder than words: Implicational schemata and the attribution of ability. *Journal of Experimental Social Psychology, 16*, 33–46.

Reeder, G. D., & Spores, J. M. (1983). The attribution of morality. *Journal of Personality and Social Psychology, 44*, 736–745.

Reeder, G. D., Kumar, S., Hesson-McInnis, M. S., & Trafimow, D. (2002). Inferences about the morality of an aggressor: The role of perceived motive. *Journal of Personality and Social Psychology, 83*, 789–803.

Reeder, G. D., Vonk, R., Ronk, M. J., Ham, J., & Lawrence, M. (2004). Dispositional attribution: Multiple inferences about motive-related traits. *Journal of Personality and Social Psychology, 86*, 530–544.

Rescorla, R. A., & Wagner, A. R. (1972). A theory of Pavlovian conditioning: Variations in the effectiveness of reinforcement and nonreinforcement. In A. H. Black & W. F. Prokasy (Eds.), *Classical conditioning II: Current research and theory* (pp. 64–98). New York: Appleton-Century-Crofts.

Riketta, M., & Dauenheimer, D. (2003). Manipulating self-esteem with subliminally presented words. *European Journal of Social Psychology, 33*, 679–699.

Riolo, R. L., Cohen, M. D., & Axelrod, R. (2000). Evolution of cooperation without reciprocity. *Nature, 414*, 441–443.

Rosch, E. H. (1978). Principles of categorization. In E. H. Rosch & B. B. Lloyds (Eds.), *Cognition and categorization* (pp. 27–48). Hillsdale, NJ: Lawrence Erlbaum Associates, Inc.

Rosenberg, M. J., & Hovland, C. I. (1960). Cognitive, affective and behavioral components of attitudes. In C. I. Hovland & M. J. Rosenberg (Eds.), *Attitude organization and change: An analysis of consistency among attitude components* (pp. 1–14). New Haven, CT: Yale University Press.

Rosenfield, D., & Stephan, W. G. (1977). When discounting fails: An unexpected finding. *Memory and Cognition, 5*, 97–102.

Roskos-Ewoldsen, D. R., Bichsel, J., & Hoffman, K. (2002). The influence of accessibility of source likeability on persuasion. *Journal of Experimental Social Psychology, 38*, 137–143.

Ross, L. (1977). The intuitive psychologist and his shortcomings: Distortions in the attribution process. In L. Berkowitz (Ed.), *Advances in experimental social psychology* (Vol. 10, pp. 173–220). New York: Academic Press.

Rothbart, M. (1981). Memory processes and social beliefs. In D. L. Hamilton (Ed.), *Cognitive processes in stereotyping and intergroup behavior* (pp. 145–182). Hillsdale, NJ: Lawrence Erlbaum Associates, Inc.

Rothbart, M., & John, O. (1985). Social categorization and behavioral episodes: A cognitive analysis of the effects of intergroup contact. *Journal of Social Issues, 41*, 81–104.

Rudolph, U., & Försterling, F. (1997). The psychological causality implicit in verbs: A review. *Psychological Bulletin, 121*, 192–218.

Rumelhart, D. E., & McClelland, J. L. (1986). *Parallel distributed processing: Explorations in the microstructure of cognition: Vol. 1. Foundations.* Cambridge, MA: MIT Press/Bradford Books.

Rumelhart, D. E., Smolensky, P., McClelland, J. L., & Hinton, G. E. (1986). Schemata and sequential thought processes in PDP models. In J. L. McClelland & D. E. Rumelhart (Eds.), *Parallel distributed processing: Explorations in the microstructure of cognition* (Vol. 2, pp. 7–57). Cambridge, MA: MIT Press.

Schacter, D. L., & Tulving, E. (Eds.). (1994). *Memory systems 1994.* Cambridge, MA: MIT Press.

Schank, R. C., & Abelson, R. P. (1977). *Scripts, plans, goals and understanding.* Hillsdale, NJ: Lawrence Erlbaum Associates, Inc.

Schuette, R. A., & Fazio, R. H. (1995). Attitude accessibility and motivation as determinants of biased processing: A test of the MODE model. *Personality and Social Psychology Bulletin, 21*, 704–710.

Schumann, D. W., Petty, R., & Clemons, D. S. (1990). Predicting the effectiveness of different strategies of advertising variation. A test of the repetition-variation hypothesis. *Journal of Consumer Research, 17*, 192–201.

Schwarz, N. (1990). Feelings as information: Informational and motivational functions of affective states. In E. T. Higgins & R. Sorrentino (Eds.), *Handbook of motivation and cognition: Foundations of social behavior* (Vol. 2, pp. 527–561). New York: Guilford Press.

Schwarz, N., & Clore, G. L. (1983). Mood, misattribution, and judgments of well-being: Informative and directive functions of affective states. *Journal of Personality and Social Psychology, 45*, 513–523.

Schwarz, N., Bless, H., & Bohner, G. (1991). Mood and persuasion: Affective states influence the processing of persuasive communications. *Advances in Experimental Social Psychology, 24*, 161–199.

Seidenberg, M. S. (1993). Connectionist models and cognitive theory. *Psychological Science, 4*, 228–235.

Shanks, D. R. (1985). Forward and backward blocking in human contingency judgment. *Quarterly Journal of Experimental Psychology, 37b*, 1–21.

Shanks, D. R. (1987). Acquisition functions in contingency judgment. *Learning and motivation, 18*, 147–166.

Shanks, D. R. (1991). Categorization by a connectionist network. *Journal of Experimental Psychology: Learning, Memory and Cognition, 17*, 433–443.

Shanks, D. R. (1993). Human instrumental learning: A critical review of data and theory. *British Journal of Psychology, 84*, 319–354.

Shanks, D. R. (1995). Is human learning rational? *Quarterly Journal of Experimental Psychology, 48a*, 257–279.

Shanks, D. R., Lopez, F. J., Darby, R. J., & Dickinson, A. (1996). Distinguishing associative and probabilistic contrast theories of human contingency judgment. In

D. R. Shanks, K. J. Holyoak, & D. L. Medin (Eds.), *The psychology of learning and motivation* (Vol. 34, pp. 265–311). New York: Academic Press.

Shavitt, S., Sanbonmatsu, D. M., Smittipatana, S., & Posavac, S. S. (1999). Broadening the conditions for illusory correlation formation: Implications for judging minority groups. *Basic and Applied Social Psychology, 21*, 263–279.

Sherman, J. W. (1996). Development and mental representation of stereotypes. *Journal of Personality and Social Psychology, 70*, 1126–1141.

Shoda, Y., LeeTiernan, S., & Mischel, W. (2002). Personality as a dynamical system: Emergence of stability and distinctiveness from intra- and interpersonal interactions. *Personality and Social Psychology Review, 6*, 316–325.

Shultz, T., & Lepper, M. (1996). Cognitive dissonance reduction as constraint satisfaction. *Psychological Review, 2*, 219–240.

Siebler, F. (2002). *Connectionist modeling of social judgment processes.* Unpublished PhD Thesis, University of Kent, Canterbury, UK.

Simon, B., & Brown, R. J. (1987). Perceived homogeneity in minority–majority contexts. *Journal of Personality and Social Psychology, 53*, 703–711.

Simon, B., & Hamilton, D. L. (1994). Self-stereotyping and social context: The effects of relative in-group size and in-group status. *Journal of Personality and Social Psychology, 66*, 699–711.

Simon, B., & Pettigrew, T. F. (1990). Social identity and perceived group homogeneity. *European Journal of Social Psychology, 20*, 269–286.

Sinclair, R. C., Mark, M. M., & Clore, G. L. (1994). Mood-related persuasion depends on (mis)attributions. *Social Cognition, 12*, 309–326.

Skowronski, J. J., & Carlston, D. E. (1987). Social judgment and social memory: The role of cue diagnosticity in negativity, positivity and extremity biases. *Journal of Personality and Social Psychology, 52*, 689–699.

Skowronski, J. J., & Carlston, D. E. (1989). Negativity and extremity biases in impression formation: A review of explanations. *Psychological Bulletin, 105*, 131–142.

Skowronski, J. J., & Gannon, K. (2000). Raw conditional probabilities are a flawed index of associative strength: Evidence from a single trait expectancy paradigm. *Basic and Applied Social Psychology, 22*, 9–18.

Skowronski, J. J., & Welbourne, J. (1997). Conditional probability may be a flawed measure of associative strength. *Social Cognition, 15*, 1–12.

Slusher, M. P., & Anderson, C. A. (1987). When reality monitoring fails: The role of imagination in stereotype maintenance. *Journal of Personality and Social Psychology, 52*, 653–662.

Smith, E. R. (1998). Mental representation and memory. In D. T. Gilbert, S. T. Fiske, & G. Lindzey-Gardner (Eds.), *The handbook of social psychology: Vol. 2* (4th ed., pp. 391–445). Boston: McGraw-Hill.

Smith, E. R. (1991). Illusory correlation in a simulated exemplar-based memory. *Journal of Experimental Social Psychology, 27*, 107–123.

Smith, E. R. (1996). What do connectionism and social psychology offer each other? *Journal of Personality and Social Psychology, 70*, 893–912.

Smith, E. R., & DeCoster, J. (1998). Knowledge acquisition, accessibility, and use in person perception and stereotyping: Simulation with a recurrent connectionist network. *Journal of Personality and Social Psychology, 74*, 21–35.

Smith, E. R., & DeCoster, J. (2000). Associative and rule-based processing: A connectionist interpretation of dual-process models. In S. Chaiken & Y. Trope

(Eds.), *Dual-process theories in social psychology* (pp. 323–338). London: Guilford Press.

Smith E. R., & Zárate, M. A. (1992). Exemplar-based model of social judgment. *Psychological Review, 99,* 3–21.

Smith, E. R., Osherson, D. N., Rips, L. J., & Keane, M. (1988). Combining prototypes: A modification model *Cognitive Science, 12,* 485–528.

Smolensky, P. (1989). Connectionist modeling: Neural computation/mental connections. In L. Nadel, L. A. Cooper, P. Culicover, & R. M. Harnish (Eds), *Neural connections, mental computation* (pp. 49–67). Cambridge, MA: MIT Press.

Snyder, M., & Jones, E. E. (1974). Attitude attribution when behavior is constrained. *Journal of Experimental Social Psychology, 10,* 585–600.

Spears, R., van der Pligt, J., & Eiser, J. R. (1985). Illusory correlation in the perception of group attitudes. *Journal of Personality and Social Psychology, 48,* 863–875.

Spears, R., Eiser, J. R., & van der Pligt, J. (1987). Further evidence for expectancy-based illusory correlations. *European Journal of Social Psychology, 17,* 253–258.

Spellman, B. A., & Holyoak, K. J. (1992). If Saddam is Hitler who is George Bush? Analogical mapping between systems of social roles. *Journal of Personality and Social Psychology, 62,* 913–933.

Spellman, B. A., Ullman, J. B., & Holyoak, K. J. (1993). A coherence model of cognitive consistency: Dynamics of attitude change during the Persian Gulf War. *Journal of Social Issues, 49,* 147–165.

Srull, T. K. (1981). Person memory: Some tests of associative storage and retrieval models. *Journal of Experimental Psychology: Human Learning and Memory, 7,* 440–463.

Srull, T. K., Lichtenstein, M., & Rothbart, M. (1985). Associative storage and retrieval processes in person memory. *Journal of Experimental Psychology: Learning, Memory, and Cognition, 11,* 316–345.

Staats, A. W., & Staats, C. K. (1958). Attitudes established by classical conditioning. *Journal of Abnormal and Social Psychology, 57,* 37–40.

Stangor, C., & Duan, C. (1991). Effects of multiple task demands upon memory for information about social groups. *Journal of Experimental Social Psychology, 27,* 357–378.

Stangor, C., & McMillan, D. (1992). Memory for expectancy-congruent and expectancy-incongruent information: A review of the social and social developmental literatures. *Psychological Bulletin, 111,* 42–61.

Stapel, D. A., Koomen, W., & van der Pligt, J. (1997). Categories of category accessibility: The impact of trait concept versus exemplar priming on person judgments. *Journal of Experimental Social Psychology, 33,* 47–76.

Stewart, R. H. (1965). Effect of continuous responding on the order effect in personality impression formation. *Journal of Personality and Social Psychology, 1,* 161–165.

Storms, M. D. (1973). Videotape and the attribution process: Reversing actor's and observer's point of view. *Journal of Personality and Social Psychology, 27,* 165–175.

Strack, F., & Deutsch, R. (2004). Reflective and impulsive determinants of social behavior. *Personality and Social Psychology Review, 8,* 220–247.

Stroessner, S. J., Hamilton, D. L., & Mackie, D. M. (1992). Affect and stereotyping: The effect of induced mood on distinctiveness-based illusory correlations. *Journal of Personality and Social Psychology, 62,* 564–576.

Sun, R. (2001). Cognitive science meets multi-agent systems: A prolegomenon. *Philosophical Psychology, 14,* 5–28.

Sutton, R. S. (1992). Introduction: The challenge of reinforcement learning. *Machine Learning, 8*, 225–227.

Swim, J. K., Scott, E. D., Sechrist, G. B., Campell, B., & Stangor, C. (2003). The role of intent and harm in judgments of prejudice and discrimination. *Journal of Personality and Social Psychology, 84*, 944–959.

Tajfel, H. (1969). Cognitive aspects of prejudice. *Journal of Social Issues, 25*, 79–97.

Tajfel, H., & Wilkes, A. L. (1963). Classification and quantitative judgment. *British Journal of Psychology, 54*, 101–114.

Taylor, S. E. (1981). A categorization approach to stereotyping. In D. L. Hamilton (Ed.), *Cognitive processes in stereotyping and intergroup behavior* (pp. 145–182). Hillsdale, NJ: Lawrence Erlbaum Associates, Inc.

Taylor, S. E., & Fiske, S. T. (1975). Point of view and perceptions of causality. *Journal of Personality and Social Psychology, 32*, 439–445.

Thagard, P. (1989). Explanatory coherence. *Behavioral and Brain Sciences, 12*, 435–467.

Thagard, P. (1992). *Conceptual revolutions*. Princeton, NJ: Princeton University Press.

Thorpe, S. (1995). Localized and distributed representations. In M. A. Arbib (Ed.), *Handbook of brain theory and neural networks* (pp. 549–552). Cambridge, MA: MIT Press.

Tormala, Z. L., Petty, R. E., & Briñol, P. (2002). Ease of retrieval effect in persuasion: A self-validation analysis. *Personality and Social Psychology Bulletin, 28*, 1700–1712.

Touretzky, D. S. (1995). Connectionist and symbolic representation. In M. A. Arbib (Ed.), *Handbook of brain theory and neural networks* (pp. 243–247). Cambridge, MA: MIT Press.

Trope, Y. (1986). Identification and inferential processes in dispositional attribution. *Psychological Review, 93*, 239–257.

Trope, Y., & Gaunt, R. (2000). Processing alternative explanations of behavior: Correction or integration? *Journal of Personality and Social Psychology, 79*, 344–354.

Tulving, E. (1972). Episodic and semantic memory. In E. Tulving and W. Donaldson (Eds.), *Organization of memory* (pp. 381–403). New York, Academic Press.

Tversky, A., & Kahneman, D. (1974). Judgment under uncertainty: Heuristics and biases. *Science, 185*, 1124–1131.

Uleman, J. S. (1999). Spontaneous versus intentional inferences in impression formation. In S. Chaiken & Y. Trope (Eds.), *Dual-process theories in social psychology* (pp. 141–160). New York: Guilford Press.

Vallée-Tourangeau, F., Baker, A. G., & Mercier, P. (1994). Discounting in causality and covariance judgments. *Quarterly Journal of Experimental Psychology, 47B*, 151–171.

Van Duynslaeger, M., & Van Overwalle, F. (2004). *Do persuasive heuristics need abstract rules?* Unpublished manuscript. Free University of Brussels, Belgium.

van Gelder, T. (1991). What is the "D" in "PDP"? A survey of the concept of distribution. In W. Ramsey, S. P. Stich, & D. E. Rumelhart (Eds.), *Philosophy and connectionist theory* (pp. 33–60). Hillsdale, NJ: Lawrence Erlbaum Associates, Inc.

Van Hamme, L., & Wasserman, E. A. (1994). Cue competition in causality judgments: The role of nonpresentation of compound stimulus elements. *Learning and Motivation, 25*, 127–151.

Vanhoomissen, T., De Haan, J., & Van Overwalle, F. (2001). *Accentuation between groups and memory: A test of a recurrent connectionist model*. Unpublished data.

Van Oudenhoven, J. P., Groenewoud, J. T., & Hewstone, M. (1996). Cooperation, ethnic salience and generalization of ethnic attitudes. *European Journal of Social Psychology*, *26*, 649–661.

Van Overwalle, F. (1996). The relationship between the Rescorla–Wagner associative model and the probabilistic joint model of causality. *Psychologica Belgica*, *36*, 171–192.

Van Overwalle, F. (1997). A test of the Joint model of causal attribution. *European Journal of Social Psychology*, *27*, 221–236.

Van Overwalle, F. (1998). Causal explanation as constraint satisfaction: A critique and a feedforward connectionist alternative. *Journal of Personality and Social Psychology*, *74*, 312–328.

Van Overwalle, F. (2003). Acquisition of dispositional attributions: Effects of sample size and covariation. *European Journal of Social Psychology*, *33*, 515–533.

Van Overwalle, F. (2004). Multiple person inferences: A view of a connectionist integration. In H. Bowman & C. Labiouse (Eds.), *Connectionist models of cognition and perception II: Proceedings of the Eighth Neural Computation and Psychology Workshop*. London: World Scientific.

Van Overwalle, F. (2006). Discounting and augmentation of dispositional and causal attributions. *Psychologica Belgica*, *46*, 211–234.

Van Overwalle, F., & Heylighen, F. (2006). Talking nets: A multi-agent connectionist approach to communication and trust between individuals, *Psychologica Review*, *113*, 606–627.

Van Overwalle, F., & Jordens, K. (2002). An adaptive connectionist model of cognitive dissonance. *Personality and Social Psychology Review*, *3*, 204–231.

Van Overwalle, F., & Labiouse, C. (2004). A recurrent connectionist model of person impression formation. *Personality and Social Psychology Review*, *8*, 28–61.

Van Overwalle, F., & Siebler, F. (2005). A connectionist model of attitude formation and change. *Personality and Social Psychology Review*, *9*, 231–274.

Van Overwalle, F., & Timmermans, B. (2001). Learning about an absent cause: Discounting and augmentation of positively and independently related causes. In R. M. French & J. P. Sougné (Eds.) *Connectionist models of learning, development and evolution: Proceedings of the sixth neural computation and Psychology Workshop, Liege, Belgium, 16–18 September 2000*. Springer Verlag.

Van Overwalle, F., & Timmermans, B. (2005). Discounting and the Role of the Relation between Causes. *European Journal of Social Psychology*, *35*, 199–224.

Van Overwalle, F., & Van Rooy, D. (1998). A connectionist approach to causal attribution. In S. J. Read & L. C. Miller (Eds.), *Connectionist models of social reasoning and social behavior* (pp. 142–171). New York: Lawrence Erlbaum Associates, Inc.

Van Overwalle, F., & Van Rooy, D. (2001a). When more observations are better than less: A connectionist account of the acquisition of causal strength. *European Journal of Social Psychology*, *31*, 155–175.

Van Overwalle, F., & Van Rooy, D. (2001b). How one cause discounts or augments another: A connectionist account of causal competition. *Personality and Social Psychology Bulletin*, *27*, 1613–1626.

Van Overwalle, F., Drenth, T., & Marsman, G. (1999). Spontaneous trait inferences: Are they linked to the actor or to the action? *Personality and Social Psychology Bulletin*, *25*, 450–462.

Van Rooy, D. (2001). *A connectionist learning model of illusory correlation*. Unpublished PhD Dissertation.

Van Rooy, D., Van Overwalle, F., Vanhoomissen, T., Labiouse, C., & French, R. (2003). A recurrent connectionist model of group biases. *Psychological Review, 8,* 28–61.

Wänke, M., & Bless, H. (2000). The effects of subjective ease of retrieval on attitudinal judgments: The moderating role of processing motivation. In H. Bless & J. P. Forgas (Eds.), *The message within: The role of subjective experience in social cognition and behavior* (pp. 143–161). Philadelphia: Taylor & Francis.

Wänke, M., Bless, H., & Biller, B. (1996). Subjective experience versus content of information in the construction of attitude judgments. *Personality and Social Psychology Bulletin, 22,* 1105–1113.

Wänke, M., Bohner, G., & Jurkowitsch, A. (1997). There are many reasons to drive a BMW: Does imagined ease of argument generation influence attitudes? *Journal of Consumer Research, 24,* 170–177.

Wasserman, E. A., Elek, S. M., Chatlosh, D. L., & Baker, A. G. (1993). Rating causal relations: Role of probability in judgments of response-outcome contingency. *Journal of Experimental Psychology: Learning, Memory, and Cognition. 19,* 174–188.

Wasserman, E. A., Kao, S-F., Van Hamme, L., Katagiri, M., & Young, M. E. (1996). Causation and association. *The psychology of learning and motivation, 34,* 207–264.

Watson, D. (1982). The actor and the observer: How are their perceptions of causality divergent? *Psychological Bulletin, 92,* 682–700.

Weber, R., & Crocker, J. (1983). Cognitive processes in the revision of stereotypic beliefs. *Journal of Personality and Social Psychology, 45,* 961–977.

Wegner, D. M. (1994). Ironic processes of mental control. *Psychological Review, 101,* 34–52.

Wegener, D. T., & Petty, R. E. (1996). Effects of mood on persuasion processes: Enhancing, reducing and biasing scrutiny of attitude-relevant information. In L. L. Martin & A. Tesser (Eds.), *Striving and feeling: Interactions among goals, affect and self-regulation* (pp. 329–362). Hillsdale, NJ: Lawrence Erlbaum Associates, Inc.

Weiner, B. (1985). "Spontaneous" causal thinking. *Psychological Bulletin, 97,* 74–84.

Weiner, B. (1986). *An attributional theory of achievement motivation and emotion.* New York: Springer-Verlag.

Welbourne, J. L. (1999). The impact of perceived entativity on inconsistency resolution for groups and individuals. *Journal of Experimental Social Psychology, 35,* 481–508.

Wells, G. L., & Ronis, D. L. (1982). Discounting and augmentation: Is there something special about the number of causes? *Personality and Social Psychology Bulletin, 8,* 566–572.

Whitney, P., Davis, P. A., & Waring, D. A. (1994). Task effects on trait inference: Distinguishing categorization from characterization. *Social Cognition, 12,* 19–35.

Wilensky, R. (1983). *Planning and understanding: A computational approach to human reasoning.* Reading, MA: Addison-Wesley.

Wilkerson, I. (1992). The tallest fence: Feelings on race in a White neighborhood. *The New York Times,* pp. A1, A12.

Wilson, T. D., & Hodges, S. D. (1992). Attitudes as temporary constructions. In L. L. Martin & A. Tesser (Eds). *The construction of social judgments* (pp. 37–65). Hillsdale, NJ: Lawrence Erlbaum Associates, Inc.

Wilson, T. D., Lindsey, S., & Schooler, T. Y. (2000). A model of dual attitudes. *Psychological Review, 107,* 101–126.

Wittenbrink, B., Judd, C. M., & Park, B. (2001). Spontaneous prejudice in context: Variability in automatically activated attitudes. *Journal of Personality and Social Psychology*, *81*, 815–827.

Wojciszke, B., Brycz, H., & Borkenau, P. (1993). Effects of information content and evaluative extremity on positivity and negativity biases. *Journal of Personality and Social Psychology*, *64*, 327–335.

Wood, W., Kallgren, C. A., & Preisler, R. M. (1985). Access to attitude-relevant information in memory as a determinant of persuasion: The role of message attributes. *Journal of Experimental Social Psychology*, *21*, 73–85.

Worth, L. T., & Mackie, D. M. (1987). Cognitive mediation of positive affect in persuasion. *Social Cognition*, *5*, 76–94.

Wyer, R. S., & Srull, T. K. (1989). *Memory and cognition in its social context*. Hillsdale, NJ: Lawrence Erlbaum Associates, Inc.

Wyer, R. S., & Srull, T. K. (Eds.). (1994). *Handbook of social cognition* (2nd ed.). Hillsdale, NJ: Lawrence Erlbaum Associates, Inc.

Yzerbyt, V. Y., Coull, A., & Rocher, S. J. (1999). Fencing off the deviant: The role of cognitive resources in the maintenance of stereotypes. *Journal of Personality and Social Psychology*, *77*, 449–462.

Zanna, M. P., Kiesler, C. A., & Pilkonis, P. A. (1970). Positive and negative attitudinal affect established by classical conditioning. *Journal of Personality and Social Psychology*, *14*, 321–328.

Author index

Subject index

Subject terms in ***bold italic*** refer to terms in equations, but may appear elsewhere in the book. Subjects terms in **bold** refer to FIT instructions that appear only in the exercises or the FIT manual (in the appendix).

www.ingramcontent.com/pod-product-compliance
Ingram Content Group UK Ltd.
Pitfield, Milton Keynes, MK11 3LW, UK
UKHW020403010325
455677UK00021B/597